ENDURING TENSIONS IN URBAN POLITICS

ENDURING TENSIONS IN URBAN POLITICS

Edited, and with Introductions by

Dennis Judd
University of Missouri—St. Louis

Paul Kantor
Fordham University

Macmillan Publishing Company
NEW YORK

Maxwell Macmillan Canada
TORONTO

Editor: Bruce Nichols

Production Supervisor: bookworks

Production Manager: Jennifer Mallon

Cover Designer: Eileen Burke

Cover Photograph: Donald Johnson/The Stock Market

Illustrations: Precision Graphics

This book was set in Times Roman by Digitype, Inc.
and was printed and bound by Book Press.
The cover was printed by New England Book Components.

Macmillan Publishing Company
866 Third Avenue, New York, New York 10022

Macmillan Publishing Company is
part of the Maxwell Communication
Group of Companies.

Maxwell Macmillan Canada, Inc.
1200 Eglinton Avenue East
Suite 200
Don Mills, Ontario M3C 3N1

Library of Congress Cataloging-in-Publication Data

Judd, Dennis R.
   Enduring tensions in urban politics / Dennis Judd, Paul Kantor.
      p.   cm.
   ISBN 0-02-361455-2
   1. Urban policy—United States.   2. Municipal government—United
States.   3. Metropolitan government—United States.   4. Urban
renewal—United States.   5. City planning—United States.
I. Kantor, Paul P.   II. Title.
HT123.J83   1992
320.8'0973—dc20   91-25625
                                                            CIP

Printing: 2   3   4   5   6   7   Year: 3   4   5   6   7   8

To the memory of Phil Meranto
—Dennis Judd

To my daughter, Elizabeth, and her future
—Paul Kantor

Brief Contents

Contents

Preface

As we taught courses in urban politics over the years we routinely recommended books and articles in addition to the required reading list. Sometimes these materials came easily to hand, but often enough they were difficult to find; this proved frustrating to us and to the students. We hope that the readings collected together in this volume will help solve this recurring problem.

We are tempted to assert that this volume brings together the "best" writing on the various topics that today constitute the study of urban politics. There are, however, two reasons why we cannot make such a claim. First, the literature on urban politics is now so rich, the scholarship of the past few years has been of such quality, that for many of the selections one or several substitutes also would have worked just fine. No publisher would have tolerated inclusion of all the readings that we thought merited space in this book. Wherever possible we attempted to include classic articles as well as more recent research in order to display the richness of writing in this field of politics. Second, the selections in this book constitute a significant theoretical or empirical contribution to knowledge about urban politics — and, at the same time, they are accessible to students. As in any discipline, there is a considerable literature in urban politics that that is of immense importance to specialists that cannot be appreciated without previous formal training. Even though such work is essential to advances in the field, we have not included it in this volume.

Nevertheless, accessibility does not mean "watered down." The selections gathered together in this book constitute some of the most important writing on urban government and politics; indeed, we believe that these readings are so influential and focus on issues that are so central to the study of the field that advanced students and scholars, as well as beginning students, ought to find this volume useful.

As we explain in the four editors' essays that introduce the sections of this book, the readings can be profitably understood from a political economy perspective. Nevertheless, this reader can be used as a supplement to any urban politics textbook or to complement a series of books in an urban politics course. Of course, this volume is particularly appropriate alongside our own books on urban politics, *The Politics of American Cities*, by Dennis Judd and *The Dependent City*, by Paul Kantor (both published by HarperCollins). We strived to create a reader that can stand alone — one that can be read and used independently of a textbook and even outside of the classroom. The editors' essays are the means to this end. In these essays we place individual selections in the context of the themes and debates that are central to the contemporary study of urban politics. In particular, our discussion explains how the readings are suggestive of enduring tensions and issues that have permeated urban politics in the past and which continue to do so today.

When we first began to work on this project we shared the misapprehension that a reader could be put together as a sideline to our "real" research. After all, we reasoned, hadn't our previous research acquainted us intimately with the literature in the field? Our frequent and lengthy discussions, sometimes arguments, about what selections to include, the dawning realization that we were dealing with a rapidly moving target (a remarkable number of selections were published only after we started work on this book), and the difficult task of editing the pieces—all these steps—woke us to the realization that completing a reader is a major undertaking in its own right. This is because the collection actually constitutes a description and evaluation of the disciplinary field as a whole. Although not all users of this volume will completely agree with our depiction of the field of urban politics, we hope that our work helps precipitate further thought and debate about it.

It is our pleasure to thank many people who helped us in the three years that we spent completing this project. We thank Bruce Nichols, Macmillan's political science editor, for his enthusiastic support for our project and for his helpful advice. Dennis Judd wants to recognize the very considerable assistance of Carter Whitson, who is a doctoral student at the University of Missouri—St. Louis. Carter spent many, many hours xeroxing possible selections; perhaps more important, he helped identify particular readings and persuasively argued the case for some that might well have been overlooked. Others in the political science department helped as well, John Kalinowski, Jan Frantzen and Lana Vierdag helped with a multitude of typing and other tasks, and T.J. Sanders, Jennifer Bays, Shane Rodgers, and Melanie McGuire, very capable work study students, assisted with such important assignments as xeroxing, page counts, and faxing.

Paul Kantor wishes to thank Haisook Song and Germain Paulo, doctoral students in the political science department at Fordham University. Both were of very considerable assistance in obtaining library materials, searching for elusive references, duplicating, page counting, and sundry other tasks of real importance. Caryn Dunleavy, a most dependable and conscientious work study student, was always helpful in getting materials typed, duplicated, and mailed when time was of the essence. Finally, Anna Kantor deserves recognition for patiently listening to ideas about "the reader," making helpful suggestions and for sometimes taking over crucial family tasks in order to permit one of the editors to have time to do his editing.

ENDURING TENSIONS IN URBAN POLITICS

THE STUDY OF URBAN POLITICS

The scholarship on urban politics has changed so fundamentally in recent years that this reader could not have been organized in its present format a decade ago. City politics has come to be understood as a continuous, complex interaction between public and private institutions, between the marketplace and the public sphere, between private goals and collective purposes. The scholarship that is devoted to a study of these interactions has been labeled the "political economy" approach, which we believe encompasses most, though certainly not all, of the research on urban politics today.

As Michael Walzer argues (in the selection that follows this essay),* the line between economic and political power is unclear in a society where control and the use of property is largely a private matter. He describes how businessmen such as George Pullman, the sleeping car manufacturer, made crucial decisions about jobs, incomes, and peoples' residence and their quality of life. Private decisions of these sorts have public consequences. Private ownership is not entirely private; indeed, in a capitalist system the political process often revolves around issues of what is private and what is not private, and the distinction between the two spheres is subject to constant negotiation. In the absence of an officially defined public sector, business institutions invariably acquire de facto political power to make the consequential decisions in a community—though they cannot act *for* the community. This is the unique capacity of governments.

In national politics and in local communities as well, governments in the twentieth century have vastly increased their responsibilities. Governments are invested with the legitimacy to act in the name of citizens collectively—a crucial political resource that private actors and institutions do not possess. Governmental authority springs from the claim to "make and apply decisions that are binding upon any and all segments of society"

*Each of the four editors' essays in this book discusses the various selections, often by the conventional "[the author] states," argues, asserts, and so forth; or "according to [the author]" and so on. It is important to note, however, that none of the authors wrote these selections specifically for this book; all the selections have previously been published elsewhere.

1

(Nordlinger, 1981; cf. also Weber, 1947). In a democratic system, governmental decisions are legitimated primarily through processes that are intended to allow for participation by citizens and their representatives. The claim to act in behalf of citizens gives government a considerable autonomy to act. Nevertheless, however much it may appear that all political interests can make a claim on public authority, business has a privileged position in every capitalist country (Domhoff 1986; Elkin 1985; Lindblom 1977, 1982). In all capitalist nations society depends on the ability of the private sector to provide employment and income for citizens and revenues for government. Governments are held accountable for how they use public resources—and also, in a general sense, for the level of prosperity. Government policy makers therefore must be very careful to maintain good relations with those institutions that can invest or disinvest.

The Political Economy Perspective

The basic assumption that defines the political economy approach is the notion that power in cities can be understood by observing the interaction between private and public institutions and actors. Few urban scholars would any longer imagine that the politics of cities are mediated solely by governmental institutions, actors, and policies. Governments possess very significant resources, but in the United States they rarely, if ever, have the capacity to implement significant policies on their own, that is, without the cooperation or active assistance of private institutions and actors. Most of the critical decisions involving jobs, land use, and investment are made by marketplace institutions and individuals. It follows, therefore, that urban politics is not the exclusive province of governmental institutions.

In local communities, governments are particularly dependent on marketplace institutions, and this dependence is made particularly plain because cities are not closed systems. In the Paul E. Peterson reading, he stresses that cities are unable to control the movement of capital and labor across their borders. In contrast to the national government, city governments lack authority to regulate immigration, currency, prices, and wages, or the import and export of goods and services. City governments, therefore, are constrained to compete for capital investment or suffer decline in the economic well-being of the community. Peterson asserts that all factions within cities share a "unitary" interest in promoting their community's economic growth because all cities compete for jobs and investment. Because a community's success in this competition defines its well-being, he says, growth is the first imperative of local politics.

A lively and sometimes contentious debate has been waged over the question of how much room for maneuver city governments have in defining their politics. Several scholars have joined the debate by arguing that Peterson has oversimplified the nature of city politics. They point out that economic growth does not benefit everyone equally; that cities too often "give away the store" by granting tax and other concessions to business, thereby creating public poverty in the midst of private plenty; and that there usually are a variety of alternative policies that cities can undertake to promote growth. How to promote the economic well-being of the community is, therefore, ultimately a political question. This issue has taken on particular urgency since the 1960s because many local economies, primarily those built on heavy manufacturing, have been adversely impacted by the restructuring of the global economy. Cities have been forced to adopt aggressive policies to attract outside investment and to provide a hospitable environment for service-sector growth—chiefly corporate headquarters, office buildings, high-technology industries, and tourism.

In the last few years the political economy literature has evolved to the point that the particular pattern of interactions between public and private institutions are becoming better understood. There is an economic and political logic in urban politics (Swanstrom 1988). The logic of the marketplace treats cities solely as locations for private economic activity—commerce, industry, finance, land, transactions, and jobs. The economic behavior of business and entrepreneurs is rarely, if ever, influenced significantly by a concern for the public at large because the discipline of the market does not reward—and may actually penalize—business for doing so. The business of business is to make a profit, not to look out for everyone else. In contrast, the political logic of democratic institutions motivates public officials to maintain and expand political support for what they do, and to get reelected. This disciplines elected officials to at least make some appearance of looking beyond single interests.

As several selections in Part I suggest, before the industrial revolution city governments lacked much capability to interpose political as distinguished from private concerns, basically because public and private ends were almost indistinguishable. Public services were provided in these cities only when the merchant elites that ran them were confronted with an immediate crisis, or when social conditions threatened their economic well-being. Thus, in the early years of the nineteenth century Philadelphia began constructing a public water supply system, but only after a series of epidemics threatened the very future of the city. In midcentury, several large cities began to organize uniformed city police forces—after crime rates had reached crisis proportions. There was no compelling philosophy that guided elites in defining what city government ought to do. Local public affairs were dominated by the basically negative understanding that government ought to do as little as possible.

As American economic and political institutions have become clearly separate and distinct, however, a tension has developed between the institutions and processes of the market and the institutions and processes of local democracy. Because local political leaders must act to protect and enhance the base from which they derive their legitimate authority, it is important that they mobilize sufficient political support, or, alternatively, not provoke the mobilization of significant opposition. At the same time, they must be constantly mindful that they must induce businesses and entrepreneurs to invest their energy and capital locally — and at a minimum they must not adopt policies that drive capital away. Failure in the local economy means that population, jobs, and wealth migrate elsewhere. It is often difficult for politicians to maintain popular support and to keep local business happy simultaneously.

The contradiction between political and economic logic is illustrated by the controversy surrounding New York City's fiscal crisis in the 1970s (Shefter 1985). In the decades leading up to the city's near-bankruptcy in 1975, local political leaders, in alliance with Democratic officials at the national level, succeeded in building a pluralist political system that delivered social programs and services to a large variety of groups — each of which helped deliver Democratic votes on election day in local, state, and congressional and presidential elections. Stimulated by the Great Society's social programs, the city's expenditures rose rapidly relative to its tax revenues. The only way the growing deficits could be managed was through massive borrowing, which eventually precipitated the city's fiscal crisis. Leaders in the financial and corporate community seized the opportunity of impending insolvency to place the city's budget into their own hands, by creating a new public authority dominated by members of the financial community. The Municipal Assistance Corporation and an Emergency Financial Control Board were empowered to determine the city's revenue guidelines. Public spending quickly fell, and the city's priorities shifted away from social expenditures and toward subsidies and incentives to businesses. In other words, an economic logic, which dictated that the city would become a more favorable environment for business investment (lower tax rates combined with active financial support for investors), eclipsed the political logic that had driven the city's municipal agenda for years.

The tension between public and private purposes normally is not as dramatically displayed as it was in New York City in the 1970s, but it is nevertheless always present. It is visually evident in contemporary cities in the stark contrast between gleaming skyscrapers and office towers, luxury hotels and enclosed malls, and homeless people roaming the streets and the devastated neighborhoods a few blocks away. Driven by an economic logic — the need to promote investment — city governments abate taxes, provide low-interest loans, and provide other subsidies to businesses willing to locate within city boundaries. Meanwhile, those same governments frequently find themselves unable to provide an adequate level of infrastructure and services to the city's neighborhoods and residents. For now, the political logic that might force city governments to distribute resources significantly beyond business constituencies has been eclipsed. It surely would be revived, however, if these populations were able to mobilize effectively and back up their demands at the ballot box or in the streets.

Urban Regimes

In recent years, a literature on "urban regimes" has emerged to explain the specific mechanisms for managing the tensions between local democracy and the marketplace. Local regimes are composed of both political and economic actors who constantly negotiate settlements among contending interests. Although a variety of groups may have a voice in deciding how particular struggles will be resolved (for example, a neighborhood association may require more off-street parking than a business may want to provide, and a compromise is struck), the two pivotal and most powerful components that make up regimes in cities include city hall—the officials who (at least nominally if not always in reality) are most motivated by a political logic— and the city's business elite. Thus, in Clarence Stone's account of politics in Atlanta he notes that, "What makes governance in Atlanta effective is not the formal machinery of government, but rather the informal partnership between city hall and the downtown business elite. This informal partnership and the way it operates constitutes the city's regime; it is the same means through which major policy decisions are made" (Stone 1989, 3).

In his selection, Stephen Elkin asserts that local democracy is often eclipsed by the demands of economic actors because there is a systematic bias that gives economic vitality, often symbolized by building and land-use projects, an "inside track" in local politics. He also points to the failure of "social intelligence"—the difficulty of connecting popular control to political authority in such a way that policy preferences not expressed through economic actors can be given political weight in public decisions. He argues that economic determinism is not to blame for this failure so much as structural features of city politics that make public officials aware that their success is immediately tied to development projects more than to any other actions or accomplishments.

We agree with Elkin that politics looks similar in city after city—almost everywhere issues of land use and development are transcendent. Nevertheless, the economic pressures on local governments to accommodate interests promoting economic growth vary across time and from place to place. The political composition of central city regimes vary widely. Regimes are inclusionary in some cities, meaning that many groups and political interests are allowed to participate actively in making policy. They may be remarkably closed in other cities, with public officials merely fronting for or being drawn from the ranks of a sector of the business community.

Regimes may be inclusionary during some historical periods and exclusionary at other times. For example, twenty years ago there were few black or Hispanic mayors in city halls in the United States. Today minority mayors —as well as judges, city councilors, commissioners, and other officials—are commonplace. These regimes are caught in the middle, however, between a political logic that requires them to reward their supporters, if possible, and an economic logic that drives them to maintain an environment for investment by keeping taxes and public expenditures low. Minority mayors are forced to walk a tightrope between these two poles.

Historically, central city regimes have differed systematically by region. From the New Deal until the 1980s, northern industrial cities were governed by Democratic mayors, who generally relied on the electoral support of labor unions, ethnics, and black voters. City hall was forced to balance the interests of business (which generally preferred lower taxes and freedom from regulations) against an electoral coalition that demanded attention to neighborhoods, and a high level of neighborhood and social services. Sometimes city hall has leaned in one direction, sometimes in another. There was a different political balance in southern and southwestern cities, the region of the country now called the Sunbelt. Business elites in that region traditionally held a stranglehold on local politics, with the result that local governments have been relatively impermeable. Only in the last decade or so have these regimes begun to open up.

There are also systematic differences between local regimes within metropolitan areas. The contrast between central city and suburban regimes has been particularly sharp in the older urban areas on the Northeast and Midwest, where the central cities are typically ringed by scores of suburban jurisdictions. Suburban regimes tend to be remarkably closed. As a consequence, political issues are often very narrowly defined, typically focusing on the preservation of property values, the maintenance of segregated neighborhoods, the quality of city services, and little else.

The options available to local regimes for managing political tensions is linked to the intergovernmental system because federal and state governments have been able to intervene through the use of grants-in-aid or via regulatory programs to shape the economic and political pressures that challenge local governments. For instance, federal civil rights programs and court decisions have powerfully enhanced the political organization and influence of minority groups in local politics. Since the late 1970s federal policy has pushed cities to pursue economic growth above all other goals.

Regimes and Urban Crises: The Organization of This Book

Transformations in local governmental regimes are likely to be precipitated when the tensions between economic and political logic cannot be successfully managed. During such periods public officials confront a crisis of legitimacy; often they are thrown out of office or are forced to adopt new policy priorities. Crises may be provoked either by a failure by local elites to promote the collective public interest sufficiently or by their inability to promote the private-sector development that underlies the economic well-being of the community — or by a failure to accomplish either objective. A caveat should be noted, however: For local regimes to suffer a crisis of legitimacy, they must be seen as having the ability to respond and as having failed to do what was in their power to accomplish.

The readings that we have reprinted in this book suggest that at least three eras — or cycles — of regime politics have emerged in response to urban crises in American history. This pattern is reflected in the organization of this book. In Part I we have selected readings that describe the character of urban politics during the mercantile and industrial eras of city government. The first urban crisis materialized in the years after the Civil War, when cities were fully into a transition from mercantile to industrial economies.

The aristocratic, merchant elites that had wielded autocratic control over city affairs since the constitutional period were undermined by the rise of a class of politicians who contested aristocratic rule by appealing to a mass electorate. A generation of full-time politicians emerged in the industrial cities who were skilled at brokering the political interests of both immigrants and business.

Powerful party machines were constructed on the basis of these political skills. City electorates were themselves fragmented, however; the political loyalty of immigrants could be secured by appeals to ethnic solidarity and by patronage jobs and other material inducements, whereas upper-class elites and middle-class voters increasingly saw the machines as corrupt and inefficient, and in any case not sufficiently attentive to their interests. By the late nineteenth century a political struggle ensued between machines and reformers to manage the pressures of democratic politics and to respond to the social problems created by the new industrial economy.

These political struggles were eclipsed by the Great Depression of the 1930s. Widespread destitution and unemployment reached such levels that it became obvious that these problems could not be solved by local governments acting alone. The economic problems of the depression affected everyone — middle class and poor — and it threatened business as well. City officials forged an alliance with national politicians that lasted for forty years. From the 1930s to the 1970s the New Deal coalition defined the policies and priorities of the national Democratic party, and cities were central to that coalition. Successful city regimes used the resources of the national government to build local electoral coalitions, and they used these same resources to promote the redevelopment of business districts. We describe the regimes produced by this kind of politics in the essay introducing the readings that make up Part II.

The regimes that governed cities from the 1930s through the 1970s struggled to find a balance between the political and economic logics. During the 1950s, federal programs were used primarily to rebuild central business districts and revitalize the economy of the cities. In the 1960s, blacks and other constituencies were able to demand that city regimes use federal programs for social purposes. This phase ran its course by the late 1970s, with the dissolution of the New Deal coalition.

Part III is composed of readings that describe our current phase of urban development, and the consequences of a politics that is singularly focused on promoting economic growth. Since the 1970s business coalitions have become ascendant in defining municipal priorities; consequently, many cities in the 1990s, especially the older and declining cities of America's Frostbelt, are nearly obsessed with policies to promote economic growth. Fiscal retrenchment and decentralization of social responsibilities have become the guiding themes for national policy and for cities alike. The social problems of the cities have grown alarmingly, but governmental services are inadequate to the task. Federal social programs have been cut, and cities have compounded the effect of these cuts by reducing expenditures for public health, city services, and basic infrastructure.

A political logic will once again become ascendant when the groups that want more attention to public problems are able to mobilize effectively, or when the social and economic consequences of growth politics becomes damaging to the private sector. The fact that the political pendulum has swung in the past does not mean that it inevitably will at this time; it is hazardous to use history for the purposes of prediction. As described in the last group of readings, one result of the contraction of public power and responsibility is that American cities in the 1990s are places where extremes of wealth and poverty exist side by side in visible and dramatic juxtaposition.

It is important to acknowledge that although the readings in this book illustrate the themes we have outlined, the individual authors of the selections chosen for this reader would not necessarily agree in all respects with our understanding of how urban politics works. Considered as a whole, however, we believe that the selections provide substantial support for the idea that there is a political dynamic and a historical unfolding in urban politics that can be usefully viewed through the lens of the political economy tradition.

REFERENCES

Domhoff, G. William. "State Autonomy and the Privileged Position of Business: An Empirical Attack on a Theoretical Fantasy." *Journal of Political and Military Sociology* (Spring 1986): 149–162.

Elkin, Stephen L. 1985. "Pluralism in Its Place: State and Regime in the Liberal Democracy." In *The Democratic State*, edited by Roger Benjamin and Stephen L. Elkin, 179–211. Lawrence: University Press of Kansas.

Lindblom, Charles A. 1977. *Politics and Markets: The World's Political Economic Systems.* New York: Basic Books.

———. "The Market as Prison." *Journal of Politics* 44, no. 2 (May 1982): 324–336.

Nordlinger, Eric. 1981. *On the Autonomy of the Democratic State.* Cambridge: Harvard University Press.

Shefter, Martin. 1985. *Political Crisis/Fiscal Crisis: The Collapse and Revival of New York City.* New York: Basic Books.

Stone, Clarence N. 1989. *Regime Politics: Governing Atlanta 1946–1988.* Lawrence: University Press of Kansas.

Swanstrom, Todd. "Semi-Sovereign Cities: The Politics of Urban Development." *Polity* 21, no. 1 (Fall 1988): 83–110.

Weber, Max. 1947. *The Theory of Social and Economic Organizations.* New York: Free Press.

1

Property and Power*

Michael Walzer

Ownership is properly understood as a certain sort of power over things. Like political power, it consists in the capacity to determine destinations and risks — that is, to give things away or to exchange them (within limits) and also to keep them and use or abuse them, freely deciding on the costs in wear and tear. But ownership can also bring with it various sorts and degrees of power over people. The extreme case is slavery, which far exceeds the usual forms of political rule. I am concerned here, however, not with the actual possession, but only with the control, of people — mediated by the possession of things; this is a kind of power closely analogous to that which the state exercises over its subjects and disciplinary institutions over their inmates. Ownership also has effects well short of subjection. People engage with one another, and with institutions too, in all sorts of ways that reflect the momentary inequality of their economic positions. I own such-and-such book, for example, and you would like to have it; I am free to decide whether to sell or lend or give it to you or keep it for myself. We organize a factory commune and conclude that so-and-so's skills do not suit him for membership. You gather your supporters and defeat me in the competition for a hospital directorship. Their company squeezes out ours in intense bidding for a city contract. These are examples of brief encounters. I see no way to avoid them except through a political arrangement that systematically replaces the encounters of men and women with what Engels once called "the administration of things" — a harsh response to what are, after all, normal events in the spheres of money and office. But what sovereignty entails, and what ownership sometimes achieves (outside its sphere), is sustained control over the destinations and risks of other people; and that is a more serious matter.

It's not easy to make out just when the free use of property converts into the exercise of power. There are difficult issues here, and much political and academic controversy.[1] Two further examples, very much of the kind that figure in the literature, will illuminate some of the problems.

1. Beset by market failures, we decide to close down or relocate our cooperatively owned factory, thereby causing considerable harm to local merchants. Are we exercising power over the merchants? Not in any sustained way, I think, though our decision may well have serious effects on their lives. We certainly don't control their response to the new conditions we have created (nor are the new conditions entirely our creation: we didn't decide to fail on the market). Still, given our commitment to democratic politics, it might be argued that we should have included the merchants in our decision making. Inclusion is suggested by the medieval maxim, much favored by modern democrats, *What touches all should be decided by all.* But once one begins including all the people who are touched or affected by a given decision, and not just those whose daily activities are directed by it, it is hard to know where to stop. Surely the merchants in the various towns where the factory might relocate must be included as well. And all the people affected by the well-being of all the merchants, and so on. So power is drained away from local associations and communities and comes more and more to reside in the one association that includes all the affected people — namely, the state (and ultimately, if we pursue the logic of "touching," the global state). But this argument only suggests that affecting others cannot be a sufficient basis for distributing inclusion rights. It doesn't amount to exercising power in the relevant political sense.

By contrast, the state's decision to relocate the district offices of one of its bureaucracies must, if challenged, by fought through the political process. These are public offices, paid for out of public funds, providing public services. Hence the decision is clearly an exercise of power over the men and women who are taxed to make up the funds and who depend upon the services. A private firm, whether individually or collectively owned, is different. Its relations with its customers are more like brief encounters. If we tried to control these relations, insisting, for example, that every decision to locate or relocate had to be fought out politically, the sphere of money and commodities would effectively be eliminated, together with its attendant freedoms. All such attempts lie beyond the rightful range of (limited) government. But what if our factory is the only one, or by far the largest one, in town? Then our decision to close down or relocate might well have devastating effects; and in any genuine democracy, the political authorities would be pressed to step in. They might seek to alter market conditions (by subsidizing the factory, for example), or they might buy us out, or they might look for some way to attract new industry to the town.[2] These choices, however, are a matter more of political prudence than of distributive justice.

2. We run our factory in such a way as to pollute the air over much of the town in which we are located and so to endanger the health of its inhabitants. Day after day, we impose risks on our fellow citizens, and we decide, for technical and commercial reasons, what degree of risk to impose. But to impose risks, or at least risks of this sort, is precisely to exercise power in the political sense of the phrase. Now the authorities will have to step in, defending the health of their constituents or insisting on the right to determine, on behalf of those constituents, the degree of risk they will accept.[3] Even here, however, the authorities won't involve themselves in any sustained way in factory decision making. They will simply set or reset the limits within which decisions are made. If we (the members of the factory commune) were able to stop them from doing that—by threatening to relocate, for example—and so maintain an unlimited ability to pollute, then it would make sense to call us tyrants. We would be exercising power in violation of the common (democratic) understanding of what power is and how it is to be distributed. Would it make a difference if we weren't aiming to maintain our profit margins but just struggling to keep the factory afloat? I am not sure; probably we would be bound, either way, to inform the local authorities of our financial condition and to accept their view of acceptable risks.[4]

These are hard cases, the second more so than the first; and I shall not attempt any detailed resolution of them here. In a democratic society, the boundary of the sphere of money and commodities is likely to be drawn, roughly, between the two, so as to include the first but not the second. I have, however, radically simplified my accounts of the cases by assuming a cooperatively owned factory; and I need now to consider, at rather greater length, the more common example of private ownership. Now the workers in the factory are no longer economic agents, licensed to make a set of decisions; only the owners are agents of that sort; and the workers, like the townspeople, are threatened by the factory's failures and by its pollution. But they aren't merely "touched," more or less seriously. Unlike the townspeople, they are participants in the enterprise that causes the effects; they are bound by its rules. Ownership constitutes a "private government," and the workers are its subjects.* So I must take up again, as in my earlier discussion of wage determination, the character of economic agency.

*There is an extensive literature on private governments, much of it the work of contemporary political scientists, reaching (rightly) for new fields.[5] But I think the decisive words were written by R. H. Tawney in 1912: "What I want to drive home is this, that the man who employs, governs, to the extent of the number of men employed. He has jurisdiction over them. He occupies what is really a public office. He has power, not of pit and gallows . . . but of overtime and short time, full bellies and empty bellies, health and sickness. The question *who* has this power, how is he qualified to use it, how does the state control his liberties . . . this is the question which really matters to the plain man today."[6]

The classic setting for private government was the feudal system, where property in land was conceived to entitle the owner to exercise direct disciplinary (judicial and police) powers over the men and women who lived on the land — and who were, moreover, barred from leaving. These people were not slaves, but neither were they tenants. They are best called "subjects"; their landlord was also their lord, who taxed them and even conscripted them for his private army. It took many years of local resistance, royal aggrandizement, and revolutionary activity before a clear boundary was drawn between the estate and the realm, between property and polity. Not until 1789 was the formal structure of feudal rights abolished and the disciplinary power of the lords effectively socialized. Taxation, adjudication, and conscription: all these dropped out of our conception of what property means. The state was emancipated, as Marx wrote, from the economy.[7] The entailments of ownership were redefined so as to exclude certain sorts of decision making that, it was thought, could only be authorized by the political community as a whole. This redefinition established one of the crucial divisions along which social life is organized today. On one side are activities called "political," involving the control of destinations and risks; on the other side are activities called "economic," involving the exchange of money and commodities. But though this division shapes our understanding of the two spheres, it does not itself determine what goes on within them. Indeed, private government survives in the post-feudal economy. Capitalist ownership still generates political power, if not in the market, where blocked exchanges set limits at least on the legitimate uses of property, then in the factory itself, where work seems to require a certain discipline. Who disciplines whom? It is a central feature of a capitalist economy that owners discipline non-owners.

What justifies this arrangement, we are commonly told, is the risk taking that ownership requires, and the entrepreneurial zeal, the inventiveness, and the capital investment through which economic firms are founded, sustained, and expanded. Whereas feudal property was founded on armed force and sustained and expanded through the power of the sword (though it was also traded and inherited), capitalist property rests upon forms of activity that are intrinsically non-coercive and non-political. The modern factory is distinguished from the feudal manor because men and women come willingly to work in the factory, drawn by the wages, working conditions, prospects for the future, and so on that the owner offers, while the workers on the manor are serfs, prisoners of their noble lords. All this is true enough, at least sometimes, but it doesn't satisfactorily mark off property rights from political power. For everything that I have just said of firms and factories might also be said of cities and towns, if not always of states. They, too, are created by entrepreneurial energy, enterprise, and risk taking; and they, too, recruit and hold their citizens, who are free to come and go, by offering them an attractive place to live. Yet we should be uneasy about any claim to own a city or a town; nor is ownership an acceptable basis for political power within cities and towns. If we consider deeply why this is so, we shall have to conclude, I think, that it shouldn't be acceptable in firms or factories either. What we need is a story about a capitalist entrepreneur who is also a political founder and who tries to build his power on his property.

The Case of Pullman, Illinois

George Pullman was one of the most successful entrepreneurs of late nine-teenth century America. His sleeping, dining, and parlor cars made train travel a great deal more comfortable than it had been, and only somewhat more expensive; and on this difference of degree, Pullman established a company and a fortune. When he decided to build a new set of factories and a town around them, he insisted that this was only another business venture. But he clearly had larger hopes: he dreamed of a community without politi-cal or economic unrest — happy workers and a strike-free plant.[8] He clearly belongs, then, to the great tradition of the political founder, even though, unlike Solon of Athens, he didn't enact his plans and then go off to Egypt, but stayed on to run the town he had designed. What else could he do, given that he owned the town?

Pullman, Illinois, was built on a little over four thousand acres of land along Lake Calumet just south of Chicago, purchased (in seventy-five indi-vidual transactions) at a cost of eight hundred thousand dollars. The town was founded in 1880 and substantially completed, according to a single unified design, within two years. Pullman (the owner) didn't just put up factories and dormitories, as had been done in Lowell, Massachusetts, some fifty years earlier. He built private homes, row houses, and tenements for some seven to eight thousand people, shops and offices (in an elaborate arcade), schools, stables, playgrounds, a market, a hotel, a library, a theater, even a church: in short, a model town, a planned community. And every bit of it belonged to him.

> A stranger arriving at Pullman puts up at a hotel managed by one of Mr. Pullman's employees, visits a theater where all the attendants are in Mr. Pullman's service, drinks water and burns gas which Mr. Pullman's water and gas works supply, hires one of his outfits from the manager of Mr. Pullman's livery stable, visits a school in which the children of Mr. Pullman's employees are taught by other employees, gets a bill charged at Mr. Pullman's bank, is unable to make a purchase of any kind save from some tenant of Mr. Pullman's, and at night he is guarded by a fire department every member of which from the chief down is in Mr. Pullman's service.[9]

This account is from an article in the *New York Sun* (the model town attracted a lot of attention), and it is entirely accurate except for the line about the school. In fact, the schools of Pullman were at least nominally run by the elected school board of Hyde Park Township. The town was also subject to the political jurisdiction of Cook County and the State of Illinois. But there was no municipal government. Asked by a visiting journalist how he "governed" the people of Pullman, Pullman replied, "We govern them in the same way a man governs his house, his store, or his workshop. It is all simple enough."[10] Government was, in his conception, a property right; and despite the editorial "we," this was a right singly held and singly exercised. In his town, Pullman was an autocrat. He had a firm sense of how its inhabitants should live, and he never doubted his right to give that sense practical force. His concern, I should stress, was with the appearance and the behavior of the people, not with their beliefs. "No one was required to subscribe to any set of ideals before moving to [Pullman]." Once there, however, they were required to live in a certain way. Newcomers might be seen "lounging on their doorsteps, the husband in his shirtsleeves, smoking a pipe, his untidy wife darning, and half-dressed children playing about them." They were soon made aware that this sort of thing was unacceptable. And if they did not mend their ways, "company inspectors visited to threaten fines."[11]

Pullman refused to sell either land or houses — so as to maintain "the harmony of the town's design" and also, presumably, his control over the inhabitants. Everyone who lived in Pullman (Illinois) was a tenant of Pullman (George). Home renovation was strictly controlled; leases were terminable on ten days' notice. Pullman even refused to allow Catholics and Swedish Lutherans to build churches of their own, not because he opposed their worship (they were permitted to rent rooms), but because his conception of the town called for one rather splendid church, whose rent only the Presbyterians could afford. For somewhat different reasons, though with a similar zeal for order, liquor was available only in the town's one hotel, at a rather splendid bar, where ordinary workers were unlikely to feel comfortable.

I have stressed Pullman's autocracy; I could also stress his benevolence. The housing he provided was considerably better than that generally available to American workers in the 1880s; rents were not unreasonable (his profit margins were in fact quite low); the buildings were kept in repair; and so on. But the crucial point is that all decisions, benevolent or not, rested with a man, governor as well as owner, who had not been chosen by the people he governed. Richard Ely, who visited the town in 1885 and wrote an article about it for *Harper's Monthly*, called it "unAmerican . . . benevolent, well-wishing feudalism."[12] But that description wasn't quite accurate, for the men and women of Pullman were entirely free to come and go. They were also free to live outside the town and commute to work in its factories, though in hard times Pullman's tenants were apparently the last to be laid off. These tenants are best regarded as the subjects of a capitalist enterprise that has simply extended itself from manufacturing to real estate and duplicated in the town the discipline of the shop. What's wrong with that?

I mean the question to be rhetorical, but it is perhaps worthwhile spelling out the answer. The inhabitants of Pullman were guest workers, and that is not a status compatible with democratic politics. George Pullman hired himself a metic population in a political community where self-respect was closely tied to citizenship and where decisions about destinations and risks, even (or especially) local destinations and risks, were supposed to be shared. He was, then, more like a dictator than a feudal lord; he ruled by force. The badgering of the townspeople by his inspectors was intrusive and tyrannical and can hardly have been experienced in any other way.

Ely argued that Pullman's ownership of the town made its inhabitants into something less than American citizens: "One feels that one is mingling with a dependent, servile people." Apparently, Ely caught no intimations of the great strike of 1894 or of the courage and discipline of the strikers.[13] He wrote his article early on in the history of the town; perhaps the people needed time to settle in and learn to trust one another before they dared oppose themselves to Pullman's power. But when they did strike, it was as much against his factory power as against his town power. Indeed, Pullman's foremen were even more tyrannical than his agents and inspectors. It seems odd to study the duplicated discipline of the model town and condemn only one half of it. Yet this was the conventional understanding of the time. When the Illinois Supreme Court in 1898 ordered the Pullman Company (George Pullman had died a year earlier) to divest itself of all property not used for manufacturing purposes, it argued that the ownership of a town, but not of a company, "was incompatible with the theory and spirit of our institutions."[14] The town had to be governed democratically — not so much because ownership made the inhabitants servile, but because it forced them to fight for rights they already possessed as American citizens.

It is true that the struggle for rights in the factory was a newer struggle, if only because factories were newer institutions than cities and towns. I want to argue, however, that with regard to political power democratic distributions can't stop at the factory gates. The deep principles are the same for both sorts of institution. This identity is the moral basis of the labor movement — not of "business unionism," which has another basis, but of every demand for progress toward industrial democracy. It doesn't follow from these demands that factories can't be owned; nor did opponents of feudalism say that land couldn't be owned. It's even conceivable that all the inhabitants of a (small) town might pay rent, but not homage, to the same landlord. The issue in all these cases is not the existence but the entailments of property. What democracy requires is that property should have no political currency, that it shouldn't convert into anything like sovereignty, authoritative command, sustained control over men and women. After 1894, at least, most observers seem to have agreed that Pullman's ownership of the town was undemocratic. But was his ownership of the company any different? The unusual juxtaposition of the two makes for a nice comparison.

They are not different because of the entrepreneurial vision, energy, inventiveness, and so on that went into the making of Pullman sleepers, diners, and parlor cars. For these same qualities went into the making of the town. This, indeed, was Pullman's boast: that his "'system' which had succeeded in railroad travel, was not being applied to the problems of labor and housing.'"[15] And if the application does not give rise to political power in the one case, why should it do so in the other?*

Nor are the two different because of the investment of private capital in the company. Pullman invested in the town, too, without thereby acquiring the right to govern its inhabitants. The case is the same with men and women who buy municipal bonds: they don't come to own the municipality. Unless they live and vote in the town, they cannot even share in decisions about how their money is to be spent. They have no political rights; whereas residents do have rights, whether they are investors or not. There seems no reason not to make the same distinction in economic associations, marking off investors from participants, a just return from political power.

Finally, the factory and the town are not different because men and women come willingly to work in the factory with full knowledge of its rules and regulations. They also come willingly to live in the town, and in neither case do they have full knowledge of the rules until they have some experience of them. Anyway, residence does not constitute an agreement to despotic rules even if the rules are known in advance; nor is prompt departure the only way of expressing opposition. There are, in fact, some associations for which these last propositions might plausibly be reversed. A man who joins a monastic order requiring strict and unquestioning obedience, for example, seems to be choosing a way of life rather than a place to live (or a place to work). We would not pay him proper respect if we refused to recognize the efficacy of his choice. Its purpose and its moral effect are precisely to authorize his superior's decisions, and he can't withdraw that authority without himself withdrawing from the common life it makes possible. But the same thing can't be said of a man or a woman who joins a company or comes to work in a factory. Here the common life is not so all-encompassing and it does not require the unquestioning acceptance of authority. We respect the new worker only if we assume that he has not sought out political subjection. Of course, he encounters foremen and company police, as he knew he would; and it may be that the success of the enterprise requires his obedience, just as the success of a city or a town requires that citizens obey public officials. But in neither case would we want to say (what we might say to the novice monk): if you don't like these officials and the orders they give, you can always leave. It's important that there be options short of leaving, connected with the appointment of the officials and the making of the rules they enforce.

Other sorts of organizations raise more difficult questions. Consider an example that Marx used in the third volume of *Capital* to illustrate the nature of authority in a communist factory. Cooperative labor requires, he

---

*But perhaps it was Pullman's expertise, not his vision, energy, and so on, that justified his autocratic rule. Perhaps factories should be assimilated to the category of disciplinary institutions and run by scientific managers. But the same argument might be made for towns. Indeed, professional managers are often hired by town councils; they are subject, however, to the authority of the elected councilors. Factory managers are subject, though often ineffectively, to the authority of owners. And so the question remains: Why owners rather than workers (or their elected representatives)?

wrote, "one commanding will," and he compared this will to that of an orchestra conductor.[16] The conductor presides over a harmony of sounds and also, Marx seems to have thought, over a harmony of musicians. It is a disturbing comparison, for conductors have often been despots. Should their will be commanding? Perhaps it should, since an orchestra must express a single interpretation of the music it plays. But patterns of work in a factory are more readily negotiated. Nor is it the case that the members of an orchestra must yield to the conductor with regard to every aspect of the life they share. They might claim a considerable voice in the orchestra's affairs, even if they accept when they play the conductor's commanding will.

But the members of an orchestra, like the workers in a factory, while they spend a great deal of time with one another, don't live with one another. Perhaps the line between politics and economics has to do with the difference between residence and work. Pullman brought the two together, submitted residents and workers to the same rule. Is it enough if residents rule themselves while only workers are submitted to the power of property, if the residents are citizens and the workers metics? Certainly the self-rule of residents is commonly thought to be a matter of the first importance. That's why a landlord has so much less power over his tenants than a factory owner over his workers. Men and women must collectively control the place where they live in order to be safe in their own homes. *A man's home is his castle.* I will assume that this ancient maxim expresses a genuine moral imperative. But what the maxim requires is not political self-rule so much as the legal protection of the domestic sphere—and not only from economic but also from political interventions. We need a space for withdrawal, rest, intimacy, and (sometimes) solitude. As a feudal baron retired to his castle to brood over public slights, so I retire to my home. But the political community is not a collection of brooding places, or not only that. It is also a common enterprise, a public place where we argue together over the public interest, where we decide on goals and debate acceptable risks. All this was missing in Pullman's model town, until the American Railway Union provided a forum for workers and residents alike.

From this perspective, an economic enterprise seems very much like a town, even though—or, in part, because—it is so unlike a home. It is a place not of rest and intimacy but of cooperative action. It is a place not of withdrawal but of decision. If landlords possessing political power are likely to be intrusive on families, so owners possessing political power are likely to be coercive of individuals. Conceivably the first of these is worse than the second, but this comparison doesn't distinguish the two in any fundamental way; it merely grades them. Intrusiveness and coercion are alike made possible by a deeper reality—the usurpation of a common enterprise, the displacement of collective decision making, by the power of property. And for this, none of the standard justifications seems adequate. Pullman exposed their weaknesses by claiming to rule the town he owned exactly as he ruled the factories he owned. Indeed, the two sorts of rule are similar to one another, and both of them resemble what we commonly understand as authoritarian politics. The right to impose fines does the work of taxation; the right to evict tenants or discharge workers does (some of) the work of punishment. Rules are issued and enforced without public debate by appointed rather than by elected officials. There are no established judicial procedures, no legitimate forms of opposition, no channels for participation or even for protest. If this sort of thing is wrong for towns, then it is wrong for companies and factories, too.

Imagine now a decision by Pullman or his heirs to relocate their factory/town. Having paid off the initial investment, they see richer ground elsewhere; or, they are taken with a new design, a better model for a model town, and want to try it out. The decision, they claim, is theirs alone since the factory/town is theirs alone; neither the inhabitants nor the workers have anything to say. But how can this be right? Surely to uproot a community, to require large-scale migration, to deprive people of homes they have lived in for many years; these are political acts, and acts of a rather extreme sort. The decision is an exercise of power; and were the townspeople simply to submit, we would think they were not self-respecting citizens. What about the workers?

What political arrangements should the workers seek? Political rule implies a certain degree of autonomy, but it's not clear that autonomy is possible in a single factory or even in a group of factories. The citizens of a town are also the consumers of the goods and services the town provides; and except for occasional visitors, they are the only consumers. But workers in a factory are producers of goods and services; they are only sometimes consumers, and they are never the only consumers. Moreover, they are locked into close economic relationships with other factories that they supply or on whose products they depend. Private owners relate to one another through the market. In theory, economic decisions are non-political, and they are coordinated without the interventions of authority. Insofar as this theory is true, worker cooperatives would simply locate themselves within the network of market relations. In fact, however, the theory misses both the collusions of owners among themselves and their collective ability to call upon the support of state officials. Now the appropriate replacement is an industrial democracy organized at national as well as local levels. But how, precisely, can power be distributed so as to take into account both the necessary autonomy and the practical linkage of companies and factories? The question is often raised and variously answered in the literature on workers' control. I shall not attempt to answer it again, nor do I mean to deny its difficulties; I only want to insist that the sorts of arrangements required in an industrial democracy are not all that different from those required in a political democracy. Unless they are independent states, cities and towns are never fully autonomous; they have no absolute authority even over the goods and services they produce for internal consumption. In the United States today, we enmesh them in a federal structure and regulate what they can do in the areas of education, criminal justice, environmental use, and so on. Factories and companies would have to be similarly enmeshed and similarly regulated (and they would also be taxed). In a developed economy, as in a developed polity, different decisions would be made by different groups of people at different levels of organization. The division of power in both these cases is only partly a matter of principle; it is also a matter of circumstance and expediency.

The argument is similar with regard to the constitutional arrangements within factories and companies. There will be many difficulties working these out; there will be false starts and failed experiments exactly as there have been in the history of cities and towns. Nor should we expect to find a single appropriate arrangement. Direct democracy, proportional representation, single-member constituencies, mandated and independent representatives, bicameral and unicameral legislatures, city managers, regulatory commissions, public corporations — political decision making is organized and will continue to be organized in many different ways. What is important is that we know it to be political, the exercise of power, not the free use of property.

Today, there are many men and women who preside over enterprises in which hundreds and thousands of their fellow citizens are involved, who direct and control the working lives of their fellows, and who explain themselves exactly as George Pullman did. I govern these people, they say, in the same way a man governs the things he owns. People who talk this way are wrong. They misunderstand the prerogatives of ownership (and of foundation, investment, and risk taking). They claim a kind of power to which they have no right.

To say this is not to deny the importance of entrepreneurial activity. In both companies and towns, one looks for people like Pullman, full of energy and ideas, willing to innovate and take risks, capable of organizing large projects. It would be foolish to create a system that did not bring them forward. They are of no use to us if they just brood in their castles. But there is nothing they do that gives them a right to rule over the rest of us, unless they can win our agreement. At a certain point in the development of an enterprise, then, it must pass out of entrepreneurial control; it must be organized or reorganized in some political way, according to the prevailing (democratic) conception of how power ought to be distributed. It is often said that economic entrepreneurs won't come forward if they cannot hope to own the companies they found. But this is like saying that no one would seek divine grace or knowledge who did not hope to come into hereditary possession of a church or "holy commonwealth," or that no one would found new hospitals or experimental schools who did not intend to pass them on to his children, or that no one would sponsor political innovation and reform unless it were possible to own the state. But ownership is not the goal of political or religious life, and there are still attractive and even compelling goals. Indeed, had Pullman founded a better town, he might have earned for himself the sort of public honor that men and women have sometimes taken as the highest end of human action. If he wanted power as well, he should have run for mayor.

NOTES

1. See the useful discussions of Steven Lukes, *Power: A Radical View* (London, 1974); and William E. Connolly, *The Terms of Political Discourse* (Lexington, Mass., 1974), chap. 3.

2. For an example, see Martin Carnoy and Derek Shearer, *Economic Democracy: The Challenge of the 1980s* (White Plains, N.Y., 1980), pp. 360–61.

3. For an argument that we should rely on the market and the courts rather than on executive or legislative action, see Robert Nozick, *Anarchy, State, and Utopia* (New York 1974), pp. 79–81; cf. the case study of Matthew Crenson, *The Unpolitics of Air Pollution: A Study of Non-Decisionmaking in Cities* (Baltimore, 1971).

4. For a possible further complication, see Connolly on threats and predictions, *Political Discourse*, pp. 95–96.

5. For an excellent beginning, see Grant McConnell, *Private Power and American Democracy* (New York, 1966).

6. *R. H. Tawney's Commonplace Book*, ed. J. M. Winter and D. M. Joslin (Cambridge, England, 1972), pp. 34–35.

7. Karl Marx, "On the Jewish Question," in *Early Writings*, trans. T. B. Bottomore (London, 1963), pp. 12–13.

8. Stanley Buder, *Pullman: An Experiment in Industrial Order and Community Planning, 1880–1930* (New York, 1967).

9. Ibid., pp. 98–99.

10. Ibid., p. 107.

11. Ibid., p. 95; see also William M. Carwardine, *The Pullman Strike*, intro. Virgil J. Vogel (Chicago, 1973), chaps. 8, 9, 10.

12. Richard Ely, quoted in Buder, *Pullman*, p. 103.

13. Ibid.; see also Carwardine, *Pullman Strike*, chap. 4.

14. Carwardine, *Pullman Strike*, p. xxxiii.

15. Buder, *Pullman*, p. 44.

16. Karl Marx, *Capital* (New York, 1967), vol. III, pp. 383, 386. Lenin repeats the argument, suggesting "the mild leadership of a conductor of an orchestra" as an example of communist authority; see "The Immediate Tasks of the Soviet Government," in *Selected Works* (New York, n.d.), vol. VII, p. 342.

2
The Interests of the Limited City*

Paul E. Peterson

Like all social structures, cities have interests. Just as we can speak of union interests, judicial interests, and the interests of politicians, so we can speak of the interests of that structured system of social interactions we call a city. Citizens, politicians, and academics are all quite correct in speaking freely of the interests of cities.[1]

Defining the City Interest

By a city's interest, I do not mean the sum total of the interests of those individuals living in the city. For one thing, these are seldom, if ever, known. The wants, needs, and preferences of residents continually change, and few surveys of public opinion in particular cities have ever been taken. Moreover, the residents of a city often have discordant interests. Some want more parkland and better schools; others want better police protection and lower taxes. Some want an elaborated highway system; others wish to keep cars out of their neighborhood. Some want more inexpensive, publicly subsidized housing; others wish to remove the public housing that exists. Some citizens want improved welfare assistance for the unemployed and dependent; others wish to cut drastically all such programs of public aid. Some citizens want rough-tongued ethnic politicians in public office; others wish that municipal administration were a gentleman's calling. Especially in large cities, the cacophony of competing claims by diverse class, race, ethnic, and occupational groups makes impossible the determination of any overall city interest — any public interest, if you like — by compiling all the demands and desires of individual city residents.

Some political scientists have attempted to discover the overall urban public interest by summing up the wide variety of individual interests. The earlier work of Edward Banfield, still worth examination, is perhaps the most persuasive effort of this kind.[2] He argued that urban political processes — or at least those in Chicago — allowed for the expression of nearly all the particular interests within the city. Every significant interest was represented by some economic firm or voluntary association, which had a stake in trying to influence those public policies that touched its vested interests. After these various groups and firms had debated and contended, the political leader searched for a compromise that took into account the vital interests of each,

*Peterson, Paul E. 1981. "The Interests of the Limited City." Pp. 17–30 and 231–232 in *City Limits*. Chicago: University of Chicago Press. Copyright © 1981. Reprinted by permission of University of Chicago Press.

and worked out a solution all could accept with some satisfaction. The leader's own interest in sustaining his political power dictated such a strategy.

Banfield's argument is intriguing, but few people would identify public policies as being in the interest of the city simply because they have been formulated according to certain procedures. The political leader might err in his judgment; the interests of important but politically impotent groups might never get expressed; or the consequences of a policy might in the long run be disastrous for the city. Moreover, most urban policies are not hammered out after great controversy, but are the quiet product of routine decision making. How does one evaluate which of these are in the public interest? Above all, this mechanism for determining the city's interest provides no standpoint for evaluating the substantive worth of urban policies. Within Banfield's framework, whatever urban governments do is said to be in the interest of their communities. But the concept of city interest is used most persuasively when there are calls for reform or innovation. It is a term used to evaluate existing programs and to discriminate between promising and undesirable new ones. To equate the interests of cities with what cities are doing is to so impoverish the term as to make it quite worthless.

The economist Charles Tiebout employs a second approach to the identification of city interests.[3] Unlike Banfield, he does not see the city's interests as a mere summation of individual interests but as something which can be ascribed to the entity, taken as a whole. As an economist, Tiebout is hardly embarrassed by such an enterprise, because in ascribing interests to cities his work parallels both those orthodox economists who state that firms have an interest in maximizing profits and those welfare economists who claim that politicians have an interest in maximizing votes. Of course, they state only that their model will assume that firms and politicians behave in such a way, but insofar as they believe their model has empirical validity, they in fact assert that those constrained by the businessman's or politician's role must pursue certain interests. And so does Tiebout when he says that communities seek to attain the optimum size for the efficient delivery of the bundle of services the local government produces. In his words, "Communities below the optimum size seek to attract new residents to lower average costs. Those above optimum size do just the opposite. Those at an optimum try to keep their populations constant."[4]

Tiebout's approach is in many ways very attractive. By asserting a strategic objective that the city is trying to maximize—optimum size—Tiebout identifies an overriding interest which can account for specific policies the city adopts. He provides a simple analytical tool that will account for the choices cities make, without requiring complex investigations into citizen preferences and political mechanisms for identifying and amalgamating the same. Moreover, he provides a criterion for determining whether a specific policy is in the interest of the city—does it help achieve optimum size? Will it help the too small city grow? Will it help the too big city contract? Will it keep the optimally sized city in equilibrium? Even though the exact determination of the optimum size cannot presently be scientifically determined in all cases, the criterion does provide a most useful guide for prudential decision making.

The difficulty with Tiebout's assumption is that he does not give very good reasons for its having any plausibility. When most economists posit a certain form of maximizing behavior, there is usually a good commonsense reason for believing the person in that role will have an interest in pursuing this strategic objective. When orthodox economists say that businessmen maximize profits, it squares with our understanding in everyday life that people engage in commercial enterprises for monetary gain. The more they make, the better they like it. The same can be said of those welfare economists who say politicians maximize votes. The assumption, though cynical, is in accord with popular belief—and therefore once again has a certain plausibility.

By contrast, Tiebout's optimum size thesis diverges from what most people think cities are trying to do. Of course, smaller communities are often seeking to expand—boosterism may be the quintessential characteristic of small-town America. Yet Tiebout takes optimum size, not growth or maximum size, as the strategic objective. And when Tiebout discusses the big city that wishes to shrink to optimum size, his cryptic language is quite unconvincing. "The case of the city that is too large and tries to get rid of residents is more difficult to imagine," he confesses. Even more, he concedes that "no alderman in his right political mind would ever admit that the city is too big." "Nevertheless," he continues, "economic forces are at work to push people out of it. Every resident who moves to the suburbs to find better schools, more parks, and so forth, is reacting, in part, against the pattern the city has to offer."[5] In this crucial passage Tiebout speaks neither of local officials nor of local public policies. Instead, he refers to "economic forces" that may be beyond the control of the city and of "every resident," each of whom may be pursuing his own interests, not that of the community at large.

The one reason Tiebout gives for expecting cities to pursue optimum size is to lower the average cost of public goods. If public goods can be delivered most efficiently at some optimum size, then migration of residents will occur until that size has been reached. In one respect Tiebout is quite correct: local governments must concern themselves with operating local services as efficiently as possible in order to protect the city's economic interests. But there is little evidence that there is an optimum size at which services can be delivered with greatest efficiency. And even if such an optimum did exist, it could be realized only if migration occurred among residents who paid equal amounts in local taxes. In the more likely situation, residents pay variable prices for public services (for example, the amount paid in local property taxes varies by the value of the property). Under these circumstances, increasing size to the optimum does not reduce costs to residents unless newcomers pay at least as much in taxes as the marginal increase in costs their arrival imposes on city government.[6] Conversely, if a city needs to lose population to reach the optimum, costs to residents will not decline unless the exiting population paid less in taxes than was the marginal cost of providing them government services. In most big cities losing population, exactly the opposite is occurring. Those who pay more in taxes than they receive in services are the emigrants. Tiebout's identification of city interests with optimum size, while suggestive, fails to take into account the quality as well as the quantity of the local population.

The interests of cities are neither a summation of individual interests nor the pursuit of optimum size. Instead, policies and programs can be said to be in the interest of cities whenever the policies maintain or enhance the economic position, social prestige, or political power of the city, taken as a whole.[7]

Cities have these interests because cities consist of a set of social interactions structured by their location in a particular territorial space. Any time that social interactions come to be structured into recurring patterns, the structure thus formed develops an interest in its own maintenance and enhancement. It is in that sense that we speak of the interests of an organization, the interests of the system, and the like. To be sure, within cities, as within any other structure, one can find diverse social roles, each with its own set of interests. But these varying role interests, as divergent and competing as they may be, do not distract us from speaking of the overall interests of the larger structural entity.[8]

The point can be made less abstractly. A school system is a structured form of social action, and therefore it has an interest in maintaining and improving its material resources, its prestige, and its political power. Those policies or events which have such positive effects are said to be in the interest of the school system. An increase in state financial aid or the winning of the basketball tournament are events that, respectively, enhance the material well-being and the prestige of a school system and are therefore in its interest. In ordinary speech this is taken for granted, even when we also recognize that teachers, pupils, principals, and board members may have contrasting interests as members of differing role-groups within the school.

Although social roles performed within cities are numerous and conflicting, all are structured by the fact that they take place in a specific spatial location that falls within the jurisdiction of some local government. All members of the city thus come to share an interest in policies that affect the well-being of that territory. Policies which enhance the desirability or attractiveness of the territory are in the city's interest, because they benefit all residents—in their role as residents of the community. Of course, in any of their other social roles, residents of the city may be adversely affected by the policy. The Los Angeles dope peddler—in his role as peddler—hardly benefits from a successful drive to remove hard drugs from the city. On the other hand, as a resident of the city, he benefits from a policy that enhances the attractiveness of the city as a locale in which to live and work. In determining whether a policy is in the interest of a city, therefore, one does not consider whether it has a positive or negative effect on the total range of social interactions of each and every individual. That is an impossible task.

To know whether a policy is in a city's interest, one has to consider only the impact on social relationships insofar as they are structured by their taking place within the city's boundaries.

An illustration from recent policy debates over the future of our cities reveals that it is exactly with this meaning that the notion of a city's interest is typically used. The tax deduction that homeowners take on their mortgage interest payments should be eliminated, some urbanists have argued. The deduction has not served the interests of central cities, because it has provided a public subsidy for families who purchase suburban homes. Quite clearly, elimination of this tax deduction is not in the interest of those central city residents who wish to purchase a home in the suburbs. It is not in the interest of those central city homeowners (which in some cities may even form a majority of the voting population), who would then be called upon to pay higher federal taxes. But the policy might very well improve the rental market in the central city, thereby stimulating its economy—and it is for this reason that the proposal has been defended as being in the interest of central cities.

To say that people understand what, generally, is in the interest of cities does not eliminate debate over policy alternatives in specific instances. The notion of city interest can be extremely useful, even though its precise application in specific contexts may be quite problematic. In any policy context one cannot easily assert that one "knows" what is in the interest of cities, whether or not the residents of the city agree. But city residents do know the kind of evidence that must be advanced and the kinds of reasons that must be adduced in order to build a persuasive case that a policy is in the interest of cities. And so do community leaders, mayors, and administrative elites.

Economic Interests

Cities, like all structured social systems, seek to improve their position in all three of the systems of stratification—economic, social, and political—characteristic of industrial societies. In most cases, improved standing in any one of these systems helps enhance a city's position in the other two. In the short run, to be sure, cities may have to choose among economic gains, social prestige, and political weight. And because different cities may choose alternative objectives, one cannot state any one overarching objective—such as improved property values—that is always the paramount interest of the city. But inasmuch as improved economic or market standing seems to be an objective of great importance to most cities, I shall concentrate on this interest and only discuss in passing the significance of social status and political power.

Cities constantly seek to upgrade their economic standing. Following Weber, I mean by this that cities seek to improve their market position, their attractiveness as a locale for economic activity. In the market economy that characterizes Western society, an advantageous economic position means a competitive edge in the production and distribution of desired commodities relative to other localities. When this is present, cities can export goods and/or services to those outside the boundaries of the community.

Some regional economists have gone so far as to suggest that the welfare of a city is identical to the welfare of its export industry.[9] As exporters expand, the city grows. As they contract, the city declines and decays. The economic reasoning supporting such a conclusion is quite straightforward. When cities produce a good that can be sold in an external market, labor and capital flow into the city to help increase the production of that good. They continue to do so until the external market is saturated — that is, until the marginal cost of production within the city exceeds the marginal value of the good external to the city. Those engaged in the production of the exported good will themselves consume a variety of other goods and services, which other businesses will provide. In addition, subsidiary industries locate in the city either because they help supply the exporting industry, because they can utilize some of its by-products, or because they benefit by some economies of scale provided by its presence. Already, the familiar multiplier is at work. With every increase in the sale of exported commodities, there may be as much as a four- or fivefold increase in local economic activity.

The impact of Boeing Aircraft's market prospects on the economy of the Seattle metropolitan area illustrates the importance of export to regional economies. In the late sixties defense and commercial aircraft contracts declined, Boeing laid off thousands of workmen, the economy of the Pacific Northwest slumped, the unemployed moved elsewhere, and Seattle land values dropped sharply. More recently, Boeing has more than recovered its former position. With rapidly expanding production at Boeing, the metropolitan area is enjoying low unemployment, rapid growth, and dramatically increasing land values.

The same multiplier effect is not at work in the case of goods and services produced for domestic consumption within the territory. What is gained by a producer within the community is expended by other community residents. Residents, in effect, are simply taking in one another's laundry. Unless productivity increases, there is no capacity for expansion.

If this economic analysis is correct, it is only a modest oversimplification to equate the interests of cities with the interests of their export industries. Whatever helps them prosper redounds to the benefit of the community as a whole — perhaps four and five times over. And it is just such an economic analysis that has influenced many local government policies. Especially the smaller towns and cities may provide free land, tax concessions, and favorable utility rates to incoming industries.

The smaller the territory and the more primitive its level of economic development, the more persuasive is this simple export thesis. But other economists have elaborated an alternative growth thesis that is in many ways more persuasive, especially as it relates to larger urban areas. In their view a sophisticated local network of public and private services is the key to long-range economic growth. Since the world economy is constantly changing, the economic viability of any particular export industry is highly variable. As a result, a community dependent on any particular set of export industries will have only an episodic economic future. But with a well-developed infrastructure of services the city becomes an attractive locale for a wide variety of export industries. As older exporters fade, new exporters take their place and the community continues to prosper. It is in the city's interest, therefore, to help sustain a high-quality local infrastructure generally attractive to all commerce and industry.

I have no way of evaluating the merits of these contrasting economic arguments. What is important in this context is that both see exports as being of great importance to the well-being of a city. One view suggests a need for direct support of the export industry; the other suggests a need only for maintaining a service infrastructure, allowing the market to determine which particular export industry locates in the community. Either one could be the more correct diagnosis for a particular community, at least in the short run. Yet both recognize that the future of the city depends upon exporting local products. When a city is able to export its products, service industries prosper, labor is in greater demand, wages increase, promotional opportunities widen, land values rise, tax revenues increase, city services can be improved, donations to charitable organizations become more generous, and the social and cultural life of the city is enhanced.

To export successfully, cities must make efficient use of the three main factors of production: land, labor, and capital.[10]

Land

Land is the factor of production that cities control. Yet land is the factor to which cities are bound. It is the fact that cities are spatially defined units whose boundaries seldom change that gives permanence to their interests. City residents come and go, are born and die, and change their tastes and preferences. But the city remains wedded to the land area with which it is blessed (or cursed). And unless it can alter that land area, through annexation or consolidation, it is the long-range value of that land which the city must secure — and which gives a good approximation of how well it is achieving its interests.

Land is an economic resource. Production cannot occur except within some spatial location. And because land varies in its economic potential, so do the economic futures of cities. Historically, the most important variable affecting urban growth has been an area's relationship to land and water routes.

On the eastern coast of the United States, all the great cities had natural harbors that facilitated commercial relations with Europe and other coastal communities. Inland, the great industrial cities all were located on either the Great Lakes or the Ohio River–Mississippi River system. The cities of the West, as Elazar has shown, prospered according to their proximity to East-West trade flows.[11] Denver became the predominant city of the mountain states because it sat at the crossroads of land routes through the Rocky Mountains. Duluth, Minnesota, had only limited potential, even with its Great Lakes location, because it lay north of all major routes to the West.

Access to waterways and other trade routes is not the only way a city's life is structured by its location. Its climate determines the cost and desirability of habitation; its soil affects food production in the surrounding area; its terrain affects drainage, rates of air pollution, and scenic beauty. Of course, the qualities of landscape do not permanently fix a city's fate—it is the intersection of that land and location with the larger national and world economy that is critical. For example, cities controlling access to waterways by straddling natural harbors at one time monopolized the most valuable land in the region, and from that position they dominated their hinterland. But since land and air transport have begun to supplant, not just supplement, water transport, the dominance of these once favored cities has rapidly diminished.

Although the economic future of a city is very much influenced by external forces affecting the value of its land, the fact that a city has control over the use of its land gives it some capacity for influencing that future. Although there are constitutional limits to its authority, the discretion available to a local government in determining land use remains the greatest arena for the exercise of local autonomy. Cities can plan the use of local space; cities have the power of eminent domain; through zoning laws cities can restrict all sorts of land uses; and cities can regulate the size, content, and purpose of buildings constructed within their boundaries. Moreover, cities can provide public services in such a way as to encourage certain kinds of land use. Sewers, gas lines, roads, bridges, tunnels, playgrounds, schools, and parks all impinge on the use of land in the surrounding area. Urban politics is above all the politics of land use, and it is easy to see why. Land is the factor of production over which cities exercise the greatest control.

Labor

To its land area the city must attract not only capital but productive labor. Yet local governments in the United States are very limited in their capacities to control the flow of these factors. Lacking the more direct controls of nation-states, they are all the more constrained to pursue their economic interests in those areas where they do exercise authority.

Labor is an obvious case in point. Since nation-states control migration across their boundaries, the industrially more advanced have formally legislated that only limited numbers of outsiders—for example, relatives of citizens or those with skills needed by the host country—can enter. In a world where it is economically feasible for great masses of the population to migrate long distances, this kind of restrictive legislation seems essential for keeping the nation's social and economic integrity intact. Certainly, the wage levels and welfare assistance programs characteristic of advanced industrial societies could not be sustained were transnational migration unencumbered.

Unlike nation-states, cities cannot control movement across their boundaries. They no longer have walls, guarded and defended by their inhabitants. And as Weber correctly noted, without walls cities no longer have the independence to make significant choices in the way medieval cities once did.[12] It is true that local governments often try to keep vagrants, bums, paupers, and racial minorities out of their territory. They are harassed, arrested, thrown out of town, and generally discriminated against. But in most of these cases local governments act unconstitutionally, and even this illegal use of the police power does not control migration very efficiently.

Although limited in its powers, the city seeks to obtain an appropriately skilled labor force at wages lower than its competitors so that it can profitably export commodities. In larger cities a diverse work force is desirable. The service industry, which provides the infrastructure for exporters, recruits large numbers of unskilled workers, and many manufacturing industries need only semiskilled workers. When shortages in these skill levels appear, cities may assist industry in advertising the work and living opportunities of the region. In the nineteenth century when unskilled labor was in short supply, frontier cities made extravagant claims to gain a competitive edge in the supply of ordinary labor.

Certain sparsely populated areas, such as Alaska, occasionally advertise for unskilled labor even today. However, competition among most cities is now for highly skilled workers and especially for professional and managerial talent. In a less than full-employment economy, most communities have a surplus of semiskilled and unskilled labor. Increases in the supply of unskilled workers increase the cost of the community's social services. Since national wage laws preclude a decline in wages below a certain minimum, the increases in the cost of social services are seldom offset by lower wages for unskilled labor in those areas where the unemployed concentrate. But even with high levels of unemployment, there remains a shortage of highly skilled technicians and various types of white collar workers. Where shortages develop, the prices these workers can command in the labor market may climb to a level where local exports are no longer competitive with goods produced elsewhere. The economic health of a community is therefore importantly affected by the availability of professional and managerial talent and of highly skilled technicians.

When successfully pursuing their economic interests, cities develop a set of policies that will attract the more skilled and white collar workers without at the same time attracting unemployables. Of course, there are limits on the number of things cities can do. In contrast to nation-states they cannot simply forbid entry to all but the highly talented whose skills they desire. But through zoning laws they can ensure that adequate land is available for middle-class residences. They can provide parks, recreation areas, and good-quality schools in areas where the economically most productive live. They can keep the cost of social services, little utilized by the middle class, to a minimum, thereby keeping local taxes relatively low. In general, they can try to ensure that the benefits of public service outweigh their costs to those highly skilled workers, managers, and professionals who are vital for sustaining the community's economic growth.

Capital

Capital is the second factor of production that must be attracted to an economically productive territory. Accordingly, nation-states place powerful controls on the flow of capital across their boundaries. Many nations strictly regulate the amount of national currency that can be taken out of the country. They place quotas and tariffs on imported goods. They regulate the rate at which national currency can be exchanged with foreign currency. They regulate the money supply, increasing interest rates when growth is too rapid, lowering interest rates when growth slows down. Debt financing also allows a nation-state to undertake capital expenditures and to encourage growth in the private market. At present the powers of nation-states to control capital flow are being used more sparingly and new supranational institutions are developing in their place. Market forces now seem more powerful than official policies in establishing rates of currency exchange among major industrial societies. Tariffs and other restrictions on trade are subject to retaliation by other countries, and so they must be used sparingly. The economies of industrialized nations are becoming so interdependent that significant changes in the international political economy seem imminent, signaled by numerous international conferences to determine worldwide growth rates, rates of inflation, and levels of unemployment. If these trends continue, nation-states may come to look increasingly like local governments.

But these developments at the national level have only begun to emerge. At the local level in the United States, cities are much less able to control capital flows. In the first place, the Constitution has been interpreted to mean that states cannot hinder the free flow of goods and monies across their boundaries. And what is true of states is true of their subsidiary jurisdictions as well. In the second place, states and localities cannot regulate the money supply. If unemployment is low, they cannot stimulate the economy by increasing the monetary flow. If inflationary pressures adversely affect their competitive edge in the export market, localities can neither restrict the money supply nor directly control prices and wages. All of these powers are reserved for national governments. In the third place, local governments cannot spend more than they receive in tax revenues without damaging their credit or even running the risk of bankruptcy. Pump priming, sometimes a national disease, is certainly a national prerogative.

Local governments are left with a number of devices for enticing capital into the area. They can minimize their tax on capital and on profits from capital investment. They can reduce the costs of capital investment by providing low-cost public utilities, such as roads, sewers, lights, and police and fire protection. They can even offer public land free of charge or at greatly reduced prices to those investors they are particularly anxious to attract. They can provide a context for business operations free of undue harassment or regulation. For example, they can ignore various external costs of production, such as air pollution, water pollution, and the despoliation of trees, grass, and other features of the landscape. Finally, they can discourage labor from unionizing so as to keep industrial labor costs competitive.

This does not mean it behooves cities to allow any and all profit-maximizing action on the part of an industrial plant. Insofar as the city desires diversified economic growth, no single company can be allowed to pursue policies that seriously detract from the area's overall attractiveness to capital or productive labor. Taxes cannot be so low that government fails to supply residents with as attractive a package of services as can be found in competitive jurisdictions. Regulation of any particular industry cannot fall so far below nationwide standards that other industries must bear external costs not encountered in other places. The city's interest in attracting capital does not mean utter subservience to any particular corporation, but a sensitivity to the need for establishing an overall favorable climate.

In sum, cities, like private firms, compete with one another so as to maximize their economic position. To achieve this objective, the city must use the resources its land area provides by attracting as much capital and as high a quality labor force as is possible. Like a private firm, the city must entice labor and capital resources by offering appropriate inducements. Unlike the nation-state, the American city does not have regulatory powers to control labor and capital flows. The lack thereof sharply limits what cities can do to control their economic development, but at the same time the attempt by cities to maximize their interests within these limits shapes policy choice.

Local Government and the Interests of Cities

Local government leaders are likely to be sensitive to the economic interests of their communities. First, economic prosperity is necessary for protecting the fiscal base of a local government. In the United States, taxes on local sources and charges for local services remain important components of local government revenues. Although transfers of revenue to local units from the federal and state governments increased throughout the postwar period, as late as 1975–76 local governments still were raising almost 59 percent of their own revenue.[13] Raising revenue from one's own economic resources requires continuing local economic prosperity. Second, good government is good politics. By pursuing policies which contribute to the economic prosperity of the local community, the local politician selects policies that redound to his own political advantage. Local politicians, eager for relief from the cross-pressures of local politics, assiduously promote goals that have widespread benefits. And few policies are more popular than economic growth and prosperity. Third, and most important, local officials usually have a sense of community responsibility. They know that, unless the economic well-being of the community can be maintained, local business will suffer, workers will lose employment opportunities, cultural life will decline, and city land values will fall. To avoid such a dismal future, public officials try to develop policies that assist the prosperity of their community — or, at the very least, that do not seriously detract from it. Quite apart from any effects of economic prosperity on government revenues or local voting behavior, it is quite reasonable to posit that local governments are primarily interested in maintaining the economic vitality of the area for which they are responsible.

Accordingly, governments can be expected to attempt to maximize this particular goal — within the numerous environmental constraints with which they must contend. As policy alternatives are proposed, each is evaluated according to how well it will help to achieve this objective. Although information is imperfect and local governments cannot be expected to select the one best alternative on every occasion, policy choices over time will be limited to those few which can plausibly be shown to be conducive to the community's economic prosperity. Internal disputes and disagreements may affect policy on the margins, but the major contours of local revenue policy will be determined by this strategic objective.

NOTES

1. Flathman, R. E. 1966. *The public interest* (New York: John Wiley).

2. Banfield, E. C. 1961. *Political influence* (Glencoe, Illinois: Free Press). Ch. 12.

3. Tiebout, C. M. 1956, A pure theory of local expenditures. *Journal of Political Economy* 64: 416–24.

4. Ibid., p. 419.

5. Ibid., p. 420.

6. Bruce Hamilton, "Property Taxes and the Tiebout Hypothesis: Some Empirical Evidence," and Michelle J. White, "Fiscal Zoning in Fragmented Metropolitan Areas," in Mills, E. S., and Oates, W. E. 1975. *Fiscal zoning and land use controls* (Lexington, Massachusetts: Lexington Books). Chs. 2 and 3.

7. See Weber, "Class, Status, and Power," in Gerth, H. H., and Mills, C. W., trans. 1946. *From Max Weber* (New York: Oxford University Press).

8. For a more complete discussion of roles, structures, and interests, see Greenstone, J. D., and Peterson, P. E. 1976. *Race and authority in urban politics.* Phoenix edition. (Chicago: University of Chicago Press). Ch. 2.

9. cf. Thompson, W. R. 1965. *A preface to urban economics* (Baltimore, Maryland: Johns Hopkins University Press).

10. I treat entrepreneurial skill as simply another form of labor, even though it is a form in short supply.

11. Elazar, D. J. 1976. *Cities of the prairie.* New York: Basic Books.

12. Weber, M. 1921. *The city.* New York: Collier Books.

13. United States Department of Commerce, Bureau of the Census. 1977. *Local government finances in selected metropolitan areas and large counties: 1975–76.* Government finances: GF 76, no. 6.

3
City and Regime*
Stephen L. Elkin

It is unlikely that the workings of any political order are neutral if by this is meant that, at any given moment, its configuration advantages no interest or interests. The important question is whether such advantages are general, so that the workings of the political arrangements consistently favor some interests and impede others. If this is so, it is appropriate to speak of systematic bias. Such bias is particularly offensive under popular government since, by its very nature, it promises that the benefits and burdens of political life will not be systematically skewed. What is the case with the operation of popular control in the city?

It is most revealing to address the question of systematic bias by looking at the shape of the public agenda. What gets discussed logically precedes what actually gets decided on. To know which viewpoints are regularly advanced, which find it hard going, and which are not considered at all—as well as why these things occur—is to know a good deal more than how particular decisions are made and how controversies are resolved. For the decisions will reflect the kinds of viewpoints regularly advanced; bias in the agenda will be reflected by bias in decision.

Much political activity is, in fact, not directed at making decisions at all (i.e., at allocating goods and services and issuing regulations) but at maintaining existing patterns of access and excluding formulations of the public's business that will impede policies. Just as much effort is likely to be expended, for example, in ensuring that those neighborhood groups who might resist large-scale growth projects will find it difficult to mount serious electoral challenges as is expended in putting together the political and economic pieces of the project itself. This is the principal point of the Dallas study: virtuoso political talent was displayed in keeping control of the public agenda. Indeed, the premiere form of controlling the public agenda is to

*Elkin, Steven L. 1987. "City and Regime." Pp. 85–101 in *City and Regime in the American Republic.* Chicago: University of Chicago Press. Copyright © 1987 University of Chicago Press. Reprinted by permission of University of Chicago Press.

establish that the position and benefactions of those who dominate political pathways are not considered a fit subject for public discussion but are instead part of the natural order of things.

Decision making, in the sense of making and/or ratifying conscious choices through formal decision procedures, hardly exhausts what governments do, for much of what they do is routine. Indeed, the cumulation of these routine actions is likely to have marked consequences on the well-being of the urban citizenry, consequences perhaps even more marked than the results of public decision making. Again, a focus on the public agenda will be more revealing than an examination of particular decisions. Much government activity is a matter of following standard operating procedures, rules of thumb, professional practice, and the advice of valued clienteles or other interested parties who are regularly consulted. The attention to bond ratings by city financial officers, and their regular reminders to elected officials of the need to be able to market bonds at reasonable rates, is not a matter of decision making, as this is ordinarily understood. It is simply a matter of professionals doing their jobs. In the same way, much of the effort to facilitate growth in Dallas comes from the city manager and his staff following the canons of good professional practice. The content of the public agenda of course reflects these designations of what is routine and properly a matter for experts and what is suitable for public decision. But to say that something is best decided on by bureaucratic rule does not mean that there are no regular beneficiaries of such practices. Systematic bias may result from the mundane workings of city bureaucracies and the definition of expertise as well as from the more obvious stuff of political struggle.

A comprehensive analysis of systematic bias should not stop with an analysis of the public agenda. To guard against missing something significant, it is important to look at what is known about the actual pattern of results. We want, then, to look at the distribution of goods and services across population groups, for example, or at the direct impact of policy decisions, for example at the number of people displaced by land-use changes. But a focus on such outcomes is not enough for the assessment of systematic bias. Individual citizens will make various kinds of choices in response to their perceptions of how existing political arrangements work. They are likely to believe that the political arrangements that are responsible for the shape of public policy are difficult and expensive to alter. As a consequence they will, for example, sell their houses and change jobs because they sense that the drift of public policy makes this either advantageous or at least prudent. But the ability to adapt is differentially distributed. The result is that some citizens are more at risk from the shape of the public agenda and thus more regularly in need of having to adapt their behavior. These may also be the citizens least well equipped to do so. It is necessary only to add that the effects may well be cumulative. Every effort to adapt and every failure to do so may drain resources and morale. The cumulative effect of having to adapt one's behavior and of occasional or regular failures to do so will also affect the resources available for political activity. In short, the shape of the public agenda can have significant effects on who can participate effectively in the political life of the city.

Given the above understanding of systematic bias and the importance of the public agenda, we are in a position to interpret the analysis presented in the preceding chapters. Its main theme is that certain viewpoints and interests are regularly included on the agenda of city politics, others excluded, and yet others considered routine. What remains to be done is to draw out the implications in terms of systematic bias of what by now should, in any case, be reasonably apparent. For present purposes, the most important consideration is not the variety of urban political economies but their commonalities.

The discussion can be conveniently divided into three parts: city services, land-use control, and city jobs. These are the principal domains in which systematic bias, if it exists, can be expected. The distinction between city services and land-use control reflects the central role that the latter plays in the growth-oriented politics of the city.

City Services

The implication of the analysis in the preceding chapters is that there is no central directing force at work shaping the behavior of city bureaucracies. By and large, elected officials are willing to allow them substantial autonomy—and, in many cases, have no choice—while land-use interests have no continuing need to pay attention to the workings of the police department or the school board, for example. There are two principal exceptions: when major land-use changes require the special attentions of a service bureaucracy, for example, the police department, to make them successful and when periods of intense fiscal strain may prompt the natural alliance between elected officials and businessmen to exert substantial control over the service bureaucracies.

Rather than a central directing force being at work, the politics of most city services is dominated by the bureaucracies themselves, acting in concert with groups that are particularly attentive to their workings. Considerable effort goes into fending off the attentions of outside politicians and businessmen, and, in the manner of bureaucracies at other levels of government, what is sought is a secure environment in which to operate.[1] The agenda of each bureaucracy is likely to be shaped by some combination of professional criteria, the demands of interest groups, organizational maintenance requirements, and the givens of the service area. Although this is likely to mean that some groups are going to be favored by the politics of a particular bureaucracy, it also suggests that they will not be the same groups in each case. If nothing else, those bureaucracies whose professional criteria include a strong ethic of concern for low-income clienteles and those bureaucracies in which street-level personnel deal regularly with such clientele are likely to be more attentive than are other agencies to the concerns of the worse off. The combination of a lack of strong central direction and variation in the politics of the bureaucracies themselves suggests that the overall public agenda in this domain will evidence no systematic bias.

The inequalities associated with the impact of bureaucratic routines and with the content of the public agenda are unlikely, than, to cumulate. This being so, it is also unlikely that the politics of service delivery in the city will cause the same groups of people to see themselves at risk from the general pattern of service politics. Although there will be plenty of adaptive behavior by low-income residents aimed at avoiding what is thought to be the regular manner in which police behave, for example, these sorts of adaptations probably do not occur across the board.

Studies of the distribution of municipal services also support the conclusion that there is no systematic bias in service delivery. To date, there have been major investigations of the distribution of city services across major population groupings in Oakland, San Antonio, Detroit, Houston, and Chicago. They all come to essentially the same conclusion: in the words of one of the leading students of the subject, "distributional decision making is routinized and largely devoid of explicit political content."[2] It is, instead, the impact of past decisions, population shifts, technological changes, rational technical criteria, and professional values that is largely at work. In short, the givens of the situation in which the bureaucracy operates and its character as a particular kind of bureaucracy are largely crucial. None of this adds up to systematic bias. Perhaps the best way to characterize service delivery in the city is to say that it is a matter of unpatterned inequalities: those who come out on the short end in one case do not do so in all cases. And a little reflection suggests that it would be odd if it were otherwise. Bureaucracies are, after all, defined by their efforts to operate according to rules. Systematic bias is unlikely to spring from such soil.

City Jobs

The comments on the distribution of city jobs can be brief. The two principal devices for allocating them are the civil service system and the politics of coalition building in the city, with the mix between them varying by the type of city political economy. Both, however, point in the same direction: new entrants into the city political arena will find it difficult to gain a share of city jobs that corresponds with either their absolute numbers or their voting strength. The reasons are not far to seek. More or less by definition, the civil service system will slow the entry of new groups into the city bureaucracy. As for coalition building, the leaders of politically dominant groups are usually adept at doling out relatively large favors to the leadership of the new groups while at the same time giving little in the way of tangible benefits to the mass of new claimants.[3] The politics of city jobs is not an engine of redistribution from those who have to those who want. The claims of the latter must wait a long time before they become the subject of public discussion and decision.[4]

This having been said, ethnic and racial succession does occur and over a period of time substantial voting strength does convert into the material benefits of jobs. And if we add to this the more obvious point that city jobs have not been the object of burning desire by the better off, the case for the city as an engine of inequality is not easy to sustain. City politics is perhaps not the great equalizer that it is sometimes made out to be, but, at least in the case of city jobs, if new claimants are sufficiently numerous and willing to wait around long enough, they will eventually get their share.

The organization of the public agenda of city politics works, then, against city jobs for newcomers, and in its early stages the bias will be systematic. But eventually members of poorer racial and ethnic groups do get access. This is confirmed by detailed studies of the allocation of city jobs. For example, Browning et al., in their investigation of black and Hispanic political struggles in cities, conclude that from 1966 to 1978 minority employment in city jobs in ten cities increased faster than minority population. This was as true for lower-level jobs as for administrative positions. Particularly suggestive are the differences between black and Hispanic populations: the latter, who are comparative newcomers, lagged behind the former in the speed with which they entered the city employment force.[5]

Land-Use Control

The situation with land use is different. Here systematic bias is strongly and persistently evident, and thus there is a substantial failure of popular control. The extent of the failure is that much greater because land-use patterns are not just like the other "outputs" of city governments. They are more important to the shape of people's lives than variations in the quality of the services provided by the city. Spatial location means, among other things, access to jobs, friends, facilities, entertainment—in short to a whole environment. The importance of this access might be captured by saying that land-use patterns are not like commodities that are incidental to a life; they are, at a minimum, important contexts in which a life develops. More expansively considered, land-use patterns are integral to a person's conception of himself, to how he wishes to carry on his life: his life is *defined* by access to certain kinds of persons and activities. As such, access cannot be easily substituted for, as can a commodity. The loss of the environment in which the self has taken shape is likely to be an especially painful experience. Since in most cities city politics is now and for some time has been a matter of rearranging land use, the shape of the public agenda is a fundamental matter to the citizens of the city. Which powers and resources are to be brought to bear to influence land-use patterns matters in a way that few other public choices do.

The implication of the last three chapters is that the land-use agenda is, in fact, heavily tilted toward the land interests of the city. It is to their views that public officials are most attentive, and even when land interests are poorly organized, officials will have strong reasons to think about rearranging land use to promote city growth. As the Dallas case makes clear in a particularly vivid way, officials themselves happily will focus on city growth and, as circumstances demand, on rearranging land use. The concerns of those who can be expected to bear the principal burden of such changes are given less attention as are those who wish to argue that the growth of the city might be pursued in other ways or through other sorts of land-use projects.

Land use in the city is at the convergence of three streams of forces, and the public agenda represents the balance between them. Land is capital for those who own it or manage it, a context for the day-to-day lives of the citizens who live in the city, and a source of political benefits and revenues for the officials who govern the city. Once the mutuality of interest between those for whom land is capital and those for whom it is a benefit and revenue stream is noted, it is no great mystery that the city as community receives so little attention. Those for whom the city is a setting for their lives can of course make their concerns known to officials in their role as voters and members of interest groups, but in this they are competing not only with those for whom the city is capital but with officials who also are not focused on the city as community.

It only needs to be added that the bias of the land-use agenda also follows from what is considered to be a technical and legal matter not subject to public decision at all. If it were necessary to argue at every turn that a principal task of city government is to promote economic growth and to induce new investment, then the land-use agenda would undoubtedly look different. But the very jobs of many officials are defined in terms of responsibility for saying just these things. The principal reason why their jobs are defined this way resides in the division of labor between state and market and in the concomitant ability of capital to relocate relatively easily across regions. Said less abstractly, there would be fewer officials whose jobs are defined in terms of concern with investment and revenue—and thus fewer routine actions such as city promotional campaigns and studies of tax rebates—if the city did not need to compete for resources in the fashion that it does. The land-use agenda of the city is, at least in part, simply a question of public officials following their job specifications.

Not surprisingly, the record of the results of land-use projects parallels this characterization of the land-use agenda. There are several studies of the effects of land-use changes across the full range of cities, but their focus has been largely confined to the impact of the urban renewal program.[6] To get a sense of the full scale of land-use changes undertaken and the size of the effects on city residents, it will be more helpful to look briefly at two cities—San Francisco and Atlanta—that have been intensively studied. First, consider San Francisco.[7] As in many other older cities, one key to rearranging the land-use patterns in San Francisco was the effort to expand the central business district into the surrounding areas of lower-intensity use that typically housed the small businesses and the poorer residents of the city. Expansion to the west was impossible since this was the location of major hotels, and, in any case, the topography was difficult. To the north, lay the politically well-organized area of Chinatown, in addition to other difficulties, and to the east lay the Bay and wholesale-produce market. The latter proved easy to move. But the difficult and important part of the exercise was the move south into what became known as the Yerba Buena Center. At its core was to be a convention center and sports facility surrounded by office blocks. The convention center has, in fact, been built, along with some office buildings and housing for the elderly. The project, still not completed, has resulted in the displacement of some 4,000 people, the vast majority of whom were low- or modest-income residents, and some 700 businesses.

The other key to promoting the growth of the city was to rework some of the residential land-use patterns at the edge of the downtown.[8] The Western Addition (A-2) project was on land near the downtown, west of the city hall and within walking distance. The urban renewal plan called for clearing 103 of 276 acres of the project area, including two-thirds of the acres then in residential use. By 1970, some 2,000 housing units had been demolished and some 7,000 people, a substantial number of whom were low-income blacks, had been displaced. The A-2 project followed on the A-1 Western Addition project and displaced some 4,000 (mostly low-income) households and built some 1,800 new housing units, 65 percent of which were rented or sold at market rates and the rest of which were subsidized for middle-income people.[9]

The scale of these projects is suggested by the fact that they demolished 10,000 low-income housing units[10] in a city whose total population is now just over 700,000. Most of the units were either replaced by those at higher rents or not replaced at all. The answer to the question of whether the displaced residents might have gained from enhanced employment generated by the new office development is suggested by the fact that from 1965 to 1980 office growth in San Francisco created 16,000 new jobs but the number of employed residents of the city dropped by 18,000. This suggests that most of the jobs went to those who lived out of the city. So, unless taxes went down or services went up as a result of the land-use changes, the displaced residents gained little if anything. It is difficult to say much about the impact of the changes on city services, but we do know that the central business district's share of property taxes for the period 1965 to 1980 *fell* from 21.3 percent to 13.3 percent of the total. The question of compensation is not so easily disposed of and will be picked up again in a moment, but it is worth emphasizing that these figures are hardly comforting to those who wish to argue that significant changes in land use generate benefits for virtually all residents of the city.

The outline of Atlanta's alteration of its land-use patterns is not markedly different from that of San Francisco's; the same themes of expanding the central business district and eliminating low-income residences from the core of the city appear. In the case of Atlanta, however, there is an estimate available of the impact of all major public projects, not just of several large ones, as in San Francisco. It is estimated that from 1956 to 1966 21,000 families were displaced by governmental action in the city. This is on the order of one-fifth of the population of the city during that period.[11] This is simply an extraordinary figure—and any discussion of the supposed benefits of city-growth strategies built around land-use change must come to terms with it.

Those not yet convinced that both the land-use agenda and its results evidence systematic bias might also wish to contemplate that New York City has recently awarded $500 million in tax abatements to encourage businesses to remain in the city.[12] What is taken away with one hand—residences—is also taken away with the other, namely, potential tax revenues to support city services.

The effects of land-use changes are not confined to those that are a direct consequence of the exercise of governmental authority. Although large numbers of residents of the city will not be directly affected by land-use changes (though many more will be than typically is supposed), they will not be equally well placed to adapt to these changes. So, while one's home and job may remain intact, shops may be moved or their nature changed. For those with resources, reasonable and not markedly more expensive substitutes are available, whereas for those with limited resources, this is unlikely to be the case.

The question of compensation for the various sorts of burdens discussed up to this point must now be faced. After all, land-use changes are not advertised as being for the benefit of a selected few. They are presented in the language of the common good, and those who are inclined to believe—or, indeed, to make—such claims cannot be dismissed out of hand as being either deeply cynical or hopelessly naive. Might it not be true that one gives up one's home in the service of some future benefit—perhaps for a better job or for more city taxes, which will come back in the form of a safer neighborhood? Thus, the argument might go, however important land-use patterns are to the lives of city residents and however much the land-use agenda reflects projects that are to the taste of land interests, it is either wrong or incomplete to conclude that this is a case of systematic bias. Some of these considerations have been addressed above, but there are some general remarks that can be made about the nature of such arguments.

It seems reasonable to assume that people do not wish to move house or change jobs except as they choose to do so. So the question of whether someone can be said to approve of being displaced because he looks to future benefits (which is the form that the argument most often takes) depends on the understanding of "choice" in this context. The easiest way to make the point is to say that compensation for what one loses may assuage one's pain at a loss but is not the same thing as choosing to undergo the pain in order to get the prospective benefit. Of course, a person may in fact weight up what he is losing and his prospective gain and in a meaningful sense choose to undergo the present loss for the future gain. The crucial point is simply that we cannot infer that he has made such a choice from the fact that he has in fact received a gain great enough to bring him out ahead (which, in the present context, is doubtful in any case). People who accept post-facto compensation for automobile accidents that make them rich cannot be said to have chosen to undergo the accident. In much the same way, rational individuals who are thinking about the promised gain of relinquishing their homes will be aware that the gain is in the long run. And even if they have not heard of Keynes, they will no doubt reflect, with him, that in the long run we are all dead. In this they will be more realistic than those who argue that in the end benefits will be widely distributed.

The bias in the land-use agenda persists even if major land-use projects have come to a halt, as they probably have in many cities. Bias consists of the difficulty of substituting some other conception of how the powers and resources of the city shall be used in shaping land-use patterns—some conception that less closely follows the preferences of land interests and their allies among city officials. The flaw in the workings of popular control is that even if the land-use alliance is not for the moment in a position to engineer major land-use changes, it is still in a position to prevent the emergence of any other conception of the use of city powers. The new cannot be born even if the old is, for the moment, less ambitious than it has been.

PROBLEM SOLVING

The success or failure of popular control is not confined to matters of systematic bias, since the benefits of government are not confined to parceling out goods and services to particular persons and groups. City residents face collective problems, difficulties that, if not dealt with, will reduce the well-being of all. The distinction made by economists between private and public goods captures what is at issue.

What is the connection between effective problem solving and popular control? The simplest answer is that popular control is itself an organized way of solving social problems. Popular control is a mode of coordination, the way in which some collectivity is organized to consider the alternatives before it and decide on them. Of course, it may not do either of these in a conscious way, constructing a decision-making process designed to array the alternatives and choose among them. The point is simpler: coordination can take place without a central, directing mind, and thus problem solving is a generic aspect of all sorts of interactions. What from one viewpoint are relations of political control are, from another viewpoint, efforts at coordination as a means of coping with social problems.[13] Politics here meets problem solving.

An important implication of the coincidence of control and coordination is that, if the operation of popular control is systematically biased, problem solving is also likely to be ineffective, simply because some desirable alternatives will go unexplored. This is, of course, what is happening in cities: one version of how to make cities grow dominates and others—which might either spread the costs differently or involve something different than rearranging land use with an eye particularly to downtown development—are given little or no consideration.[14]

Any of the cities heretofore mentioned could provide an example of the domination of one solution to the problem of how to make cities grow economically, since a principal point of the preceding discussion has been that this is fundamental to what cities have in common. But a little detail, in the form of a brief description of Detroit, will prove useful here. First, consider that Detroit has been experiencing a significant decline in employment, from 630,000 in 1968 to 421,000 in 1977, a fall of 33 percent.[15] This correlates with an increase in both permanent unemployment and the welfare case load. Additionally, there has been a major fiscal crunch, with capital leaving the city, budget shortfalls, and property evaluations falling behind revenue needs.[16] Here, then, is a city with more than the usual need to promote city growth, and one in which doing so will have large collective benefits. Not doing anything will make virtually everyone worse off, not least by making the city an increasingly unpleasant place to be as a consequence of the resulting concentration of misery and anger.

In common with other cities, Detroit has adopted what might be termed a corporate-center strategy.[17] The underlying conception is to transform an aging industrial city into a modern headquarters city with the latter's attendant service sector, young professionals, and luxury consumption. This is, in short, the sort of city that corporate elites would like to work in, that they possibly might want to live in, and that they assume that their managers will also prefer. In other cities, the energy for promoting this conception is less likely to come from corporate leaders and more likely to come from the variety of other land interests, but the results are much the same. The centrality of the automobile industry to the Detroit economy explains the difference.[18]

Two comments are worth making about the strategy adopted. First, even if the overall conception of how to promote economic growth is granted, the mix of projects chosen is not exactly self-evident. The emphasis on the Renaissance Center, a development of hotels, shops and offices, betrays more a taste for making business decisions in pleasant surroundings than a serious concern for generating jobs. Beyond the short-lived construction jobs, it is hard to see how a local economy with a skilled industrial work force is going to gain very much.[19]

More telling, perhaps, is that the strategy itself is so oriented to restructuring land use. The model is one of building infrastructure and providing attractive parcels of land, along with attendant incentives to build on them. There is, of course, some connection between such construction and city economic activity, but it is not as obvious as the actions taken would suggest. At a minimum, there is some evidence—and certainly much belief—that fostering educational and entrepreneurial skills might do a good deal more to promote growth. But such nonphysical approaches receive little attention. Like some other cities, Detroit is like nothing so much as a third-world country that equates wealth with physical structures. This is, to say the least, strange in an economy whose managers (at some level) certainly know better. Popular control as it operates in cities does not allow such knowledge to shape the agenda of problem solving. Not surprisingly, it does not work much better in Detroit than in Africa.

As Lisa Peattie and her colleagues comment, development planning is difficult to do and far from generally supported. There are, they comment, a number of competing conceptions of what city planning should be about, but "development planning—i.e., planning for business—consistently remains the central concern of city government."[20] Increasingly, even in newer cities such as Dallas—where perhaps it once might have been argued that the strategies adopted for promoting growth made a good deal of sense—the signs are now apparent that they are starting on or are already well into the bricks-and-mortar version of city politics. The workings of popular control strongly dispose cities to such limited conceptions of the economic vitality of the city.

CONCLUSION

The promise of popular control of political authority is that it will make the benefits of collective life widely available and will draw on the intelligence of a wide range of citizens. Focusing particularly on the use of land—which is so central both to the politics of cities and to the lives of its citizens—cities evidence serious failings of popular control because they do not honor these promises. Of paramount importance are the common roots of these failings of city political institutions: both systematic bias and limited social intelligence stem from the historically constructed political-economic arrangements that strongly shape how city politics is carried on. Thus the failings are, in large part, systemic and can be traced to, among other things, that definition of property rights that provides significant incentives for public officials to join in alliance with city businessmen. The question of property rights will occupy our attention again below. Here I want to emphasize that efforts to improve political equality in the city will be doubly rewarded. Because of the common roots just noted, the result will be not only that the benefits and burdens of collective life will not be systematically skewed but also that there will be an increased chance for canvassing a wider range of views regarding how to make the city vital economically and in other ways. In the same vein, leaving the political institutions of the city as they are is to incur two losses. To talk, then, of a trade-off between equality and efficiency is to employ a misleading abstraction. When the actual political arrangements by which equality and efficiency are generated are entered into the equation, it is apparent that we are dealing neither with distinct processes nor distinct results. Not surprisingly, at least in this regard, political life is all of a piece. Benefits cumulate as do failures.

The reasons for systematic bias and limited social intelligence are not to be found in a kind of economic determinism in which cities are assumed to respond to the economic facts of life in the only way that makes sense. The argument here is more complex: things look as they do because of a complex of inherited structural factors, important among which is how officials get and stay elected. Officials pursue the policies that they do because the structural features within which they work dispose them to certain interpretations. The facts of economic life for the city offer choices regarding how to respond, but some kinds of choices—particularly a bricks-and-mortar strategy—have the inside track. A belief in the supposedly inexorable march of economic reality is the basis for arguments that, to get equality, some efficiency must be sacrificed. One must, that is, do something other than what the facts of economic life supposedly dictate. The discussion of the last several chapters points in a different direction—not to the reign of necessity, but to that of interpretation. The roots of the city's failures are not in the necessity of earning its keep but in how that impulse gets translated into action.

The political life of the city has, then, its own very important weight. Moreover, this conclusion, and the reasoning on which it rests, have a significance beyond the present discussion. The same worries about economic determinism and trade-offs will emerge in the later analysis of the city and citizenship. There too it will become apparent that, in the pursuit of a secure material foundation for the city, we need not trade off some measure of concern for the kind of citizenship necessary for a commercial republic to flourish. The sad thing in all this is that it is thought to be necessary to exchange the coin of political equality (and of appropriate citizenship) for that of effective problem solving. It is doubly sad because the supposed gains are mostly chimerical.[21]

Others have reached more benign conclusions about city politics. It would be tedious to inquire at length into why this is so. At the core of such views, however, are probably two beliefs. The first belief is that, since businessmen play so important a role in the politics of the city—and, indeed, are crucial to deciding on and carrying out a wide range of the most important policy choices, in short because they are much like public officials—they should be similarly understood. That is, it is appropriate to see them as actors whose concerns are citywide rather than parochial. That many businessmen have such large concerns is true. And indeed, at their best, they may act, as the Dallas case shows, in ways that are not overwhelmingly tainted by naked self-interest. But there is as much reason to inquire into such claims as there is to inquire into the claims of clubhouse political hacks that they speak for the commonweal even while they put in their bids for more patronage.

The second belief is that, since the benefits of at least some land-use schemes are immediate and large and the costs difficult to see, an inference can be made about the full run of development projects. Notions about compensation and long-run benefits smooth the way. In much the same way, since it seems that officials and businessmen are so naturally drawn to each other, the slide between what is natural and what is acceptable is easily made. The preceding discussion has offered at least some reasons why such convenient transitions need to be treated skeptically. More generally, it has offered reasons why skepticism is the appropriate response to arguments that cities must devote themselves to growth strategies while other levels of government handle whatever problems of inequality are to be found in the city. The difficulty is simply that the two cannot be so neatly separated. There is good reason to believe that growth strategies themselves contribute to inequality.

Resistance to these arguments about the shortcomings of popular control in cities might also come from those who would point to the efforts in some cities to alter systematic bias and to advance more effective strategies for promoting city growth. They might point to recent efforts in Boston to link downtown development to aid for the city's poor[22] or to innovative planning efforts in Hartford and other cities, where those calling themselves progressives have attempted to reorganize the way in which city politics is practiced.[23] There is nothing in such efforts that is inconsistent with the analysis offered here. Electoral coalitions that have at their heart something other than rearranging land use to favor downtown interests are certainly possible. Politicians in the cities *are* independent, not in the employ of land interests, and if there is sufficient public interest they can and will attempt to join their fate to that of other forces.

The problem is not whether aspiring politicians can run for office on some other platform and get elected. It is not easy, but they can. The problem, instead, is to sustain such efforts over any period of time. The difficulty is that eventually even officials otherwise committed will be drawn to large land-use schemes. This will be not so much because of the influence that land interests can wield and the campaign contributions they can offer, although these will help. But there are other forces at work as well: the exigencies of coalition building make large land-use projects attractive; and land interests and their schemes will look like an appealing way to keep mobile investors in the city and to attract new ones. Officials thus are likely to find their attention wandering down the paths suggested by land interests.

The battlefield of city politics is not flat but is tilted toward an alliance of public officials and land interests. Those who want it any other way must push uphill, whereas such an alliance only has to sit still and wait until the task of pushing the rock up the incline grows too burdensome. This alliance is the status quo. Others who seek new political arrangements are thereby considered to be radical. And, in addition, they must sustain their efforts and win at most if not at every turn. They must also build electoral coalitions, maintain them, and make them do some work. The natural order of things in city politics, therefore, is for the alliance between public officials and land interests to be in business.

The shortcomings of popular control in cities contribute to failings in the national political economy, and this is perhaps the saddest comment of all. It is in cities that the relative concentration of the have-nots might be expected to count politically, for numbers are, after all, their prime resource, as theorists from Aristotle to Dahl have pointed out. But the structural factors that make city politics what it is strongly militate against a politics that is attentive to those with limited resources. Thus, to the systematic bias characteristic of national politics must be added that of cities. In much the same way, the limits on intelligent social problem solving in cities are especially unsettling, since city governments provide the services that, in a day-to-day way, most affect the lives of the citizenry. A high order of social problem solving by city officials and citizens is, then, particularly important. But what one notices instead is a dreary sameness: cities do much the same things for much the same reasons. Again, structural factors are at work.

NOTES

1. See James Q. Wilson, *The Investigators: Managing FBI and Narcotics Agents.*

2. Kenneth Mladenka, "The Urban Bureaucracy and the Chicago Political Machine: Who Gets What and the Limits of Political Control," *American Political Science Review* 74, no. 4 (December 1980): 996.

3. See Stephen L. Elkin, "Political Structure, Political Organization and Race," *Politics and Society* 8, no. 2 (1978): 225–51.

4. See the discussions in Steven P. Erie, "Rainbow's End: From the Old to the New Urban Ethnic Politics," in Joan W. Moore and Lionel A. Maldonado (eds.), *Urban Ethnicity: A New Era*; and Raymond Wolfinger, *The Politics of Progress*, esp. chap. 3.

5. Rufus P. Browning et al., *Protest Is Not Enough: The Struggle of Blacks and Hispanics for Equality in Urban Politics*, chap. 5.

6. See, among others, Martin Anderson, *The Federal Bulldozer: A Critical Analysis of Urban Renewal, 1949–1962*; Scott A. Greer, *Urban Renewal and American Cities*; Heywood Sanders, "The Politics of City Redevelopment," Ph.D. diss., Harvard, 1977; and James Q. Wilson, ed., *Urban Renewal: The Record and the Controversy.*

7. For background on San Francisco politics and land-use trends, see Frederick M. Wirt, *Power in the City: Decision Making in San Francisco*; and Susan S. Fainstein et al., *Restructuring the City: The Political Economy of Urban Redevelopment.* The following discussion is based on Chester H. Hartman's, *The Transformation of San Francisco.*

8. The discussion here is based on John H. Mollenkopf, *The Contested City*, chaps. 4 and 5.

9. Susan S. Fainstein, Norman I. Fainstein, and P. Jefferson Armistead, "San Francisco: Urban Transformation and the Local 'State'" in Fainstein et al., *Restructuring the City*, 218.

10. Hartman, *The Transformation of San Francisco*, 231.

11. Clarence N. Stone, *Economic Growth and Neighborhood Discontent: System Bias in the Urban Renewal Program of Atlanta*, 237.

12. *New York Times*, May 4, 1983. The Industrial and Commercial Investment Board, which awards the abatements, began operating in 1977.

13. The premier statement in this regard is by Charles E. Lindblom. See *The Intelligence of Democracy* and *Politics and Markets.*

14. For some other possibilities and comments on the shortcomings of presently employed strategies, see Jane Jacobs, *Cities and the Wealth of Nations*; Katharine L. Bradbury et al., *Urban Decline and the Future of American Cities*; and Todd Swanstrom, *The Crisis of Growth Politics.* See also the discussion in chap. 9 below.

15. Richard Child Hill, "Crisis in the Motor City," in Fainstein et al., *Restructuring the City*.

16. See the account of some of the roots of Detroit's fiscal dilemma in *Business Week*, June 19, 1981.

17. Robert Fitch, "Planning New York," in Roger A. Alcaly and David Mermelstein (eds.), *The Fiscal Crisis of American Cities*.

18. On Detroit politics, in addition to Hill, see Thomas J. Anton, *Federal Aid to Detroit*; and Bryan Jones and Lynn Bachelor, *The Sustaining Hand*.

19. Two extensive reviews of the financial difficulties of the Center can be found in the *New York Times* for July 4, 1983, and September 1, 1986. The Center has had difficulty holding major retailers, and its owners have twice defaulted on mortgages.

20. Lisa Peattie et al., "Development Planning as the Only Game in Town," *Journal of Planning, Education and Research* 5, no. 1 (Autumn 1985): 17.

21. See Todd Swanstrom, "Semi-Sovereign Cities: The Political Logic of Urban Development"; and Marie Howland, "Property Taxes and the Birth and Intraregional Location of New Firms."

22. Which, it must be noted, has recently been overturned by the Massachusetts Superior Court. The decision was, however, overturned on appeal (*Bonan et al. v. City of Boston et al.* 398 Mass. 315, 496 N.E. ad. 640 [1986]), but the substantive merits of the linkage concept were not adjudicated. The Supreme Judicial Court suggested that the City of Boston seek authorization from the state legislature, where the matter now rests. In San Francisco similar efforts have been made to tie downtown development to neighborhood investment. Some cities have also started to impose exactions for purposes in addition to housing.

23. See Pierre Clavel, *The Progressive City*.

4

Urban Regimes:
A Research Perspective*

Clarence N. Stone

> *I have come across men of letters who have written history without taking part in public affairs, and politicians who have concerned themselves with producing events without thinking about them. I have observed that the first are always inclined to find general causes, whereas the second, living in the midst of disconnected daily facts, are prone to imagine that everything is attributable to particular incidents, and that the wires they pull are the same as those that move the world. It is to be presumed that both are equally deceived.*
> —*Alexis de Tocqueville*

What makes governance in Atlanta effective is not the formal machinery of government, but rather the informal partnership between city hall and the downtown business elite. This informal partnership and the way it operates constitute the city's regime; it is the means through which major policy decisions are made.

The word "regime" connotes different things to different people, but in this book regime is specifically about the *informal arrangements* that surround and complement the formal workings of governmental authority. All governmental authority in the United States is greatly limited—limited by the Constitution, limited perhaps even more by the nation's political tradition, and limited structurally by the autonomy of privately owned business enterprise. The exercise of public authority is thus never a simple matter; it is almost always enhanced by extraformal considerations. Because local governmental authority is by law and tradition even more limited than authority at the state and national level, informal arrangements assume special importance in urban politics. But we should begin our understanding of regimes by realizing that informal arrangements are by no means peculiar to cities or, for that matter, to government.

Even narrowly bounded organizations, those with highly specific functional responsibilities, develop informal governing coalitions.[1] As Chester Barnard argued many years ago, formal goals and formal lines of authority are insufficient by themselves to bring about coordinated action with sufficient energy to accomplish organizational purposes;[2] commitment and co-operation do not just spring up from the lines of an organization chart. Because every formal organization gives rise to an informal one, Barnard concluded, successful executives must master the skill of shaping and using informal organization for their purposes.

Attention to informal arrangements takes various forms. In the analysis of business firms, the school of thought labeled "transaction cost economics" has given systematic attention to how things actually get done in a world full of social friction—basically the same question that Chester Barnard considered. A leading proponent of this approach, Oliver Williamson,[3] finds that what he terms "private orderings" (as opposed to formal and legal agreements) are enormously important in the running of business affairs. For many transactions, mutual and tacit understanding is a more efficient way of conducting relations than are legal agreements and formal contracts. Williamson quotes a business executive as saying, "You can settle any dispute if you keep the lawyers and accountants out of it. They just do not understand the give-and-take needed in business."[4] Because informal understandings and arrangements provide needed flexibility to cope with nonroutine matters, they facilitate cooperation to a degree that formally defined relationships do not. People who know one another, who have worked together in the past, who have shared in the achievement of a task, and who perhaps have experienced the same crisis are especially likely to develop tacit understandings. If they interact on a continuing basis, they can learn to trust one another and to expect dependability from one another. It can be argued, then, that transactions flow more smoothly and business is conducted more efficiently when a core of insiders form and develop an ongoing relationship.

A regime thus involves not just any informal group that comes together to make a decision but an informal yet relatively stable group *with access to institutional resources* that enable it to have a sustained role in making governing decisions. What makes the group informal is not a lack of institutional connections, but the fact that the group, *as a group*, brings together institutional connections by an informal mode of cooperation. There is no all-encompassing structure of command that guides and synchronizes everyone's behavior. There is a purposive coordination of efforts, but it comes about informally, in ways that often depend heavily on tacit understandings.

If there is no overarching command structure, what gives a regime coherence? What makes it more than an "ecology of games"?[5] The answer is that the regime is purposive, created and maintained as a way of facilitating action. In a very important sense, *a regime is empowering*. Its supporters see it as a means for achieving coordinated efforts that might not otherwise be realized. A regime, however, is not created or redirected at will. Organizational analysis teaches us that cognition is limited, existing arrangements have staying power, and implementation is profoundly shaped by procedures in place.[6] Shrewd and determined leaders can effect purposive change, but only by being attentive to the ways in which existing forms of coordination can be altered or amplified.[7]

We can think of cities as organizations that lack a conjoining structure of command. There are institutional sectors within which the power of command may be much in evidence, but the sectors are independent of one another.[8] Because localities have only weak formal means through which coordination can be achieved, informal arrangements to promote coordination are especially useful. *These informal modes of coordinating efforts across institutional boundaries are what I call "civic cooperation."* In a system of weak formal authority, it holds special importance. Integrated with the formal structure of authority into a suprainstitutional capacity to take action, any informal basis of cooperation is empowering. It enables community actors to achieve cooperation beyond what could be formally commanded.

Consider the case of local political machines. When ward politicians learned to coordinate informally what otherwise was mired in institutional fragmentation and personal opportunism, the urban political machine was created and proved to have enormous staying power.[9] "Loyalty" is the shorthand that machine politicians used to describe the code that bound them into a cohesive group.[10] The political machine is in many ways the exemplar of governance in which informal arrangements are vital complements to the formal organization of government. The classic urban machines brought together various elements of the community in an informal scheme of exchange and cooperation that was the real governing system of the community.

The urban machine, of course, represents only one form of regime. In considering Atlanta, I am examining the governing coalition in a nonmachine city. The term "governing coalition" is a way of making the notion of regime concrete. It makes us face the fact that informal arrangements are held together by a core group—typically a body of insiders—who come together repeatedly in making important decisions. Thus, when I refer to the governing coalition in Atlanta, I mean the core group at the center of the workings of the regime.

To talk about a core group is not to suggest that they are of one mind or that they all represent identical interests—far from it. "Coalition" is the word I use to emphasize that a regime involves bringing together various elements of the community and the different institutional capacities they control. "Governing," as used in "governing coalition," I must stress, does not mean rule in command-and-control fashion. Governance through informal arrangements is about how some forms of coordination of effort prevail over others. It is about mobilizing efforts to cope and to adapt; it is not about absolute control. Informal arrangements are a way of bolstering (and guiding) the formal capacity to act, but even this enhanced capacity remains quite limited.

Having argued that informal arrangements are important in a range of circumstances, not just in cities, let me return to the specifics of the city setting. After all, the important point is not simply that there are informal arrangements; it is the particular features of urban regimes that provide the lenses through which we see the Atlanta experience. For cities, two questions face us: (1) Who makes up the governing coalition—who has to come together to make governance possible? (2) How is the coming together accomplished? These two questions imply a third: What are the consequences of the *who* and *how*? Urban regimes are not neutral mechanisms through which policy is made; they shape policy. To be sure, they do not do so on terms solely of the governing coalition's own choosing. But regimes are the mediating agents between the ill-defined pressures of an urban environment and the making of community policy. The *who* and *how* of urban regimes matter, thus giving rise to the further question of *with what consequences*. These three questions will guide my analysis of Atlanta.

URBAN REGIMES

As indicated above, an urban regime refers to the set of arrangements by which a community is actually governed. Even though the institutions of local government bear most of the formal responsibility for governing, they lack the resources and the scope of authority to govern without the active support and cooperation of significant private interests. An urban regime may thus be defined as *the informal arrangements by which public bodies and private interests function together in order to be able to make and carry out governing decisions.* These governing decisions, I want to emphasize, are not a matter of running or controlling everything. They have to do with *managing conflict* and *making adaptive responses* to social change. The informal arrangements through which governing decisions are made differ from community to community, but everywhere they are driven by two needs: (1) institutional scope (that is, the need to encompass a wide enough scope of institutions to mobilize the resources required to make and implement governing decisions) and (2) cooperation (that is, the need to promote enough cooperation and coordination for the diverse participants to reach decisions and sustain action in support of those decisions).

The mix of participants varies by community, but that mix is itself constrained by the accommodation of two basic institutional principles of the American political economy: (1) popular control of the formal machinery of government and (2) private ownership of business enterprise.[11] Neither of these principles is pristine. Popular control is modified and compromised in various ways, but nevertheless remains as the basic principle of government. Private ownership is less than universal, as governments do own and operate various auxiliary enterprises from mass transit to convention centers. Even so, governmental conduct is constrained by the need to promote investment activity in an economic arena dominated by private ownership. This political-economy insight is the foundation for a theory of urban regimes.[12]

In defining an urban regime as the informal arrangements through which public bodies and private interests function together to make and carry out governing decisions, bear in mind that I did not specify that the private interests are business interests. Indeed, in practice, private interests are not confined to business figures. Labor-union officials, party functionaries, officers in nonprofit organizations or foundations, and church leaders may also be involved.[13]

Why, then, pay particular attention to business interests? One reason is the now well-understood need to encourage business investment in order to have an economically thriving community. A second reason is the sometimes overlooked factor that businesses control politically important resources and are rarely absent totally from the scene. They may work through intermediaries, or some businesses may even be passive because others represent their interests as property holders, but a business presence is always part of the urban political scene. Although the nature of business involvement extends from the direct and extensive to the indirect and limited, the economic role of businesses *and the resources they control* are too important for these enterprises to be left out completely.

With revived interest in political economy, the regime's need for an adequate institutional scope (including typically some degree of business involvement) has received significant attention. However, less has been said about the regime's need for cooperation—and the various ways to meet it.[14] Perhaps some take for granted that, when cooperation is called for, it will be forthcoming. But careful reflection reminds us that cooperation does not occur simply because it is useful.

Robert Wiebe analyzed machine politics in a way that illustrates an important point: "The ward politician . . . required wider connections in order to manage many of his clients' problems. . . . Therefore clusters of these men allied to increase their bargaining power in city affairs. But if logic led to an integrated city-wide organization, the instinct of self-preservation did not. The more elaborate the structure, the more independence the ward bosses and area chieftains lost."[15] Cooperation can thus never be taken as a given; it must be achieved and at significant costs. Some of the costs are visible resources expended in promoting cooperation—favors and benefits distributed to curry reciprocity, the effort required to establish and maintain channels of communication, and responsibilities borne to knit activities together are a few examples. But, as Wiebe's observation reminds us, there are less visible costs. Achieving cooperation entails commitment to a set of relationships, and these relationships limit independence of action. If relationships are to be ongoing, they cannot be neglected; they may even call for sacrifices to prevent alienating allies. Forming wider connections is thus not a cost-free step, and it is not a step that community actors are always eager to take.

Because centrifugal tendencies are always strong, achieving cooperation is a major accomplishment and requires constant effort. Cooperation can be brought about in various ways. It can be induced if there is an actor powerful enough to coerce others into it, but that is a rare occurrence, because power is not usually so concentrated. More often, cooperation is achieved by some degree of reciprocity.

The literature on collective action focuses on the problem of cooperation in the absence of a system of command. For example, the "prisoner's dilemma" game instructs us that noncooperation may be invited by a number of situations.[16] In the same vein, Mancur Olson's classic analysis highlights the free-rider problem and the importance of selective incentives in inducing cooperation.[17] Alternatively, repeated interactions permit people to see the shortcomings of mutual noncooperation and to learn norms of cooperation.[18] Moreover, although Robert Axelrod's experiments with TIT FOR TAT computer programs indicate that cooperation can be instrumentally rational under some conditions, the process is not purely mechanical.[19] Students of culture point to the importance of common identity and language in facilitating interaction and promoting trust.[20] Size of group is also a consideration, affecting the ease of communication and bargaining among members; Michael Taylor, for example, emphasizes the increased difficulty of conditional cooperation in larger groups.[21]

What we can surmise about the urban community is thus twofold: (1) cooperation across institutional lines is valuable but far from automatic; and (2) cooperation is more likely to grow under some circumstances than others. This conclusion has wide implications for the study of urban politics. For example, much of the literature on community power has centered on the question of control, its possibilities and limitations: to what extent is domination by a command center possible and how is the cost of social control worked out. The long-standing elitist-pluralist debate centers on such questions. However, my line of argument here points to another way of viewing urban communities; it points to the need to think about cooperation, its possibilities and limitations — not just any cooperation, but cooperation of the kind that can bring together people based in different sectors of a community's institutional life and that enables a coalition of actors to make and support a set of governing decisions.

If the conventional model of urban politics is one of social control (with both elitist and pluralist variants), then the one proposed here might be called "the social-production model." It is based on the question of how, in a world of limited and dispersed authority, actors work together across institutional lines to produce a capacity to govern and to bring about publicly significant results.

To be sure, the development of a system of cooperation for governing is something that arises, not from an unformed mass, but rather within a structured set of relationships. Following Stephen Elkin, I described above the basic configuration in political-economy terms: popular control of governmental authority and private ownership of business activity. However, both of these elements are subject to variation. Populations vary in characteristics and in type of political organization; hence, popular control comes in many forms. The economic sector itself varies by the types of businesses that compose it and by the way in which it is organized formally and informally. Hence there is no one formula for bringing institutional sectors into an arrangement for cooperation, and the whole process is imbued with uncertainty. Cooperation is always somewhat tenuous, and it is made more so as conditions change and new actors enter the scene.

The study of urban regimes is thus a study of who cooperates and how their cooperation is achieved across institutional sectors of community life. Further, it is an examination of how that cooperation is maintained when confronted with an ongoing process of social change, a continuing influx of new actors, and potential break-downs through conflict or indifference.

Regimes are dynamic, not static, and regime dynamics concern the ways in which forces for change and forces for continuity play against one another. For example, Atlanta's governing coalition has displayed remarkable continuity in the post-World War II period, and it has done so despite deep-seated forces of social change. Understanding Atlanta's urban regime involves understanding how cooperation can be maintained and continuity can prevail in the face of so many possibilities for conflict.

STRUCTURE, ACTION, AND STRUCTURING

Because of the interplay of change and continuity, urban regimes are perhaps best studied over time. Let us, then, take a closer look at historical analysis. Scholars make sense out of the particulars of political and social life by thinking mainly in terms of abstract structures such as democracy and capitalism. Although these are useful as shorthand, the danger in abstractions is that they never capture the full complexity and contingency of the world. Furthermore, "structure" suggests something solid and unchanging, yet political and social life is riddled with contradictions and uncertainties that give rise to an ongoing process of change and adjustment. Much of the change that occurs is at the margins of basic and enduring relationships, making it easy to think in terms of order and stability. Incrementalists remind us that the present is the best predictor of the near future. But students of history, especially those accustomed to looking at longer periods of time, offer a different perspective. They see a world undergoing change, in which various actors struggle over what the terms of that change will be. It is a world shaped and reshaped by human efforts, a world that never quite forms a unified whole.

In historical light, social structures are less solid and less fixed than social scientists have sometimes assumed. Charles Tilly has argued that there is no single social structure. Instead, he urges us to think in terms of multiple structures, which "consist of shifting, constructed social relations among limited numbers of actors."[22] Philip Abrams also sees structures as relationships, relationships that are socially fabricated and subject to purposive modification.[23]

Structures are real but not fixed. Action does not simply occur within the bounds set by structures but is sometimes aimed at the structures themselves, so that a process of reshaping is taking place at all times. Abrams thus argues that events have a two-sided character, involving both structure and action in such a way that action shapes structures and structures shape actions. Abrams calls for the study of a process he labels as "structur*ing*," by which he means that events occur in a structured context and that events help reshape structure.[24]

Abrams therefore offers a perspective on the interplay of change and continuity. This continuity is not so much a matter of resisting change as coping with it. Because the potential for change is ever present, regime continuity is a remarkable outcome. Any event contains regime-altering potential—perhaps not in sudden realignment, but in opening up a new path along which subsequent events can cumulatively bring about fundamental change.[25] The absence of regime alteration is thus an outcome to be explained, and it must be explained in terms of a capacity to adapt and reinforce existing structures. Events are the arena in which the struggle between change and continuity is played out, but they are neither self-defining nor free-formed phenomena. They become events in our minds because they have some bearing on structures that help shape future occurrences. It is the interplay of event and structure that is especially worthy of study. To identify events, one therefore needs to have some conception of structure. In this way, the researcher can focus attention, relieved of the impossible task of studying everything.

There is no escaping the necessity of the scholar's imposing some form of analysis on research. The past becomes known through the concepts we apply. Abrams sees this as the heart of historical sociology: "The reality of the past is just not 'there' waiting to be observed by the resurrectionist historian. It is to be known if at all through strenuous theoretical alienation."[26] He also reminds us that many aspects of an event cannot be observed in a direct sense; too much is implicit at any given moment.[27] That is why the process, or the flow of events over time, is so important to examine. That is also why events are not necessarily most significant for their immediate impact; they may be more significant for their bearing on subsequent events, thus giving rise to modifications in structure.

PROLOGUE TO THE ATLANTA NARRATIVE

Structuring in Atlanta is a story in which race is central. If regimes are about who cooperates, how, and with what consequences, one of the remarkable features of Atlanta's urban regime is its biracial character. How has cooperation been achieved across racial lines, particularly since race is often a chasm rather than a bridge? Atlanta has been governed by a biracial coalition for so long that it is tempting to believe that nothing else was possible. Yet other cities followed a different pattern. At a time when Atlanta prided itself on being "the city too busy to hate," Little Rock, Birmingham, and New Orleans pursued die-hard segregation and were caught up in racial violence and turmoil. The experience of these cities reminds us that Atlanta's regime is not simply an informal arrangement through which popular elections and private ownership are reconciled, but is deeply intertwined with race relations, with some actors on the Atlanta scene able to overcome the divisive character of race sufficiently to achieve cooperation.

Atlanta's earlier history is itself a mixed experience, offering no clear indication that biracial cooperation would emerge and prevail in the years after World War II. In 1906, the city was the site of a violent race riot apparently precipitated by inflammatory antiblack newspaper rhetoric.[28] The incident hastened the city's move toward the economic exclusion and residential segregation of blacks, their disenfranchisement, and enforcement of social subordination; and the years after 1906 saw the Jim Crow system fastened into place. Still, the riot was followed by modest efforts to promote biracial understanding, culminating in the formation in 1919 of the Commission on Interracial Cooperation.

Atlanta, however, also became the headquarters city for a revived Ku Klux Klan. During the 1920s, the Klan enjoyed wide support and was a significant influence in city elections. At this time, it gained a strong foothold in city government and a lasting one in the police department.[29] In 1930, faced with rising unemployment, some white Atlantans also founded the Order of Black Shirts for the express purpose of driving blacks out of even menial jobs and replacing them with whites. Black Shirt protests had an impact, and opportunities for blacks once again were constricted. At the end of World War II, with Atlanta's black population expanding beyond a number that could be contained in the city's traditionally defined black neighborhoods, another klanlike organization, the Columbians, sought to use terror tactics to prevent black expansion into previously all-white areas. All of this occurred against a background of state and regional politics devoted to the subordination of blacks to whites—a setting that did not change much until the 1960s.

Nevertheless, other patterns surfaced briefly from time to time. In 1932, Angelo Herndon, a black Communist organizer, led a mass demonstration of white and black unemployed protesting a cutoff of work relief. Herndon was arrested, and the biracial following he led proved short-lived. Still, the event had occurred, and Atlanta's city council did in fact accede to the demand for continued relief.[30] In the immediate postwar period, a progressive biracial coalition formed around the successful candidacy of Helen Douglas Mankin for a congressional seat representing Georgia's fifth district. That, too, was short-lived, as ultra-conservative Talmadge forces maneuvered to reinstitute Georgia's county-unit system for the fifth district and defeat Mankin with a minority of the popular vote.[31]

It is tempting to see the flow of history as flux, and one could easily dwell on the mutable character of political alignments. The Atlanta experience suggests that coalitions often give expression to instability. Centrifugal forces are strong, and in some ways disorder is a natural state. What conflict does not tear asunder, indifference is fully capable of wearing away.

The political incorporation of blacks into Atlanta's urban regime in tight coalition with the city's white business elite is thus not a story of how popular control and private capital came inevitably to live together in peace and harmony. It is an account of struggle and conflict—bringing together a biracial governing coalition at the outset, and then allowing each of the coalition partners to secure for itself an advantageous position within the coalition. In the first instance, struggle involved efforts to see that the coalition between white business interests and the black middle class prevailed over other possible alignments. In the second instance, there was struggle over the terms of coalition between the partners; thus political conflict is not confined to "ins" versus "outs." Those on the inside engage in significant struggle with one another over the terms on which cooperation will be maintained, which is one reason governing arrangements should never be taken for granted.

Atlanta's urban regime therefore appears to be the creature of purposive struggle, and both its establishment and its maintenance call for a political explanation. The shape of the regime was far from inevitable, but rather came about through the actions of human agents making political choices. Without extraeconomic efforts by the city's business leadership, Atlanta would have been governed in a much different manner, and Atlanta's urban regime and the policies furthered by that regime might well have diverged from the path taken. History, perhaps, is as much about alternatives not pursued as about those that were. . . .

THE POLITICAL RAMIFICATIONS
OF UNEQUAL RESOURCES

From Aristotle to Tocqueville to the present, keen political observers have understood that politics evolves from and reflects the associational life of a community. How people are grouped is important—so much so that, as the authors of the *Federalist* essays understood, the formation and reformation of coalitions is at the heart of political activity. Democracy should be viewed within that context; i.e., realizing that people do not act together simply because they share preferences on some particular issue.

Overlooking that long-standing lesson, many public-choice economists regard democracy with suspicion. They fear that popular majorities will insist on an egalitarian redistribution of benefits and thereby interfere with economic productivity. As worded by one economist, "The majority (the poor) will always vote for taxing the minority (the rich), at least until the opportunities for benefiting from redistribution run out."[32] In other words, majority rule will overturn an unequal distribution of goods and resources. This reasoning, however, involves the simple-minded premise that formal governmental authority confers a capacity to redistribute at the will of those who hold office by virtue of popular election. The social-production model of politics employed here offers a contrasting view. Starting from an assumption about the costliness of civic cooperation, the social production model suggests that an unequal distribution of goods and resources substantially modifies majority rule.

In operation, democracy is a great deal more complicated than counting votes and sorting through the wants of rational egoists. In response to those who regard democracy as a process of aggregating preferences within a system characterized by formal equality, a good antidote is Stein Rokkan's aphorism, "Votes count by resources decide."[33] Voting power is certainly not insignificant, but policies are decided mainly by those who control important concentrations of resources. Hence, governing is never simply a matter of aggregating numbers, whether for redistribution or other purposes.

How governing coalitions are put together is the focus of this book. An underlying question throughout has been why one alignment has prevailed over others. The Atlanta case suggests that a key factor is control of resources in a quantity and of a kind that can lead groups to ally with one set of arrangements instead of another. Thus any element of the community that has a unique capacity to promote action—whether by making side payments, affording small opportunities, or some other means—has a claim on membership in the governing coalition.

Of course, the election of key public officials provides a channel of popular expression. Since democracy rests on the principle of equal voting power, it would seem that all groups do share in the capacity to become part of the governing regime. Certainly the vote played a major role in the turnaround of the position of blacks in Atlanta. Popular control, however, is not a simple and straightforward process. Much depends on how the populace is organized to participate in a community's civic life. Machine politics, for example, promotes a search for personal favors. With electoral mobilization dependent upon an organizational network oriented toward patronage and related considerations, other kinds of popular concerns may have difficulty gaining expression.[34] The political machine thus enjoys a type of preemptive power, though the party organization is only one aspect of the overall governing regime.

On the surface, Atlanta represents a situation quite different from machine politics. Nonpartisan elections and an absence of mass patronage have characterized the city throughout the post-World War II era. Yet it would hardly be accurate to describe civic life in Atlanta as open and fluid. Nonpartisanship has heightened the role of organizations connected to business, and the newspapers have held an important position in policy debate. At the same time, working-class organizations and nonprofit groups unsupported by business are not major players in city politics.

Within Atlanta's civic sector, activities serve to piece together concerns across the institutional lines of the community, connecting government with business and each with a variety of nonprofit entities. The downtown elite has been especially adept at building alliances in that sector and, in doing so, has extended its resource advantage well beyond the control of strictly economic functions. Responding to its own weakness in numbers, the business elite has crafted a network through which cooperation can be advanced and potential cleavages between haves and have-nots redirected.

Consider what Atlanta's postwar regime represents. In 1946, the central element in the governing coalition was a downtown business elite organized for and committed to an active program of redevelopment that would transform the character of the business district and, in the process, displace a largely black population to the south and east of the district. At the same time, with the end of the white primary that same year, a middle-class black population, long excluded from power, mobilized its electoral strength to begin an assault on a firmly entrenched Jim Crow system. Knowing only those facts, one might well have predicted in 1946 that these two groups would be political antagonists. They were not. Both committed to an agenda of change, they worked out an accommodation and became the city's governing coalition. The alliance has had its tensions and even temporary ruptures, but it has held and demonstrated remarkable strength in making and carrying out policy decisions.

To understand the process, the Atlanta experience indicates that one must appreciate institutional capacities and the resources that various groups control. That is why simple preference aggregation is no guide to how coalitions are built. The downtown elite and the black middle class had complementary needs that could be met by forming an alliance, and the business elite in particular had the kind and amount of resources to knit the alliance together.

Politics in Atlanta, then, is not organized around an overriding division between haves and have-nots. Instead, unequally distributed resources serve to destabilize opposition and encourage alliances around small opportunities. Without command of a capacity to govern, elected leaders have difficulty building support around popular discontent. That is why Rokkan's phrase, "Votes count but resources decide," is so apt.

UNEQUAL RESOURCES AND URBAN REGIMES

Regimes, I have suggested, are to be understood in terms of (1) who makes up the governing coalition and (2) how the coalition achieves cooperation. Both points illustrate how the unequal distribution of resources affects politics and what differences the formation of a regime makes. That the downtown elite is a central partner in the Atlanta regime shapes the priorities set and the trade-offs made. Hence, investor prerogative is protected practice in Atlanta, under the substantial influence of the business elite *within* the governing coalition. At the same time, the fact that the downtown elite is part of a governing coalition prevents business isolation from community affairs. Yet, although "corporate responsibility" promotes business involvement, it does so in a way that enhances business as patron and promoter of small opportunities.

Similarly, the incorporation of the black middle class into the mainstream civic and economic life of Atlanta is testimony to its ability to use electoral leverage to help set community priorities. The importance of the mode of cooperation is also evident. Although much of what the regime has done has generated popular resistance, the black middle class has been persuaded to go along by a combination of selective incentives and small opportunities. Alliance with the business elite enabled the black middle class to achieve particular objectives not readily available by other means. This kind of enabling capacity is what gives concentrated resources its gravitational force.

The pattern thus represents something more than individual cooptation. The black middle class as a group benefited from new housing areas in the early postwar years and from employment and business opportunities in recent years. Some of the beneficiaries have been institutional—colleges in the Atlanta University system and a financially troubled bank, for example. Because the term "selective incentives" implies individual benefits (and these have been important), the more inclusive term "small opportunities" provides a useful complement. In both cases, the business elite is a primary source; they can make things happen, provide needed assistance, and open up opportunities. At the same time, since the downtown elite needs the cooperation of local government and various community groups, the elite itself is drawn toward a broad community-leadership role. Although its bottom-line economic interests are narrow, its community role can involve it in wider concerns. Selective incentives, however, enable the elite to muffle some of the pressure that might otherwise come from the larger community.

Once we focus on the regime and the importance of informally achieved cooperation, we can appreciate better the complex way in which local politics actually functions. Public-choice economists, fearful that democracy will lead to redistribution, misunderstand the process and treat politics as a causal force operating in isolation from resources other than the vote. That clearly is unwarranted. Atlanta's business elite possesses substantial slack resources that can be and are devoted to politics. Some devotion of resources to political purposes is direct, in the form of campaign funds, but much is indirect; it takes on the character of facilitating civic cooperation of those efforts deemed worthy.

The business elite is small and homogeneous enough to use the norms of class unity and corporate responsibility to maintain its cohesion internally. In interacting with allies, the prevailing mode of operation is reciprocity, reinforced in many cases by years of trust built from past exchanges. The biracial insiders have also been at their tasks long enough to experience a sense of pride in the community role they play. Even so, the coalition is centered around a combination of explicit and tacit deals. Reciprocity is thus the hallmark of Atlanta's regime, and reciprocity hinges on what one actor can do for another. Instead of promoting redistribution toward equality, such a system perpetuates inequality.

Reciprocity, of course, occurs in a context, and in Atlanta, it is interwoven with a complex set of conditions. The slack resources controlled by business corporations give them an extraordinary opportunity to promote civic cooperation. Where there is a compelling mutual interest, as within Atlanta's downtown elite, businesses have the means to solve their own collective-action problem and unite behind a program of action. Their resources also enable them to create a network of cooperation that extends across lines of institutional division, which makes them attractive to public officials and other results-oriented community groups. In becoming an integral part of a system of civic cooperation, Atlanta's business elite has used its resource advantage to shape community policy and protect a privileged position. Because the elite is useful to others, it attracts and holds a variety of allies in its web of reciprocity. The concentration of resources it has gathered thus enables the elite to counter demands for greater equality.

SOCIAL LEARNING VERSUS PRIVILEGE

Instead of understanding democratic politics as an instance of the equality (redistribution)/efficiency (productivity) trade-off, I suggest an alternative. Policy actions (and inactions) have extensive repercussions and involve significant issues that do not fit neatly into an equality-versus-efficiency mold. There is a need, then, for members of the governing coalition to be widely informed about a community's problems, and not to be indifferent about the information. That is what representative democracy is about.

For their part, in order to be productive, business enterprises need a degree of autonomy and a supply of slack resources. It is also appropriate that they participate in politics. However, there are dangers involved in the ability of high-resource groups, like Atlanta's business elite, to secure for themselves a place in the governing coalition and then use that inside position along with their own ample resources to shape the regime on their terms. Elsewhere I have called this "preemptive power,"[35] and have suggested that it enables a group to protect a privileged position. The ability to parcel out selective incentives and other small opportunities permits Atlanta's business elite to enforce discipline on behalf of civic cooperation by vesting others with lesser privileges—privileges perhaps contingently held in return for "going along."

The flip side of discipline through selective incentives is a set of contingent privileges that restrict the questions asked and curtail social learning. Thus one of the trade-offs in local politics can be phrased as social learning versus privilege. Some degree of privilege for business may be necessary to encourage investment, but the greater the privilege being protected, the less the incentive to understand and act on behalf of the community in its entirety.

The political challenge illustrated by the Atlanta case is how to reconstitute the regime so that both social learning and civic cooperation occur. The risk in the present situation is that those who govern have only a limited comprehension of the consequences of their actions. Steps taken to correct one problem may create or aggravate another while leaving still others unaddressed. Those who govern can discover that only, it seems, through wide representation of the affected groups. Otherwise, choices are limited by an inability to understand the city's full situation.

No governing coalition has an inclination to expand the difficulties of making and carrying out decisions. Still, coalitions can be induced to attempt the difficult. For example, Atlanta's regime has been centrally involved in race relations, perhaps the community's most difficult and volatile issue. Relationships within the governing coalition have been fraught with tension; friction was unavoidable. Yet the coalition achieved a cooperative working relationship between the black middle class and the white business elite. In a rare but telling incident, black leaders insisted successfully that a 1971 pledge to build a MARTA spur to a black public-housing area not be repudiated. The newspaper opined that trust within the coalition was too important to be sacrificed on the altar of economizing. Thus the task of the governing regime was expanded beyond the narrow issue of serving down-town in the least expensive manner possible; concerns *can* be broadened.

Although no regime is likely to be totally inclusive, most regimes can be made more inclusive. Just as Atlanta's regime was drawn into dealing with race relations, others can become sensitive to the situations of a larger set of groups. Greater inclusiveness will not come automatically nor from the vote alone. Pressures to narrow the governing coalition are strong and recurring. Yet, if civic cooperation is the key to the terms on which economic and electoral power are accommodated, then more inclusive urban regimes can be encouraged through an associational life at the community level that reflects a broad range of perspectives. The problem is not an absence of associational life at that level but how to lessen its dependence on business sponsorship, how to free participation in civic activity from an overriding concern with protecting insider privileges, and how to enrich associational life so that nonprofit and other groups can function together as they express encompassing community concerns.

This step is one in which federal policy could make a fundamental difference. In the past, starting with the urban-redevelopment provision in the 1949 housing act and continuing through the Carter administration's UDAG program, cities have been strongly encouraged to devise partnerships with private, for-profit developers, thus intensifying already strong leanings in that direction. Since these were matters of legislative choice, it seems fully possible for the federal government to move in another direction and en-courage nonprofit organizations. The federal government could, for exam-ple, establish a program of large-scale assistance to community development corporations and other nonprofit groups. Some foundations now support such programs, but their modest efforts could be augmented. Programs of community service required by high schools and colleges or spawned by a national-level service requirement could increase voluntary participation and alter the character of civic life in local communities. It is noteworthy that neighborhood mobilization in Atlanta was partly initiated by VISTA (Volunteers in Service to America) workers in the 1960s and continued by those who stayed in the city after completing service with VISTA. This, however, is not the place to prescribe a full set of remedies; my aim is only to indicate that change is possible but will probably require a stimulus external to the local community.

SUMMING UP

If the slack resources of business help to set the terms on which urban governance occurs, then we need to be aware of what this imbalance means. The Atlanta case suggests that the more uneven the distribution of resources, the greater the tendency of the regime to become concerned with protecting privilege. Concurrently, there is a narrowing of the regime's willingness to engage in "information seeking" (or social learning). Imbalances in the civic sector thus lead to biases in policy, biases that electoral politics alone is unable to correct.

A genuinely effective regime is not only adept at promoting cooperation in the execution of complex and nonroutine projects, but is also able to comprehend the consequences of its actions and inactions for a diverse citizenry. The promotion of this broad comprehension is, after all, a major aim of democracy. Even if democratic politics were removed from the complexities of coordination for social production, it still could not be reduced to a set of decision rules. Arrow's theorem shows that majority choices cannot be neutrally aggregated when preference structures are complex,[36] as indeed they are bound to be in modern societies.

Democracy, then, is not simply a decision rule for registering choices; it has to operate with a commitment to inclusiveness. Permanent or excluded minorities are inconsistent with the basic idea of equality that underpins democracy. That is why some notion of social learning is an essential part of the democratic process; all are entitled to have their situations understood. Thus, to the extent that urban regimes safeguard special privileges at the expense of social learning, democracy is weakened.

Those fearful that too much community participation will lead to unproductive policies should widen their own understanding and consider other dangers on the political landscape. Particularly under conditions of an imbalance in civically useful resources, the political challenge is one of preventing government from being harnessed to the protection of special privilege. The social-production model reminds us that only a segment of society's institutions are under the sway of majority rule; hence, actual governance is never simply a matter of registering the preferences of citizens as individuals.

The character of local politics depends greatly on the nature of a community's associational life, which in turn depends greatly on the distribution of resources other than the vote. Of course, the vote is significant, but equality in the right to vote is an inadequate guarantee against the diversion of politics into the protection of privilege. If broad social learning is to occur, then other considerations must enter the picture. "One person, one vote" is not enough.

NOTES

1. James G. March, "The Business Firm as a Political Coalition," *Journal of Politics* 24 (November 1962): 662–678.

2. Chester I. Barnard, *The Functions of the Executive* (Cambridge, Mass.: Harvard University Press, 1968).

3. Oliver E. Williamson, *The Economic Institutions of Capitalism* (New York: Free Press, 1985).

4. Ibid., 10.

5. See Norton E. Long, "The Local Community as an Ecology of Games," *American Journal of Sociology* 64 (November 1958): 251–261.

6. Cf. Graham T. Allison, *Essence of Decision* (Boston: Little, Brown, 1971).

7. See Philip Selznick, *Leadership in Administration* (New York: Harper & Row, 1957).

8. Cf. Bryan D. Jones and Lynn W. Bachelor, *The Sustaining Hand* (Lawrence: University Press of Kansas, 1986).

9. See especially Martin Shefter, "The Emergence of the Political Machine: An Alternative View." in *Theoretical Perspectives on Urban Politics*, by Willis D. Hawley and others (Englewood Cliffs, N.J.: Prentice-Hall, 1976).

10. Clarence N. Stone, Robert K. Whelan, and William J. Murin, *Urban Policy ana Politics in a Bureaucratic Age*, 2d ed. (Englewood Cliffs, N.J.: Prentice-Hall, 1986), 104.

11. Stephen L. Elkin, *City and Regime in the American Republic* (Chicago: University of Chicago Press, 1987).

12. See ibid.

13. Cf. Jones and Bachelor, *The Sustaining Hand*, 214–215.

14. But see Elkin, *City and Regime*; Martin Shefter, *Political Crisis/Fiscal Crisis: The Collapse and Revival of New York City* (New York: Basic Books, 1985); and Todd Swanstrom, *The Crisis of Growth Politics* (Philadelphia: Temple University Press, 1985).

15. Robert H. Wiebe, *The Search for Order, 1877–1920* (New York: Hill and Wang, 1967), 10.

16. Russell Hardin, *Collective Action* (Baltimore: Johns Hopkins University Press, 1982); and Michael Taylor, *The Possibility of Cooperation* (Cambridge: Cambridge University Press, 1987).

17. Mancur Olson, Jr., *The Logic of Collective Action* (Cambridge, Mass.: Harvard University Press, 1965).

18. Hardin, *Collective Action*.

19. Robert Axelrod, *The Evolution of Cooperation* (New York: Basic Books, 1984).

20. Hardin, *Collective Action*; and David D. Laitin, *Hegemony and Culture* (Chicago: University of Chicago Press, 1986).

21. Taylor, *Possibility of Cooperation*.

22. Charles Tilly, *Big Structures, Large Processes, Huge Comparisons* (New York: Russell Sage Foundation, 1984), 27.

23. Philip Abrams, *Historical Sociology* (Ithaca, N.Y.: Cornell University Press, 1982). For a similar understanding applied to urban politics, see John R. Logan and Harvey L. Molotch, *Urban Fortunes* (Berkeley and Los Angeles: University of California Press, 1987).

24. Cf. Anthony Giddens, *Central Problems in Social Theory* (Berkeley and Los Angeles: University of California Press, 1979).

25. Cf. James G. March and Johan P. Olsen, "The New Institutionalism," *American Political Science Review* 78 (September 1984): 734–749.

26. Abrams, *Historical Sociology*, 331.

27. Ibid.

28. Michael L. Porter, "Black Atlanta: An Interdisciplinary Study of Blacks on the East Side of Atlanta, 1890–1930" (Ph.D. diss., Emory University, 1974); Walter White, *A Man Called White* (New York: Arno Press and the New York Times, 1969); and Dana F. White, "The Black Sides of Atlanta," *Atlanta Historical Journal* 26 (Summer/Fall 1982): 199–225.

29. Kenneth T. Jackson, *The Ku Klux Klan in the City 1915–1930* (New York: Oxford University Press, 1967); and Herbert T. Jenkins, *Forty Years on the Force: 1932–1972* (Atlanta: Center for Research in Social Change, Emory University, 1973).

30. Charles H. Martin, *The Angelo Herndon Case and Southern Justice* (Baton Rouge: Louisiana State University Press, 1976); Kenneth Coleman, ed., *A History of Georgia* (Athens: University of Georgia Press, 1977), 294; and Writer's Program of the Works Progress Administration, *Atlanta: A City of the Modern South* (St. Clairshores, Mich.: Somerset Publishers, 1973), 69.

31. Lorraine N. Spritzer, *The Belle of Ashby Street: Helen Douglas Mankin and Georgia Politics* (Athens: University of Georgia Press, 1982).

32. John Bonner, *Introduction to the Theory of Social Choice* (Baltimore: Johns Hopkins University Press, 1986), 34.

33. Stein Rokkan, "Norway: Numerical Democracy and Corporate Pluralism," in *Political Oppositions in Western Democracies*, ed. Robert A. Dahl (New Haven, Conn.: Yale University Press, 1966), 105; see also Erie, *Rainbow's End*.

34. Matthew A. Crenson, *The Un-Politics of Air Pollution* (Baltimore: Johns Hopkins University Press, 1971); see also Edwin H. Rhyne, "Political Parties and Decision Making in Three Southern Counties," *American Political Science Review* 52 (December 1958): 1091–1107.

35. Clarence N. Stone, "Preemptive Power: Floyd Hunter's 'Community Power Structure' Reconsidered," *American Journal of Political Science* 32 (February 1988): 82–104.

36. Norman Frohlich and Joe A. Oppenheimer, *Modern Political Economy* (Englewood Cliffs, N.J.: Prentice-Hall, 1978), 19–31.

PART I

THE EVOLUTION OF REGIMES IN AMERICAN CITIES, 1789–1933

The century and a half from the constitutional era to the 1930s encompassed fundamental transformations in American society. During the nineteenth century the Western world underwent urbanization on a scale unprecedented in history. In the United States, the impact of this development was magnified by the fact that the nation was being carved from the wilderness; in just a few decades a rural society that had substantially defined its national character by reference to the frontier and westward expansion was transformed into an urban and industrial culture. Cities were themselves the leading symbols of these extraordinary changes. The relatively small, homogeneous, commercial cities that characterized the new nation eventually gave way to the complex, chaotic, rapidly growing industrial cities of the post–Civil War period.

Of course, these extraordinary changes were expressed in the political realm. The commercial cities were run by merchant elites who ruled as much by their social prestige as by any formal claims to political office. Indeed, the demarcation between their private affairs and their public activities were hardly distinguishable. The basic political development in nineteenth-century cities was the gradual building of democratic political systems and formal mechanisms of governance. By the latter decades of the century the aristocrats and merchants had lost power to full-time politicians who had successfully learned how to manage a mass electorate and to assume political power over city affairs. The politicians who built the party machines became enduring symbols of corruption in American political life. The machine was soon challenged by reformers who struggled to establish their own vision of city government, however. From the 1890s to the 1930s urban politics was defined by a tug of war between the machines and a generation of reformers who sought to mobilize middle-class voters in the cause of "nonpolitical" and "efficient" local government.

Entrepreneurial City

Until the waning years of the nineteenth century, to most Americans cities and towns must have seemed completely overshadowed by a vast landscape of wilderness and agriculture. On the occasion of the first decennial census of 1790, only 5 percent of the nation's population lived in cities of twenty-five hundred or more. More than a century later, when the census of 1920 revealed that more than half the population had become urban, Americans still indulged in the notion (by then, the fantasy) that cities did not define the national culture; the most popular books of the decade were Zane Grey's novels.

In reality, cities had always been pivotal in shaping national economic and cultural development. Even before the age of industry, the nation's cities prospered by presiding over an economic system wherein agricultural and extractive products were exchanged for goods shipped from abroad or produced by craftsmen located mostly in cities. In the commercial cities, the streets "led past the warehouse to the piers," and later also to the rail lines (Glaab and Brown 1967, 27). Frontiersmen and farmers alike participated in the trade and commerce that gave the cities their reason for being.

The prime mover in a city's commercial and trading activities was the merchant capitalist, an entrepreneur whose activities encompassed almost every aspect of commercial trade (Taylor 1951, 11). As cities grew in size and complexity, the local economic community became increasingly fragmented and specialized. The movement of European and domestic goods was handled by retailers, wholesalers, manufacturer's representatives, auctioneers, and shipping agents. A strata of occupations provided services to support these activities: insurance brokers, accountants, printing shops that produced accounting ledgers, handbills, and legal documents. Most manufacturing was devoted to supporting these activities, or to items of personal consumption; there were the breweries and distillers, shoemakers, hatters, bakers, carpenters, blacksmiths, potters, and butchers, and whole occupations that built and maintained containers and conveyances for moving goods from dock to warehouse. By the middle of the nineteenth century larger investors such as railway promoters, land speculators, and small industrialists began to emerge as important local entrepreneurs.

The merchant entrepreneur's status at the apex of the local economy translated into a similar position in local politics. Even when the Jacksonian reforms of the 1830s ushered in universal male suffrage and mass involvement in political parties, the chief effect in most cities was to replace the colonial-era patricians, who asserted their authority by their education and social standing, with merchant and professional elites, who defined cities solely by their economic function. For this generation of municipal leaders, the purpose of cities was to provide an environment for making money.

The idea of a popular government separate from an autonomous private local economy emerged only gradually during the nineteenth century. The merchants who dominated the economic life of the city found that their power and position were easily translated into public leadership. These individuals typically worked alongside other notables such as respected preachers, lawyers, and the occasional patrician gentleman to run the public affairs of the city. Public affairs were easily reconciled with private affairs: City governments provided services sufficient to maintain a level of safety and order necessary to sustain the local economy.

Indeed, in his selection Daniel J. Boorstin observes that businessmen presumed during the commercial era that public and private prosperity were inseparable. He colorfully describes how businessmen such as William B. Ogden made little distinction between the public affairs of the city and their private business lives. They believed and acted as though boosting the fortunes of the local community was as much a public matter as a private one—if the community prospered, they also benefited—and vice versa.

Accordingly, mercantile regimes helped establish what Sam Bass Warner describes as a tradition of "privatism" in urban politics and city building. By espousing the notion that cities mainly existed to serve private economic activities, the dominant regimes permitted the agenda of local politics and even the physical character of cities to be driven by the market decisions of traders, builders, land speculators, and investors. Warner believes that the culture of privatism made it difficult for public authorities to respond with much effectiveness to the problems of cities as they grew in size, complexity, and social composition. He describes the frustrations that Philadelphia civic leaders faced in efforts to improve the city's water supply to protect its citizens from public health threats. Although the city's economic prosperity was becoming closely intertwined with the need to provide clean water, the city's political leaders struggled to avoid the public consequences of this reality.

Merchant elites were indefatigable promoters of local growth because they instinctively understood that some cities—but not all—would prosper. The major obstacles to local economic growth were physical barriers that impeded the exchange of goods between a rural hinterland and the city, and between the city and other commercial centers. Those cities that were most successful at breaking down barriers to commerce gained a competitive advantage, and of course their local merchants stood to profit. Consequently, during several decades of the nineteenth century the singular dynamic driving city politics was a competition among merchant elites who found their destinies tied to particular cities.

The building of the Erie Canal was a landmark event that precipitated several decades of interurban rivalry. Prodded by entrepreneurs in New York City, the state of New York authorized construction of the 364-mile waterway in 1817 to connect the Hudson River with Lake Erie. By giving New York access to the vast agricultural hinterland of the old Northwest, national trade patterns were fundamentally altered. After completion of the canal in 1825 it often was cheaper and quicker for producers and shippers to send their bulk freight through the Great Lakes than down the Ohio, Mississippi, and Missouri River systems and through New Orleans. New York's tremendous economic power now reached more securely beyond the confines of its East Coast location.

The success of the Erie Canal dramatically altered the politics of the mercantile cities. By 1840 there were 3,326 miles of canals in the United States, most of them constructed between 1824 and 1840. Urban proponents of canals almost invariably turned to their state governments to raise the massive capital needed for their construction. Private sources of capital, which eventually provided about 30 percent of the investment in these projects, could not by itself have been sufficient (Goodrich 1960, 266–271; 1961, 49).

Similarly, in subsequent decades railroad building transformed the economic competition among cities into a truly national phenomenon. Cities everywhere, big and small, new or old, could use the railroad to penetrate their hinterland in the expectation that they could gather up the trade of the back country and channel it through their own commercial streets. Local business leaders tried to outbid one another to secure rail connections. Cities gave land to the railroads, bought their bonds, and even financed construction, often, but not always, with the help of state legislatures. As plans for railroads extended west, rivalry among city promoters and real estate speculators intensified. Railroad entrepreneurs were adept at bargaining with competing towns for the best possible terms in stock subscriptions, bond issues, rights of way, and other subsidies. Private capital combined in complex ways with public resources to fuel the railway wars.

Individual cities, as public corporations, provided massive assistance for railroad promotion. Although precise figures for local government aid are difficult to estimate, overall assistance probably totaled more than that of state assistance; by 1870, it equaled one-fifth of the construction costs of the railroads then in existence (Taylor 1951, 92). Such a powerful use of municipal resources could only have occurred behind strong, united leadership within the cities.

Mercantile cities were characterized, for the most part, by a remarkable degree of political consensus. The economic interests of merchant elites were so closely tied to the growth of their cities that it drove them to close ranks and unite behind even the most ambitious and risky plans to promote local development. The same drive tended to mute opposition from other groups. Local political leadership became virtually defined as the task of convincing all the factions in the community that it was in everybody's interest to support or contribute to some specific public works, harbor improvement, railway venture, or whatever. Most voters followed the lead of the merchants, often sharing the belief that a growing economy would, indeed, benefit everyone. As a result, the regimes that governed the mercantile cities were extremely closed, and the dominant political issues reflected the degree of autonomy and authority commanded by an elite that exerted both political and economic leadership.

The spirit of this intercity rivalry is captured by Richard C. Wade, who portrays the commercial struggles among frontier cities during the first decades of the nineteenth century. In his selection, Wade notes that in these contests the prizes were rich, but the penalties for losing could be devastating: "the economically strongest survived and flourished . . . smaller places were trampled in the process, some being swallowed up by ambitious neighbors, others being overwhelmed before they could attain a challenging position."

The stability of the entrepreneurial regimes rested very much on excluding nonbusiness interests from governmental power to keep urban agendas limited. In the end, regimes constructed in this way could not last; they constantly had to struggle with the spread of democratizing reforms that enlarged urban electorates and forced political leaders to develop mass party systems to organize voters. This gave birth to professional politicians who capitalized on their superior ability to organize the electorate and win voter support. Amy Bridges's essay about this "new house of power in town" in New York City suggests how these politicians affected the position of the city's wealthy business elites. She documents how the new career politicians forged a division of labor with men of wealth that forced aristocrats to limit their political involvement and to compromise their demands regarding the purposes of government.

Although the entry of ordinary people into local politics and the expansion of the electorate helped to overturn rule by merchant elites, class conflict rarely emerged as a dominating theme in city politics. Ira Katznelson's essay describes how the dominant political and social conflicts, the "city trenches" of the antebellum period, were more apt to be related to matters of residence than to work and occupation. His survey of New York City suggests that party politicians of the period sought to organize workers not as laborers (members of an economic class) but as residents of particular neighborhoods or ethnic groups and religious groups. Consequently, the process of regime change in nineteenth-century cities did not entail a change from business-dominated government to a working-class politics emphasizing radical changes in governmental responsibilities.

The final blow that ended the Entrepreneurial Era (as we have labeled it) was precipitated by the excesses occasioned by intercity competition. Although canals, railroads, and other transportation improvements promoted by local and state governments often, but not always, brought economic growth in their wake, they sometimes did so at the cost of ruining the governments that funded them. Competition among cities for railroads was so fierce that they frequently bid up the subsidies beyond what was economically rational. Railroad promoters played one town against the other in search of better subsidy "deals," predicting rapid town growth, rising real estate values, and overflowing municipal treasuries. They sometimes promised that profits on railroad stocks would even eliminate the need for local taxes. Many cities never realized the economic bonanza they expected from their subsidies; indeed, most cities lost more money than they invested (Goodrich 1960, 272). The frenzy of railroad building meant that many lines were built that could never be profitable; in any case, not all cities could win the competition for growth and prosperity. When the six-year depression of the 1870s was ushered in by the panic of 1873, hundreds of cities were driven into bankruptcy.

Municipal bond railroad defaults broke the spell that merchant elites had cast over city politics and over some legislatures. Several states curbed the power of their cities to buy railroad stocks or to provide other subsidies. In many cities merchant elites were thrown out of office, to be replaced by a new generation of municipal officials (sometimes also local businessmen) who were less interested in using municipal powers for commercial promotion. An ideology of laissez faire replaced the mercantilist habit of seeing public powers and private resources as almost inseparable.

CONTESTING POWER IN THE AGE OF INDUSTRY

Machine Politics

The industrial revolution and the development of mass democratic institutions transformed the politics of cities. After the Civil War most larger cities established a commanding market position over vast hinterlands, and they became the leading centers for manufacturing. Only in the nation's larger cities could business find access to port facilities, rail terminals and cheap freight rates, huge and reliable labor forces, and the infrastructure needed to support large-scale manufacturing. Consequently, the intercity competition that characterized the enterpreneurial era gave way to an urban hierarchy in which cities occupied distinct niches. This new reality changed the relationship of city governments to their business communities: Local political leaders no longer had to compete vigorously to attract business investment because businesses were already becoming tied to the downtowns, factory districts, and rail heads of the larger cities.

Wide-open political struggle to shape the institutions of mass democracy became crucial in building the urban regimes of the industrial era. New sources of social conflict and new political arrangements emerged in this struggle. City populations burgeoned when waves of immigrants from abroad and migrants from rural areas were drawn by jobs in the cities; they dramatically changed the social and political complexion of the cities and eventually sought to win some of the prizes of local politics. The advent of industrialization intensified social conflicts. The disintegration of oligarchic control by business elites left a vacuum that was replaced, although often slowly and chaotically, by unstable coalitions of politicians held together by little more than a mutual desire to use the political system for personal advancement. Public officials and those seeking favorable governmental action became accustomed to buying loyalty and favors with cash, jobs, contracts, and other material inducements.

Centralized party machines gradually evolved from this political factionalism. In New York City "rapacious individualism" characterized machine politics in its early period (Shefter 1976). In the years leading up to the fall of the Tweed Ring in 1871, the Democratic party nominally dominated the city's politics. It was riven by competing factions that made up the party's leading political club, however. The Tweed Ring extended this mode of politics. Tweed was able to win the cooperation of members of the party, those who became part of the Ring, through a system of bribes and payoffs. The huge costs of winning cooperation required Tweed to raid the municipal treasury to the point of almost driving the city into bankruptcy.

By the late nineteenth century, a system of politics that relied on material incentives became regularized in most larger American cities. As machines became the dominant urban political institution, its survival became closely tied to two constituencies: voters and business. Machine politicians traded jobs and favors, and traded on symbols of ethnic identity and solidarity, for votes. They also made themselves useful — for a price, of course — to business entrepreneurs who wanted an orderly operation of the city's economy and politics. Government officials routinely made important decisions granting franchises and setting utility rates; they approved contracts for the installation of street lights, gas, telephones, and trolley lines. They could also smooth things over for small businessmen and for those occupying the seamier side of city life, the operators of gambling parlors and houses of prostitution.

This style of politics is colorfully rendered in the reading by William L. Riordon about George Washington Plunkett, who climbed out of poverty to become a millionaire during his forty years of service as a Tammany boss. Note that Plunkett's secret for political success did not depend on winning the minds or appealing to the ideals of voters, but in gaining the voters' loyalty through petty favors or, when necessary, giving them jobs. Conveying lovable cynicism, Plunkett even saw how it was possible to convert treats to little children into votes on election day!

Though Plunkett's ideas were recorded (and perhaps embellished a bit) by newspaperman William L. Riordan just after the turn of the century, his lessons have continued to influence city politicians. In particular, the political art of winning votes by tending to the individual needs of voters has flourished. The selection from Milton Rakove's book describes how during the 1970s Chicago ward politicians like Vito Marzullo could no longer rely very much on providing illegitimate favors, such as fixing traffic tickets, bribing officials, and the like to win votes. Instead, Marzullo learned the individual needs of people in the precincts and then provided friendly advice, services, and other forms of legitimate help to those voters who encounter difficulties coping with the layers of bureaucracy in modern government. Note how Marzullo regards elections as events that are won or lost in the precincts well before election day rolls around.

The machine's capacity to reduce political conflicts by the granting of petty favors was, in general, highly exploitive. By representing the immigrants' individual rather than collective interests as a disadvantaged class, the machines effectively undermined any tendency for immigrants to focus on business practices or class relationships as a cause of poverty and other social ills. Indeed, by using the distribution of jobs and favors and playing on ethnic and neighborhood rivalries in exchange for votes, machine politicians made it difficult for low-income groups or reformers to promote social reforms that offered collective benefits of any kind. Thus bosses' main interest was in avoiding issues and reducing all political conflicts to individual problems. Machine politicians derived their power from their ability to manipulate the political and economic system, not by trying to change it. In exchange for their tribute, machine government enabled business to operate freely in its own sphere of influence; the politicians expected in exchange that they would be allowed to operate freely within theirs. For this reason, urban businessmen were often supporters of machine governments during the nineteenth century.

The United States stands virtually alone among Western industrial democracies in producing machine-style politics on a large scale. Why did such organizations arise in American cities? Robert K. Merton's answer to this question influenced scholarship on machines for decades. In his classic formulation, Merton asserts that the machines were "functional" in several respects, and that the functions that the machines performed were not always obvious because they were "latent" (or unintended) outcomes of the way the machines operated. Merton asserts that the machine's ability to centralize power informally served as an antidote to the constitutional dispersal of power that made governing cities difficult. The machine also humanized and personalized assistance to the needy—particularly to immigrants who liked the no-questions-asked help of the ward boss to the impersonal, professional, and frequently paternalistic assistance offered by charity organization workers who often disdained the immigrants' ethnicity and religion. The machine also provided business, including illicit businesses, with the privileges they needed to survive. Finally, the machine offered social mobility to some immigrants who found that job discrimination in the private sector limited their opportunities.

This functionalist explanation for the rise of the machines has been challenged in recent research. Alan DiGaetano suggests that there is little evidence that the machines actually functioned to overcome a weak or fragmented local governmental system. Rather, he argues that party bosses survived by harnessing the power that was centralized into strong executive institutions prior to and coincident with the appearance of political machines. In effect, by suggesting that the machine exploited the development of a more powerful administrative state rather than compensating for a lack of one, he seems to turn part of Merton's thesis on its head.

In his selection, Martin Shefter also questions whether the origins of machine politics are to be found in the social character and political preferences of immigrants. His description of the beginnings of machine politics in New York City points to the pivotal role of the city's business community in supporting the construction of a centralized party organization. Shefter believes that New York business interests supported boss politics as a means of containing the fiscal excesses of mass democratic politics. Business leaders also found that a well-organized boss system enabled them to avoid the uncertainties of honest electoral competition for the immigrant vote. Thus, although the existence of a large impoverished immigrant electorate may have been a necessary condition for the rise of machine politics, Shefter asserts that it was not a sufficient condition for it. The Irish, for example, supported nationalist movements and reform leagues in Ireland, but those who came to America often supported machines. Did this happen, as Shefter suggests, because business leadership refused to accept more democratic kinds of regimes as alternatives?

In the end, how much did immigrants benefit from what machine politics had to offer? Steven P. Erie questions Merton's assessment that the machine provided an important route to social mobility. Even though many machines were dominated by Irish politicians who favored Irish constituents in their distribution of jobs, contracts, and other rewards, Erie suggests that the machines actually retarded the upward mobility of Irish-Americans as a group. Party bosses were inclined to spread patronage as thinly as possible to maximize votes, creating many relatively blue-collar and poorly paid public jobs at a time when there were better employment opportunities in the private sector. Erie also believes that entrenched machine politicians did little to facilitate economic assimilation among southern and eastern Europeans. He points out that in cities where Irish bosses had secure power bases they found it more advantageous to exclude newer immigrant groups from voting and participating in the machine to preserve Irish political domination. The newer immigrants were incorporated into the machines only in the cases in which exclusionary strategies no longer worked. Erie thinks that the lessons of the Irish machines should give pause to many of today's minority politicians who might believe that a "rainbow" strategy of ethnic group politics, at least if it operates through material inducements, offers their constituents an effective means of political advancement.

Reform Politics

The machines created their own opposition because they were often remarkably exclusionary: They represented some immigrant groups but not others, they were useful only to that fraction of the business community that was willing or able to engage in deal making and privilege buying. Machine politicians often affronted middle- and upper-class sensibilities, and they tended toward corruption. The fledgling reform efforts that arose in the last years of the nineteenth century mostly met with failure because they did not succeed at articulating a vision of the city that could unite enough groups behind a compelling cause. During the Progressive Era, however, the agenda that defined municipal reform became well articulated within a national movement. A protracted fight for the city's soul was joined.

The system of boss politics found its most potent challenge in a municipal reform movement that became increasingly well coordinated at the national level. Particularly after the turn of the century, when national business corporations and organizations moved to the reform cause, reform victories often led to electoral reform and investigations to root out corruption. In principle, the reformers could have challenged the machines by destroying the machine's social base of support through appeals and programs designed to attract immigrants away from the machines—for instance, relief and housing programs could have competed with the bosses' unreliable dispensing of favors; taxes could have been imposed on business, the middle-class, and the wealthy to pay for such programs. In reality, however, those who dominated the reform movement sought not only to limit the influence of the bosses but also of the immigrants, and they certainly did not imagine that the role of city government was to redistribute resources.

Quite the opposite. The essay by Samuel P. Hays, a historian, describes how the reform agenda was intended to bring about a redistribution of power in urban politics. Reformers, suggests Hays, "wished not simply to replace bad men with good; they proposed to change the occupational and class origins of decision makers." The reformers artfully obfuscated this agenda behind a rhetoric of "good government" in which they proposed that the "public interest" could be objectively defined, and that this interest dictated only one objective: the delivery of basic city services at the lowest possible cost. This theory was directly related to local democratic politics in the reformers' assertion that elections and representation should be strictly separated from the day-to-day administration of services. To protect municipal government from "politics," the reformers said that experts with training, experience, and ability should run the public's business. Implementing efficiency in government was, in sum, a question of mechanics, not of politics.

The spirit and substance of this approach to local government is eloquently stated in the essay by Andrew D. White, who was the first president of Cornell University. White believed that cities could be run just like a business and that its affairs were nonpartisan in character, having nothing to do with politics. Note that White's advocacy of nonpartisanship was intimately linked to his belief that removing the party label from election ballots could help remove local government from the influences of immigrants. Like nonpartisanship, the reformers' catchall phrase, "efficiency," served as a useful cover for a political agenda to wrest political control from the immigrants. Though they constantly harped on the wastefulness and corruption of the machines and promised to replace partisan politics with minimalist government, they were as interested as the machine politicians in city building—but they wanted a different class of people to be in charge of it. Behind the complex struggle between machine and reform lay an agenda shared by both: to use government as an instrument to cope with the demands of industrial urbanization.

To put power back into the hands of the "better classes," the reformers could not return to the halcyon days of the mercantile city when politics was run by patricians. The industrial city was simply too big and complex; it required a high level of services, the building of a public infrastructure sufficient to cope with rapid urban growth, and the political management of the social conflicts precipitated by industrialization and immigration. For this reason most reform governments invested in the public sector as much as did the machines. Jon C. Teaford contends that, given the enormous stresses and challenges faced by city governments of the time, municipal governance in this period should be considered an "unheralded triumph." American city governments served their residents without suffering financial collapse. More important, he concludes that messy-looking local political systems were able to incorporate in uneasy balance among the myriad interests that held very different and conflicting conceptions of city politics and policy priorities. Political tensions might well have rendered the municipal polity impotent, but they did not.

Industrial Urban Crisis and Regime Failure

Though city governments succeeded in brokering among political interests, there were fundamental flaws in both the machines' and the reformers' approach to city building and governance. Neither bosses nor reformers made significant efforts to address the urgent social problems connected to overcrowded slums and widespread urban poverty. The essays by Melvin G. Holli, Michael B. Katz, and Lewis Mumford describe why they believe the governmental responses of the industrial era were ultimately inadequate for the challenges of the twentieth century.

Holli says that most reformers were uninterested in social reform. Commonly they offered programs that focused on tinkering with the machinery of government and finding cost-containment measures, programs that had little appeal to the masses of poor immigrants whose needs were neglected. Even reformers who were most inclined to promote attention to the problems of the poor were unwilling to accept very substantial public intervention to achieve changes. Historian Michael B. Katz describes how housing reformers, appalled by turn-of-the-century social conditions in the tenement slums, relied on limited housing programs, such as model tenements and housing code regulation, because they would not "cross the fictive boundary between public responsibility and private prerogative." That is, these programs would not significantly interfere with the private housing market. Katz describes how housing reformers in New York City and in Chicago thus not only failed to improve housing for the poor, but also helped build the black ghetto.

Social critic and historian Lewis Mumford's classic essay "The City" was written in 1922, when he was only twenty-six years old. He addressed a fundamental question: What has American city building contributed to civilization? In this excerpt he concludes that city builders have emphasized using the city to facilitate commercial movement and economic exchange rather than making cities serve human settlement and community values. Mumford believes that the limited conception of the city has dehumanized and degraded the urban environment, making cities unattractive as places where people are able to enjoy life as members of a genuine community. Mumford's assessment raises discomforting doubts about the capacity of such cities to adapt in order to serve people over the long run.

The limitations of both machine and reform regimes helped precipitate their undoing during the economic crisis of the 1930s. When the Great Depression hit, city governments were unprepared to deal with the miseries caused by this economic catastrophe. The widespread unemployment, poverty, and other hardships triggered by the depression outstripped the fiscal and governmental capacities of city governments, forcing them to turn to state and federal governments for assistance. For more than half a century the industrial cities had wrestled with the problem of growth. For the next half century they would try to cope with the problems of decline.

REFERENCES

Glaab, Charles N., and A. Theodore Brown. 1967. *A History of Urban America*. New York: Macmillan.

Goodrich, Carter. 1960. *Government Promotion of American Canals and Railroads, 1800–1890*. New York: Columbia University Press.

——, ed. 1961. *Canals and American Economic Development*. New York: Columbia University Press.

Shefter, Martin. 1976. "The Emergence of the Political Machine: An Alternative View." In *Theoretical Perspectives on Urban Politics*, edited by Willis D. Hawley and Michael Lipsky, pp. 18–32. Englewood Cliffs, NJ: Prentice Hall.

Taylor, George Rogers. 1951. *The Transportation Revolution, 1815–1860*. New York: Rinehart and Co.

Entrepreneurial Cities

5
The Businessman as City Booster*

Daniel J. Boorstin

The American businessman—a product (and a maker) of the upstart cities of the American West between the Revolution and the Civil War—was not an American version of the enterprising European city banker or merchant or manufacturer. Not an American Fugger or Medici or Rothschild or Arkwright, he was something quite different. His career and his ideals are an allegory of an American idea of community, for he was born and bred in the dynamic American urbanism in the period the our greatest growth.

The changing meaning of his very name, "businessman," gives us a clue. In 18th-century England to say someone was a "man of business' was primarily to say he engaged in public affairs. Thus David Hume in 1752 described Pericles as "a man of business." Before the end of the 18th century the expression had begun to lose this, its once primary meaning, and instead to describe a person engaged in mercantile transactions; it became a loose synonym for "merchant." But our now common word "businessman" seems to have been American in origin. It came into use around 1830 in the very period when the new Western cities were founded and were growing most rapidly. Even a casual look at this early American businessman, who he was, what he was doing, and how he thought of his work, will show how inaccurate it would be to describe him as simply a man engaged in mercantile transactions. We might better characterize him as a peculiarly American type of community maker and community leader. His starting belief was in

*Boorstin, Daniel J. 1965. "The Businessman as City Booster." Pp. 115–123 in *The Americans: The National Experience*. New York: Random House. Copyright © 1965 by Daniel J. Boorstin. Reprinted by permission of Random House, Inc.

the interfusing of public and private prosperity. Born of a social vagueness unknown in the Old World, he was a distinctive product of the New.

The new fast-growing city, where nothing had been before, a city with no history and unbounded hopes, was the American businessman's first natural habitat. In the period when he first appeared, his primary commodity was land and his secondary commodity transportation. This transformation of land rights and transport rights from political symbols and heirlooms into mere commodities was also an American phenomenon.

The businessman's characteristics would appear in the story of any one of the thousands who made their fortunes in the early 19th century. "I was born close by a saw-mill," boasted William B. Ogden (1805–77), "was early left an orphan, was cradled in a sugar-trough, christened in a mill-pond, graduated at a log-school-house, and at fourteen fancied I could do any thing I turned my hand to, and that nothing was impossible, and ever since, madame, I have been trying to prove it, and with some success." He was destined to be an upstart businessman on a heroic scale. Born into a leading local family in a small town in the Catskills in New York, he was actively dealing in real estate before he was fifteen. Before thirty he was elected to the New York Legislature on a program to construct the New York & Erie Railroad with State aid. He was a great booster for his State, to whose growth he called the new railroad essential. "Otherwise," he argued "the sceptre will depart from Judah. The Empire State will no longer be New York. . . . Philadelphia is your great rival, and, if New York is idle, will gather in the trade of the great west."

But Ogden's enthusiasm for New York was not immovable. In 1835, the very year when the money was appropriated for the New York & Erie Railroad, he met some Eastern investors who had formed the American Land Company. They had already shown the foresight to invest heavily in Chicago real estate. One of these was Charles Butler, a politically and philanthropically minded lawyer of Albany, who married Ogden's sister. Butler himself (once a clerk in the law office of Martin Van Buren) was an energetic promoter of real estate and railroads. A man of wide public interests, he was a founder of Hobart College and of Union Theological Seminary, and an early supporter of New York University, among his other community works. He asked Ogden to go to Chicago to manage his interests. Ogden then joined in the purchase of considerable tracts there.

William B. Ogden arrived in Chicago in June, 1835. The town census showed a population of 3265, almost all of whom had come since 1832 (when the settlement had numbered under a hundred). Quickly Ogden transferred his extravagant hopes from the Empire State to the City of Chicago. In 1837, when Chicago was incorporated, Ogden was elected its first mayor, and the city census counted 4170—an increase of almost thirty percent in two years.

"He could not forget," one of Ogden's fellow businessmen observed, "that everything which benefitted Chicago, or built up the great West, benefitted him. Why should he?" His commodity was land, whose value rose with the population. And Chicago now grew as few cities had ever grown before. The population approximately trebled, decade after decade: from 29,963 in 1850, to 109,260 in 1860, and to 298,977 in 1870. Chicago held over half a million people in 1880 and over a million by 1890, when it was already the second city on the continent. Meanwhile, real-estate values, especially in choice locations such as those Ogden was shrewd enough to buy, rose even more spectacularly. Men like Ogden proudly recorded their business success as the best evidence of their faith in their city. "In 1844," Ogden recalled, "I purchased for $8000, what 8 years thereafter, sold for 3 millions of dollars, and these cases could be extended almost indefinitely." Property he had bought in 1845 for $15,000 only twenty years later was worth ten million dollars. Successes were so common and so sudden, it was hard to know where fact ended and where fable began. Some of this purchasing was, of course, sheer speculative mania. The Chicago *American* (April 23, 1836) boasted of a piece of city property sold for $96,700 which, in romanticized arithmetic, they said had "risen in value at the rate of *one hundred per cent per* DAY, on the original cost ever since [1830], embracing a period of *five years* and a half."

Not to boost your city showed both a lack of community spirit and a lack of business sense. "Perhaps, the most striking trait of his character," a contemporary remembered of Ogden, "was his absolute faith in Chicago. He saw in 1836, not only the Chicago of today, but in the future the great City of the continent. From that early day, his faith never wavered. Come good times—come bad times—come prosperity or adversity—Chicago booming, or Chicago in ashes, its great future was to him a fixed fact." Quite naturally Ogden became a leader in community affairs, and within a few years Chicagoans called him their "representative man."

There was hardly a public improvement in which he did not play a leading role. He built the first drawbridge across the Chicago river, laid out and opened many miles of streets in the north and west parts of the city, promoted the Illinois and Michigan Canal and advocated laws for its construction and enlargement, projected and built thousands of miles of railroads serving Chicago, and did a great deal to develop Chicago's water supply, sewage system, and parks. More than a hundred miles of streets and hundreds of bridges were built at the private expense of Ogden and his real-estate clients. He helped introduce the McCormick reaping and mowing machines into the West, and helped build the first large factory for their manufacture. He was the first president of Rush Medical College (the first institution of its kind in Chicago), a charter member of the Chicago Historical Society, president of the Board of Trustees of the first "University of Chicago," and one of the first directors of the Merchants Loan and Trust Company (1857). He was elected to the Illinois Senate by the Republicans in 1860. He supported the Theological Seminary of the Northwest, the Academy of Sciences, and the Astronomical Society. The French historian Guizot only slightly exaggerated when he said Ogden had built and owned Chicago.

Characteristic also was Ogden's interest in improving transportation.

An upstart community, a community of boosters measuring itself by its rate of growth, depended on transportation in a new way. Settled communities of the Old World — Bordeaux, Lyon, Manchester, or Birmingham — especially when, as in the early 19th century, they were fast becoming industrial towns, needed transportation to feed raw materials and labor to their factories and to take away finished products. But Chicago and the other upstart cities of the American West needed it for their very lifeblood. In the Old World a city might grow or decline, prosper or languish, depending on its transportation, among other facilities. But here, without transportation there was no city at all.

An American city had to "attract" people. The primary community service was to make it easier, cheaper, and pleasanter for people to join your community. In all this, too, William B. Ogden was a paragon, for he pioneered the railroads. One of the first to run out of Chicago was the Galena & Chicago Union Railroad, built to connect Chicago with the great Mississippi River traffic. Chicago businessmen bought a controlling interest in 1846, and tried to raise money from local citizens to complete the railroad. Ogden worked hard to obtain numerous individual subscriptions in small amounts. This, its first railroad, opened a new era in the life and expansion of Chicago. Citizens subscribed its stock "as a public duty, and not as an investment." "Railroads," one of Ogden's collaborators later boasted, "were built as public enterprises, and not as money-making speculations. They were regarded as great highways constructed by the people, either at the expense of the government or by means of private capital, to accommodate the public, and not for the especial benefit of the stockholders." In April, 1849, the first locomotive started west from Chicago on the Galena line.

Ogden took the lead in promoting many more railroads for Chicago. In 1853 he was a director of the Pittsburg, Ft. Wayne & Chicago Railroad; in 1857, president of the Chicago, St. Paul & Fond-du-Lac Railroad which later became part of the Chicago & Northwestern Railroad, of which he was also president (1859–68). A transcontinental railroad with Chicago as the great junction was, of course, his dream. In 1850 he presided over the National Railway Convention and, on the organization of the Union Pacific Company in 1862, its first president was William B. Ogden.

The Ogden story was re-enacted a thousand times all over America — wherever there were upstart cities. Scenes were different, stakes smaller, and dimensions less heroic, but the plot everywhere was much the same. Here was a new breed: the community builder in a mushrooming city where personal and public growth, personal and public prosperity intermingled.

Another example was Dr. Daniel Drake (1785–1852), born in New Jersey, and raised in Kentucky, whose family sent him when he was only fifteen to study in the offices of a leading physician of the small town of Ft. Washington (later called Cincinnati). Within a few years he himself became the town's most prominent practitioner. He opened a drug store where, in 1816, he pioneered in the sale of artificial mineral water; soon he was also running a general store. His *Picture of Cincinnati in 1815*, with its full statistics, and its vivid account of the archaeology, topography, climate, and promise of the city, was translated and circulated widely abroad. Drake, in his own way, was as much a booster as Ogden; using subtler techniques of precise and calculated understatement, he produced the first detailed account of an upstart city. Many believed him when he concluded that small towns like Cincinnati were "destined, before the termination of the present century, to attain the rank of populous and magnificent cities." Drake had established himself in the high noon of Cincinnati prosperity, before the Panic of 1819.

Drake's boosterism was as energetic as Ogden's. Hoping to make Cincinnati a great medical center in 1819, he founded the Ohio Medical College (later the Medical College of the University of Cincinnati). He did a great deal to promote all kinds of community enterprises: the Commercial Hospital and Lunatic Asylum, the eye infirmary, the circulating library, the teacher's college. He helped plan and develop canals and he promoted railroads leading toward the South, which included the successful municipal line, the Cincinnati Southern Railway.

Still another example with a more western habitat was General William Larimer (1809–75). Born and raised in Pennsylvania, he tried many different businesses around Pittsburgh: a general store, a freight service, horse trading, a coal company, a wholesale grocery, his father's hotel, railroads, and banking. When he lost everything in the depression of 1854, Larimer, quickly resolving to start afresh farther west, was in Nebraska the very next spring. There he too became the instantaneous booster of a town which did not yet exist. We have an intimate record in letters he sent east. On May 23, 1855:

> I have taken two claims at La Platte, Nebraska Territory . . . and we are laying out a town. I am elected President of the Company, and secured ⅓ of the town. . . . I like this country very much indeed. . . . I think I can make a big raise here in a few years.

Already he claimed a good chance of being elected to Congress from Nebraska. Within a week his optimism had risen still higher: he planned to pay off his creditors with town lots, for he owned a thousand acres within the proposed city.

> Now my plan is this: I intend to live in La Platte City. I intend to open up a large farm. I can raise hemp, corn or anything. . . . I will go on with the farm and if the land is ever wanted for a town it is ready. . . . I intend not only to farm simply but I will open a Commission House. I expect to supply the Territory with iron nails, lumber, etc., this will not only be profitable in itself but will be the great means of building up the city. If I go there I can build the city if I do not go only to sell lots as the city may never rise.

Larimer expected the transcontinental railroad to go through La Platte, but this proved a miscalculation. Then, after a heavy winter, the town suffered deep spring floods. "We were not long in coming to the conclusion that La Platte was doomed as a town site." The pattern of western hope was all-or-nothing.

From La Platte, Larimer moved on to Omaha. There he lived in a prefabricated house that had actually been framed in Pittsburgh, knocked down and shipped out in 1856. When Omaha, too, looked unpromising (as it did within less than two years) he moved to Leavenworth, Kansas. This was in 1858, just in time for him to learn of the discovery of gold at Cherry Creek by Pike's Peak. Unwilling to wait for the better traveling conditions of the following spring, Larimer and his son immediately made up a party and left that fall. After a forty-seven-day trip, the Larimers were among the first to arrive at the mouth of Cherry Creek, where they found two dozen cabins under construction.

This, the first settlement in Colorado, was named Auraria. Larimer's son recorded the events of November 17, 1858:

> On our very first night here, my father, without consulting anyone outside of our own Leavenworth Party, packed his blankets and some provisions, left camp and crossed the Creek to pick out a new site. He left instructions for us to get up the oxen and join him, as he believed the east side of the Creek was much the best location for a town and no one in the country laid claim to it, or if so had abandoned it and left the country. . . . When we finally reached the eastern side of Cherry Creek, we found him near the bank with a camp fire awaiting us. He had 4 cottonwood poles crossed, which he called the foundation of his settlement and claimed the site for a town, — for *the* town which has now grown into the one of which Colorado is the proudest.

This time Larimer chose well. He had located on the site of Denver.

At first there was competition between the sites on either side of Cherry Creek. Then the stockholders combined and became a single city named Denver (in honor of the Virginian who had become Governor of the Kansas Territory) in 1860. "I am Denver City," Larimer wrote in a letter in February 1859. And his whole later career proved the extraordinary ability of the American businessmen of these upstart cities to fuse themselves and their destiny with that of their community — at least so long as the community remained prosperous or promising.

At the beginning Larimer had been put in charge of the town and made "Donating Agent," which authorized him to give two city lots to anyone who would build a cabin there measuring at least 16 by 16 feet. He promoted a good hotel and gave valuable shares to men "who were already or could be induced to become interested in the welfare of the city and might be influential in bringing a stage line into the country with Denver as its objective point." He encouraged the founding of drugstores, general stores, sawmills, and newspapers. Complaining that the town lacked the ultimate convenience, he finally helped organize a cemetery.

Examples could be multiplied. But even these three — Ogden, Drake, and Larimer — suggest the variety of opportunities, motives, and attitudes which created the new species *Businessman Americanus.* None of the characteristics of his American habitat was quite unique but their extreme American form and their American combination were.

Cities with No History. The upstart western cities were the rare examples of a dynamic urban environment where almost nothing had been pre-empted by history. Cities were proverbially the centers of institutions, where records were kept and the past was chronicled, hallowed, and enshrined. They were sites of palaces, cathedrals, libraries, archives, and great monuments of all kinds. The American upstart city, by contrast, had no past. At its beginning, it was free of vested interests, monopolies, guilds, skills, and "No Trespassing" signs. Here was the fluidity of the city—the spatial dimension of cosmopolitanism, movement, diversity, and change—but without the historical dimension. There were no ancient walls between classes, occupations, neighborhoods, and nationalities. The American upstart cities began without inherited neighborhood loyalties, without ghettos. "Everything," recalled Larimer, "was open to us."

Quick Growth and High Hopes. The pace of growth of the upstart cities fired imaginations. A town where nobody was ten years ago, but which today numbered thousands, might be expected to number tens or hundreds of thousands in a few decades. Mankind had required at least a million years to produce its first urban community of a million people; Chicagoans accomplished this feat in less than a century. Within a few days' wagon ride of Drake's Cincinnati, hundreds of towns were laid out, all guaranteed to have unrivalled advantages. Precisely one week after Larimer cut his four cottonwood poles on the future site of Denver, he wrote his wife back east that "we expect a second Sacramento City, at least." In 1834, H. M. Brackenridge noted, his Pittsburgh was changing so fast that anyone returned after ten years felt himself a stranger. He confidently foresaw that the settlement which had grown from village to big city in a quarter-century would very soon reach half a million. He could not be surprised that Cincinnati had grown from a forest to a city in thirteen years. He himself had hopes "of attaining, on the Ohio or Mississippi, distinction and wealth, with the same rapidity, and on the same scale, that those vast regions were expanding into greatness." The centennial history of St. Louis in 1876 called the city's site superior to that of any other in the world, and predicted that, when its railroad network was completed, it would outstrip Chicago and the eastern metropolises. "And yet, when this has been said, we have but commenced to tell of the wonders of a city destined in the future to equal London in its population, Athens in its philosophy, art and culture, Rome in its hotels, cathedrals, churches and grandeur, and to be the central commercial metropolis of a continent."

Community before Government. On this landscape too it was normal to find communities before governments. Men in sudden urban proximity, bound together by specific, concrete purposes, first felt their common needs. Afterwards they called governments into being. From force of circumstance, then, government became functional. Early Chicagoans, and their upstart counterparts elsewhere, were not confronted with the problem of evading obsolete regulations or of transmuting time-honored tyrannies. They simply combined to provide their own water, their own sewage system, their own sidewalks, streets, bridges, and parks. They founded medical schools and universities and museums. Eager for these and other services, they created municipal governments and enlisted state and federal government aid. An upstart government had neither the odor of sanctity nor the odium of tyranny. It was a tool serving personal and community prosperity at the same time.

Intense and Transferable Loyalties. In upstart cities the loyalties of people were in inverse ratio to the antiquity of their communities, even to the point of absurdity. Older towns could point only to the facts of limited actual accomplishment, while the uncertain future was, of course, ever more promising. Ogden removed his enthusiasm from New York to Chicago; Larimer removed his from La Platte to Omaha to Leavenworth to Auraria to Denver. Men could do this in the twinkling of an eye, and without so much as a glance over the shoulder. Promise, not achievement, commanded loyalty and stirred the booster spirit. One was untrue to oneself and to the spirit of expanding America if one remained enslaved to a vision which had lost its promise. The ghost town and the booster spirit were opposite sides of the same coin.

Competition among Communities. The circumstances of American life in the upstart cities of the West produced a lively competitive spirit. But the characteristic and most fertile competition was a competition among communities. We have been misled by slogans of individualism. Just as the competition among colonial seaboard cities helped diffuse American culture and kept it from becoming concentrated in a European-style metropolis, so the competition among western upstart cities helped create the booster spirit. Where there had been no cities before, where all were growing fast, there was no traditional rank among urban centers. If Lexington, Kentucky, could quickly arise by 1800 to be the most populous city of the West, if St. Louis and Cincinnati and Chicago had so suddenly arisen, might not some new Lexington displace them all? Many of each community's institutions had been founded to give it a competitive advantage. Dr. Drake's medical college helped Cincinnati keep ahead of Lexington, just as Ogden's streets and bridges and parks helped Chicago lead Cincinnati. Where individual and community prosperity were so intermingled, competition among individuals was also a competition among communities.

The emerging businessman of the upstart cities had much in common with the energetic American of an earlier generation. He was the Franklin of the West. He was the undifferentiated man of the colonial period, but in a more expansive setting. The new language of that day called him a "businessman"; the retrospective language of our century calls him the booster.

He thrived on growth and expansion. His loyalties were intense, naive, optimistic, and quickly transferable.

Versatility was his hallmark. He usually had neither the advantages nor the disadvantages of specialized skills or monopolistic protection. In Dr. Drake's Cincinnati, physicians became merchants, clergymen became bankers, lawyers became manufacturers. "The young lawyer," H. M. Brackenridge shrewdly advised the Western seeker after fortune (in one of the first recorded uses of the word "businessman") "should think more of picking up his crumbs, than of flying like a balloon. He must be content to become a *business man*, and leave the rest to fortune." For success in this environment, the specialized skills — of lawyer, doctor, financier, or engineer — had a new unimportance. Rewards went to the organizer, the persuader, the discoverer of opportunities, the projector, the risk-taker, and the man able to attach himself quickly and profitably to some group until its promise was tested.

6
The Environment of Private Opportunity*

Sam Bass Warner

American cities have grown with the general culture of the nation, not apart from it. Late eighteenth-century Philadelphia was no exception. Its citizens, formerly the first wave of a Holy Experiment, had been swept up in the tides of secularization and borne on by steady prosperity to a modern view of the world. Like the Puritans of Massachusetts and Connecticut, the Quakers of Pennsylvania had proved unable to sustain the primacy of religion against the solvents of cheap land and private opportunity. Quaker, Anglican, Presbyterian, Methodist, Pietist — each label had its social and political implications — but all congregations shared in the general American secular culture of privatism.[1]

Already by the time of the Revolution privatism had become the American tradition. Its essence lay in its concentration upon the individual and the individual's search for wealth. Psychologically, privatism meant that the

*Warner, Sam Bass. 1968. "The Environment of Private Opportunity." Pp. 3–4 and 99–109 in *The Private City: Philadelphia in Three Periods of Its Growth*. 1st ed. Copyright © 1968 by the University of Pennsylvania Press. Reprinted by permission of the University of Pennsylvania Press.

individual should seek happiness in personal independence and in the search for wealth; socially, privatism meant that the individual should see his first loyalty as his immediate family, and that a community should be a union of such money-making, accumulating families; politically, privatism meant that the community should keep the peace among individual money-makers, and, if possible, help to create an open and thriving setting where each citizen would have some substantial opportunity to prosper.

To describe the American tradition of privatism is not to summarize the entire American cultural tradition. Privatism lies at the core of many modern cultures; privatism alone will not distinguish the experience of America from that of other nations. The tradition of privatism is, however, the most important element of our culture for understanding the development of cities. The tradition of privatism has always meant that the cities of the United States depended for their wages, employment, and general prosperity upon the aggregate successes and failures of thousands of individual enterprises, not upon community action. It has also meant that the physical forms of American cities, their lots, houses, factories, and streets have been the outcome of a real estate market of profit-seeking builders, land speculators, and large investors. Finally, the tradition of privatism has meant that the local politics of American cities have depended for their actors, and for a good deal of their subject matter, on the changing focus of men's private economic activities.[2]

In the eighteenth century the tradition of privatism and the social and economic environment of colonial towns nicely complemented each other. Later as towns grew to big cities, and big cities grew to metropolises, the tradition became more and more ill-suited to the realities of urban life. The tradition assumed that there would be no major conflict between private interest, honestly and liberally viewed, and the public welfare. The modes of eighteenth-century town life encouraged this expectation that if each man would look to his own prosperity the entire town would prosper. . . .

The goals of the nineteenth-century municipality remained those of the Revolutionary era. The city was to be an environment for private money-making, and its government was to encourage private business. At the same time the city was to be an equalitarian society; its government should endeavor to maintain an open society where every citizen would have some chance, if not an equal chance, in the race for private wealth. These traditional goals worked upon the settled forms of the municipal corporation; they set the framework of the new municipal institutions, and they directed the attention and the efforts of the city's leaders, both the merchant amateurs and the new professionals.

The enduring effects of the interaction of these traditional goals with the demands of big city life can be summarized in the history of . . . the municipal corporation [and] the waterworks. . . . The history of the municipal corporation is best known and therefore can be sketched briefly. The story of Philadelphia's pioneer municipal waterworks demands more attention since it shows the permanent constraints that the city's tradition of privatism placed upon what was to be a universal public health program. . . .

MUNICIPAL CORPORATION

The Philadelphia municipal corporation grew directly out of the Revolution. The moderate merchant-artisan faction which had resumed control of the city and state at the end of the Revolution wrote the 1789 Philadelphia city charter, the first since independence was gained. It blended the traditional offices of colonial municipal government with the federalist fashion for bicameral legislatures. The taxpayer franchise established in 1776 by the radicals for all of Pennsylvania remained the electoral base of the city. The taxpayers of the city elected at-large both select and common councils which, together, voted appropriations, levied taxes, and enacted local ordinances. The mayor, not popularly elected, but chosen by the councils, as in colonial times, was the chief executive officer. With the approval of the councils he appointed a board of commissioners and together the mayor and the board carried on the executive business of the city government.

Despite domination by merchants, in the years following the 1789 charter, the demands of radical equalitarianism continued to press upon Philadelphia's corporation and thereby to hold it to a weak executive, to increase local control, and to expand both the franchise and the number of elected offices.[3] Philadelphia's municipal history, thus, ran directly counter to the trends of centralization and large-scale activity which characterized the contemporaneous industrialization of the city.

The radical fears of strong executives, inherited from the conflicts of the Revolution and continued by the Jacksonians in the nineteenth century, prevented the mayor and commissioners of the Philadelphia corporation from exercising much independence of action. When new municipal functions were added, like responsibilities for municipal water and gas, the councils created independent committees which did not report to the mayor but to the councils themselves. The patronage of the new activities, thus, fell to the councilors, not to the mayor, and therefore the effectiveness of the municipal corporation throughout the first half of the nineteenth century depended on the quality of the elected councilors and the volunteers who served on the council's committees.

Localism also gained with successive reforms of the post-Revolutionary Philadelphia and Pennsylvania governments. In 1834, when the basic public school statute for Pennsylvania was enacted it stipulated that three citizens be elected from each ward of Philadelphia to serve as school directors. The colonial tradition of having resident tax collectors and assessors in each ward was continued on an elected basis until just before the Civil War. The pressures of neighborhood partisan politics upon these officials produced widely fluctuating assessments and ultimately great confusion in the tax rolls. In 1854, when all the boroughs and districts of Philadelphia County joined into one consolidated city, to preserve the strength of past localisms, the select and common councillors were hereafter chosen on a ward basis, not at-large as formerly.

State and municipal election reforms expanded the number of voters and the number of elected offices. In 1838, state judges became elected officials. At the same time the franchise, which had been restricted to all taxpayers, was redefined to include all white males who had reached the age of twenty-one. This franchise reform, one of the few genuinely popular accomplishments in a deeply divided constitutional convention (1837–1838), reflected an important current in American equalitarianism: An enthusiasm for the uniform political status of whites was often accompanied by a heavy prejudice against Negroes. By the time the state constitutional convention convened in Philadelphia the city had already experienced its first major race riot. In 1841 the mayorality became a popularly elected office, while the ballot for Philadelphia county positions grew steadily longer.[4]

By mid-century the city of Philadelphia had grown to a big city and the functions of its government had kept pace with this growth. The cost of half a century of political change which ran against the trends of the city's industrialization now stood out clearly. The committee system of the councils, the extreme localism of politics, and the large number of elected offices appeared as handicaps to effective government. The consolidation of all the county into one municipal corporation in 1854 brought unity of management to the major functions of government, but it did not bring with it imagination or high quality of service.

The authors of the 1854 consolidation charter had voiced concern for effective control over municipal departments and sought devices for protecting the corporation from looting by predatory local political groups. To these ends they considerably enlarged the powers of the mayor at the expense of the councils' committees, and they created new executives in the offices of comptroller and receiver of taxes. So strong was the tradition of elected officials, however, that both these new executives had to be elected, not appointed by the mayor. Altogether, the reforms of 1854 could make but little progress. Bigness and industrialization had already destroyed both the source of competent leadership and the informed community which would have been necessary for the city to have enjoyed a future of strong, efficient, and imaginative government. Instead, a century of weakness and corruption lay ahead.[5]

DEVELOPMENT OF WATERWORKS

Philadelphia pioneered in building America's first municipal waterworks and thus operated for forty years an experimental water supply project for all other large cities in the nation. The success of Philadelphia's water program stands as a tribute to its old merchant-led committee system of government. Indeed, in the beginning, its success was as much a product of an aggressive committee as it was the result of sponsorship by the municipal corporation.[6]

The yellow fever epidemic of 1793 forced Philadelphians into their pioneering public water system. In that epidemic, the city's first major plague, one in twelve Philadelphians perished. More than 23,000 persons fled the city, and all business with the outside world ceased for a month.[7] It was clear to those who tasted the well water of different neighborhoods that in crowded blocks the contents of privies penetrated the wells.[8] Although doctors debated repeatedly the causes of the fever, all sides agreed that the cleansing of the streets, yards, and houses of filth and an abundant supply of cool, clear water for drinking were essential requirements if the city was to be preserved.

During these years a private company was digging a canal to connect the Schuylkill River to the Delaware River. It therefore seemed reasonable to add to these transportation plans a branch water supply canal through the center of the city. The canal company, however, soon went bankrupt. In 1797 another serious epidemic of yellow fever struck the city and carried away over 3,000 citizens. Extended negotiations between the canal company and the city were renewed, but satisfactory financial arrangements could not be worked out. The issue then moved to the state legislature, where the company proved a more powerful lobbyist than the municipal corporation. The fever returned in 1798.

In 1799 the immigrant English engineer and architect, Benjamin Latrobe (1764–1820), visited Philadelphia on a commission to design the Bank of Pennsylvania. While in town he heard of the problem and published a pamphlet proposing a quick solution. He suggested, as an alternative to the slow and expensive program of a dam and canals, that the city build two steam pumps, a culvert from the Schuylkill to the edge of the city's dense settlement (then Pennsylvania Square), and a distribution system of wooden pipes and street hydrants. To capture popular support he added the provision of free water to the poor at the street hydrants. The cost of construction and operation of the system, Latrobe maintained, could be met by rents charged to businesses and private homes that were directly connected to the system. Although there had been a steam engine in Philadelphia before the Revolution, Latrobe's scheme was a bold innovation.[9]

At this point, as in the later expansion of Fairmount Dam, the strength of the city's merchant-led committee system of government proved itself. During the years from 1799 to 1837 very able leaders of the city served on the Watering Committee of the City Councils. Henry Drinker, Jr. (1757–1822), son of the well-known Quaker merchant and himself cashier of the Bank of North America, Thomas P. Cope (1768–1854), then at the beginning of his successful merchant career, and Samuel M. Fox (1763–1808) of the Bank of Pennsylvania led the campaign for the Latrobe plan. In subsequent years William Rush (1766–1833), the famous sculptor; Joseph S. Lewis (1778–1836), prominent attorney and son of a wealthy china merchant; and John P. Wetherill (1794–1853), of the old Philadelphia paint manufacturing company Wetherill and Brother, all served on the Watering Committee and directed its aggressive policies.[10]

The city councils and their watering committee fought free of the canal interests and arranged their own financing without state aid. Despite setbacks in construction and periodic shortages of funds which the committee sometimes met by the members' advancing money out of their own pockets, they pushed the project through to completion by 1801. Henceforth Philadelphians enjoyed a reasonably adequate supply of water to cleanse themselves and to fight fires. The trials of the watering committee, however, did not cease. It continued to suffer all the pains of innovation. Engineering problems hampered the Committee until the twenties, financial problems until the thirties. The steam engines for the pumps, though good examples of Watt's low-pressure engine, broke down frequently and consumed mountains of cordwood. After sixteen years of difficulty they were replaced with high-pressure engines but these, though steady and powerful, used even more fuel. The original hydrants rarely shut off completely and in the winter froze solid. After two seasons the hydrants had to be entirely replaced by a new design. The hollow wooden logs used to distribute the water from the tank above the second pump leaked badly and after a few years a program of replacement by cast iron pipe was instituted.[11]

The original Latrobe scheme for financing the works was based on the assumption that many families would want direct water connections to their houses and that these private subscriptions would carry the cost of building and operating the system. Except for the boldest thinkers, however, Philadelphians in 1801 used water sparingly. By 1811 only 2,127 Philadelphians subscribed for water. Most of the city's 54,000 residents (city proper in 1810) depended for water on street hydrants or private wells. There were only two bath-houses in the entire city. As for home bathrooms, American inventors did not turn their attention to sanitary appliances until the 1830's. Thus over the first three decades of operation the watering committee struggled against heavy deficits while continuing to supply its product at a loss in advance of popular usage, for public health reasons.

Having established abundant clear water as part of the city's health services, the watering committee could not turn back even in the face of heavy financial deficits. During the second decade of the nineteenth century the city grew at the rate of about 2,200 persons per year. By 1820 Philadelphia and its immediate environs held a population of 114,000. The lawyer Joseph S. Lewis led the committee to seek a lasting solution to its problems of high operating costs and inadequate supply for the enlarging city. In 1819, in the midst of a severe depression, he proposed, and the City Councils accepted, a plan to invest another $400,000, this time in a dam across the Schuylkill and a series of water-powered pumps to raise the water to adjacent Fairmount Hill, where large reservoirs for a gravity-fed system could be built. The waterpowered pumps would cut the operating costs to a mere fraction of the former steam costs. Also, the dam was to be constructed for eight water wheels, although only three would be needed immediately. Thus it was hoped that the Fairmount scheme afforded enough surplus capacity for years to come. Within four years the works were completed.

The Fairmount works met every economic and engineering expectation. They also stand as a lasting memorial to the era of Philadelphia's merchant-led committee government. The watering committee had sufficient taste, standing in the city, and pride in its accomplishment to finish the works and lay out the grounds as a beautiful park. Although only a beginning, like the works themselves, the park was an extremely valuable project. With its 1844 additions, it became the first large urban park in America, and, as such, was an essential link in the chain of outstanding landscapes that included Boston's Mt. Auburn Cemetery, New York's Central Park, and Chicago's lake front. Over the years Philadelphians expanded the original waterworks layout to create the greatest civic monument of Philadelphia, the Fairmount Park system.[12]

The excess capacity of the Fairmount works soon disappeared. Since public waterworks with their abundant supply of water for domestic and commercial users offered a novel product, there was no way to predict its future use. The growth of Philadelphia during the years 1830–1850 exceeded its rate for any other period (1820–1830 38 percent, 1830–1840 37 percent, 1840–1850 58 percent, Philadelphia only). Such a pace of growth, occurring for the first time in large American cities, likewise could not be expected to yield reliable future estimates. Both the sustained, rapid growth in Philadelphia's population and the increase in per capita consumption of water must have surprised contemporaries.[13]

In 1837 the committee issued a triumphant report. It had $100,000 in the bank, six wheels running at the dam, and the number of paying customers had jumped to 20,000. Of equal significance, consumption had begun its rise toward modern levels; doubling since 1823, it now equaled twenty gallons per person per day. The system as a whole—street hydrants, house and commercial connections—served a total population of 196,000. The report noted that 1,500 Philadelphians had installed bathrooms with running water. That critical moment in the history of any social innovation, the time when a fashion of the rich becomes an imperative for the middle class, seemed to have arrived.[14]

Though public enthusiasm for bathing and water closets grew apace, after 1837 the watering committee began to lose the imagination and largeness of view which had characterized its early performance. It seems reasonable to detect in this falling off of the quality of the committee the beginning of the decline in the quality of Philadelphia's municipal officers and a weakening of the committee system of government. Perhaps the very triumph of the Fairmount works in routinizing the water supply of the city, at least for a few years, made the watering committee unattractive to the most imaginative city leaders. Whatever the cause, the committee began to falter and in one way or another failed to keep pace with the growing needs of the city.

During the 1840's, spurred by immigration and industrial expansion, Philadelphia filled up rapidly and the towns and districts outside its boundaries grew at unprecedented rates. Spring Garden, Kensington, and Northern

Liberties, districts which had joined the Philadelphia system, now used water in enormous amounts and demanded an equalization of their rates with those of Philadelphia customers. In addition, Spring Garden requested a high-pressure reservoir to give more adequate service on its hills. The watering committee, forgetting the essential public health purpose of its undertaking, now responded like a short-sighted monopolist by refusing to lower its rates. Spring Garden countered by securing legislative authorization to build its own works. Negotiations continued for a time, and ultimately the rates were conceded by the watering committee, but no satisfactory long-term contract could be worked out among Philadelphia and its neighbors. Spring Garden, Northern Liberties, and Kensington joined together to build their own pumping station in 1844. Ironically, they drew their water from behind the Fairmount Dam. In 1850 Kensington set up its own station, drawing from the Delaware River.

By 1850 only Southwark remained connected to the Philadelphia system. Yet such had been the decade's increase in per capita consumption that with all eight wheels working at the dam, and all the reservoirs filled, only three day's supply of water could be stored. In the summer 160,000 people drew forty-four gallons per person per day. Fifteen thousand houses had water closets, and 3,500 had baths. Clearly, the middle class of Philadelphia had adopted modern plumbing as an essential in its standard of living. The modern urban rate of water usage had arrived.

The subsequent history of the Philadelphia Water Works is inglorious. In 1851 inadequate capacity forced the watering committee to refuse West Philadelphia's request for service. The consolidation of all Philadelphia County into one city government in 1854 reunited all the water systems of the city, but union did not revive the old policy of aggressive building to meet future needs and to popularize higher standards of consumption. In the 1870's the city erected new steam pumping stations, but droughts brought shortages. Increasing pollution of the Schuylkill and Delaware rivers destroyed the former quality of the water. Such were the popular priorities of the city that the citizens taxed themselves with disease and dirty drinking water in order to allow private pollution of the rivers to continue unabated. In the years from 1880 to 1910 the typhoid fever rate in Philadelphia exceeded that of New York and Boston. Though filter systems had been demonstrated for over a decade, Philadelphia purchased its filters late and proceeded slowly. As late as 1906, 1,063 persons died of typhoid in Philadelphia in one season. In 1910–1911 filters and chlorine brought relief from these recurrent epidemics.[15]

The early history of the Philadelphia's water works does more than help to date the mid-nineteenth century decline in the effectiveness of its municipal government. Its history shows how the city's general culture of privatism stopped a universal public health program short of full realization. Fear of epidemics had created the water system, but once this fear had abated, little or no public support remained to bring the benefits of the new technology to those who could not afford them. The popular goal of the private city was a goal to make Philadelphia a moderately safe place for ordinary men and women to go about conducting their own business; the goal was never to help raise the level of living of the poor.

NOTES

1. Quaker historians agree that the Holy Experiment died from materialism and secularization during the eighteenth century, Frederick B. Tolles, *Meeting House and Counting House* (Chapel Hill, 1948), 240–243; Sydney V. James, *A People Among Peoples* (Cambridge, 1963), 37–43, 211–215; and see the charges against his contemporaries in John Woolman, *The Journal of John Woolman* (F. B. Tolles, Introduction, New York, 1961).

2. Howard Mumford Jones, *O Strange New World* (New York, 1964), 194–272, treats with this tradition as a blend of Christian and classical ideas.

3. Philadelphia's experience in these years appears to have been part of a general national trend, Ernest S. Griffith, *Modern Development of City Government in the United Kingdom and the United States* (London, 1927), I, 3–29.

4. The history of the municipal corporation is taken from Edward P. Allinson and Boies Penrose, *City Government of Philadelphia (Johns Hopkins Studies in Historical and Political Science*, Fifth Series, I–II, Baltimore, 1887), 33–61; J. Thomas Scharf and Thompson Westcott, *History of Philadelphia 1606–1884* (Philadelphia, 1884), III, 1703, 1737, 1936.

5. Eli K. Price, *The History of the Consolidation of the City of Philadelphia* (Philadelphia, 1873), 82–89. Compare with Lincoln Steffens, "Philadelphia: Corrupt and Contented," *The Shame of Cities* (N.Y., 1904, 1957 ed.), 134–161.

6. Public water supplies were established in Philadelphia in 1801, in New York in 1842, Boston 1848, Baltimore, a small private system in 1808, expanded in 1838, and a full public system in 1857.

7. The first U.S. Census returned 44,096 persons for Philadelphia, the Liberties and Southwark. Therefore the population of the city on the eve of the plague must have been about 48,000. The epidemic is recounted in detail in John H. Powell, *Bring Out Your Dead: The Great Plague of Yellow Fever in Philadelphia in 1793* (Philadelphia, 1949).

8. Latrobe noted the seepage of wastes through the Philadelphia sand in his journal, Talbot Hamlin, *Benjamin Henry Latrobe* (New York, 1955), 157.

9. Hamlin, *Latrobe*, 134–135, 157–167; John A. Kouwenhoven, *Made in America* (New York, 1948), 41.

10. For the narrative of the Philadelphia waterworks I have relied on Nelson M. Blake, *Water for the Cities* (Syracuse, 1956), Ch. II, V.

11. There is some evidence that the Philadelphia waterworks may be a case of provincial technological backwardness caused by the imperfect communication of engineering technique in the Atlantic world. W. H. Chaloner, "John Wilkinson, Ironmaster," *History Today*, I (May, 1951), 67 reports shipments of cast iron water pipe from England to Paris in 1780–1781 but does not indicate whether these pipes were for a Paris waterworks or for the Versailles fountain system. Whichever the case it would seem that French engineering and specifications would have saved Philadel-

phia the grief it experienced with faulty hydrants and fittings. The changeover to cast iron pipe went slowly. Scharf and Westcott claim replacement did not begin until 1818 and that in 1822 there were still thirty-two miles of wooden pipe in the city, *History of Philadelphia,* I, 605.

12. Commissioners of Fairmount Park, *First Annual Report* (Philadelphia, 1869), 6–12; George B. Tatum, "The Origins of Fairmount Park," *Antiques* LXXXII (November, 1962), 502–507.

13. Today planners struggle with the identical problem which faced the Philadelphia Watering Committee. How much extra capacity should be built into the works in the case when capital is in short supply and a city is growing at an indeterminate pace? The size of the Fairmount Works, and hence the amount of extra capacity for the entire system was set by a combination of engineering considerations and prior private property rights. The design of the dam and its wheels followed the plans of an English engineer who had formerly built mills along the nearby Brandywine River. He estimated the possible height of the dam and hence the available power at the site on the basis of contemporary rules of thumb. To guard against an underestimate on his part of the efficiency of the pumps the Watering Committee purchased additional upstream riparian rights so that the height of the dam could be raised to carry its lake to the Manyunk mills upstream. No further height was possible since to purchase the Manyunk mill rights would have been enormously expensive. Thus the efficiency of the overshot wheels at the Fairmount Dam and the presence of the Manyunk mills determined the capacity of the Philadelphia system for the next thirty years. Thomas Gilpin, "Fairmount Dam and Waterworks, Philadelphia," *Pennsylvania Magazine* XXXVII (October, 1913), 471–479; Select and Common Councils of Philadelphia, *Report of the Watering Committee on the Propriety of Raising the Dam at Fair Mount* (Philadelphia, 1820), 4–6.

14. A great enthusiasm for bathing seized the public at this moment and even suggested to an editorial writer that public bathhouses would improve the moral habits of the poor by lessening the jealousy between classes. *Public Ledger,* July 10, 1838. Purity of the water had not been entirely satisfactory. The same paper complained that the hydrant system meant impure water. It reported an "animal, like a centipede" in a glass of hydrant water, *Public Ledger,* October 6, 1836.

15. Philadelphia Bureau of Water, *Description of the Filtration Works and History of Water Supply 1789–1900* (Philadelphia, 1909), 3–4, 50–51, 70–71; City of Philadelphia, *Third Annual Message of Mayor Harry A. Mackey* (Philadelphia, 1931), 388; pollution, Blake, *Water for the Cities,* 97–98, 255–256, 259–261.

7

The Urban Frontier*

Richard C. Wade

Part of Philadelphia's appeal to towndwellers was its leadership among the nation's cities, for nearly every young metropolis . . . coveted a similar primacy in the West. Indeed, one of the most striking characteristics of this period was the development of an urban imperialism which saw rising young giants seek to spread their power and influence over the entire new country. The drive for supremacy, furthermore, was quite conscious, infusing an extraordinary dynamic into city growth, but also breeding bitter rivalries among the claimants. In the ensuing struggles, the economically strongest survived and flourished, while the less successful fell behind. Smaller places were trampled in the process, some being swallowed up by ambitious neighbors, others being overwhelmed before they could attain a challenging position. The contest, however, produced no final victor. In fact, the lead changed three times, and though Cincinnati commanded the field in 1830, Pittsburgh, Louisville, and St. Louis were still in the running.

The rivalries developed very early. Lexington jumped off to a quick start, but by 1810 Pittsburgh, enjoying a commercial and manufacturing boom, forged ahead. The postwar depression undermined its leadership, however, and Cincinnati moved forward to take its place. The fierce competition led to widespread speculation about the outcome. Most of the prophecy was wishful, stemming from the hopes of boosters and involving doubtful calculations. In 1816, for instance, a Pittsburgher summed up many of the elements of this competition in a chart (with ratings presumably on a scale of excellence from one to ten) designed to illustrate the inevitability of the Iron City's supremacy:[1]

	Pittsburgh	Lexington	Cincinnati
Situation for inland trade and navigation......	9	2	6
Adaptness for manufacturers	9	3	5
Fertility of surrounding soil	2	7	4
Salubrity.................................	9	7	5
Pleasantness and beauty....................	.3	1	.6
Elegance of scite [sic] and environs	1	.3	.6
	30.3	20.3	21.2

*Wade, Richard C. 1959. "The Urban Dimension." Pp. 322–336 in *The Urban Frontier: The Rise of Western Cities*. Cambridge, MA: Harvard University Press. Copyright © 1959 by the President and Fellows of Harvard College. Reprinted by permission of Harvard University Press.

Not only did the author work out the estimates in scientific detail, but he also predicted that the totals represented the population (in thousands) which each would reach in 1830.

Before a city could hope to enter the urban sweepstake for the largest prize, it had to eliminate whatever rivals arose in its own area. In many instances the odds in these battles were so uneven that smaller places gave in quickly. In others, a decision came only after a bitter and prolonged struggle. Edwardsville, Illinois, fell easily before St. Louis, but Wheeling's submission to Pittsburgh followed a decade of acrimony. Sometimes defeat meant the end of independence for a town. Louisville, for example, ultimately annexed Shippingport and Portland, while Pittsburgh reached across the river to take in Allegheny. In other cases, the penalty for failure was the lessening of power and prestige. Steubenville and Wheeling, unable to sustain their position against Pittsburgh in the Upper Ohio, had to settle for a much reduced pace of development. The same fate befell Ste. Genevieve, an early challenger of St. Louis's domination of the Mississippi and Missouri. Occasionally a victor reduced its competitor to a mere economic appendage. This is what happened to Jeffersonville and New Albany, Indiana, after Louisville captured the trade of the Falls.

Though struggles for regional primacy characterized the urban growth of the entire West, the most celebrated was Pittsburgh's duel with Wheeling. Both were situated on the Ohio and both hoped to capture its flourishing commerce. Wheeling's great advantage lay in its down-river position, where it outflanked the shoals and rapids which dominated the approach to Pittsburgh. During the late summer, low water made navigation difficult and at times impossible, inducing some merchants to use the Virginia town as a transshipment point to the East. This fact alone made Wheeling a competitor, for in no other department could it match the Iron City. Pittsburgh's detractors saw this situation as early as 1793, when the Army considered establishing a post at Wheeling. Isaac Craig complained that "this new arrangement, . . . has Originated in the Brain of the Gentlemen in Washington who envy Pittsburgh, and . . . have represented to General Knox, that Navigation is practicable from Wheeling in the dry season."[2] The same consideration made Wheeling a stop in the mail route to the West and the Ohio River terminus of the National Road.

Despite these advantages, Wheeling's population barely reached 1,000 by 1815, while Pittsburgh had become the new country's leading metropolis. A serious rivalry seemed almost ridiculous. But the postwar depression, felling the Iron City, gave its smaller neighbor the hope of rising on the ruins. This prospect brightened in 1816, when, after many abortive attempts to change the terminus, the National Road was completed to Wheeling. Optimism about the town's future abounded throughout the valley. A Steubenville editor caught the spirit in verse:

> Wheeling has secured her roads,
> Come waggoners, come and bring your loads.

> Emigrants, come hither, and build a town,
> And make Wheeling a place of renown.

By 1822, 5,000 wagons were arriving annually in the booming settlement. "Wheeling is a thriving place," a traveler observed; "it bids fair to rival Pittsburgh in the trade of the Western country."[3]

The Iron City, troubled by a stagnant economy and worried about its future, warily watched the progress of this upstart. Actually, Wheeling's challenge was only a small part of Pittsburgh's total problem, but its very ludicrousness made the situation all the more intolerable. "A miserable Virginia country town, which can never be more than two hundred yards wide, having the mere advantage of a free turnpike road and a warehouse or two, to become rivals of this *Emporium* of the West!" exclaimed the incredulous editor of the *Statesman*. As Wheeling continued to prosper, Pittsburgh accused its competitor of unfair practices, particularly of circulating the rumor that ships could not go up the river to "the Point." "They have taken to lying," the *Statesman* snapped. "We cannot believe this report," the *Gazette* asserted with more charity; "the citizens with whom we are acquainted in that place, are too honorable to countenance such childish, hurtless falsehood," especially since "everybody acquainted with the river knows that the water is as good if not better above than for 100 miles below."[4]

Civic leaders in Wheeling, feeling their oats and certain that the National Road provided a secure base for unlimited growth, continually goaded the stricken giant. "Strange that a 'miserable Virginia Country Town,' a 'mere village,' should have attracted so much attention at the 'emporium of the West,'" the *Northwestern Gazette* observed. Moreover, it asserted that the difficulty of navigation on the Upper Ohio was not mere rumor. "During the drier part of the season the greater part of the Western Merchants order their goods to Wheeling and *not* to Pittsburgh. This fact is a stubborn and decisive one. It speaks volumes. It is a demonstration." A patronizing condescension expressed an increasing confidence. "Pittsburgh may, if she will, be a large and respectable manufacturing town. She may also retain a portion of the carrying trade," the same source graciously conceded. There seemed no limit to Wheeling's assurance. Travelers reported that its residents were "actually doing nothing but walking about on stilts, and stroking their chins with utmost self-complacency. Every man who is so fortunate as to own about 60 feet front and 120 feet back, considers himself . . . snug."[5]

The next few years demonstrated, however, that history was only teasing. Wheeling's hopes for greatness were soon dashed. The National Road proved disappointing as a freight carrier, and Pittsburgh recovered from its depression, once again becoming the urban focus of the Upper Ohio. Though the Virginia town could boast over 5,000 inhabitants in 1830, its rate of growth lagged and its future prospects dimmed. To some shrewd observers the outcome was not unexpected. A Steubenville editor, consoling his readers in 1816 after their efforts to get the National Road had failed, asserted that cities could not be reared on mere highway traffic. "Rely on agriculture and manufactures," he counseled, "and you will do well without the mail or the turnpike bubble—it is not the sound of the coachman's horn that will make a town flourish."[6]

Though Pittsburgh beat back Wheeling's challenge, it could not maintain its Western leadership. Cincinnati, less affected by the postwar collapse, surged by the Iron City and established its primacy throughout the new country. It was not content, however, to win its supremacy by another's injury. Rather it developed its own positive program to widen its commercial opportunities and spread its influence. In fact, the city was so alive with ideas that one visitor referred to it as "that hot bed of projects," and another observed "great plans on foot; whenever two or three meet at a corner nothing is heard but schemes." In broad terms the object of Cincinnati's statesmanship was threefold: to tap the growing trade on the Great Lakes by water links to the Ohio, to facilitate traffic on the river by a canal around the Falls, and to reach into the hinterland with improved roads. Later another canal—this time down the Licking "into the heart of Kentucky" —a bridge across the Ohio, and a railway to Lexington were added.[7] Success would have made the entire valley dependent upon this urban center, and given the Ohio metropolis command of the strategic routes of trade and travel.

This ambitious program caused great concern in Pittsburgh. "We honestly confess," the *Gazette* admitted, that "a canal from the lakes either into the Ohio or the Great Miami . . . adds another item to the amount of our present uneasiness." By tipping the commerce of the valley northward, Cincinnati would substantially reduce the Iron City's importance as the central station between East and West. "Without this trade," the *Statesman* warned, "what can Philadelphia and Pittsburgh become but deserted villages, compared with their great rivals?"[8] Pennsylvania responded to this threat by improving the turnpike between its urban centers and ultimately constructing an elaborate canal across the mountains. In addition, Pittsburgh proposed to head off Cincinnati by building a water route to Lake Erie or tying into the Ohio system below Cleveland.

The challenge to Cincinnati's supremacy, however, came not only from a resurgent Pittsburgh, but also from a booming downriver neighbor, Louisville. As early as 1819 a visitor noted this two-front war. "I discovered two ruling passions in Cincinnati; enmity against Pittsburgh and jealousy of Louisville." In one regard the Falls City was the more serious rival, because as a commercial center it competed directly with the Ohio emporium. In fact, guerilla warfare between the two towns for advantage in the rural market began early in the century.[9] But the great object of contention was the control and traffic on the river—the West's central commercial artery.

In this contest Louisville held one key advantage. Its strategic position at the Falls gave it command of both parts of the Ohio. All passengers and goods had to pass through the town, except during the few months of high water when even large vessels could move safely over the rapids. It was a clumsy system, and from the earliest days many people envisaged a canal around the chutes. Nothing came of these plans until the coming of the steamboat immensely expanded traffic and made the interruption seem intolerable. Though nearly every shipper favored a canal, it was not until Cincinnati, anxious both to loosen river commerce and weaken a rival city, put its weight behind the improvement that any real activity developed.

Cincinnati had a deep stake in this project. A canal would not only aid the town generally but also advance the interests of some powerful groups. The mercantile community was anxious to get freer trade, and many residents had large investments in companies which hoped to dig on either the Kentucky or Indiana side of the Falls.[10] Others owned real estate in the area. William Lytle, for example, had large holdings around Portland of an estimated value of between $100,000 and $500,000.[11] Moreover, ordinary Cincinnatians had come to the conclusion that a canal would serve a broad public purpose. Hence in 1817 a town meeting was called to discuss the issue. An editor provided the backdrop: "No question was ever agitated here that involved more important consequences to this town." And from the beginning Louisville was cast as the villain of the piece. *Liberty Hall* referred to it as "a little town" trying to make "all the upper country tributary to it, by compelling us to deposit our goods in its warehouses and pay extravagant prices for transportation around or over the Falls."[12]

Since the Falls City could frustrate any project on Kentucky soil, Cincinnati's first move was to build on the opposite side. The Indiana legislature incorporated the Jeffersonville Ohio Canal Company in 1817, empowering it to sell 20,000 shares of stock at $50 apiece, and authorizing a lottery for $100,000 more. From the outset it was clear that the scheme stemmed from the Queen City. Not only did that town provide more than half the concern's directors, but also the campaign for funds emphasized its role. "The public may be assured that the wealth, influence, enterprise and talents of Cincinnati are at the head of this measure," *Liberty Hall* declared in 1818. Moreover, advocates underlined the stake of the Ohio metropolis, warning residents that if they did not support the drive they "deserved to be hewers of wood and drawers of water" for Louisville. In May 1819 a prominent Cincinnatian gave the ceremonial address as digging began on the Indiana side.[13]

Louisville hesitated to support any canal. The city had flourished on the transportation break, and many inhabitants felt that facilitating travel over the rapids would destroy the very *raison d'être* of the place. That view was probably extreme, but in the short run no one could deny that certain interests were jeopardized. "It must be admitted that the business of a portion of our population would be affected," the *Public Advertiser* confessed. "The storage and forwarding business would probably be diminished —and there might be less use for hacks and drays."[14] Tavern and hotel owners shared this anxiety, while the pilots who guided the ships through the chutes faced almost certain unemployment.

Unwilling to sacrifice these interests and uneasy about the town's future, Louisville leaders tried to deflect the mounting enthusiasm for a canal. Their first strategy was to suggest a small cut around the Falls which would accomodate keelboats and lesser craft. This expedient found few supporters, and Louisville next tried to reduce the pressure by paving the road to Portland and Shippingport, thus, facilitating the transshipment process.[15] But this, too, was inadequate, and within a few years the clamor for a canal became irresistible.

Yet the city still hoped to salvage something out of defeat, to find some compensation for the loss of its strategic position. In 1824 a local editor laid down the conditions. "It is true that we could feel but little interest in opening a canal merely for the purpose of navigation," he conceded. "A canal to be useful . . . should be constructed to give us ample water power, for various and extensive manufacturing establishments; and a sufficient number of dry docks for the building and . . . repair of nearly all the steamboats employed on western waters, should be constructed as necessary appendages." If the project included these items, he declared, then "the citizens of Louisville will be found among its most zealous advocates."[16]

The Falls City could afford to take its pound of flesh, because building on the Indiana side was much less feasible than the Kentucky route. The engineering problems were immensely more complicated, and the cost was nearly three times as great. In 1819 an official committee, comprised of delegates from Virginia, Pennsylvania, Ohio, and Kentucky, estimated the expense of the northern plan at $1,100,000 and the southern one at $350,000.[17] Hence few people acquainted with the situation took seriously the Jeffersonville Ohio Canal Company's enterprise. Yet the disadvantages of the Indiana route were not insurmountable, and Louisvillians realized that in the long run the Falls would be skirted on one side or the other. If they dragged their feet too much, their opponents would press for action regardless of the cost or difficulty. This possibility ultimately brought the Kentucky emporium to its knees.[18]

While Louisville reluctantly yielded at the Falls, Cincinnati pursued the rest of its expansion program. By 1822 the Miami Canal to Dayton was open, and work had begun on the state system which ultimately connected the Great Lakes with the Ohio River. Though the Queen City could claim less success in the Kentucky area, its economic supremacy in the West was not questioned. The new country's largest urban center, it had corralled the bulk of the region's mounting commerce and become the nexus of trade lines that reached from the Atlantic Ocean to the Gulf of Mexico.

Cincinnati's economic primacy, however, did not yet carry with it cultural leadership. This honor still belonged to Lexington, whose polish and sophistication were the envy of every transmontane town. "Cincinnati may be the Tyre, but Lexington is unquestionably the Athens of the West," *Liberty Hall* conceded in 1820. This admission reflected a sense of inadequacy which constantly shadowed the Queen City and compromised its claim to total supremacy. One resident suggested an ambitious lecture program to overcome the deficiency and "convince those persons at a distance who pronounce us as a *Commercial* people alone, that we have here, both the *Tyre* and the *Athens* of the West." Another observer, though not armed with a remedy, made the same point. "It may be well for us," he counseled, "when we can catch a moment from the grovelling pursuits of commercial operations, to cull and admire the varied sweets of those literary and scientific effusions, which have stamped Lexington as the headquarters of *Science and Letters* in the Western country."[19]

The establishment and success of Transylvania University aggravated this inferiority complex. Not only did it lend prestige to another place, but it also lured local youths to its classrooms. The *Western Spy* admitted that it was "particularly mortifying to see the College of a neighboring state attract both Students and Professors" from the Ohio metropolis. In the early twenties Cincinnati countered with a medical school which it hoped would become a "powerful rival" and "ultimately go beyond" the Kentucky institution.[20] But it was not until financial difficulties and fire brought down Transylvania that the Queen City could claim cultural parity with its Blue Grass rival.

Lexington's position also bred jealousy in Louisville. Though the larger and more prosperous of the two by 1825, the Falls City had to concede that intellectual primacy rested with its Kentucky neighbor. This admission was not easy to make, because the two towns had been bitter foes for many years. They contended for political leadership in the state; earlier, in fact, each had hoped to become its capital. Moreover, their economic interests often collided, with Lexington depending upon manufacturing and protection and Louisville emphasizing commerce and wanting freer trade. Neither yielded readily to the other on any issue. Yet the cultural leadership of the Blue Grass town was too obvious to be denied, and, from the Falls City viewpoint, it was certainly too important to be permanently surrendered.

There was, however, something of a family quarrel about this rivalry. Despite their differences, both professed love for mother Kentucky, and occasionally one deferred to the other out of filial pride. In 1820, for example, Louisville's *Public Advertiser* supported state aid to Transylvania, explaining that "distinguished institutions of learning in our own state, where education from its cheapness, shall be within the reach of the poor, is the *pivot* on which the grandeur of the state depends." In addition, the Falls City stood to gain by its success. "Louisville cannot be jealous of Lexington," the same newspaper declared; "her future interest is measurably blended with that of Transylvania University; for as that flourishes Lexington will become a more extensive and important customer to her in a commercial point of view." Likewise, when Lexington tried to get money for a hospital, its old foe offered support, but for perhaps less elevated reasons. If the Blue Grass got such an institution, "one of the same kind at this place cannot, consistently, be refused," the editor observed.[21]

And nothing forced the two to discover common interests more quickly than the appearance of a hostile outsider. When Cincinnati planned a medical school to compete with Transylvania, Louisville stood behind the testimony of the university, whose spokesman urged the state to give additional money to the institution. Otherwise, he warned, "in the struggle that must ensue, we of Transylvania will be compelled to enter the lists naked and defenceless, our opponents of Cincinnati being . . . armed. The issue of such a conflict cannot be doubted. We shall certainly be vanquished and your young men will . . . repair to the eastern schools for medical education, or Kentucky must become tributary to the state of Ohio."[22] Lexington reciprocated when the Queen City threatened a canal on the Indiana side of the river.

Kind words were few, however, and mutual aid sporadic. Usually the two communities did little to conceal their animosity. In fact, Louisville had no sooner supported Transylvania's expansion than it began again its vicious barrage on the school and its town. The attack stemmed from a mixture of political, economic, and urban motives, but it centered on the university because it was at once the symbol of Lexington's importance and its most vulnerable spot. The city's economy never recovered from the postwar depression and only its cultural renaissance kept stores and shops open. If the college failed, all failed. This was understood in the Falls City. Indeed, the *Public Advertiser* noted that the "ablest and best citizens" of the Blue Grass metropolis had tried to give a "new impetus" to the place by the encouragement of its "literary establishments."[23] Knowingly, then, Louisville struck at Lexington where it would hurt most.

Nor was there anything gentle about the tactics. In 1816, during the first debate over state assistance to Transylvania, John Rowan from the Falls City argued that the institution ought to be moved elsewhere to keep it from "improper influence" and the "many means of corrupting the morals of youth," which existed in the town. Four years later the criticism had become more barbed. "If you wish to jeopardize every amiable trait in the private character of your son, send him to Lexington," the *Public Advertiser* contended, linking the college to radical politics. "If you wish him to become a Robespierre or a Murat, send him to Lexington to learn the rudiments of Jacobinism and disorganization." By 1829 a Louisville editor was warning parents that at the university their children would be "surrounded by political desperadoes" and that "the very atmosphere of the place has been calculated to pollute the morals and principles of the youth attending it."[24]

Lexington, though an old veteran of urban rivalries, had not anticipated this bitterness. "We thought of all our institutions, it was the pride and boast of the town; and the least calculated to excite the envy, and stir up the opposition of any individual or section of the country." But the assault threatened the city's very life, and it fought back. The defense was generally constructive, detailing the achievements of Transylvania and extolling its influence on students and the new country. Graduates wrote testimonials and local citizens publicized the healthfulness and "literary atmosphere" of the community, while officials dispelled rumors about the snobbery of the college.[25]

The case was good, but Lexington strategists bungled in several respects. In 1829 not a single Jacksonian was appointed to the Board of Trustees, and not enough was done to quiet the uneasiness of either the farmers or the highly religious.[26] As a result, when Transylvania needed support most, it was almost friendless. By 1830 the campaign instituted by Louisville had destroyed Kentucky's brightest ornament and pulled the most substantial prop from Lexington's economy.

Even before Transylvania's demise Lexington felt itself slipping economically, and it tried to steady itself by better connections with the trade of the Ohio River. Canals and roads proved either impractical or inadequate, and in 1829 civic leaders planned a railroad. The act of incorporation in the next year left the northern terminus undecided, with the understanding that it would be either Louisville or Cincinnati. The uncertainty set off a curious kind of competition between those two cities. Neither could foresee the impact that a railroad might have on its own importance, yet they equally feared that it would give their rival a substantial advantage.

Louisville was especially wary. This looked like the canal issue in another form, and many people thought it wise to wait for the results of the first project. Moreover, some of the same local interests seemed to be threatened. The hack and dray owners protested that their $125,000 business would be jeopardized. And since the railroad would pass through the city and continue on to Portland, others feared the growth of a "rival town" on the Western end of the Falls. The city council, walking gingerly because of this opposition, appointed a committee to look into the question, and called a public hearing to sound out local opinion. The meeting attracted over three hundred people, and after a lively debate, it voted to keep the tracks out of Louisville.[27]

Very quickly, however, civic leaders realized that any alternative terminus was more perilous to the Falls City than the possible dislocations occasioned by accepting the railroad. Thus "S" wrote that if "we are to have a rival town, the nearer to us the less dangerous," and a "Gentleman in Lexington" warned that its "great rival, Cincinnati" was "straining every nerve" to induce the company to build in that direction. By December 1830 the tide had turned, and the council invited the Lexington and Ohio Railroad to come to Louisville.[28]

Cincinnati, despite its official policy, had many qualms about a railroad from Lexington. "Why should the citizens of Cincinnati be so anxious to create a rival town across the river?" asked the editor of the *Advertiser*. Yet the same logic which drove Louisville to change its mind sustained the Queen City's original decision. On December 7, 1830, a public meeting declared that the project "would conduce to the prosperity of this city, in an eminent degree," and a committee of prominent civic leaders invited the company's directors to come to Cincinnati to discuss details.[29] These events, coupled with Louisville's acceptance, brought great rejoicing to Lexington, for it now looked as though the railroad would bring it a share of the Ohio's commerce and arrest at last the economic decay which had brought the "Athens of the West" to the very brink of disaster.

The struggle for primacy and power—and occasionally survival—was one of the most persistent and striking characteristics of the early urban history of the West. Like imperial states, cities carved out extensive dependencies, extended their influence over the economic and political life of the hinterland, and fought with contending places over strategic trade routes. Nor was the contest limited to the young giants, for smaller towns joined the scramble. Cleveland and Sandusky, for example, clashed over the location of the northern terminus of the Ohio canal, the stakes being nothing less than the burgeoning commerce between the river and the lakes. And their instinct to fight was sound, for the outcome shaped the future of both.

Like most imperialisms, the struggle among Western cities left a record of damage and achievement. It trampled new villages, smothered promising towns, and even brought down established metropolises. Conflicting ambitions infused increasing bitterness into the intercourse of rivals, and made suspicion, jealousy, and vindictiveness a normal part of urban relationships. Yet competition also brought rapid expansion. The fear of failure was a dynamic force, pushing civic leaders into improvements long before they thought them necessary. The constant search for new markets furnished an invaluable stimulus to commercial and industrial enterprise. And, at its best, urban imperialism bred a strong pride in community accomplishment. As one resident put it, "there exists in our city a spirit . . . which may render any man proud to being called a Cincinnatian."[30]

NOTES

1. *Pittsburgh Mercury*, February 3, 1816.

2. I. Craig to J. O'Hara, June 15, 1793, MS, Isaac Craig Papers, Carnegie Library of Pittsburgh.

3. C. B. Smith, "The Terminus of the Cumberland Road on the Ohio River" (M.A. Thesis, University of Pittsburgh, 1951), 69; *Western Herald* (Steubenville), April 12, 1816; Smith, "Cumberland Road," 71; Woods, *Illinois Country*, 75.

4. *Pittsburgh Statesman* June 2, 1821; *Pittsburgh Gazette*, May 4, 1821.

5. *Northwestern Gazette* (Wheeling), June 16, 1821; *Pittsburgh Gazette*, December 18, 1818.

6. Smith, "Cumberland Road," 69; *Western Herald* (Steubenville), September 20, 1816.

7. *Pittsburgh Gazette*, January 22, 1819; February 5, 1819; *Liberty Hall* (Cincinnati), January 21, 1823; November 25, 1825.

8. *Pittsburgh Gazette*, January 22, 1819; *Pittsburgh Statesman*, November 26, 1818.

9. *Pittsburgh Gazette*, February 5, 1819; *Louisville Public Advertiser*, June 21, 1820.

10. For example, see the account of the Ohio Canal Company in *Liberty Hall* (Cincinnati), March 24, 1817.

11. The William Lytle Collection in the Historical and Philosophical Society of Ohio library includes a series of letters which explain his stake in the canal. He owned most of the land in the Portland area through which the canal ultimately passed. For a statement of its value, see D. McClellan to W. Lytle, October 21, 1817, Lytle Collection.

12. *Liberty Hall* (Cincinnati), December 29, 1817; March 26, 1817.

13. *Liberty Hall* (Cincinnati), June 5, 1818; Felbruary 26, 1818; May 20, 1818; May 6, 1818; May 14, 1819.

14. *Louisville Public Advertiser*, February 7, 1824.

15. *Liberty Hall* (Cincinnati), March 18, 1816; *Louisville Public Advertiser*, October 16, 1819.

16. *Louisville Public Advertiser*, January 21, 1824.

17. *Louisville Public Advertiser*, November 17, 1819.

18. *Louisville Public Advertiser*, February 7, 1824.

19. *Liberty Hall* (Cincinnati), May 27, 1820; December 17, 1819; May 27, 1820.

20. *Western Spy* (Cincinnati), October 13, 1817; *Liberty Hall* (Cincinnati), January 14, 1823.

21. *Louisville Public Advertiser*, September 20, 1820; September 27, 1820; December 20, 1820.

22. *Louisville Public Advertiser*, November 27, 1820.

23. *Louisville Public Advertiser*, August 23, 1820.

24. *Kentucky Reporter*, February 14, 1816; *Louisville Public Advertiser*, September 9, 1820; October 13, 1829.

25. *Kentucky Reporter*, March 7, 1827; March 10, 1823, February 21, 1827, September 8, 1828.

26. For these problems see, for example, *Louisville Public Advertiser*, October 29, 1829.

27. *Louisville Public Advertiser*, December 8, 1830; November 2, 1830; Louisville, City Journal, October 20, 1830; October 29, 1830; *Louisville Public Advertiser*, November 4, 1830.

28. *Louisville Public Advertiser*, November 3, 1830; November 5, 1830; Louisville, City Journal, December 3, 1830.

29. *Cincinnati Advertiser*, December 11, 1830; *Liberty Hall* (Cincinnati), December 10, 1830.

30. *Liberty Hall* (Cincinnati), January 9, 1829.

8

A House of Power in Town*

Amy Bridges

A historical exploration of city government in the United States reveals a set of recurrent if not constant themes: corruption and extravagance, the sacrifice of the public weal to private ends, the abuse of patronage. These outrages are denounced, evils bemoaned, opportunities seen and taken, scurrilities unmasked, men in office declared unfit, and defenders of the common good put forward and defeated with depressing regularity. Yet by accounts both contemporary and retrospective something in particular, something extraordinary and surely something worse, happened in the antebellum city. By the 1850s, reformers were declaring that the issue was not who would govern the city but whether the city could be governed at all.

Some elements of this "ungovernedness" are readily apparent. The antitemperance riot of 1857 and the mass demonstrations of 1854–57 marked a dramatic escalation in political protest and collective violence. There was more bribery and more talk of corruption than in the prior two decades. The institutional coherence of the city government was torn by the interventions of the state legislature. Factionalized parties offered voters three, four, five, or six slates to choose from, and the tabulated votes in some wards significantly exceeded the size of the registered electorate.

In addition to the popular causes of disorder, there was disorder among the leading men of New York's economic and political life. For the better part of the antebellum period, there were broad areas of agreement among politicians and men of wealth. Within the second American party system, politicians and men of wealth created an amicable division of labor, the former organizing grass-roots support and running for office and the latter providing funding for the parties and being active in the councils of party governance and the maintenance of ties to the state ad national parties. When the second American party system dissolved under the impact of national divisions, the discipline that bound plutocrats and politicians to one another dissolved with it.

At the same time, the expansion of city government increased both the temptations and the possibilities for career politicians to go it alone. Seeing their opportunities and taking them, career politicians alienated their erstwhile partners, and plutocrats responded by launching the City Reform movement. That movement was a declaration of war on politicians by men of wealth, a war that the plutocrats decisively lost at the polls. Thus the 1850s

*Bridges, Amy 1984. "A House of Power in Town." Pp. 125–137 and 189–192 in *A City in the Republic: Antebellum New York and the Origins of Machine Politics.* New York: Cambridge University Press. Copyright © 1984. Reprinted by permission of Cambridge University Press.

witnessed the emergence of the characteristic antagonists of American city politics, the boss and the reformer.

PLUTOCRACY AND POLITICS AGAIN

In 1860, reflecting on a decade of corruption and misrule, Horace Greeley asked why New York City could not return to government by the few, the "best citizens." "Our City is fearfully misgoverned and despoiled, and Corruption has been growing worse for years," Greeley argued, "mainly because her substantial citizens . . . have too generally neglected or slighted their public duties." The wealthy, he went on to say, had been allowed to abandon the ship of state for too long and should be pressed back into service.[1] Similarly, Henry J. Raymond lamented in the *Times* that businessmen were too busy making money to pay attention to politics. When August Belmont and others formed the Fifth Avenue Hotel Committee in October of 1859, James Gordon Bennett's *Herald* applauded the "revolt of the awakened respectability and integrity of the Democratic Party in New York" against "the atrocious tyranny of ruffian plunderers" from Tammany Hall.[2]

Later observers have sometimes thought, as the newspapermen did, that the conflict and insurgency of the 1850s might have been avoided, and the order and community of the older city restored, if the "best men" had not turned from public to private pursuits.[3] Indeed, the exodus of the wealthy from politics is a familiar theme in the accounts of antebellum cities. Robert Dahl presented one version of this theme in *Who Governs?*, which argued that patricians, entrepreneurs, and ex-plebes successively governed the city.[4] Sam Bass Warner, Jr., saw the emergence of the career politician in Philadelphia as a part of a more general process of specialization and the division of labor. Businessmen turned their attention to national and regional matters as the larger economic environment became more relevant to profit making; as "businessmen abandoned the city's affairs and its politics new specialists assumed their former tasks."[5] Gabriel Almond's historical study of New York documented a continuous decline in the status of New York City's officeholders from the late eighteenth to the early twentieth centuries. Almond found that, although New York's wealthy men in the pre–Civil War period were not as decadent as their postwar successors, neither were they as public spirited as their forebears. Wealthy New Yorkers were active in philanthropic organizations of various kinds, but "the wealthier groups of New Yorkers . . . engaged in politics hardly at all,"[6] and in fact "developed an attitude of contempt for politics."[7] Documenting again the retreat of men of wealth from office holding, Edward Pessen concluded that "rich men appear to have gained what they need from municipal government without exercising direct influence over it."[8] Finally, when Frank Otto Gatell sought to investigate the partisan affiliations of New York's wealthiest men, he discovered that "only a few were lured into participating in political meetings."[9]

Despite the unanimity of these studies, a nagging doubt remains. Histories of nineteenth-century enterprise and party histories seem to share a familiar list of names. An effort to concretize the sense of *déjà vu* bears fruit: Patronage beneficiaries and saloonkeepers aside, it would be hard to find *any* group of New Yorkers more politically active than the rich. Compiling a list of New York's wealthiest men in 1828, 1845, and 1856, and comparing it to the list of politicians I constructed from party histories and newspaper accounts, I found that of the city's wealthiest 470 men, 103 — or 21 percent —were active in party politics.[10] Although this finding is, on the basis of past studies, a surprise, it is very probably an understatement of the political activity of wealthy men. For one thing, the list of politicians is obviously incomplete. Second, the representation of wealth in politics would be greater if the activity or representation of families or firms rather than individuals was examined. Although the individual Thornes, Rhinelanders, Schermerhorns, and Schiefellins on the list of the wealthiest were not politically active, among their uncles, brothers, sons, in-laws, and business partners were men who devoted a good part of their energies to politics.

Who were the wealthy partisans? The 103 wealthy partisans represent all the important sources of wealth, and are not very different from the apolitical men of the same class. Included among the partisans are industrialist James P. Allaire; shipbuilders William Webb and Henry Eckford; bankers Stephen Allen, Saul Alley, J. Q. Jones, James Gore King, and Edward Prime; manufacturers Alonzo Alvord, William Colgate, and Peter Cooper; financiers John J. and William B. Astor and August Belmont; merchants William H. Aspinwall, Philip, John, and Isaac Hone, Samuel Judd, Moses Grinnell, Anson Phelps, and A. T. Stewart; and men of diversified interests like Samuel Ruggles and George Law. Peter Cooper is one of the very few men on the list who was a self-made man. The entrepreneur-industrialist who, as Robert Dahl saw, was taking the reigns of office up when the patricians were laying them down simply did not have as much money as the men on this list. Mayors Havemeyer, Harper, and Fernando Wood, for example, were affluent men, but they were not possessors of fortunes on the scale of the Grinnells, Posts, Schieffellins, Primes, and Astors.

The politically active among the wealthy were a minority group, but it is clearly not the case that only the extraordinary man of wealth took time from making money to engage in politics. The retreat from office is, to be sure, marked: In the years from 1828 to 1840, 32 of these men ran for office (and more had held office before 1828), whereas in the years from 1850 to 1863 only 12 did so. There was no comparable retreat from party politics, nor was there a retreat into a single party. If all the affiliations of wealthy partisans are examined (some changed parties and are counted more than once here), 51 were Democrats, 30 were Whigs, 2 were Workingmen, 11 were American Republicans or Know-Nothings, 22 were Reformers, 10 were Republicans, and 4 were men who ran for office before 1834 and therefore cannot be properly said to have had a party affiliation. Looking only at that affiliation that lasted longest does not change the distribution much: The 103 partisans included 46 Democrats, 25 Whigs, 6 nativists, 18 Reformers, 4 Republicans, and the 4 men without party identification.

The predominance of Democrats here is in part an artifact of the longevity of that party, and a better sense of party affiliations and shift in affiliations can be gained by looking at the figures for partisanship by decade. In the 1830s, plutocrats, like the city's electorate, favored the Democrats: Of the 20 men with party affiliations between 1834 and 1840, 12 were Democrats and 8, Whigs. In the forties, and probably beginning in the late 1830s, with the revolt of the conservative Democrats against the removal of deposits in 1838, plutocrats distinguished themselves from the electorate as a whole by favoring the Whigs 16 to 9. This finding accords well with Frank Otto Gatell's affirmation of the "basic assumption" of "olden times" that the Whigs were the party of wealth,[11] though the party's hold on them may not have been as great as the "basic assumption" claimed. In the 1850s, particularly as the struggle for control of the national government grew intense toward the end of the decade, the Democrats experienced a new infusion of wealth, claiming 17 of the very wealthy to the 4 Republicans and one die-hard Whig.

This Democratic predominance did not mean unity, for during most of the 1850s New York's wealthy partisans were as much affected by the disarray of the national party system as were the career politicians. Philip Foner has emphasized the bipartisan efforts of the wealthy during the decade before the Civil War to stop, in George Templeton Strong's words, "Billy Seward and his gang of incendiaries who wanted to set the country on fire with Civil War."[12] Foner's *Business and Slavery* demonstrates the fear of "black Republicanism" among New York's business leaders, their desire to avert a break with the South, and their bipartisan efforts to maintain the Union. The other side of support for the Missouri Compromise, the Union Safety Committee, the petitions to Washington, the assurances to the South, and the great Castle Garden Meetings was a series of partisan efforts to which Foner is less attentive. For, finally, the fate of the Union depended on who ran the national government. Only twice, in the state elections of 1850 and at the last moment, in the presidential election of 1860, did this unity transform itself from the meeting ground to the electoral ticket. For most of the 1850s, men of wealth like other men differed on the best candidate and the party to implement their consensus. John A. Thomas, Myndert Van Schaick, and Prosper Wetmore worked for William Marcy's nomination for the presidency on the Democratic ticket in 1852; Belmont worked for Buchanan; "steamboat Democrats" supported Douglas.[13] Whigs Ketchum, Grinnell, and Minturn hoped Webster would be the candidate of the Whigs; Henry Brevoort, Shepherd Knapp, and Hugh Maxwell worked for Fillmore.[14] In 1856, some former Whigs were so fearful of Republican victory that they supported Buchanan,[15] Ruggles and other die-hard anti-Republican Whigs worked for Fillmore.[16] In city contests, Francis B. Cutting, Thomas Suffern, and John Anderson supported the Hard Shells,[17] and Edward Phillips and Royal Phelps the Soft Shells.[18] Ruggles and others worked to keep the Silver Grey Whigs alive. The greatest number of wealthy partisans however, twenty-two, worked for the Reformers in city contests.

Wealthy men helped their parties in a variety of ways. Men of wealth could demonstrate their support of partisan efforts by being present at party meetings. At public meetings, the parties generally appointed a group of vice-presidents and secretaries. These positions of honor were ways to advertise who supported the party. At the same time, from this honorary vantage point the man of wealth could demonstrate his approval of the democratization (such as it was) of intraparty processes, thereby proving themselves Gentleman Democrats. Stephen Whitney and John L. Lawrence were prominent in this role at Whig meetings in the 1840s, and John G. Rohr and James P. Allaire served as vice-presidents of meetings of Whig mechanics![19] Saul Alley and John L. Graham in the 1830s, Henry Brevoort in the 1840s, and Isaac Lawrence and George Law in the 1850s were among those who supported Tammany in this way.[20] J. C. Green and George Folsom lent their energy and prestige to the emergent Republican Party;[21] Solomon P. Townsend and Anson Phelps showed their approval of the Temperance Party in 1854, and in the succeeding year Phelps appeared at a Know-Nothing meeting.[22] George Law also played an active role in the Know-Nothing organization, and the earlier nativist party, the American Republicans, also had the help of wealthy men. Edward Prime, Thomas Woodruff, and Waldron Post helped found and endorsed the American Republicans. In addition, Post and one of the Schieffelin brothers ran for alderman on the American Republican ticket.[23]

Men of wealth also acted as ward leaders and organizers for their parties. In the 1830s, wealthy men commonly served as chairmen of ward meetings. Though this kind of activity on the part of the wealthy declined, in the 1840s we find Richard Carman organizing for the Whigs in the twelfth ward,[24] and Jonathon I. Coddington[25] and Francis B. Cutting[26] worked for Tammany in the wards in the 1840s and 1850s, respectively. In general, until the appearance of the City Reform League in the 1850s, when wealthy men once again took to ward organizing, few of the wealthy are found at ward meetings outside of the first, second, third, and fifteenth wards (where many of them lived) after 1840.

Wealthy men were prominent, however, in citywide organizing and in maintaining communications with party members elsewhere in the state or in Washington. Philip Hone and Samuel Ruggles were indefatigable workers for the Whigs in this capacity, and the Whigs could also claim Robert Minturn, Hamilton Fish, the Hones, Richard Blatchford, and Simeon Draper. Similarly, the Democrats relied over the antebellum period on James Boorman, Moses B. Taylor, James R. Whiting, William B. Astor, Anson Phelps, Myndert Van Schaick, Alexander T. Stewart, Francis B. Cutting, Peter Cooper, and, toward the end, August Belmont. Men like Hone, Ruggles, Verplanck, Cooper, and Grinnell were exceptional in the consistency and prominence of their political roles. Of the 100 men examined here, perhaps 20 were consistently politically active over a long period;

a few, like George Law or Charles Henry Hall, changed affiliation often and were opportunistic; the majority were active over periods of about ten years.

In addition to their time, organizing ability, and status, wealthy men could of course give money to their parties, money that was needed for broadsides and newspapers, campaign and travel.[27] Thurlow Weed tells the story of a trip to Albany, conducted with the greatest secrecy, so that Minturn, Grinnell, Draper, Blatchford, and James Bowen could deliver $8,000 to aid Weed in securing a Whig victory Upstate.[28] In 1838, Grinnell, Blatchford, Wetmore, and others hired an estimated 200 Philadelphians to vote for the Whigs in New York City.[29] Henry Eckford offered to buy the state legislature to ensure Crawford's victory in the presidential campaign of 1824.[30] And much later, in 1859, August Belmont organized the Democratic Vigilant Association to unify the power of wealth and coerce faction-ridden Democratic politicians into line.

If, then, businessmen had abandoned older roles of patrician social leadership, and they were heavily involved in the newer forms of gaining and maintaining fortunes, they had not abandoned politics. The attachment of wealthy men to the parties is only surprising because the contrary tale has been told so many times. Even a little reflection argues that the idea that the wealthy could renounce partisan activity in the antebellum period does not square with common sense. The parties were vehicles for fixing tariffs, chartering banks, managing the currency, securing or abandoning investments in land at the frontier, and making the hinterland accessible through internal-improvement programs. Parties, for the wealthy as for others, were the institutions through which allies were or were not secured and government moved or not moved in desired directions. Men of wealth could not abandon politics for profits, if only because the latter depended in part on government policy. Moreover, among the wealthy as among citizens in general there were those who cared passionately about democracy or republicanism, religion, slavery, or the immigrant presence. To further these values, they engaged in party politics.

Although wealthy men funded parties, organized ties with state and national party organizations, and pressed for a nationally oriented political life in the city, the work of running for office, grass-roots party organizing, and a good part of local governance were left to career politicians. At the same time, politicians and wealthy men insisted, contrary to the facts of their association, that they were not the same men at all. It is not difficult to speculate on the incentives underlying this insistence. For the politicians, the same decline of deference or even outright hostility to wealth that made wealthy men poor candidates and organizers was an incentive to emphasize their own distinctiveness and their likeness to their supporters. For the wealthy, in a general situation of low stateness, and in repeated particular situations of scandal, theft, and sacrifice of the common good to private gain (in which the wealthy were as often as not implicated), there was every reason to trumpet their contempt for politics. In the 1830s and 1840s, this made for an amicable division of labor between men of wealth and career politicians. Their tasks were different, but they shared an orientation to federal and state levels of government that wed them to the parties of the second American party system and, as a result, to one another. There was, however, tension in this division of labor, and in the 1850s that tension became open conflict. In that decade, there would be intense efforts to capitalize on the distinction between the wealthy and politicians. The "best men" would put their virtue to the service of the City Reform movement, and politicians would use their popularity to coerce wealth and attempt independence of party. The conflict between career politicians and men of wealth shaped the city politics of the 1850s.

THE SECOND AMERICAN PARTY SYSTEM AND THE ROAD TO REFORM

In the 1830s and 1840s, politicians and plutocrats created an amicable division of labor. Politicians organized the machinery of local party politics and political life in the wards, mobilized grass-roots support, and held most local offices. Men of wealth funded the parties, worked to maintain ties with the state and national party apparatus, and worked in the citywide councils of party governance. Politicians and men of wealth were bound together by their shared commitment to the second American party system. For men of wealth, the policies associated with party politics in the state and nation were the politics of importance. Gideon Lee and Prosper Wetmore, for example, were Jacksonians because their "democracy and their interests had coincided in enthusiastic support of the Jacksonian assault on the 'monster monopoly.'"[31] In 1838, many wealthy Democrats became Whigs in opposition to Van Buren's Independent Treasury proposal.[32] Banks, internal improvements, tariffs, and trade were all the business of state and federal government. There were things at stake in the city—franchises and real estate, for example—but for the most part partisan dominance in the city was a means to state and national goals.

There was good reason for career politicians to share that orientation, for the patronage resources of city government had not kept pace with the growth of the electorate. In the 1780s and 1790s, when the electorate numbered about 4,000, the number of appointees—put thoroughly to use by the Federalists—was about 1,500.[33] Fifty years later, politicians faced an electorate of 40,000 with perhaps 2,000 jobs.[34] For the most part patronage was divided among the aldermen, each of whom was responsible for maintaining party organization in his ward. Readily available patronage resources were regarded as inadequate, and council members attempted various strategies in an effort to increase the number of city employees. A Whig council in the 1840s passed an ordinance to reduce the salaries of the 1,000-man municipal watch in order to increase the number of watchmen without increasing the budget. The watchmen, of course, immediately protested. Threatening to ensure Whig defeat if their salaries were not restored, the men presented the council with a petition of 3,860 signatures to demonstrate the public support they had and succeeded in regaining their former rate of pay.[35] In 1850, the Whigs attempted the same ploy with Customs House employees, with a similar lack of success.[36] For their part, the Democrats increased the pace of work on the Croton Aqueduct in the 1840s, giving rise to the term "pipe laying" to refer to public work undertaken for partisan purposes. The Democrats also tried, unsuccessfully, to use the fire department in a partisan way. . . . These strategies were not only clumsy in their particular application but also generally contentious. Workers resented being made "political creatures" and wanted government to be an exemplary employer by recognizing skill rather than partisanship, limiting the work day to ten hours, and paying good wages.

The less contentious means to increase the patronage at the disposal of local politicians was partisan control of the state or federal government. The state appointed port wardens, judges, surrogates, county clerks, weighers of merchandise, measurers of grain, and other inspectors of commodities, totaling perhaps 1,400 New York City jobs controlled by the state government in the late 1830s.[37] The national government had even larger resources at its disposal. The great prize was the Customs House. From a partisan point of view, the Customs House's attraction lay in its staff of 750 appraisers, clerks, weighers, inspectors, and the like. These were relatively well-paying positions that could be and were filled by men with some grade-school education and "rather humble origin."[38] That employment there had a four- rather than a one-year tenure was also attractive. As a result, the Customs House was an important concern of New York politicians for nearly the whole of the antebellum period. When, for example, Jackson appointed a collector not approved of by the local Democratic organization, and who did not use jobs to build it, C. C. Cambreleng wrote to the president that "we have driven from our ward meetings a body of strong republicans who for twenty or thirty years have been the back-bone of our party."[39] There were in addition 1,500 civilian jobs at the Brooklyn Navy Yard, and jobs controlled by the U.S. Marshall in the city, the subtreasurer, and the postmaster, all federal appointees. In 1853, the federal payroll in the city totaled 1.5 million dollars. In the same year, Customs House employees contributed nearly $7,000 to the Tammany treasury.[40]

None of these benefits were available if one's own party was not in power, and the existence of a significant state and even larger federal payroll in New York was a tremendous incentive to local politicians to mobilize the electorate along national lines. In this, they were in perfect agreement with those who provided partisan warchests, with nativists who wanted immigration restrictions, with those who had become convinced that general prosperity was dependent on national policy, and with organized labor desirous of ten-hours legislation and other forms of relief not in the power of local government. The success of the parties at mobilizing the electorate along national lines may be seen in turnout statistics. Voters consistently turned out in larger numbers for presidential (even, according to partial data, congressional) elections than they did for local ones. On average, the presidential elections of 1836 through 1848 drew 15 percent more votes from the city than mayoral elections. The vote for governor, though it was smaller than the vote for president, was also greater than the vote cast for mayor in the 1830s and 1840s. In the 1850s, these gaps would be appreciably narrowed. . . .

If there were good reasons for politicians and men of wealth to share a national orientation, there were also tensions between the things politicians needed to do to get elected and the policy preferences of the wealthy men with whom they were in partnership. The partnership gave rise to a series of unpopular policy positions. Politicians of both parties denounced landlords, but neither party supported legislation for a residential building code. Neither party supported popular demands for democratized control of the city's school system, nor did either party support workingmen demanding an end to contract labor. Both parties agreed with the view that charity undermined independence and caused vice and that government should retreat from economic management and the offering of succor to the unfortunate.

At the same time that these were the official positions, the behavior of politicians was at variance with them in response to popular pressure. Thus, if in their role as aldermen it was agreed to cut back on charity, as politicians the same men offered it. If as officials they insisted that state legislation like the Main Law had to be enforced, as politicians they refrained from doing so. If officials of city government denounced disorder and rowdyism by gangs and fire companies, as politicians they offered patronage to gang leaders and joined the fire companies themselves. While both parties endorsed governmental frugality, both parties engaged in pipe laying. This divergence of behavior from policy was early evidence that, by forsaking the offices of government and distancing themselves from the populace, the wealthy had lost control of city government. There was more direct evidence as well. Loss of control of public policy was demonstrated by Seward's successful promotion of the common-school system and by Fernando Wood's outrageous relief proposals.

More concretely, loss of control of public policy was evidenced in the rapid growth of the city budget, which endangered the security of wealth against taxation and the security of investments in city bands against overissue and overspending. The dimensions of the city budget are not altogether clear (and the standard source of the history of New York's finances argues that this is no accident), but the general outlines of the situation are. First, the tax rate was rising. In 1853, after making appropriations beyond the originally proposed budget, the Common Council raised the rate from $.97 per $100 to $1.23. The reform council of 1853–4 succeeded in lowering the rate, but by 1856 it was $1.38, by 1857, $1.56, and by 1863, $2.03.[41]

While taxes were going up, the tax revenue and the fees collected by the city accounted for a shrinking proportion of the city's income. In the 1830s and 1840s the city sold Croton Aqueduct and other special bonds to fund large projects, but beginning in 1843 the city sold bonds to meet current expenses as well.[42] In the 1850s, these revenue-anticipation bonds accounted for greatly increased proportions of current "income."[43] In 1844, the tax levied (when the rate was $.86) covered 67 percent of all expenditures.[44] In 1853, the tax covered 49 percent of the city's expenditures; in 1856, the levy covered 32 percent of the city's expenditures.[45] In 1844, revenue-anticipation bonds covered 27 percent of the city's expenditures;[46] in 1853 and 1856 the figures were, respectively, 32 percent and 47 percent.[47] Small wonder that reformers argued the city was having trouble selling its bonds.[48]

Wealthy men also lost direct access to the profitable areas of government that were franchised or regulated. It is this aspect of the loss of control that readers of urban history are most familiar with, for the most frequent cry of the reformer is "corruption!" In the 1850s, the accusation of corruption meant in particular taking bribes. If "much of what we consider . . . corruption is simply the 'uninstitutionalized' influence of wealth in a political system," and if, as Namier pointed out, "no one bribes where he can bully,"[49] then corruption itself is testimony to the loss of control of government decisions. Bribery, of course, was an old story in the city and an older one in the state legislature. Indeed, some of the men who became prominent in the reform movement were themselves involved in efforts to bribe the city council. In the 1850s, however, politicians seemed to stop playing by the rules. The council of 1852–3 took bribes and then did not deliver contracts.[50] They and their successors made deals and subsequently upped the ante. Offices were sold and the buyer not appointed. The "best men" could honestly react with horror when men "guilty of dishonesty in business" were nominated for office in a city that "looked to commerce for its lifeblood."[51] The council of 1852–3 may at least be credited with a fine sense of how to add insult to injury: If the Sixth and Eighth Avenues railroad franchise had to be illegally bought, the Third Avenue railroad franchise was granted to a group of men who were prominent not in business, but in politics.[52]

None of this passed unnoticed. As early as 1845, there was concern that uncontrolled city spending and the issue of revenue-anticipation bonds be curtailed. It was thought at the time that the concentration of power in the common council, the nearly powerless role of the city's executive, and the absence of executive departments were responsible for overspending. As a result, there was a flurry of reform activity in the city in the mid-1840s, including a charter-reform convention, to reorganize the city government. Nothing came of this effort[53] and in April 1849 Robert Jones (a former Whig alderman of the fifth ward counted as one of the city's wealthiest men in 1845) chaired a meeting at Vauxhall Gardens. Cambridge Livingston served as secretary; Joseph Blunt, later a prominent Republican, and Democrat James B. Murray were speakers.[54] Ward meetings were held as well,[55] and a petition was drawn up and taken to the state legislature, demanding reorganization of the city government. The legislature passed the new charter, and it was ratified by the city's electorate later in the same year.

The new arrangements created by reformers with the assistance of the state legislature did not provide any relief from corruption, overspending, and demagoguery and indeed made things worse. Reformers wanted to remove powers from the city council; they were assisted by the state legislature because the legislature, largely Republican, wanted to remove patronage resources from Democratic hands. These joint efforts succeeded in constraining the power of the city council, but at the cost of shattering the institutional coherence of the city government and increasing entrepreneurial opportunities for politicians.

The charter revisions of 1849 created ten (later seven) municipal departments with elected commissioners. Throughout the 1850s, citizens elected seven "little mayors": the comptroller; the street commissioner; the commissioners of repairs and supplies, streets and lamps, and the almshouse; the counsel to the corporation; and the city inspector (whose province was public health).[56] Appointment of the police was moved from the aldermen to the office of the mayor.[57] Later the influence of the best men in combination with Republican dominance of the statehouse led the state government to create a series of commissions with appointed chiefs. The metropolitan police board (discussed in Chapter 5), the Central Park Commissioners, and the Croton Aqueduct Board were removed from the control of the city government and made available to Republican partisans. The Board of Education had been separate from the city council for some time. Each of these boards made up its own budget and demanded funds from the city council.[58] To further reduce the fiscal control of the city council, the legislature in 1857 made the Board of County Supervisors distinct from charter officials and arranged for it to be bipartisan.

The multiplicity of relatively independent city departments provided opportunities for enterprising politicians to create their own organizations, and in doing so to make themselves independent both of the parties and of partnership with men of wealth. It was not possible, when each of the independent departments was run by an elected official, to coordinate their policies. The functioning of the almshouse—whether criteria for relief were stringent or relaxed, whether inmates were exploited or not—depended on who was almshouse commissioner. The work life of city employees (whether they would be subject to political taxes, whether there would be much work or little, whether foremen would be knowledgeable workmen or political "creatures," and the size and certitude of the paychecks) depended on who was elected commissioner of repairs and supplies, who was appointed to the Central Park Board, and who ran the street department (that last, according to the *Times*, the "El Dorado of municipal offices"). Candidates boasted of their generosity or Americanness and accused others of bigotry, partisan abusiveness, or tight-fistedness. Emphasis on personality fueled the disintegration of parties, already factionalized by national differences. Thus the 1850s and 1860s witnessed a series of entrepreneurial efforts by men declaring themselves anti-Tammany Democrats. Daniel F. Tiemann, who was the reform candidate for mayor in 1857, could bring a part of the Democratic organization with him to the reform effort because he had been an alderman and also an almshouse governor.[59] John McKeon, who organized the

"McKeon Democracy" in 1862–3, had been alderman, district attorney, and almshouse governor.[60] Henry W. Genet, who tried to take Tammany over from within, had built his own "ring" of supporters in a career as alderman, president of the board of aldermen, and county clerk.[61] The most successful of these insurgencies, of course, was that of Fernando Wood.

The efforts of reformers to diffuse the powers of the common council and the efforts of upstate Republicans to gain control of certain institutions of municipal governance were both made more intense by the fact that the expansion of city government had as its natural concomitant the expansion of resources available for organization building in the city. Entrepreneurial efforts by politicians were inviting prospects not only because of the increased independence of municipal departments but also because the pot was much larger than it had been five or ten years before. Central Park alone, for example, employed as many as 1,000 men a day.[62] By 1858, Isaac Fowler was writing to a friend, "It is hardly necessary . . . to tell you that city patronage is greater than the Customs House."[63] Three years later, a Tammany official declared: "No man should have power in this state if that power is to be swayed by the authorities in Washington. . . ."[64] It was now possible for the first time to build an elegant house of power in town, and politicians were working away at it.

NOTES

1. *NYTr*, 16 October 1860, p. 4.

2. *NYT*, 11 November 1857, p. 4; *NYH*, 1 October 1850, p. 4.

3. Warner, *Private City*, for example, argued that "professional politics" produced "weak, corrupt, unimaginative municipal government" because without business leadership in office "voters . . . would not trust their government with large sums of money, big projects, or major innovations"; p. 98.

4. Robert A. Dahl, *Who Governs? Democracy and Power in an American City* (New Haven, Conn.: Yale University Press, 1961), chapter 1.

5. Warner, *Private City*, p. 86.

6. Gabriel Almond, "Plutocracy and Politics in New York City," Ph.D. dissertation, University of Chicago, 1938, p. 52.

7. Ibid., p. 48.

8. Pessen, *Riches*, pp. 283–7.

9. Gatell, "Money and Party," p. 263.

10. Edward Pessen's *Riches* provides a list of New York's 200 wealthiest citizens in 1828 and 300 wealthiest citizens in 1845. In addition, I constructed a list of New York's wealthiest 200 citizens from William H. Boyd, *Boyd's New York City Tax Book 1856 and 1857* (New York: William H. Boyd, 1857), which lists assessor's valuations of personal and real property for those who paid taxes in 1856. The three lists, totaling 700 names, reduce by redundancy and the elimination of a few widows

to 470 men. I compared this list to a list of politicians compiled from newspaper accounts of partisan meetings, the party histories, and other secondary sources. These sources generated a Politicians' List of 1,067 names. In addition, lists as complete as sources allowed were constructed of men who ran for alderman and state assemblyman, and these generated an additional 916 names.

11. Gatell, "Money and Party," p. 257.
12. Nevins and Thomas, *George Templeton Strong*, 2:19 (5 October 1860).
13. Foner, *Business and Slavery*, pp. 82–3.
14. Ibid., pp. 81–2, n. 82; 152; 153.
15. Ibid., p. 132.
16. Ibid., pp. 100ff.
17. *NYH*, 2 November 1854.
18. *NYH*, 26 October, 1855, p. 1.
19. Whitney, *NYTr*, 19 February 1845, p. 2; Lawrence, *NYTr*, 6 April 1842, p. 2, and 19 March 1845, p. 2; Allaire and Rohr, *JC*, 7 February 1838, p. 2.
20. On Alley, see *EP*, 28 March 1834, and Myers, *Tammany Hall*, p. 106. On Graham, see *EP*, 28 March 1834, p. 2; Graham was also the second-ward aldermanic candidate for the party in 1835. Henry Brevoort ran for alderman of the twelfth ward on the Democratic ticket in 1842 and 1843. Isaac Lawrence was a Mozart Hall activist; see *NYH*, 17 November 1859, p. 1. George Law was a member of the Democratic Vigilant Association in 1860; see *NYH*, 27 November 1857, p. 8; and *NYTr* 1 December 1859, p. 4.
21. On Green, see Foner, *Business and Slavery*, p. 248. On Folsom, see *NYTr*, 2 December 1859, p. 5.
22. On Temperance, see *NYH*, 5 November 1854, p. 5. On Phelps as a Know-Nothing, see *NYH*, 8 October 1855, p. 5.
23. On Law as a Know-Nothing, see Scisco, *Political Nativism*, p. 219. On Prime, see ARP *Address*. On Woodruff, see ARP *Address* and Leonard, "Nativism and Reform" p. 382. On Post, see Politicians' List (fifteenth ward). On Schieffelin, see *NYTr*, 19 March 1845, p. 2. Schieffelin won, Post lost.
24. *NYTr*, 6 April 1842, p. 2.
25. Mushkat, *Tammany*, pp. 115, 215, 225.
26. *NYH*, 2 November 1854.
27. New York money was important in maintaining Whig, Republican, and Democratic parties in the West. Weed, *Autobiography*, p. 476; De Alva S. Alexander, *A Political History of the State of New York*, 4 vols. (New York: Holt, 1906), 2:282ff. Both authors felt that Seward lost the Republican nomination in 1860 in part because Republicans feared a dominance of New York in their party since New York money had given New York a dominant role in the Whig Party. New York played a similar financial role in the Democratic Party, particularly at the approach of the elections of 1856 and 1860. See Irving Katz, *August Belmont, A Political Biography* (New York: Columbia University Press, 1968), pp. 18–22, 74–83.
28. Weed, *Autobiography*, p. 476.

29. D. R. Fox, *The Decline of the Aristocracy in the Politics of New York, 1801–1840* (New York: Harper Torchbooks, 1965 [orig. pub. 1917]), p. 417, n. 3.

30. Weed, *Autobiography*, p. 124.

31. Trimble, "Diverging Tendencies," p. 404.

32. Gatell, "Money and Party," p. 265; *JC*, 4 January 1838, and the week following; *NYH*, 3 January 1838, p. I.

33. Sidney Pomerantz, *New York, An American City, 1783–1803* (New York: Columbia University Press, 1938), pp. 37, 51, 63. Staughton Lynd and Alfred Young, "After Carl Becker: The Mechanics and New York City Politics, 1774–1801," *Labor History* 5 (1964):221.

34. Leo Hershkowitz estimated the patronage available to the city council in 1838 as 1,200 positions, and Ira Leonard estimated the official patronage available in the early 1840's as 2,000. Hershkowitz, "Local Politics," p. 318. Leonard, "The Politics of Charter Revision in New York City, 1845–1847," *New York Historical Society Quarterly* 62 (1978):51.

35. Leonard, "New York City Politics," pp. 243–4.

36. *NYH*, 25 October 1850, p. 2.

37. Alexander, *Political History*, p. 38.

38. William Hartman, "The New York Custom House: Seat of Spoils Politics," *New York History* 34 (April 1953): 156.

39. Mushkat, *Tammany*, p. 116.

40. Chalmers, "Tammany Hall," pp. 48–9. As each new president assumed office, delegates and petitions demanding that particular individuals be rewarded with these posts left New York for Washington. After 1845, the factiousness of both parties put presidents in positions that had to be handled with great skill. For example, when New York's Democrats turned against Fernando Wood, part of their effort to isolate him involved convincing Buchanan not to give Wood any patronage. As a result, federal patronage in the city was divided between Hard Shells and the New York Hotel Committee, Ibid., p. 167.

41. Edward Dana Durand, *The Finances of New York City* (New York: Macmillan, 1898), gives an annual listing of the tax rate, pp. 372–3.

42. There was concern about this almost immediately. See Leonard, "Charter Revision," p. 66. New York City Board of Aldermen, *Documents*, vol. 12, doc. 1 (1845), p. 8.

43. In 1852, an additional kind of revenue-anticipation bond was created, the "assessment bond." Residents were required to contribute a portion of the costs for grading their streets, and these charges were special assessments. Contractors refused to wait to be paid until the special assessments were collected. Revenue from special assessments was pledged against the assessment bonds and revenue from bond sales was used to pay the contractors. Durand, *Finances*, p. 168.

44. Computed for 1844 from New York City Board of Aldermen, *Documents*, vol. 12, doc. 1 (1845), p. 8.

45. Computed for 1853 from Valentine, *Manual . . . 1854*, pp. 198–9, and for 1856 from Valentine, *Manual . . . 1857*, pp. 180–1.

46. The amount of bond revenue is in Valentine, *Manual . . . 1844–5*, p. 167, and the total budget is in Valentine, *Manual . . . 1854*, pp. 198–9 and Valentine, *Manual . . . 1857*, pp. 180–1.

47. Ibid.

48. James R. Whiting claimed the city could not sell its bonds when he ran as the reform candidate for mayor. *NYH*, 30 October 1856, p. 1.

49. James C. Scott, *Comparative Political Corruption* (Englewood Cliffs, N.J.: Prentice-Hall, 1972), pp. 33, 99.

50. The Sixth- and Eighth-Avenue railroad contract, the contract investigated by the grand jury, was originally awarded to John Pettigrew and his associates, on payment of a bribe. When Kipp et al. were awarded the contract, the bribe was not returned to Pettigrew and his business partners. Carman, *Street Surface Railway*, p. 47.

51. This was an objection to Fernando Wood's candidacy. Wood had been sued by a former business partner.

52. Carman, *Street Surface Railway*, pp. 59–60.

53. Leonard, "Charter Revision," passim.

54. *NYTr*, 7 April 1849, p. 3.

55. *NYTr*, 9 April 1849, p. 3.

56. Chalmers, "Tammany Hall," p. 77.

57. Richardson, "Fernando Wood," p. 6.

58. "How New York is Going to be Punished," *Harpers Weekly*, 28 March 1857, p. 194; Chalmers, "Tammany Hall," pp. 146–8; Durand, *Finances*, pp. 80–8.

59. Myers, *Tammany Hall*, p. 179.

60. Mushkat, *Tammany*, pp. 252, 309.

61. Ibid., pp. 336–7.

62. *NYH*, 12 November 1857, p. 1.

63. Chalmers, "Tammany Hall," p. 162.

64. Mushkat, *Tammany*, p. 369.

9

City Trenches*

Ira Katznelson

It is hard to find the right words to discuss politics and the American working class without reaching for the clinical language of schizophrenia. The main element of what Raymond Williams calls the "selective tradition"[1] of the working class in the United States has been a stark split between the ways workers in the major industrial cities think, talk, and act when they are at work and when they are away from work in their communities. When was this disconnected pattern first formed? How did it differ from the ways working classes developed in other Western societies at comparable moments? What were the main causes of the political dissociation between work and home?[2]

The eighteenth-century northern mercantile port cities of Boston, Philadelphia, and New York were urban enclaves in a rural world. Their internal organizations of space; the character of production; class relations between merchants, the property-owning middle classes, and a small but growing group of propertyless unskilled laborers and some artisans; their rates of growth; their economic prosperity; and their relations to other units of government—all these were determined largely by the commercial and transport functions they performed by linking internal and external markets for the agrarian economy. Three kinds of economic activities were predominant: trade with Britain, the Continent, Africa, and the West Indies (furs, tobacco, rice, lumber, wheat, fish, indigo, and livestock for export, and the importation of manufactured goods, sugar, immigrants, and slaves); production in industries like flour milling and shipbuilding (sails, ropes, and barrels) that directly supported this commerce; and crafts of baking, carpentry, weaving, and tailoring, among others, which provided goods and services for the local population. "The prevailing mode of production in the colonial towns was the workshop craft, employing generally one or two journeymen and a like number of apprentices." Most frequently the household provided the place of production.[3]

In the forty years from 1820 to the outbreak of the Civil War, the economic context within which these cities functioned changed radically. In the 1830s and 1850s especially, there was an extraordinary increase in the tempo of investment in canals, roads, and railways, the internal improvements that created an extended domestic market and provided the infra-

*Katznelson, Ira. 1981. "City Trenches." Pp. 45–58 in *City Trenches: Urban Politics and the Patterning of Class in the United States.* New York: Pantheon Books. Copyright © 1981. Reprinted by permission of Pantheon Books, a division of Random House, Inc.

structure for subsequent industrial development. A recognizably modern business cycle of boom and bust, closely tied to the pattern of these expenditures, replaced oscillations of food prices as the dominant feature of economic life. The labor force that was engaged in manufacturing grew from 3 percent in 1810 to 14 percent by 1860. . . . [4]

. . . The U.S. economy remained chiefly agrarian and commercial throughout the antebellum period. But the explosive expansion in commerce, domestic and overseas, qualitatively transformed economic patterns of exchange. After the conclusion of the War of 1812, domestic trade displaced foreign trade in importance. Allan Pred has carefully documented the consequences of the "great turnabout" of 1810–1820. In 1810 approximately two tons were shipped abroad for every one that was carried on vessels engaged in domestic trade. By 1820 parity had been reached, and by 1840 the ratio of 1810 had nearly been reversed. Commodities were exchanged in growing volume between Northeast and South, between the major northeastern cities of New York, Boston, Philadelphia, and Baltimore, and between these cities and the newer lake and river cities west of the Allegheny Mountains.[5] The geographic points of exchange were cities; the expanded pattern of trade was interurban. Rapid urbanization and commercial expansion went hand in hand.[6]

Until the 1840s manufacturing clearly had a subsidiary role in the older port cities. Local markets were too small and the national transportation system too primitive to support large-scale manufacturing independent of mercantile imperatives. Rather, the urban economy was characterized by highly diversified industrial production in small handicraft and unmechanized firms that had relatively low output. "An overwhelming portion," Pred observes, "perhaps virtually all, of the industrial activities located within the confines of New York, Boston, Philadelphia, and Baltimore were either directly or indirectly linked to the mercantile functions of those cities." Tobacco milling, tanning and leather processing, and sugar refining were among the largest industries in these cities. Only in Philadelphia was manufacturing on a significant scale divorced from either direct or indirect dependence on merchants' requirements and commercial capital. Its cotton, locomotive, and iron works were atypical.[7]

Although virtually all the major industries of the mercantile cities had roots that reached back at least a century or more, their growth in number produced major alterations. Chandler observes that in the first four decades of the nineteenth century the traditional enterprise in commerce changed under the impact of economic expansion and business specialization. General merchants presided over the colonial and early-postcolonial economy. The family was the basic unit of commerce. The general merchant was a "grand distributor," who "bought and sold all types of products and carried out all the basic commercial functions. He was an exporter, wholesaler, importer, retailer, shipowner, banker, insurer." He presided not only over overseas and domestic intercity trade, but over the local distribution and marketing of the products of the city's many small enterprises. "In all these activities, the colonial merchant knew personally most of the individuals involved." By 1840 the general merchant had virtually disappeared. The earliest distinction was between shopkeepers and merchants; then the merchant was replaced by the "impersonal world of the jobber, importer, factor, broker, and the commission agent." Commercial enterprises grew increasingly specialized, as they came to deal exclusively in a specific genre of goods—china, glass, hardware, dry goods, watches, wines, clothing. Market forces replaced personal contact in the management of the growing volume and complexity of trade. And in finance and transportation the joint-stock finance company superseded more traditional family and partnership forms of ownership. These enterprises came to cluster more and more in specialized portions of the city, divorced from residence communities.[8]

Change came more slowly to the traditional organization of production, but it came nevertheless. Victor Clark's classic study of manufacturing in early America documents at some length the family basis of manufacturing; at the turn of the century, manufacturers were skilled artisans who lived at, or very near, the premises where they worked at highly specialized trades. Before 1840 urban production expanded in three distinctive ways. First, traditional shops were enlarged, as "craftsmen added more apprentices and journeymen to their work force." Work was still performed in or near the home of the master, though more and more laborers lived away from the workplace. Second, work was distributed for processing in the homes of nearby families. Third, large industrial factor establishments wholly divorced from the home were created; before 1840 factories employing more than fifty workers were common only in the textiles.[9]

After 1840, in the last two antebellum decades, the factory system began to expand. By the late 1850s foreign observers regularly took note of the "American system of manufacturing." Primarily, but not exclusively, in southern New England,

> in the light metalworking industries, notably in firearms, clocks, watches, locks, and tools of various kinds, and then spreading into neighboring states and a broadening range of industries, there came into being the basic elements and patterns of modern mass manufacturing; that is, the principles and practice of quantity manufacture of standardized products characterized by interchangeable parts and the use of a growing array of machine tools and specialized jigs and fixtures, along with power, to substitute simplified, and as far as possible, mechanized operations for craftsman's arts.[10]

In this period, Mohl notes, "commerce began to give way to manufacturing in eastern cities. New York and Philadelphia led the way. Factories . . . proliferated and became typical places of work for urban laborers.[11] After the 1840s what Pred calls an "industrial threshold" was reached in cities, as accumulated capital came to be invested more and more in large-scale urban manufacturing, rather than in the traditional wholesaling-trading complex.[12] In these ways the economic base of the major cities before the Civil War was transformed. By the outbreak of hostilities, they had developed a mix of manufacturing and nonmanufacturing employment that remained roughly stable, in spite of continuing city growth, for the subsequent century. Thus, Williamson stresses that we should take note of

the general similarity in the economic structure of cities between 1860, 1870, and 1950. Especially for those in the northeastern tier of states . . . the ratio of manu-facturing employment to total employment is not very different from that of the "industrial" cities of 1950. . . . Even relative to their industrial maturity in 1950, by 1860 most of the cities in the Northeast and many in the Midwest fully qualified as industrial-urban complexes.[13]

Interpreting the precise extent to which the social and spatial structures of these industrializing cities differed from the prevailing patterns of the late-eighteenth century is made difficult by disputes about the character of the mercantile city. Recent scholarship indicates that in the port cities of the Revolutionary era, workplaces and residence spaces had begun to segment; small neighborhoods became increasingly segregated by class; inequality between the classes may have become more acute.[14] In his study of New York, Carl Abbott argues that the mercantile city was not an integrated jumble of work and residence with little differentiation of neighborhoods. Rather, a new built form was being created in which different kinds of functional spaces could be distinguished:

Proceeding on the basis of economic function, one can discover a commercial district along the lower East River, a sector devoted to light manufacturing and retailing in the middle part of town, and a heavier manufacturing sector on its northern edge. The city was similarly split into residential neighborhoods of differ-ent status and characteristics. Its upper classes lived within the commercial district and adjacent to it west of Broad Street. Artisans and tradesmen . . . lived as well as worked in a broad band across the center of the city. Areas with the poorest housing, worst physical conditions, and most undesirable and transient population were found on the fringes.[15]

Nevertheless, in spite of these emerging divisions in space, the mercan-tile cities in the Revolutionary era stood, from the vantage point of 1860, rather closer to the level of differentiation characteristic of medieval cities than to that typical of the modern commercial-industrial city. The incipient divisions — which Abbott, among others, rightly emphasizes and sets against overromanticized notions of the mercantile city — were more in the nature of a combination of emerging tendencies and traditional patterns. The cities were very compact and crowded. A complete, or even a terribly well-defined, separation of land uses and activities was virtually impossible, given the ecology and topography of the cities. The latter developed close to their shores (their "hinge" to the world market) and hugged the coast. Philadel-phia in 1780 was nine blocks square and had a population of 16,500. New York's 22,000 residents lived and worked in a triangle only four thousand feet wide and six thousand feet from apex to base.[16] This crowding expressed and helped reproduce the ideology and reality of an integrated community. Thus, Warner has insisted that late-eighteenth-century Philadelphia

> was a community. Graded by wealth and divided by distinctions of class though it was, it functioned as a single community. The community had been created out of a remarkably inclusive network of business and economic relationships and it was maintained by the daily interactions of trade and sociability . . . every man and occupation lived jumbled together in a narrow compass.[17]

By the time of Civil War, the ambiguous status of "community" in the older port cities had been resolved, by the impact of capitalist development. Between 1800 and 1850 Philadelphia grew in population from 69,000 to 340,000; and New York City from 60,000 to 516,000.[18] The cities were becoming unmistakably divided into distinctive districts of work and home.[19] The "unity of everyday life, from tavern to street, to workplace, to housing," of the late-eighteenth-century city shattered; Philadelphia was by 1860 "a city of closed social cells." One manufacturing worker in four labored in the principal downtown ward (the sixth) in a city of twenty-four wards:

> The garment industry in all its branches, boot and shoe makers, bookbinders, printers, and paper box fabricators, glass manufacturers, machinists, coopers, sugar refiners, brewers, and cigar makers especially concentrated here. Thousands of workers walked to the downtown every day, while omnibuses, and just before the Civil War, horse-drawn streetcars brought shopkeepers and customers. No tall office buildings yet outlined the downtown, no manufacturing lofts filled entire blocks, but the basic manufacturing-wholesale-retail-financial elements had already been assembled by 1860 for the future metropolis.[20]

New manufacturing clusters radiated "out from the original urban core like a crude spiderweb spun through the blocks of little houses." Although the incompleteness of street directories and census data makes it very difficult to know precisely how many workers left their homes to labor, documented commutation patterns for Philadelphia and New York indicate unmistakably that "work began to be separated from home neighborhood."[21] Even before the rapid industrial development of the 1840s, there were "significant alterations in the propensity to commute and in the average length of commutation that did occur." Pred very conservatively estimates that in New York City in 1840 approximately one-fourth of the *industrial* workers were already working outside their homes.[22] The increasing separation of work and home was matched by the growing segregation of residence communities by class, ethnicity, and race. New York City in this era, Robert Ernst reports, became increasingly differentiated in these ways:

Whether in shanty towns or in the commercial districts, whether along the waterfront or in the Five Points, immigrant settlers drew to their area others having the same nationality, language, religion, or race. Once a nucleus was established toward which later arrivals were attracted, the cohesive bond resulting from consciousness of similarity tended to replace the magnetic forces of cheap shelter and ready employment. Native prejudice against foreigners furthered the isolation of these communities, and white prejudice against Negroes similarly produced well-defined colored settlements. . . . [23]

This new urban system of "city trenches" had three main elements: trade unions at the workplace; a quite separate decentralized party system; and an array of new government services that were delivered to citizens in their residential communities.

The trade unions that developed at the workplace in the antebellum period sought to protect the traditional prerogatives of skilled workers, struggled for better working conditions, and, above all, fought for higher wages. These unions were prepared to be quite militant, especially in periods of prosperity and labor scarcity. Urban unions called many strikes, which were notably successful in raising pay scales. Between 1850 and 1857 skilled unionized workers in New York secured a 25 percent increase in wages. The unions of the 1850s collected dues systematically and accumulated strike funds. Their most important progressive achievement was their ability "to apply the principles of collective bargaining to the whole trade in order to establish a uniform wage scale for all workers." [24] More than any other institution of the period, the trade unions overcame the differences between native and immigrant workers to forge a common consciousness of class. Many unions, including those of the bakers, smiths, and wheelwrights, actively recruited immigrants. "Quite often," Foner writes,

> several nationalities united within the same labor organization, as in the Upholsterers Union in New York which had among its membership in 1850 German-American, Irish-American, French-Canadian, English, and native American workers. The Tailors Union of New York was made up of native American and German-American workers. At first they were not on the best of terms, but police brutality, impartial as to a worker's national origin, during a strike made for greater understanding. [25]

Although most of these unions were shattered by the economic crisis of 1857, they left a legacy of a class-conscious labor movement and of the familiar paraphernalia of the union shop, strike funds, and collective bargaining. They also left the legacy of restricting their attention to immediate trade-union demands and eschewing party activity and political action outside the workplace.

The antebellum party system complemented the limited focus of the unions because it was grounded exclusively in the residence community. The main political parties in the three decades before the Civil War were less interested in ideology than in mobilizing voters. Their attempts to garner votes in the big cities were organized on the geographical basis of the ward by professional politicians who used new kinds of patronage to woo supporters.

Although the parties competed in national presidential elections, party organizations were intensely *local* territorial institutions. Seen from the bottom of party hierarchies, party life in this period, especially with respect to local offices, gave the overwhelming impression of factional fluidity, individual initiative, clientalistic ties between leaders and followers, and the isolation of organizations in one ward from those in other parts of the large cities. The centralized urban machines date from the 1870s and beyond. In the antebellum years the urban party structures especially were decentralized and enmeshed in the organizational life of neighborhoods—their gangs, firehouses, secret societies, saloons.[26] The ward, as community and as the juridical unit of politics, was the core of the political community.

In these wards, indeed at all levels of the political system, the professional politician (whose prototype can be found in the Albany Regency of the 1820s)[27] superseded the older governing elite of patrician merchants. The sheer number of elections and the organizational skills and time required "put a premium on the efforts of men who were willing to devote all, or almost all, of their time to politics, and who did not expect leadership to fall to them as a matter of deference, celebrity, or wealth."[28] For these new organizers the perpetuation of the party took precedence over ideological commitments. They sought to prosper by organizing political life. And they reflected in their diverse social backgrounds and ties to neighborhood institutions the increasingly heterogeneous class and ethnic character of the urban mosaic. Not all these politicians, of course, came from working-class wards. But those who did were, from the vantage point of working-class neighborhoods, a part of "us," not "them."[29]

The new political organizations that they led bound voters to the party by distributing patronage. Traditional patron-client forms of patronage, in which family and personal ties determined job distribution, came to be replaced by more instrumental bases of distribution. At the national level this transformation was achieved most importantly by the Jacksonians who "established a party system and built a system of public administration which were independent of the informal social hierarchies upon which the Jeffersonians had relied." Locally, too, patronage became the principal instrument of party cohesion. In his important work on the subject, Shefter notes the shift in the character of patronage in New York City in the antebellum years. In the early decades of the nineteenth century, local politics was a politics of low participation. The Tammany elite that governed in close association with the merchant elite pursued a politics "centered chiefly around the competitive quest for patronage and mercantile privileges —charter franchises, supply contracts—and these leaders had no incentive to distribute the fruits of power more widely." When, under the impact of the franchise extension and the appeals of the Workingmen's party, new voters without ties to Tammany were brought into the electorate, Tammany responded by soliciting support on the basis of a new kind of patronage network. Patronage was distributed to leaders of indigenous working-class associations in the wards who could utilize these new resources to secure and expand their followings.[30] . . .

. . . In the antebellum years a new kind of political system was created there; at its center were municipal *services*. The systematic organization of disciplined professional policemen at the city level was unknown in the West before the creation of a police force in London in 1829. The London system was introduced in the major cities of the United States in the three decades before the Civil War. This period is also characterized by the bureaucratization of municipal charity and poor relief and by the establishment of modern mass public school systems. These organizations, together with the massive expansion in the budgets and the capacities of local governments to license, award contracts, and shape the tempo and spatial direction of city growth, put unprecedented distributive resources in the hands of local government and party officials.[31] These tangible resources provided the largesse needed to organize the world's first mass urban political parties that were working-class based. By the 1850s, it is important to stress, local political parties at the community level were genuinely working-class institutions, rooted deeply in the local institutions and cultural life made possible by the development of class-homogeneous neighborhoods separate from workplaces.

Significantly, however, these parties at the neighborhood-ward level organized workers not as workers, but as residents of this or that ward, as members of this or that ethnic group; and they did not intrude on workplace concerns. Although throughout the antebellum period such class-related economic issues as banking, tariffs, internal improvements, and slavery dominated the national and state political agendas, votes were increasingly solicited on the basis of ethnic and religious affiliations. It is striking that in a society undergoing very rapid change, and offering many possible points of conflict between groups and classes, the party system exploited locality-based ethnic divisions in the older cities more than anything else.

NOTES

1. Raymond Williams, *Culture and Society* (New York: Columbia University Press, 1950).

2. Remarkably, with the exception of Susan Hirsch, in her first-rate study of Newark, New Jersey, scholars have left these issues unexamined. Hirsch's work, moreover, for all its merits, is rather more descriptive of the split between work and community than analytical. Susan G. Hirsch, *Roots of the American Working Class* (Philadelphia: University of Pennsylvania Press, 1978).

3. Richard Morris, *Government and Labor in Early America* (New York: Columbia University Press, 1946), p. 42; Howard P. Chudacoff, *The Evolution of American Urban Society* (Englewood Cliffs, N.J.: Prentice-Hall, 1975), p. 14; and Allan R. Pred, *The Spatial Dynamics of U.S. Urban-Industrial Growth, 1800–1914* (Cambridge, Mass.: MIT Press, 1966), chap. 4.

4. Douglas C. North, *The Economic Growth of the United States, 1790–1860* (Englewood Cliffs, N.J.: Prentice-Hall, 1961); William N. Parker and Franklee Whartenby, "The Growth of Output Before 1840," Conference on Research in Income and Wealth, *Trends in the American Economy in the Nineteenth Century* (Princeton, N.J.: Princeton University Press, 1961); Stanley Lebergott, "Labor Force and Employment, 1800–1960," Conference on Research in Income and Wealth, *Output, Employment, and Productivity in the United States after 1800* (New York: Columbia University Press, 1966); Thomas C. Cochran, "The Business Revolution," *American Historical Review* 79 (December 1974); and J. R. T. Hughes and Nathan Rosenberg, "The United States Business Cycle Before 1860: Some Problems of Interpretation," *Economic History Review* 15, no. 3 (1963).

5. Allan R. Pred, *Urban Growth and the Circulation of Information: The United States System of Cities, 1790–1840* (Cambridge, Mass.: Harvard University Press, 1973), chap. 4.

6. Jeffrey Williamson, "Antebellum Urbanization in the American Northeast," *Journal of Economic History* 25 (December 1965): 598–99.

7. Pred, *Spatial Dynamics*, pp. 168, 176.

8. Chandler, *Visible Hand*, pp. 15, 18, 27.

9. Ibid., pp. 51, 57; Victor S. Clark, *History of Manufacturers in the United States*, 3 vols. (New York: Carnegie Institution, 1929).

10. John Sawyer, "The Social Basis of the American System of Manufacturing," *Journal of Economic History* 14 (1954): 369.

11. Raymond A. Mohl, "The Preindustrial American City," in Raymond A. Mohl and James F. Richardson, eds., *The Urban Experience: Themes in American History* (Belmont, Cal.: Wadsworth, 1973), p. 7.

12. Pred, *Spatial Dynamics*, p. 183; see also Douglass C. North, "Location Theory and Regional Economic Growth," *Journal of Political Economy* 63 (June 1955).

13. Williamson, "Antebellum Urbanization," pp. 603–4.

14. David Montgomery, "The Working Classes of the Pre-Industrial American City, 1780–1830," *Labor History* 9 (winter 1968).

15. Carl Abbott, "The Neighborhoods of New York, 1760–1775," *New York History* 55 (January 1974): 51.

16. Ibid.; Sam Bass Warner, Jr., *The Private City: Philadelphia in Three Periods of Its Growth* (Philadelphia: University of Pennsylvania Press, 1968), pp. 2, 11.

17. Ibid., p. 11.

18. Ira Rosenwaike, *Population History of New York City* (Syracuse, N.Y.: Syracuse University Press, 1972), p. 16.

19. It is tempting to overstate the extent of change in the internal organization of city space that economic change entailed. As late as 1860, Warner cautions, most areas of Philadelphia were still "a jumble of occupations and classes, shops, homes, immigrants and native Americans." Yet the direction of change was unmistakable, and its degree quite dramatic. Warner, *Private City*, p. 50.

20. Ibid., pp. 58–59.

21. Ibid., p. 59.

22. Pred, *Spatial Dynamics*, p. 208.

23. Robert Ernest, *Immigrant Life in New York City* (New York: King's Crown Press, 1949), p. 38

24. Philip Foner, *History of the Labor Movement in the United States,* vol. 1 (New York: International Publishers, 1972), pp. 221, 223. See also John Commons et al., *History of Labor in the United States,* vol. 1 (New York: Macmillan, 1918), chap. 7.

25. Foner, *Labor Movement,* p. 224.

26. The best discussion is Amy Bridges, "The Working Classes in Ante-Bellum Urban Politics, New York City, 1828–1863," unpublished ms., June 1977.

27. Cf. Michael Wallace, "Changing Concepts of Party in the United States: New York, 1815–1828," *American Historical Review* 74 (December 1968).

28. Richard Hofstadter, *The Idea of a Party System* (Berkeley and Los Angeles: University of California Press, 1965), p. 211.

29. For a rich, if flawed, Beardian discussion of these issues, see Gabriel Almond, "Plutocracy and Politics in New York City" (Ph.D. diss., University of Chicago, Department of Political Science, 1938), esp. chap. 4.

30. Ronald P. Formisano, "Deferential-Participant Politics: The Early Republic's Political Culture, 1789–1840," *American Political Science Review* 68 (June 1974): 47; Martin Shefter, "Party Bureaucracy and Political Change in the United States," in Louis Maisel and Joseph Cooper, eds., *The Development of Political Parties: Patterns of Evolution and Decay,* Sage Electoral Studies Yearbook, vol. 4 (Beverly Hills, Cal.: Sage Publications, 1979).

31. Diane Ravitch, *The Great School Wars* (New York: Basic Books, 1974); David Rothman, *The Discovery of the Asylum* (Boston: Little, Brown, 1971); Wilbur R. Miller, *Cops and Bobbies: Police Authority in New York and London, 1830–1870* (Chicago: University of Chicago Press, 1977); Frank Goodnow, *Municipal Government* (New York: Century, 1909), pp. 234–324. Cf. Matthew Holden, "Ethnic Accommodation in a Historical Case," *Comparative Studies in Society and History* 8 (January 1966).

Machine Politics

10

CHAPTER THREE

To Hold Your District: Study Human Nature and Act Accordin'*

William L. Riordon

There's only one way to hold a district: you must study human nature and act accordin'. You can't study human nature in books. Books is a hindrance more than anything else. If you have been to college, so much the worse for you. You'll have to unlearn all you learned before you can get right down to human nature, and unlearnin' takes a lot of time. Some men can never forget what they learned at college. Such men may get to be district leaders by a fluke, but they never last.

To learn real human nature you have to go among the people, see them and be seen. I know every man, woman, and child in the Fifteenth District, except them that's been born this summer—and I know some of them, too. I know what they like and what they don't like, what they are strong at and what they are weak in, and I reach them by approachin' at the right side.

For instance, here's how I gather in the young men. I hear of a young feller that's proud of his voice, thinks that he can sing fine. I ask him to come around to Washington Hall and join our Glee Club. He comes and sings, and he's a follower of Plunkitt for life. Another young feller gains a reputation as a baseball player in a vacant lot. I bring him into our baseball club. That fixes him. You'll find him workin' for my ticket at the polls next election day. Then there's the feller that likes rowin' on the river, the young feller that makes a name as a waltzer on his block, the young feller that's handy with his dukes—I rope them all in by givin' them opportunities to

---

*Riordin, William L. 1963. "To Hold Your District: Study Human Nature and Act Accordin'." Pp. 25–28 in *Plunkett of Tammany Hall*. New York: Penquin USA.

show themselves off. I don't trouble them with political arguments. I just study human nature and act accordin'.

But you may say this game won't work with the hightoned fellers, the fellers that go through college and then join the Citizens' Union. Of course it wouldn't work. I have a special treatment for them. I ain't like the patent medicine man that gives the same medicine for all diseases. The Citizens' Union kind of a young man! I love him! He's the daintiest morsel of the lot, and he don't often escape me.

Before telling you how I catch him, let me mention that before the election last year, the Citizens' Union said they had four hundred or five hundred enrolled voters in my district. They had a lovely headquarters, too, beautiful roll top desks and the cutest rugs in the world. If I was accused of havin' contributed to fix up the nest for them, I wouldn't deny it under oath. What do I mean by that? Never mind. You can guess from the sequel, if you're sharp.

Well, election day came. The Citizens' Union's candidate for Senator, who ran against me, just polled five votes in the district, while I polled something more than 14,000 votes. What became of the 400 or 500 Citizens' Union enrolled voters in my district? Some people guessed that many of them were good Plunkitt men all along and worked with the Cits just to bring them into the Plunkitt camp by election day. You can guess that way, too, if you want to. I never contradict stories about me, especially in hot weather. I just call your attention to the fact that on last election day 395 Citizens' Union enrolled voters in my district were missin' and unaccounted for.

I tell you frankly, though, how I have captured some of the Citizens' Union's young men. I have a plan that never fails. I watch the City Record to see when there's civil service examinations for good things. Then I take my young Cit in hand, tell him all about the good thing and get him worked up till he goes and takes an examination. I don't bother about him any more. It's a cinch that he comes back to me in a few days and asks to join Tammany Hall. Come over to Washington Hall some night and I'll show you a list of names on our rolls marked "C.S." which means, "bucked up against civil service."

As to the older voters, I reach them, too. No, I don't send them campaign literature. That's rot. People can get all the political stuff they want to read—and a good deal more, too—in the papers. Who reads speeches, nowadays, anyhow? It's bad enough to listen to them. You ain't goin' to gain any votes by stuffin' the letter boxes with campaign documents. Like as not you'll lose votes, for there's nothin' a man hates more than to hear the letter carrier ring his bell and go to the letter box expectin' to find a letter he was lookin' for, and find only a lot of printed politics. I met a man this very mornin' who told me he voted the Democratic State ticket last year just because the Republicans kept crammin' his letter box with campaign documents.

What tells in holdin' your grip on your district is to go right down among the poor families and help them in the different ways they need help. I've got a regular system for this. If there's a fire in Ninth, Tenth, or Eleventh Avenue, for example, any hour of the day or night, I'm usually there with some of my election district captains as soon as the fire engines. If a family is burned out I don't ask whether they are Republicans or Democrats, and I don't refer them to the Charity Organization Society, which would investigate their case in a month or two and decide they were worthy of help about the time they are dead from starvation. I just get quarters for them, buy clothes for them if their clothes were burned up, and fix them up till they get things runnin' again. It's philanthropy, but it's politics, too—mighty good politics. Who can tell how many votes one of these fires bring me? The poor are the most grateful people in the world, and, let me tell you, they have more friends in their neighborhoods than the rich have in theirs.

If there's a family in my district in want I know it before the charitable societies do, and me and my men are first on the ground. I have a special corps to look up such cases. The consequence is that the poor look up to George W. Plunkitt as a father, come to him in trouble—and don't forget him on election day.

Another thing, I can always get a job for a deservin' man. I make it a point to keep on the track of jobs, and it seldom happens that I don't have a few up my sleeve ready for use. I know every big employer in the district and in the whole city, for that matter, and they ain't in the habit of sayin' no to me when I ask them for a job.

And the children—the little roses of the district! Do I forget them? Oh, no! They know me, every one of them, and they know that a sight of Uncle George and candy means the same thing. Some of them are the best kind of vote-getters. I'll tell you a case. Last year a little Eleventh Avenue rosebud, whose father is a Republican, caught hold of his whiskers on election day and said she wouldn't let go till he'd promise to vote for me. And she didn't.

11

Don't Makes No Waves . . . Don't Back No Losers: An Insider's Analysis of the Daley Machine*

Milton Rakove

Patronage jobs are usually parceled out to precinct captains in a ward organization on the basis of their efficiency in their precincts, and their qualifications. Young attorneys seeking to climb the political ladder by manning a precinct in a ward organization can be appointed as an assistant state's attorney, assistant corporation counsel, or work in the state attorney general's office, if the office is held by a Democrat. The college graduate with accounting skills can work in the county comptroller's office, or in a comparable position in the city bureaucracy. A high school graduate without any particular skills or training can work on a highway crew, can be a sidewalk inspector, a house-drain inspector, a forest ranger, a tree cutter, a sewer inspector, or a street sign wiper.

A classic example of how the system works was recounted to me by a Chicago alderman. According to the alderman, Committeeman Bernard Neistein of the 29th Ward sponsored a man who was a minister in a storefront church for a position with a city department. The irate department head called Neistein to complain that the prospective job candidate could neither read nor write adequately. "Put him to work. I need him." Neistein told the bureaucrat. Turning to the alderman, Neistein showed him a picture of the minister's podium, where, facing the audience, was a sign bearing the following information for the edification of the worshipers: "——— Baptist Church. ———Minister. Bernard Neistein, Ward Committeeman." ("Bernie Neistein," one high-level local bureaucrat told me, "is reasonable. If he sends you five guys to put to work, only two are illiterate. But Matt Bieszczat sends you five illiterates and wants you to take them all!")

In most cases, a precinct captain holds his patronage position as long as he delivers his precinct or covers the precinct to the satisfaction of his ward committeeman. Like his committeeman, a precinct captain is expected to carry his share of the burden for the party in his ward, as his committeeman is expected to carry the ward's share in city or county elections. Thus, power is delegated from the county central committee to the ward committeemen,

*Rakove, Milton. 1975. Pp. 114–125 in *Don't Make No Waves . . . Don't Back No Losers: An Insider's Analysis of the Daley Machine*. Bloomington: Indiana University Press. Copyright © 1975. Reprinted by permission of Indiana University Press.

and from the ward committeemen to the precinct captains. The entire system operates on the principle of autonomy of authority at each level in the political pyramid. When a man is given a precinct, it is his to cover, and it is up to him to produce for the party. If he cannot produce for the party, he cannot expect to be rewarded by the party. "Let's put it this way," Alderman Marzullo told me. "If your boss has a salesman who can't deliver, who can't sell his product, wouldn't he put someone else in who can?"

Like the ward committeeman, a precinct captain is required to estimate the results of the coming election in his precinct. And, like the ward committeeman, he is expected to predict accurately. Whereas losing a precinct may result in losing a patronage job, a captain who overestimates or underestimates the vote totals in his precinct also could be in trouble with his committeeman. Being unable to predict vote totals indicates to the ward committeeman that the precinct captain either is not working his precinct well or does not know what the voters in his precinct are thinking. Either reason is sufficient cause for disciplinary action such as the following incident recounted to me by a friend who spent election night, 1964, in the ward headquarters of former Alderman and Committeeman Mathias ("Paddy") Bauler of the 43rd Ward as the precinct captains came in to report. On the wall of Bauler's office was a tally board indicating which precincts had been carried and which had been lost in that day's election. A captain, who had lost his precinct that day, appeared before Bauler. "What kind of a job are you going to look for now?" asked Bauler of the abject precinct captain standing before him. As the unfortunate miscreant went out the door of the office, the next precinct captain appeared before the committeeman. "Your brother didn't vote," said Bauler to the precinct captain. "My brother didn't vote!" exclaimed the captain. "I'll kill him!" "Okay," said Bauler to the captain, "bring in the evidence, and you'll keep your job."

The party policy by which each captain or committeeman is expected to carry his precinct or ward, of suffer the consequences of failure regardless of the overall result of the election, forces each individual in the party's organization to concern himself only with his part of the action, not with the total result. For, even if the party wins the election, and he does poorly in his ward or precinct, the electoral victory will have little significance for him personally. Conversely, if he does well in his ward or precinct, he will stand well with the party hierarchy, even if the party loses the election. This policy forces every individual in the organization to think locally, to concern himself almost exclusively with his bit of turf, and to leave broad policy matters and directions for the party leadership. As a consequence, the machine in Chicago is not really one citywide organization but, rather, a composite of approximately 3148 local precinct organizations, each under the control of an individual responsible for his organization. There is no room in such a system for ideology, philosophy, or broad social concern. There is, instead, a pragmatic recognition of the need to concern oneself with one's little corner of the world, not with the interest of society as a whole, or mankind in general.

I became aware of this psychology in the election of 1968, when I worked a precinct for the Democratic organization in one of the North Side wards in Chicago. On election night at ward headquarters, I stood with my precinct co-captain before the big tally board which indicated the results in each of the ward's ninety-five precincts. Over the radio came the news of the developing results of the national and statewide elections for the Democratic party. It was clear that Vice-President Hubert Humphrey was losing the presidency to Richard Nixon, that Democratic Governor Sam Shapiro was losing the gubernatorial election to Republican Richard B. Ogilvie, and that Democratic senatorial candidate William Clark was losing the United States Senate seat from Illinois to incumbent Republican Senator Everett McKinley Dirksen. That night, even though I did not hold, and had no interest in securing a patronage job, and had taught political science for sixteen years, I found myself in the ward headquarters, my eyes intently fixed on the board carrying the tallies of my precinct, uninterested in the results in any other precinct in the ward, and almost totally unconcerned with the results of the city, county, state, and national elections for the Democratic party.

WORKING THE PRECINCT

How does a good precinct captain carry a precinct in cities like Chicago? Not by stressing ideology or party philosophy, not by stuffing mailboxes with party literature, not by debating issues with his constituents, but rather by ascertaining individual needs and by trying to serve those needs. Good precinct captains know that most elections are won or lost, not on great national, ideological issues, but rather on the basis of small, private, individual interests and concerns. If they don't know this or have forgotten it, their ward committeemen remind them in ward organization meetings. "Distinguished citizens," Alderman Marzullo addressed his precinct captains on the eve of the 1971 mayoralty election, "civic leaders, and religious leaders. This ward is not depending on the kind of publicity given to troublemakers and the nitwits and crackpots. This ward is depending on the record for sixteen years of our great mayor and the people who will put their shoulder to the wheel because they love Richard J. Daley and what he has done for the city of Chicago with the help of the Democratic party. Bring this message to your neighbors in your own language. You don't have to be an intellectual. I'm not an intellectual and I don't intend to be one."

Four months after the mayoralty election, in which Marzullo carried his ward for the mayor by a heavy majority, Marzullo leaned back in the high-back leather chair in his City Hall office and told *Sun-Times* columnist Tom Fitzpatrick, "I ain't got no axes to grind. You can take all your news media and all the do-gooders in town and move them into my 25th Ward, and do you know what would happen? On election day we'd beat you fifteen to one. The mayor don't run the 25th Ward. Neither does the news media or the do-gooders. Me, Vito Marzullo. That's who runs the 25th Ward, and on election day everybody does what Vito Marzullo tells them."

What kinds of goods and services do precinct captains in ward organizations provide? According to Marzullo, his captains work 365 days a year providing "service and communication" to his people. This includes free legal service for the destitute, repair of broken street lights, intensified police squad patrol, special anti-rodent clean-ups in the alleys, new garbage cans for tenants provided for them by their landlords, and talks with the probation officers of youngsters who are in trouble. "Anybody in the 25th needs something, needs help with his garbage, needs his street fixed, needs a lawyer for his kid who's in trouble, he goes first to the precinct captain," says Marzullo. "If the captain can't deliver, that man can come to me. My house is open every day to him." New residents moving into Marzullo's ward get a welcoming letter from the alderman on 25th Ward letterhead stationery:

February 11, 1971

Dear Friend:

As you know, the City Council of Chicago has redistricted the Wards, and you are now a resident of the 25th Ward. As the Ward Committeeman and Alderman of the 25th Ward, I take pride in welcoming you into the official family of our Ward.

The 25th Ward is fortunate in being represented at all levels of government by people of all ethnic backgrounds. We are truly a cosmopolitan organization. As members of our organization, we have the Honorable Frank Annunzio, who is Congressman for the Seventh Congressional District; Honorable Thaddeus V. Adesko, Judge of the Appellate Court; Honorable Charles S. Bonk, County Commissioner; Honorable Anthony Kogut, Judge of the Circuit Court of Cook County; Honorable Sam Romano, State Senator; Honorable Matt Ropa, State Representative; and Madison Brown, Con-Con Delegate.

I would like to point out to you that the next nonpartisan aldermanic election will be held on February 23, 1971. At that time I am sure you will be visited by your Democratic Precinct Captain who will be most anxious to discuss any problems of mutual interest.

Our organization has always endeavored to meet the needs and wants of our people. I personally await the opportunity on behalf of all the officials of the 25th Ward and myself, to be of assistance. Do not hesitate to let us know what your problems are, and if we can help, we are more than willing to extend our services.
    With every best wish, I am

Sincerely,
Alderman Vito Marzullo
25th Ward Committeeman

Marzullo is a five-feet-six-inches seventy-seven-year-old grandfather, an Italian immigrant who came to Chicago at age twelve, who has spent fifty-five years in politics on the city's west side, who went only as far as the fourth grade in school but who lectures on politics at the University of Illinois, and who is one of the last authentic old-line ward bosses in the Democratic machine which has governed Chicago for more than forty years. On a winter night, in November 1974, I spent an evening with Marzullo in his ward headquarters on Chicago's west side. Seated behind his desk, Marzullo looked and sounded like Marlon Brando as the Godfather. "I always say, 'Vito, put yourself on the other side of the table. How would you like to be treated?'" Marzullo told me. "I'm not an intellectual, but I love people. I'm not elected by the media, the intellectuals or do-gooders. I'm elected by my people. Service and communication. That's how my ward is run."

Marzullo has run for office 18 times. Only once has he had an opponent. "I beat him 15,000 to 1000," Vito said. "I carried his precinct 3 and a half to 1. In 1940, when I first ran for state representative, I carried my precinct 525 to 14. The Republican precinct captain's mother and father voted for me."

"We got the most cosmopolitan ward in Chicago," said Marzullo. "Thirty percent black, twenty percent Polish, twelve to fifteen percent Mexican, five percent Italian, Slovenians, Lithuanians, Bohemians. We got them all."

"But I take care of all my people. Many politicians are like groundhogs. They come out once a year. On November fifth [election day], I visited every precinct polling place. On November sixth, I was in my office at City Hall at nine A.M. I'm there five days a week. On November seventh, I was here in my ward office at six-thirty P.M., ready to serve my people. My home is open twenty-four hours a day. I want people to come in. As long as I have a breathing spell, I'll go to a wake, a wedding, whatever. I never ask for anything in return. On election day, I tell my people, 'Let your conscience be your guide.'"

Marzullo's precinct captains were assembled in the rear room. After State Senator Sam Romano called the roll of the forty-eight precincts in the 25th Ward, Marzullo took the podium to remind his captains to maintain their efforts. "No man walks alone. Mingle with the people. Learn their way of life. Work and give service to your people."

After the meeting with the captains, Marzullo moved to the front office to greet his constituents. A precinct captain ushered in a black husband and wife. "We got a letter here from the city," the man said. "They want to charge us twenty dollars for rodent control in our building." "Give me the letter. I'll look into it," Marzullo replied. The captain spoke up. "Your daughter didn't vote on November fifth. Look into it. The alderman is running again in February. Any help we can get, we can use." "I'm looking for a job," the woman said. "I don't have anything right now," said the alderman.

The telephone rang. Marzullo listened and said, "Come to my office tomorrow morning." He hung up. "She's a widow for thirteen years. She wants to put her property in joint tenancy with her daughter. The lawyer wants a hundred dollars. I'll have to find someone to do it for nothing."

"Some of those liberal independents in the city council, they can't get a dog out of a dog pound with a ten-dollar bill," Marzullo snorted. "Who's next?"

Another captain ushered in a constituent. "Frank has a problem. Ticket for a violation of street sweeping." "Tell John to make a notation," Marzullo said. "You'll have to go to court. We'll send Freddy with you." The constituent thanked Marzullo and left. The captain said, "Alderman, how about that job in the Forest Preserves?" "You'll have to wait until after the first of the year," Marzullo responded.

The captain from the 16th precinct brought in a young black man who had just graduated from college and was looking for a job. "I just lost fifteen jobs with the city," Marzullo said. "How about private industry?" said the captain. "His family has been with us a long time." "Bring him downtown tomorrow," Marzullo instructed the captain. "I'll give him a letter to the ———— Electric Company. They may have something." The young man left. "What about a donation to the Illinois Right to Life Committee?" asked the captain. "Nothing doing," said Marzullo. "I don't want to get into any of those controversies. People for it and people against it."

"We give a donation to thirty-five churches in the ward every year," Marzullo said. "One election day, I saw the priest from St. Roman's serving coffee and cake in the polling place. 'What are you doing?' I asked him. 'What the hell do you think I'm doing?' the priest replied. 'I'm trying to get some Democratic votes.'"

"Last time I ran, the Polish priest from St. Anne's took my petitions and got all the nuns to sign them," Marzullo said. "He had a paralyzed woman in a wheelchair who couldn't go to Mass because she couldn't get her chair over the curb in front of the church. I had the city build a ramp over the curb for her."

Marzullo pulled the ward organization's checkbook out of the desk. "Look at some of these donations—$100 to the City of Hope, $20 to St. Stephen's Holy Name Society, $20 to the Bennett Playground, $200 to St. Michael's Church, $100 to the American Legion, $125 to the West Chicago Florists, $600 for tickets to the Mike Howlett dinner, $25 to the New Trier Baseball Club."

"On election day, every captain gets $50 to $200 for expenses in his precinct," Marzullo explained. "We buy eight tables for the $100-per-plate Cook County central committee dinner. That's $8,000. We make contributions to all of our candidates and pay assessments for people running from our ward. When the mayor runs we carry the ward for him by at least five to one. He's a great family man. A great religious person. We've been together all the way. I got six married children. He came to every one of their weddings. He invited me to the weddings of every one of his kids. You don't go back on people like that."

"The money comes from our annual ward dinner dance," Marzullo explained. "We don't charge our patronage workers any dues, or take kickbacks. We sell ads for our ad book for the dance and clear about $35,000 from the ad book." Marzullo's ad book looks like a fair-size telephone book.

A Polish truck driver came in. "I was laid off three weeks ago," he told Marzullo. "I've got six children." Marzullo countered, "I lost two truck drivers and three laborers this week. The city budget is being held down. We have to keep taxes down. But come down to my office in City Hall tomorrow morning. I'll see if there is an opening in street sweeping or snow plowing." "We got ten votes in my building," said the man. "If we get you a job, let your conscience be your guide," the alderman advised.

Two more captains came in. "Can you do anything about garbage cans?" said one. "I need two." "I don't have anything yet," said Marzullo. "But we'll get forty or fifty soon as a donation from Trilla Cooperage." The second captain spoke up. "I got two goddamn sewers caving in. That goddamn Quigley!" (referring to City Sewer Commissioner Edward Quigley). "What are you yelling about?" asked Marzullo. "Give them to Johnny Domogala" (his efficient ward secretary).

More people came in. A Mexican crane operator who was getting his hours cut back, a captain who wanted a transfer from the blacksmith shop to an easier job, a woman computer operator who was being mistreated by her supervisor. To each of them, Marzullo said, "I'll see what I can do."

The last captain came in with a sickly looking black woman. "Mamie, he said, "I want you to meet my great alderman and your great alderman. If he can help you, he'll do it."

"Alderman," Mamie said, "I need food stamps. I've been in the hospital three times this year. They're giving me pills, but I can't afford to eat."

"You have to get food stamps from your case worker," Marzullo explained. "I can't help on that." Turning to County Commissioner Charley Bonk, "Charley, give her a check for fifty dollars for food." And to Mamie, "If you need more come back again." "God bless you!" Mamie responded as she went out the door. "I guess that's it for tonight," sighed Bonk wearily. "If you meet them head-on every day, you wear them all out."

In middle-class wards on the northwest and southwest sides of the city, precinct captains can help get tax bills appealed, curbs and gutters repaired, scholarships for students to the University of Illinois, summer jobs for college students, and directions and assistance to those who need some help in finding their way through the maze of government bureaucracy with a grievance. "See the four men on this wall to the right?" Marzullo once asked Tom Fitzpatrick. "There's Mayor Daley, Congressman Frank Annunzio, County Commissioner Charles Bonk, and the other man is Vito Marzullo. We put a lot of other judges on the bench, too. And don't think that these people are ingrates. They always cooperate with the party that put them on the bench whenever they can. You see what I mean? The 25th Ward has a voice in every branch of government. That's a hobby we have in the 25th. It's our way of providing service to our people."

Most of the work of a good precinct captain in providing services to his constituents is not fixing tickets, bribing officials, or getting special favors for people, but rather ascertaining the individual needs of his people, communicating those needs through proper channels to the proper authorities, and providing help to those who are unable to find their way through the massive layers of bureaucracy in twentieth-century American government.

"The days when you went to the ward committeeman for a bucket of coal or a sweater for Johnny were on the way out when we went to the welfare programs of a more compassionate society under Roosevelt," according to the number-two man in the Cook County Democratic organization, Committeeman Tom Keane of the 31st Ward. "The political organization today [in the 1970s] is a service organization, an ombudsman and an inquiry department. I consider my ward has fifty-seven community organizations doing public service," says Keane, who calls his fifty-seven precinct captains "community representatives." Keane's analysis is echoed by county board president George Dunne, the Democratic committeeman in the 42nd Ward. "To a great extent the service we offer now is referral," says Dunne. "People ask, 'How do I get this? Where do I go to get that?' In some instances a letter from me helps and I never turn them down. Some people feel a letter always helps, but I think they would get what they need without it in most cases. . . . Even though over the years times have changed, the success of a political organization depends on giving service to the people."[1]

For a good precinct captain, a patronage position is only one of the reasons for staying on the job. Precinct work, especially before an election, is hard work and sometimes sheer drudgery. The annual or semi-annual all-important canvass and registration drive requires a check of every house and apartment in the precinct to find out who moved out and who moved in, getting recalcitrant and uninterested voters registered, an on-the-spot psychological evaluation of every new voter who has come into the precinct, and a quick decision as to whether the new voter is a potential Democrat or Republican. If he is probably a Democrat, or might be encouraged to become one, he has to be registered. If he sounds like a Republican, he had best be ignored (who wants to register Republican voters?). Precinct work requires calculation of the way in which every potential voter in the precinct is likely to vote in the coming election. Good precinct work requires climbing stairs at night and on weekends, timing the visit properly so as not to interfere with the popular television programs, and learning the names, relationships, and attitudes of the voters. "Cover every home! Don't take nothing for granted!" Marzullo exhorted his captains at a ward meeting I attended. Good precinct work requires also an ability to blunt ideological prejudices, establish personal relationships, and adapt to the voters' peripatetic political perambulations. It further requires an ability to measure the depth of the voter's feelings, to push for the whole ticket when you can, but to be able to retreat gracefully when necessary. If the voters are angry at Hubert Humphrey or Richard J. Daley, will they at least vote for Matt Danaher for clerk of the circuit court and Edward Hanrahan for state's attorney of Cook County? If they don't like gubernatorial candidate Sam Shapiro's religion or vice-presidential candidate Edmund Muskie's ethnicity, can their hostility be overcome by appealing to their loyalty to the Democratic party, castigating the iniquitous Republican opposition, or asking them to help save the precinct captain's job by voting right this time? A good precinct captain, according to Alderman Marzullo, "is a salesman, selling the party every day of the year."

After the sovereign voters are canvassed and registered, and after an estimate is made of the vote tally, the precinct captain still has the formidable task of getting the forgetful, uninterested, and lazy voters to the polls. Elections are won or lost in the precincts on election day after the preparatory work has been done. A precinct captain had better be in good physical condition to undergo the rigors of delivering the vote. "I've been on the street since 4 A.M.," precinct captain Al Chesser of the 31st Precinct in the 24th Ward told *Sun Times* columnist Tom Fitzpatrick on election day, November 4, 1970. "You know how it is. Polls open at 6 A.M. I've got to get out and put reminders on car windows of my voters that I know go to work early." By 6:30 A.M., Chesser's fifteen precinct helpers are working the neighborhood, knocking on doors, bringing out the voters, and reporting to Chesser at his station near the polling place. "I stand at this spot every election," Chesser told Fitzpatrick. "Everyone knows where I am. They all come this way and stop by so that I can give them advice on how to fill out their ballots." In Marzullo's neighboring 25th Ward, "The sun will rise over the 25th on Tuesday at 5:26 A.M.," a *New York Times* reporter told his eastern constituency after an interview with Alderman Marzullo. "By that time Mr. Marzullo's precinct captains will already be at the polling places in their precincts, ready to check the voters as they begin arriving at 6 A.M.. On every major street corner their assistants will be posted, voices at the ready, to remind each resident as he starts to work that it is his duty to vote and vote right that day." "Politics," explained Marzullo, "is a matter of communicating. The people got to get the word. The 25th is ready to get it to them."

NOTES

1. In 1950, when I was a graduate student at the University of Chicago and a full-time clerk with civil service status at the United States Post Office in Chicago, working forty hours a week on the night shift, I requested a change in status at the post office to substitute clerk, so that I could work only four or five hours a night. After going through all the proper channels in the post office, I was told repeatedly by the authorities that such a request could not be granted, that a regular clerk could not be reduced to a substitute mail handler, even at his request. A subsequent brief conversation with my Democratic precinct captain resulted in a note from the precinct captain to the ward committeeman, a letter from the ward committeeman to my congressman, who was on the House of Representatives Post Office Committee, a letter from the congressman to the Postmaster of the Chicago Post Office, and a letter from the postmaster to me, notifying me of my immediate reduction to substitute mail handler.

12

The Latent Functions of the Machine*

Robert K. Merton

. . . In large sectors of the American population, the political machine or the "political racket" are judged as unequivocally "bad" and "undesirable." The grounds for such moral judgment vary somewhat, but they consist substantially in pointing out that political machines violate moral codes: political patronage violates the code of selecting personnel on the basis of impersonal qualifications rather than on grounds of party loyalty or contributions to the party war-chest; bossism violates the code that votes should be based on individual appraisal of the qualifications of candidates and of political issues, and not on abiding loyalty to a feudal leader; bribery and "honest graft" obviously offend the proprieties of property; "protection" for crime clearly violates the law and the mores; and so on.

In view of these manifold respects in which political machines, in varying degrees, run counter to the mores and at times to the law, it becomes pertinent to inquire how they manage to continue in operation. The familiar "explanations" for the continuance of the political machine are not here in point. To be sure, it may well be that if "respectable citizenry" would carry through their political obligations, if the electorate were to be alert and enlightened; if the number of elective officers were substantially reduced from the dozens, even hundreds, which the average voter is now expected to appraise in the course of local, county, state and national elections, if the electorate were activated by the "wealthy and educated classes without whose participation," as the not-always democratically oriented Bryce put it, the best-framed government must speedily degenerate," if these and a plethora of similar changes in political structure were introduced, perhaps the "evils" of the political machine would indeed be exorcized. But it should be noted that these changes are not typically introduced, that political machines have the phoenix-like quality of arising strong and unspoiled from their ashes, that, in short, this structure exhibits a notable vitality in many areas of American political life.

Proceeding from the functional view, therefore, that we should *ordinarily* (not invariably) expect persistent social patterns and social structures to perform positive functions *which are at the same time not adequately fulfilled by other existing patterns and structures*, the thought occurs that perhaps this publicly maligned organization is, *under present conditions*, satisfy-

*Merton, Robert K. 1957. "The Latent Functions of the Machine." Pp. 71–81 in *Social Theory and Social Structure*. Rev. ed. New York: The Free Press. Copyright © 1957 by the Free Press; renewed 1985 by Robert K. Merton. Reprinted by permission of The Free Press, a division of Macmillan, Inc.

ing basic latent functions. A brief examination of current analyses of this type of structure may also serve to illustrate additional problems of functional analysis.

Some Functions of the Political Machine.   Without presuming to enter into the variations of detail marking different political machines — a Tweed, Vare, Crump, Flynn, Hague are by no means identical types of bosses — we can briefly examine the functions more or less common to the political machine, as a generic type of social organization. We neither attempt to itemize all the diverse functions of the political machine nor imply that all these functions are similarly fulfilled by each and every machine.

The key structural function of the Boss is to organize, centralize and maintain in good working condition "the scattered fragments of power" which are at present dispersed through our political organization. By this centralized organization of political power, the boss and his apparatus can satisfy the needs of diverse subgroups in the larger community which are not adequately satisfied by legally devised and culturally approved social structures.

To understand the role of bossism and the machine, therefore, we must look at two types of sociological variables: (1) the *structural context* which makes it difficult, if not impossible, for morally approved structures to fulfill essential social functions, thus leaving the door open for political machines (or their structural equivalents) to fulfill these functions and (2) the subgroups whose distinctive needs are left unsatisfied, except for the latent functions which the machine in fact fulfills.

Structural Context.   The constitutional framework of American political organization specifically precludes the legal possibility of highly centralized power and, it has been noted, thus "discourages the growth of effective and responsible leadership. The framers of the Constitution, as Woodrow Wilson observed, set up the check and balance system 'to keep government at a sort of mechanical equipoise by means of a standing amicable contest among its several organic parts.' They distrusted power as dangerous to liberty: and therefore they spread it thin and erected barriers against its concentration." This dispersion of power is found not only at the national level but in local areas as well. "As a consequence," Sait goes on to observe, "when *the people or particular groups* among them demanded positive action, no one had adquate authority to act. The machine provided an antidote."[1]

The constitutional dispersion of power not only makes for difficulty of effective decision and action but when action does occur it is defined and hemmed in by legalistic considerations. In consequence, there develops "a much *more human system* of partisan government, whose chief object soon became the circumvention of government by law. . . . The lawlessness of the extra-official democracy was merely the counterpoise of the legalism of the official democracy. The lawyer having been permitted to subordinate democracy to the Law, the Boss had to be called in to extricate the victim, which he did after a fashion and for a consideration."[2]

Officially, political power is dispersed. Various well-known expedients were devised for this manifest objective. Not only was there the familiar separation of powers among the several branches of the government but, in some measure, tenure in each office was limited, rotation in office approved. And the scope of power inherent in each office was severely circumscribed. Yet, observes Sait in rigorously functional terms, "Leadership is necessary; and *since* it does not develop readily within the constitutional framework, the Boss provides it in a crude and irresponsible form from the outside."[3]

Put in more generalized terms, *the functional deficiencies of the official structure generate an alternative (unofficial) structure to fulfill existing needs somewhat more effectively.* Whatever its specific historical origins, the political machine persists as an apparatus for satisfying otherwise unfulfilled needs of diverse groups in the population. By turning to a few of these subgroups and their characteristic needs, we shall be led at once to a range of latent functions of the political machine.

Functions of the Political Machine for Diverse Subgroups.   It is well known that one source of strength of the political machine derives from its roots in the local community and the neighborhood. The political machine does not regard the electorate as a vague, undifferentiated mass of voters. With a keen sociological intuition, the machine recognizes that the voter is primarily a man living in a specific neighborhood, with specific personal problems and personal wants. Public issues are abstract and remote; private problems are extremely concrete and immediate. It is not through the generalized appeal to large public concerns that the machine operates, but through the direct, quasi-feudal relationships between local representatives of the machine and voters in their neighborhood. Elections are won in the precinct.

The machine welds its link with ordinary men and women by elaborate networks of personal relations. Politics is transformed into personal ties. The precinct captain "must be a friend to every man, assuming if he does not feel sympathy with the unfortunate, and utilizing in his good works the resources which the boss puts at his disposal."[4] The precinct captain is forever a friend in need. In our prevailingly impersonal society, the machine, through its local agents, fulfills the important social *function of humanizing and personalizing all manner of assistance* to those in need. Foodbaskets and jobs, legal and extra-legal advice, setting to rights minor scrapes with the law, helping the bright poor boy to a political scholarship in a local college, looking after the bereaved—the whole range of crises when a feller needs a friend, and, above all, a friend who knows the score and who can do something about it—all these find the ever-helpful precinct captain available in the pinch.

To assess this function of the political machine adequately, it is important to note not only the fact that aid is provided but *the manner in which it is provided*. After all, other agencies do exist for dispensing such assistance. Welfare agencies, settlement houses, legal aid clinics, medical aid in free hospitals, public relief departments, immigration authorities—these and a multitude of other organizations are available to provide the most varied types of assistance. But in contrast to the professional techniques of the welfare worker which may typically represent in the mind of the recipient the cold, bureaucratic dispensation of limited aid following upon detailed investigations of *legal* claims to aid of the "client," are the unprofessional techniques of the precinct captain who asks no questions, exacts no compliance with legal rules of eligibility and does not "snoop" into private affairs.

For many, the loss of "self-respect" is too high a price for legalized assistance. In contrast to the gulf between the settlement house workers who so often come from a different social class, educational background and ethnic group, the precinct worker is "just one of us," who understands what it's all about. The condescending lady bountiful can hardly compete with the understanding friend in need. In *this struggle between alternative structures for fulfilling the nominally same functions* of providing aid and support to those who need it, it is clearly the machine politician who is better integrated with the groups which he serves than the impersonal, professionalized, socially distant and legally constrained welfare worker. And since the politician can at times influence and manipulate the official organizations for the dispensation of assistance, whereas the welfare worker has practically no influence on the political machine, they only add to his greater effectiveness. More colloquially and also, perhaps, more incisively, it was the Boston ward-leader, Martin Lomasny, who described this essential function to the curious Lincoln Steffens: "I think," said Lomasny, "that there's got to be in every ward somebody that any bloke can come to—no matter what he's done—and get help. *Help, you understand; none of your law and justice, but help.*"[5]

The "deprived classes," then, constitute one subgroup for whom the political machine clearly satisfies wants not adequately satisfied in the same fashion by the legitimate social structure.

For a second subgroup, that of business (primarily "big" business but also "small") the political boss serves the function of providing those political privileges which entail immediate economic gains. Business corporations, among which the public utilities (railroads, local transportation companies, communications corporations, electric light) are simply the most conspicuous in this regard, seek special political dispensations which will enable them to stabilize their situation and to near their objective of maximizing profits. Interestingly enough, corporations often want to avoid a chaos of uncontrolled competition. They want the greater security of an economic czar who controls, regulates and organizes competition, providing this czar is not a public official with his decisions subject to public scrutiny and public control. (The latter would be "government control," and hence taboo.) The political boss fulfills these requirements admirably.

Examined for a moment apart from any "moral" considerations, the political apparatus of the Boss is effectively designed to perform these functions with a minimum of inefficiency. Holding the strings of diverse governmental divisions, bureaus and agencies in his competent hands, the Boss rationalizes the relations between public and private business. He serves as the business community's ambassador in the otherwise alien (and sometimes unfriendly) realm of government. And, in strict business-like terms, he is well-paid for his economic services to his respectable business clients. In an article entitled, "An Apology to Graft," Steffens suggested that "Our economic system, which held up riches, power and acclaim as prizes to men bold enough and able enough to buy corruptly timber, mines, oil fields and franchises and 'get away with it,' was at fault."[6] And, in a conference with a hundred or so of Los Angeles business leaders, he described a fact well known to all of them: the Boss and his machine were an *integral part* of the organization of the economy. "You cannot build or operate a railroad, or a street railway, gas, water, or power company, develop and operate a mine, or get forests and cut timber on a large scale, or run any privileged business, without corrupting or joining in the corruption of the government. You tell me privately that you must, and here I am telling you semipublicly that you must. And that is so all over the country. And that means that we have an organization of society in which, *for some reason*, you and your kind, the ablest, most intelligent, most imaginative, daring, and resourceful leaders of society, are and must be against society and its laws and its all-around growth."[7]

Since the demand for the services of special privileges are built into the structure of the society, the Boss fulfills diverse functions for this second subgroup of business-seeking-privilege. These "needs" of business, as presently constituted, are not adequately provided for by "conventional" and "culturally approved" social structures; consequently, the extra-legal but more-or-less efficient organization of the political machine comes to provide these services. To adopt an *exclusively* moral attitude toward the "corrupt political machine" is to lose sight of the very structural conditions which generate the "evil" that is so bitterly attacked. To adopt a functional outlook on the political machine is not to provide an apologia, but a more solid base for modifying or eliminating the machine, *providing* specific structural arrangements are introduced either for eliminating these effective demands of the business community or, if that is the objective, of satisfying these demands through alternative means.

A third set of distinctive functions fulfilled by the political machine for a special subgroup is that of providing alternative channels of social mobility for those otherwise excluded from the more conventional avenues for personal "advancement." Both the sources of this special "need" (for social mobility) and the respect in which the political machine comes to help satisfy this need can be understood by examining the structure of the larger culture and society. As is well known, the American culture lays enormous emphasis on money and power as a "success" goal legitimate for all members of the society. By no means alone in our inventory of cultural goals, it still remains among the most heavily endowed with positive affect and value. However, certain subgroups and certain ecological areas are notable for the relative absence of opportunity for achieving these (monetary and power) types of success. They constitute, in short, sub-populations where "the cultural emphasis upon pecuniary success has been absorbed, but where there is *little access to conventional and legitimate* means for attaining such success. The conventional occupational opportunities of persons in (such areas) are almost completely limited to manual labor. Given our cultural stigmatization of manual labor, and its correlate, the prestige of white-collar work, it is clear that the result is a tendency to achieve these culturally approved objectives *through whatever means are possible*. These people are on the one hand, "asked to orient their conduct toward the prospect of accumulating wealth [and power] and, on the other, they are largely denied effective opportunities to do so institutionally."

It is within this context of social structure that the political machine fulfills the basic function of providing avenues of social mobility for the otherwise disadvantaged. Within this context, even the corrupt political machine and the racket "represent the triumph of amoral intelligence over morally prescribed 'failure' when the channels of vertical mobility are closed or narrowed *in a society which places a high premium on economic affluence, [power] and social ascent for* all its members."[8] As one sociologist has noted on the basis of several years of close observation in a "slum area":

> The sociologist who dismisses racket and political organizations as deviations from desirable standards thereby neglects some of the major elements of slum life. . . . *He does not discover the functions they perform for the members* [of the groupings in the slum]. The Irish and later immigrant peoples have had the greatest difficulty in finding places for themselves in our urban social and economic structure. Does anyone believe that the immigrants and their children could have achieved their present degree of social mobility without gaining control of the political organization of some of our largest cities? The same is true of the racket organization. *Politics and the rackets have furnished an important means of social mobility for individuals, who, because of ethnic background and low class position,* are blocked from advancement in the "respectable" channels.[9]

This, then represents a third type of function performed for a distinctive subgroup. This function, it may be noted in passing, is fulfilled by the *sheer* existence and operation of the political machine, for it is in the machine itself that these individuals and subgroups find their culturally induced needs more or less satisfied. It refers to the services which the political apparatus provides for its own personnel. But seen in the wider social context we have set forth, it no longer appears as *merely* a means of self-aggrandizement for profit-hungry and power-hungry *individuals*, but as an organized provision for *subgroups* otherwise excluded or restricted from the race for "getting ahead."

Just as the political machine performs services for "legitimate" business, so it operates to perform not dissimilar services for "illegitimate" business: vice, crime and rackets. Once again, the basic sociological role of the machine in this respect can be more fully appreciated only if one temporarily abandons attitudes of moral indignation, to examine with all moral innocence the actual workings of the organization. In this light, it at once appears that the subgroup of the professional criminal, racketeer, gambler, has basic similarities of organization, demands and operation to the subgroup of the industrialist, man of business, speculator. If there is a Lumber King or an Oil King, there is also a Vice King or a Racket King. If expansive legitimate business organizes administrative and financial syndicates to "rationalize" and to "integrate" diverse areas of production and business enterprise, so expansive rackets and crime organize syndicates to bring order to the otherwise chaotic areas of production of illicit goods and services. If legitimate business regards the proliferation of small enterprises as wasteful and inefficient, substituting, for example, the giant chain stores for the hundreds of corner groceries, so illegitimate business adopts the same businesslike attitude, and syndicates crime and vice.

Finally, and in many respects, most important, is the basic similarity, if not near-identity, of the economic role of "legitimate" business and "illegitimate" business. *Both are in some degree concerned with the provision of goods and services for which there is an economic demand.* Morals aside, they are both business, industrial and professional enterprises, dispensing goods and services which some people want, for which there is a market in which goods and services are transformed into commodities. And, in a prevalently market society, we should expect appropriate enterprises to arise whenever there is a market demand for given goods or services.

As is well known, vice, crime and the rackets *are* "big business." Consider only that there have been estimated to be about 500,000 professional prostitutes in the United States, and compare this with the approximately 200,000 physicians and 200,000 nurses. It is difficult to estimate which have the larger clientele: the professional men and women of medicine or the professional men and women of vice. It is, of course, difficult to estimate the economic assets, income, profits and dividends of illicit gambling in this country and to compare it with the economic assets, income, profits and dividends of, say, the shoe industry, but it is altogether possible that the two industries are about on a par. No precise figures exist on the annual expenditures on illicit narcotics, and it is probable that these are less than the expenditures on candy, but it is also probable that they are larger than the expenditure on books.

It takes but a moment's thought to recognize that, *in strictly economic terms*, there is no relevant difference between the provision of licit and of illicit goods and services. The liquor traffic illustrates this perfectly. It would be peculiar to argue that prior to 1920 (when the 18th amendment became effective), the provision of liquor constituted an economic service, that from 1920 to 1933, its production and sale no longer constituted an economic service dispensed in a market, and that from 1934 to the present, it once again took on a serviceable aspect. Or, it would be *economically* (not morally) absurd to suggest that the sale of bootlegged liquor in the dry state of Kansas is less a response to a market demand than the sale of publicly manufactured liquor in the neighboring wet state of Missouri. Examples of this sort can of course be multiplied many times over. Can it be held that in

European countries, with registered and legalized prostitution, the prostitute contributes an economic service, whereas in this country, lacking legal sanction, the prostitute provides no such service? Or that the professional abortionist is in the economic market where he has approved legal status and that he is out of the economic market where he is legally taboo? Or that gambling satisfies a specific demand for entertainment in Nevada, where it is one of the largest business enterprises of the largest city in the state, but that it differs essentially in this respect from movie houses in the neighboring state of California?

The failure to recognize that these businesses are only *morally* and not *economically* distinguishable from "legitimate" businesses has led to badly scrambled analysis. Once the economic identity of the two is recognized, we may anticipate that if the political machine performs functions for "legitimate big business" it will be all the more likely to perform not dissimilar functions for "illegitimate big business." And, of course, such is often the case.

The distinctive function of the political machine for their criminal, vice and racket clientele is to enable them to operate in satisfying the economic demands of a large market without due interference from the government. Just as big business may contribute funds to the political party war-chest to ensure a minimum of governmental interference, so with big rackets and big crime. In both instances, the political machine can, in varying degrees, provide "protection." In both instances, many features of the structural context are identical: (1) market demands for goods and services; (2) the operators' concern with maximizing gains from their enterprises; (3) the need for partial control of government which might otherwise interfere with these activities of businessmen; (4) the need for an efficient, powerful and centralized agency to provide an effective liaison of "business" with government.

Without assuming that the foregoing pages exhaust either the range of functions or the range of subgroups served by the political machine, we can at least see that *it presently fulfills some functions for these diverse subgroups which are not adequately fulfilled by culturally approved or more conventional structures.*

Several additional implications of the functional analysis of the political machine can be mentioned here only in passing, although they obviously require to be developed at length. First, the foregoing analysis has direct implications for *social engineering.* It helps explain why the periodic efforts at "political reform," "turning the rascals out" and "cleaning political house" are typically short-lived and ineffectual. It exemplifies a basic theorem: *any attempt to eliminate an existing social structure without providing adequate alternative structures for fulfilling the functions previously fulfilled by the abolished organization is doomed to failure.* (Needless to say, this theorem has much wider bearing than the one instance of the political machine.) When "political reform" confines itself to the manifest task of "turning the rascals out," it is engaging in little more than sociological magic. The reform may for a time bring new figures into the political limelight; it may serve the casual social function of re-assuring the electorate that the moral virtues remain intact and will ultimately triumph; it may actually effect a turnover in the personnel of the political machine; it may even, for a time, so curb the activities of the machine as to leave unsatisfied the many needs it has previously fulfilled. But, inevitably, unless the reform also involves a "reforming" of the social and political structure such that the existing needs are satisfied by alternative structures or unless it involves a change which eliminates these needs altogether, the political machine will return to its integral place in the social scheme of things. *To seek social change, without due recognition of the manifest and latent functions performed by the social organization undergoing change, is to indulge in social ritual rather than social engineering.* The concepts of manifest and latent functions (or their equivalents) are indispensable elements in the theoretic repertoire of the social engineer. In this crucial sense, these concepts are not "merely" theoretical (in the abusive sense of the term), but are eminently practical. In the deliberate enactment of social change, they can be ignored only at the price of considerably heightening the risk of failure.

A second implication of our analysis of the political machine also has a bearing upon areas wider than the one we have considered. The "paradox" has often been noted that the supporters of the political machine include both the "respectable" business class elements who are, of course, opposed to the criminal or racketeer and the distinctly "unrespectable" elements of the underworld. And, at first appearance, this is cited as an instance of very strange bedfellows. The learned judge is not infrequently called upon to sentence the very racketeer beside whom he sat the night before at an informal dinner of the political bigwigs. The district attorney jostles the exonerated convict on his way to the back room where the Boss has called a meeting. The big business man may complain almost as bitterly as the big racketeer about the "extortionate" contributions to the party fund demanded by the Boss. Social opposites meet — in the smoke-filled room of the successful politician.

In the light of a functional analysis all this of course no longer seems paradoxical. Since the machine serves both the businessman and the criminal man, the two seemingly antipodal groups intersect. This points to a more general theorem: *the social functions of an organization help determine the structure (including the recruitment of personnel involved in the structure), just as the structure helps determine the effectiveness with which the functions are fulfilled.* In terms of social status, the business group and the criminal group are indeed poles apart. But status does not fully determine behavior and the interrelations between groups. Functions modify these relations. Given their distinctive needs, the several subgroups in the large society are "integrated," whatever their personal desires or intentions, by the centralizing structure which serves these several needs. In a phrase with many implications which require further study, *structure affects function and function affects structure.*

NOTES

1. Edward M. Sait, "Machine, Political," *Encyclopedia of the Social Sciences,* IX, 658b [italics supplied].
2. Herbert Croly, *Progressive Democracy* (New York, 1914), p. 254, cited by Sait, *op. cit.,* 658b.
3. Sait, *op. cit.,* 659a.
4. *Ibid.*
5. *The Autobiography of Lincoln Steffens* (Chautauqua, N.Y.: Chantauqua Press. 1931), 618.
6. *Autobiography of Lincoln Steffens,* 570.
7. *Ibid.,* 572–573.
8. Merton, *op. cit.,* 146.
9. William F. Whyte, "Social Organization in the Slums," *American Sociological Review,* Feb. 1943, 8, 34–39 (italics supplied).

13
The Rise and Development of Urban Political Machines: An Alternative to Merton's Functional Analysis*

Alan DiGaetano

MERTON'S FUNCTIONAL ANALYSIS
OF POLITICAL MACHINES

To transcend the "prevailing moral evaluations" of machine politics, Merton (1968: 71) examined the political machine as a "generic type of social organization." Merton claimed that normative explanations and judgments fail to comprehend the true nature of the political machine because they are couched "largely in terms of the *manifest* consequences" of machine politics—graft, bribery, and protection rackets (p. 71). Functionalist inquiry, in contrast, focuses attention on the latent consequences of machine

*DiGaetano, Alan. 1988. "The Rise and Development of Urban Political Machines: An Alternative to Merton's Functional Analysis." *Urban Affairs Quarterly,* 24, no. 2 (December 1988): 243–267.

politics. Latent consequences, as defined by Merton, are unrecognized and unintended, and manifest consequences are recognized and intended (p. 51). The objective of functional analysis, according to Merton's interpretation, is to discern whether social organizations, like the machine, perform the essential manifest and latent functions of a society. Reflecting on the possibility that reformers misunderstood the deeper significance of the political machine, Merton mused: "the thought occurs that perhaps this publicly maligned organization [the machine] is, under present conditions, satisfying basic latent functions" (pp. 71–72). It is this notion of "latent functions" that sets Merton's explanation apart from other theoretical perspectives on the political machine.

Latent Functions of the Machine

Merton's functional analysis of the machine hinges on the interaction of "two types of sociological variables" (1968: 72): the first is "the *structural context* which makes it difficult, if not impossible, for morally approved structures to fulfill essential social functions"; the second variable consists of "the subgroups whose distinctive needs are left unsatisfied, except for the latent functions which the machine in fact fulfills." The interplay between the structural context and unmet social needs determines the functional requisites for the development of social organizations.

The structural context of the machine was established by the constituting principle of separation of powers. The division of political authority between various units "is found not only at the national level but in the local areas as well" (Merton, 1968: 73). Moreover, limited terms of office and "approved" rotation in office compounded the "dispersion of power" resulting from the formally fragmented governmental structure (p. 72). In this context the "key structural function of the boss [was] to organize, centralize and maintain in good working condition the 'scattered fragments of power' which [were] dispersed through our political organization" (p. 72). Thus, for Merton, urban political machines sprang to life in order to compensate for the functional deficits of official governmental institutions.

Merton (1968) then explained how governmental fragmentation and the unmet social needs of urban subgroups, his second sociological variable, necessitated the formation of political machines. The functional deficiencies of the American local state apparatus, in Merton's view, prevented the adequate satisfaction of "needs of diverse subgroups in the larger community" (p. 68). Merton identified four subgroups whose needs were not adequately met by the official governmental structure. These included the "deprived classes," disadvantaged groups "excluded from the conventional avenues for personal advancement," legitimate businesses, and illegitimate businesses (pp. 74–76). In each case, Merton contended that the machine performed the latent functions necessary to fulfill the unsatisfied needs of these subgroups. As Merton (1968: 73) explicated,

> the *functional deficiencies* of the official structure generate an alternative (unofficial) structure to fulfill existing needs somewhat more effectively. Whatever its *specific historical origins*, the political machine persists as an apparatus of satisfying otherwise unfulfilled needs of diverse groups in the population [emphasis added].

The political boss, it seems, welded together a strong and centralized machine organization in a structural context of dispersed power because it was latently necessary to "fulfill essential social functions" (p. 72).

The acceptance of Merton's theoretical link between social needs and the rise of urban political machines has become part of the received wisdom on machine politics. As the historian Zane Miller (1981: 59) noted, "Most now accept . . . sociologist Robert K. Merton's functional model of the machine, the notion that it originated as a response to needs and demands which other institutions failed to satisfy." Similarly, the political scientists Edward Banfield and James Q. Wilson (1963: 126) wholeheartedly endorsed Merton's analysis of the latent functions of the political machine:

> The machine served certain latent social functions, functions which no one intended but which presumably would have had to be served by another means if not by that one. According to Merton . . . it was an antidote to the constitutional dispersion of authority.

Also, the sociologist Thomas Guterbock (1980), in his work on the contemporary Chicago machine, employed an analysis with "a similar logic" to Merton's functional approach. For many, or perhaps most, students of the machine, Merton's functional theory constitutes a point of embarcation.

A Critique of Merton's Functional Analysis

Despite the apparent tidiness of Merton's theory of the machine, a number of methodological and empirical problems stem from its underlying assumptions. Functional analysis posits that social institutions like the machine must arise to meet the social needs in any society. The heretofore undetected causes of the machine, reasoned Merton, lay in its latent, rather than manifest, properties. Because of his emphasis on the latency of the machine's purpose in satisfying social needs, Merton inextricably tied the functional raison d'être of the machine to the larger need of maintaining the stability, or perhaps the very existence, of the social order. Without intending to do so, and without anybody realizing it, machines maintained the social order by meeting those needs left unattended by the official institutions of society. In this sense, functional analysis is akin to Adam Smith's (1937) "invisible hand," implying some hidden self-correcting mechanism in society that serves to preserve social order. Merton therefore propounded a teleological explanation of the political machine, whereby the latent consequences of maintaining a social order determined the creation of this particular institutional form (see also Hempel, 1959; Lehman, 1966).

A second conceptual problem is rooted in the tautological nature of functional analysis. Merton reasoned that if the machine had not performed the necessary latent functions that maintained social order in urban industrial society, some functionally equivalent institution would have stepped in as a substitute. As he elaborated, "any attempt to eliminate an existing social structure without providing adequate alternative structures for fulfilling the functions previously fulfilled by the abolished organization is doomed to failure" (Merton, 1968: 81). Functional theory of this sort can never be disproven. Whatever exists is necessary and functional (see also Giddens, 1981). . . .

AN ALTERNATIVE APPROACH TO THE STUDY OF POLITICAL MACHINES

The period of machine emergence can be demarcated as the last three decades of the nineteenth century. Rapid industrialization, burgeoning urban growth, and massive waves of immigration, among other things, converged in the making of American urban life during the machine era. To make some sense of this clutter of social patterning, Katznelson (1981) recently recommended that we peer through the interpretive lens of "American Exceptionalism." This approach is aptly suited to the study of machine politics for the simple reason that the big-city machine proved to be a distinctly North American political institution.[1]

To understand the exceptional nature of the American political machine, it is essential to remember that machine politics represent a special form of the general social structuring principle known as clientelism. What distinguishes the clientelistic mode of structuring political relationships is the method of intertwining specific and generalized motifs. The hard-edged and rather cold instrumentalities of market-like exchanges and power are softened by the warmer relations of trust, loyalty, and solidarity. Political clientelism, therefore, bridges the gap between the structural and symbolic spheres of social ordering.

At the core of clientelism lies the patron-client relationship. The trenchant analysis of clientelism developed by Eisenstadt and Roniger in their comparative study *Patrons, Clients and Friends* (1984) reveals the deeper significance of patron-client relations. First, clientelistic relations entail both specific (market-like, simple) and generalized (symbolic) principles of social exchange. Patron-client relations are predicated on the "simultaneous exchange of different resources—above all, instrumental and economic as well as political ones (support, loyalty, votes, protection) on the one hand, and promises of reciprocity, solidarity and loyalty on the other" (p. 48). Secondly, patron-client relationships involve "a strong element of interpersonal obligation" that binds patrons and clients into a nexus of "personal loyalty or reciprocity" (p. 48). Patron-client relations tend to be "informal understandings" that are not completely "contractual or legal" in nature (p. 48). Finally, patron-client relations, whether taking the form of dyadic couplings or complex networks, are structured vertically and contain a "very strong element of inequality and of differences in power between patrons and clients" (pp. 48–49). In sum, patron-client exchanges evince personalized, particularistic, reciprocal, and hierarchical relations.

The political machine, simply put, is a political party organization that mobilizes voters and, if successful, governs a polity on the basis of patron-client relations. Katznelson (1976), among others (Judd, 1984; Piven and Cloward, 1971), imputed to urban party machines a "dual broker, buffer role" in performing the tasks of urban governance.

> At the local level the machine substituted institutional and reward mechanisms of control for traditional deference; in turn, the particularistic activities of the machine created a *new "political formula"* for urban *legitimacy.* In any event, so long as the political energies of the new entrants into the political system were absorbed by the particularistic politics of the machines, stability and order were relatively assured [Katznelson, 1976: 225, emphasis added].

At the heart of this "new formula for urban legitimacy" lay the clientelistic mode of structuring social and political relationships. The electoral success or failure of political bosses depended on their ability to cultivate patron-client relations with urban constituencies-working-class voters and economic entrepreneurs. Political machines, then, were party institutions that maintained governing power by legitimizing the rule of local clientelistic regimes. . . .

What differentiates American city politics from other Western industrial democracies in the late nineteenth century is the interclass character of political party organization—the machine. Without going into great detail, it can be said that the early extension of suffrage to the working classes played a significant part in molding the character of American politics. In her work on the formation of working-class politics in the United States, Bridges (1986) sheds some light on the relationship between the timing of the elimination of property qualifications for voting and the rise of the urban political machine. According to Bridges, the antebellum structure of American party politics did not collapse in the turbulence of the Industrial Revolution. Instead, the "mutualist" politics of Jacksonian Democracy, which Bridges defines as the potential "to mobilize . . . voters into cross-class political coalitions emphasizing shared interests," persisted well into the post-Civil War period (p. 186). . . .

A second distinctive feature of the American political machine . . . was its local character. That is, the ubiquitous spread of machine politics in the United States, in contrast to those developing nations where political clientelism took root, assumed the institutional form of locally based and autonomous party organizations. . . .

The exceptional elements of the American political machine, then, were the *local* character and the *interclass* governing coalition it forged out of ostensibly opposing forces in an industrializing society. These distinctive attributes serve as markers for tracing the historical origins of the urban political machine in the United States. The urban party machine's exceptional characteristics were linked to two features of nineteenth-century American political development: (1) the extension of universal male suffrage prior to the period of industrialized urbanization, and (2) a federal political structure. These two distinctive arrangements, as argued here, provided the context necessary for the creation of locally based and largely autonomous political-patronage organizations in the United States. I accept Bridge's argument about how early democratization effected a "cross-class" character for American partisan politics and concentrate instead on the second distinctive feature of American political development—federalism.

HISTORICAL ANALYSIS OF URBAN POLITICAL MACHINES

American federalism deviates from the pattern of centralized nation-state structures developed in Western European countries. The more centralized authority of the unitary political systems in nineteenth-century France and England, for instance, led to nationally centralized party organizations. Power and patronage emanated from the central state apparatus in these countries, and, as a consequence, the structure of political party organizations adhered to the contours of centralized state authority (Goldsmith, 1979; Huntington, 1968; Machin, 1979).

Federalism, conversely, partitions political authority vertically into national and subnational governmental strata. The decentralized American state structure produced autonomous pockets of power and authority at the state and local levels of government. The structuring principle of federalism, as a result, permitted urban political leaders to carve out an autonomous region of political power and authority for the local state in the United States. From this perspective, machine bosses fashioned their organizations to fit the federated structure of the American state. As Piven and Cloward (1982: 93–94) explained:

> The exceptional vitality of machine politics in the United States was itself encouraged by the unusual degree of decentralization that characterized the American state structure. Decentralization provided a fertile ground for the development of client relations, for it yielded the patronage that made possible the rapid growth of machines in the immigrant wards without the need to capture a central state bureaucracy. Finally, a decentralized state structure also provided protected enclaves within which the machine could weather attempts to dislodge it.

Cities in the United States, then, as separate islands of political power and resources, furnished urban politicians with locally generated political authority and patronage well out of the reach of national political leaders. In this sense, local political autonomy provided a shielded space within which locally based party organizations could be established.

Local State-Building and the Rise of the Political Machine

Although federalism created a political environment that encouraged the formation of locally based party organizations, the building and maintenance of *machine-style* party organizations depended on a regular supply of political power and patronage. What this means is that urban party leaders required a local state apparatus that possessed adequate resources and authority for constructing their machines from the ground up.

This raises a central question about Merton's thesis: Was the local state apparatus functionally deficient during the period when centralized political machines dominated urban politics? A useful method for addressing this problem has been developed in the study of national political development. Tilly (1975) and others employed the concept of *state-building* to trace the pattern of institutional development in nation states over time. The idea of state-building is adopted here to ascertain the character of institutional development of American urban governance during the period of political machine formation. "Local" state-building is measured here, first, by gauging the degree of bureaucratization in the execution of local state authority over a wider range of governmental responsibilities and, second, by assessing the extent to which that political authority had become consolidated.

The local state in the antebellum period governed in a minimal fashion. The "government-by-committee" style of the preindustrial local state confined itself, for the most part, to matters of commerce (Judd, 1984; Teaford, 1972). At the onset of the Industrial Revolution, however, municipal government started to enlarge the purview of its authority. Mounting concerns about public safety, social order, public health, and urban growth forced municipal officials to retool the machinery or urban government. Urban political leaders, under the pressures imposed by an industrializing society, undertook the task of modernizing the local state apparatus.

Was the institutionalization of the local state, wherein urban governmental activities had become regularized and routinized, associated with the rise of urban political machines? If historical evidence reveals that substantial local state-building activities preceded the formation of the urban political machine, this would cast doubt on the functionalist argument that machines arose to compensate for the functional deficiency of urban government.

One way of clarifying the relationship between local state-building and the growth of political machines is to analyze the extent of organizational development in urban government during the period of machine emergence for individual cities. The historical development of the six selected municipal functions for 25 cities is outlined in Table 1. Information pertaining to both local state-building and political machine origins for other major cities could not be found.

Table 1 indicates that institutionalization of two out of the three public agencies (police, fire, and public works) antedated or coincided with the emergence of a machine organization in 23 of the 25 cities. These service

TABLE 1. Local State-Building and the Rise of Political Machines

City	Fire	Police	Public Works	Water System	Sewage Disposal	Mass Transit	Machine Origins	No. of Municipal Functions
Baltimore	1859	1857	1824	1804	1860	n.a.	1880s	5
Boston	1837	1854	1911	1823	1846	1852	1880s	5
Buffalo	1880	1866	1891	1854	n.a.	1860	1870s	3
Chicago	1858	1837	1861	1840	1856	1859	1890s	6
Cincinnati	1853	1859	1876	1821	1861	n.a.	1880s	5
Cleveland	1897	1866	1852	1856	1870s	1859	1880s	5
Denver	1899	1899	1890s	1904	1880s	1870s	1880s	2
Detroit	1851	1865	1873	1852	1857	1862	1880s	6
Grand Rapids	1872	1871	1873	1873	1865	1875	1890s	6
Indianapolis	1893	1891	n.a.	1871	1860s	1860s	1880s	3
Jersey City	1871	1871	1871	n.a.	n.a.	n.a.	1870s	3
Kansas City	1871	1874	1925	1895	n.a.	1869	1890s	4
Lynn, MA	1860s	1866	n.a.	1860s	n.a.	n.a.	1870s	3
Memphis	1860	1848	1909	1860	1880	1866	1890s	5
Milwaukee	1845	1855	1869	1873	1880	1859	1860s	4
New Orleans	1891	1852	1881	1899	1899	1850s	1880s	3
New York	1865	1844	1870	1842	1866	1875	1860s	4
Omaha	1871	1866	1857	n.a.	n.a.	1880s	1900s	4
Paterson, NJ	1890	1866	1857	1855	1868	1888	1870s	4
Philadelphia	1870	1854	1887	1799	1887	1857	1860s	3
Portland	1883	1870	1913	1885	1873	1868	1870s	3
Providence	1866	1866	1866	n.a.	1888	n.a.	1920s	4
Richmond, VA	1858	1860s	1919	1832	1836	1865	1870s	5
St. Louis	1857	1861	1914	1835	1863	1859	1880s	5
San Francisco	1866	1847	n.a.	1804	1858	1860	1970s	5
							Average	4.2

SOURCE: Questionnaire sent to mayoral offices of the 25 cities; historical literature (see Appendix).

Note: The dates listed under the categories of Fire, Police, and Public Works indicate the years when these municipal services were first established as administrative departments of the municipal executive. The columns headed by the titles Water Systems, Sewage Disposal, and Mass Transit contain the dates when these infrastructural systems were first constructed. The dates under the heading of Machine Origins identify the decade when machine politics originally appeared in organizational form. The last column consists of the total number of municipal functions that had been introduced before or during the decade of machine emergencies for each city.

functions in most of the cities became regularized and routinized before or during the period of machine formation. Municipal police forces, previously irregular "night watchman" operations, were converted into professional, bureaucratically organized departments. The voluntary fire brigades of the antebellum era were likewise abandoned for trained and bureaucratically administered fire departments. Finally, public works departments replaced ad hoc supervision over the maintenance and repair of the municipal infrastructure by city councils (Teaford, 1972). The establishment of police, fire, and public works departments, in other words, represented a bureaucratization and expansion of the local state apparatus. These local state-building activities, which increased the regularization and routinization of local state institutions, marked a qualitative shift away from the less formalized operations of antebellum urban government. This was the first step in building an *administrative* local state, where executive institutions began supplanting legislative bodies in a number of pivotal policy-making arenas.

The other three local state-building activities have less to do with bureaucratic development, at least during the period of machine emergence, and more to do with the expansion of local state authority and responsibility. Rapid urbanization and industrial growth forced local political leaders to enlarge the scope of local state authority and responsibility. The construction and maintenance of municipal infrastructure posed larger and more complex problems in the industrializing period after the Civil War. Although municipal governments in the latter half of the nineteenth century almost always contracted out the jobs of constructing water systems or sewer systems, authorization for these sorts of projects could be issued only by those who controlled the local state apparatus. The same was true of mass transit systems. The local state awarded franchises to operate trolley lines within the corporate boundaries of the city. Power to dispense contracts, franchises, or licenses, as with the establishment of public safety and public works agencies, augmented the local state's power of surveillance over its territorially defined jurisdiction.

Overall, the growth in local state authority is clear. In all cases but one (Denver), three or more municipal functions had been introduced before or during the decade of machine emergence. In the 1880s and 1890s, loosely configured "rings" vied for power in Denver, but never consolidated into a dominant machine organization. Robert Speer did not construct a powerful machine organization in Denver until after 1900, when he used as building blocks the recently established police, fire, and public works departments. More important, perhaps, is the fact that the average number of functions adopted before or during the period of machine origins is 4.2. This suggests that a rough cumulative threshold of local state-building may have existed as a precondition for political machine formation. That is, a local state that had not institutionalized and expanded its administrative apparatus probably could not have supported a centralized machine organization.

As it turned out, local party organizations in control of the governmental institutions responsible for the allocation of these principal municipal services established themselves as pivotal brokerage agencies. Party bosses doled out public employment to loyal ward heelers as a reward for political work and dispensed city franchises and contracts in exchange for financial support from urban capitalists involved in urban development and service delivery. Those machine politicians with sufficient acumen and skill mastered the art of political brokering and spun expansive webs of clientelistic relationships throughout the urban polity.

The argument proffered here is that nineteenth-century restructuring of the local state yielded a regularization of governmental activity and an expansion of political resources; the resultant administrative local state, in turn, furnished the materials and power necessary for constructing party machines. In this sense, Merton misread the role of urban government in the formation of machine organizations. The enriched governing capacity of the American local state, not its deficiency, permitted local party politicians to forge their loosely knit clientelistic networks into powerful political institutions.

Local State-Building and the Centralization of Political Machines

Merton's basic thesis, nonetheless, does not necessarily founder on the above evidence alone. The structural principle that produced urban governmental deficiency, according to Merton, is the separation of powers. The dispersion of formal power engendered by this type of authority structure, so the argument runs, meant that an informal centralization of power was necessary to hold the urban polity together. The centralized party machine served to fulfill this function.

This elicits a second empirical question: Was the authority structure of the American local state consolidated or fragmented during the period that party bosses centralized their machine organizations? If the direction of local state-building moved toward the consolidation of political authority, the functionalist argument would appear less tenable.

Shefter (1976), in his careful study of the Tammany Hall machine in New York City, identified three stages of machine development—rapacious individualism, centralization of party organization, and the rise of the dominant machine. Shefter portrayed the centralization of machine organization as a product of changes in the urban economic structure. His argument posited that businessmen in the emerging corporate sector of the urban economy demanded that order be imposed on lower echelon party officials by Tammany bosses to assure regularity in machine-business relations. Instability caused by William Marcy Tweed's[2] reign of "rapacious individualism" would no longer be tolerated by the emergent corporate businessmen known as the Swallowtails (p. 28). The profligate party bosses under Tweed welshed on deals and exacted exorbitant kickbacks; these actions were construed by the Swallowtails as threatening market stability (pp. 32–33). In Shefter's view, the impetus for centralization of the Tammany Hall machine, which followed the downfall of the Tweed ring in 1872, originated with that disgruntled group of corporate businessmen who wished to instill a sense of order in Tammany's operations.

Shefter's analysis represented a benchmark in the study of political machines because he cast his explanation in terms of political development. This is a point that was missed or ignored by Merton (1968: 72), who simply characterized the machine as centralized. Although many machines matured into centralized organizations, most early versions were merely loose coalitions of ward bosses.

The last quarter of the nineteenth century saw changes not only in the nature of the local economy, but also in the structure of urban government. Municipal charters originally empowered local legislative bodies with substantial governing authority, while sharply curtailing the powers of municipal executives (Klebanow et al., 1977). Furthermore, numerous state-appointed boards and commissions, coupled with large and often bicameral local legislatures and weak mayors, made the local state apparatus into a labyrinth of autonomous institutions. This Byzantine structure of the local state, however, eventually gave way to a more modern form by the turn of the century (Klebanow et al., 1977). Mayors gained the power to veto legislation and the authority to appoint and remove heads of city departments; their terms of office were lengthened as well. This consolidation of authority in the executive branch of urban government was usually accompanied by a reduction in the size and power of the city council (Klebanow et al., 1977; Griffith, 1974). The mayor's office, in other words, moved to the center stage of urban politics. This shift, in conjunction with the local state-building activities discussed earlier, represented an embryonic stage in the development of the administrative local state.

The reforms instituted during the Progressive era carried this modernization process even further. Commission government fused legislative and executive powers into a single decision-making body. City-manager forms of government streamlined executive decision making. In sum, strong-mayor, commission, city-manager forms, all of which placed executive authority at the center of local governmental power, encouraged the development of the administrative local state.

Cacophonous boards and commissions, in conjunction with a large and often unwieldly legislative council, governed most American cities prior to 1880. However, the freewheeling and sometimes unscrupulous style of politicking that surfaced from this decentralized structure of government rarely, if ever, crystalized into a centralized machine organization. Big city bosses like Tweed in New York, Colonel Edward Butler in St. Louis, "King" James McManes in Philadelphia, and John Chris Jacob in Detroit never managed to forge their loosely fashioned political rings into organizationally centralized party machines. For most cities, in fact, centralized machines appeared only after the institutional arrangements of local state authority had been organized.

The direction of governmental reorganization, it would seem, is the key to understanding the formation of centralized machines. A lengthy search of historical sources yielded the information found in Table 2. Table 2 compares the timing of charter reforms that strengthened mayors or instituted commission or city-manager forms of government with the consolidation of city party organizations into centralized party machines in 15 major cities. Again, information for both machine centralization and local state-building was not available for other cities. Table 2 presents striking evidence that the consolidation of machine organizations coincided with or followed charter reforms that established strong-mayor or commission forms of local government.

TABLE 2. Comparisons of Machine Centralization and Consolidation of the Local State in Sixteen Cities

City	Decade of Machine Consolidation	Centralization of Local State Apparatus		
		Strong Mayor	Commission	City Manager
Albuquerque	1910s		1917	
Baltimore	1900s	1899		
Boston	1880s	1885		
Cleveland	1890s	1891		
Denver	1900s	1903		
Indianapolis	1890s	1891		
Jersey City	1910s		1913	
Kansas City	1920s			1925
Lowell	1910s		1911	
Memphis	1920s		1908	
New Orleans	1900s	1896		
New York	1870s	1875		
Philadelphia	1880s	1885		
Pittsburgh	1880s	1887		
Rochester	1900s	1900		

SOURCE: See Appendix, Sources for Data on Local State-Building and Political Machines.

Strong-mayor charters extended the mayor's control over municipal administration by granting appointment and removal power to the mayor and by enlarging the mayor's role in the legislative process. This meant that control over political patronage distribution, the lifeblood of machine politics, had been centralized under the authority of the executive branch.

In the 11 cities that had adopted strong-mayor forms of municipal government, political bosses built their machine organizations around the centralized administrative authority vested in the mayor's office. In New Orleans, for instance, the Crescent Club (Democratic machine), which dominated city politics before 1900, failed to unify its members under the leadership of a single boss. Each ward boss or elected administrative official ruled independently over his own neighborhood satrapy (Jackson, 1969). Martin Behrman, elected to the mayor's office in 1903, molded the various factions of New Orleans' local Democracy into a highly centralized machine. This was made possible by the institution of a strong-mayor form of government in 1896. Behrman wielded his newly found administrative authority to discipline, and in some cases to oust, uncooperative city officials and ward bosses. The centralized machine organization built by Behrman, known as the Choctaw Club, was so well constructed that it outlived him by more than two decades (Hass, 1974). Other mayor-bosses who used their office to consolidate their machine organizations include Thomas Taggert of Indianapolis, Robert McKisson of Cleveland, and Robert Speer of Denver. As with the Choctaw Club, machine organizations in each of these cases rested on the foundation of a strong mayor's office (Dorsett, 1976; Leary, 1970; Warner, 1964).

In the other machine-dominated cities, party bosses harnessed the power radiating from a strong executive by manipulating mayoral nominations to ensure that their own henchmen would ultimately control municipal administration. Richard Croker of New York, Rochester's George Aldridge, Pittsburgh's dual bosses (Christopher Magee and William Flinn), Patrick Maguire of Boston, and Edwin "Duke" Vare of Philadelphia were all reputed for their skill in pulling the strings of marionette-like mayors (Allswang, 1977; Blodgett, 1982; Mosher, 1940; Steffens, 1957; Zink, 1930).

Table 2 also points to a close association between the adoption of a commission form of government and the formation of centralized machine organizations. This occurrence deals a particularly severe blow to Merton's functional explanation. The commission form of government abrogates the principle of separation of powers by fusing legislative and executive authority into a single governing body, the city commission. Commission government empowers a small number of elected officials, usually five, with both legislative and administrative duties. As a group, commissioners were lawmakers, and, as individual commissioners, they directed the activities of municipal departments. Local party leaders who controlled a city commission, then, gained ready access to both legislative and executive power. Moreover, a small body of commissioners could more easily coordinate a patronage system because they held all the reins of municipal authority. This concentration of governing power enabled political bosses to discipline party minions into well-oiled political machines in a number of cities.

The story of Frank Hague's iron-fisted rule in Jersey City exemplifies how commission government provided the means to erect a powerful citywide machine organization (McKean, 1940). Hague won a seat on the city commission as director of public safety in 1913. Shortly after the election, Hague's allies on the commission appointed him mayor. Using his control over the police and fire departments, Hague assembled an army of political workers loyal to him alone. Combining his administrative authority over public safety activities and his political authority over the commission, Hague skillfully wrought a highly disciplined machine out of a previously fractionalized Democratic party in Jersey City. As Table 2 indicates, Hague's accomplishment did not represent an isolated incident. Edward Crump in Memphis, James E. O'Donnel in Lowell, Massachusetts, and Clyde Tingley in Albuquerque all engineered centralized and durable political machines by plying the political tools forged by the fusion of legislative and executive powers in commission government (Blewett, 1976; Miller, 1964; Rabinowitz, 1983).

Only one case of a direct relationship between the adoption of a city-manager form of government and the formation of a dominant machine could be tracked down in the historical literature (Dorsett, 1968). Jim Pendergast organized a powerful Democratic ward-based machine in Kansas City in the late 1890s. Pendergast's machine, however, never really held sway over the entire city. When Jim's brother Tom slipped into the driver's seat of the Pendergast machine after Jim's death in 1911, the Pendergast organization still only controlled a minority of wards in Kansas City. It was not until after the installment of a city-manager form of government in 1925 that the Pendergast machine achieved citywide dominance. Tom Pendergast, through his influence over the city council's legislative agenda and the city manager's appointive powers, consolidated his machine into a centralized, citywide, patronage organization.

In some cities the adoption of city-manager charters did not necessarily lead to the demise of a dominant machine. For instance, machine politics did not ebb in Cleveland (1924) or Rochester (1927) when confronted by newly instituted city-manager systems (Allen, 1969; Mosher, 1940). The reigning political bosses simply took advantage of the situation, like Pendergast in Kansas City, by orchestrating the distribution of patronage through the city manager's office.

In a nutshell, Merton's functional analysis of the machine, premised on the argument that the dispersion of power in the American local state necessitated the formation of centralized political machines to coordinate the latent functions of governance, is not substantiated. The centralized machines identified here appeared during or after the consolidation of local state authority through such reforms as strong-mayor, commission, or, in one case, city-manager government. This suggests that the rise of the administrative local state, where executive authority was enhanced and the power of the city council curtailed, afforded local party bosses the means to organize centralized political machines. A local party leader in control of a strong executive could impose order on lower level party officials by threatening to cut off their supply of patronage. The consolidation of administrative authority enabled city-wide party bosses to orchestrate the distribution of patronage from above and thus united previously autonomous ward bosses into a single, centralized machine.

AN ALTERNATIVE TO THE FUNCTIONAL EXPLANATION OF CITY MACHINES

Robert Merton propounded a theory of political machines that rests on a functional understanding of the social and political world. Merton's discussion provided a useful heuristic framework for describing *how* the political machine operated. That is, Merton's careful analysis unveiled a clear picture of the machine's coalition-building practices. The uniqueness of Merton's explanation, however, lies in its functional interpretation of machine politics. This functional explanation, it has been argued here, has taken undue hold of the scholarly discourse about urban political machines. To counter this bit of conventional wisdom, I have endeavored to mark out an alternative explanation for the rise and development of urban political machines in the United States.

Theories of the political machine that rely on functional analysis, by invoking social needs and dispersed power as explanatory concepts, fail to account adequately for the actual historical conditions that set the stage for big city machines. Indeed, the historical evidence presented here paints an entirely different picture of machine politics than the one depicted by the conventional wisdom. Federalism, which established a decentralized structure for the American state, accorded the local state an exceptional degree of autonomy in governing affairs within its territorial jurisdiction.

In the context of federalism, extensive local state-building activities in the second half of the nineteenth century, propelled largely by rapid industrialization and urban growth, engendered the formation of an inchoate administrative local state. The expansion and institutionalization of local state authority, in conjunction with the concentration of power within the local state apparatus, preceded or coincided with the appearance of political machines in all cities considered in this study. The emergence of the administrative local state was crucial for the rise and development of urban political machines. Therefore, the building up of urban governmental institutions and authority, not their deficiencies, occasioned the formation of urban political machines in the United States.

NOTES

1. Political machines also appeared in a number of Canadian cities during the same era as the American machine, because the Canadian political system is also organized around the principle of federalism. For discussions pertaining to political machines in Canada see Stetler and Artibise (1977), Artibise and Stetler (1979), Magussen and Sancton (1983), and Kaplan (1982).

2. Tweed was the first citywide political boss of New York City. Tweed rose to power through his control over Tammany Hall, a prominent Democratic political club. His reign was rather short, however, lasting from 1869 to 1872. For detailed accounts of Tweed's political career see Callow (1966) and Mandelbaum (1965).

REFERENCES

Allen, R. S. [ed.] (1969) Our Fair City. New York: Oxford.

Allswang, J. (1977) Bosses, Machines, and Urban Voters. Baltimore, MD: Johns Hopkins Univ. Press.

Artibise, A. and G. A. Stetler [eds.] (1979) The Urban Usable Past: Planning and Politics in the Modern Canadian City. Toronto: McMillan.

Banfield, E. and J. Q. Wilson (1963) City Politics. New York: Vintage.

Blewett, M. (1976) "The mills and the multitudes: a political history," pp. 161–189 in A. Eno (ed.) Cotton Was King: A History of Lowell, Massachusetts. Lowell, MA: Lowell Historical Society.

Blodgett, G. (1982) "Yankee leadership in a divided city: Boston 1860–1910." J. of Urban History 8 (August): 371–397.

Bridges, A. (1986) "Becoming American: the working classes in the United States before the Civil War," pp. 157–196 in I. Katznelson and A. R. Zolberg (eds.) Working Class

Formation: Nineteenth Century Patterns in Western Europe and the United States. Princeton, NJ: Princeton Univ. Press.

Bryce, J. (1888) The American Commonwealth. New York: AMS.

Callow, A. (1966) The Tweed Ring. New York: Oxford Univ. Press.

Cornwell, Jr., E. (1964) "Bosses, machines, and ethnics." Annals of the Amer. Academy of Pol. and Social Sci. (May): 27–39.

Dorsett, L. (1968) The Pendergast Machine. Lincoln: Univ. of Nebraska Press.

Dorsett, L. (1976) The Queen City: A History of Denver. Boulder, CO: Pruett.

Eisenstadt, E. S. and L. Roniger (1984) Patrons, Clients, and Friends: Interpersonal Relations and the Structure of Trust in Society. Cambridge, MA: Cambridge Univ. Press.

Fraser, D. (1976) Urban Politics in Victorian England: The Structure of Politics in Victorian Cities. Leicester, England: Leicester Univ. Press.

Giddens, A. (1981) A Contemporary Critique of Historical Materialism. Berkeley: University of California.

Goldsmith, M. (1979) "The changing system of English local government," pp. 10–27 in J. LaGroye and V. Wright (eds.) Local Governments in Britain and France: Problems and Prospects. London: George Allen & Unwin.

Greenstein, F. I. (1969) "The changing patterns of urban politics," pp. 154–170 in A. Shank (ed.) Political Power and the Urban Crisis. Boston: Holbrook.

Griffith, E. (1974) A History of the American City: The Conspicuous Failure, 1870–1900. New York: Praeger.

Guterbock, T. (1980) Machine Politics in Transition: Party and Community in Chicago. Chicago: Univ. of Chicago Press.

Hass, E. F. (1974) Delesseps S. Morrison and the Image of Reform: New Orleans Politics 1946–1961. Baton Rouge: Louisiana State Univ. Press.

Hempel, C. (1959) "The logic of functional analysis," pp. 271–307 in L. Gross (ed.) Symposium on Social Theory. New York: Harper & Row.

Hofstadter, R. (1955) The Age of Reform. New York: Vintage.

Huntington, S. (1968) Political Order in Changing Societies. New Haven: Yale Univ. Press.

Jackson, J. J. (1969) New Orleans in the Gilded Age: Politics and Urban Progress, 1880–1896. Baton Rouge: Louisiana State Univ. Press.

Judd, D. (1984) The Politics of American Cities: Private Power and Public Policy (2nd ed.). Boston: Little, Brown.

Kaplan, H. (1982) Reform, Planning, and City Politics: Montreal, Winnipeg, Toronto. Toronto: University of Toronto.

Katznelson, I. (1976) "The crisis of the capitalist city: urban politics and social control," pp. 214–229 in W. Hawley and M. Lipsky (eds.) Theoretical Perspectives on Urban Politics. Englewood Cliffs, NJ: Prentice-Hall.

Katznelson, I. (1981) City Trenches: Urban Politics and the Patterning of Class in the United States. New York: Pantheon.

Klebanow, D., F. L. Jonas, and I. M. Leonard (1977) Urban Legacy: The Story of American Cities. New York: Mentor.

Leary, E. A. (1970) Indianapolis: The Story of a City, Indianapolis: Bobbs-Merrill.

Lehman, H. (1966) "R. K. Merton's concept of function and functionalism." Inquiry 9 (5): 274–283.

Machin, H. (1979) "Traditional patterns of French local government," pp. 29–41 in J. LaGroye and V. Wright (eds.), Local Governments in Britain and France: Problems and Prospects. London: George Allen & Unwin.

Magussen, W. and A. Sanction [eds.] (1983) City Politics in Canada. Toronto: Univ. of Toronto Press.

Mandelbaum, S. (1965) Boss Tweed's New York. New York: John Wiley.

McKean, D. D. (1940) The Boss: The Machine in Action. Boston: Houghton Mifflin.

Merton, R. K. (1968) Social Structure and Social Theory. New York: Free Press.

Miller, W. D. (1964) Mr. Crump of Memphis. Baton Rouge: Louisiana State Univ. Press.

Miller, Z. (1981) "Bosses, machines, and the urban political process," pp. 51–84 in S. Greer (ed.) Ethnics, Machines and the American Urban Future. Cambridge, MA: Schenkman.

Moore, B., Jr. (1966) Social Origins of Dictatorship and Democracy: Lord and Peasant in the Making of the Modern World. Boston: Beacon.

Mosher, F. (1940) "Rochester," pp. 3–97 in City Manager Government in Seven Cities. Chicago: Public Administration Service.

Nelson, J. (1979) Access to Power: Politics and the Urban Poor. Princeton, NJ: Princeton Univ. Press.

Piven, F. F. and R. Cloward (1971) Regulating the Poor: The Functions of Public Welfare, New York: Vintage.

Piven, F. F. and R. Cloward (1982) The New Class War: Reagan's Attack on the Welfare State and its Consequences. New York: Pantheon.

Rabinowitz, H. M. (1983) "Albuquerque: a city at a crossroads," pp. 255–267 in R. M. Bernard and B. Rice (eds.) Sunbelt Cities: Politics and Growth Since World War II. Austin: Univ. of Texas Press.

Scott, J. C. (1969) "Corruption, machine politics, and political change." Amer. Pol. Sci. Rev. 63 (December): 1142–1158.

Shefter, M. (1976) "The emergence of the political machine: an alternative view," pp. 14–44 in W. Hawley and M. Lipsky (eds.) Theoretical Perspectives on Urban Politics. Englewood Cliffs, NJ: Prentice-Hall.

Shefter, M. (1984) "Political parties, political mobilization and political demobilization," pp. 140–148 in T. Ferguson and J. Rogers (eds.) The Political Economy: Readings in the Politics and Economics of American Public Policy. Armonk, NY: M. E. Sharpe.

Smith, A. (1937) An Inquiry into the Nature and Causes of the Wealth of Nations. New York: Modern Library.

Steffens, L. (1957) The Shame of Cities. New York: Hill & Wang.

Stetler, G. A. and A. Artibise [eds.] (1977) The Canadian City: Essays in Urban History. Toronto: McClelland and Stewart.

Teaford, J. (1972) The Municipal Revolution in America: The Origins of Urban Government, 1650–1825. Chicago: Univ. of Chicago Press.

Tilly, C. [ed.] (1975) The Formation of Nation States in Western Europe. Princeton, NJ: Princeton Univ. Press.

Warner, H. L. (1964) Progressivism in Ohio, 1897–1917. Columbus: Ohio State Univ. Press.

Zink, H. (1930) City Bosses in the United States: A Study of Twenty Municipal Bosses. Durham: Duke Univ. Press.

Zolberg, A. R. (1986) "How many exceptionalisms?," pp. 397–455 in I. Katznelson and A. R. Zolberg (eds.) Working-Class Formation: Nineteenth-Century Patterns in Western Europe and the United States. Princeton, NJ: Princeton Univ. Press.

14
The Emergence of the Political Machine: An Alternative View*

Martin Shefter

It is unfortunate that the literature on urban politics is of little use in helping one fashion an explanation for the development of the New York machine. Although political scientists, sociologists, and historians have written about the machine, one strategy of explanation tends to prevail in these writings, a mode of explanation which, despite appearances to the contrary, is profoundly ahistorical. First, it is noted (quite properly) that a distinguishing characteristic of mature political machines is the peculiar organizational cement that binds them together: machine politicians are linked to their supporters and to one another through a web of particularistic loyalties and individual payoffs. The question, "How can one account for the emergence of political machines?" is then interpreted to mean, "Under what circum-

*Shefter, Martin. 1976. "The Emergence of the Political Machine: An Alternative View." Pp. 18–32 in *Theoretical Perspectives on Urban Politics*, ed. Willis D. Hawley and Michael Lipsky, Englewood Cliffs. NJ: Prentice Hall. Copyright © 1976. Reprinted by permission of Prentice Hall.

stances will a party so constituted be able to command the support of a majority of the electorate?" and an answer is sought in social characteristics which distinguish those voters who support machine candidates from those who do not. The emergence of machines is then attributed to the growth in the city of groups with the indicated characteristics.

Proceeding in this way, Banfield and Wilson, for example, argue that citizens who are willing to exchange their votes for the favors and the "friendship" offered by the functionaries of political machines are expressing thereby a "private-regarding" or "individualist" conception of politics, one that regards the advancement of individual or family-based interests as *the* purpose of politics.[1] Voters who reject such blandishments indicate by their actions that they have a "public-regarding" or "unitarist" conception of politics — a view that government should be conducted according to general principles, that considerations of personal loyalty and individual advancement are illegitimate in public life, and that the purpose of politics is to advance a broadly defined and abstractly conceived public interest. Second, Banfield and Wilson observe that during the height of machine rule, those who affiliated with political machines tended to be of lower- or working-class immigrant background, while the opponents of the machine were on the whole middle- and upper-class native Protestants. From these two observations Banfield and Wilson conclude three things: (1) the tendency of various groups to support (or oppose) the machine is to be explained by the political ethos of the group in question; (2) the political ethos of a group is a function of its income and ethnicity — the more heavily immigrant and the poorer a city's population, the more prevalent will be those attitudes and orientations that support machine politics; and (3) the emergence of political machines is to be explained by the influx of poor immigrants into American cities, and their decline is explained by the movement of these groups up the class scale and their consequent assimilation into the middle-class political ethos.[2]

Other theorists of the machine focus upon different characteristics that plausibly can be said to motivate and hence, it is argued, to explain support for, or opposition to, the machine. Robert Merton, for example, claims that the "needs" of the poor and of businesses in an expanding city (and the absence of alternative structures to serve these needs) accounted for the tendency of these groups to support the machine.[3] James Scott attributes the willingness of the machine's supporters to pursue individual interests in politics to the social disorganization produced by migration, urbanization, and economic change.[4] Daniel Moynihan and Elmer Cornwell suggest that the attachment of voters to the machine was an expression of primordial ethnic loyalties.[5] Richard Wade focuses upon the relationship of the machine to the patterns of social life in the city's tenement districts.[6] And Samuel P. Hays suggests that support for, and opposition to, the party organization was an expression of the cleavage between those whose personal attachments were to their neighborhood communities and those who were attached to citywide or even more broadly based institutions.[7] But in all these cases the mode of explanation is similar. A more or less elaborate description of the ties that bind machine politicians to their supporters, and to one another, is presented; the sentiments or interests that would motivate participation in (and opposition to) such a nexus of bonds are suggested; the groups who support (and oppose) the mature political machine are then identified, and this support is attributed to their being moved by the appropriate sentiments and motives; and from this static correlation a dynamic explanation for the emergence of the political machine is inferred, with the engine, the pace, and the direction of change being attributed to, and determined by, one or another autonomous social process (population movements and the growth of cities; cultural persistence, anomie, and acculturation; economic mobility and immobility; the development, persistence, and decay of ethnic identifications, and so on).

When the logical structure of the conventional explanations for the emergence of the political machine is explicitly stated, the problems with these theories become clear. These explanations assume that the meaning of the question, "What explains the emergence of the political machine?" is exhausted by the answer to the question, "When a machine exists, who supports and opposes it?" But the meaning of these two questions is identical only if one is willing to introduce two assumptions, neither of which is tenable. The first is an assumption of fact: that the political alignments that prevail subsequent to the emergence of a dominant machine are identical to those that existed prior to its emergence. There is, of course, no reason to believe *a priori* that the prevailing cleavage patterns in the premachine and the machine eras will be identical. As Lipset and Rokkan note, the setting of political choices and the choice among a relatively fixed set of political alternatives are two distinct processes.[8]

The second problem with the conventional arguments for the machine's emergence involves a matter of explanatory sufficiency. To consider that once one has discerned the social bases of a political institution and has offered a plausible account of the motives, the sentiments, and the inducements that link that institution to its supporters, one has provided a sufficient explanation for the existence of that institution is to commit oneself to a species of social determinism that is the reverse of, but as strict as, that employed by only the most vulgar of Marxists. Such a mode of reasoning rests upon the implicit assumptions that political institutions mechanically reflect, and are uniquely determined by, an underlying configuration of social forces. For as soon as one admits the possibility that alternative political structures can exist in a given social environment, one is driven to ask why one of these has triumphed over its equally plausible alternatives — or, at least, why the possible alternatives were, in fact, less plausible than the one that did emerge triumphant.

The problems with, and the assumptions implicit in, the conventional explanations for the emergence of the political machine can perhaps most clearly be illustrated if one represents this argument in diagrammatic form (Figure 1). At some point subsequent to the emergence of the political machine, a correlation is perceived between the maintenance of a political

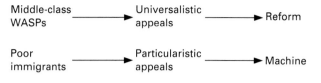

institution (the "Machine") and the support of a social group (such as "poor immigrants"), the relationship being mediated by the observation that the former offers a set of inducements ("particularistic appeals") to which the latter, for one or another of the abovementioned reasons, responds. At this time it is also observed that the opponents of the machine ("Reform") stage a rather different set of appeals ("universalistic appeals") and draw their support from a different social group (such as "middle-class WASPs").

Even granting the accuracy of this account of the structure of political competition subsequent to the emergence of the machine, the effort to draw dynamic inferences from these static associations involves ignoring the possibility that alternative causal paths may exist. In Figure 2, I have shown only a few of the alternatives that the evidence from New York indicates were, at various points in time, live options. For example, as I shall note, the quest for specific material benefits in politics can be subversive of the very political order that such leaders of the Tammany machine as John Kelly were struggling to establish. While in the last decades of the nineteenth century the leadership of Tammany managed to create a political structure that, as it were, harnessed and harmonized these motivations, and organized and monopolized these inducements, in earlier decades these same individual motivations and behaviors, so to speak, "summed" to a radically different political structure—indeed to one that scarcely could be called a "structure." In other words, a politics of particularism is not a sufficient condition for the existence of a political machine (any more than the quest for material gain by individuals is a sufficient condition for the existence of a capitalistic economic order). Nor is the fact that a given social group such as the poor immigrants *can* be mobilized by particularistic appeals sufficient to establish

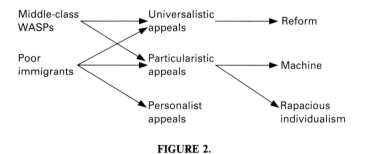

FIGURE 2.

that they *will* be mobilized in this way. The example of the political behavior of blacks in recent years should alert us to the recognition that among recently urbanized groups, leaders who stage ideological appeals, on the one hand, and those who stage personalist ones, on the other, are social types as authentic as those who distribute specific material benefits, and that the process through which such groups get incorporated into the polity frequently involves a struggle among leaders who stage radically different appeals for the loyalty of the same mass base. By the same token, elements of the very groups—such as the Irish—that supported Tammany so fervently at the end of the century, at earlier times supported leaders who staged entirely different appeals. Finally, being middle- or upper-class in income and Protestant in religion was not a sufficient condition for participating in politics out of universalistic motives. Well before the immigrants became the preponderant element in New York's population, the city's politics were quite corrupt, and the massive corruption of the Tweed era might best be seen as the way in which a linkage was established between the members of a rising entrepreneurial class (most of whom were of native origins) and the city's politicians (who themselves, and whose constituents, were of both immigrant and native stock).

If conventional theories of the political machine are inadequate—if they fail to explain what requires explanation how can one account for the emergence of a dominant machine in New York? In order to do so it is necessary to analyze in some detail the salient characteristics of New York's party system at various stages of its development.

THE POLITICS OF RAPACIOUS INDIVIDUALISM

A brief account of the structure of party politics in New York prior to the downfall of the Tweed Ring is sufficient to indicate how poorly the model of urban political competition outlined above describes the character of political life in New York during the middle decades of the nineteenth century. The dominant fact about New York politics during the era of rapacious individualism was the weakness of political organizations in the city and the fluidity of local political alignments—a pattern of politics that, if anything, resembles more closely that of an underdeveloped polity than it does the highly organized politics of the machine era. Far from being structured around an overriding cleavage between two well-organized forces that differed both in their fundamental orientations towards politics and in their social composition, political competition in New York during this period was characterized rather by, first, the multiplicity of formations that contended for power in the city; second, the failure of the cleavages among these formations to map out the distinction between machine and reformist political orientations; and, finally, the considerable social and ethnic heterogeneity of the major political factions.

During the era of rapacious individualism the Democratic party in New York was rent by factionalism. In the late 1810s Tammany Democrats divided into Hunkers and Barnburners and then, in the early 1850s, into Hardshells and Softshells. Over the next decade a number of anti-Tammany Democratic factions such as the Mozart Hall and the McKeon Democracy —arose.[9] The years of Tweed's preeminence in New York politics—which roughly extended from 1866 to 1871—were ones in which Tammany men managed to win most of the significant public offices in New York, but before the collapse of the Ring, Tammany Hall itself was the scene of intense rivalry. A grouping known as the Young Democracy managed at one point in 1870 to seize control of the Tammany General Committee away from Tweed and his confederates. Tweed was able to remain in control of Tammany Hall only because a majority of the sachems of the Tammany Society remained loyal to him. The Tammany Society, which ostensibly was a fraternal and benevolent association, owned the building—Tammany Hall —in which New York City's Democratic General Committee met. On five occasions prior to its reinstating Tweed, the Council of Sachems, which was the executive committee of the Tammany Society, had settled factional struggles by the simple procedure of locking out the faction it did not favor and permitting only the General Committee whose claims to regularity it endorsed to use Tammany Hall.[10]

The lines along which these factions and groupings divided did not map onto a cleavage between machine and reformist political styles—a cleavage that emerged only much later in the city's political history. Mozart Hall, for example, was founded by Fernando Wood not as a vehicle for reform but rather as a means of promoting Wood's career after Tammany refused to renominate him for mayor. The reports of a succession of investigating committees suggest that corruption was as rife when Tammany's opponents were in office as during periods of Tammany rule.[11] The willingness of various factions to at times nominate common slates of candidates, and the movement of politicians among these factions, indicate that the factions were not distinguished from one another by fundamentally different orientations to politics. Rather than being united by a common ideology, these factions, like the parties in many underdeveloped political systems today, were simply coalitions of politicians who shared nothing but a common desire for power and who were prepared to change their allegiance as their career interests dictated.[12]

Finally, the major political factions of this period did not divide along readily discernible lines of nativity, religion, ethnicity, or social class. During the era of rapacious individualism, wealthy, native-born Protestants appear to have been as willing as poor, foreign-born Irish Catholics to participate in politics out of a quest for particularistic benefits. The ethnic and religious heterogeneity of the Tweed Ring is especially striking: the Ring was a veritable melting pot. Two of the Tweed Ring's four central leaders, Peter Sweeney and Richard Connolly, were Irish. Tweed's forebears were Scots who came to America in the eighteenth century, and A. Oakey Hall's were English. The Ring's three major representatives on the judiciary—McCunn, Barnard, and Cardozo—were respectively a Catholic, a Protestant, and a Jew. Participation in, and support for, the schemes of the Ring cut across class as well as ethnic lines. The Ring was closely allied with important segments of New York's business and financial community. Tweed, for example, used his influence in the state legislature and with the judiciary to assist Jay Gould and Jim Fiske in their struggles against Cornelius Vanderbilt for control of the Erie Railroad, and many of New York's wealthiest men signed petitions supporting various of Tweed's reorganization plans for the city government.[13] Indeed, the city's financial community played such an active (and anxious) role in the overthrow of the Tweed Ring in 1871 for the very reason that through the purchase of municipal bonds during the period of Ring rule, their interests and their fate had become intimately intertwined with that of the city government.[14]

Although the quest for specific material benefits played a major role in binding political followings together, political parties during the era of rapacious individualism were loosely structured and ill-disciplined. In contrast to the situation that was to prevail after the development of the mature political machine, party organizations, as such, did not dominate the city's electoral process. Politicians relied upon their personal followings to secure nominations—which frequently were captured by the leader who brought the largest number of brawlers to a primary meeting. Tweed, for example, received his first nomination to public office in 1850, the year he became foreman of a volunteer fire company: although he had performed no previous party service, his leadership of a band of seventy-five men was enough to get the Tammany committee in his ward to nominate him for assistant alderman.[15] Twenty years later, when Tweed was its leader, Tammany's district committees still were not very strong. During the severe winter of 1870–71 Tweed spent $50,000 of his personal funds in his own ward and gave each of the city's aldermen $1,000 out of his own pocket to buy coal for the poor: the provision of those storied hods of coal had yet to become institutionalized.[16]

Because during the era of rapacious individualism the party apparatus was weak, party leaders were unable to control the behavior of elected officials. The groupings formed by officials in the governmental arena consequently bore little relation to those that prevailed in the city's electoral arena. The combine that, for example, dominated the Common Council of 1851 — one whose operations were so blatantly corrupt that its affairs were subject to considerable scrutiny—was organized by a group of aldermen subsequent to, rather than prior to the election, and its membership cut across party and factional lines. The leaders of the combine negotiated for the sale of public favors—franchises, leases of city property, and city contracts—and they distributed the proceeds to their associates. They were quite willing to extort money from other public officials (such as the coroners) and to insist that party leaders and luminaries (such as Myndert Van Schaick, a former Tammany mayoral candidate), as much as anyone else, had to pay for the favors they received.[17]

The Tweed Ring extended this system but did not transcend it: The

Ring departed from the pattern set by earlier combines of public officials only to the extent that its members occupied positions in each of the major branches and boards of the municipal government. Tweed, being unable to command the support of other public officials, was compelled to purchase it. Five percent of the proceeds of the Ring was placed in a "sinking fund" to bribe legislators. The measures whose passage Tweed secured in this way indicate how little confidence the Ring was willing to place in its ability to control elections. Tweed attached to the Tax Levy of 1870 a "joker clause" that amended the city charter that just had been adopted by authorizing the mayor, five days after the passage of the Tax Levy, to appoint a city comptroller for a term that would not expire until January 1, 1875. This clause enabled the incumbent mayor (Oakey Hall) to reappoint the incumbent comptroller (Richard Connolly) and thus ensured — or so it was believed — that whatever the outcome of the next municipal election, the Ring would control the city's finance department through 1874.[18] A piece of legislation passed the following year created a Board of Apportionment, which had authority over the appropriation of city revenues. The composition of the board, as mandated by the bill, indicates how narrow was the group Tweed felt he could trust or control. The legislation provided that the board was to be composed of Tweed, Connolly, Hall, and Sweeney![19] Finally, an amendment to the Tax Levy of 1871 introduced by Tweed extended the life of the incumbent Board of Aldermen for a year beyond the point provided in the new city charter. Tweed was not confident that he could control the aldermanic elections required by the new charter and hence wanted the current aldermen — a majority of whom he had on his payroll — continued in office.[20]

The Tweed Ring, then, was essentially an *intragovernmental* formation of remarkably narrow scope. It was a combine within Tammany, whose membership was considerably narrower than the party's and whose corrupt activities did not serve to strengthen the party. And the Ring did not command a disciplined electoral organization. Much as the fact that a few colonels can so easily overthrow governments in Asia, Africa, and Latin America is a token of the antecedent regime's structural fragility, the fact that a group of bankers could by cutting off the city's credit bring about the *total* collapse of the Tweed Ring (in the mayoral election of 1872 there was no mayoral candidate identified with Tweed) was a token and a consequence of the Ring's essential fragility.

This comparison between the politics of rapacious individualism and that of underdeveloped politics can be extended beyond the domain of political *structure*. One cannot but be struck by the resemblances between political *processes* in New York during the third quarter of the nineteenth century and those that prevail in many third world nations today. Much as in contemporary developing nations, the political system of mid-nineteenth-century New York was easily penetrated by external authorities. And political actors who could deploy violence and wealth were both willing to employ such resources to the hilt and frequently found it efficacious to do so: party loyalties were weaker than the appeal of cash, and when conflicts occurred between those who mobilized incomensurable political resources — numbers, wealth, authority, notability, and violence — it frequently turned out that the forces commanding the latter prevailed.

The permeability of New York's political system to external authority was demonstrated most starkly in 1857. In that year the newly formed Republican party gained power in the state and proceeded immediately to strip New York City (which generally was run by Democrats) of control over many important and patronage-rich municipal functions. The city's police department was abolished and a state-appointed metropolitan police board was established in its place. A state appointed Central Park Commission (which had authority over public works other than parks in the northern portion of the city) was also created in 1857. (State-appointed metropolitan fire and health departments were established in the mid-1860s.) The legislature also created an independent Board of Supervisors to supervise taxation and county functions and provided that it be elected in a manner that guaranteed that half its members would be Republicans.[21]

The use of public authority by external authorities was supplemented, and at times countered, by the deployment of force. One such violent confrontation occurred in 1857 when Mayor Fernando Wood refused to disband the municipal police department after the creation of the metropolitan police force. For a time the city was patrolled by two police forces, the members of one frequently releasing the prisoners arrested by the other. This conflict was settled only when the state militia was called to the scene to quell a battle between the two forces in City Hall Park.[22] In 1863 the "dangerous classes" of New York rose up against the enforcement of the federal conscription act. The great New York draft riot was the largest outburst of civil disorder in American urban history — an outburst that Democratic officials did little to suppress and much to stimulate[23] — and was put down only after federal troops were brought to the city and as many as 2,000 persons had been killed. (It is a token of how weak was the sense of political community at the time that the troops fired *artillery* shells directly into the mobs.) In 1864 federal troops were called by fearful Republicans to the city again, in anticipation of Democratic election violence and frauds.[24]

Finally, and most obviously, the prevalence of corruption in New York politics during the era of rapacious individualism also suggests parallels to the politics of developing nations today. During this period party and factional loyalties — to say nothing of the force of institutional loyalties and of norms of public probity — were so weak that political actors both found it necessary to bribe their nominal co-partisans in order to secure and to maintain cooperation and found it possible to secure the support of their nominal party and factional opponents with cash payments. Tweed's predecessor as Tammany's Grand Sachem, Elijah Purdy, for example, had to bribe Tammany aldermen in order to get them to do his bidding,[25] and Tweed himself had to meet the incessant demands of his confederates in order to preserve their loyalty. Comptroller Connolly, for example, insisted in 1870 that his share of the Ring's take be increased as the price for his continued cooperation, and ex-sheriff James O'Brien joined in the founding of the Young Democracy after Tweed's Board of Audit refused to approve $250,000 in claims he had presented to it.[26] Examples of bribery being used to induce politicians to cross party and factional lines also abound. Tweed, for example, overcame the equal party division on the Board of Supervisors by bribing one of its Republican members.[27] And Tweed induced two of the three senators who belonged to the Young Democracy to vote in favor of the city charter he favored by paying them cash bribes.[28] Indeed, during the era of rapacious individualism, corruption appears to have done as much to subvert as to strengthen party ties.

Three indications of the fragmentation and the fragility of political structures in New York during the era of rapacious individualism, and of the volatility of methods of political competition and control, suggest how far New York City was from being governed by a political machine during the middle decades of the nineteenth century. The construction of a dominant machine in New York during the last decades of the century required (as does the emergence of dominant parties in developing nations today) that a system of political order be created out of a system of political chaos.[29]

THE EMERGENCE OF PARTY ORGANIZATION

During the years immediately following the collapse of the Tweed Ring New York's party system changed in a number of crucial respects. In the decades prior to 1872, . . . the most significant political formations in the city were the personal followings of politicians and the combines formed by public officials. These formations were plentiful in number, short in duration, amorphous in structure, and each operated primarily in either the city's governmental or its electoral arena. During the 1870s and 1880s, by contrast, a set of party organizations emerged that were few in number, fairly stable in duration, substantially more coherent in their structure, and *did* provide a linkage between the city's electoral and governmental arenas. Moreover, during the 1870s and 1880s a number of intraorganizational and interorganizational processes most notably, the purge, threat of "exit,"[30] and the competitive quest for voters supplanted (though they did not entirely replace) the mobilization of wealth and violence and the appeal to external authority, as the dominant means through which the struggle for power in the city was conducted.

The elaboration of party organization—the development of a measure of structural complexity and organizational coherence—is a precondition for a party's becoming a dominant machine. But the existence of a number of such organizations the fragmentation of party and the persistence of factionalism is subversive of central control in the polity. During the 1870s and 1880s, then, New York City moved substantially towards, though it did not fully achieve, machine government. I shall first briefly describe the emergence of party organization and of factional multiplicity in New York during this period and then consider how one can account for these two developments.

The individual most responsible for engineering these changes was John Kelly, who, in the words of one contemporary, "found Tammany a horde [and] left it a political army."[31] Kelly, who assumed the leadership of Tammany after the overthrow of Tweed, immediately undertook to bolster his position within the party by purging Tammany of Tweed's allies and by centralizing the party organization. During the first decade of his leadership Kelly engineered the adoption of a set of reforms in party structure and established a series of precedents that strengthened the Tammany organization in a number of ways. First, control over entry into and exit from the organization was centralized. The Committee on Organization, which was chained by Kelly and which served as his politburo, assumed the power to expel members from Tammany's district committees and to reorganize delegations to the Tammany General Committee.[32] A specialized control organ, which evolved into the standing Committee on Discipline, was also established to investigate, and if need be to recommend the expulsion of, party cadres accused of aiding the organization's enemies.[33] Second, the decisions, as well as the membership, of the organization's local units were subject to central review. For example, in 1873 the Committee on Organization asserted its claim to reject the nominations for public office made by Tammany district conventions.[34] Third, efforts were made to establish the principle that powers attached to party roles and offices rather than to the individuals who at the moment happened to occupy them. In 1875 the Committee on Organization decreed that thenceforth patronage would be distributed through the district committees of the party (in proportion to the vote they turned out) rather than being allocated to individual leaders, and in 1881, as mentioned above, Kelly purged two district leaders (one of whom was a personal protégé of his) for accepting patronage appointments without having had their names tendered to the mayor by the organization.[35] Fourth and finally, public officials as well as party politicians were subjected to the control and discipline of the organization. The Tammany members of the state legislative delegation began meeting with the Committee on Organization in 1875 to discuss pending legislation, and in 1879, when the Democratic state convention renominated for the governorship a man who had aided Tammany's factional opponents, the Tammany delegation bolted and nominated Kelly for governor, thereby ensuring the defeat of the Democratic nominee.[36]

Kelly's efforts to centralize control over the party did not, however, go unchallenged. Contrary to Daniel P. Moynihan's claim that the political culture of the Irish inclines them to respect hierarchy,[37] a group of ward politicians under the leadership of John Morrissey strenuously objected to Kelly's efforts to subject the party to central direction. When Kelly in 1875 purged several of the district organizations in which the dissidents were strong. Morrissey and his associates left Tammany and joined another Democratic faction, the Bixby-Hart group. Over the next three years other prominent Democrats—most notably, a large segment of the wealthier element of the party—deserted or were expelled from Tammany and organized other independent factions. These factions coalesced into the Irving Hall Democracy in 1879. In 1881 many of the leading figures in Irving Hall abandoned it and founded a third major faction, the New York County Democracy.

During the fifteen years following 1875, then, the Democratic party in New York again was factionalized. But the factionalism of this period differed essentially from the variety which prevailed prior to 1872: the major political formations of this era were not loose confederations of politicians but rather were recognizably party *organizations*. Irving Hall and the County Democracy each survived for about ten years; both, significantly, outlived their initial leaders. Upon their founding both Irving Hall and the County Democracy conducted primaries in each of the city's hundreds of election districts (more than 20,000 voters participated in the first County Democratic primary), and each established an elaborate structure of assembly district and city committees to link their mass followings to the minor politicians who affiliated with the faction and thence to the organization's leaders.[38] Although these factions were well organized, the very multiplicity of factional organizations impeded the efforts of the leaders of each to establish discipline internally: the threat of deserting to an opposing faction —and such desertions were not uncommon—enhanced the bargaining power of subleaders in their dealings with their nominal superiors. And if the impermeability of organizational boundaries to penetration at the middle and upper levels be accepted as a criterion of institutionalization, then the party organizations of the 1870s and 1880s in New York must be considered imperfectly institutionalized: Henry Purroy, for example, was elevated to the chairmanship of the Executive Committee of the County Democracy shortly after he brought his personal following into that faction.

Though the party factions of the 1870s and 1880s in New York were as yet imperfectly institutionalized, the changes in party structure that occurred in the years immediately following Tweed's downfall were great enough so as fundamentally to transform the character of political competition in New York. Party organizations became the poles around which the struggle for power in the city centered. If the deployment of wealth and of violence were major strategies in the struggle for power during the era of rapacious individualism, the formation of new organizations, and efforts either to maintain control of an existing organization by purging one's opponents or to enhance one's influence within an organization by threatening to withdraw from it were major strategies in the period 1872–1890. The pattern of organizational formation and schism, of purges and power plays, of factional competition and alliances that emerged during these years can be regarded as a process of testing, through which those who contended for influence in the city sought to secure control over a political vehicle and to gauge their relative power. And it is important to note that during these years, in contrast to the "count" politics of the Tweed era, the focus of political competition shifted towards the electoral arena. In the negotiations and competition between the party factions, and in the dealings between other political organizations and the party factions, the control over votes was a major bargaining counter.

How can one account for these transformations in the structure and conduct of party politics in New York? Any such explanation must acknowledge the central role that John Kelly played in these developments: it was under Kelly's leadership that Tammany strengthened and centralized its organization and, though they denounced Kelly as a tyrant, the other Democratic factions found it necessary to copy his methods in order to compete successfully with Tammany. And one cannot account for Kelly's having fostered the various organizational innovations he did without reference to the simple fact that his intentions differed fundamentally from those of Tweed. Whatever their ultimate ends, Kelly and his lieutenants pursued them by attempting to build a party organization; Tweed and his confederates were interested primarily in maximizing their personal wealth over the short run and were too impatient to undertake the burdens that the task Kelly set for himself entailed. But simply to say that Kelly was an organizational entrepreneur who set out to build on organization, while Tweed made no such attempt, does not constitute a satisfactory explanation for the development of party organization in New York.[39] We must, further, specify the conditions that enabled an organizational entrepreneur such as Kelly to rise to a position of leadership in the party; the interests and values that would be served, and those that would be threatened, by the process of party building; and the conditions of and the constraints upon the success of this endeavor.

Who, then, supported Kelly's efforts to strengthen the Tammany organization, and how can one account for their supporting his reforms? Kelly was elevated to the leadership of Tammany by the "swallowtail" (frock-coated) element of the Tammany Society,[40] and at crucial junctures in the years immediately following his accession Kelly relied upon the backing of the swallowtails to sustain his program of centralization. (In 1872, for example, a leader of the swallowtails threatened to withdraw his followers from Tammany unless Kelly's Committee on Organization were permitted to purge Tweed's allies from Tammany's district committees.) The swallowtails were prominent in the city's business community: many of them also were major figures in the national Democratic Party. The Tammany sachems upon whom Kelly could rely in 1872 included, for example, Samuel Tilden, one of the city's most accomplished corporation lawyers and the Democratic presidential nominee in 1876; Abram Hewitt, an iron manufacturer and future chairman of the Democratic National Committee; Wheeler Peckham, whom President Cleveland later nominated to the United States Supreme Court; Sanford Church, who was to become chief judge of the New York Court of Appeals; and Augustus Schell and Horace Clark, both directors of the nation's largest railroad, the New York Central. In retrospect, the early and mid 1870s might be termed the N.F.P. phase of Tammany's development. Much like the leadership of the Soviet Communist party in the mid-1920s. Kelly during the 1870s endorsed a rather conservative approach to public policy while devoting himself to the task of building the party organization.[41] Kelly, for example, as city comptroller vigorously pursued the policy of municipal retrenchment that was demanded by the party's respectable element during the depression of the 1870s.

Besides being backed from this quarter, Kelly's leadership was supported by many Irish ward politicians in Tammany Hall. Clearly, then, the image of nineteenth century urban politics presented in much of the literature on the machine—an image of a public-spirited Protestant upper class aligned against a private-regarding leadership drawn from the immigrant lower classes—does not accurately depict the patterns of alignment and opposition during Kelly's regime any more than it does during Tweed's. But if Kelly's supporters did not share a common background or political ethos, how can one account for their uniting behind his efforts to strengthen the Tammany organization?

To the ward politicians who allied with Kelly, the construction of a mechanism capable of sanctioning those who would violate party discipline was something of a collective benefit. So long as the Democratic party remained a loose confederation of patronage-seeking politicians—as it had been under Tweed—the only feasible leadership strategy was a highly inflationary one. Unable to command the obedience of those whose cooperation he required, or to discipline those who possessed the authority to injure him, Tweed was compelled to purchase the support of other politicians, and in the process he increased the scale of the Ring's depredations. This process increased the visibility of the Ring's methods of governance and thereby threatened the city's credit, shocked the moral sensibilities of a large segment of the community, and consequently mobilized into political activity a congeries of forces that, as the events of 1871 proved, were capable of overthrowing the entire system. The experience of the Tweed era indicated, then, that it is in the interest of patronage-seeking politicians as a class that municipal corruption be kept within reasonable limits. Yet it is not in the interest of any single politician to exercise self-restraint: such behavior on the part of one individual is personally costly, and in the absence of like behavior on the part of his colleagues, will not significantly reduce the probability of his party's defeat. The only way in which the interests of each can be made compatible with the interests of all is by establishment of a mechanism capable of sanctioning those whose behavior threatens the collective good and of rewarding those whose behavior is collectivity-serving.[42]

The swallowtails also saw party organization as a way to control the excesses of the politics of rapacious individualism. In an age when cant was less prevalent in public discourse than it is today, they explained their reasoning forthrightly. For example, Hugh J. Hastings, the editor of the *Commercial Advertiser*, said of Kelly: "Kelly has ruled the fierce Democracy in such a manner that life and property are comparatively safe. . . . It requires a great man to stand between the City Treasury and this most dangerous mass. . . . dethrone Kelly, and where is the man to succeed him?"[43] One thus might say of the elaboration of party organization in New York under Kelly something akin to what Walter Dean Burnham has said was the function of the "system of 1896" in national politics: it was a way of making democracy safe for capitalism.[44] Kelly's centralizing reforms were a means of reconciling, in the context of an industrializing city (in which the ownership of property was not widely diffused), the security of wealth with a system of mass suffrage.

As neat as it may be, however, one's account of the interests served by the strengthening of party organization in New York requires some further specification. If Kelly's regime served the interests of men of property in the 1870s, how can one account for the support that Tweed's regime — which differed in many important respects from Kelly's — received from substantial elements of the city's business elite in the 1860s? . . . How, in other words, can one account for *changes* in the public conduct of, and in the character of the regimes supported by, the politically most active elements of the city's business elite? . . .

A full account of the sources of the behavior of the politically active members of the New York business community must await further studies of their economic and institutional affiliations, but a preliminary survey of the evidence suggests the following hypothesis. First, with regard to the question of who precisely supported the Tweed regime and why, it appears that the most prominent of Tweed's wealthy allies — those whose schemes he aided and whose support he received in return — can best be described as speculators: Jay Gould, Jim Fiske, Cornelius Vanderbilt, John Jacob Astor, and perhaps also August Belmont and the Seligmans. They made their fortunes through the rapid acquisition and sale of assets — be they commodities (as in Gould and Fiske's efforts to corner the gold market in 1869), franchises, land, public bonds, or corporate securities — and through the capitalization of anticipated monopoly profits. They used the state in their efforts to secure and inflate the value of choice properties, and in these endeavors politicians such as Tweed were useful allies. The most dramatic example of this occurred during the struggle between Gould and Fiske, on the one side, and Vanderbilt, on the other, over control of the Erie Railroad: Gould and Fiske bribed the state legislature to amend the Erie's charter so that the procedure for selecting the railroad's board of directors would be advantageous to them, and each side induced the judges it controlled to issue injunctions against the activities of its opponents.

Those who supported Kelly were of a rather different stamp. In contrast to the speculators who participated in the politics of rapacious individualism, the most prominent of Kelly's allies fell into one of three major categories: corporation laywers (such as Samuel Tilden, Abraham Lawrence, and William Whitney); entrepreneurs who managed as well as owned the firms with which they were associated (such as Abram Hewitt and Edward Cooper, of Cooper, Hewitt & Co., and William Grace of W. R. Grace & Co.); or merchants who supervised or traded in markets and exchanges whose maintenance depended upon the assumption of good faith among the parties to transations (such as Franklin Edson, president of the Produce Exchange, William Wickham, a diamond merchant, and Smith Ely, a leather merchant). The entrepreneurs associated with Tweed and those associated with Kelly prospered under two rather different modes of business competition, modes that rewarded different skills, fostered different virtues, and were, in several respects, in fundamental conflict. If the former acquired their fortunes through great speculative ventures—by virtue of their willingness to assume risks—the latter did so through holding on to their enterprises and managing them well. If the former served their ends by bribing legislators to change, and judges to ignore, the law, the latter did so by drafting and relying upon instruments whose value depended upon the predictability of the law. If the former sought to crush their competitors and to deceive those on the other side of the market, the business of the latter depended upon the preservation of markets.

In the light of the magnitude of these differences, it is not surprising that the political preferences and affiliations of the speculators and the swallowtails were at odds. But the cleavage in the political realm between these two forces derived from more than conflicts between the economic interests, narrowly conceived, of those individuals who supported Tweed and those individuals who allied with Kelly. Such narrow conflicts, to be sure, were present (the lawyers who fought Tweed might well have reasoned that if judges and legislators could be bribed, corporations would hire bag men rather than retain them), but they can account for neither the willingness of the swallowtails to undertake the burdens of collective action to serve common ends nor the expressions of disgust that the politics of rapacious individualism evoked from them—expressions whose sincerity there is no reason to question. (Banfield and Wilson's WASP ethos cannot account for these differences between those who allied with Tweed and those who rallied behind Kelly, for the two groups did not differ in their wealth, their nativity, or their religion.) To explain the full range and depth of the cleavage between the two in the political realm, one has to take note of the ways in which the interests of the speculators and the swallowtails as a class, and the values that informed their behavior in civil society, were of a piece with their political ideas and behavior.

The interests and the orientations of the speculators and the swallowtails implied distinctive preferences concerning both the general shape of public policy and the appropriateness of various forms of public conduct. As for the speculators, it is evident that entrepreneurs will best be able to gain competitive advantages through political connections if the government has a Whiggish and expansionist orientation towards economic development and if public officials are open to manipulation. Businessmen who do not seek public franchises, subsidies, and contracts, by contrast, have nothing to gain, and through taxation, much to lose from such a pattern of public policy. And businessmen who had undertaken (or, what amounts to the same thing, could convince themselves that they had undertaken) whatever personal sacrifices are required in order to pursue one's fortune through diligent activity in the firm, the exchange, or at the bar, naturally regarded the get-rich-quick schemes of Tweed's business and political associates as scandalous.

The political orientations of the swallowtails and the speculators differed in one additional respect. Just as they believed that diligence, character, and accomplishment should be rewarded in civil society, the swallowtails believed that the commonweal would best be served if men who embodied these virtues (namely, themselves) were elevated to public office. The swallowtails, in other words, were a political class as well as an economic one. They sought to govern, not simply to prosper as individuals. Tilden aspired to the presidency; Whitney, Cleveland's secretary of the Navy, was a president-maker; Cooper, Edson, and Hewitt all sought and were elected to the mayoralty. Or perhaps it would be most useful to say that by governing they sought to make it possible for their class to prosper. Abram Hewitt, for example, asserted that he regarded it as his life's work to strive to eliminate the fetters upon industry — be it the protective tariff or confiscatory taxation that hindered the prosperity of the industrious classes.[45] The speculators who participated in the politics of rapacious individualism, by contrast, were interested chiefly in lining their own pockets. They did not seek public office for themselves, nor is there any indication that they were concerned with the identity of other than the corruptibility of public officials.

For these reasons the swallowtails, much more than the speculators, were inclined to support the strengthening of party organization. The creation of a centralized party apparatus provided the means whereby the rapacity of ward politicians could be controlled, making it possible for the city government to pursue a policy of economy and retrenchment. And by increasing the control the party leader exercised over the behavior of his subordinates, it enabled Kelly to secure nominations for candidates of the appropriate character; certainly Tammany's mayoral nominees in the years of Kelly's active leadership were all of impeccable stature. The importance of party centralization to the swallowtails was underlined by William Whitney who, in explaining his support of Kelly's leadership in 1876, asserted that Kelly was a man of "too valuable influence, and of too efficient control over certain elements of the party, to make it a matter of policy, to say nothing else, to dispense with his services."[46]

Granted that the political orientations of the speculators and the swallowtails differed substantially, what conditions enabled the former to prevail in the 1860s and the latter to do so in the 1870s? In order to answer this question one must take note of those factors whose consideration we earlier had laid aside: the state of the city's economy as a whole and the character of its political institutions.

The 1860s were years of sustained economic growth and prosperity in New York, as in the nation at large. Profits clearly were to be made and fortunes accumulated by those who were not overly prudent or scrupulous in their economic and political dealings, and consequently entrepreneurs who proposed new ventures be they wholly commercial or partly political as well—were able to enlist large numbers of their fellow businessmen in their plans. The promoters of the New York Viaduct Railway Company—an especially ambitious and blatant piece of Whiggery—managed, for example, to enroll many of the city's most prominent commercial, financial, and political leaders as incorporators.[47]

Those who in the pursuit of wealth were prepared to corrupt public officials found it relatively easy to do so because the political system was so poorly institutionalized—party ties were weak, public authority was highly fragmented, institutional loyalties among public officials were low. But the very political conditions that enabled Tweed and his allies to rise to prominence in the city and state were responsible for their undoing. Politicians were as willing to extort money from Tweed as they were from businessmen, and hence Tweed was compelled to expand the scope of his activities. To protect his interests in the city Tweed found it necessary to extend his operations to Albany: the great election and naturalization frauds of 1868— through which the number of registered voters in the city was increased by one third in a few weeks' time—were engineered by Tweed's judges to secure the gubernatorial mansion for Tweed's candidate.[48] But the claims of these newly enfranchised voters had thereafter to be satisfied. Mass suffrage became more costly after 1868 than it previously had been. And to maintain the allegiance of his associates in government, Tweed sponsored ever new schemes and projects. As municipal indebtedness grew—it increased three-fold between 1867 and 1871—the number and the weight of those who had a stake in the city's credit rating grew. When the size of the city's debt and rumors of fiscal chicanery threatened to undermine the value of New York municipal bonds (and hence the survival of many of the city's financial institutions), the city's bondholders staged what essentially was a *coup*: New York bankers refused to extend short-term credit to the city (so that current expenses could be met) until an individual of their choosing was given control over the city's financial management.[49]

The revelation that the excesses of the politics of rapacious individualism could threaten the interests of the business community at large discredited those elements most closely associated with this pattern of political activity and enabled the swallowtails—whose counsels of caution earlier had not been heeded—to establish their hegemony among businessmen. This hegemony was confirmed by the onset of the Depression of 1873. Municipal retrenchment was widely demanded and hence the policies of, and the claims to leadership of, the swallowtails gained general support.

The swallowtails were initially able to parlay this hegemony into political power through the Tammany Society. The society's membership was skewed towards the Democratic party's wealthier elements and, since Tweed had failed to strengthen the party apparatus during his reign, the swallowtails were able to use their position in the society to elevate Kelly to the leadership of Tammany Hall. And so long as mechanisms to control the electorate remained relatively underdeveloped, the swallowtails, by threatening to withdraw from Tammany, could threaten to wreak serious injury to it at the polls, and hence they were able to maintain their influence in Tammany Hall. . . .

NOTES

1. Edward Banfield and James Q. Wilson, *City Politics* (Cambridge, Mass.: Harvard University Press, 1963), Chap. 9.

2. In their most recent restatement of the ethos theory Wilson and Banfield suggest that the two ethoses were held most distinctly by politically influential leadership "cliques" (as opposed to the population at large) in American cities and that this fact, if anything, enhances the "historical importance" and the "explanatory value" of the ethos concept. Most of the evidence I shall present in this essay bears directly upon their most recent claim. James Q. Wilson and Edward Banfield, "Political Ethos Revisited," *American Political Science Review* 65 (December 1971), 1062.

3. Robert Merton, *Social Theory and Social Structure* (New York: Free Press, 1957), pp. 72–82.

4. James C. Scott, "Corruption, Machine Politics, and Political Changes," *American Political Science Review* 65 (December 1969): 1146–1148.

5. Daniel P. Moynihan, "The Irish," in Nathan Glazer and Daniel P Moynihan, *Beyond the Melting Pot* (Cambridge, Mass.: M.I.T. Press, 1963), pp. 221–229; Elmer Cornwell, "Bosses, Machines, and Ethnic Group," *The Annals of the American Academy of Political and Social Sciences* 353 (May 1964): 27–39.

6. Richard Wade, "Urbanization," in C. Vann Woodward, ed., *The Comparative Approach to American History* (New York: Basic Books, 1968), pp. 196 f.

7. Samuel P. Hays, "Political Parties and the Community Society Continuum," in William Chambers and Walter Dean Burnham, *The American Party Systems* (New York: Oxford University Press, 1967). pp. 173–181.

8. S. M. Lipset and Stein Rokkan, *Party Systems and Voter Alignments* (New York: Free Press, 1967), p. 53.

9. Gustavus Myers, *The History of Tammany Hall* (New York: Boni and Liveright, 1917). Chaps. 16–22.

10. Jermone Mushkat, *Tammany: The Evolution of a Political Machine, 1789–1865* (Syracuse, N.Y.: The Syracuse University Press, 1971), p. 2. On the overthrow of Tweed by the Young Democracy and his reinstatement by the Tammany Society, see Alexander Callow, *The Tweed Ring* (New York: Oxford University Press, 1966), Chap. 15.

11. Myers, *History of Tammany Hall*, pp. 167–171, 181–182.

12. See, e.g., Carl Landé, "Networks and Groups in Southeast Asia: Some Observations on the Group Theory of Politics," *American Political Science Review* 67 (March 1975): 115.

13. For the Erie War see Charles Francis Adams, Jr., and Henry Adams, *Chapters of Erie and Other Essays* (New York: Henry Holt, 1886). Those who signed petitions endorsing the Tweed Charter and Tweed's Board of Apportionment bill are listed in John D. Townsend, *New York in Bondage* (New York: 1901), Chaps. 6 and 8.

14. Seymour Mandelbaum, *Boss Tweed's New York* (New York: John Wiley, 1965), Chap. 8.

15. Dennis T. Lynch, *"Boss" Tweed* (New York: Boni and Liveright, 1927), p. 59.

16. Myers, *History of Tammany Hall*, p. 230.

17. *Ibid.*, Chap. 19.

18. Werner, *Tammany Hall*, p. 171.

19. Townsend, *New York in Bondage*, p. 49.

20. *New York Times*, April 21, 1871, p. 5.

21. Bryce, *American Commonwealth*, pp. 379–381. See also, Charles Mohr, *The Radical Republicans and Reform in New York During Reconstruction* (Ithaca: Cornell University Press, 1973).

22. Herbert Asbury, *The Gangs of New York* (New York: Alfred Knopf, 1928), pp. 108–111.

23. Edward Banfield, "Roots of the Draft Riots," *New York Magazine* 1 (July 29, 1968): 55–57.

24. John I. Davenport, *The Election and Naturalization Frauds in New York City, 1860–1870* (New York: 1894), pp. 59–65.

25. Myers *History of Tammany Hall*, pp. 167 f.

26. Werner, *Tammany Hall*, pp. 187, 208 f.

27. Alexander Callow, *The Tweed Ring* (New York: Oxford University Press, 1966), p. 22.

28. *Ibid*, p. 234.

29. Cf. Aristede Zolberg, *Creating Political Order: The Party States of West Africa* (Chicago: Rand McNally, 1967).

30. Albert Hirschman, *Exit, Voice and Loyalty* (Cambridge, Mass.: Harvard University Press, 1970).

31. Werner, *Tammany Hall*, p. 276.

32. Mandelbaum, *Boss Tweed's New York*, pp. 95, 111.

33. *New York Times*, September 20, 1972, p. 5.

34. Mandelbaum, *Boss Tweed's New York*, p. 111.

35. *New York Times*, March 14, 1875, p. 1.

36. *New York Times*, February 7, 1875, p. 7: Roscoe Brown and Ray Smith, *Political and Governmental History of the State of New York* (Syracuse, N.Y.: Sycracuse Press, 1922), Vol. III, pp. 232–236.

37. Moynihan, *Beyond the Melting Pot*, pp. 226–228.

38. The founding and the structure of the County Democracy is described in some detail in Mark Hirsch, *William Whitney, Modern Warwick* (New York: Dodd, Mead, 1948), pp. 160–167.

39. Cf. Norman Frolick, Joe Oppenheimer, and Oran Young, *Political Leadership and Collective Goods* (Princeton, N.J.: Princeton University Press, 1971), pp. 18–25.

40. Mandelbaum, *Boss Tweed's New York*, p. 93.

41. Merle Fainsod, *How Russia is Ruled* (Cambridge, Mass.: Harvard University Press, 1965), pp. 97–99.

42. On sanctioning mechanisms as collective goods see Frohlich et al., *Political Leadership*, p. 18.

43. Townsend, *New York in Bondage*, p. 154.

44. Walter Dean Burnham, "Party Systems and the Political Process," in Chambers and Burnham, *American Party Systems*, p. 301.

45. Louis Freeland Post and Fred C. Leubuscher, *An Account of the George Hewitt Mayoral Campaign in the New York City Municipal Election of 1886* (New York: John W. Lovell Co., 1886), p. 41.

46. Mandelbaum, *Boss Tweed's New York*, p. 138.

47. Townsend, *New York in Bondage*, p. 59 f.

48. Davenport, *Election and Naturalization Frauds*, p. 20.

49. Mandelbaum, *Boss Tweed's New York*, pp. 79–84.

15

Big-City Rainbow Politics: Machines Revividus?*

Steven P. Erie

MACHINES AND ETHNIC ASSIMILATION

The Pluralist Approach

In the postwar era, social scientists eulogized the dying and much-maligned machine. In the 1940s and 1950s, a new generation of empirically trained sociologists such as William Foote Whyte, Robert K. Merton, and Daniel Bell used the machine as a test case to critique the middle-class Protestant value orientation that had dominated social analysis. Buttressing their claims for a value-neutral, functional approach to social science, the Young Turks argued that the censorious view of machine politics ignored the positive functions performed by lower-class ethnic institutions offering unconventional mobility routes. Finding their career opportunities blocked in the Protestant-controlled business world, the Irish had turned to the machine; the Italians, to the mob. Because it served the material needs of the immi-

*Erie, Steven P. 1988. "Machines and Ethnic Assimilation; Today's Big-City Rainbow Politics: Machines Revividus?" Pp. 238–246, 298, 299, and 301–303 in *Rainbow's End: Irish-Americans and the Dilemmas of Urban Machine Politics, 1840–1985*. Berkeley: University of California Press. Copyright © 1988 by The Regents of the University of California. Reprinted by permission of University of California Press.

grant working class, machine politics persisted, despite middle-class Protestant opposition.[1]

By the 1960s, political scientists such as Dahl, Fred Greenstein, Elmer Cornwell, and Edgar Litt had joined the chorus of machine defenders, arguing that the big-city party bosses had been both ethnic integrators and system stabilizers-transformers.[2] In the hands of the pluralists, the machine became a local precursor to the New Deal ethnic coalition and the welfare state; the boss, a new paradigm of democratic leadership and mass politics.

The pluralist locus classicus was *Who Governs?*, Robert Dahl's 1961 survey of New Haven's political development over two centuries. Dahl's treatment of the Irish party bosses represented part of a larger analysis of successful regime transformation. In nineteenth-century New Haven, an oligarchic system of cumulative inequalities and overlapping privileges (the same hands holding wealth, social standing, and power) gradually and peacefully gave way to a pluralist system of dispersed inequalities and advantages (in which different people controlled different resources).[3]

By the mid-nineteenth century, a new breed of Yankee businessmen-politicians had displaced the "Old Standing Order" of leading Federalist and Congregationalist families. From humble origins, the new self-made entrepreneurs fought to end property restrictions on voting in order to mobilize a new electoral majority of native-born artisans and laborers. But this insurgent elite's primary weapon of victory—the vote—would soon be turned against them. Successfully challenging Yankee leadership at century's end, Irish Democratic politicians naturalized, registered, and claimed the votes of their countrymen in order to forge a new electoral majority.[4]

The Irish bosses then turned to the task of group economic uplift. According to Dahl, politics and city jobs served as "major springboards" for the Irish into the middle class. Controlling the levers of urban power, the Irish traded votes for patronage, accelerating their movement out of the laboring classes. The early machine's patronage cache awaiting capture appeared sizable indeed. In the pre–New Deal era, the big-city machines controlled thousands of public sector and private sector patronage jobs. Tammany Hall, for example, had more than 40,000 patronage jobs at its disposal in the late 1880s. Furthermore, the public sector offered greater social mobility opportunities than did the private sector. In San Francisco at the turn of the century, nearly one-quarter of all public employees were in professional and managerial positions compared with only 6 percent of the privately employed workforce.[5]

Using machine patronage, the Irish supposedly built a middle class with surprising rapidity considering their meager job skills and the discrimination they encountered. In the big cities, the proportion of first- and second-generation Irish in white-collar jobs rose from 12 percent to 27 percent between 1870 and 1900. Among the non-Irish, the white-collar increase was smaller, from 27 percent to 34 percent. As Andrew Greeley has shown, Irish-Americans are now the most affluent of the country's non-Jewish ethnic groups, having translated their apparently early white-collar job gains into a solid middle and upper middle class anchored in business and the professions in the post–World War II era.[6]

Dahl's account of the rise of the Irish "ex-plebes" and the accompanying systemic shift from cumulative to dispersed inequalities is central to a larger pluralist theory of American politics. Placing himself in an Aristotelian-Machiavellian tradition, Dahl highlighted the creative role of political elites such as the Irish party bosses in promoting both change and stability in the modern city-state. In the hands of gifted leaders, the mechanisms of political equality — popular sovereignty, universal suffrage, competitive parties, and the patronage system — could be used to reduce social and economic inequalities.

Our case studies support the pluralist argument regarding the machine's *political* assimilation of the Irish. The English-speaking famine Irish arrived as the competitive second party system was entering its modern or mobilization phase. As the Irish allegiance to the Democratic party solidified, the embryonic machines actively worked to naturalize and enroll Irish voters. Group mobilization allowed the Irish to infiltrate and take over the helm of the big-city Democratic machines.

Yet the machine's *economic* assimilation of the Irish — and its redistributional potential generally — was smaller than pluralists allow. For one thing, early Irish economic progress was slower and more uneven than the growth in white-collar jobholders indicates. As Stephan Thernstrom has carefully shown for Boston, many middle-class gains by first- and second-generation Irish were marginal at best, signaling entry into poorly paid clerical and sales work rather than into business and the professions.[7]

Thernstrom also cautions that it is misleading to compare Irish economic progress with the sluggish performance of the new immigrants. The new immigration was made up of successive waves of impoverished Southern and Eastern Europeans. More instructive is his comparison of the progress of the politically powerful Irish in Boston's labor market relative to that of other early-arriving but politically weaker immigrant groups. First- and second-generation Germans, Scandinavians, and English all climbed the economic ladder more quickly than did their Irish counterparts.

Our case studies of the classic Irish machines suggest that the pluralist model overestimates the magnitude of machine resources and the Irish ability to use them for sizable group economic gain. The Democratic machines of the late nineteenth century offered impressive channels of advancement for *individual* Irish politicians and contractors. But the early machines could do only so much for Irish *group* mobility.

Political and class constraints hampered the early bosses in their search for greater resources. Middle-class Yankee Republicans had not yet migrated to the suburbs. They vigorously contested local elections, demanding fiscal retrenchment. The early Irish bosses like John Kelly also had to contend with opponents in their own ranks: Democratic businessmen-reformers advocating "tight-fisted" economic policies. This bipartisan conservative coalition forced the nascent Celtic machines to pursue cautious fiscal policies, limiting their patronage take.

Republicans dominated state politics during much of this era, reinforcing the fiscal conservatism of the early Irish machines. Republican governors and legislators imposed constitutional restrictions, severely limiting the bosses' ability to raise taxes, increase municipal debts, and reward their working-class ethnic followers. Consequently, . . . only a small minority of the Irish working class in the late nineteenth century could crowd into the machine's patronage enclave.

The twentieth-century machines did a better job of economically aiding the Irish. Political and legal constraints on the bosses' ability to raise and spend money—and thus to create patronage jobs—began to ease as the machine's middle-class Republican and reform opponents moved to the suburbs, as home rule lifted state fiscal restraints, and as the millions of Southern and Eastern Europeans filling the cities demanded new services. Machines directly and indirectly controlled more than 20 percent of post-1900 urban job growth, double their pre-1900 share. In the Irish-run machine cities of New York, Jersey City, and Albany, the Irish were rewarded with more than 60 percent of this newly created patronage. As a result, on the eve of the Depression, at least one-third of the Irish-stock workforce toiled in machine-sponsored jobs.

The second-generation machine's patronage policies appear to support the pluralist argument that politics served as an important conduit of Irish economic advancement. Compared with Yankees, Germans, and Jews, though, the Irish were slow to build a middle class in business and the professions. Today's Irish affluence was latecoming, postdating the heyday of the machine. As even Greeley admits, the Irish middle class was only emerging on the eve of the Depression; its arrival would not occur until after World War II.[8]

In light of Irish political success, why was Irish middle-class status so slow in coming? Was there an *inverse* relation between political success and economic advancement? The Irish crowded into the largely blue-collar urban public sector in the late nineteenth and early twentieth centuries. Yet as low-paid policemen, firemen, and city clerks, the Irish were solidly lower-middle- rather than middle-class. The relative security of blue-collar jobs in public works, police, and fire departments may have hindered the building of an Irish middle class by encouraging long tenure in poorly paid bureaucratic positions. The pluralist machine's apparent cornucopia of resources could turn into a blue-collar cul-de-sac.[9]

It can be argued that by channeling so much of their economic energy into the public sector, the Irish forsook opportunities in the private sector save for industries such as construction that depended on political connections. As Moynihan has accurately observed, the economic rewards of America have gone to entrepreneurs, not to functionaries. Moreover, the Irish public sector job gains were fragile. The Depression forced the cities to cut their payrolls. The 1930s also witnessed the long-awaited revolt of the Southern and Eastern Europeans against their Irish overlords. Thousands of Irish-American payrollers lost their jobs as a result of retrenchment and machine overthrow. Only with lessened job dependence on the machine in the prosperous post–World War II era were the third- and fourth-generation Irish able to move rapidly into business and the professions.

The puzzling question is why the Irish embraced the machine's blue-collar patronage system with such enthusiasm. Dahl has advanced a "blocked mobility" explanation. In his account, the Irish quickly assimilated the American value of upward mobility. However, limited job skills and anti-Catholicism blocked Irish advancement in the private sector. Thus, the Irish, in Dahl's words, "eagerly grabbed the 'dangling rope' [of politics] up the formidable economic slope."[10]

If the Irish so easily assimilated the American success ethic, why did they allow the dangling rope of politics to become a noose? There are both cultural and resource explanations for the Irish overreliance on the patronage system. Moynihan has taken issue with Dahl, arguing that the Irish displayed a "distaste for commerce," valuing security over entrepreneurial success. Seeking safe bureaucratic havens, the Irish settled for marginal advancement through politics.[11]

Borrowing a page from Max Weber, Edward Levine similarly argues that the Irish working class consciously rejected the middle-class Protestant value of economic achievement. Alienated from Protestant values and institutions, the Irish constructed the Democratic party and the Catholic church as mutually reinforcing institutions rooted in working-class Irish Catholic values. For the Irish, power and security, not money or status, represented the highest values. In this scheme of things, social and geographical mobility meant apostasy. Reinforcing their separateness from the Protestant mainstream, politics enveloped the Irish, becoming *the* approved secular career. As the machines have declined, however, the Irish have gradually replaced the values of power and security with those of money and status.[12]

A resource explanation for limited Irish patronage mobility looks to the machine's maintenance needs. To win the jurisdictional battles for working-class support, machines quickly realized the potency of economic appeals. Yet scarce economic benefits had to be spread as widely as possible to realize their full vote-getting value. Thus the Irish bosses stretched patronage, creating large numbers of poorly paid blue-collar positions to maximize the number of working-class voters rewarded. The machine's job growth strategy created ever more blue-collar public employment for the Irish at a time when the cities were moving from a manufacturing to a service economy and when the greatest increases in private sector employment occurred in white-collar ranks.

The party's maintenance needs conflicted with the long-run goal of Irish prosperity. But patronage had short-run economic advantages. The machine's job system allowed unskilled and semiskilled Irish workers to move to the next rung above the working class. In fact, the ready availability of blue-collar patronage helped to *shape* Irish economic horizons, encouraging the values of security, seniority, and slow bureaucratic advancement.

The pluralist view of the machine as an integrator of the immigrants has been applied to the Southern and Eastern Europeans. Elmer Cornwell, for example, argues that the Irish bosses in the northern cities were forced to politically assimilate the second-wave immigrants in order to continue to win elections.[13] Competitive electoral pressures encouraged the Irish bosses to naturalize and register the newer arrivals. Our survey of the classic Irish machines found that the machine's invisible hand did not automatically embrace the newcomers. Mature machines were one-party regimes lacking the political incentive to mobilize the second-wave immigrants. The Irish Democratic bosses had already constructed winning electoral coalitions among early-arriving ethnic groups. The newcomers' political assimilation would only encourage demands for a redistribution of power and patronage.

In entrenched machine cities like New York and Jersey City, naturalization and voter registration rates for the Southern and Eastern Europeans remained quite low until the late 1920s. Electoral participation rates for the second-wave immigrants increased thereafter in response to national candidates and issues rather than to sponsorship by local party bosses.

In competitive party cities, however, the Irish party chieftains worked energetically to mobilize the Southern and Eastern Europeans. The fledgling Democratic machines of Chicago and Pittsburgh most successfully mobilized the newcomers. As the minority party in these cities in the 1920s, the Democrats were forced into actively courting the new ethnics. Chicago's Democratic precinct captains naturalized and registered the new immigrants far more quickly than did their counterparts in one-party New York, Jersey City, and Boston.

Entrenched machines did little to further economic assimilation among the Southern and Eastern Europeans before the latter mobilized in the 1930s. With so much of Irish well-being and group identity dependent on continued control of the machines, Irish politicos were understandably loath to share power and patronage. To preserve their hegemony, the Irish accommodated the slowly mobilizing newcomers in parsimonious fashion, dispensing social services, symbolic recognition, and collective benefits rather than the organization's core resources of power and patronage.

At critical moments the Irish were forced by electoral pressures to enter tactical alliances with some groups for a greater share of the machine's jealously guarded core resources. As Jews flexed their political muscle in New York in the 1920s, the Irish offered them minor offices and a greater share of municipal employment, particularly in the rapidly expanding school system. The Celtic bosses worked as actively to reduce Italian influence by gerrymandering Italian neighborhoods.

Postwar machines such as the Daley organization accommodated the Southern and Eastern Europeans in different and less costly ways than those in which the prewar machines had rewarded the Irish. Wartime and postwar prosperity benefited the second-wave immigrants and their children, propelling large numbers into the property-owning middle class. As homeowners, white ethnics objected to high property taxes to pay for patronage jobs they did not need. The Southern and Eastern Europeans demand a different set of machine policies: low property taxes, the preservation of property values and white neighborhoods, and homeowner rather than welfare services. The postwar Irish-led machines accommodated these taxation and service demands—as long as the Irish maintained control over key party positions and those city offices with major policy-making and patronage-dispensing responsibilities.

Machines did little to assimilate blacks and Hispanics. In the pre-1960 period, black sub-machines to the white machines had emerged in cities such as Chicago and Pittsburgh. Congressman William Dawson, the only black in the Daley machine's inner circle, ran the black sub-machine in the South Side ghetto. To counter the threat of Polish insurgency, Dawson and his lieutenants mobilized the minority vote for Mayor Daley. As the threat of white revolt diminished in the 1960s, the threat of black revolt grew. Using welfare-state benefits, the machine systematically demobilized the black vote.

Contrary to pluralist theory, the big-city machine's political and economic incorporation of ethnic groups was limited. The Irish represent the theory's par excellence case. The nascent Democratic machines actively assisted the Irish in acquiring citizenship, in voting, and in securing patronage jobs. Yet pluralist theory exaggerates the ability of the Irish to turn political into economic success. The economic disadvantages suffered by the Irish could not readily be overcome by politics; they may even have been aggravated. Celtic economic success came *after* the machine's heyday. Failing to consider the class and political constraints on the machine's creation and distribution of resources, pluralists overestimate the old-style party organization's redistributional capacity.

The pluralist case is further weakened when we consider the machine's limited assimilation of other ethnic groups. The entrenched Democratic machines did little to mobilize and reward the new arrivals from Southern and Eastern Europe, the South, the Caribbean, and Latin America. Deprived of machine sponsorship, the newcomers would have to rely on internal group resources to contest urban power. . . .

TODAY'S BIG-CITY RAINBOW POLITICS: MACHINES REVIVIDUS?

In the past twenty years the baton of urban power has slowly been passed to the third- and fourth-generation ethnic arrivals—blacks, Hispanics, and Asians. Black mayors have been elected in Los Angeles, Chicago, Philadelphia, Detroit, Atlanta, Washington, Cleveland, Gary, Newark, and New Orleans. Blacks have also been elected in large numbers to city councils and school boards. The new black power is bureaucratic as well as electoral. In the big cities, black administrators have been appointed to such top policy-making positions as city manager, police chief, and school superintendent.[14]

In the Sunbelt, Hispanics and Asians are beginning to transform urban political life. San Antonio's voters in 1981 elected Henry Cisneros as the first Mexican-American mayor of a major U.S. city. Miami has a Cuban-American mayor and a Hispanic majority on the city council. Reversing a century-old legacy of racism and discrimination against Asians, California's cities are witnessing the first stirrings of Asian-American power. Los Angeles's voters elected Michael Woo to the city council, and San Francisco Mayor Dianne Feinstein appointed Thomas Hsieh to the city's Board of Supervisors.[15]

As the new minorities mobilize, particularly the black and Mexican-American communities with large lower-class populations, they have searched for strategies of group uplift. The viability of the machine model was problematic for the new groups. Before the 1960s, minorities were deliberately kept out of the established system of "city trenches." Except for a few independent politicians such as New York's Adam Clayton Powell, the legacy of the machine era for blacks was "plantation politics" Chicago-style. When the minority assault finally came, the old-style party organizations were in the last stages of decline.[16]

In the postmachine era, the prizes of urban politics seemed hollow indeed. The northern cities where blacks had migrated in massive numbers had experienced economic decline, their treasuries nearing bankruptcy. The rapidly growing Sunbelt cities had small, lean public sectors (the legacy of conservative reformers), limiting government job opportunities. To make matters worse, white civil service commissioners and municipal union stewards zealously guarded the prerogatives of the heavily white public sector workforce, making it difficult for minorities to translate political gains into economic advancement.[17]

Even the means of ethnic capture were more difficult. The new minorities were the victims of reform. In the process of wresting power from the Irish, the Southern and Eastern Europeans had created additional barriers for later-arriving groups. The second-wave ethnics joined Yankee reformers in bringing to the eastern cities the reforms first implemented by progressives in the West and South: at-large city council elections, nonpartisanship, educational requirements for public employment, and expanded civil service coverage. At-large electoral systems, in particular, made it harder for blacks to gain representation on city councils. Designed to prevent the machine's reemergence, reforms also made it more difficult for working-class blacks and Hispanics to gain group influence and benefits.[18]

In this bleak age of reform, a possible return to machine politics didn't seem so bad after all. Black politicians in particular called for the machine's resurrection in part or in toto. During the 1960s, black moderates committed to "working within the system" had embraced the Irish model of group electoral politics to counter radical separatist demands. The radical rhetoric of militant nationalism and community control ultimately proved an empty threat, revealing an incrementalist and patronage core that could be accommodated as the emerging black bourgeoisie took over such community institutions as schools and health clinics. By the 1970s, blacks of diverse ideological inclinations had moved "from protest to politics," emulating the strategy of ethnic group mobilization—registration, turnout, and bloc voting en masse—first perfected by the Irish.[19]

To appeal to both militants and moderates in the minority community, contemporary black politicians disingenuously coupled radical-reformist rhetoric with venerable machine-building techniques designed to enhance group influence and payoffs. Claiming that at-large electoral systems discriminated against racial minorities, followers of rainbow "reformer" Jesse Jackson in cities such as Pittsburgh and Cincinnati have pursued the machine gambit of reviving the ward system. Chicago's "antimachine" Mayor Harold Washington ransacked city hall and special district governments for additional patronage to pay off his supporters and consolidate power. Reformer Washington also vigorously opposed a move to make the city's elections nonpartisan.[20]

Are black politicians correct in looking to the machine past? What lessons could the departed Irish bosses offer today's minorities about group influence, electoral coalition building, and economic advancement through local politics? Moynihan has argued that the twentieth-century black experience needs to be understood in terms of a critical comparison with the nineteenth-century Irish experience.[21]

Both groups have tried their hand at public sector politics, seeking governmental channels of group mobility. The Irish political experience cannot fully be emulated by blacks because the big-city machines—centralized party structures—are unlikely to be revived in anything like their historical form. Yet machine politics—the trading in divisible benefits—has staying power in local politics. The Irish bosses were the undisputed masters of this game. Can their example educate today's minority power brokers about both the possibilities and the limits of ethnic politics?

On the positive side, the Irish experience demonstrates some potential for group economic uplift through the local political process. The votes of the Irish working class could be translated into group power and a major share of city jobs and services. The twentieth-century Celtic municipal engines served as modest redistributional devices, reallocating economic burdens and benefits within the middle of the class structure. To the extent that the Irish bosses were Robin Hoods, they were selective about their victims and beneficiaries. Rather than taking from the very rich and giving to the very poor, the Irish politicos took from the Yankee middle class and gave to the lower-middle-class payroll Irish.

On the negative side, the Irish machines were as much instruments of social control as of economic reward. The nineteenth-century Irish bosses imposed retrenchment on their followers as the price of keeping power. Black mayors are under the same fiscal constraints today. Retrenchment produced ideological-class schisms among the Irish in the 1880s and is doing the same for blacks in the 1980s. The conflict between Tammany's conservative "long-hair" Irish faction and the militant working-class "short-hairs" finds contemporary expression in the tensions between moderate black mayors and militant followers of the Jacksonian rainbow.

The early Irish bosses parsimoniously accommodated later arrivals on the rainbow bandwagon. With limited resources and pressing group demands, black politicians may have to do the same with Hispanics and Asians. The down-side risk of today's slow-growth politics is that the new rainbow coalition may produce a small pot of gold for the black political elite, while browns, yellows, and even the black underclass are left chasing the mirage.

Concluding the Irish-black comparison on an even more pessimistic note, what will urban politics look like at century's end if present trends in conservative national politics and uneven regional economic development continue? Will big-city minority politicians in declining Frostbelt cities be called on to implement an updated "System of '96" — for 1996? Will black leaders soothe the "mixed multitudes" with populist rhetoric while cutting deals with conservative national politicians? And will federally funded "urban enterprise zones" prove to be the newest species of "plantation politics" designed to discipline the have-nots? Big-city minority politicians might have to take a lesson from the Christian Democratic party bosses of stagnant Palermo after all.

Blacks are now emulating the Irish by using political strategies of group uplift. The means employed, however, are different. The Irish used the big-city party organizations; blacks use local and national bureaucracies. The locus of urban power has shifted from political machines to independent and semiautonomous bureaucracies, organized along functional lines. Furthermore, urban politics has been nationalized. In the post–New Deal era, the political access and economic distribution functions once monopolized by local machines now are nationally performed by the Democratic party and federal welfare-state bureaucracies.[22]

Peter Eisinger finds black mayors pursuing a dual strategy of group advancement in this new arena of urban politics. The first prong consists of the politics of public sector bureaucracies. Black leaders in cities such as Detroit and Atlanta have used their appointment powers to name minorities to head city personnel departments and other major agencies. Minority administrators, in turn, have launched aggressive affirmative action programs, producing a dramatic increase in the minority share of public employment. Black mayors are also using affirmative action to award city contracts to minority businesses. Newark's former Mayor Kenneth Gibson, for example, set aside 25 percent of all federal public works project monies for minority contractors.[23]

The second prong consists of a strategy of "trickle down" from private sector economic growth. Black mayors in Los Angeles, Chicago, Detroit, Washington, Atlanta, and Newark have formed alliances with the white business community to promote downtown redevelopment, hoping to create private sector job opportunities for minorities.

The Irish experience suggests the limits of this dual strategy. On the public sector side, the approach has a major down-side risk — retrenchment. The Irish were the principal beneficiaries of city payroll growth from 1900 to 1929; after 1929, however, they were also the victims of retrenchment. Blacks clearly benefited from the halcyon municipal employment growth of the 1960s and early 1970s. The late 1970s, however, brought municipal austerity, threatening to reverse black city payroll gains. As the last hired, minorities were frequently the first victims of budgetary cutbacks. Detroit's black Mayor Coleman Young, for example, was forced by budget-balancing pressures to fire hundreds of minority police, undoing in a single afternoon ten years of hard-fought affirmative action in police hiring.

Black politicians and civil servants may also face a political challenge to their power and prerogatives. In the 1930s and 1940s, the Irish machine's jerry-built rainbow coalition unraveled as the new immigrants countermobilized, jeopardizing the jobs of thousands of Irish payrollers. In the 1990s, Asian-Americans and Hispanics could challenge blacks for control of the big cities, particularly if black politicians are unable or unwilling to share power and patronage. With a large and prosperous middle class, Asian-Americans in particular might assume the broker role, financing and leading an Asian-Hispanic coalition that could threaten today's black municipal workers.

The Irish experience also suggests caution regarding the extent of "trickle-down" to the black masses from publicly subsidized private sector growth. Public investment in urban infrastructure was the early equivalent of today's publicly assisted downtown redevelopment projects. Public works contracts benefited individual Irish contractors while providing temporary low-wage employment for the masses of unskilled and semiskilled Irish workers.

Today, black mayors offer public seed money, tax and zoning abatements, and lease-back arrangements to downtown developers. Ambitious redevelopment projects like Detroit's Renaissance Center and Atlanta's Peachtree Plaza are sold to minorities and the poor on the premise that economic benefits—primarily in the form of job opportunities—will filter down to them. But new convention centers, hotels, and shopping centers are not a viable vehicle of group uplift. Too few jobs are created to make an appreciable dent in inner-city poverty. The limited pool of high-paying professional and managerial positions disproportionately goes to upper-middle-class white suburbanites. Minority "trickle down" has primarily taken the form of a limited number of low-wage service jobs.[24]

There is a vital third element to today's black advancement strategy—federal social programs. Both Irish and black politicians have used the expanding welfare state to consolidate power. The nascent Irish Democratic machines of the 1930s fused with New Deal programs. A generation later, the Great Society served as a catalyst for black power. Studying minority politics in ten northern California cities, Rufus Browning, Dale Marshall, and David Tabb argue that the Great Society programs "provided the functional equivalent of earlier forms of patronage." In the Bay Area cities, federal social initiatives encouraged minority political mobilization, promoted their incorporation into local governing coalitions, and secured greater local governmental responsiveness to minority job and service demands.[25]

The expanding welfare state was more than a vehicle for black assimilation into local politics. It was a primary route of group *economic* advancement. Where the Irish had used machine patronage, blacks now relied on federally funded social programs. In the 1960s and early 1970s, the new black middle class found jobs in the expanding federally funded human services sector—health, education, and welfare. By the late 1970s, nearly half of all black professionals and managers worked in the social welfare sector, compared with less than one-quarter of comparably situated whites.[26]

The welfare state meant more than jobs for the black middle class; it also represented cash and in-kind welfare payments for the underclass. From the mid-1960s onward, the black poor increasingly relied on transfer payments. Two-thirds of poor black families received welfare in the late 1970s, up from one-third in the late 1960s. Economically, blacks were more integrated into the public sector in the late 1970s than the Irish had been during the machine's heyday—but under *federal* and *bureaucratic* auspices.[27]

But black politicians lack integrating mechanisms like the machine that can fuse together the disparate elements of today's urban politics—national versus local, bureaucratic versus electoral. As a result, big-city and minority politics reflect their unreconciled imperatives. The continued flow of welfare-state jobs, transfer payments, and social services, which sustain the black middle class and underclass, depend on group influence and alliance building at the national and state levels where social policy is made and funded. Blacks, however, are not as well organized to press their claims outside the local political arena.

In the absence of local machines capable of mobilizing voters, bureaucratic politics has acted as a depressant on electoral participation. The relationship between the bureaucratic service provider and the recipient differs from the relationship between the party cadre and the voter. Precinct workers are encouraged to mobilize loyal voters on election day. Human service workers, however, have little incentive to politically mobilize their clientele—as long as social programs and budgets grow. In the 1970s, minority service providers increasingly involved themselves in bureaucratic politics within the intergovernmental grant system rather than in mobilizing their clientele in local electoral politics. The expansion of means-tested programs such as AFDC depoliticized welfare recipients by isolating them from the work experiences encouraging political participation.[28]

Whatever the Great Society's initial mobilization effect, it soon acted as a brake on black voter turnout. During the period of welfare-state expansion, from 1964 to 1976, the mass electoral base of black politics in the northern cities eroded. The voting rate for young urban blacks plummeted, from 56 percent to 29 percent, while the rate for unemployed blacks dropped nearly as sharply, from 62 percent to 37 percent. Low turnout hurt big-city black politicians seeking to challenge white-controlled machine and reform regimes.[29]

Welfare-state contraction in the 1980s, however, reversed the bureaucratic expansion-electoral decline cycle. Threatened with job and benefit loss by the Reagan cutbacks, minority social service providers and recipients quickly rediscovered the value of electoral politics. Though primarily generated by national forces, the remobilization drive could be used in local politics. In machine Chicago and reform Philadelphia, black mayoral candidates rode the electoral surge to victory.

It is ironic that the policies of a president who points to his Irish ancestry during campaigns helped to produce the last hurrah for the Irish Democratic machines. Black mayors have ridden the turbulent waves of Reaganite austerity into office. Yet the practitioners of the new ethnic politics are trying to consolidate power with limited local resources and diminished welfare-state largesse. Lacking the tangible benefits demanded by their supporters, the new minority power brokers may discover what was learned the hard way by the now-departed Irish bosses: the real lessons at rainbow's end.

NOTES

1. William Foote Whyte, "Social Organization in the Slums," pp. 34–39; William Foote Whyte, *Street Corner Society: The Social Structure of an Italian Slum*, pp. 194–252; Robert K. Merton, *Social Theory and Social Structure*, pp. 125–136; Daniel Bell, "Crime as an American Way of Life," pp. 131–154; Jerome K. Myers, "Assimilation in the Political Community," pp. 175–182.

2. Fred I. Greenstein, "The Changing Pattern of Urban Party Politics," pp. 1–13; Elmer E. Cornwell, "Party Absorption of Ethnic Groups: The Case of Providence, Rhode Island," pp. 87–98; Elmer E. Cornwell, "Bosses, Machines, and Ethnic Groups," pp. 27–39; Edgar Litt, *Beyond Pluralism: Ethnic Politics in America*, esp. pp. 60–74, 155–168.

3. Robert A. Dahl, *Who Governs? Democracy and Power in an American City*, pp. 2–86.

4. Ibid., pp. 11–31. In support of his "springboard" thesis, Dahl cites a 1933 sample survey of 1,600 New Haven families conducted by Yale's Institute of Human Relations. Constituting 13 percent of the sample, Irish-Americans held nearly half of the public service jobs. Yet the city's public sector constituted only 5 percent of the local economy and employed only 15 percent of the Irish-stock workforce. The 1930 census reports that blue-collar jobs accounted for nearly half of all public employment. See John W. McConnell, *The Evolution of Social Classes*, pp. 84–85; and U.S. Bureau of the Census, *Fifteenth Census of the United States, 1930*, vol. 4, Table 12, pp. 280–283.

5. Dahl, *Who Governs?* pp. 40–44; Eric L. McKitrick, "The Study of Corruption," pp. 502–514; Steven P. Erie, "Two Faces of Ethnic Power," pp. 262–263.

6. U.S. Census Office, *Ninth Census, 1870*, vol. 1, Tables 29, 32; U.S. Bureau of the Census, *Special Reports: Occupations at the Twelfth Census*, Tables 41, 43; Andrew Greeley, *That Most Distressful Nation: The Taming of the American Irish*, pp. 122–128; Andrew Greeley, *Ethnicity, Denomination, and Inequality*, pp. 54–55.

7. Stephan Thernstrom, *The Other Bostonians*, pp. 132–133, 232.

8. Greeley, *That Most Distressful Nation*, pp. 122–128; Greeley, *Ethnicity*, pp. 54–55.

9. Dennis P. Ryan, *Beyond the Ballot Box: A Social History of the Boston Irish, 1845–1917*, pp. 106, 149.

10. Dahl, *Who Governs?* pp. 33–34, 40–41. Oscar Handlin argues that the acculturated second-generation Irish, not the transplanted first generation, saw politics as a route of personal and group advancement; see Handlin, *The Uprooted*, pp. 201–216.

11. Daniel Patrick Moynihan, "The Irish," in Nathan Glazer and Daniel Patrick Moynihan, *Beyond the Melting Pot*, pp. 229, 259–260.

12. Edward M. Levine, *The Irish and Irish Politicians: A Study of Cultural and Social Alienation*, pp. 134–138.

13. Cornwell, "Bosses."

14. Regarding urban black politics, see Leonard A. Cole, *Blacks in Power: A Comparative Study of Black and White Elected Officials*; William E. Nelson, Jr., and Philip J. Meranto, *Electing Black Mayors: Political Action in the Black Community*; John R. Howard and Robert C. Smith, eds., "Urban Black Politics," pp. 1–150; Peter K. Eisinger, *The Politics of Displacement: Racial and Ethnic Transition in Three American Cities*; Albert Karnig and Susan Welch, *Black Representation and Urban Policy*; and Michael B. Preston et al., eds., *The New Black Politics: The Search for Political Power*.

15. On Hispanic and Asian-American politics, see F. Chris Garcia and Rudolpho de la Garza, *The Chicano Political Experience: Three Perspectives*; Raymond A. Mohl, "Miami: The Ethnic Cauldron," in Richard M. Bernard and Bradley R. Rice, eds., *Sunbelt Cities: Politics and Growth Since World War Two*, pp. 58–99; David L. Clark, "Los Angeles: Improbable Los Angeles," in Bernard and Rice, eds., *Sunbelt Cities*, pp. 268–308; Joan Moore and Harry Pachon, *Hispanics in the United States*; Bruce E. Cain and D. Roderick Kiewiet, *Minorities in California*; and Judy Tachibana, "California's Asians: Power from a Growing Population," pp. 534–543.

16. Martin Kilson, "Political Change in the Negro Ghetto, 1900–1940s," in Nathan Huggins et al., eds., *Key Issues in the Afro-American Experience*, pp. 182–189; Hanes Walton, Jr., *Black Politics: A Theoretical and Structural Analysis*, pp. 56–69.

17. Roger E. Alcaly and David Mermelstein, eds., *The Fiscal Crisis of American Cities*; George Sternlieb and James W. Hughes, "The Uncertain Future of the Center City," pp. 455–572; Marilyn Gittell, "Public Employment and the Public Service," in Alan Gartner et al., eds., *Public Service Employment: An Analysis of Its History, Problems, and Prospects*, pp. 121–142.

18. Leonard Sloan, "Good Government and the Politics of Race," pp. 171–174; Albert Karnig, "Black Representation on City Councils: The Impact of District Elections and Socioeconomic Factors," pp. 223–242; Theodore P. Robinson and Thomas R. Dye, "Reformism and Black Representation on City Councils," pp. 133–142; Richard L. Engstrom and Michael D. McDonald, "The Election of Blacks to City Councils: Clarifying the Impact of Electoral Arrangements on the Seats/Population Relationship," pp. 344–354; Peggy Heilig and Robert J. Mundt, "Changes in Representational Equity: The Effect of Adopting Districts," pp. 393–397.

19. Joyce Gelb, "Blacks, Blocs, and Ballots: The Relevance of Party Politics to the Negro," pp. 44–69; Charles V. Hamilton, "Blacks and the Crisis of Political Participation," pp. 191–193; Robert C. Smith, "The Changing Shape of Urban Black Politics: 1960–1970," pp. 16–28.

20. Linda M. Watkins, "Pittsburgh Blacks' Paucity of Political Clout Stirs Struggle over the City's At-Large Election System," p. 58; Marty Willis, "Jan. 6 Demonstration to Greet All-White City Council," pp. A-1, A-4; Gilbert Price, "Skirmish Begins 'At

Large' Battle" [Cincinnati], p. H-8; Larry Green, "Chicago's Mayor Finally Grasps Power and Spoils," pp. 1, 18; Chinta Strausberg, "Mayor Seizes Control of Park Board," pp. 1, 18; Robert Davis and Joseph Tybor, "Mayor Wins Election Ruling," pp. 1, 10.

21. Daniel Patrick Moynihan, "Foreward" to Greeley, *That Most Distressful Nation*, p. xi.

22. Ira Katznelson, "The Crisis of the Capitalist City: Urban Politics and Social Control," in Willis D. Hawley et al., eds., *Theoretical Perspectives on Urban Politics*, pp. 223–226.

23. Peter K. Eisinger, "Black Employment in Municipal Jobs: The Impact of Black Political Power," pp. 380–392; Peter K. Eisinger, "The Economic Conditions of Black Employment in Municipal Bureaucracy," pp. 754–771; Peter K. Eisinger, "Black Mayors and the Politics of Racial Economic Advancement," in William C. McReady, ed., *Culture, Ethnicity, and Identity*, pp. 95–109; John J. Harrigan, *Political Change in the Metropolis*, pp. 129–139. For evidence that minority gains in elective office have not been translated into significant minority policy payoffs, see Susan Welch and Albert Karnig, "The Impact of Black Elected Officials on Urban Social Expenditures," pp. 707–714; and Edmond J. Keller, "The Impact of Black Mayors on Urban Policy," pp. 40–52.

24. Clarence N. Stone, *Economic Growth and Neighborhood Discontent: System Bias in the Urban Renewal Program of Atlanta*, pp. 90–185; Clarence N. Stone, "Atlanta: Protest and Elections Are Not Enough," in Rufus P. Browning and Dale Rogers Marshall, eds., "Black and Hispanic Power in City Politics: A Forum," pp. 618–625; Dennis R. Judd, *The Politics of American Cities: Private Power and Public Policy*, pp. 373–407; John Helyar and Robert Johnson, "Tale of Two Cities: Chicago's Busy Center Masks a Loss of Jobs in Its Outlying Areas," pp. 1, 22.

25. Rufus P. Browning et al., *Protest Is Not Enough: The Struggle of Blacks and Hispanics for Equality in Urban Politics*, pp. 207–238 (quote at p. 214).

26. Michael K. Brown and Steven P. Erie, "Blacks and the Legacy of the Great Society: The Economic and Political Impact of Federal Social Policy," pp. 302–309, esp. Table 3, p. 308; U.S. Equal Employment Opportunity Commission, *Minorities and Women in State and Local Government, 1977*, vol. I; U.S. Civil Service Commission, *Minority Group Employment in the Federal Government*, 1975.

27. Steven P. Erie, "Public Policy and Black Economic Polarization," pp. 311–315, esp. Table 1, p. 313.

28. Charles V. Hamilton, "Public Policy and Some Political Consequences," in Marguerite R. Barnett and James A. Hefner, eds., *Public Policy for the Black Community*, p. 245; and Charles V. Hamilton, "The Patron-Recipient Relationship and Minority Politics in New York City," p. 224.

29. U.S. Bureau of the Census, *Voter Participation in the National Election, November, 1964*, pp. 11–13, 21–22; U.S. Bureau of the Census, *Voting and Registration in the Election of November, 1976*, pp. 14–23, 61–62.

Reform Politics

16
City Affairs Are Not Political*
Andrew D. White

Without the slightest exaggeration we may assert that, with very few exceptions, the city governments of the United States are the worst in
Christendom—the most expensive, the most inefficient, and the most corrupt. No one who has any considerable knowledge of our own country and
of other countries can deny this.. . . .

What is the cause of the difference between municipalities in the old
world and in the new? I do not allow that their populations are better than
ours. What accounts, then, for the better municipal development in their
case and for the miserable results in our own? My answer is this: we are
attempting to govern our cities upon a theory which has never been found to
work practically in any part of the world. Various forms of it were tried in the
great cities of antiquity and of the middle ages, especially in the mediaeval
republics of Italy, and without exception they ended in tyranny, confisca-
tion, and bloodshed. The same theory has produced the worst results in
various countries of modern Europe, down to a recent period.

What is this evil theory? It is simply that the city is a political body; that
its interior affairs have to do with national political parties and issues. My
fundamental contention is that a city is a corporation; that as a city it has
nothing whatever to do with general political interests; that party political
names and duties are utterly out of place there. The questions in a city are
not political questions. They have reference to the laying out of streets; to the
erection of buildings; to sanitary arrangements, sewerage, water supply, gas
supply, electrical supply; to the control of franchises and the like; and to
provisions for the public health and comfort in parks, boulevards, libraries,
and museums. The work of a city being the creation and control of the city

*White, Andrew D., "City Affairs Are Not Political"; originally titled "The Government of Ameri-
can Cities." *Forum* (December 1890): 213–216. Copyright © 1890.

property, it should logically be managed as a piece of property by those who have created it, who have a title to it, or a real substantial part in it, and who can therefore feel strongly their duty to it. Under our theory that a city is a political body, a crowd of illiterate peasants, freshly raked in from Irish bogs, or Bohemian mines, or Italian robber nests, may exercise virtual control. How such men govern cities, we know too well; as a rule they are not alive even to their own most direct interests. . . .

The difference between foreign cities and ours, is that all these well-ordered cities in England, France, Germany, Italy, Switzerland, whether in monarchies or republics, accept this principle — that cities are corporations and not political bodies; that they are not concerned with matters of national policy; that national parties as such have nothing whatever to do with city questions. They base their city governments upon ascertained facts regarding human nature, and upon right reason. They try to conduct them upon the principles observed by honest and energetic men in business affairs. We, on the other hand, are putting ourselves upon a basis which has always failed and will always fail — the idea that a city is a political body, and therefore that it is to be ruled, in the long run, by a city proletariat mob, obeying national party cries.

What is our safety? The reader may possibly expect me, in logical consonance with the statement I have just made, to recommend that the city be treated strictly as a corporate body, and governed entirely by those who have a direct pecuniary interest in it. If so, he is mistaken. I am no doctrinaire; politics cannot be bent completely to logic — certainly not all at once. A wise, statesmanlike view would indicate a compromise between the political idea and the corporate idea. I would not break away entirely from the past, but I would build a better future upon what we may preserve from the past.

To this end I would still leave in existence the theory that the city is a political body, as regards the election of the mayor and common council. I would elect the mayor by the votes of the majority of all the citizens, as at present; I would elect the common council by a majority of all the votes of all the citizens; but instead of electing its members from the wards as at present — so that wards largely controlled by thieves and robbers can send thieves and robbers, and so that men who can carry their ward can control the city — I would elect the board of aldermen on a general ticket, just as the mayor is elected now, thus requiring candidates for the board to have a city reputation. So much for retaining the idea of the city as a political body. In addition to this, in consideration of the fact that the city is a corporation, I would have those owning property in it properly recognized. I would leave to them, and to them alone, the election of a board of control, without whose permission no franchise should be granted and no expenditure should be made. This should be the rule, but to this rule I am inclined to make one exception; I would allow the votes of the board of control, as regards expenditures for primary education, to be overridden by a two-thirds majority of the board of aldermen. I should do this because here alone does the city policy come into direct relations with the general political system of the nation at large. The main argument for the existence of our public schools is that they are an absolute necessity to the existence of our Republic; that without preliminary education a republic simply becomes an illiterate mob, that if illiterate elements control, the destruction of the Republic is sure. On this ground, considering the public-school system as based upon a national political necessity, I would have an exception made regarding the expenditures for it, leaving in this matter a last resort to the political assembly of the people.

A theory resulting in a system virtually like this, has made the cities of Europe, whether in monarchies or republics, what they are, and has made it an honor in many foreign countries for the foremost citizens to serve in the common councils of their cities. Take one example: It has been my good fortune to know well Rudolf Von Gneist, councilor of the German Empire. My acquaintance with him began when it was my official duty to present to him a testimonial, in behalf of the government of the United States, for his services in settling the north-west boundary between the United States and Great Britain. The Emperor William was the nominal umpire; he made Von Gneist the real umpire—that shows Von Gneist's standing. He is also a leading professor of law in the University of Berlin, a member of the Imperial Parliament and of the Prussian Legislature, and the author of famous books, not only upon law, but upon the constitutional history of Germany and of England. This man has been, during a considerable time, a member of what we should call the board of aldermen of the city of Berlin, and he is proud to serve in that position. With him have been associated other men the most honored in various walks of life, and among these some of the greatest business men, renowned in all lands for their enterprise and their probity. Look through the councils of our cities, using any microscope you can find, and tell me how many such men you discern in them. Under the system I propose, it is, humanly speaking, certain that these better men would seek entrance into our city councils. Especially would this be the case if our citizens should, by and by, learn that it is better to have in the common council an honest man, though a Republican, than a scoundrel, though a Democrat; and better to have a man of ability and civic pride, though a Democrat, than a weak, yielding creature, though a Republican.

Some objections will be made. It will be said, first, that wealthy and well-to-do people do not do their duty in city matters; that if they should, they would have better city government. This is true to this extent, that even well-to-do men are in city politics strangely led away from their civic duties by fancied allegiance to national party men and party issues. But in other respects it is untrue; the vote of a single tenement house, managed by a professional politician, will neutralize the vote of an entire street of well-to-do citizens. Men in business soon find this out; they soon find that to work for political improvement under the present system is time and labor and self-respect thrown away. It may be also said that the proposal is impracticable. I ask, why? History does not show it to be impracticable; for we have before us, as I have shown, the practice of all other great civilized nations on earth, and especially of our principal sister republics.

But it will be said that "revolutions do not go backward." They did go backward in the great cities of Europe when these rid themselves of the old bad system that had at bottom the theory under which ours are managed, and when they entered into their new and better system. The same objection, that revolutions do not go backward, was made against any reform in the tenure of office of the governor and of the higher judiciary in the State of New York; and yet the revolution did go backward, that is, it went back out of doctrinaire folly into sound, substantial, common-sense statesmanship. In 1847 the State of New York so broke away from the old conservative moorings as to make all judgeships elective, with short terms, small pay, and wretched accommodations, and the same plan was pursued as regards the governor and other leading officials; but the State, some years since, very wisely went back to much of its former system — in short, made a revolution backward, if any one chooses to call it so — resuming the far better system of giving our governor and higher judges longer terms, larger salaries, better accommodations, and dignified surroundings. We see, then, that it is not true that steps in a wrong direction in a republic cannot be retraced. As they have been retraced in State affairs, so they may be in municipal affairs.

But it will be said that this change in city government involves a long struggle. It may or it may not. If it does, such a struggle is but part of the price which we pay for the maintenance of free institutions in town, State, and nation. For this struggle, I especially urge all men of light and leading to prepare themselves. As to the public at large, what is most needed in regard to municipal affairs, as in regard to public affairs generally, is the quiet, steady evolution of a knowledge of truth and of proper action in view of it. That truth, as regards city government, is simply the truth that municipal affairs are not political; that political parties as such have nothing to do with cities; that the men who import political considerations into municipal management are to be opposed. This being the case, the adoption of some such system as that which I have sketched would seem likely to prove fruitful of good.

17

The Politics of Reform in Municipal Government in the Progressive Era*

Samuel P. Hays

In order to achieve a more complete understanding of social change in the Progressive Era, historians must now undertake a deeper analysis of the practices of economic, political, and social groups. Political ideology alone is no longer satisfactory evidence to describe social patterns because generalizations based upon it, which tend to divide political groups into the moral and the immoral, the rational and the irrational, the efficient and the inefficient, do not square with political practice. Behind this contemporary rhetoric concerning the nature of reform lay patterns of political behavior which were at variance with it. Since an extensive gap separated ideology and practice, we can no longer take the former as an accurate description of the latter, but must reconstruct social behavior from other types of evidence.

Reform in urban government provides one of the most striking examples of this problem of analysis. The demand for change in municipal affairs, whether in terms of over-all reform, such as the commission and city-manager plans, or of more piecemeal modifications, such as the development of the city-wide school boards, deeply involved reform ideology. Reformers loudly proclaimed a new structure of municipal government as more moral, more rational, and more efficient and, because it was so, self-evidently more desirable. But precisely because of this emphasis, there seemed to be no need to analyze the political forces behind change. Because the goals of reform were good, its causes were obvious; rather than being the product of particular people and particular ideas in particular situations, they were deeply imbedded in the universal impulses and truths of "progress." Consequently, historians have rarely tried to determine precisely who the municipal reformers were or what they did, but instead have relied on reform ideology as an accurate description of reform practice.

The reform ideology which became the basis of historical analysis is well known. It appears in classic form in Lincoln Steffens' *Shame of the Cities*. The urban political struggle of the Progressive Era, so the argument goes, involved a conflict between public impulses for "good government" against a corrupt alliance of "machine politicians" and "special interests."

During the rapid urbanization of the late 19th century, the latter had been free to aggrandize themselves, especially through franchise grants, at the expense of the public. Their power lay primarily in their ability to manipulate the political process, by bribery and corruption, for their own ends. Against such arrangements there gradually arose a public protest, a demand by the public for honest government, for officials who would act for the public rather than for themselves. To accomplish their goals, reformers sought basic modifications in the political system, both in the structure of government and in the manner of selecting public officials. These changes, successful in city after city, enabled the "public interest" to triumph.[1]

Recently, George Mowry, Alfred Chandler, Jr., and Richard Hofstadter have modified this analysis by emphasizing the fact that the impulse for reform did not come from the working class.[2] This might have been suspected from the rather strained efforts of National Municipal League writers in the "Era of Reform" to go out of their way to demonstrate working-class support for commission and city-manager governments.[3] We now know that they clutched at straws, and often erroneously, in order to prove to themselves as well as to the public that municipal reform was a mass movement.

The Mowry-Chandler-Hofstadter writings have further modified older views by asserting that reform in general and municipal reform in particular sprang from a distinctively middle-class movement. This has now become the prevailing view. Its popularity is surprising not only because it is based upon faulty logic and extremely limited evidence, but also because it, too, emphasizes the analysis of ideology rather than practice and fails to contribute much to the understanding of who distinctively were involved in reform and why.

Ostensibly, the "middle-class" theory of reform is based upon a new type of behavioral evidence, the collective biography, in studies by Mowry of California Progressive party leaders, by Chandler of a nationwide group of that party's leading figures, and by Hofstadter of four professions— ministers, lawyers, teachers, editors. These studies demonstrate the middle-class nature of reform, but they fail to determine if reformers were distinctively middle class, specifically if they differed from their opponents. One study of 300 political leaders in the state of Iowa, for example, discovered that Progressive party, Old Guard, and Cummins Republicans were all substantially alike, the Progressives differing only in that they were slightly younger than the others and had less political experience.[4] If its opponents were also middle class, then one cannot describe Progressive reform as a phenomenon, the special nature of which can be explained in terms of middle-class characteristics. One cannot explain the distinctive behavior of people in terms of characteristics which are not distinctive to them.

Hofstadter's evidence concerning professional men fails in yet another way to determine the peculiar characteristics of reformers. For he describes ministers, lawyers, teachers, and editors without determining who within these professions became reformers and who did not. Two analytical distinctions might be made. Ministers involved in municipal reform, it appears, came not from all segments of religion, but peculiarly from upper-class churches. They enjoyed the highest prestige and salaries in the religious community and had no reason to feel a loss of "status," as Hofstadter argues. Their role in reform arose from the class character of their religious organizations rather than from the mere fact of their occupation as ministers.[5] Professional men involved in reform (many of whom — engineers, architects, and doctors — Hofstadter did not examine at all) seem to have come especially from the more advanced segments of their professions, from those who sought to apply their specialized knowledge to a wider range of public affairs.[6] Their role in reform is related not to their attempt to defend earlier patterns of culture, but to the working out of the inner dynamics of professionalization in modern society.

The weakness of the "middle-class" theory of reform stems from the fact that it rests primarily upon ideological evidence, not on a thoroughgoing description of political practice. Although the studies of Mowry, Chandler, and Hofstadter ostensibly derive from behavioral evidence, they actually derive largely from the extensive expressions of middle-ground ideological position, of the reformers' own descriptions of their contemporary society, and of their expressed fears of both the lower and the upper classes, of the fright of being ground between the millstones of labor and capital.[7]

Such evidence, though it accurately portrays what people thought, does not accurately describe what they did. The great majority of Americans look upon themselves as "middle class' and subscribe to a middle-ground ideology, even though in practice they belong to a great variety of distinct social classes. Such ideologies are not rationalizations of deliberate attempts to deceive. They are natural phenomena of human behavior. But the historian should be especially sensitive to their role so that he will not take evidence of political ideology as an accurate representation of political practice.

In the following account I will summarize evidence in both secondary and primary works concerning the political practices in which municipal reformers were involved. Such an analysis logically can be broken down into three parts, each one corresponding to a step in the traditional argument. First, what was the source of reform? Did it lie in the general public rather than in particular groups? Was it middle class, working class, or perhaps of other composition? Second, what was the reform target of attack? Were reformers primarily interested in ousting the corrupt individual, the political or business leader who made private arrangements at the expense of the public, or were they interested in something else? Third, what political innovations did reformers bring about? Did they seek to expand popular participation in the governmental process?

There is now sufficient evidence to determine the validity of these specific elements of the more general argument. Some of it has been available for several decades; some has appeared more recently; some is presented here for the first time. All of it adds up to the conclusion that reform in municipal government involved a political development far different from what we have assumed in the past.

Available evidence indicates that the source of support for reform in municipal government did not come from the lower or middle classes, but from the upper class. The leading business groups in each city and professional men closely allied with them initiated and dominated municipal movements. Leonard White, in his study of the city manager published in 1927, wrote:

> The opposition to bad government usually comes to a head in the local chamber of commerce. Business men finally acquire the conviction that the growth of their city is being seriously impaired by the failures of city officials to perform their duties efficiently. Looking about for a remedy, they are captivated by the resemblance of the city-manager plan to their corporate form of business organization.[8]

In the 1930s White directed a number of studies of the origin of city-manager government. The resulting reports invariably begin with such statements as, "the Chamber of Commerce spearheaded the movement," or commission government in this city was a "businessmen's government."[9] Of thirty-two cases of city-manager government in Oklahoma examined by Jewell C. Phillips, twenty-nine were initiated either by chambers of commerce or by community committees dominated by businessmen.[10] More recently James Weinstein has presented almost irrefutable evidence that the business community, represented largely by chambers of commerce, was the overwhelming force behind both commission and city-manager movements.[11]

Dominant elements of the business community played a prominent role in another crucial aspect of municipal reform: the Municipal Research Bureau movement.[12] Especially in the larger cities, where they had less success in shaping the structure of government, reformers established centers to conduct research in municipal affairs as a springboard for influence.

The first such organization, the Bureau of Municipal Research of New York City, was founded in 1906; it was financed largely through the efforts of Andrew Carnegie and John D. Rockefeller. An investment banker provided the crucial support in Philadelphia, where a Bureau was founded in 1908. A group of wealthy Chicagoans in 1910 established the Bureau of Public Efficiency, a research agency. John H. Patterson of the National Cash Register Company, the leading figure in Dayton municipal reform, financed the Dayton Bureau, founded in 1912. And George Eastman was the driving force behind both the Bureau of Municipal Research and city-manager government in Rochester. In smaller cities data about city government was collected by interested individuals in a more informal way or by chambers of commerce, but in larger cities the task required special support, and prominent businessmen supplied it.

The character of municipal reform is demonstrated more precisely by a brief examination of the movements in Des Moines and Pittsburgh. The Des Moines Commercial Club inaugurated and carefully controlled the drive for the commission form of government.[13] In January, 1906 the Club held a so-called "mass meeting" of business and professional men to secure an enabling act from the state legislature. P. C. Kenyon, president of the Club, selected a Committee of 300, composed principally of business and professional men, to draw up a specific proposal. After the legislature approved their plan, the same committee managed the campaign which persuaded the electorate to accept the commission form of government by a narrow margin in June, 1907.

In this election the lower-income wards of the city opposed the change, the upper-income wards supported it strongly, and the middle-income wards were more evenly divided. In order to control the new government, the Committee of 300, now expanded to 530, sought to determine the nomination and election of the five new commissioners, and to this end they selected an avowedly businessman's slate. Their plans backfired when the voters swept into office a slate of anticommission candidates who now controlled the new commission government.

Proponents of the commission form of government in Des Moines spoke frequently in the name of the "people." But their more explicit statements emphasized their intent that the new plan be a "business system" of government, run by businessmen. The slate of candidates for commissioner endorsed by advocates of the plan was known as the "businessman's ticket." J. W. Hill, president of the committees of 300 and 530, bluntly declared: "The professional politician must be ousted and in his place capable businessmen chosen to conduct the affairs of the city." I. M. Farle, general counsel of the Bankers Life Association and a prominent figure in the movement, put the point more precisely: "When the plan was adopted it was the intention to get businessmen to run it."

Although reformers used the ideology of popular government, they in no sense meant that all segments of society should be involved equally in municipal decision-making. They meant that their concept of the city's welfare would be best achieved if the business community controlled city government. As one businessman told a labor audience, the businessman's slate represented labor "better than you do yourself."

The composition of the municipal reform movement in Pittsburgh demonstrates its upper-class and professional as well as its business sources.[14] Here the two principal reform organizations were the Civic Club and the Voters' League. The 745 members of these two organizations came primarily from the upper class. Sixty-five percent appeared in upper-class directories which contained the names of only 2 percent of the city's families. Furthermore, many who were not listed in these directories lived in upper-class areas. These reformers, it should be stressed, comprised not an old but a new upper class. Few came from earlier industrial and mercantile families. Most of them had risen to social position from wealth created after 1870 in the iron, steel, electrical equipment, and other industries, and they lived in the newer rather than the older fashionable areas.

Almost half (48 percent) of the reformers were professional men: doctors, lawyers, ministers, directors of libraries and museums, engineers, architects, private and public school teachers, and college professors. Some of these belonged to the upper class as well, especially the lawyers, ministers, and private school teachers. But for the most part their interest in reform stemmed from the inherent dynamics of their professions rather than from their class connections. They came from the more advanced segments of their organizations, from those in the forefront of the acquisition and application of knowledge. They were not the older professional men, seeking to preserve the past against change; they were in the vanguard of professional life, actively seeking to apply expertise more widely to public affairs.

Pittsburgh reformers included a large segment of businessmen; 52 percent were bankers and corporation officials or their wives. Among them were the presidents of fourteen large banks and officials of Westinghouse, Pittsburgh Plate Glass, U.S. Steel and its component parts (such as Carnegie Steel, American Bridge, and National Tube), Jones and Laughlin, lesser steel companies (such as Crucible, Pittsburgh, Superior, Lockhart, and H. K. Porter), the H. J. Heinz Company, and the Pittsburgh Coal Company, as well as officials of the Pennsylvania Railroad and the Pittsburgh and Lake Erie. These men were not small businessmen; they directed the most powerful banking and industrial organizations of the city. They represented not the old business community, but industries which had developed and grown primarily within the past fifty years and which had come to dominate the city's economic life.

These business, professional, and upper-class groups who dominated municipal reform movements were all involved in the rationalization and systematization of modern life; they wished a form of government which would be more consistent with the objectives inherent in those developments. The most important single feature of their perspective was the rapid expansion of the geographical scope of affairs which they wished to influence and manipulate, a scope which was no longer limited and narrow, no longer within the confines of pedestrian communities, but was now broad and city-wide, covering the whole range of activities of the metropolitian area.

The migration of the upper class from central to outlying areas created a geographical distance between its residential communities and its economic institutions. To protect the latter required involvement both in local ward affairs and in the larger city government as well. Moreover, upper-class cultural institutions, such as museums, libraries, and symphony orchestras, required an active interest in the larger municipal context from which these institutions drew much of their clientele.

Professional groups, broadening the scope of affairs which they sought to study, measure, or manipulate, also sought to influence the public health, the educational system, or the physical arrangements of the entire city. Their concerns were limitless, not bounded by geography, but as expansive as the professional imagination. Finally, the new industrial community greatly broadened its perspective in governmental affairs because of its new recognition of the way in which factors throughout the city affected business growth. The increasing size and scope of industry, the greater stake in more varied and geographically dispersed facts of city life, the effect of floods on many business concerns, the need to promote traffic flows to and from work for both blue-collar and managerial employees—all contributed to this larger interest. The geographically larger private perspectives of upper-class, professional, and business groups gave rise to a geographically larger public perspective.

These reformers were dissatisfied with existing systems of municipal government. They did not oppose corruption per se—although there was plenty of that. They objected to the structure of government which enabled local and particularistic interests to dominate. Prior to the reforms of the Progressive Era, city government consisted primarily of confederations of local wards, each of which was represented on the city's legislative body. Each ward frequently had its own elementary schools and ward-elected school boards which administered them.

These particularistic interests were the focus of a decentralized political life. City councilmen were local leaders. They spoke for their local areas, the economic interests of their inhabitants, their residential concerns, their educational, recreational, and religious interests—i.e., for those aspects of community life which mattered most to those they represented. They rolled logs in the city council to provide streets, sewers, and other public works for their local areas. They defended the community's cultural practices, its distinctive languages or national customs, its liberal attitude toward liquor, and its saloons and dance halls which served as centers of community life. One observer described this process of representation in Seattle:

> The residents of the hill-tops and the suburbs may not fully appreciate the faithfulness of certain downtown ward councilmen to the interests of their constituents. . . . The people of a state would rise in arms against a senator or representative in Congress who deliberately misrepresented their wishes and imperiled their interests, though he might plead a higher regard for national good. Yet people in other parts of the city seem to forget that under the old system the ward elected councilmen with the idea of procuring service of special benefit to that ward.[15]

In short, pre-reform officials spoke for their constituencies, inevitably their own wards which had elected them, rather than for other sections or groups of the city.

The ward system of government especially gave representation in city affairs to lower- and middle-class groups. Most elected ward officials were from these groups, and they, in turn, constituted the major opposition to reforms in municipal government. In Pittsburgh, for example, immediately prior to the changes in both the city council and the school board in 1911 in which city-wide representation replaced ward representation, only 24 percent of the 387 members of those bodies represented the same managerial, professional, and banker occupations which dominated the membership of the Civic Club and the Voters' League. The great majority (67 percent) were small businessmen—grocers, saloonkeepers, livery-stable proprietors, owners of small hotels, druggists—white-collar workers such as clerks and bookkeepers, and skilled and unskilled workmen.[16]

This decentralized system of urban growth and the institutions which arose from it reformers now opposed. Social, professional, and economic life had developed not only in the local wards in a small community context, but also on a larger scale had become highly integrated and organized, giving rise to a superstructure of social organization which lay far above that of ward life and which was sharply divorced from it in both personal contacts and perspective.

By the late 19th century, those involved in these larger institutions found that the decentralized system of political life limited their larger objectives. The movement for reform in municipal government, therefore, constituted an attempt by upper-class, advanced professional, and large business groups to take formal political power from the previously dominant lower- and middle-class elements so that they might advance their own conceptions of desirable public policy. These two groups came from entirely different urban worlds, and the political system fashioned by one was no longer acceptable to the other.

Lower- and middle-class groups not only dominated the pre-reform governments, but vigorously opposed reform. It is significant that none of the occupational groups among them, for example, small businessmen or white-collar workers, skilled or unskilled artisans, had important representation in reform organizations thus far examined. The case studies of city-manager government undertaken in the 1930s under the direction of Leonard White detailed in city after city the particular opposition of labor. In their analysis of Jackson, Michigan, the authors of these studies wrote:

> The *Square Deal*, oldest Labor paper in the state, has been consistently against manager government, perhaps largely because labor has felt that with a decentralized government elected on a ward basis it was more likely to have some voice and to receive its share of privileges.[17]

In Janesville, Wisconsin, the small shopkeepers and workingmen on the west and south sides, heavily Catholic and often Irish, opposed the commission plan in 1911 and in 1912 and the city-manager plan when adopted in 1923.[18] "In Dallas there is hardly a trace of class consciousness in the Marxian sense," one investigator declared, "yet in city elections the division has been to a great extent along class lines."[19] The commission and city-manager elections were no exceptions. To these authors it seemed a logical reaction, rather than an embarrassing fact that had to be swept away, that workingmen should have opposed municipal reform.[20]

In Des Moines working-class representatives, who in previous years might have been council members, were conspicuously absent from the "businessman's slate." Workingmen acceptable to reformers could not be found. A workingman's slate of candidates, therefore, appeared to challenge the reform slate. Organized labor, and especially the mineworkers, took the lead; one of their number, Wesley Ash, a deputy sheriff and union member, made "an astonishing run" in the primary, coming in second among a field of more than twenty candidates.[21] In fact, the strength of anticommission candidates in the primary so alarmed reformers that they frantically sought to appease labor.

The day before the final election they modified their platform to pledge both an eight-hour day and an "American standard of wages." They attempted to persuade the voters that their slate consisted of men who represented labor because they had "begun at the bottom of the ladder and made a good climb toward success by their own unaided efforts."[22] But their tactics failed. In the election on March 30, 1908, voters swept into office the entire "opposition" slate. The business and professional community had succeeded in changing the form of government, but not in securing its control. A cartoon in the leading reform newspaper illustrated their disappointment; John Q. Public sat dejectedly and muttered, "Aw, What's the Use?"

The most visible opposition to reform and the most readily available target of reform attack was the so-called "machine," for through the "machine" many different ward communities as well as lower- and middle-income groups joined effectively to influence the central city government. Their private occupational and social life did not naturally involve these groups in larger city-wide activities in the same way as the upper class was involved; hence they lacked access to privately organized economic and social power on which they could construct political power. The "machine" filled this organizational gap.

Yet it should never be forgotten that the social and economic institutions in the wards themselves provided the "machine's" sustaining support and gave it larger significance. When reformers attacked the "machine" as the most visible institutional element of the ward system, they attacked the entire ward form of political organization and the political power of lower- and middle-income groups which lay behind it.

Reformers often gave the impression that they opposed merely the corrupt politician and his "machine." But in a more fundamental way they looked upon the deficiencies of pre-reform political leaders in terms not of their personal shortcomings, but of the limitations inherent in their occupational, institutional, and class positions. In 1911 the Voters' League of Pittsburgh wrote in its pamphlet analyzing the qualifications of candidates that "a man's occupation ought to give a strong indication of his qualifications for membership on a school board."[23] Certain occupations inherently disqualified a man from serving:

> Employment as ordinary laborer and in the lowest class of mill work would naturally lead to the conclusion that such men did not have sufficient education or business training to act as school directors. . . . Objection might also be made to small shopkeepers, clerks, workmen at many trades, who by lack of educational advantages and business training, could not, no matter how honest, be expected to administer properly the affairs of an educational system, requiring special knowledge, and where millions are spent each year.

These, of course, were precisely the groups which did dominate Pittsburgh government prior to reform. The League deplored the fact that school boards contained only a small number of "men prominent throughout the city in business life . . . in professional occupations . . . holding positions as managers, secretaries, auditors, superintendents and foremen" and exhorted these classes to participate more actively as candidates for office.

Reformers, therefore, wished not simply to replace bad men with good; they proposed to change the occupational and class origins of decision-makers. Toward this end they sought innovations in the formal machinery of government which would concentrate political power by sharply centralizing the processes of decision-making rather than distribute it through more popular participation in public affairs. According to the liberal view of the Progressive Era, the major political innovations of reform involved the equalization of political power through the primary, the direct election of public officials, and the initiative, referendum, and recall. These measures played a large role in the political ideology of the time and were frequently incorporated into new municipal charters. But they provided at best only an occasional and often incidental process of decision-making. Far more important in continuous, sustained, day-to-day processes of government were those innovations which centralized decision-making in the hands of fewer and fewer people.

The systematization of municipal government took place on both the executive and the legislative levels. The strong-mayor and city manager types become the most widely used examples of the former. In the first decade of the 20th century, the commission plan had considerable appeal, but its distribution of administrative responsibility among five people gave rise to a demand for a form with more centralized executive power; consequently, the city-manager or the commission-manager variant often replaced it.[24]

A far more pervasive and significant change, however, lay in the centralization of the system of representation, the shift from ward to city-wide election of councils and school boards. Governing bodies so selected, reformers argued, would give less attention to local and particularistic matters and more to affairs of city-wide scope. This shift, an invariable feature of both commission and city-manager plans, was often adopted by itself. In Pittsburgh, for example, the new charter of 1911 provided as the major innovation that a council of twenty-seven, each member elected from a separate ward, be replaced by a council of nine, each elected by the city as a whole.

Cities displayed wide variations in this innovation. Some regrouped wards into larger units but kept the principle of areas of representation smaller than the entire city. Some combined a majority of councilmen elected by wards with additional ones selected at large. All such innovations, however, constituted steps toward the centralization of the system of representation.

Liberal historians have not appreciated the extent to which municipal reform in the Progressive Era involved a debate over the system of representation. The ward form of representation was universally condemned on the grounds that it gave too much influence to the separate units and not enough attention to the larger problems of the city. Harry A. Toulmin, whose book, *The City Manager*, was published by the National Municipal League, stated the case:

> The spirit of sectionalism had dominated the political life of every city. Ward pitted against ward, alderman against alderman, and legislation only effected by "long-rolling" extravagant measures into operation, molding the city, but gratifying the greed of constituents, has too long stung the conscience of decent citizenship. This constant treaty-making of factionalism has been no less than a curse. The city manager plan proposes the commendable thing of abolishing wards. The plan is not unique in this for it has been common to many forms of commission government. . . . [25]

Such a system should be supplanted, the argument usually went, with city-wide representation in which elected officials could consider the city "as a unit." "The new officers are elected," wrote Toulmin, "each to represent all the people. Their duties are so defined that they must administer the corporate business in its entirety, not as a hodge-podge of associated localities."

Behind the debate over the method of representation, however, lay a debate over who should be represented, over whose views of public policy should prevail. Many reform leaders often explicitly, if not implicitly, expressed fear that lower- and middle-income groups had too much influence in decision-making. One Galveston leader, for example, complained about the movement for initiative, referendum, and recall:

> We have in our city a very large number of negroes employed on the docks; we also have a very large number of unskilled white laborers; this city also has more barrooms, according to its population, than any other city in Texas. Under these circumstances it would be extremely difficult to maintain a satisfactory city government where all ordinances must be submitted back to the voters of the city for their ratification and approval.[26]

At the National Municipal League convention of 1907, Rear Admiral F. E. Chadwick (USN Ret.), a leader in the Newport, Rhode Island, movement for municipal reform, spoke to this question even more directly:

> Our present system has excluded in large degree the representation of those who have the city's well-being most at heart. It has brought, in municipalities . . . a government established by the least educated, the least interested class of citizens.
>
> It stands to reason that a man paying $5,000 taxes in a town is more interested in the well-being and development of his town than the man who pays no taxes. . . . It equally stands to reason that the man of the $5,000 tax should be assured a representation in the committee which lays the tax and spends the money which he contributes. . . . Shall we be truly democratic and give the property owner a fair show or shall we develop a tyranny of ignorance which shall crush him?[27]

Municipal reformers thus debated frequently the question of who should be represented as well as the question of what method of representation should be employed.

That these two questions were intimately connected was revealed in other reform proposals for representation, proposals which were rarely taken seriously. One suggestion was that a class system of representation by substituted for ward representation. For example, in 1908 one of the prominent candidates for commissioner in Des Moines proposed that the city council be composed of representatives of five classes: educational and ministerial organizations, manufacturers and jobbers, public utility corporations, retail merchants including liquor men, and the Des Moines Trades and Labor Assembly. Such a system would have greatly reduced the influence in the council of both middle- and lower-class groups. The proposal revealed the basic problem confronting business and professional leaders: how to reduce the influence in government of the majority of voters among middle- and lower-income groups.[28]

A growing imbalance between population and representation sharpened the desire of reformers to change from ward to city-wide elections. Despite shifts in population within most cities, neither ward district lines nor the apportionment of city council and school board sets changed frequently. Consequently, older areas of the city, with wards that were small in geographical size and held declining populations (usually lower and middle class in composition), continued to be overrepresented, and newer upper-class areas, where population was growing, became increasingly underrepresented. This intensified the reformers' conviction that the structure of government must be changed to give them the voice they needed to make their views on public policy prevail.[29]

It is not insignificant that in some cities (by no means a majority) municipal reform came about outside the urban electoral process. The original commission government in Galveston was appointed rather than elected. "The failure of previous attempts to secure an efficient city government through the local electorate made the business man of Galveston willing to put the conduct of the city's affairs in the hands of a commission dominated by state-appointed officials."[30] Only in 1903 did the courts force Galveston to elect the members of the commission, an innovation which one writer described as "an abandonment of the commission idea," and which led to the decline of influence of the business community in the commission government.[31]

In 1911 Pittsburgh voters were not permitted to approve either the new city charter or the new school board plan, both of which provided for city-wide representation; they were a result of state legislative enactment. The governor appointed the first members of the new city council, but thereafter they were elected. The judges of the court of common pleas, however, and not the voters, selected members of the new school board.

The composition of the new city council and new school board in Pittsburgh, both of which were inaugurated in 1911, revealed the degree to which the shift from ward to city-wide representation produced a change in group representation.[32] Members of the upper class, the advanced professional men, and the larger business groups dominated both. Of the fifteen members of the Pittsburgh Board of Education appointed in 1911 and the nine members of the new city council, none were small businessmen or white-collar workers. Each body contained only one person who could remotely be classified as a blue-collar worker; each of these men filled a position specifically but unofficially designed as reserved for a "representative of labor," and each was an official of the Amalgamated Association of Iron, Steel, and Tin Workers. Six of the nine members of the new city council were prominent businessmen, and all six were listed in upper-class directories. Two others were doctors closely associated with the upper class in both professional and social life. The fifteen members of the Board of Education included ten businessmen with city-wide interests, one doctor associated with the upper class, and three women previously active in upper-class public welfare.

Lower- and middle-class elements felt that the new city governments did not represent them.[33] The studies carried out under the direction of Leonard White contain numerous expressions of the way in which the change in the structure of government produced not only a change in the geographical scope of representation, but also in groups represented. "It is not the policies of the manager or the council they oppose," one researcher declared, "as much as the lack of representation for their economic level and social groups."[34] And another wrote:

> There had been nothing unapproachable about the old ward aldermen. Every voter had a neighbor on the common council who was interested in serving him. The new councilmen, however, made an unfavorable impression on the less well-to-do voters. . . . Election at large made a change that, however desirable in other ways, left the voters in the poorer wards with a feeling that they had been deprived of their share of political importance.[35]

The success of the drive for centralization of administration and representation varied with the size of the city. In the smaller cities, business, professional, and elite groups could easily exercise a dominant influence. Their close ties readily enabled them to shape informal political power which they could transform into formal political power. After the mid-1890s the widespread organization of chambers of commerce provided a base for political action to reform municipal government, resulting in a host of small-city commission and city-manager innovations. In the larger, more heterogeneous cities, whose subcommunities were more dispersed, such community-wide action was extremely difficult. Few commission or city-manager proposals materialized here. Mayors became stronger, and steps were taken toward centralization of representation, but the ward system or some modified version usually persisted. Reformers in large cities often had to rest content with their Municipal Research Bureaus through which they could exert political influence from outside the municipal government.

A central element in the analysis of municipal reform in the Progressive Era is governmental corruption. Should it be understood in moral or political terms? Was it a product of evil men or of particular sociopolitical circumstances? Reform historians have adopted the former view. Selfish and evil men arose to take advantage of a political arrangement whereby unsystematic government offered many opportunities for personal gain at public expense. The system thrived until the "better elements," "men of intelligence and civic responsibility," or "right-thinking people" ousted the culprits and fashioned a political force which produced decisions in the "public interest." In this scheme of things, corruption in public affairs grew out of individual personal failings and a deficient governmental structure which could not hold those predispositions in check, rather than from the peculiar nature of social forces. The contestants involved were morally defined: evil men who must be driven from power, and good men who must be activated politically to secure control of the municipal affairs.

Public corruption, however, involves political even more than moral considerations. It arises more out of the particular distribution of political power than of personal morality. For corruption is a device to exercise control and influence outside the legal channels of decision making when those channels are not readily responsive. Most generally, corruption stems from an inconsistency between control of the instruments of formal governmental power and the exercise of informal influence in the community. If powerful groups are denied access for formal power in legitimate ways, they seek access through procedures which the community considers illegitimate. Corrupt government, therefore, does not reflect the genius of evil men, but rather the lack of acceptable means for those who exercise power in the private community to wield the same influence in governmental affairs. It can be understood in the Progressive Era not simply by the preponderance of evil men over good, but by the peculiar nature of the distribution of political power.

The political corruption of the "Era of Reform" arose from the inaccessibility of municipal government to those who were rising in power and influence. Municipal government in the United States developed in the 19th century within a context of universal manhood suffrage which decentralized political control. Because all men, whatever their economic, social, or cultural conditions, could vote, leaders who reflected a wide variety of community interests and who represented the views of people of every circumstance arose to guide and direct municipal affairs. Since the majority of urban voters were workingmen or immigrants, the views of those groups carried great and often decisive weight in governmental affairs. Thus, as Herbert Gutman has shown, during strikes in the 1870s city officials were usually friendly to workingmen and refused to use police power to protect strikebreakers.[36]

Ward representation on city councils was an integral part of grass-roots influence, for it enabled diverse urban communities, invariably identified with particular geographical areas of the city, to express their views more clearly through councilmen peculiarly receptive to their concerns. There was a direct, reciprocal flow of power between wards and the center of city affairs in which voters felt a relatively close connection with public matters and city leaders gave special attention to their needs.

Within this political system the community's business leaders grew in influence and power as industrialism advanced, only to find that their economic position did not readily admit them to the formal machinery of government. Thus, during strikes, they had to rely on either their own private police, Pinkertons, or the state militia to enforce their use of strikebreakers. They frequently found that city officials did not accept their views of what was best for the city and what direction municipal policies should take. They had developed a common outlook, closely related to their economic activities, that the city's economic expansion should become the prime concern of municipal government, and yet they found that this view had to compete with even more influential views of public policy. They found that political tendencies which arose from universal manhood suffrage and ward representation were not always friendly to their political conceptions and goals and had produced a political system over which they had little control, despite the fact that their economic ventures were the core of the city's prosperity and the hope for future urban growth.

Under such circumstances, businessmen sought other methods of influencing municipal affairs. They did not restrict themselves to the channels of popular election and representation, but frequently applied direct influence—if not verbal persuasion, then bribery and corruption. Thereby arose the graft which Lincoln Steffens recounted in his *Shame of the Cities*. Utilities were only the largest of those business groups and individuals who requested special favors, and the franchises they sought were only the most sensational of the prizes which included such items as favorable tax assessments and rates, the vacating of streets wanted for factory expansion, or permission to operate amid antiliquor and other laws regulating personal behavior. The relationships between business and formal government because a maze of accommodations, a set of political arrangements which grew up because effective power had few legitimate means of accomplishing its ends.

Steffens and subsequent liberal historians, however, misread the significance of these arrangements, emphasizing their personal rather than their more fundamental institutional elements. To them corruption involved personal arrangements between powerful business leaders and powerful "machine" politicians. Just as they did not fully appreciate the significance of the search for political influence by the rising business community as a whole, so they did not see fully the role of the "ward politician." They stressed the argument that the political leader manipulated voters to his own personal ends, that he used constituents rather than reflected their views.

A different approach is now taking root, namely, that the urban political organization was an integral part of community life, expressing its needs and its goals. As Oscar Handlin has said, for example, the "machine" not only fulfilled specific wants, but provided one of the few avenues to success and public recognition available to the immigrant.[37] The political leader's arrangements with businessmen, therefore, were not simply personal agreements between conniving individuals; they were far-reaching accommodations between powerful sets of institutions in industrial America.

These accommodations, however, proved to be burdensome and unsatisfactory to the business community and to the upper third of socioeconomic groups in general. They were expensive; they were wasteful; they were uncertain. Toward the end of the 19th century, therefore, business and professional men sought more direct control over municipal government in order to exercise political influence more effectively. They realized their goals in the early 20th century in the new commission and city-manager forms of government and in the shift from ward to city-wide representation.

These innovations did not always accomplish the objectives that the business community desired because other forces could and often did adjust to the change in governmental structure and reestablish their influence. But businessmen hoped that reform would enable them to increase their political power, and most frequently it did. In most cases the innovations which were introduced between 1901, when Galveston adopted a commission form of government, and the Great Depression, and especially the city-manager form which reached a height of popularity in the mid-1920s, served as vehicles whereby business and professional leaders moved directly into the inner circles of government, brought into one political system their own power and the formal machinery of government, and dominated municipal affairs for two decades.

Municipal reform in the early 20th century involves a paradox: the ideology of an extension of political control and the practice of its concentration. While reformers maintained that their movement rested on a wave of popular demands, called their gatherings of business and professional leaders "mass meetings," described their reforms as "part of a world-wide trend toward popular government," and proclaimed an ideology of a popular upheaval against a selfish few, they were in practice shaping the structure of municipal government so that political power would no longer be broadly distributed, but would in fact be more centralized in the hands of a relatively small segment of the population. The paradox became even sharper when new city charters included provisions for the initiative, referendum, and recall. How does the historian cope with this paradox? Does it represent deliberate deception or simply political strategy? Or does it reflect a phenomenon which should be understood rather than explained away?

The expansion of popular involvement in decision-making was frequently a political tactic, not a political system to be established permanently, but a device to secure immediate political victory. The prohibitionist advocacy of the referendum, one of the most extensive sources of support for such a measure, came from the belief that the referendum would provide the opportunity to outlaw liquor more rapidly. The Anti-Saloon League, therefore, urged local option. But the League was not consistent. Towns which were wet, when faced with a county-wide local-option decision to outlaw liquor, demanded town or township local option to reinstate it. The League objected to this as not the proper application of the referendum idea.

Again, "Progressive" reformers often espoused the direct primary when fighting for nominations for their candidates within the party, but once in control they often became cool to it because it might result in their own defeat. By the same token, many municipal reformers attached the initiative, referendum, and recall to municipal charters often as a device to appease voters who opposed the centralization of representation and executive authority. But, by requiring a high percentage of voters to sign petitions—often 25 to 30 percent—these innovations could be and were rendered relatively harmless.

More fundamentally, however, the distinction between ideology and practice in municipal reform arose from the different roles which each played. The ideology of democratization of decision-making was negative rather than positive; it served as an instrument of attack against the existing political system rather than as a guide to alternative action. Those who wished to destroy the "machine" and to eliminate party competition in local government widely utilized the theory that these political instruments thwarted public impulses, and thereby shaped the tone of their attack.

But there is little evidence that the ideology represented a faith in a purely democratic system of decision-making or that reformers actually wished, in practice, to substitute direct democracy as a continuing system of sustained decision-making in place of the old. It was used to destroy the political institutions of the lower and middle classes and the political power which those institutions gave rise to, rather than to provide a clear-cut guide for alternative action.[38]

The guide to alternative action lay in the model of the business enterprise. In describing new conditions which they wished to create, reformers drew on the analogy of the "efficient business enterprise," criticizing current practices with the argument that "no business could conduct its affairs that way and remain in business," and calling upon business practices as the guides to improvement. As one student remarked:

> The folklore of the business elite came by gradual transition to be the symbols of governmental reformers. Efficiency, system, orderliness, budgets, economy, saving, were all injected into the efforts of reformers who sought to remodel municipal government in terms of the great impersonality of corporate enterprise.[39]

Clinton Rodgers Woodruff of the National Municipal League explained that the commission form was "a simple, direct, businesslike way of administering the business affairs of the city . . . an application to city administration of that type of business organization which has been so common and so successful in the field of commerce and industry."[40] The centralization of decision-making which developed in the business corporation was now applied in municipal reform.

The model of the efficient business enterprise, then, rather than the New England town meeting, provided the positive inspiration for the municipal reformer. In giving concrete shape to this model in the strong-mayor, commission, and city-manager plans, reformers engaged in the elaboration of the processes of rationalization and systematization inherent in modern science and technology. For in many areas of society, industrialization brought a gradual shift upward in the location of decision-making and the geographical extension of the scope of the area affected by decisions.

Experts in business, in government, and in the professions measured, studied, analyzed, and manipulated ever wider realms of human life, and devices which they used to control such affairs constituted the most fundamental and far-reaching innovations in decision-making in modern America, whether in formal government or in the informal exercise of power in private life. Reformers in the Progressive Era played a major role in shaping this new system. While they expressed an ideology of restoring a previous order, they in fact helped to bring forth a system drastically new.[41]

The drama of reform lay in the competition for supremacy between two systems of decision-making. One system, based upon ward representation and growing out of the practices and ideas of representative government, involved wide latitude for the expression of grass-roots impulses and their involvement in the political process. The other grew out of the rationalization of life which came with science and technology, in which decisions arose from expert analysis and flowed from fewer and smaller centers outward to the rest of society. Those who espoused the former looked with fear upon the loss of influence which the latter involved, and those who espoused the latter looked only with disdain upon the wastefulness and inefficiency of the former.

The Progressive Era witnessed rapid strides toward a more centralized system and a relative decline for a more decentralized system. This development constituted an accommodation of forces outside the business community to the political trends within business and professional life rather than vice versa. It involved a tendency for the decision-making processes inherent in science and technology to prevail over those inherent in representative government.

Reformers in the Progressive Era and liberal historians since then misread the nature of the movement to change municipal government because they concentrated upon dramatic and sensational episodes and ignored the analysis of more fundamental political structure, of the persistent relationships of influence and power which grew out of the community's social, ideological, economic, and cultural activities. The reconstruction of these patterns of human relationships and of the changes in them is the historian's most crucial task, for they constitute the central context of historical development. History consists not of erratic and spasmodic fluctuations, of a series of random thoughts and actions, but of patterns of activity and changes in which people hold thoughts and actions in common and in which there are close connections between sequences of events. These contexts give rise to a structure of human relationships which pervade all areas of life; for the political historian the most important of these is the structure of the distribution of power and influence.

The structure of political relationships, however, cannot be adequately understood if we concentrate on evidence concerning ideology rather than practice. For it is becoming increasingly clear that ideological evidence is no safe guide to the understanding of practice, that what people thought and said about their society is not necessarily an accurate representation of what they did. The current task of the historian of the Progressive Era is to quit taking the reformers' own description of political practice at its face value and to utilize a wide variety of new types of evidence to reconstruct political practice in its own terms. This is not to argue that ideology is either important or unimportant. It is merely to state that ideological evidence is not appropriate to the discovery of the nature of political practice.

Only by maintaining this clear distinction can the historian successfully investigate the structure of political life in the Progressive Era. And only then can he begin to cope with the most fundamental problem of all: the relationship between political ideology and political practice. For each of these facets of political life must be understood in its own terms, through its own historical record. Each involves a distinct set of historical phenomena. The relationship between them for the Progressive Era is not now clear; it has not been investigated. But it cannot be explored until the conceptual distinction is made clear and evidence tapped which is pertinent to each. Because the nature of political practice has so long been distorted by the use of ideological evidence, the most pressing task is for its investigation through new types of evidence appropriate to it. The reconstruction of the movement for municipal reform can constitute a major step forward toward that goal.

NOTES

1. See, for example, Clifford W. Patton, *Battle for Municipal Reform* (Washington, D.C., 1940), and Frank Mann Stewart, *A Half-Century of Municipal Reform* (Berkeley, 1950).

2. George F. Mowry, *The California Progressives* (Berkeley and Los Angeles, 1951). pp. 86–101; Richard Hofstadter, *The Age of Reform* (New York, 1955), pp. 131–260; Alfred D. Chandler, Jr., "The Origins of Progressive Leadership," in Elting Morrison *et al.*, (eds.). *Letters of Theodore Roosevelt* (Cambridge, 1951–54). VIII, Appendix III. pp. 1462–64.

3. Harry A. Toulmin, *The City Manager* (New York, 1915). pp. 156–68; Clinton R. Woodruff, *City Government by Commission* (New York, 1911). pp. 243–53.

4. Eli Daniel Potts, "A Comparative Study of the Leadership of Republican Factions in Iowa, 1904–1914." M.A. thesis (State University of Iowa, 1956). Another satisfactory comparative analysis is contained in William T. Kerr, Jr., "The Progressives of Washington, 1910–12." *PNQ* 55 (1964): pp. 16–27.

5. Based upon a study of eleven ministers involved in municipal reform in Pittsburgh, who represented exclusively the upper-class Presbyterian and Episcopal churches.

6. Based upon a study of professional men involved in municipal reform in Pittsburgh, comprising eighty three doctors, twelve architects, twenty-five educators, and thirteen engineers.

7. See especially Mowry, *The California Progressives.*

8. Leonard White, *The City Manager* (Chicago, 1927), pp. ix–x.

9. Harold A. Stone *et al., City Manager Government in Nine Cities* (Chicago, 1940); Frederick C. Mosher *et al., City Manager Government in Seven Cities* (Chicago, 1940); Harold A. Stone *et al., City Manager Government in the United States* (Chicago, 1940). Cities covered by these studies include: Austin, Texas; Charlotte, North Carolina; Dallas, Texas; Dayton, Ohio; Fredericksburg, Virginia; Jackson, Michigan; Janesville, Wisonsin; Kingsport, Tennessee; Lynchburg, Virginia; Rochester, New York; San Diego, California.

10. Jewell Cass Phillips, *Operation of the Council-Manager Plan of Government in Oklahoma Cities* (Philadelphia, 1935), pp. 31–39.

11. James Weinstein, "Organized Business and the City Commission and Manager Movements," *Journal of Southern History* XXVIII (1962): 166–182.

12. Norman N. Gill, *Municipal Research Bureaus* (Washington, 1944).

13. This account of the movement for commission government in Des Moines is derived from items in the Des Moines Register during the years from 1905 through 1908.

14. Biographical data constitutes the main source of evidence for this study of Pittsburgh reform leaders. It was found in city directories, social registers, directories of corporate directors, biographical compilations, reports of boards of education, settlement houses, welfare organizations, and similar types of material. Especially valuable was the clipping file maintained at the Carnegie Library of Pittsburgh.

15. *Town Crier* (Seattle), Feb. 18, 1911, p. 13.

16. Information derived from the same sources as cited in n. 14.

17. Stone *et al., Nine Cities,* p. 212.

18. *Ibid.,* pp. 3–13.

19. *Ibid.,* p. 329.

20. Stone *et al., City Manager Government;* 26, 237–41, for analysis of opposition to city manager government.

21. Des Moines *Register and Leader,* March 17, 1908.

22. *Ibid.,* March 30, March 28, 1908.

23. Voters' Civic League of Allegheny County, "Bulletin of the Voters' Civic League of Allegheny County Concerning the Public School System of Pittsburgh," Feb. 14, 1911, pp. 2–3.

24. In the decade 1911 to 1920, 45 percent of the municipal charters adopted in eleven home rule states involved the commission form and 35 percent the city manager form; in the following decade the figures stood at 6 percent and 71 percent respectively. The adoption of city manager charters reached a peak in the years 1918 through 1923 and declined sharply after 1933. See Leonard D. White, "The Future of Public Administration." *Public Management* XV (1933): 12.

25. Toulmin, *The City Manager,* p. 42.

26. Woodruff, *City Government*, p. 315. The Galveston commission plan did not contain provisions for the initiative, referendum, or recall, and Galveston commercial groups which had fathered the commission plan opposed movements to include them. In 1911 Governor Colquitt of Texas vetoed a charter bill for Texarkana because it contained such provisions; he maintained that they were "undemocratic" and unnecessary to the success of commission government. *Ibid.*, pp. 314–15.

27. *Ibid.*, pp. 207–8.

28. Des Moines *Register and Leader*, Jan 15, 1908.

29. Voters' Civic League of Allegheny County, "Report on the Voters' League in the Redistricting of the Wards of the City of Pittsburgh" (Pittsburgh, n.d.).

30. Horace E. Deming, "The Government of American Cities," in Woodruff, *City Government*, p. 167.

31. *Ibid.*, p. 168.

32. Information derived from same sources as cited in n. 14.

33. W. R. Hopkins, city manager of Cleveland, indicated the degree to which the new type of government was more responsive to the business community: "It is undoubtedly easier for a city manager to insist upon acting in accordance with the business interests of the city than it is for a mayor to do the same thing." Quoted in White, *The City Manager*, p. 13.

34. Stone *et al., Nine Cities*, p. 20.

35. *Ibid.*, p. 225.

36. Herbert Gutman, "An Iron Workers' Strike in the Ohio Valley, 1873–74," *Ohio Historical Quarterly*, IXVIII (1959): 353–70; "Trouble on the Railroads, 1873–1874: Prelude to the 1877 Crisis," *Labor History*, II (1961): 215–36.

37. Oscar Handlin, *The Uprooted* (Boston, 1951). pp. 209–17.

38. Clinton Rodgers Woodruff of the National Municipal League even argued that the initiative, referendum, and recall were rarely used. "Their value lies in their existence rather than in their use." Woodruff, *City Government*, p. 314. It seems apparent that the most widely used of these devices, the referendum, was popularized by legislative bodies when they could not agree or did not want to take responsibility for a decision and sought to pass that responsibility to the general public, rather than because of a faith in the wisdom of popular will.

39. J. B. Shannon, "County Consolidation," *Annals of the American Academy of Political and Social Science* 207 (1940): 168.

40. Woodruff, *City Government*, pp. 29–30.

41. Several recent studies emphasize various aspects of this movement. See, for example, Loren Baritz, *Servants of Power* (Middletown, 1960); Raymond E. Callahan, *Education and the Cult of Efficiency* (Chicago, 1962); Samuel P. Hays, *Conservation and the Gospel of Efficiency* (Cambridge, 1959); Dwight Waldo, *The Administrative State* (New York, 1948), pp. 3–61.

18
Trumpeted Failures and Unheralded Triumphs*

Jon C. Teaford

In 1888 the British observer James Bryce proclaimed that "there is no denying that the government of cities is the one conspicuous failure of the United States."[1] With this pronouncement he summed up the feelings of a host of Americans. In New York City, residents along mansion-lined Fifth Avenue, parishioners in the churches of then-sedate Brooklyn, even petty politicos at party headquarters in Tammany Hall, all perceived serious flaws in the structure of urban government. Some complained, for example, of the tyranny of upstate Republican legislators, others attacked the domination of ward bosses, and still others criticized the greed of public utility companies franchised by the municipality. Mugwump reformer Theodore Roosevelt decried government by Irish political machine hacks, the moralist Reverend Charles Henry Parkhurst lambasted the reign of rum sellers, and that pariah of good-government advocates, New York City ward boss George Washington Plunkitt, also found fault, attacking the evils of civil service. For each, the status quo in urban government was defective. For each, the structure of municipal rule needed some revision. By the close of the 1880s the litany of criticism was mounting, with one voice after another adding a shrill comment on the misrule of the cities.

During the following two decades urban reformers repeated Bryce's words with ritualistic regularity, and his observation proved one of the most-quoted lines in the history of American government. Time and again latter-day Jeremiahs damned American municipal rule of the late nineteenth century, denouncing it as a national blight, a disgrace that by its example threatened the survival of democracy throughout the world. In 1890 Andrew D. White, then-president of Cornell University, wrote that "without the slightest exaggeration . . . the city governments of the United States are the worst in Christendom — the most expensive, the most inefficient, and the most corrupt."[2] Four years later the reform journalist Edwin Godkin claimed that "the present condition of city governments in the United States is bringing democratic institutions into contempt the world over, and imperiling some of the best things in our civilization."[3] Such preachers as the Reverend Washington Gladden denounced the American city as the "smut of civilization," while his clerical colleague Reverend Parkhurst said of the

*Teaford, Jon C. 1984. "Trumpeted Failures and Unheralded Triumphs." Pp. 1–11 and 315 in *The Unheralded Triumphs*. Baltimore: Johns Hopkins University Press. Copyright © 1984. Reprinted by permission of Johns Hopkins University Press.

230

nation's municipalities: "Virtue is at the bottom and knavery on top. The rascals are out of jail and standing guard over men who aim to be honorable and law-abiding."[4] And in 1904 journalist Lincoln Steffens stamped American urban rule with an indelible badge of opprobrium in the corruption-sated pages of his popular muck-raking exposé *The Shame of the Cities.* Books, magazines, and newspapers all recited the catalog of municipal sins.

Likewise, many twentieth-century scholars passing judgment on the development of American city government have handed down a guilty verdict and sentenced American urban rule to a place of shame in the annals of the nation. In 1933 a leading student of municipal home rule claimed that "the conduct of municipal business has almost universally been inept and inefficient" and "at its worst it has been unspeakable, almost incredible."[5] That same year the distinguished historian Arthur Schlesinger, Sr., in his seminal study *The Rise of the City,* described the development of municipal services during the last decades of the nineteenth century and found the achievements "distinctly creditable to a generation . . . confronted with the phenomenon of a great population everywhere clotting into towns." Yet later in his study he returned to the more traditional position, recounting tales of corruption and describing municipal rule during the last two decades of the century as "the worst city government the country had ever known."[6] Writing in the 1950s, Bessie Louise Pierce, author of the finest biography to date of an American city, a multivolume history of Chicago, described that city's long list of municipal achievements but closed with a ritual admission of urban shortcomings, citing her approval of Bryce's condemnation.[7] Similarly, that lifelong student of American municipal history, Ernest Griffith, subtitled his volume on late-nineteenth-century urban rule "the conspicuous failure," though he questioned whether municipal government was a greater failure than state government.[8]

Historians such as Schlesinger and Griffith were born in the late nineteenth century, were raised during the Progressive era, and early imbibed the ideas of such critics as Bryce and White. Younger historians of the second half of the twentieth century were further removed from the scene of the supposed municipal debacle and could evaluate it more dispassionately. By the 1960s and 1970s, negative summations such as "unspeakable" and "incredible" were no longer common in accounts of nineteenth-century city government, and historians professing to the objectivity of the social sciences often refused to pronounce judgment on the quality of past rule. Yet recent general histories of urban America have continued both to describe the "deterioration" of city government during the Gilded Age and to focus on political bosses and good-government reformers who were forced to struggle with a decentralized, fragmented municipal structure supposedly unsuited to the fast-growing metropolises of the 1880s and 1890s. Some chronicles of the American city have recognized the material advances in public services during the late nineteenth century, but a number speak of the failure of the municipality to adapt to changing realities and of the shortcomings of an outmoded and ineffectual municipal framework. Sam Bass Warner, Jr., one of the leading new urban historians of the 1960s, has characterized the pattern of urban rule as one of "weak, corrupt, unimaginative municipal government."[9] Almost one hundred years after Bryce's original declaration, the story of American city government remains at best a tale of fragmentation and confusion and at worst one of weakness and corruption.

If modern scholars have not handed down such damning verdicts as the contemporary critics of the 1880s and 1890s, they have nevertheless issued evaluations critical of the American framework of urban rule. As yet, hindsight has not cast a golden glow over the municipal institutions of the late nineteenth century, and few historians or political scientists have written noble tributes to the achievements of American municipal government. Praise for the nation's municipal officials has been rare and grudging. Though many have recognized the elitist predilections of Bryce and his American informants, the influence of Bryce's words still persists, and the image of nineteenth-century city government remains tarnished. Historians have softened the harsh stereotype of the political boss, transforming him from a venal parasite into a necessary component of a makeshift, decentralized structure. Conversely, the boss's good-government foes have fallen somewhat from historical grace and are now typified as crusaders for the supremacy of an upper-middle-class business culture. But historians continue to aim their attention at these two elements of municipal rule, to the neglect of the formal, legal structure. They write more of the boss than of the mayor, more on the civic leagues than on the sober but significant city comptroller. Moreover they continue to stage the drama of bosses and reformers against a roughly sketched backdrop of municipal disarray. The white and black hats of the players may have shaded to gray, but the setting of the historian's pageant remains a ramshackle municipal structure.

Nevertheless, certain nagging realities stand in stark contrast to the traditional tableau of municipal rule. One need not look far to discover the monuments of nineteenth-century municipal achievement that still grace the nation's cities, surviving as concrete rebuttals to Bryce's words. In 1979 the architecture critic for the *New York Times* declared Central Park and the Brooklyn Bridge as "the two greatest works of architecture in New York . . . each . . . a magnificent object in its own right; each . . . the result of a brilliant synthesis of art and engineering after which the world was never quite the same."[10] Each was also a product of municipal enterprise, the creation of a city government said to be the worst in Christendom. Moreover, can one visit San Francisco's Golden Gate Park or enter McKim, Mead, and White's palatial Boston Public Library and pronounce these landmarks evidence of weakness or failure? Indeed, can those city fathers be deemed "unimaginative" who hired the great landscape architect Frederick Low Olmsted to design the first public park systems in human history? And were the vast nineteenth-century water and drainage schemes that still serve the cities the handiwork of bumbling incompetents unable to cope with the demands of expanding industrial metropolises? The aqueducts of Rome were among the glories of ancient civilization; the grander water systems of nineteenth-century New York City are often overlooked by those preoccupied with the more lurid aspects of city rule.

A bright side of municipal endeavor did, then, exist. American city governments could claim grand achievements, and as Arthur Schlesinger, Sr., was willing to admit in 1933, urban leaders won some creditable victories in the struggle for improved services. Certainly there were manifold shortcomings: Crime and poverty persisted, fires raged and pavements buckled; garbage and street rubbish sometimes seemed insurmountable problems. Yet no government has ever claimed total success in coping with the problems of society; to some degree all have failed to service their populations adequately. If government ever actually succeeded, political scientists would have to re-tool and apply themselves to more intractable problems, and political philosophers would have to turn to less contemplative pursuits. Those with a negative propensity can always find ample evidence of "bad government," and late-nineteenth-century critics such as Bryce, White, and Godkin displayed that propensity. In their writings the good side of the municipal structure was as visible as the dark side of the moon.

Thus, observers of the late-nineteenth-century American municipality have usually focused microscopic attention on its failures while overlooking its achievements. Scoundrels have won much greater coverage than conscientious officials. Volumes have appeared, for example, on that champion among municipal thieves, New York City's political boss William M. Tweed, but not one book exists on the life and work of a perhaps more significant figure in nineteenth-century city government, Ellis Chesbrough the engineer who served both Boston and Chicago and who transformed the public works of the latter city. Only recently has an admirable group of studies begun to explore the work of such municipal technicians who were vital to the formulation and implementation of public policy.[11] But prior to the 1970s accounts of dualistic conflicts between political bosses and good-government reformers predominated, obscuring the complexities of municipal rule and the diversity of elements actually vying for power and participating in city government. And such traditional accounts accepted as axiomatic the inadequacy of the formal municipal structure. Critics have trumpeted its failures, while its triumphs have gone unheralded.

If one recognizes some of the challenges that municipal leaders faced during the period 1870 to 1900, the magnitude of their achievements becomes clear. The leaders of the late nineteenth century inherited an urban scene of great tumult and stress and an urban population of increasing diversity and division. During the midcentury, thousands of Roman Catholic immigrants from Ireland and Germany had flooded American metropolitan areas, threatening the traditional Protestant dominance and igniting sharp ethnic conflicts. Riots between the native-born and immigrants flared in Philadelphia during the 1840s; the anti-immigrant Native American Party assumed control of both Philadelphia and Baltimore in the 1850s; and New York City's Draft Riots of 1863 pitted Irish against blacks in the nation's bitterest and most destructive urban uprising. The melting pot was coming to a boil, and yet throughout the 1870s, 1880s, and 1890s, waves of new-comers continued to enter the country, including more and more representatives of the alien cultures of southern and eastern Europe. To many in 1870, social and ethnic diversity seemed to endanger the very foundation of order and security in the nation, and municipal leaders faced the need to maintain a truce between Protestants and Catholics, old stock and new, the native business elite and immigrant workers.

The rush of migrants from both Europe and rural America combined with a high birth rate to produce another source of municipal problems, a soaring urban population. New York City, Boston, Baltimore, and Philadelphia were dynamic centers, expanding rapidly and increasing their populations at a rate of 30 percent to 40 percent each decade. Chicago, on the average, doubled in population each decade between 1870 and 1900, and elsewhere, growth rates of 50 percent or 60 percent were not unusual. During the last thirty years of the century, the nation's chief cities absorbed thousands of acres of new territory to accommodate this booming population, and once-compact cities sprawled outward from the urban core. This expansion and sprawl produced demands for the extension of services and the construction of municipal facilities. The newly annexed peripheral wards needed sewer lines and water mains; they required fire and police protection; and residents of outlying districts expected the city to provide paved streets and lighting. Municipal governments could not simply maintain their services at existing levels; instead, they had to guarantee the extension of those services to thousands of new urban dwellers.

Improved and expanded municipal services, however, required funding, and revenue therefore posed another challenge for city rulers. Municipalities markedly extended their endeavors during the midcentury, purchasing waterworks, creating paid fire brigades, establishing public school systems, and forming modern police forces. To pay for this, taxes rose and municipal indebtedness soared. Taxpayer revolts were common as early as the 1850s, with angry citizens in New York City, Chicago, Philadelphia, and Milwaukee complaining of public extravagance and corruption and already urging a more frugal, businesslike administration of municipal government. Inflation in the 1860s and economic depression in the 1870s exacerbated the financial problems of the city, leading to heightened cries for retrenchment. And throughout the 1880s and 1890s city governments faced the difficult problem of meeting rising expectations for services while at the same time satisfying demands for moderate taxes and fiscal conservatism. This was perhaps the toughest task confronting the late-nineteenth-century municipality.

During the last three decades of the century, American city government did, however, meet these challenges of diversity, growth, and financing with remarkable success. By century's close, American city dwellers enjoyed, on the average, as high a standard of public services as any urban residents in the world. Problems persisted, and there were ample grounds for complaint. But in America's cities, the supply of water was the most abundant, the street lights were the most brilliant, the parks the grandest, the libraries the largest, and the public transportation the fastest of any place in the world. American city fathers rapidly adapted to advances in technology, and New York City, Chicago, and Boston were usually in the forefront of efforts to apply new inventions and engineering breakthroughs to municipal problems. Moreover, America's cities achieved this level of modern service while remaining solvent and financially sound. No major American municipality defaulted on its debt payments during the 1890s, and by the end of the century all of the leading municipalities were able to sell their bonds at premium and pay record-low interest. Any wise financier would have testified that the bonds of those purported strongholds of inefficiency and peculation, the municipal corporations, were far safer investments than were the bonds of those quintessential products of American business ingenuity: the railroad corporations.

Not only did the city governments serve their residents without suffering financial collapse, but municipal leaders also achieved an uneasy balance of the conflicting forces within the city, accommodating each through a distribution of authority. Though commentators often claimed that the "better elements" of the urban populace had surrendered municipal administration to the hands of "low-bred" Irish saloonkeepers, such observations were misleading. Similarly incorrect is the claim that the business and professional elite abandoned city government during the late nineteenth century to decentralized lower-class ward leaders. The patrician, the plutocrat, the plebeian, and the professional bureaucrat all had their place in late-nineteenth-century municipal government; each staked an informal but definite claim to a particular domain within the municipal structure.

Upper-middle-class business figures presided over the executive branch and the independent park, library, and sinking-fund commissions. Throughout the last decades of the nineteenth century the mayor's office was generally in the hands of solid businessmen or professionals who were native-born Protestants. The leading executive officers were persons of citywide reputation and prestige, and during the period 1870 and 1900 their formal authority was increasing. Meanwhile, the legislative branch—the board of aldermen or city council—became the stronghold of small neighborhood retailers, often of immigrant background, who won their aldermanic seats because of their neighborhood reputation as good fellows willing to gain favors for their constituents. In some cities men of metropolitan standing virtually abandoned the city council, and in every major city this body was the chief forum for lower-middle-class and working-class ward politicians.

At the same time, an emerging body of trained experts was also securing a barony of power within city government. Even before the effective application of formal civil service laws, mayors and commissioners deferred to the judgment and expertise of professional engineers, landscape architects, educators, physicians, and fire chiefs, and a number of such figures served decade after decade in municipal posts, despite political upheavals in the executive and legislative branches. By the close of the century these professional civil servants were securing a place of permanent authority in city government. Their loyalty was not to downtown business interests nor to ward or ethnic particularism, but to their profession and their department. And they were gradually transforming those departments into strongholds of expertise.

The municipal professional, the downtown business leader, and the neighborhood shopkeeper and small-time politico each had differing concepts of city government and differing policy priorities. They thus represented potentially conflicting interests that could serve to divide the municipal polity and render it impotent. Yet, during the period 1870 to 1900, these elements remained in a state of peaceful, if contemptuous, coexistence. Hostilities broke out, especially if any element felt the boundaries of its domain were violated. But city governments could operate effectively if the truce between these elements was respected; in other words, if ward business remained the primary concern of the ward alderman, citywide policy was in the hands of the business elite, and technical questions were decided by experts relatively undisturbed by party politics. This was the informal détente that was gradually developing amid the conflict and complaints.

Such extralegal participants as political parties and civic leagues also exerted their influence over municipal government, attempting to tip the uneasy balance of forces in their direction. The political party organization with its ward-based neighborhood bosses was one lever that the immigrants and less affluent could pull to affect the course of government. Civic organization and reform leagues, in contrast, bolstered the so-called better element in government, the respected businessmen who usually dominated the leading executive offices and the independent commissions. Emerging professional groups such as engineering clubs and medical societies often lent their support to the rising ambitions and growing authority of the expert bureaucracy and permanent civil servants. And special-interest lobbyists like the fire insurance underwriters also urged professionalism in such municipal services as the fire department. Municipal government was no simple dualistic struggle between a city-wide party boss with a diamond shirt stud and malodorous cigar and a good-government reformer with a Harvard degree and kid gloves. Various forces were pushing and pulling the municipal corporations, demanding a response to petitions and seeking a larger voice in the chambers of city government.

State legislatures provided the structural flexibility to respond to these demands. The state legislatures enjoyed the sovereign authority to bestow municipal powers and to determine the municipal structure, but when considering local measures, state lawmakers generally deferred to the judgment of the legislative delegation from the affected locality. If the local delegation favored a bill solely affecting its constituents, the legislature usually ratified the bill without opposition or debate. This rule of deference to the locality no longer applied, however, if the bill became a partisan issue, as it occasionally did. But in most cases authorization for new powers or for structural reforms depended on the city's representatives in the state legislature, and each session the state assemblies and senates rubber-stamped hundreds of local bills. Thus, indulgent legislators provided the vital elasticity that allowed urban governments to expand readily to meet new challenges and assume new responsibilities.

Local delegations, however, responded not only to the requests of the formal rulers of the city—the board of aldermen and the mayor; they also considered the petitions of extralegal agencies eager to obtain favors and reforms. Recourse to the state legislature became an alternate route for those seeking action, a detour around the obstruction of city authorities. Indeed, many believed that the right to appeal to state lawmakers created too much flexibility in the governmental system. Early advocates of municipal home rule therefore sought to block this avenue and to create a less flexible system, but before 1900 those favoring a more rigid, less adaptable structure won few victories. In most states, then, the legislatures responded readily to urban demands, perhaps too readily, and lawmakers tinkered endlessly with the governmental mechanism.

Even so, this process of perpetual adjustment resulted in a mechanism that succeeded in performing the job of city government. Municipal leaders adapted to the need for experts trained in the new technologies and hired such technicians. Moreover, downtown businessmen and ward politicos, the native-born and the immigrants, Protestants and Catholics, loosened the lid on the melting pot and reduced the boiling hostility of the midcentury to a simmer. The cities provided services; they backed off from the brink of bankruptcy; and the municipal structure guaranteed a voice to the various elements of society in both immigrant wards and elite downtown clubs.

Why, then, all the complaints? Why did so many critics of the 1880s and 1890s indulge in a rhetoric of failure, focusing on municipal shortcomings to the neglect of municipal successes? Why was municipal government so much abused? The answer lies in a fundamental irony: The late-nineteenth-century municipal structure accommodated everyone but satisfied no one. It was a system of compromise among parties discontented with compromise. It was a marriage of convenience, with the spouses providing a reasonably comfortable home for American's urban inhabitants. But it was not a happy home. The parties to the nuptials tolerated one another because they had to. Nevertheless, the businessman-mayors and plutocrat park commissioners disliked their dependence on ward politicians, whom they frequently regarded as petty grafters, and they frowned upon the power of the immigrant voters. Likewise, the emerging corps of civil servants was irked by interference from laypersons of both high and low status. And the plebeian party boss opposed efforts to extend the realm of the civil servants who had performed no partisan duties and thus merited no power. None liked their interdependence with persons they felt to be unworthy, incompetent, or hostile.

Enhancing this dissatisfaction was the cultural absolutism of the Victorian era. The late nineteenth century was an age when the business elite could refer to itself as the "best element" of society and take for granted its "God-given" superiority. It was an age when professional engineers, landscape architects, public health experts, librarians, educators, and fire fighters were first becoming aware of themselves as professionals, and with the zeal of converts they defended their newly exalted state of grace. It was also an age when most Protestants viewed Catholics as papal pawns and devotees of Italian idolatry, while most Catholics believed Protestants were little better than heathens and doomed to a quick trip to hell with no stops in purgatory. The late nineteenth century was not an age of cultural relativism but one of cultural absolutes, an age when people still definitely knew right from wrong, the correct from the erroneous. The American municipality, however, was a heterogeneous polyarchy, a network of accommodation and compromise in an era when accommodation and compromise smacked of unmanly dishonor and unprincipled pragmatism. Municipal government of the 1870s, 1880s, and 1890s rested on a system of broker politics, of bargaining and dealing. Yet Parson Weems's panegyric of George Washington, a figure of unbending morality, had molded the political conscience of nineteenth-century American school children, and on reaching adulthood these Americans still believed in the ideal of the great statesman who could not tell a lie. Although the prefix *poly* and the term *relativism* were alien to the guiding principles of the nineteenth century, they are basic to any description of urban government in that era.

Some leaders of the period could, without troubled conscience, act as broker and bargainer, and these figures thrived in urban politics. For example, the high-born Mayor Carter Harrison, Sr., of Chicago, was a master of municipal government and a pragmatic politician who seemed to enjoy the heterogeneity of his city. Likewise, in New York City the low-born Tammany boss Richard Croker commanded his motley metropolis, though he was unable to master the mechanism sufficiently to prevent the ouster of his organization twice in a decade. And a number of high-minded gentlemen seemed capable of playing the game of politics and winning the mayoral office, though they might turn to reform periodicals and lambaste in print the very system they exploited. Still, the idea of reaching an accommodation with grafters, saloonkeepers, and other social pariahs seemed reprehensible, especially among the upper middle-class. Through its control of executive offices and independent commissions, the upper middle class was usually the dominant force within city government, and America's municipalities proved especially effective in providing services for that class, with its devotion to flush toilets, public libraries, and suburban parks. No other group, however, proved more hostile in its attacks on the existing system of municipal rule. Though often effective, city government was, according to upper-middle-class critics, almost always dishonorable.

Late-nineteenth-century urban government was a failure not of structure but of image. The system proved reasonably successful in providing services, but there was no prevailing ideology to validate its operation. In fact, the beliefs of the various participants were at odds with the structure of rule that governed them. The respectable elements believed in sobriety and government by persons of character. But the system of accommodation permitted whiskey taps to flow on the Sabbath for the Irish and for Germans, just as it allowed men in shiny suits with questionable reputations to occupy seats on the city council and in the municipal party conventions. The ward-based party devotees accepted the notions of Jacksonian democracy and believed quite literally in the maxim To the victor belong the spoils. But by the 1890s they faced a growing corps of civil servants more devoted to their profession than to any party. Although new professional bureaucrats preached a gospel of expertise, they still had to compromise with party-worshiping hacks and the supposedly diabolical forces of politics. Likewise, special-interest lobbyists such as the fire insurance underwriters were forced to cajole or coerce political leaders whom they deemed ignorant and unworthy of public office. Each of these groups worked together, but only from necessity and not because they believed in such a compromise of honor. There was no ideology of heterogeneous polyarchy, no system of beliefs to bolster the existing government structure. Thus late-nineteenth-century city government survived without moral support, and to many urban dwellers it seemed a bargain with the devil.

Twentieth-century historians also had reasons for focusing on urban failure rather than urban success. Some chroniclers in the early decades accepted rhetoric as reality and simply repeated the condemnations of critics such as Bryce, White, and Godkin. By the midcentury greater skepticism prevailed, but so did serious ills. In fact, the urban crisis of the 1960s provided the impetus for a great upsurge of interest in the history of the city, inspiring a search for the historical roots of urban breakdown and collapse. Urban problems were the scholars' preoccupation. Not until the much-ballyhooed "back-to-the-city" movement of the 1970s did the city become less an object of pity or contempt and more a treasured relic. By the late 1970s a new rhetoric was developing, in which sidewalks and streets assumed a nostalgic significance formerly reserved to babbling brooks and bucolic pastures.

The 1980s, then, seem an appropriate time to reevaluate the much-maligned municipality of the late nineteenth century. Back-to-the-city euphoria, however, should not distort one's judgment of the past. Instead, it is time to understand the system of city government from 1870 to 1900 complete with blemishes and beauty marks. One should not quickly dismiss the formal mechanisms of municipal rule as inadequate and outdated, requiring the unifying grasp of party bosses. Nor should one mindlessly laud municipal rule as a triumph of urban democracy. A serious appreciation of the municipal structure is necessary. How did it work? Who was in charge? What did it achieve?

NOTES

1. James Bryce, *The American Commonwealth*, 3 vols. (London: Macmillan & Co., 1888), 2:281.

2. Andrew D. White, "The Government of American Cities," *Forum* 10 (Dec. 1890): 357.

3. Edwin Godkin, "The Problems of Municipal Government," *Annals of the American Academy of Political and Social Science* 4 (May 1894): 882.

4. Jacob H. Dorn, *Washington Gladden: Prophet of the Social Gospel* (Columbus: Ohio State University Press, 1966), p. 303; Charles H. Parkhurst, *Our Fight with Tammany* (New York: Charles Scribner's Sons, 1895), p. 2.

5. Joseph D. McGoldrick, *Law and Practice of Municipal Home Rule, 1916–1930* (New York: Columbia University Press, 1933), p. 1.

6. Arthur M. Schlesinger, Sr., *The Rise of the City, 1878 1898* (New York: Macmillan Co.., 1933), pp. 120, 391.

7. Bessie Louise Pierce, *A History of Chicago*, 3 vols. (New York: Alfred A. Knopf, 1957), 3:380.

8. Ernest S. Griffith, *A History of American City Government: The Conspicuous Failure, 1870–1900* (New York: Praeger Publishers, 1974), p. 283.

9. Sam Bass Warner, Jr., *The Private City* (Philadelphia: University of Pennsylvania Press, 1968), p. 98.

10. Paul Goldberger, *The City Observed: New York, A Guide to the Architecture of Manhattan* (New York: Random House, 1979), p. 27.

11. See, for example: Louis P. Cain, *Sanitation Strategy for a Lakefront Metropolis: The Case of Chicago* (DeKalb: Northern Illinois University Press, 1978); Stanley K. Schultz and Clay McShane, "To Engineer the Metropolis: Sewers, Sanitation, and City Planning in Late-Nineteenth-Century America," *Journal of American History* 65 (Sept. 1978): 389–411, Joel A. Farr, "The Separate vs. Combined Sewer Problem: A Case Study in Urban Technology Design Choice," *Journal of Urban History* 5 (May 1979): 308–39; Clay McShane, "Transforming the Use of Urban Space: A Look at the Revolution in Street Pavements, 1880–1924," ibid., pp. 279–307.

The Industrial Urban Crisis and Regime Failure

19

The Empty Promise of Reform*

Melvin G. Holli

. . . [Most] prevalent in the programs of large-city mayors who earned the epithet "reformer" was the effort to change the structure of municipal government, to eliminate petty crime and vice, and to introduce the business system of the contemporary corporation into municipal government. Charter tinkering, elaborate audit procedures, and the drive to impose businesslike efficiency upon city government were the stock-in-trade of this type of urban executive. Mayors of this kind of reform persuasion could be found in New York, Brooklyn, Buffalo, San Francisco, and countless other cities.

Although most of these structural reformers did not articulate their positions as eloquently as Seth Low or attempt to install business methods as ruthlessly as John Purroy Mitchel, they all shared a certain style, a number of common assumptions about the cause of municipal misgovernment, and, in some instances, a conviction about which class was best fitted to rule the city. Few of them were as blatantly outspoken in their view of democracy as Samuel S. McClure, the publisher of the leading muckrake journal. He instructed Lincoln Steffens to prove that popular rule was a failure and that cities should be run by a dictatorship of wise and strong men, such as Samuel S. McClure or Judge Elbert Gary. Similarly New York's former reform mayor, Abram Hewitt asserted in 1901 that "ignorance should be excluded from control, [and] the city business should be carried on by trained experts selected upon some other principle than popular suffrage."[1]

*Holli, Melvin G. 1969. "The Empty Promise of Reform." Pp. 162–180 in *Reform in Detroit*. New York: Oxford University Press, Copyright © 1969 by Oxford University Press, Inc. Copyright © 1977 by Melvin G. Holli. Reprinted by permission of Melvin G. Holli.

None of the structural reformers had the unqualified faith in the ability of the masses to rule themselves intelligently that social reformers Hazen S. Pingree, Samuel "Golden Rule" Jones, or Tom L. Johnson did. "I have come to lean upon the common people as the real foundation upon which good government must rest," Pingree told the Nineteenth Century Club in 1897. In a statement that represented more than a rhetorical flourish, "Golden Rule" Jones chastised Reverend Josiah Strong for his distrust of the masses and told him that the "voice of the people is the voice of God." Tom Johnson, asserted Brand Whitlock, knew that "the cure for the ills of democracy was not less democracy, as so many people were always preaching, but more democracy." When Johnson was defeated by the Cleveland electorate at the very pinnacle of one of the most productive urban reform careers in the nation, he told Whitlock, "The people are probably right."[2]

The structural reform movement was in sharp contrast to the democratic mood of such a statement. It represented instead the first wave of prescriptive municipal government which placed its faith in rule by educated, upper class Americans and, later, by municipal experts rather than the lower classes. The installation in office of men of character, substance, and integrity was an attempt to impose middle class and patrician ideals upon the urban masses. The movement reached its height in the second and third decades of the twentieth century with the city-manager and city-commissioner forms of government, which called for the hiring of nonpartisan experts to decide questions hitherto viewed as resolvable only by the political process. Like the structural reform movement of the late-nineteenth-century, the city-manager movement reflected an implicit distrust of popular democracy.[3]

New York's Mayor William F. Havemeyer was a prototype of the twentieth-century structural reformers. Having inherited a substantial fortune, he retired from the sugar refining business at the age of forty and devoted most of his career to public service. Elected mayor in 1872 during the public exposure of the Tweed Ring, Havemeyer was a reformer who championed "clean government," "economy," and the business class point of view. Obsessed with tax cuts and retrenchment, he and his fiscal watchdog, city Treasurer Andrew H. Green, cut wages on public works and demanded elaborate procedures to account for all petty expenditures of public funds. Green's painstaking scrutiny of every claim snarled the payroll so badly that the city's laborers rioted when their pay checks got lost in an administrative tangle.[4]

To practice economy, Havemeyer sacrificed important public services and, in the process, "crippled downtown development." During a three-month period in 1874 the Mayor vetoed more than 250 bills related to street grading, paving, and widening, board of education contracts, and appropriations intended for public charities. In justifying his liquidation of work relief, Havemeyer told the Harvard Association that contributions of private individuals and Christian and charitable associations were generous enough to meet the needs of the poor. According to Seymour Mandelbaum, the lower classes and the promoters of new areas of the city suffered most from Havemeyer's policies.[5]

During his second year in office, the aging Mayor fought with the city council and accomplished nothing of lasting importance. Havemeyer and the New York Council of Political Reform were so obsessed with "honest, efficient and economical government" that they indicated every public improvement as a "job" and labeled every politician who supported such measures as an "exponent of the class against which society is organized to protect itself." The Mayor's death in 1874 mercifully ended the agony of a reform administration which was strangling the city with red tape generated by its own economy programs. Ironically, Havemeyer helped to perpetuate the widespread belief that reformers were meddling, ineffectual reactionaries, or, as George Washington Plunkitt charged, "morning glories" who wilted in the heat of urban politics. . . .[6]

Seth Low, a wealthy merchant, philanthropist, and university president, was mayor of Brooklyn (1882–85) and later of New York (1902–03). Perhaps more than any other American mayor, he possessed the qualities of a high-minded, nonpartisan structural reformer who attempted to infuse a large dose of businesslike efficiency into municipal government. He was widely recognized by his generation as one of the most prominent practicing reformers on the urban scene, but he also built a considerable reputation as a scholar of municipal affairs. In countless addresses, Low argued that the answer to urban problems was charter reform to bring nonpartisanship and a centralized administration into city government. Reform of this sort would arouse a new civic consciousness and create a cohesive corporate government that could be run along business lines, free from outside influences.[7]

Under the aegis of a silk-stocking Citizens' Committee, Low, with his refined eloquence and business support, had waged an effective campaign against political spoilsmanship and partisanship and won Brooklyn's mayoralty election in 1881. Low disregarded political affiliation and based his appointments on ability and merit. Although his two terms proved to be unspectacular, Low had advanced what he considered the cardinal principles of municipal reform: he had reduced the city's debt, tightened up the tax system, and conducted a vigorous campaign at Albany to stop special state legislation from interfering in Brooklyn's affairs. Such social questions as tenement house reform and aid to the aged, the poor, or workingmen were for Seth Low but special benefits which could not be considered until local partisanship had been wiped out and municipal government had been reorganized along the lines of authority and responsibility. Low's name had become synonymous with efficiency, responsibility, and clean government.[8]

After a particularly flagrant period of municipal corruption under Tammany Hall, a reform-minded Citizens' Union, which counted J. Pierpont Morgan and Elihu Root among its founders, asked Seth Low to enter the lists as an independent candidate for mayor of New York against the Tammany favorite in 1901. Low ran on a platform of home rule and nonpartisanship, avoided the social-welfare planks endorsed by the Citizens' Union, and discussed honesty, economy, and responsibility in his speeches. Low was known to the voters because he had assisted in drafting the first charter for Greater New York, which consolidated hundreds of small towns and three large cities into one unit. Low's victory in 1901 was probably less an endorsement of his brand of reform than a public reaction against the excesses of Tammany.[9]

As New York's mayor, Low brought in experts to operate the various departments, pared away Tammany's payroll padding, and set himself up as the businessman in office. He cut salaries, increased the length of the working day for municipal employees, and reduced the city's annual budget by $1,500,000. In the public transit and utility field, Low saw to it that franchises were carefully drafted to safeguard the city's interests and to provide for additional revenue. He failed to press for lower rates, to agitate for a public rate-making body, or to instruct his district attorney to investigate the corrupt alliances between private business and politicians. He balked at appointing one of the best-qualified housing reformers, Lawrence Veiller, to head the tenement house commission, apparently because Low did not wish to disturb the conservative real estate interests. Low was willing, however, to use the full force of law against Sunday drinking, petty gambling, and prostitution, which were commonly found in the immigrant and lower class sections of the city. The Bureau of Licenses also cracked down on the city's 6,000 pushcart peddlers who were operating without licenses, and the Department of Law prosecuted residents whose tax payments were delinquent. With similar zeal, the Department of Water raised nearly $1,000,000 in income from overdue water bills.[10]

Low's tinkering with the machinery of government, his charter revision and rewriting, his regularization of tax collections, his enforcement of the city statutes, his appointment of men of merit, and his reduction of city expenditures were laudable actions by almost anybody's test of good government. Unfortunately, these measures bore most severely upon the lower classes. Low's structural reforms were also very impolitic, as his defeat in the election of 1903 demonstrated. Low never seemed to realize that his municipal reform had nothing to offer the voters but sterile, mechanical changes and that fundamental social and economic conditions which pressed upon the vast urban masses of immigrants and poor could not be changed by rewriting charters or enforcing laws.[11]

San Francisco's reform mayor James D. Phelan, a wealthy banker and anti-Bryan Democrat who held office from 1897 to 1902, was also a structural reformer like his model, Seth Low, whom Phelan frequently quoted. Phelan's program for reform included the introduction of efficiency and economy to ensure "scientific, systematic and responsible government," which was also the goal of the San Francisco Merchants' Association. Franchise regulation, lower traction rates, municipal ownership, and equal taxation were not part of Phelan's design for a better San Francisco. The distinguishing mark of the Phelan administration was its sponsorship of a strong mayor, and a short ballot charter that provided rigid fiscal controls over expenditures, city-wide elections for the council, and a merit system. Known as a "watchdog of the treasury," Mayor Phelan supported a low tax rate that forced the city to withhold schoolteachers' salaries, suspend many of the essential functions of the city health department, subject patients at the city hospital to inadequate care, and turn off the street lights at midnight. Phelan crippled his administration when he permitted the president of the police commissioners (who was also president of the Chamber of Commerce) to protect strikebreakers and club pickets during a teamsters' and a dock-workers' strike against the open shop. Although the 18 unions lost their strike, they retaliated by forming their own political party and defeating the reformers in 1901. In the famous graft prosecutions after 1901, Phelan continued to act like a "member of his class" or, as Fremont Older put it, "a rich man toward a great business in which he is interested."[12] Like Low, Phelan failed to attack what social reformers recognized as the basic problems confronting the city.

Equally ineffectual in his attempt to make New York the best governed city in the nation was Mayor John Purroy Mitchel, who served from 1914 to 1917. He was an "oddly puritanical Catholic" who represented the foibles and virtues of patrician class reform. Mitchel's election in 1913 was the result of voter reaction to a decade of brazen looting by Tammany Hall. Like his reform predecessors, Mitchel was responsible for little of lasting importance and did not generate enthusiasm among the large mass of voters with his structural reforms.[13]

Mitchel's failure was due to his misconception that city government could be conducted by the "ledger book ethics of the corporation accountant." So dedicated was Mitchel to budgetary cutbacks that he adopted the Gary Plan of education, which enabled New York City to cram more children into the existing schools. He decreased appropriations for the city's night schools, thus seriously hampering the entire program; for the summer program, Mitchel asked the teachers to volunteer their services without remuneration. Mitchel also appointed cost-cutting charity agents who began either to return feeble-minded children to their parents or to threaten to charge the often hard-pressed parents if their children were kept in public supported institutions. In addition, he instituted an investigation of the city's religious child care organizations, hoping thus to cut the city subsidy; but this action brought the wrath of the Catholic church down upon him.[14] Mitchel, although well-intentioned, had a kind of King Midas touch in reverse: everything he touched seemed to turn to ashes.

Robert Moses dismissed the Mitchel administration's efficiency drives as "saving rubber bands" and "using both ends of the pencil," but its flaws were much greater. The Mitchel administration and the structural reform movement were not only captives of a modern business mentality but sought to impress middle and upper class social values upon the urban community and to redistribute political power to the patrician class.[15]

Built upon a narrow middle and patrician class base and a business concept of social responsibility, the structural reform movement, with its zeal for efficiency and economy, usually lacked staying power. As George Washington Plunkitt pointed out, such crusaders were usually repudiated by lower class voters after a brief tenure in office. Unlike the social reformers, who were also interested in economy, the structural reformers had a blind spot when it came to weighing the human cost of their programs. They failed to recognize that a dose of something as astringent as wage-cutting and payroll audits had to be counterbalanced with social welfare programs if the public were to be served effectively. Too often they blamed the immigrant for the city's shortcomings or directed much of the force of their administrations to exterminating low-class vices, which they saw as the underlying causes of municipal problems.[16]

Unlike the structural reformers, social reform mayors such as Hazen S. Pingree (1890–97), "Golden Rule" Jones (1897–1903), Tom Johnson (1901–09), Mark Fagan (1901–07), Brand Whitlock (1906–13), and Newton D. Baker (1912–16) began with a different set of assumptions about the basic causes of misgovernment in the cities. They shared the view, which Lincoln Steffens later publicized, that big business and its quest for preferential treatment and special privileges had corrupted municipal government. The public service corporations, the utilities, the real estate interests, and the large industrial concerns all had vested interests in urban America. They sought special tax advantages, franchises which eliminated competition, and other municipal concessions. They bought aldermen, councilmen, and mayors to protect these interests and, in the process, demoralized urban politics and city government. Mayor Tom Johnson's aide Frederic C. Howe was shocked when he was berated by his upper class friends for opposing a franchise steal; they explained that the public utilities have "millions of dollars invested" and had to "protect their investments." "But I do say emphatically," declared Mayor Pingree in 1895, "... better take [the utilities] out of private hands than allow them to stand as the greatest corruptors of public morals that ever blackened the pages of history."[17]

The programs of the social reform mayors aimed at lower gas, light, telephone, and street railway rates for the community and higher taxes for railroads and business corporations. When they were unable to obtain the regulation of public utilities, these mayors fought for municipal ownership, the only technique to redistribute economic power available to them as urban executives. Establishment of free public baths, expansions of parks, schools, and public relief were similarly attempts to distribute the amenities of middle class life to the masses. The social reformers recognized that the fight against crime in its commonly understood sense (i.e. rooting out gambling, drinking, and prostitution) was an attempt to treat the symptoms rather than the disease itself and that such campaigns would burn out the energies of a reform administration and leave the fundamental problems of the urban masses untouched. Pingree, like Jones and Johnson, believed that such binges of "Comstockery" were irrelevant to municipal reform. "The good people are always insisting upon 'moral' issues," asserted Toledo

Mayor Brand Whitlock, "urging us to turn aside from our large immediate purpose, and concentrate our official attention on the 'bad' people — and wreck our movement."[18]

The saloons where drinking, gambling, and other vices flourished, Pingree, Jones, and Johnson agreed, were but poor men's clubs and offered the workers but a few of the comforts that most rich men enjoyed. "The most dangerous enemies to good government are not the saloons, the dives, the dens of iniquity and the criminals," Pingree told the Springfield, Massachusetts, Board of Trade. "Most of our troubles can be traced to the temptations which are offered to city officials when franchises are sought by wealthy corporations, or contracts are to be let for public works." For refusing to divert public attention from the "larger and more complex immoralities" of the "privileged" interests, as Brand Whitlock put it, to the more familiar vices, the social reformers earned the bitter censure of the ministerial and "uplift" groups.[19]

The whole tone of the social reform movement was humanistic and empirical. It did not attempt to prescribe standards of personal morality nor did it attempt to draft social blueprints or city charters which had as their goals the imposition of middle class morality and patrician values upon the masses. Instead, it sought to find the basic causes of municipal misgovernment. Pingree, the first of the broad gauged social reformers, discovered the sources of municipal corruption in his day-to-day battle with the light, gas, telephone, and traction interests, the latter represented at the time by Tom Johnson. Johnson, like Mayor Newton D. Baker, knew from his own experience as a utility magnate why municipal government had been demoralized. Mayor Mark Fagan discovered that Jersey City could neither regulate nor tax the utilities and the railroads because both parties were dominated by these interests.[20]

In attempting to reform the city, Pingree, Jones, Johnson, and Whitlock lost upper class and business support and were forced to rely upon the lower classes for political power. The structural reformers, on the other hand, were frequently members of and sponsored by the very social and economic classes which most vehemently opposed social reform. "If we had to depend upon these classes for reforms," Pingree told the *Outlook* in 1897, "they could never have been brought about." "It is not so much the undercrust as the upper crust," asserted Professor Edward Bemis, who served as a Pingree aide, "that threatens the interests of the people."[21]

The inability of the structural reformers to pursue positive programs to alter the existing social and economic order was probably a reflection of their own business and class backgrounds. Their high regard for the sacrosanct nature of private property, even if obtained illegally, limited them to treating but one aspect of the municipal malaise, and then only when corruption by urban machines reached an intolerable point. This half-way attempt at urban reform prompted Brand Whitlock to observe in 1914: "The word 'reformer' like the word 'politician' has degenerated, and, in the mind of the common man, come to connotate something very disagreeable. In four terms as mayor I came to know both species pretty well, and, in the latter connotations of the term, I prefer politician. He, at least, is human."[22]

The structural reform tradition drew much of its strength from a diverse group of theorists composed of good government people, spokesmen for the business community, civic uplifters, representatives of taxpayers' associations, editors, and college professors. The most prominent and influential spokesmen of this persuasion were the Englishman James Bryce, college professors Frank J. Goodnow and William B. Munro, and the editor and scholar Albert Shaw. These theorists diagnosed problems of the city differently from the social reformers. Of fundamental importance to the models they formulated to bring about better city government was their view of the basic causes of the urban malaise. New York's problems, according to Professor Frank Goodnow, had begun in 1857, when the "middle classes, which had thus far controlled the municipal government, were displaced by an ignorant proletariat, mostly foreign born." Three decades later, James Bryce, who dealt with the problems of the city in one of the most influential books of his age, observed that the same "droves of squalid men, who looked as if they had just emerged from an emigrant ship" were herded by urban bosses before magistrates to be enrolled as voters. Such men, said Bryce, were "not fit for suffrage" and "incompetent to give an intelligent vote." Furthermore, their odious habits and demeanor had driven "cultivated" and "sensitive" men out of political life and discouraged the business classes from assuming their share of civic responsibility. One of the most able students of comparative municipal government, Albert Shaw, agreed with Bryce and Goodnow and concluded that the foreign-born had provided the opportunities for the "corruptionist and the demagogue,"[23] who had demoralized city government and lowered the tone of civic responsibility. The immigrant was central to the analyses of the theorists: although a few of them admitted other contributing factors, it is doubtful that any of them believed that the quality of civic responsibility, the level of public morality, and the honesty of urban administrations could have sunk as low had not the immigrant been present in overwhelming numbers in American cities.

Unlike the immigration restrictionists, the theorists did not distinguish between the new and old immigrants but lumped them together with the urban lower classes and attacked the political agencies that had facilitated the rise to power of these new groups. Even the newcomers from Northern Europe "knowing nothing of the institutions of the country, of its statesmen, of its political issues," Bryce argued. "Neither from Germany nor from Ireland do they bring much knowledge of the methods of free government." Lower class representatives from the wards were not welcome in municipal circles, for presumably the district system produced "inferior men" of "narrowed horizons," or as Alfred Conkling put it, permitted the balance of power to be held by the "worst class of men." "Wards largely controlled by thieves and robbers," Cornell's Andrew D. White warned, ". . . can control the city." Harvard's Professor Munro argued that the ward system elected councils that only wasted time and money in "fruitless debate" and sent to councils men "whose standing in the community is negligible." The ward system of representation was denounced by Professors Goodnow and Munro and Delos F. Wilcox for producing the worst representatives in the city. The National Municipal League's model charter called upon municipalities to abolish local representation. In Goodnow's view there were no local interests worthy of political representation anyway.[24]

In building their case against the ability of a mass urban electorate to rule itself, the theorists also drew upon psychology and history. The "craving for excitement" and the "nervous tension" of the city had a degenerative effect, Delos F. Wilcox argued, for "urban life tends to endanger the popular fitness for political power and responsibility." City populations were "radical rather than conservative," and "impulsive rather than reflective," asserted Goodnow, and far less inclined than rural populations to have "regard for the rights of private property." This was caused in part by the fact, Goodnow continued, that urban residents, unlike rural, had "no historical associations" with the cities in which they lived and thus had a poorly developed "neighborhood feeling." The elective system that depended upon familiar relationships and a cohesive community for its success was thus a failure in the city. Goodnow was also disturbed by his study of the larger contours of Western municipal history which convinced him that when city populations had been permitted to develop free of outside control, they evinced an "almost irresistible tendency to establish oligarchical or despotic government." American cities that were under Boss rule, in his opinion, showed similar tendencies.[25]

The first solutions proposed by many spokesmen of reform were hardly original. Outright disfranchisement had been suggested frequently since the end of the Civil War. Some cities had enacted stiffer registration requirements to pare down the vote of the unwashed, and some states had followed the pattern of Michigan, which revoked the alien franchise in 1894. Just as effective, although less direct, was the 1876 recommendation of the New York commissioners for the creation of an upper house with control over money bills in New York City, which was to be elected by propertied voters.[26]

The theorists, however, appear to have been inspired by a contemporary historical event. Drawing upon the Southern experience of disfranchising the Negro, Albert Shaw and Frank Goodnow suggested that such a measure might be applied to Northern cities. The "grandfather clause" apparently convinced Goodnow that the nation was not irrevocably committed to universal suffrage: once the people became convinced that "universal suffrage inevitably must result in inefficient and corrupt government, it will be abandoned," he predicted. The safeguards of suffrage, Fourteenth and Fifteenth Amendments, did not pose insurmountable obstacles, argued Goodnow. He dismissed the Fourteenth Amendment as merely an appeal to Congress, and he pointed out that the Fifteenth left room for educational and property qualifications.[27]

Accepting the Southern solution as reasonable, Shaw argued that the franchise in the North should be "absolutely" restricted to those who could read English, and "in the case of the foreign-born, to those showing positive fitness for participation in our political and governmental life." Furthermore Shaw argued that European immigrants should be directed southward where they would provide competition for Negroes which would result in a beneficial "survival of the fittest." In order to upgrade the quality of the urban electorate, Professor Munro recommended that the literacy test for the franchise should be extended throughout the nation. Universal suffrage was a "sacrifice of common sense to abstract principles," Bryce asserted. "Nobody pretends that such persons [immigrant voters] are fit for civic duty, or will be dangerous if kept for a time in pupilage, but neither party will incur the odium of proposing to exclude them."[28]

Although demands to purge the unfit elements from urban voting lists were often voiced during the 1890's, it became apparent that such a solution was too drastic. Few civic federations and even fewer politicians picked up the suggestion. Despite the prestige and influence of the theorists, it was evident that disfranchisement was unacceptable to the American public as a way to solve its urban problems. Clearly, less abrasive and more refined techniques would have to be found.

The theorists often spoke of installing into office the "better" classes, the "best" citizens and civic patriots. Excluded were labor, ethnic, or lower class representatives. As Goodnow put it, their choice was "men engaged in active business" or professionals, presumably associated with the business community. The theorists did not distinguish between big and small businessmen, or between entrepreneurs and financiers. What they wanted, as Conkling expressed it, was "any business or professional man . . . who has been successful in private life" and who was reasonably honest. As Richard T. Ely observed, the battle cries of the good government crowd in the 1890's had been: "Municipal government is business not politics." "Wanted, A municipal administration on purely business principles." If one accepted the premise it followed logically, as Ely noted, that businessmen were the "natural and inevitable directors of local affairs."[29]

The theorists argued that the business of city government was business and not politics. The "purely administrative functions—that is to say business functions—outweighed the political functions nine to one," declared Walter Arndt. They extensively used the modern business corporation as a model in their discussions of city government; some called the citizens "stockholders," and others referred to the council as the "board of directors" and the mayor as the "chairman of the board." They spoke of the pressing need for efficiency, the complexity of urban problems, and favored the use of experts to replace elected amateurs. Goodnow argued that a clear distinction must be drawn between legislative and administrative duties and that municipal departments must be staffed by experts. Munro warned that public opinion was the "worst" enemy of the expert and therefore should be rendered less influential in municipal decision-making.

In short, the theorists were arguing that the role of public opinion and political expression should be substantially reduced in governing the modern city.[30]

In urging the reconstruction of city government, the theorists called for far-reaching changes in city charters. They advocated a strong mayor system, which accorded with what most of them knew about New York City politics: at least once during each decade since the end of the Civil War, "reformers" had been able to win the mayorality, although they repeatedly failed to control the city council. The theorists also recommended that the mayor be given complete authority to appoint members to the various municipal boards. Board members, they argued, should serve without pay since this would remove the mercenary motive that prompted professional politicians to serve and, incidentally, would eliminate most of those without substantial wealth as well. If those who got their "living out of their salaries" could be excluded from municipal office, Goodnow argued, the way would be open for the "business and professional classes" to assume control of the city.[31] At the lower levels of municipal administration, Shaw, Goodnow, and Munro recommended a thoroughgoing application of the civil service system, which also tended to eliminate ethnic and lower class representatives. A professional civil service at the lower grades, the theorists argued, would create a good technical and supportive staff and, as Goodnow put it, "make it possible for the business and professional classes of the community to assume the care of public business without making too great personal sacrifices."[32]

The recommendations of the theorists aimed at weakening popular control over the legislative arm of government, the city council. Goodnow was convinced that the council system, since it provided so many "incompetent if not corrupt men," should not be a powerful force in municipal government. Goodnow was more favorably impressed by municipal arrangements in Berlin, Germany, where a propertied electorate comprising less than 10 per cent of the voters elected two-thirds of the city council. "This gives to the wealthier class the directing voice in municipal affairs," commented Professor Leo S. Rowe with approval. Andrew D. White argued that men of property should be represented by a board of control, "without whose permission no franchise should be granted and no expenditure should be made." The English system which in effect disfranchised most lower class slum residents also met with Goodnow's favor. Councils elected by a non-propertied franchise disturbed Goodnow, for such bodies often prodded cities into "undertakings which are in excess of the city's economic resources." Evidently pessimistic about changing the basis of municipal suffrage to one of property, Goodnow reversed the formula and suggested that to extend the tax-paying obligation to more citizens might produce better councils. That failing, he supported state intervention to limit taxing and spending of municipal governments. "The trouble with leaving our cities to govern themselves, at least along purely democratic lines," argued C. E. Pickard, is "that they are utterly unworthy of trust."[33]

The theorists also argued for fewer elective offices and smaller city councils. "Men of little experience and less capacity have found it easy to get themselves elected to membership in large city councils," asserted Munro. Smaller councils would presumably concentrate responsibility and produce better men. The at-large election was a favorite device of the theorists and one of the most important structural changes they proposed. City-wide elections to the council, in their opinion, could be won only by men of commanding presence and city-wide prominence. Obviously the lower class politician or the ethnic representative who served his ward well would come out second best if pitted against a prominent businessman or professional. Not until late in the Progressive period, after the at-large system began to elect the "better classes" into office, did the theorists return to decentralizing authority and to expanding the powers of councilmen who then would be known as city commissioners. The ideas of the theorists make it difficult to quibble with Frederic C. Howe's observation: "Distrust of democracy has inspired much of the literature on the city."[34]

Agencies to regulate utility rates, to investigate tax inequities, or to foster and advance social reform were not on the drawing boards of the theorists. Few of them focused their wrath and moral indignation upon the corrupting influence of privately owned utilities and the real estate interests on city councils. They were less bothered by the businessman who bribed the city council than by the machine politician who accepted the bribe. Yerkes and Whitney seldom warranted their attention in the way that Tweed did. They chose instead to focus responsibility upon the individuals who sat on councils and the political systems that elected them rather than upon the business interests that sought favorable franchises, tax favoritism, and city services, such as paving, sewers, and water, which enhanced the value of their enterprises.

The ideas of the theorists were not lost upon the practitioners and designers of good city government. The structural reformers began to design new forms of urban organization and to codify the ideas of the theorists into new city charters. Two decades of searching and theorizing produced the city commissioner and later the city manager systems.

The theorists provided the rationale for the most radical departure the American city took in all its history. The widespread adoption of the commissioner and manager systems late in the Progressive period brought about what one scholar called a "revolution in the theory and practice of city government." Although the commissioner system had its origins in an accident of nature, it and the manager plan soon became the favored devices for achieving what the old political system could not — namely, the large scale movement of businessmen and business-minded representatives into public office. Both systems were patterned after the modern business corporation and rapidly adopted its ideals. Henry Bruère, a director of the New York Bureau of Municipal Research, boasted that commission governments were often made a "part of the progressive programs of 'boosting' commercial organizations." "Money saving and efficiency" were pursued as key objectives under the manager plan. The "Godfather of City Managerism," Richard S. Childs, observed that the city managers at their fourth annual conference could "unblushingly point with pride" to an average savings of 10 per cent in tax levies in the cities under his brain child. The first city manager of the publicized "Dayton Plan," Henry M. Waite, admitted that the "main thing" the nation's fifty manager towns had accomplished up to 1917 was a "financial saving." "Economy, not service," James Weinstein correctly asserted, was the "basic principle" of both the commissioner and manager systems. As Harold A. Stone has suggested, and Weinstein has demonstrated, no important reform movement of the Progressive period was more peculiarly the captive of organized business than the commissioner and manager movements.[35]

Although the commissioner and manager systems achieved their greatest success in middle-sized and smaller cities, they represented the ultimate ideal of the earlier theorists (whose major concern had been large American cities). Commissioner and manager reorganization brought about in its finished form the structural arrangements that facilitated the movement into office of that class of people whom Bryce, Goodnow, Munro, and Shaw believed best fitted and qualified to rule the city. Chambers of commerce and the dominant business groups were the main force behind the movement, and, as James Weinstein and Samuel P. Hays have demonstrated, these new forms facilitated the inflow of the commercial and upper class elements into the centers of municipal power at the price of ethnic and lower class representation.[36] The business model of municipal government would eventually spread to nearly one-half of our cities, and the structural-reform persuasion would dominate the main stream of urban reform thought in the twentieth century.[37] This extension of the instruments and the ideology of the business world would help to return to power men with the temperaments of Havemeyer, Cleveland, and Low and considerably diminish the electoral prospects for men like Pingree, Jones, and Johnson—as well as like Tweed.

The conservative revolution in city government would also help to end the process whereby astute politicians and socially-conscious reformers used the political system to ease the shock of assimilation for newcomers into American life. The political machine may have been one of the most important institutions not only for acknowledging the immigrant's existence but for interpreting a new environment to him and helping him to adjust to a bewildering new society.

By concentrating on the mechanistic and bureaucratic aspects of city government and by throwing the weight of their influence behind the election of businessmen, the theorists grossly oversimplified the problems of the city. Wiping out lower class and foreign-born corruption unfortunately took precedence in their minds over the social needs of the city. The theorists confined themselves to dealing with the plumbing and hardware of city government and finally became narrow administrative reformers. In the process, they deceived themselves and helped to mislead a generation of reformers into thinking that they were dealing with the fundamental problems of the city, when in reality they were retooling the machinery of urban government to fit the needs of the business world. . . .

NOTES

1. Lincoln Steffens, *The Autobiography of Lincoln Steffens* (New York, 1931), pp. 374–75; Hewitt quoted in *Pilgrim*, III (December, 1901), 4.

2. Hazen S. Pingree, "Address to the Nineteenth Century Club of New York," November 11, 1897, p. 7; S. M. Jones to Josiah Strong, November 15, 1898, Jones Papers; Brand Whitlock, *Forty Years of It* (New York, 1914), pp. 172–74.

3. Frederic C. Howe, *The City: The Hope of Democracy* (New York, 1913), pp. 1, 2. For the elitist views of reformers who overthrew Boss Tweed, see Alexander B. Callow, Jr., *The Tweed Ring* (New York, 1966), pp. 69–71, 265–67. Charles R. Adrian, "Some General Characteristics of Nonpartisan Elections," Robert C. Wood, "Nonpartisanship in Suburbia," both in *Democracy in Urban America*, ed. Oliver P. Williams and Charles Press (Chicago, 1964), pp. 251–66. For an exposition of the views regarding muncipal government of one of the most prominent twentieth-century "structural" reformers, see Richard S. Childs, "The Faith of a Civic Reformer," *ibid.*, pp. 222–24. The "elitist commitments" of the city manager system (as prescribed in city government textbooks) can also be seen in Lawrence J. R. Herson, "The Lost World of Municipal Government," *American Political Science Review*, LI (June, 1957), 330–45.

4. Howard B. Furer, *William Frederick Havemeyer: A Political Biography* (New York, 1965), pp. 14, 144–54, 160; Seymour J. Mandelbaum, *Boss Tweed's New York* (New York, 1965), pp. 91, 97, 108, 111; Callow, *The Tweed Ring*, pp. 253–86.

5. Mandelbaum, *Boss Tweed's New York*, pp. 98–100, 111; Furer, *William F. Havemeyer*, pp. 156, 158, 160–61, 169.

6. *Ibid.*, p. 161; Mandelbaum, *Boss Tweed's New York*, pp. 112–13; William L. Riordin, *Plunkitt of Tammany Hall* (New York, 1963), p. 17.

7. Harold Coffin Syrett, *The City of Brooklyn 1865–1898, A Political History* (New York, 1944), p. 134; Steven C. Swett, "The Test of a Reformer A Study of Seth Low," *New York Historical Society Quarterly*, XLIV (January, 1960), pp. 8, 9; Lincoln Steffens, *The Shame of the Cities* (New York, 1966), p. 201.

8. Syrett, *Brooklyn*, pp. 104–6, 109–19, 134; Swett, "Test of a Reformer," pp. 7–9.

9. Albert Fein, "New York City Politics From 1897–1903; A Study in Political Party Leadership" (M.A. thesis, Columbia University, 1954), pp. 19–20; Swett, "Test of a Reformer," pp. 10–14, 16–18.

10. *Ibid*, pp. 21–23, 26–31, 35–36; Roy Lubove, *The Progressives and the Slums, Tenement House Reform in New York City, 1890–1917* (Pittsburgh, 1962), pp. 153–54.

11. Swett, "Test of Reformer," pp. 6, 32, 35–36, 38–41; Wallace S. Sayre and Herbert Kaufman, *Governing New York City Politics in the Metropolis* (New York, 1960), p. 695.

12. James D. Phelan, "Municipal Conditions and the New Charter," *Overland Monthly*, XXVIII (no. 163, 2nd series), pp. 104–11; Roy Swanstrom, "Reform Administration of James D. Phelan, Mayor of San Francisco, 1897–1902," (M. A.

thesis, University of California-Berkeley, 1949), pp. 77–79, 80, 83, 85, 86; Walton Bean, *Boss Ruef's San Francisco: The Story of the Union Labor Party, Big Business, and the Graft Prosecution* (Berkeley, 1952), pp. 8, 9, 16, 17, 23; George E. Mowry, *The California Progressives* (Chicago, 1963), pp. 23–25; Fremont Older, *My Own Story* (San Francisco, 1919), pp. 27, 31, 65.

13. William E. Leuchtenburg, Preface to Edwin R. Lewinson, *John Purroy Mitchel: The Boy Mayor of New York* (New York, 1965), pp. 11–13; Lewinson, *Boy Mayor,* pp. 93, 95, 100, 102, 117, 124.

14. Leuchtenburg, *ibid.,* p. 12; Lewinson, *ibid.,* pp. 18, 151–69, 175–88.

15. Leuchtenburg, *ibid.,* pp. 11–13; Samuel P. Hayes, "The Politics of Reform in Municipal Government," *Pacific Northwest Quarterly,* LV (October, 1964), pp. 157–69.

16. Lewinson, *Boy Mayor,* pp. 11–13, 18, 93, 95, 102; Riordin, *George Washington Plunkitt,* pp. 17–20; Swett, "Seth Low," pp. 8, 9; Allan Nevins, *Abram S. Hewitt: With Some Account of Peter Cooper* (New York, 1935), pp. 515–16, 529–30; Seth Low, "An American View of Municipal Government in the United States," in James Bryce, *The American Commonwealth* (New York, 1893), I, 651, 665.

17. Hoyt Landon Warner, *Progressivism in Ohio 1897–1917* (Columbus, 1964), pp. 32, 70–72; Whitlock, *Forty Years of It,* pp. 211, 252; Clarence H. Cramer, *Newton D. Baker: A Biography* (Cleveland, 1961), pp. 46–47; Steffens, *Autobiography of Lincoln Steffens,* pp. 477, 492–93; Frederic C. Howe, *The Confessions of a Reformer* (New York, 1925), pp. 98, 102–8; Pingree, *Facts and Opinions,* p. 196. For Mark Fagan, see Lincoln Steffens, *Upbuilders* (New York, 1909), pp. 28, 30, 33, 35, and Ransom E. Noble, Jr., *New Jersey Progressivism before Wilson* (Princeton, 1946), pp. 13–42. St. Louis circuit Attorney Joseph W. Folk (1901–04), who began his career by investigating and prosecuting franchise "grabs," discovered that the real despoilers of municipal government were not minor city officials but promoters, bankers, and corporation directors who profited by misgovernment. After he became governor he dropped his crime-busting and supported progressive and urban reforms. Louis G. Geiger, *Joseph W. Folk of Missouri* (Columbia, 1953), pp. 32, 41, 81, 88, 93, 99–117. Robert Wiebe's assertion that the "typical business ally of the boss, moreover, was a rather marginal operator, anathema to the chamber of commerce" is at variance with what is known about the political influence wielded in Detroit by urban capitalists such as the Hendries, McMillans and Johnson or for that matter with the role played by Yerkes and Insull in Chicago, Mark Hanna in Cleveland and the Huntington interests in Los Angeles, just to cite a few examples. *The Search for Order, 1877–1920* (New York, 1967), p. 167.

18. Steffens, *Upbuilders,* pp. 3–45; Warner, *Progressivism in Ohio, 1897–1917,* pp. 71, 74; Cramer, *Newton D. Baker,* pp. 50–52; Howe, *Confessions of a Reformer,* pp. 90–93, 108–9; Carl Lorenz, *Tom L. Johnson, Mayor of Cleveland* (New York, 1911), p. 152; Steffens, *Autobiography of Lincoln Steffens,* p. 480; Detroit *Free Press,* March 14, 1896, P.S.; Samuel M. Jones to Henry D. Lloyd, April 16, 1897, Lloyd Papers; Samuel M. Jones to James L. Cowes, April 27, 1897; Tom L. Johnson to S. M. Jones, May 3, 1902, Jones Papers; Harvey S. Ford, "The Life and Times of Golden Rule Jones" (Ph.D. thesis, University of Michigan, 1953), pp. 185, 284–85, 330; Whitlock, *Forty Years of It,* p. 212. William D. Miller has argued that "Boss" Edward H. Crump, who was Memphis mayor from 1910 to 1916, stands with "Golden Rule" Jones and Tom L. Johnson as a typical progressive of the period,

but an examination of Miller's book raises serious doubts about that judgment. Although Crump occasionally employed reform rhetoric, established a few milk stations for the poor, and put screens on public school windows, he used most of the energy of his administration to enforce the laws and instill efficiency into the municipal government in the structural-reform tradition. Crump wiped out "policy" playing by Negroes, eliminated loafing by the garbage collectors and street pavers, forced the railroads to construct eleven underpasses, lowered city taxes, reduced waste in municipal government by extending audit procedures even to the purchase of postage stamps, and increased city income by selling empty bottles, feed sacks, and scrap. William D. Miller, *Mr. Crump of Memphis* (Baton Rouge, 1964), pp. 79–113. Brooklyn's Mayor Charles A. Schieren (1894–95), who gained some stature as a reformer by defeating a venal Democratic machine, also followed a well-trodden path of cleaning out "deceit and corruption" and installing "integrity, nonpartisanship, and routine efficiency." Like most of the reform mayors of his period, Schieren failed to advance or support social reform programs. Harold C. Syrett, *The City of Brooklyn, 1865–1898, A Political History* (New York, 1944), pp. 218–32. Geoffrey Blodgett has tried to show that Boston became for "a brief time the cutting edge of urban reform in America" under Mayor Josiah Quincy (1896–1900), who established a publicly owned printing plant and expanded the city's playgrounds. Although the Dover Street Bath House may have been a "monument to municipal socialism" as Blodgett contends, Mayor Quincy stopped his programs short of anything that would have threatened the vested interests in the traction and utility business. Geoffrey Blodgett, *The Gentle Reformers: Massachusetts Democrats in the Cleveland Era* (Cambridge, 1966), pp. 240–61. For Quincy's absurd notion that regular bathing would cause the "filthy tenement house" to disappear, crime and drunkenness to decrease and the death rate to drop, see Josiah Quincy, "Municipal Progress in Boston," *Independent,* LII (February 15, 1900), 424. Henry Demarest Lloyd was critical of Mayor Quincy's failure to resist the traction interests and referred to the Mayor's public baths as Quincy's "little sops." H. D. Lloyd to Samuel Bowles, December 13, 1898, Lloyd Papers.

19. Ford, "Golden Rule Jones," pp. 151, 166, 339; Samuel M. Jones to Dr. [Graham] Taylor, October 5, 1897; S. M. Jones to L. L. Dagett, April 17, 1899, Jones Papers; Hazen S. Pingree address to Springfield, Massachusetts Board of Trade, March 3, 1894, Ralph Stone Scrapbook; Whitlock, *Forty Years of It,* pp. 252, 254.

20. Robert H. Bremner, "The Civic Revival in Ohio: The Fight Against Privilege in Cleveland and Toledo, 1890–1912," (Ph.D. thesis, Ohio State Univeristy, 1943), p. 25; Hazen S. Pingree, "The Problem of Municipal Reform. Contract by Referendum," *Arena,* XVII (April, 1897), 707–10; Cramer, *Newton D. Baker,* p. 46; Steffens, *Upbuilders,* pp. 28–30, 33, 35; Noble, *New Jersey Progressivism before Wilson,* pp. 25–26, 35, 38.

21. Tom L. Johnson, *My Story* (New York, 1911), p. 113; Ford, "Golden Rule Jones," pp. 136–37, 170, 339; Hazen S. Pingree, "Detroit: A Municipal Study," *Outlook,* LV (February 6, 1897), 437; Bemis quoted in Detroit *Evening News:* June 21, 1899, Stone Scrapbook; Whitlock, *Forty Years of It,* p. 221.

22. Whitlock, *Forty Years of It,* p. 221.

23. Frank J. Goodnow, "The Tweed Ring in New York City," in James Bryce's *The American Commonwealth* (London, 1888), II, 335; Bryce, *ibid.,* p. 67; Bryce, *ibid.,* I, 613; Albert Shaw, *Political Problems of American Development* (New York, 1907),

p. 66. According to Edwin L. Godkin, New York City's problems began with the establishment of universal suffrage in 1846 which coincided with the beginning of the great Irish migration. Edwin L. Godkin, *Problems of Modern Democracy,* ed. Morton Keller (New York, 1896, Cambridge, 1966), p. 133.

24. Bryce, *American Commonwealth,* II, 67; William B. Munro, *The Government of American Cities* (New York, 1913), pp. 308–9, 310, 312; Andrew D. White, "The Government of American Cities," *Forum,* x (December, 1890), 369; Alfred R. Conkling, *City Government in the United States* (New York, 1899), p. 49; Frank J. Goodnow, *Municipal Problems* (New York, 1897), pp. 150–53; Delos F. Wilcox, *The Study of City Government* (New York, 1897), p. 151; "Report of the Committee on Municipal Program," *Proceedings* of the Indianapolis Conference for Good City Government and Fourth Annual Meeting of the National Municipal League (Philadelphia, 1898), p. 11 (hereafter cited *Proceedings for Good City Government*).

25. Wilcox, *The Study of City Government,* pp. 237–38; Frank J. Goodnow, *Municipal Government* (New York, 1910), pp. 39, 149, 378–79; James T. Young, *Proceedings for Good City Government,* 1901, p. 230.

26. *Michigan Legislative Manual and Official directory 1899–1900* (Lansing, 1899), p. 322; *Report of the Commission to Devise a Plan for the Government of Cities in the State of New York* (New York, 1877) pp. 35–36.

27. Goodnow, *Municipal Problems,* pp, 148–49.

28. Shaw, *Political Problems of American Development,* pp. 65–67, 82, 125; Munro, *Government of American Cities,* pp. 120–21; Bryce, *American Commonwealth,* II, 67.

29. Goodnow, *Municipal Problems,* p. 278; Conkling, *City Government in the United States,* p. 34; Richard T. Ely, *The Coming City* (New York, 1902), p. 29.

30. Walter T. Arndt, *The Emancipation of the American City* (New York, 1917), p. 12; Frank M. Sparks, *Government As a Business* (Chicago, 1916), pp. 1, 7; Goodnow, *Municipal Government,* pp. 150, 381–82; Munro, *Government of American Cities,* p. 306; William H. Tolman, *Municipal Reform Movements in the United States* (New York, 1895), p. 34.

31. Conkling, *City Government in the United States,* pp. 6, 32; Goodnow, *Municipal Problems,* pp. 262–65.

32. *Ibid.,* pp. 204–5, 265; Munro, *Government of American Cities,* pp. 241, 279–80; Albert Shaw, "Civil Service Reform and Municipal Government," in *Civil Service Reform and Municipal Government* (New York, 1897), pp. 3–7.

33. Goodnow, *Municipal Government,* pp. 142–46, 385–86, and *Municipal Problems,* pp. 66–67; Leo S. Rowe, "City Government As It Should Be And May Become," *Proceedings for Good City Government, 1894,* p. 115; White, "The Government of American Cities, p. 370; John Agar, "Shall American Cities Municipalize?" *Municipal Affairs,* IV (March, 1900), 14–20; C. E. Pickard, "Great Cities and Democratic Institutions," *American Journal of Politics,* IV (April, 1894), 385. The Boston mayor Nathan Mathews, Jr., asserted that the proposal to restrict municipal suffrage to the propertied classes was one of the most common remedies for the evils of city government of his age. Nathan Mathews, Jr., *The City Government of Boston* (Boston, 1895), p. 176.

34. Munro, *Government of American Cities,* pp. 294, 308–10; Goodnow, *Municipal Problems,* pp. 150–53; Leo S. Rowe, "American Political Ideas and Institutions in

Their Relation to the Problem of the City," *Proceedings for Good City Government, 1897*, p. 77; William Dudley Foulke, *ibid., 1898*, p. 137; Frederic C. Howe, *The City, The Hope of Democracy* (New York, 1913), p. 1.

35. Henry Bruère, "Efficiency in City Government," *Annals* of the American Academy of Political and Social Science, XLI (May, 1912), 19; Richard S. Childs, "Now that We Have the City Manager Plan, What Are We Going to Do With It," *Fourth Yearbook of the City Managers' Association* (Auburn, 1918), pp. 82–83; Henry M. Waite, *ibid.*, pp. 88–89; Harold A. Stone, Don K. Price and Kathryn H. Stone, *City Manager Government in the United States* (Chicago, 1940).

36. *Ibid.*, p. 173; Samuel P. Hayes, "The Politics of Reform in Municipal Government in the Progressive Era," *Pacific Northwest Quarterly*, LV (October, 1964), 157–69.

37. Edward C. Banfield and James Q. Wilson, *City Politics* (New York, 1963), p. 148.

20

The Limits of Urban Reform: New York's Tenements and Chicago's Ghetto*

Michael B. Katz

Early in the twentieth century, housing reform finally emerged as an important national urban campaign. Because it enlisted every variety of urban expert, housing reform, even though it failed, illustrates both the style and limits of urban reform. Like health care delivery, housing reform bumped up against the boundaries between public responsibility and private prerogative; neither state legislatures, municipal governments, nor the activists who organized the national housing reform movement were willing to enter directly into the housing market. With only regulation and inspection as tools, housing reformers could not assure an adequate supply of low-cost housing to the urban poor or renovate the slums. Indeed, housing reformers, including major settlement house leaders, not only capitulated before the market; they shared the racism of their times. As a consequence, they not only failed to eradicate the slum; they helped build the ghetto.

New York City, which had the worst housing problem in the country,

*Katz, Michael B. 1986. "The Limits of Urban Reform: New York's Tenements and Chicago's Ghetto." Pp. 171–178 and 310–311. *In the Shadow of the Poorhouse: A Social History of Welfare in America.* New York: Basic Books. Copyright © 1986 by Basic Books, Inc. Reprinted by permission of Basic Books, a division of Harper Collins Publishers.

housed its poor primarily in tenements.[1] In other cities, where land was cheaper and population less congested, more of the poor still lived in small frame houses. Though often flimsy, crowded, and unsanitary, these houses were considered distinctly better than the tenements into which perhaps half of New York's population had been packed. Even though New York's housing problems were unique, the story of tenement house reform there is instructive. New Yorkers took the initial active interest in housing reform in America. They gave intellectual definition to the movement and sponsored a national campaign, headquartered in the city and led by Lawrence Veiller, the most important housing reformer in the country. New Yorkers also pioneered the strategies of housing reform adopted by other cities—model tenements and restrictive legislation—until the New Deal. Its practical influence, therefore, was very great. The reasons New York's housing reform failed, however, were not indigenous to the city. To the contrary, with special clarity, they showed how the contradictions between public responsibility and privatism played themselves out in the attempt to renovate the slums, guide the development of the city, and improve workers' housing.[2]

As in New York, revelations of Chicago's appalling housing conditions stimulated a housing reform movement. Two of its features are especially noteworthy. First, none of the discussions of housing problems mentioned living conditions among the city's black population, whose housing, by and large, was the worst in the city. Indeed, only the race riot of 1919 aroused any interest in black housing. Second, in Chicago, housing reform adopted the same tactics as in New York: a reliance on model housing and restrictive legislation.

New York had a serious housing problem as early as the 1840s when Irish immigrants crowded into the sections of Manhattan near the docks where they worked. Landlords subdivided houses and built tall new tenements wherever they chose, for the city had no regulations governing housing or land use. Appalled by the conditions it discovered, the Association for Improving the Condition of the Poor, the first organization to respond to the city's housing problem, constructed a model tenement in the 1850s. Because model tenements were supposed to demonstrate how decent working-class housing could be built and run at a profit, they represented, as Lubove points out, "less a solution to the housing problem than an evasion." Although in New York and elsewhere model tenements remained a favorite reform strategy throughout the nineteenth century, they never even dented urban housing problems. For one thing, the scale of the experiments was too small. For another, they never provided houses inexpensive enough for the very poorest people who needed help most. It simply remained impossible to construct housing that was cheap, decent, and profitable. Profit remained critical because model housing definitely was not a philanthropy. Rather, it was supposed to show how to improve the living conditions of the poor and still make money. It was, of course, an illusion.[3]

In 1879, an amendment to New York City's weak 1867 Tenement House Act permitted construction of the notoriously wretched dumbbell tenements which housed most of New York City's poor for the rest of the century. Within these six-story tenements crammed onto tiny lots, two dozen families crowded into small four-room apartments with a living room and kitchen, each about 10×11 feet and two bedrooms, perhaps 7×8, hardly more than closets. Only the living room had any direct light from the street. On each floor, two families usually shared each toilet, which was located in the hall, lighted and ventilated by the "air shaft."[4]

Housing reform drew its energy from the threat of moral collapse and social disorder. Although housing reformers had mixed moralism and fear with compassion since the 1840s, by the 1890s, their fears had escalated. Manhattan, after all, had become the most congested place in the world. Reformers observed with horror the growth of prostitution in the tenements; they had no idea how families could survive amid the dirt, smell, noise, and crowding in the slums. Nor did they forget the way the poor had exploded in the great draft riots of 1863. Jacob Riis warned, "the sea of a mighty population, held in galling fetters, heaves uneasily in the tenements." After 1890, housing reformers capitalized on the sentiment aroused by the publication of Jacob Riis's *How the Other Half Lives* to orchestrate a national housing reform movement, led by Lawrence Veiller, secretary of the COS Tenement House Committee. They also persuaded the state to appoint still another housing commission and to pass another weak tenement law.[5]

In 1900, Veiller's agitation culminated in a masterful tenement house exhibition, complete with models of tenement blocks and maps showing the correlation between high rates of disease, mortality, and bad housing. Within a year, the state had appointed yet another commission, this time with Veiller as its secretary. Its recommendations, most of which became law, outlawed the dumbbell tenement, created a municipal housing department with a staff of inspectors, and developed regulations designed to improve new buildings and encourage the renovation of old ones. Without doubt, the new law tenements were an improvement on the old dumbbells, and within two decades, many tenements had been "swept, garnished, and repaired," according to Edith Elmer Wood, a "well-informed student of housing." Although not all tenements were "immaculate," she found no "accumulations of filth," "no dilapidation or extreme disrepair." Still, the newest and best tenements remained too expensive for the very poor, who still crowded into old, unsatisfactory buildings, and no one argued that New York's working class was housed very well. By and large, New York's tenements were less dangerous, unsanitary, and unhealthful, but the great problems— how to prevent the housing situation from deteriorating again under the impact of population growth, how to assure working people housing they found satisfactory at a price they could afford, and how to provide minimally decent housing for the poor—still had not been solved.[6]

The businessmen and reformers who formed the City Homes Association in 1990, the first Chicago organization to focus on housing reform, brought in one of Veiller's closest associates, Charles Ball, to run their operation, and, in 1907, they managed to secure his appointment as head of the city's Sanitary Bureau, which he ran for the next 21 years. Although almost no model housing was built before 1920, in 1902 and 1910, the association persuaded the city council to pass tenement ordinances, which were the counterparts of the New York Tenement Act of 1901. The ordinances set out sanitary standards and building codes, which depended for enforcement on inspection. In practice, inspection proved a weak reform tool. Not only were there too few inspectors, but the system invited graft. According to Philpott, City Council members passed the 1901 ordinance so readily because they realized it was a "four-flush law," that is, "one which politicians passed for the purpose of soliciting graft in return for *not* enforcing it." The association also sponsored the Municipal Lodging House for homeless men — excluding blacks, who were not allowed to stay there — and the development of city parks and playgrounds, created by displacing thousands of poor people and leveling their homes. Neither the members of the association nor the settlement workers who supported their project showed any sympathy for the "protests of the uprooted families.[7]

In both Chicago and New York City the problem of housing for the poor remained unsolved partly because Veiller and most other influential Progressive era housing reformers refused to extend the role of government beyond restrictive legislation. Although Veiller seemed radical and dangerous to real estate and construction interests, he remained fundamentally conservative. Veiller believed that America's urban housing crisis could be solved — though not quickly — within the context of the market, and he rejected public housing on both economic and political grounds. Model municipal tenements, he argued, could never house more than a tiny fraction of the working class. Even more, public construction actually would curtail housing supply by discouraging private builders unwilling to compete with the government. Nor could government's involvement be contained. There would be no "limit to the scope of municipal building operations if once they were begun. If cities . . . are to become landlords at all, where should the wage line be drawn between those for whom they should and . . . should not provide? Where in practice, would the line be drawn in American cities where democracy reigns supreme, and the limit of public bounty would be ultimately fixed by popular vote?" Public housing would become another form of outdoor relief, demanded by everybody, generously doled out by politicians anxious to curry favor and build strong machines.[8]

For Veiller, the wretched housing that disfigured the lives of half the people who lived in New York had two great sources: greed and neglect. Regulation and inspection, he felt, could check both. Without destroying economic incentives by curtailing profits, they would insure that builders and landlords supplied the working class with safe, clean, sanitary housing. Willing to stretch, although not to cross, the fictive boundary between public responsibility and private prerogative, Veiller advocated an individual solution to a massive social problem. Government would not build, buy, or subsidize housing. Instead, it would control the behavior of individual builders and landlords. It would prevent them from doing harm (if it could), but how could it force them to do good? This is the question Veiller did not answer.[9]

Nor did any of the other serious approaches to the housing problem cross the boundary between public and private. Some reformers, appalled especially by congestion and crowding, advocated the garden city solution popularized in England by Ebenezer Howard, who wanted to uproot the working class from cities and move them into planned new towns in the countryside. But no garden cities were built in America. More important was zoning (developed first in Germany), which united housing reformers and the new city planning profession early in the twentieth century. Planners and reformers hoped "zoning would improve urban housing and living conditions by controlling population distribution." Businessmen often supported it because they felt it would "protect their financial interests." In New York City, a coalition of reformers and businessmen passed "America's first comprehensive zoning code" in 1916, but it suffered the same inherent weakness as housing reform: it was a negative policy that "could not clear slums," house the poor, or "establish criteria for satisfactory residential development."[10]

Not only builders and landlords objected to housing reform by regulation and inspection. By World War I, younger reformers familiar with European housing legislation and anxious to push state and local governments to positive, constructive action also attacked the restrictive or "negative" approach. However, until the New Deal, they had no chance to try their alternatives. In retrospect, the sorry history of public housing since then hardly makes them seem more prescient than Veiller and his colleagues. If Veiller could not recognize the contradictions between quality, cost, and profit, his critics could not foresee how the degradation of public responsibility in America would rob public housing of its potential and leave it just another form of welfare.[11]

Progressive era housing reformers not only failed to improve housing for the poor, they also helped build the ghetto. "The period between 1870 and 1915," claims Kenneth Kusmer, "may be called the formative years of the black ghetto in the United States." In these years, Southern blacks, attracted by industrial opportunity, began to drift into Northern cities. Although few "clear cut" ghettos appeared, the degree of residential segregation increased as the racism of the period, industrial relocation, and inexpensive mass transit reshaped American cities.[12]

In Chicago, before World War I, existing black neighborhoods accommodated the small but growing black population, which increased from 34,691 in 1870 to 44,103 by 1910. In each of the next two decades, the black population more than doubled; in 1920 it was 109,458 and in 1930, 233,803. After World War I, Chicago faced a housing crisis as the city's population growth exceeded its housing supply, and where the growing black population threatened to move into adjacent white neighborhoods, racial tensions flared. Whites used two tactics to prevent blacks from crossing the color line. One was violence: they beat blacks who moved into their neighborhoods and bombed their homes. Nor were the police any protection in racial clashes, because they usually sided with whites. The other tactic was forced exclusion, accomplished either through deed restrictions or racial covenants. The former, "covering a single parcel or a whole subdivision, was common" early in the century; racial covenants by which residents formally agreed not to sell their property to blacks became widespread in the 1920s.[13]

The history of Chicago's blacks, and of blacks in every other city, did not recapitulate the experience of European immigrants. No immigrant group ever lived in neighborhoods as segregated as the black ghetto. With each decade, as they left the center of cities for new homes in the suburbs, European immigrants and their children lived in less segregated surroundings. By contrast, black segregation, higher from the start, continued to increase. European immigrants were allowed, indeed encouraged, to move out of ethnic enclaves; blacks were prevented from leaving the ghetto. Even though blacks often lived closer to industrial jobs than European immigrants, they held far fewer of them, because racial discrimination concentrated them in unskilled and domestic work. In every way, blacks should have been more mobile than European immigrants. Their early migration to cities coincided with industrial expansion; they came in "moderate numbers"; they were Protestant and spoke English; they were eager for work. But they confronted racism and laws that deprived them of their civil rights. An 1853 Illinois law, abandoned only slowly, legally forbade them from entering the state. They could not vote until 1870. Schools were segregated legally until 1874. Most of all, they were relegated to menial "nigger jobs," paid badly, and often laid off. Even when they wanted to buy housing within the Black Belt, they faced special problems because banks demanded a larger down payment and charged them a higher interest rate. Indeed, their carrying charges were so high they found it "impossible to keep up repairs." Moreover, white landlords "were lax about upkeep," and the city "neglected all poor areas and all districts with Negro residents, poor or otherwise. So deterioration in Negro-occupied property continued. . . . The Black Belt was a ghetto-slum and there was no way out of it."[14]

In the summer of 1919, a terrible race riot erupted when white youths attacked and drowned a black youngster who swam across a generally acknowledged color line that divided a section of Lake Michigan. In the week-long riot that followed, 38 people were killed; 537 injured; and about 1,000 left homeless. As one way to ease the tensions that had led to racial violence, the Chicago Commission on Race Relations, created to study the riots, urged the city to improve its "housing problem by 'constructive means,'" by which it meant restrictive legislation, zoning, model homes, and, especially, "better Negro housing." Although the commission did not recommend segregation, in practice its report called for housing reform based on two principles: "the business creed and the color line."[15]

Throughout the 1920s, Chicago's housing reformers and settlement workers—often, of course, the same people—did nothing to discourage segregation. In fact, they often reinforced it. Leading settlement workers had been active in all aspects of housing reform; they had served on the Riot Commission; they had advised leading philanthropists and other civic leaders about housing problems. With their base in immigrant neighborhoods, staffed by well-educated residents with serious research interests, closely connected with the University of Chicago, their experience and data made them the leading authorities on the city's social conditions. There were, of course, shades of difference in their points of view. Jane Addams, Edith Abbott, Sophonisba Breckenridge, and Florence Kelley led the left wing of the settlement movement. They understood how blacks had been exploited and denied opportunity. Nonetheless, when it came to practical policies, no differences separated them from their more openly racist colleagues in the settlement movement. The more liberal settlement leaders advocated economic and political equality, but not social equality; worked to improve black living conditions within the ghetto; and accepted segregation either as inescapable or desirable. All of them refused to integrate their settlement houses. Even when the racial composition of their neighborhoods changed, most settlements remained white islands, and the handful of settlements opened to serve blacks were "always few, always separate, and always unequal."[16]

By 1930, what did Chicago's housing reformers and settlement workers have to show for fifty years of hard work? Chicago had over seventy settlements and boys' clubs almost all for whites only. Private developers had built three segregated, model projects that were too expensive for most of the families who lived in tenements. The city had passed tenement ordinances that it could not enforce because most families were too poor to pay the rent on houses which met the minimum standards. The advent of the automobile had begun to eliminate "the filthy stables and dreadful manure heaps," but, "For all their effort, housing reformers and neighborhood workers had not been able to unmake the slum, and they had helped to make the ghetto." Reform by regulation and model housing worked no better in Chicago than in New York. Mixed with racism, the limitation of public responsibility by the profit motive proved lethal to every attempt to build decent, low-cost housing. And so it has remained ever since.[17]

Housing reform stands as a metaphor for the reorganization of cities in the early twentieth century. Although it united new urban experts around a single issue, the limits they accepted made real solutions impossible, and, in the end, their achievements were more organizational than substantive. They adapted the structure of city government to the transformation of urban life and built new, specialized public and private organizations dedicated to the amelioration of great civic problems. Reformed city governments spent more money on public functions and probably delivered services more efficiently and with less corruption. Nonetheless, as business interests, buttressed by racism, increased their control over policy, experts retreated before the fictive boundaries between public and private and declined to propose solutions that seriously interfered with the market. As a consequence, they scarcely touched the fundamental problems of the urban poor.

NOTES

1. According to New York law, a tenement was "Any house occupied as the home or residence of three families or more, living independently of each other and doing their cooking upon the premises." To differentiate tenements from apartments, reformers drew a line marking off "those houses which in their construction and maintenance require regulation for the protection of the inmates."

2. Robert W. DeForest and Lawrence Veiller, "The Tenement House Problem," in DeForest and Veiller, eds., *The Tenement House Problem* (New York: Macmillan, 1903), p. 67.

3. Roy Lubove, *Progressives and the Slums* (Pittsburgh: University of Pittsburgh Press, 1962), pp. 9–10, 102–112.

4. Lubove, *Progressives and the Slums,* pp. 28–30; DeForest and Veiller, "Tenement House Problem," pp. 8–9.

5. Riis, quoted in Lubove, *Progressives and the Slums,* pp. 246–247. Born in Elizabeth, New Jersey, in 1872. Veiller attended City College in New York and "became interested in social problems after studying the social critics of Victorian England, Ruskin and Carlyle." In the depression of 1893, he worked for the East Side Relief Work Committee, which taught him "at the mature age of 20 years, that the improvement of the homes of the people was the starting point of everything." Between 1895 and 1897, Veiller worked in the city's Building Department as a plan examiner, where he learned a great deal about the technical aspects of the tenement problem. Then, in 1898, he became secretary of the new Tenement House Committee of the Charity Organization Society. When New York created a Tenement House Department, Veiller, also the author of several books, became its first deputy director; he virtually founded as well as directed the National Housing Association; and after 1907, he directed the COS Department for the Improvement of Social Conditions, which immersed him in the campaign against tuberculosis and in juvenile court work as well as housing. Lubove, *Progressives and the Slums,* pp. 127–128.

6. Lubove, *Progressives and the Slums,* pp. 94–166; quote from p. 166.

7. Thomas Lee Philpott, *The Slum and the Ghetto: Neighborhood Deterioration and Middle-Class Reform, Chicago, 1880–1930* (Chicago: University of Chicago Press, 1978), pp. 89, 95–102.

8. DeForest and Veiller, "Tenement House Problem," p. 44; Lubove, *Progressives and the Slums,* p. 178.

9. Lawrence Veiller, "Tenement House Reform in New York City, 1834–1900," in DeForest and Veiller, eds., *Tenement House Problem,* p. 89.

10. Lubove, *Progressives and the Slums,* pp. 221–230; 244–245.

11. Lubove, *Progressives and the Slums,* p. 179.

12. Kenneth I. Kusmer, *A Ghetto Takes Shape: Black Cleveland, 1870–1930* (Urbana: University of Illinois Press, 1976), pp. 35–36. On the development of ghettos in this period, see also Allen H. Spear, *Black Chicago: The Making of a Negro Ghetto 1890–1920* (Chicago: University of Chicago Press, 1967); Gilbert Osofsky, *Harlem: The Making of a Ghetto: Negro New York 1890–1930* (New York: Harper Torchbook edition, 1968): Howard N. Rabinowitz, *Race Relations in the Urban South 1865–1890* (Urbana: University of Illinois Press, 1980); Elisabeth Hafkin Pleck,

   Black Migration and Poverty: Boston 1865–1900 (New York; Academic Press, 1979).

13.   Philpott, *Slum and Ghetto,* pp. 119, 168–169, 189.

14.   Philpott, *Slum and Ghetto,* pp. 116–117, 159. A number of other studies also show the fundamental differences between the experiences of blacks and white immigrants. These include: Kusmer, *Ghetto Takes Shape*; Theodore Hershberg, et al., "A Tale of Three Cities: Blacks, Immigrants, and Opportunity in Philadelphia, 1850–1880, 1930, 1970," in Theodore Hershberg, ed., *Philadelphia: Work, Space, Family, and Group Experience in the 19th Century* (New York: Oxford University Press, 1981); Stanley Lieberson, *A Piece of the Pie: Blacks and White Immigrants since 1880* (Berkeley: University of California Press, 1980); and Stephen Steinberg, *The Ethnic Myth: Race, Ethnicity, and Class in America* (Boston: Beacon Press, 1981).

15.   Philpott, *Slum and Ghetto,* pp. 170, 204. For a special psychological interpretation of the riot, see Richard Sennett, *Families Against the City: Middle Class Homes of Industrial Chicago, 1872–1890* (Cambridge: Harvard University Press, 1970).

16.   Philpott, *Slum and Ghetto,* pp. 274–275, 341.

17.   Philpott, *Slum and Ghetto,* p. 346.

21
The City*

Lewis Mumford

PROVINCIAL AND COMMERCIAL ERAS

Around us, in the city, each epoch in America has been concentrated and crystallized. In building our cities we deflowered a wilderness. Today more than one-half the population of the United States lives in an environment which the jerry-builder, the real estate speculator, the paving contractor, and the industrialist have largely created. Have we begotten a civilization? That is a question which a survey of the American city will help us to answer. . . .

Now the New England town was a genuine community. In so far as the New England community had a common social and political and religious life, the town expressed it. The city which was representative of the second period, on the other hand, was in origin a trading fort, and the supreme occupation of its founders was with the goods life rather than the good life. New York, Pittsburgh, Chicago, and St. Louis have this common basis. They

*Mumford, Lewis. 1945. "The City." Pp. 5 and 8–18. In *City Development: Studies in Disintegration and Renewal.* New York: Harcourt, Brace Jovanovich. Copyright © 1945. Reprinted by permission of Harcourt, Brace Jovanovich, Inc.

were not composed of corporate organizations on the march, as it were, towards a New Jerusalem: they were simply a rabble of individuals "on the make." With such a tradition to give it momentum it is small wonder that the adventurousness of the commercial period was exhausted on the fortuities and temptations of trade. A state of intellectual anesthesia prevailed. One has only to compare Cist's Cincinnati Miscellany with Emerson's Dial to see at what a low level the towns of the Middle West were carrying on.

Since there was neither fellowship nor social stability nor security in the scramble of the inchoate commercial city, it remained for a particular institution to devote itself to the gospel of the "glad hand." Thus an historian of Pittsburgh records the foundation of a Masonic lodge as early as 1785, shortly after the building of the church, and in every American city, small or big, Odd Fellows, Mystic Shriners, Woodmen, Elks, Knights of Columbus, and other orders without number in the course of time found for themselves a prominent place. (Their feminine counterparts were the D.A.R. and the W.C.T.U., their juniors, the college Greek letter fraternities.) Whereas one will search American cities in vain for the labor temples one discovers today in Europe from Belgium to Italy, one finds that the fraternal lodge generally occupies a site of dignity and importance. There were doubtless many excellent reasons for the strange proliferation of professional fraternity in the American city, but perhaps the strongest reason was the absence of any other kind of fraternity. The social center and the community center, which in a singularly hard and consciously beatific way have sought to organize fellowship and mutual aid on different terms, are products of the last decade.

Perhaps the only other civic institution of importance that the commercial towns fostered was the lyceum: forerunner of the elephantine Chautauqua. The lyceum lecture, however, was taken as a soporific rather than a stimulant, and if it aroused any appetite for art, philosophy, a science there was nothing in the environment of the commercial city that could satisfy it. Just as church going became a substitute for religion, so automatic lyceum attendance became a substitute for thought. These were the prayer wheels of a preoccupied commercialism.

The contrast between the provincial and the commercial city in America was well summed up in their plans. Consider the differences between Cambridge and New York. Up to the beginning of the nineteenth century New York, at the tip of Manhattan Island, had the same diffident, rambling town plan that characterizes Cambridge. In this old type of city layout the streets lead nowhere, except to the buildings that give onto them: outside the main roads the provisions for traffic are so inadequate as to seem almost a provision against traffic. Quiet streets, a pleasant aspect, ample domestic facilities were the desiderata of the provincial town; traffic, realty speculation, and expansion were those of the newer era. This became evident as soon as the Empire City started to realize its "manifest destiny" by laying down, in 1811, a plan for its future development.

New York's city plan commissioners went about their work with a scarcely concealed purpose to increase traffic and raise realty values. The amenities of city life counted for little in their scheme of things: debating "whether they should confine themselves to rectilinear and rectangular streets, or whether they should adopt some of those supposed improvements, by circles, ovals, and stars," they decided, on grounds of economy, against any departure from the gridiron design. It was under the same stimulus that these admirable philistines had the complacency to plan the city's development up to 155th Street. Here we are concerned, however, with the results of rectangular plan rather than with the motives that lay behind its adoption throughout the country.

The principal effect of the gridiron plan is that every street becomes a thoroughfare, and that every thoroughfare is potentially a commercial street. The tendency towards movement in such a city vastly outweighs the tendency towards settlement. As a result of progressive shifts in population, due to the changes to which commercial competition subjects the use of land, the main institutions of the city, instead of cohering naturally—as the museums, galleries, theaters, clubs, and public offices group themselves in the heart of Westminster—are dispersed in every direction. Neither Columbia College, New York University, the Astor Library, nor the National Academy of Design—to seize but a few examples—is on its original site. Yet had Columbia remained at Fiftieth Street it might have had some effective working relation with the great storehouse of books that now occupies part of Bryant Park at Forty-second Street; or, alternatively, had the Astor Library remained on its old site it might have had some connection with New York University—had that institution not in turn moved!

What was called the growth of the commercial city was really a manifestation of the absence of design in the gridiron plan. The rectangular parceling of ground promoted speculation in land-units and the ready interchange of real property: it had no relation whatever to the essential purposes for which a city exists. It is not a little significant that Chicago, Cincinnati, and St. Louis, each of which had space set aside for public purposes in their original plans, had given up these civic holdings to the realty gambler before half of the nineteenth century was over. The common was not the center of a well-rounded community life, as in New England, but the center of land-speculation—which was at once the business, the recreation, and the religion of the commercial city. Under the influence of New York the Scaders, whom Martin Chuzzlewit encountered, were laying down their New Edens throughout the country.

BROADWAY AS SYMBOL

It was during the commercial period that the evolution of the Promenade, such as existed in New York at Battery Park, took place. The new promenade was no longer a park but a shop-lined thoroughfare, Broadway. Shopping became for the more domesticated half of the community an exciting, bewildering amusement; and out of a combination of Yankee "notions,"

Barnumlike advertisement, and magisterial organization arose that *omnium gatherum* of commerce, the department store. It is scarcely possible to exaggerate the part that Broadway—I use the term generically—has played in the American town. It is not merely the Agora but the Acropolis. When the factory whistle closes the week, and the factory hands of Camden, or Pittsburgh, or Bridgeport pour out of the buildings and stockades in which they spend the more exhausting half of their lives, it is through Broadway that the greater part of their repressions seek an outlet. Both the name and the institution extend across the continent from New York to Los Angeles. Up and down these second-hand Broadways, from one in the afternoon until past ten at night, drifts a more or less aimless mass of human beings, bent upon extracting such joy as is possible from the sights in the windows, the contacts with other human beings, the occasional or systemic flirtations, and the risks and adventures of purchase.

In the early development of Broadway the amusements were adventitious. Even at present, in spite of the ubiquitous movie, the crowded street itself, at least in the smaller communities, is the main source of entertainment. Now, under normal conditions, for a great part of the population in a factory town one of the chief instincts to be repressed is that of acquisition (collection). It is not merely that the average factory worker cannot afford the luxuries of life: the worst is that he must think twice before purchasing the necessities. Out of this situation one of Broadway's happiest achievements has arisen: the five and ten cent store. In the five and ten cent store it is possible for the circumscribed factory operative to obtain the illusion of unmoderated expenditure—and even extravagance—without actually inflicting any irreparable rent in his purse. Broadway is thus, in more than one sense, the great compensatory device of the American city. The dazzle of white lights, the color of electric signs, the alabaster architecture of the moving-picture palaces, the esthetic appeals of the shop windows—these stand for elements that are left out of the drab perspectives of the industrial city. People who do not know how to spend their time must take what satisfaction they can in spending their money. That is why, although the five and ten cent store itself is perhaps mainly an institution for the proletariat, the habits and dispositions it encourages are universal. The chief amusement of Atlantic City, that opulent hostelry-annex of New York and Philadelphia, lies not in the beach and the ocean but in the shops which line the interminable Broadway known as the Boardwalk.

Broadway, in sum, is the façade of the American city: a false front. The highest achievements of our material civilization—and at their best our hotels, our department stores, and our Woolworth towers are achievements—count as so many symptoms of its spiritual failure. In order to cover up the vacancy of getting and spending in our cities, we have invented a thousand fresh devices for getting and spending. As a consequence our life is externalized. The principal institutions of the American city are merely distractions that take our eyes off the environment, instead of instruments which would help us to mold it creatively a little nearer to humane hopes and desires.

CONSEQUENCES OF INDUSTRIALISM

The birth of industrialism in America is announced in the opening of the Crystal Palace in Bryant Park, Manhattan, in 1853. Between the Crystal Palace Exhibition and the Chicago World's Fair in 1892 lies a period whose defects were partly accentuated by the exhaustion that followed the Civil War. The debasement of the American city during this period can be read in almost every building that was erected. The influence of colonial architecture had waned to extinction during the first half of the century. There followed a period of eclectic experiment, in which all sorts of Egyptian, Byzantine, Gothic, and Arabesque ineptitudes were committed — a period whose absurdities we have only in recent years begun to escape. The domestic style, as the century progressed, became more limited. Little touches about the doors, moldings, fanlights, and balustrades disappeared, and finally craftsmanship went out of style altogether and a pretentious architectural puffery took its place. The "era of good feeling" was an era of bad taste.

. . . The industrial city did not represent the creative values in civilization: it stood for a new form of human barbarism. In the coal towns of Pennsylvania, the steel towns of the Ohio and its tributaries, and the factory towns of Long Island Sound and Narragansett Bay was an environment much more harsh, antagonistic, and brutal than anything the pioneers had encountered. Even the fake exhilaration of the commercial city was lacking.

The reaction against the industrial city was expressed in various ways. The defect of these reactions was that they were formulated in terms of an escape from the environment rather than in a reconstruction of it. . . .

. . . Almost down to the last decade the best buildings of the industrial period have been anonymous, and scarcely ever recognized for their beauty. A grain elevator here, a warehouse there, an office building, a garage — there has been the promise of a stripped, athletic, classical style of architecture in these buildings which shall embody all that is good in the Machine Age: its precision, its cleanliness, its hard illuminations, its unflinching logic. Dickens once poked fun at the architecture of Coketown because its infirmary looked like its jail and its jail like its town hall. But the joke had a sting to it only because these buildings were all plaintively destitute of esthetic inspiration. In a place and an age that had achieved a well-rounded and balanced culture, we should expect to find the same spirit expressed in the simplest cottage and the grandest public building. So we find it, for instance, in the humble market towns of the Middle Age: there is not one type of architecture for fifteenth-century Shaftesbury and another for London; neither is there one style for public London and quite another for domestic London. Our architects in America have only just begun to cease regarding the Gothic style as especially fit for churches and schools, whilst they favor the Roman mode for courts, and the Byzantine, perhaps, for offices. Even the unique beauty of the Bush Terminal Tower is compromised by an antiquely "stylized" interior.[1]

With the beginning of the second decade of this century there is some evidence of an attempt to make a genuine culture out of industrialism — instead of attempting to escape from industrialism into a culture which, though doubtless genuine enough, has the misfortune to be dead. The schoolhouses in Gary, Indiana, have some of the better qualities of a Gary steel plant. That symptom is all to the good. It points perhaps to a time when the Gary steel plant may have some of the educational virtues of a Gary school. One of the things that has made the industrial age a horror in America is the notion that there is something shameful in its manifestations. The idea that nobody would ever go near an industrial plant except under stress of starvation is in part responsible for the heaps of rubbish and rusty metal, for the general disorder and vileness, that still characterize broad acres of our factory districts. There is nothing short of the Alkali Desert that compares with the desolateness of the common American industrial town. These qualities are indicative of the fact that we have centered attention not upon the process but upon the return; not upon the task but the emoluments; not upon what we can get out of our work but upon what we can achieve when we get away from our work. Our industrialism has been in the grip of business, and our industrial cities, and their institutions, have exhibited a major preoccupation with business. The coercive repression of an impersonal, mechanical technique was compensated by the pervasive will-to-power — or at least will-to-comfort — of commercialism.

We have shirked the problem of trying to live well in a régime that is devoted to the production of T-beams and toothbrushes and T.N.T. As a result, we have failed to react creatively upon the environment with anything like the inspiration that one might have found in a group of medieval peasants building a cathedral. The urban worker escapes the mechanical routine of his daily job only to find an equally mechanical substitute for life and growth and experience in his amusements. The Gay White Way with its stupendous blaze of lights, and Coney Island, with its fear-stimulating roller coasters and chute-the-chutes, are characteristic by-products of an age that has renounced the task of actively humanizing the machine, and of creating an environment in which all the fruitful impulses of the community may be expressed. The movies, the White Ways, and the Coney Islands, which almost every American city boasts in some form or other, are means of giving jaded and throttled people the sensations of living without the direct experience of life — a sort of spiritual masturbation. In short, we have had the alternative of humanizing the industrial city or de-humanizing the population. So far we have de-humanized the population.

NOTE

1. This paragraph — like the article on Machinery and the Modern Style I published in The New Republic in 1921 — antedated the lucubrations of Le Corbusier on the same subject.

PART	**REGIME POLITICS**
II	**IN THE**
	CONTEMPORARY
	METROPOLIS

Most of America's metropolitan areas are composed of a crazy-quilt mosaic of independent governments. In 1979, for example, 1,214 governmental units made up the Chicago metropolitan area. There were 864 governments in the Philadelphia metropolitan region and 615 in the St. Louis region, which has more than ninety suburban jurisdictions in one county alone (U.S. Bureau of Census 1981, 2). Though a map of these metropolitan areas may appear to show a random and merely chaotic fracturing of political authority, there are consistent patterns in which a central city anchors the metropolitan region, surrounded by a multitude of suburban jurisdictions.

Especially in the years since World War II, the older industrial cities that occupied the core of metropolitan regions lost population, but their suburbs boomed. Racial and socioeconomic segregation between central cities and suburbs became increasingly stark, with the cities containing a disproportionate share of minority and poverty populations. A special set of constraints and political problems came to define politics in most of the larger older cities. These central city regimes learned to accommodate the demands of low-income minority populations, and they became fixated on rebuilding decaying downtowns and neighborhoods. In this cause most central city governments actively sought and ultimately most central cities became dependent on federal assistance. At the same time, suburbanites were trying to wall themselves off from the problems that beset the central cities; ironically, they also were assisted by the national government in achieving this objective. The national policies that affected urban growth and development were remarkably contradictory and perverse in their effects.

NATIONAL POLICY AND LOCAL POLITICS

The Great Depression of the 1930s created the conditions for a close relationship between the cities and the national government, one that would last for several decades. Municipal officials responded to the crisis of unemployment and destitution by appealing to the federal government for assistance. It did not take long for local and national officials in the Democratic party to discern that a continuing partnership would be in their mutual interests: Local officials could deliver the votes of blue-collar workers, ethnics, and blacks in exchange for federal programs, and national politicians could win office with the support of urban voters. A political relationship forged during the New Deal matured in the years following World War II, and bore fruit during the Democratic administrations of John F. Kennedy and Lyndon Johnson. The alliances that made up the New Deal coalition fell apart by the late 1970s, with huge consequences for cities and the regimes that governed them.

A broad alliance of urban officials, liberal Democratic congressmen, and business representatives were able to push the 1949 Housing Act through Congress to clear inner-city slums and build public housing. Though this program survived the eight years of the Eisenhower administration, urban programs were not in favor in the Republican White House. John F. Kennedy's election in 1960 signaled a new era for the cities. Federal assistance in urban areas rose from $3.9 billion in 1961, the last Republican fiscal year, to $14 billion in President Lyndon Johnson's last budget eight years later. The growth in federal commitment was accompanied by fundamental changes in the purposes of urban programs. In the 1950s urban renewal was designed exclusively to remove unsightly slums and to subsidize new investment in inner-city property; it was this basic purpose that had elicited support from business and from some conservatives. Public housing legislation received congressional support basically because it was considered a necessary adjunct to large-scale clearance programs. In the 1960s, however, the purposes of urban programs vastly expanded to embrace the social problems of the cities—juvenile delinquency, crime, poverty, education, racial conflict, and joblessness.

The Kennedy and Johnson administrations crafted their legislative agenda with an eye toward the electoral constituencies that made up the Democratic party's coalition. The new urban programs were designed to enhance the Democratic party's electoral strength among inner-city blacks. Such a choice, however, was not without its risks. Beginning with the congressional elections of 1966 a backlash against urban social programs was already evident. Southern Democrats were already in revolt against the national party concerning the issues of civil rights and voting rights. Now white blue-collar workers began to question their allegiance; they perceived favoritism toward blacks and the poor.

Other more long-term and far-reaching developments were even more important than conflicts within the New Deal constituencies in eroding the political power of the cities in national politics. Over several decades the cities have lost political clout because of the movement of people to the suburbs and to the Sunbelt states. As the older central cities lost population, the representatives of the cities could no longer deliver important blocs of votes in presidential elections.

The term "Sunbelt" was coined by Kevin Phillips in his best-selling book, *The Emerging Republican Majority,* published in 1969 (Phillips 1969). Phillips used the term to describe a broad region of the nation that has experienced economic and population growth for several decades (in most definitions, it encompasses a band of states stretching from North Carolina and Florida across the South and Southwest to California). The growth of the Sunbelt, when combined with the decline in the populations of the older cities in the states making up the Frostbelt, has fundamentally shifted the national balance of power. For the twelve states that make up the Sunbelt, reapportionment following each decennial census since World War II has increased the number of congressional seats apportioned to them. In 1950 there were 115 congressional representatives from these states, but by 1980 the number had increased to 156, a net gain of 41 seats. The adjustment as a result of the 1990 census will increase Sunbelt representation still more to 177 seats. The eight largest states of the Frostbelt, in contrast, have experienced a steady erosion in their collective congressional representation, having lost 30 seats from 1950 to 1980. They stand to lose 14 more seats as a result of reapportionment that will occur in 1992. Overall, from 1940 to 1990 the number of congressional representatives from these states will have declined from 185 to 139.

This changing political balance helps to explain why national urban policy has become a thing of the past. The central strategy of John Kennedy's campaign of 1960 required him to capture big blocs of votes in the big cities of the industrial states. Today, such a strategy would not be sensible; in the 1984 presidential election, cities more than fifty thousand in population accounted for only 12 percent of the national vote (Pomper 1985, 68–69).

Neither national party now emphasizes urban issues. Against this background it is not difficult to explain why, or how, President Ronald Reagan cut urban and social programs in the 1980s, or why we are unlikely to see a new round of urban programs in the 1990s. At the 1988 Republic convention, rural, but not urban, development rated a subcommittee in the platform debates. The Democratic convention was not much different. The word "city" was used twenty-three times in the 1968 Democratic platform but not at all in the 1988 version.

The readings in this section examine the evolution of national urban policies and then probe the federal presence in the cities. The readings by Mark I. Gelfand, Norton E. Long, and Michael J. Rich primarily look at the experience of the first several postwar decades when there was increasing federal attention to urban problems. Many of the federal initiatives of this period can be credited with success in helping local governments cope with their difficulties; for example, federal social service programs lifted significant numbers of inner-city residents out of poverty (Kantor 1988, 346–368; Schwartz 1983).

Many national programs fell short of achieving their goals, however, and sometimes even made matters worse for the people the programs were supposed to help. Mark I. Gelfand explains how the 1949 Housing Act, which funded both public housing and urban renewal, was a logical expression of the postwar alliance between the federal government and the cities. Congress committed itself to a policy of underwriting slum clearance and the construction of publicly funded housing for low-income people. At the local level the idea of slum clearance proved to be popular, but public housing construction was another matter: middle-class residents did not want projects close by, and politicians tended to want them only in areas where poor people and blacks already lived. Gelfand describes how public housing often was drab, poor in quality, and racially segregated; these features ultimately weakened political support for public housing and for the urban renewal program of which it was a part.

A generation of activist mayors built their careers on urban renewal by building broad coalitions of support behind a vision of civic renewal. The programs were popular with corporate and business leaders, labor leaders (who promised their members jobs in the reconstruction of the city), and with voters, who were happy to see a flow of national dollars, rather than their own, into the city. There were contradictions, however. The poor, and a disproportionate number of blacks, lived in the path of the bulldozer. Because so much of the land previously occupied by slum housing was converted to other uses, far more units of low-income housing were destroyed than constructed. Opposition to displacement became the principal source of tension in many cities. Over time, it became clear that supporting urban renewal was not a sure path to every mayor's political success nor was it an effective way of helping inner-city residents.

Norton E. Long offers an explanation for why national urban programs often failed to do much to revitalize cities or help their citizens. Long observes that there is a powerful tendency to respond to urban problems in a piecemeal fashion at all levels in our political system. Particular federal agencies deal only with specific parts of urban social problems (such as housing or downtown redevelopment); at the same time, urban areas typically are fragmented into political jurisdictions, and national programs are therefore unable to address the metropolis as a whole. Consequently, Long contends that governmental intervention often serves little more purpose than to support vested interests in maintaining their stake in some aspect of the status quo. He concludes that political leadership must take a more comprehensive view of the metropolis and its needs; otherwise, programs of urban aid will continue to fail.

Michael Rich provides evidence that federal assistance for community and economic development was spread far too thinly during the postwar decades to have much impact on the cities where it was needed most. Federal funds were distributed far beyond distressed cities to cities of all levels of social and economic hardship. Federal urban assistance is only loosely related to serving the worst-off jurisdictions; what best explains the distribution of federal assistance to localities is the aggressiveness of local governments seeking funds. Funding cutbacks could be accomplished by eliminating less needy jurisdictions, but traditionally there has been resistance to this in Congress and among local governments. Thus, the politics of federal grants seems to have much to do with the preservation of existing patterns of entitlements.

The readings by Kenneth K. Wong and Paul E. Peterson, Susan and Norman Fainstein, and William R. Barnes evaluate some of the important changes in federal urban policy that have occurred since President Richard M. Nixon launched his "New Federalism" in the late 1960s. Guided by the rationale that local people know best how to address local problems, the New Federalism calls for limiting the federal presence in local affairs. In general, this has been interpreted to mean the elimination of categorical grants-in-aid (funds for specific programs and purposes) in favor of block grants with fewer restrictions. The ideal of political decentralization has been seized on not only as a justification for changing how programs are administered; it also has been used to cut and sometimes entirely eliminate federal urban assistance.

Wong and Peterson's discussion of how the Community Development Block Grant Program was implemented in two cities, Milwaukee and Baltimore, points out that the block grant procedure for delivering assistance to localities is not politically neutral. The Community Development Block Grant Program permitted considerable discretion at the local level in deciding how federal monies would be spent. Local officials in both cities gave higher priority to using federal funds to stimulate economic growth and expand mayoral power and patronage than to improving social services for lower-income citizens. Wong and Peterson believe that this resulted because local governments are constrained by the pressures of intercity economic competition to promote business investment and growth in the local economy. Unless federal restrictions limit the purposes for which intergovernmental aid is spent, local governments are motivated to favor using funds for these economic objectives rather than for social programs that might help the poor. Political pressures reinforce this tendency; spending for economic development projects generates patronage and other benefits that mayors use to increase their power, popularity, and authority. Thus, Wong and Peterson conclude that the block grant approach, whatever the professed purposes, cannot do much to address the needs of impoverished residents.

According to Susan and Norman Fainstein, decentralization and retrenchment in federal programs was not an end in itself, but a means of forcing local governments to favor business interests. The New Federalism was, in effect, a cloak for cutting back on assistance to the poor in favor of other objectives. Federal retrenchment did not reduce governmental activities at the local and state levels so much as it precipitated an increase in local and state governmental efforts to promote economic development. Economic competition among local and state jurisdictions pressured these governments to give high priority to mercantilist programs that were intended to promote capital investment.

William R. Barnes explains why President George Bush will continue to carry forward Reagan's urban policies with little change. The most recent version of the New Federalism serves President Bush's Sunbelt and suburban constituencies rather well. Barnes suggests that federal programs to assist the nation's inner cities are likely to come about only as a by-product of domestic programs that do not carry a specific urban focus.

SUBURBAN REGIMES

Throughout American history, there has been a tendency for affluent people to segregate themselves from the less well-off. When these people spilled beyond the boundaries of the central cities and created their own political jurisdictions, an important new dimension was added to the previous patterns of neighborhood segregation that existed in the cities. The development of the suburbs permitted upper-income and middle-class whites to segregate themselves from the people and problems of the central cities and to maintain low taxes, high property values, and amenities not available elsewhere. Of course not all suburbs fit this profile. Working-class industrial suburbs can be found, especially at the edges of large cities, that look similar to the central cities to which they are tied. In the 1970s and 1980s blacks also moved to the suburbs in large numbers. Though the suburbs are being urbanized, however, they remain highly segregated.

It is possible that urban America would have ended up as segregated as it is without the existence of suburbs. It is unlikely, however, that the mismatch between social needs and governmental resources would have become so severe in the absence of governmental fragmentation. Hard-pressed central cities and a few poorer suburbs must cope with the greatest demands for public services, whereas significant public and private resources remain walled off in wealthier jurisdictions.

The development of suburbia as a bastion of segregated living did not occur by accident. Developers, financial institutions, and the federal government all played a part. Herbert J. Gans describes how the planners of Levittown, New Jersey, pioneered in using industrial building techniques and mass marketing to construct suburban housing on a mass scale, housing that was affordable to middle-class home buyers (but was sometimes depreciated by others for its cookie-cutter appearance). Levittown planners were successful in part because they managed to create their new developments out of whole cloth and on a large scale because they were relatively free of restrictive local land-use restrictions. It is important to note, however, that the town's planners were not against all restrictions. It did not trouble them at all to exclude blacks.

State laws in the twentieth century usually made municipal incorporation as a village, town, or other local governmental unit easy—even by relatively small communities. Once incorporated, local governments obtained the power to regulate land uses within their borders. Michael N. Danielson describes the far-reaching political consequences of this legal arrangement for the development of segregated urban areas. He describes how families moving to suburbia almost universally sought incorporation and then used their new governmental authority to exclude people unlike themselves. He observes that when so much power and independence was given to so many small political constituencies, an insular, parochial-minded, and discriminatory politics of community development almost invariably followed.

The main strategy was to use zoning, building codes, and other land-use regulations to screen out "undesirables"—usually meaning lower-income families and racial minorities—and "bring in the tax ratables," the people who would be able to buy costly single-family housing. The exclusionary enclaves created through such policies were also attractive to "clean industries," such as office parks and shopping centers, which residents might choose to tolerate to help lower the local tax bill.

Local government actions remain a powerful factor in preserving racial segregation in metropolitan areas. Yale Rabin suggests that racially segregated neighborhoods are no accident, nor are they simply the outcome of the choices made by suburban residents. Rather, highway planning, housing clearance and relocation, school districting, zoning, and other local governmental activities profoundly affect the choices that are available to people who move to the suburbs. In principle, local government policies could be used to promote racial integration; however, local governments usually have chosen to use their powers to accomplish exactly the opposite.

Suburban regimes tend to be very closed systems, despite electoral processes that symbolize the possibilities of local democracy. United by concerns about protecting property values, maintaining the status of home and family, keeping taxes low, and keeping people out, consensus on most local policy issues is the norm. Except in suburban communities that have failed to control their own development successfully or in those that did not have exclusion as a viable option, the relatively homogeneous, predominantly residential political constituencies of taxpayers and property owners almost always support discriminatory development policies. In these regimes a gatekeeper process screens out groups who might otherwise challenge established political norms.

Political disagreements are likely to revolve around project-by-project development or service issues: Will a new shopping mall lower residential values? Should clustered housing be allowed, and what kinds of people will live in them? Should the refuse service be changed to encourage recycling? Will an expansion of a gas station increase traffic? A style of politics exists in many suburbs that has the appearance of an ideal New England democracy —a politics in which individual preferences and individual civic initiative count a great deal in running local affairs. Yet, as Robert C. Wood brilliantly points out, appearance should not be confused with reality. He suggests that the local bureaucrats rather than suburban citizens tend to dominate politics in the suburbs. Most matters are considered noncontroversial and thus are defined as nonpolitical. Consequently, there is a vast scope for treating issues as "merely administrative." Because there are few mechanisms in most suburbs for scrutinizing and criticizing official activities (such as professional politicians and party organizations), full-time bureaucrats such as school superintendents and town managers find that they are free to decide public actions, and they are able to marginalize or ignore what little opposition they encounter.

In recent decades scarcity of land, the escalating costs of suburban housing, and the drift of employers to suburban locations have pressured more and more suburban communities to abandon the preferred policies of exclusion, which in the past took the form of excluding all but single-family housing. Multifamily housing is no longer identified automatically with poor people and minorities. Indeed, condominiums and townhouses, frequently built as self-contained, essentially privatized "communities," have themselves become havens for the affluent.

Changes in residential styles have not altered the insularity of suburban regimes. Quite the opposite: Self-contained, relatively high-density communities have become a new means of accomplishing social class segregation. Evan McKenzie describes "common interest developments" (CIDs), which have mushroomed across urban America. CIDs are composed of living spaces such as condominiums or single-family units built together with amenities held "in common" by the residents, often including swimming pools, small parks, and community centers. CIDs usually provide their own security and are governed by community associations so that they are, in effect, private municipalities.

In exchange for a privatized, controlled environment, CID residents achieve a sense of safety and exclusion. There is, however, a price—they must abide by various covenants, conditions, and restrictions regarding how they live and express themselves. This raises important issues of personal freedom. As McKenzie notes, there is "a generation of kids who don't know you should be able to paint your house any color you want." Perhaps even more significant, in the new privatized environments residents become detached from political rights and responsibilities. They are denied even the limited form of citizenship available, at least in principle, in the public suburb. In addition, those who live in these private complexes often have a stake in opposing public spending in the community beyond the CID.

The ultimate expression of the privatization of public space is the suburban shopping mall. It is often claimed that the mall is the replacement for the downtown shopping district of yesteryear. There is something suspect in such a claim. The urban streets of the past were not separated from the ethnic and racial diversity of the city itself. In contrast, the essence of the mall is, like so many suburbs, exclusion and segregation. William Severini Kowinsky describes malls as veritable fortresses against the outside world. Many of today's shoppers leave their defended enclaves to drive to an enclosed, climate-controlled environment that is meticulously planned and constructed as an exclusionary realm—no pawn shops, beer halls, seedy secondhand stores, or homeless are going to be encountered there.

CENTRAL CITY REGIMES

Governing coalitions of shifting composition and political purposes have emerged to cope with the political realities and the adverse economic circumstances of central cities. Internally, the central cities have themselves experienced increasing political fragmentation. The party machines that once imposed discipline on rival political interests and assured governmental leaders a relatively stable base of political power disappeared from most large cities decades ago. Yet, declining partisanship, factional rivalries, and the rise of the media as an important tool in elections have limited the development of cohesive local party organizations.

At the same time, new political interests have emerged in cities; they compete for power, reinforcing the trend toward factionalism within city political systems. The civil servants who make up professional bureaucracies have become a political force. In many cities civil service unions that have collective bargaining rights work to promote their interests in city governmental affairs. Further, city populations have undergone important demographic changes that have encouraged political rivalry. As older ethnic groups fled to suburban areas during the postwar decades, these people were more often than not replaced by black, Latino, Asian, or other racial and nationality groups seeking political recognition and power.

The readings by Theodore J. Lowi, Paul Kleppner, and William E. Nelson address the consequences of these new political divisions. Theodore Lowi suggests that in many big cities a "New Machine" has arisen. Drawing on the New York City experience, Lowi describes how the triumph of reform has left little alternative political power base for office holders than the creation of ad hoc coalitions of powerful organized special interests. Lowi believes that professional autonomous bureaucracies have stepped in to fill the void left by the decline of parties. As a result, Lowi says that "the modern city is now well run but ungoverned because it comprises islands of functional power before which the modern mayor stands impoverished."

Until the early 1970s minority mayors, city councilors, judges, and other public officials were relatively few. During the past twenty years, however, the number of elected and appointed black and Latino officials has virtually exploded in number. Today it is the exception rather than the rule for a large city in the United States not to have experienced a minority administration in city hall. In some cities, such as Atlanta, the transition to black power in city hall has resulted in the creation of biracial regimes that are characterized by compromise and cooperation between white and black power brokers.

In other cities the race issue has cut so deep that a biracial politics has not been possible. Paul Kleppner describes how racial polarization characterized the coming to power of Chicago's first black mayor, Harold Washington, in 1983. In Chicago, black politicians were always junior partners in the white-run party machines. Kleppner shows that black electoral success has not been a product of compromise and bargaining. Rather, the mobilization of black voters and a divided white opposition enabled Harold Washington to win election in a highly polarized contest in which racial voting was the norm. He describes the efforts by white politicians to contain and undermine Mayor Washington's power even after the election; their access to position, patronage, and power depended on the success of these efforts.

It is ironic that blacks and Hispanics have been able to capture the top public office in major cities just at the time that the fiscal problems of cities are most severe. Minority mayors almost inevitably feel pressure to respond positively to the needs of their minority constituents, and at the same time they must keep together a biracial or multiracial electoral coalition, and they are constrained by the difficult economic circumstances that face their cities. How they have responded to these cross pressures during the past twenty years is evaluated by William E. Nelson. Although Nelson can point to significant gains for blacks living in cities — especially regarding a gain in political access and a larger share of jobs in the public sector — he concludes that the record thus far is disappointing. Nelson points out that many of the resources that are needed to address the social and economic plight of people in the inner cities are out of the reach of mayors and in the hands of Congress, state legislators, suburban governments, and, of course, the private sector. He also asserts that some black mayors have too readily accepted notions of progress and good politics championed by important members of their governing coalitions, such as business, who benefit from a system of racial subordination.

Most disappointing to Nelson is that black mayors have not established powerful, stable political organizations, as earlier ethnics did when they ran city governments. Blacks have not succeeded at establishing a power base sufficient for winning valuable political prizes and reforms. Thus even the most successful black politicians are unable to deliver on their promises.

The character of central city regimes cannot be understood as simply the result of the internal politics of cities. Governing regimes are powerfully constrained to deal with the political consequences of the central city situation within the larger urban economy. As business and people dispersed to locations in suburbia and in the Sunbelt, new challenges were presented to central city political leaders. Typically, northeastern and midwestern city governments had to face decline in their market position as businesses left town, and their populations began to shrink. These cities also found that the growing segments of their populations were disproportionately lower income, older, and poorer. These regimes faced the most unenviable of tasks. Having a declining resource base from which to fund public services, their populations and economies have required greater expenditures and public intervention. Meanwhile, Sunbelt cities were experiencing a transformation of their own. Rapid growth was changing the character of their politics; the closed regimes of the past were being replaced by a new politics that reflected their service-based economies and new population profile.

The reading by John R. Logan and Harvey L. Molotch and the contribution by Carl Abbott highlight the political and economic underpinnings of postwar central city regimes. Logan and Molotch describe the coalition of political interests that typically participates in land-use decisions. They suggest that the pro-growth coalitions that actively participate—and often dominate—central city regimes reach well beyond the businesses that are likely to gain economic benefits directly from programs that stimulate the local economy. Politicians find that such programs help build their careers by generating jobs, campaign contributions, and votes; the media, particularly local newspapers, seek larger circulations and more advertising revenues; utilities build customer bases; universities seek a symbiotic relationship with new businesses looking for technical help; labor leaders see the prospect for more jobs; and even theaters, museums, and other community interests often believe that growth will generate payoffs and profits. The agenda of this "growth machine" is indeed compelling. It cannot and does not speak for all interests, however. For example, who in the growth coalition speaks out for the environment, the poor, or neighborhoods?

Carl Abbott surveys the enormous political and economic changes in Sunbelt regimes that have occurred during the last forty years. Traditionally, Sunbelt cities were ruled by closed business-dominated regimes that excluded most groups, especially minorities, from exerting a political voice. Over time, however, the political and economic systems of the Sunbelt cities have come to resemble more closely those of northern cities. Metropolitan politics has changed as well. Suburban development has occurred beyond the reach of and at the expense of many central cities in the Sunbelt. Equally important, the growth and increasing diversity of their populations have forced local governments to become more inclusive of blacks, Latinos, women, and other groups, though businessmen and civic notables still operate at the center of Sunbelt regimes.

REFERENCES

Kantor, Paul, with Stephen David. 1988. *The Dependent City: The Changing Political Economy of Urban America.* New York: Harper Collins.

Phillips, Kevin. 1969. *The Emerging Republican Majority.* New Rochelle, NY: Arlington House.

Pomper, Gerald. 1985. "The Presidential Election." In *The Election of 1984: Reports and Interpretations,* edited by Gerald Pomper. Chatham, NJ: Chatham House.

Schwartz, John E. 1983. *America's Hidden Success: A Reassessment of Twenty Years of Public Policy.* New York: Norton.

U.S. Bureau of the Census. 1981. *Local Government Finances in Selected Metropolitan Areas and Large Counties: 1970–1980.* Washington, DC: U.S. Government Printing Office.

National Policy and Local Politics

22

The Federal Government and the Postwar American City*

Mark I. Gelfand

The federal-municipal partnership neared its thirtieth birthday in 1960. Much to Eisenhower's chagrin, the helping hand the New Deal had hesitantly held out to urban government and urban residents in the 1930s was now an established feature of American political life. As one mayor told a House subcommittee investigating federal-state-local relations in 1957, big-city officials and interest groups knew their "way around fairly well down in Washington." The Federal Government, however, had by then become far different from the pre-Depression institution of that name. In the nation's attempt to cope with the challenges of modern industrial society and world peace, the authorities in Washington had greatly expanded their range of activities and administrative apparatus. Just as in the first half of the nineteenth century, cities again found federal decisions on such matters as internal improvements (for example, grants for airport construction), and contracts and installations (for example, military procurement and bases) important determinants of local economic health. But if practically everything the central government did—from giving price supports to agricultural products to fostering collective bargaining—affected metropolitan development, four federal programs instituted after 1933—public housing, urban renewal, home mortgage insurance, and large-scale highway build-

*Gelfand, Mark I. 1975. "Federal Programs and the Cities." Pp. 198–213 in *A Nation of Cities: The Federal Government and Urban America, 1933–1965*. New York: Oxford University Press. Copyright © 1975 by Oxford University Press, Inc. Reprinted by permission of Oxford University Press, Inc.

ing—left the greatest mark on the urban landscape. [In this selection, Gelfand discusses public housing and urban renewal.]

No federal endeavor in large cities aroused more political controversy than public housing.[1] Initiated as a recovery measure in a period of economic depression, the low-rent program represented one of the most radical legacies of the New Deal. Unlike social security, for example, which served the middle class, operated on actuarial principles and was immune from partisan criticism by 1952, public housing entailed government subsidies to the bottom third of the population and, consequently, never won wide popular support. The private American city could not take public housing to its heart.

Public housing met opposition in both Washington and the cities. Hardly a year passed between 1935 and 1960 without a congressional vote on public housing's fate; only the farm program could match that track record. Those fighting public housing at the national level fell into two groups: rural conservatives who disliked federal spending, especially in urban areas; and urban businessmen—particularly realtors and home builders—who felt government aid to the poor raised their property and income taxes and reduced their profits. The rural congressmen provided most of the votes against the program, but the financing of the intense anti-public housing lobbying campaign was assumed by the urban elements of the coalition. This alliance succeeded in virtually halting the program from 1939 to 1949 and keeping appropriations far below authorized limits from 1950 to 1960. The program's foes had also been able to add debilitating amendments to public housing legislation. What they could not accomplish in the national arena —killing the program completely—the realtors and home builders sought to bring about on the local scene. They supported candidates pledged to reject offers of federal housing aid, forced popular referenda on the question of proposed public housing construction, and encouraged neighborhood groups in their efforts to prevent the placement of projects in their midst. Thanks to these tactics, less than 440,000 public housing units, about one-tenth of the number needed to satisfy the housing requirements of the urban poor, were completed between 1939 and 1960.[2]

Those units actually built did not return their highest possible dividends to the cities. Crippling regulations in the law, unsatisfactory and often unsympathetic administration, community hostility, and socio-economic changes significantly reduced public housing's ability to help the poor and the cities. The program represented a net plus to the urban environment, but by 1960 few of its friends—social workers, labor unions, liberal mayors and congressmen—doubted that it could use an overhaul.

Typical of the statutory limitations on public housing were the curbs on construction expenses and tenant income. Proponents of the program had to accept these restrictions to blunt their opponents' allegations of extravagance with the taxpayers' money and competition with private enterprise. These concessions to America's laissez-faire heritage did not stop the local housing authorities (LHA) from building sound structures with provisions for air and light far superior to what private firms had constructed, but it did prevent the LHAs from supplying some basic amenities. Closets without doors, elevators that did not stop at every floor, bare lobbies and hallways were the penalty the poor paid for public landlordism. Compared to what they had left behind in their dark and dirty hovels this price was indeed small, but the psychological costs of the big, skyscraper-type projects (building large and up was supposed to be more economical) that were characteristic of public housing in Eastern and Midwestern cities could sometimes be overwhelming. "Visually they [i.e., projects] may be no more monotonous than a typical suburban tract," Catherine Bauer wrote in 1957,[3]

> but their density makes them seem much more institutional, like veterans' hospitals or old-fashioned orphan asylums. The fact that they are usually designed as islands—"community units" turning their back to the surrounding neighborhood, which looks entirely different—only adds to this institutional quality. Any charity stigma that attaches to subsidized housing is thus reinforced. Each project proclaims, visually, that it serves the "lowest-income group."

The drabness of the projects' milieu—one critic likened it to a well-kept cemetery—continuously reminded possibly forgetful tenants of their dependent position in society. To both resident and taxpayer, public housing became the "modern symbol of the poorhouse."[4]

Public housing's rules on income further isolated its beneficiaries from the rest of society. Families faced eviction once their earnings exceeded federally prescribed levels; after 1949, these limits were kept very low to avoid the charge of interference with the private housing market. Although this made more public housing available to the desperately poor, stricter enforcement of the income regulations also had some less positive results. The crackdown on over-income tenants deprived projects of their most successful residents and natural leaders; continued dislodgements obstructed the emergence of replacements. For those compelled to leave, the next move was often back to the slums. Their incomes might be above the public housing limits but far from the minimum necessary for decent private housing; for those remaining, the income limits slapped a "cast-iron top" on the incentive to improve. "Nothing," one housing official noted in 1956, "could be more murderous to the simple earthly American pattern of bettering oneself by little ingenious ways than the present regulations and rigmaroles on income eligibility."[5] A person had to refuse to earn more or to cheat to stay in public housing. In 1948, the median income of public housing families was 44 per cent below the median for all urban families; nine years later, the figure was 58 per cent.[6] Public housing was achieving its goal of serving the poverty-stricken, but in the process it was making itself more unpalatable to the rest of urban—and affluent—America, which associated the poor with rising crime rates and lower property values.[7]

The problems of race also burdened the public housing effort. Thanks to the dedicated work of Harold Ickes, the program's first director and a former president of the Chicago branch of the National Association for the Advancement of Colored People, Negroes had fared exceptionally well in the beginnings of the public housing endeavor. Ickes required localities to give blacks an equitable share of the new dwellings his agency constructed—about 30 per cent were so reserved—and inaugurated the practice of appointing racial relations advisers whose job was to protect minority group interests in all phases of the public housing venture. His successors continued these policies.[8] This unusual record did not go unnoticed: "The United States Housing Authority," declared Gunnar Myrdal in his classic study, *An American Dilemma* (1944), "has given him [the Negro] a better deal than has any other major federal public welfare agency." By the 1950s, however, public housing was so closely identified with Negro housing that the program could not be sustained in some big cities and could be continued in others only if public housing was kept away from white neighborhoods. Because of the large post-war migration of Negroes to Northern central cities and the blacks' inability to match the income gains of whites in this period, Negroes accounted for an increasingly large proportion of the population eligible for public housing. In Detroit, for example, 90 per cent of the people who fell within the law's income limits were black; in Chicago, 80 per cent. As the presence of blacks in projects became more marked, poor whites tended to shun public housing. By 1960, Negroes occupied nearly 50 per cent of all public housing units, and in cities like Los Angeles and Chicago 80 per cent of the tenants were non-white.[9]

The identification of public housing in the middle-class mind with overcrowded projects, the culture of poverty, and the invasion of racial minorities made the location of subsidized dwellings a volatile issue in local politics. Cities that rejected the realtor-home builder arguments about taxes and socialism—and most of the big ones did—were still divided about the best place to put these unpopular but necessary projects. The social workers and planners who staffed many of the LHAs favored vacant land sites. These offered the advantage of being cheaper and quicker to build on than slum properties; furthermore, with housing in short supply, it appeared to make no sense to destroy existing homes, slum or otherwise. But since vacant land was usually to be found only in outlying working- and middle-class neighborhoods, the LHAs' schemes were unacceptable to a majority of politically active city residents. They would support public housing only on the condition that it remained out of their communities. Elected municipal officials accepted these terms and set up informal arrangements for their implementation. In New York City, for example, no project could be approved by the Board of Estimate unless the borough president of the area involved gave his consent; the approval of the local alderman was required before the Chicago City Council would agree to a LHA proposal. The winning candidate in the 1949 Detroit mayoralty election rode into City Hall on his pledge to build public housing "where it is needed—in the slums." And that was where it was constructed in most large cities, thus helping to perpetuate the segregation of the poor and the Negro ghetto.[10]

Public housing's capacity to improve the central city environment was also diminished by the mechanics of the federal system. After 1937 the Federal Government itself did not build another public housing unit; it merely supplied funds for that purpose to those communities that wanted it. This change occurred in response to lower court decisions that had brought up the issue of the legality of Washington's use of its eminent domain powers to raze slums and construct low-cost housing. Afraid that a hostile Supreme Court might declare the entire PWA operation unconstitutional in adjudicating appeals of these cases from the lower courts, Roosevelt decided to rely upon the well-recognized police powers of the states and municipalities in the housing field. Good politics also dictated the switch. Conservatives who opposed the extension of national power might be appeased, and the reformers who chafed at Ickes's tight centralized direction of the program could be satisfied. Local control undoubtedly eased public housing's path through the courts and Congress, but it fostered the dichotomy between core cities and their suburbs in metropolitan areas. Most of the large central cities joined the program; very few of the suburbs, however, followed suit. Unlike the older core areas, the vast majority of suburbs had no serious slum problem and very few people below the poverty line. Constructing public housing, suburbanites believed, would only encourage other impoverished families to move in, driving up taxes and making their communities less attractive. Thus, at the same time that public housing and other federal programs were influencing many in the middle class to flee beyond the city limits, suburban zoning laws and the non-existence of public housing kept the poor bottled up in core cities, away from the growing job market in the suburbs and on the municipal welfare rolls.[11] . . .

II

Urban redevelopment-renewal, the first national legislation to deal explicitly with the central city, generated little of the political bitterness that plagued public housing in the 1950s, but it, too, had its human problems. The financial stringencies that kept the low-rent program from fulfilling the hopes of its sponsors also hindered the renewal effort; although in the latter instance, it was not a shortage of public funds so much as a lack of private capital. Federal subsidies were available, but the cities found it difficult to use them profitably and, at the same time, equitably. "Architecturally or socially," admitted Title I's supporters at the editorial board of *Architectural Forum* in 1958, urban renewal's accomplishments "do not match the political ingenuity that made them possible."

At the close of the 1950s, what stood out most about urban renewal was how little it had changed the face of American cities. When Title I cleared Congress in 1949 "there was a widespread expectation that a great redevelopment blitzkrieg was going to hit the country, that the scent of Federal money would nerve local planners and builders to undertake great things."[12] And, indeed, some startling transformations did take place. The grimy St. Louis riverfront received a thorough housecleaning in preparation for the construction of the graceful Gateway Arch and a new sports stadium; Philadelphia's historic downtown area, thanks to some imaginative federal-municipal cooperation, regained some of its former elegance; and New Haven's rat-infested Oak Street slum gave way to a gleaming complex of modern office buildings and fancy apartment houses. But behind the glitter, stark figures told another story. After more than a decade of action, less than ten square miles of blighted land had been acquired and only three square miles redeveloped. At urban renewal's "death-step pace" the job of salvaging the hundreds of square miles of slums would take centuries and even then might not be finished since new blight was forming at least as fast as the old disappeared. Instead of a blitzkrieg, the cities found themselves in a war of attrition, which they appeared to be losing.[13]

Urban renewal lagged for a variety of reasons. An important cause of the delay was the very complexity of the task. The demolition and rebuilding of entire city districts could not be done overnight; it required extensive consultations and deliberations at the local level. What was to be ripped down? What was to be put up in its place? Who would do it? How was it to be paid for? These questions all had to be decided before the city could begin protracted negotiations with the federal bureaucracy. Detailed and cumbersome procedures did nothing to ease the agony. As one mayor complained to a Senate committee in 1958, referring to the 1949 act and the scores of amendments to it, the law "is so full of 'provided thats' and 'notwithstandings' that it is a nightmare to track down just what is provided for." The paperwork entailed was stupefying, the steps in the planning and review process endless. On the average, more than two years elapsed between receipt of an application in HHFA offices and final approval of the federal grant. Total time consumed on projects, from beginning to completion, often ran as high as six to nine years.[14]

This dilatory schedule reduced the program's appeal to private investors. Yet their capital was essential to the success of the endeavor. Under the law, federal funds were available only for the purchase and clearance of blighted properties; rebuilding was to be the task of private enterprise. Realtors and construction firms had fought for this arrangement, but they proved hesitant in taking advantage of it. Although government subsidies in the form of "write-downs" made urban renewal a potentially lucrative outlet for investment, the long and uncertain incubation period scared many people away. "Redevelopment is a fine opportunity for profits served on a silver platter," observed a leading mortgage banker, "but the platter has a tight lid and is surrounded by mousetraps."[15] In 1960, over 5,000 acres of the 7,700 acres acquired by local renewal agencies remained unsold.[16]

Important consequences flowed from Title I's dependence upon a small pool of private funds. The 1949 act had been worked out as a compromise between those housing reformers who wished to use the new device to "help remove the impact of slums on human lives," and businessmen interested in restoring central city property values. As passed by the Democratic-controlled Congress, the measure seemed to favor the reformers: it contained a "predominantly residential" requirement to insure action against the slums and vested administration with the Housing and Home Finance Agency. Title I had been purposely drawn flexible so that it could contribute to city betterment, but in HHFA's mind, "the dog was slum clearance and the tail was community development."[17] Urban redevelopment's troubles in getting started in the early 1950s, however, gave businessmen a chance to reverse these priorities. Using their influence with the Eisenhower administration, they succeeded in easing the "predominantly residential" rule and converting urban redevelopment into the more economically oriented urban renewal whose goal was to rebuild the cities. Also, the Republican-led HHFA was philosophically inclined to allow local authorities greater discretion on how to proceed.[18]

Municipal officials quickly turned urban renewal to their own advantage. They found it politically profitable and financially expedient to channel the federal largesse into ambitious programs to revive downtown shopping and business centers and build conveniently located luxury housing so as to attract middle- and upper-class families back from the suburbs. They had little choice, given the realities of the electoral and real estate marketplace. Bankers could be induced to risk their money only if the rewards were to be large and reasonably secure; providing housing for the slum dweller obviously met neither of these standards under existing legislation. Furthermore, the reconstruction of central business districts and the erection of expensive apartments promised to add to the cities' sorely pressed property-tax base. And as an extra dividend, redevelopment permitted politicians to forge close ties with their communities' financial leaders; both groups possessed a common interest in fostering their city's image as a dynamic, vital, and growing metropolis. Instead of helping the ill-housed, urban renewal was used to enhance political reputations, provide profitable investment opportunities for lending institutions and builders, and indirectly improve the cities' economic foundations.[19]

Severe distortions were created in the slum clearance process by the subordination of urban renewal to the laws of supply and demand. Areas that could not objectively be called blighted were nonetheless demolished because their desirable locations made them ripe for "higher uses," such as office buildings and civic centers. Stable and decent neighborhoods, like Boston's West End and Los Angeles's Bunker Hill, fell below the wrecker's ball while truly deteriorated districts were allowed to stand because no one saw a way of making money out of them except as slums.[20] Urban renewal carried out beneath the banner of city betterment only aggravated the agony of being poor. In ten years, Title I was responsible for the destruction of over 140,000 units of housing, some standard, most substandard, but nearly all low-rent. Over that same period, in contrast, the redevelopment program built less than 40,000 units, of which only about 5 per cent were within the means of a low-income family.[21] Private, unsubsidized developers could not service this market, and by a quirk in the law, public housing was virtually excluded from renewal areas.[22] At a cost of hundreds of millions of dollars, urban renewal succeeded in materially reducing the supply of low-cost housing in American cities. Just as the liberals had feared, slum clearance cleared the slums without helping the slum resident. . . .[23]

No group suffered as much as did racial minorities. From the start, black leaders had feared that urban renewal might turn into "Negro removal." "Under the guise of 'city planning' and under the name of a 'reclamation' program," a black expert on housing wrote in 1940, "minority groups may be forced to relinquish areas in which they have established themselves at considerable sacrifice."[24] Urban redevelopment presented a triple threat to the Negro: it could be used to displace him from desirable neighborhoods; it could force the break-up of integrated neighborhoods; and it could reduce the supply of living space open to black occupancy. The policies followed in tenanting the nation's first redevelopment project, New York's Stuyvesant Town, built immediately after the end of World War II under state law, sharpened the Negroes' anxiety. Acting on the premise that "Negroes and whites don't mix," the life insurance company that owned the property barred Negroes as "a matter of business and economics." If similar considerations guided future projects, then Negroes would find themselves shut out from all the benefits of the pending federal subsidy. To prevent this, Negro spokesmen demanded inclusion of a non-discrimination clause in the 1949 legislation; they also urged that site occupants be given first preference in renewal areas.[25] Neither proposal received much support in Congress, however; few in the civil rights contingent on Capitol Hill wanted to imperil urban redevelopment by burdening it with the explosive racial issue.[26] Title I was thus silent on this crucial matter, but HHFA officials recognized that the measure's relocation requirements obliged them to find a solution to the "important and delicate minority housing problems which will arise in connection with the great majority of redevelopment projects."[27]

HHFA did not find that solution in the 1950s. Housing Administrator Albert Cole delivered numerous speeches arguing that the success of urban renewal depended upon the fair treatment of minorities, and the agency laid down several regulations for the protection of Negro rights. The talk and the rules, however, accomplished practically nothing, because an honest commitment to the protection of black interests might lead to a slowdown in the pace of the program.[28] Federal officials stood idly by as local authorities converted slum clearance into "Negro clearance" along the very lines minority leaders had predicted. Non-whites accounted for over two-thirds of those uprooted; Southern and border cities demolished integrated slums for reuse only by Caucasians; Northern communities constructed new housing far beyond the rent-paying capabilities of most blacks. Relocation arrangements, inadequate to begin with, degenerated still further when minorities were involved. Low incomes plus residential discrimination confined Negroes to the ghettos, placed severe strains on transitional areas, and tipped the shaky racial balance in public housing. Urban renewal, concluded the Commission on Civil Rights in 1959, "is accentuating or creating partners of clear-cut racial separation."[29] Those opportunities urban redevelopment had presented initially for improving the living conditions of Negroes vanished in the cause of "municipal progress" and private property. . . .

NOTES

1. Welfare programs were not a major issue in federal-municipal politics after 1940 and prior to the 1960s, because the relief rolls stayed fairly stable and manageable in the post-war era thanks to the generally good economic picture and the tractability of the poor. Also, in many instances, relief was a county, not a city responsibility. In either case, states, not the Federal Government, were the instrumentality localities had to deal with in this program.

2. Leonard Freedman, *Public Housing: The Politics of Poverty* (New York, 1969), pp. 15–57.

3. Catherine Bauer, "The Dreary Deadlock of Public Housing," *Architectural Forum,* CVI (May 1957), 141–42.

4. National Federation of Settlements and Neighborhood Centers, *A New Look at Public Housing* (New York, 1958), p. 4.

5. Elizabeth Wood, "Public Housing and Mrs. McGee," *Journal of Housing,* XIII (Dec. 1956), 427–28.

6. Robert M. Fisher, *Twenty Years of Public Housing* (New York, 1959), pp. 164–70.

7. William G. Grigsby, *Housing Markets and Public Policy* (Philadelphia, 1963), pp. 282–83; H. Warren Dunham and Nathan D. Grundstein, "The Impact of a Confusion of Social Objectives in Public Housing: A Preliminary Analysis," *Marriage and Family Living,* XVII (May 1955), 110–12.

8. For examples of Ickes's insistence upon fairness, see Ickes memo for Roosevelt, July 3, 1935; A. R. Clas memo for Ickes, Dec. 12, 1935, OF 63, Franklin D. Roosevelt MSS., Franklin D. Roosevelt Library; Robert C. Weaver, "Racial Policy in Public Housing," *Phylon,* I (Second Quarter 1940), 149–61.

9. Davis McEntire, *Residence and Race* (Berkeley, 1960), p. 329; Commission on Civil Rights, *Report* (Washington, D.C., 1959), p. 475.

10. The classic study of the issues involved in site selection is Martin Meyerson and Edward C. Banfield, *Politics and Planning, and the Public Interest: The Case of Public Housing in Chicago* (New York, 1955). Also see Elizabeth Wood, "Public Housing," *Planning 1958* (Chicago, 1958), p. 198.

11. for a good discussion of "the implications of the new Federal system," see Charles Abrams, *The City Is the Frontier* (New York, 1965), pp. 238–49. Civil rights groups filed a suit in federal court in 1971 contesting the constitutionality of the local control provisions of the 1937 Housing Act.

12. Daniel Seligman, "The Enduring Slums," in The Editors of *Fortune, The Exploding Metropolis* (Garden City, N.Y., 1958), p. 103.

13. Housing and Home Finance Agency, *14th Annual Report: 1960* (Washington, D.C., 1961), p. 287; "The Halting Progress of Urban Renewal," *Architectural Forum,* CVII (Oct. 1957), 240.

14. Richard H. Leach, "The Federal Urban Renewal Program: A Ten-Year Critique," *Law and Contemporary Problems,* XV (Autumn 1960), 779–80; Commission on

Urban Problems, *Building the American City*, pp. 165–69; Frederick O'R. Hayes to Roscoe C. Martin, Sept. 27, 1960, R 4–23/57.1, Bureau of the Budget Files, Executive Office of the President, Washington, D.C. One member of HHFA's legal staff called Title I "the most complicated grant-in-aid program in the Federal Government." Quoted in "Our Confused Housing Program," *Architectural Forum*, CVI (April 1957), 236.

15. Cited in Jeanne R. Lowe, *Cities in a Race With Time* (New York, 1967), p. 172.

16. Lyman Brownfield, "The Disposition Problem in Urban Renewal," *Law and Contemporary Problems*, XXV (Autumn (1960), 740.

17. Raymond Foley to Elmer Staats, Jan. 27, 1949; R. E. Neustadt/J. E. Reeve memor for the director, March 3, 1949, R 2–3/48.4, Records of the Bureau of the Budget, Record Group 51, National Archives; B. T. Fitzpatrick memo for Foley, Sept. 28, 1950, HHFA Administrators' Files, Box 2, Records of the Department of Housing and Urban Development, Record Group 207, National Archives.

18. See *supra*, pp. 171–75.

19. Grigsby, *Housing Markets and Public Policy*, pp. 323–25; Raymond Vernon, *The Myth and Reality of Our Urban Problems* (Cambridge, Mass., multilithed, 1962), pp. 69–71; Scott Greer, *Urban Renewal and American Cities* (Indianapolis, 1965), pp. 82–84, 91–97. The National Commission on Urban Problems found that most municipalities conceived of urban renewal "as a federally financed gimmick to provide relatively cheap land for a miscellany of profitable, prestigious enterprises"; *Building the American City*, p. 153.

20. Herbert J. Gans, "The Human Implications of Current Redevelopment and Relocation Policy," *Journal of the American Institute of Planners*, XXV (Feb. 1959), 16–18; Abrams, *City Is the Frontier*, pp. 116–23.

21. HHFA, *14th Annual Report: 1960*, p. 287; National Commission on Urban Problems, *Building the American City*, p. 125; Greer, *Urban Renewal*, p. 3; John H. Staples, "Urban Renewal: A Comparative Study of Twenty-Two Cities, 1950–1960," *Western Political Quarterly*, XXIII (June 1970), 294–304.

22. Public housing could be built on renewal sites, but the cities would have to pay more of the costs than if it was built in other areas. Besides having to pick up the normal local share of public housing subsidies, municipalities also had to contribute one-third of the write-down expense for renewal land. Rather than contract for this "double-subsidy," most cities put their low-rent housing elsewhere or, as sometimes happened, built none at all. Thus Title I, which public housers had hoped would solve many of the land price problems of their program, only made public housing construction more difficult.

23. "My present theme song," Catherine Bauer declared in 1949, "is that 25 years from now someone will write a book proving that the thing that finally ruined our cities was passing a big clearance program in the middle of a chronic housing shortage." Bauer to Warren J. Vinton, Oct. 30, 1949, Box 4, Warren J. Vinton MSS., Collection of Regional History and University Archives, Cornell University Library. Cf. Merlin Smelker memor for R. E. Neustadt, Jan. 14, 1949, R 2–3/48.4, Bureau of the Budget Records.

24. Robert C. Weaver, "Racial Minorities and Public Housing," *Proceedings, National Conference of Social Work 1940* (New York, 1940), p. 290.

25. Robert C. Weaver, *The Negro Ghetto* (New York, 1948), p. 324; George B. Nesbitt,

"Relocating Negroes from Urban Slum Clearance Sites," *Journal of Land Economics*, XXV (Aug. 1949), 275–88; Joseph B. Robison, "The Story of Stuyvesant Town," *Nation*, CLXXII (June 2, 1951), 514–16.

26. The fact that the Bricker-Cain amendment barring segregation applied only to public housing and not to urban redevelopment is confirmation both of its authors' lack of sincerity and Title I's wide popularity even among conservatives. See Charles Abrams, "Human Rights in Slum Clearance," *Survey*, LXXXVI (Jan. 1950), 28.

27. Memo comparing federal Works Agency proposal and Title I of S. 138, undated [early 1949], R 2–3/48.4, Budget Bureau Records. The HHFA's race relations advisor wrote that the urban redevelopment program "will be made or broken largely by the caliber of the appreciation of governmental representatives to the minority group considerations involved." Frank S. Horne memo for Raymond Foley, Sept. 12, 1949, HHFA Administrators' Files, Box 2, HUD Records.

28. The 1959 study of the Commission on Civil Rights noted that the Urban Renewal Administration required local agencies to submit detailed data on their plans to rehouse minorities, but that URA never checked to see that these promises were carried out. Unlike PHA, URA had no racial relations service of its own; Commission on Civil Rights, *Report*, pp. 483–88.

29. *Ibid.*, p. 459. For a case study, see Theodore J. Lowi, *The End of Liberalism* (New York, 1969), pp. 251–63.

23
Local Government and Renewal Policies*

Norton E. Long

Mounting concern is expressed by public officials, publicists and an odd assortment of businessmen, liberals and others over the alleged decay and decline of the central city and the older suburb. Causes of alarm are as varied as fear for the decline of our culture if central cities cease to provide propitious locations for museums, universities, symphonies and operas, and anxiety over the social consequences of the central city's becoming the segregated container of poverty and color increasingly alienated from the affluent white suburbs that surround it.

Clear thinking about the congeries of problems that are bundled to-

*Long, Norton E. 1966. "Local Government and Renewal Policies. Pp. 422–434 in *Urban Renewal: The Record and the Controversy*, edited by James Q. Wilson. Cambridge, MA: The MIT Press. Copyright © 1966 The MIT Press. Reprinted by permission of The MIT Press.

gether is made difficult by propagandist hysteria and muddled metaphors that raise emotions but fail to enlighten. Thus the core city is treated as a heart of a metropolitan area that may become diseased and thus suffer dire ill not only to itself but extending to the whole metropolitan body. No vital statistics on central city heart attacks are offered, however, nor any evidence on metropolitan bodies suffering from central city heart disease. The metaphor sometimes presents itself as the central city in the role of a tree and the suburbs as clinging parasitic vines who are destined to fall with the tree in a common fate. Again the metaphor is not designed to lead to factual translation but to poetic and evocative conviction. The rhetoric of political persuasion and nostalgic sentimental mysticism is designed to avoid both facts and rational analysis.

The assumed healthy state of the city is never spelled out. Unlike humans, cities rarely die, though they do decline and some fail to grow. The vital statistics of cities are as yet undeveloped. Accordingly it is difficult to make meaningful comparisons with past states in their history. In terms of what dimensions can we say they are getting better or worse? Impressionism is rife, and the literary imagination has free rein. Since those who view with alarm the present trends are short on reliable statistics or documentation, the debate takes on a character that defies decision by reference to objectively verifiable facts. A melange of fact, fancy and ideology creates conditions in which the putative virtue of intentions counts for more than reasoned argument and evidence.

What has clearly happened to many central cities is that they have built up the greatest part of their available land and have been prevented from expanding by the resistance of other local government units. As a result the ecology of growth and decay which used to coexist in the growing city tends to become more and more divided between city and suburbs with the city as the oldest, most built-up area, usually accounting for far more of the decay than the growth. However, the condition of the central city may be duplicated in an even more aggravated form in older declining suburbs.

The imbalance between growth and decay in the territorially constricted city has serious consequences for the city and perhaps for the society generally. Aging city real estate has rising maintenance costs with declining revenues. Residential and other demand turns toward the more modern and attractive structures built beyond central city borders. The attractiveness of these newer structures economically and otherwise produces a selective migration of population and industry from the central city. The net result of this is to increase central city costs while at the same time reducing central city resources. To the extent this becomes significantly the case, the process might be expected to feed on itself. Those who can move out, escaping the rising taxes the declining base necessitates, and those seeking a high level of public goods transfer their residence from the central city, whose financial squeeze must result in service deficiencies.

Looking at this process one may distinguish between what happens as a result of the earliest settlement's being largely populated with the oldest and most obsolescent structures and what happens because the earliest settlement is largely built up and tightly hemmed in by political boundaries. Conceivably local government might have been so designed that it would have contained all or most metropolitan growth within it, as was the case at one time with the early central city. In such a case the local fiscal disparities and population segregations that now confront us could not have taken their present form. Differences between growth and decay, suburb and slum, would have been the differences in neighborhoods observable in all cities. If growth and decay were balanced off, they might indeed be regarded as complementary and the panic over the decline of the central city seen in a perspective of regional change and development.

But the political isolation of the central city and the older suburb from the rest of the metropolitan area represents more than a mere line on a map. It represents significant differences in available resources for the provision of public goods. It represents likely frictions and rigidities in the labor and housing markets. It represents a structuring of identifications and values that have major consequences for the political decision-making process. Each corporate community develops its own political and economic nationalism, and its public officials and leadership tend to score success and failure in terms of narrowly selfish particularistic and parochial concerns. It is a race for corporate survival and a place in the sun in which "every man for himself and devil take the hindermost" is a maxim built into the system.

Public urban renewal policy has been built on an acceptance of the jurisdictional divisions of the urban status quo. It has sought remedies for urban blight and decay in terms of measures designed piecemeal for each segmented urban jurisdiction. This policy was initially based on the supposition that relatively minor hindrances stood in the way of a natural process of renewal by which a city, like a forest, would replace its decay with new growth covering the same territory. The failure of this beneficent process to take place was ascribed to difficulties in land assemblage requiring powers of eminent domain not possessed by private developers. However, despite the supposed economics of natural renewal, public policy went beyond the use of eminent domain for land assemblage to the use of subsidy for land write-down. It was thus clearly recognized that natural renewal with eminent domain would not work. Had genuine concern with economics been a major criterion of decision, the necessity of subsidy would have forced rethinking of the argument. However, claims were made that the renewed area would, like a beneficent cancer in reverse, uplift surrounding land values and, like some Keynesian multiplier, permit the natural renewal to proceed elsewhere once the locational pump had been primed. That landowners should demand prices comparable to those paid by renewal authorities and that these prices without writedown subsidies should inhibit new construction outside the renewal area seems economic logic.

Nonetheless the theory of urban renewal has historic warrant. Neighborhoods and cities have in fact renewed themselves and are now, in the vast majority of cases where renewal is going on, doing so without subsidy under private auspices and the profit motive. Bernard Frieden's *The Future of Old Neighborhoods* gives eloquent testimony to the vitality of the renewal process. But as Frieden's study abundantly shows, there is an economics to the natural renewal process. It doesn't occur everywhere, equally, at all times and under all circumstances.

In a sense the official theory of urban renewal refused to admit the possibility of permanent locational obsolescence. Agricultural land, mines, even whole states, may fall victim to technological change and population movements, but not central business districts. Ponce de Leon's fountain of eternal youth was supposed to apply to them even though the fountain had to be found in the federal treasury.

The history of many cities had made the theory of natural renewal highly plausible. The deficiency of the theory was its failure to recognize the dependence of locational values on the effects of transport technology. The dynamism of this technology, opening up a wide range of competing locational choices, has upset the stable pattern of the city of the pedestrian and the horse, and even that of the age of steam and the trolley. The motor car and the truck have invaded the locational Garden of Eden, and the world will never be the same. To change the figure, one may suspect that not all urban renewal's horses nor all its men will ever restore the central city to what it was again.

As Herbert Gans has pointed out, our public policy has been much as if we regarded our aging motor cars as a mobile slum and thus a public eyesore and perhaps, to use the ubiquitous figure applied to slums of blight and disease, a health hazard on the highways. Thus public policy would be to subsidize the destruction of these vehicles and reduce the mobile slums. General Motors, Ford, and Chrysler might find much to applaud in such a policy if the used car market gets inconvenient. Absurd as it might seem to subsidize the destruction of aging motor cars and thereby deprive people of their means of transport, it has not seemed absurd to subsidize the destruction of much-needed scarce low-rental housing.

The metaphors that have substituted for facts and theory in dealing with slums, housing occupied by the poor, have made it possible to follow a policy with houses that would have been readily seen to be absurd with respect to motor cars.

Absurd as the policy has been, looked at from a public, federal objective which was initially concerned with housing low-income groups, it has not been absurd from the point of view of central city mayors, the Housing and Home Finance Agency, or the constellation of interests that have found urban renewal useful or profitable. The tragedy of the nation's housing program was that its support was always more as public works for countercyclical purposes than as a broadly accepted program of redistribution to the poor. When after World War II the New Deal coalition broke up, public housing became less and less politically viable. Given the income limitations on public housing residence and the position of the Negro in the economy, it was inevitable that public housing should emerge as Negro housing, with all the consequent hostility that fact was bound to engender.

The late Senator Taft feared that the urban renewal program would mean that instead of subsidizing the housing of those who could not afford it we would end up by subsidizing housing for those who could. In this he has proved prophetic.

Central city mayors strapped for funds have found a public relations gold mine in renewing central city business districts, providing luxury apartments and new capital investment with federal subsidy. Harassed federal housing officials have found new and heretofore unlooked for allies in downtown businessmen, banks, the real estate industry, and the metropolitan press. To this new-found business respectability they could add the continuing ideological support of liberals and labor. While some years ago a symposium in *Law and Contemporary Problems* in which federal officials themselves took part sounded a warning note, it is only now that a swelling chorus of critics as various as Michael Harrington and Martin Anderson point to the program's devastating impact on the supply of housing for the poor. The bureaucracy reacts with outraged protestations of its good intentions and cries of foul.

It is grossly unfair to point the finger of moral blame at bureaucracies because they respond to the survival interests of their agencies, which are to please the customers who can generate effective political demand for their wares. A major misfortune of our federal system is that the national government, because of its constitutional limitations, intervenes in local affairs through single-purpose agencies. While it can spend for the general welfare, it spends through a housing agency or through a bureau of public roads. As a result its single-purpose impacts are uncoordinated by any effective or well thought out concern for the local community as a whole. "My job is housing, not education or employment. My job is to build roads, not to plan for social welfare." This seems to be the no-nonsense philosophy of the single-purpose agency. The result is an unplanned, unforeseen impact. Frequently, in the case of the housing agency, it amounts to a subsidizing of the internecine warfare that fragments a metropolitan housing and labor market.

Mayors, like bureaucracies, respond to the forces that seem likely to elect and re-elect them. It is not surprising that beefing up the central city business district, attracting middle-class luxury apartment dwellers, and reducing the numbers of the poor and Negroes should have its appeal. This is more the case since the federal government picks up a large share of the tab. Democratic Mayor Richard Lee of New Haven became a folk hero by persuading the Eisenhower Administration to subsidize Republican businessmen to remain in New Haven rather than relocate outside the city. Mayor Lee's exploit has set a fashion. Unfortunately, the arithmetic of the sums spent in New Haven makes the generalization of its experience astronomically costly and hence unlikely. However, far lesser sums can keep an urban lottery going in which any mayor with the right political arithmetic may win.

What has happened with federal subsidies in urban renewal appears likely to be extended to the field of transport. Mass transit, in its extended form at least, is sick and getting sicker. Fare box revenues have to be supplemented with tax dollars. The federal government is being asked as that jurisdiction most capable of raising revenue to pick up part and perhaps down the road a very large share of the bill. Again the justification of this proposal largely depends on the supposed ill effects on downtown and the central city of the failure or lack of rail mass transit. Despite the unpromising experience of the Long Island Railroad in what would appear to be the classically favorable high-density to high-density situation, the San Francisco Bay area has embarked on a new rail mass transit program with only an ultimate hope of federal aid.

Concern with urban change has led to the typical political response, an attempt to halt the threat to vested values by untoward market forces through government subsidy of those values. With billions invested in central city real estate and rich legacies of attached sentiment, it would be idle to expect anything but an attempt to offset the operation of the economy by political means. The farm program is the model of governmental intervention to impede market reallocation of resources. At this point, however, federal intervention in cities more resembles a rivers and harbors grab bag than a policy as developed as the farm program.

From the foregoing it should appear that there are two main competing methods of resource allocation with their variants at work. On the one hand there is the market, in its varied forms with their limitations; on the other there is the political decision-making process. Both decision-making processes need to be considered on their merits as they produce socially desirable results. The merit of the market is the likelihood that competing possibilities will be considered. That is, in the process of market allocation alternatives in terms of profitability, market demand and opportunity costs are built into the decision-making process. For a variety of purposes market determinations are inadequate to achieve the appropriate ends of public policy. The range of values represented by market forces may not include or at least adequately weight those considered important by public policy. Education and welfare are clearly of this sort, though a mixture of market and public forces might need considering rather than exclusive reliance on one or the other. What is crucial about the decision-making process, public or market, is the policy outcome it produces. Here one of the major differences between market and political decision-making is that we have a theory of the coordinative operation of the market, whereas in political decision-making we know that purposive, planned coordination to secure a general intended result is rare and difficult. In political decision-making we are likely to have the unintended piecemeal cumulation of the impacts of single-purpose agencies. This latter is especially true of federal impacts, since there is no local budgetary process or planning process to harmonize them in terms of any conception of the local community as a whole.

The lack of any structure in the federal government to consider, at the very least, the likely but unintended cumulative effect of federal programs on cities has been pointed out by Robert Connery and Richard Leach. Given the structure of interests and power, it is unlikely that even a cabinet office of urban affairs would achieve coordination in the present system. However, there is at least a chance that we might develop a theory of what we were about in the large as opposed to the present unthought-out historical accumulation of piecemeal vested interventions. This to be sure would amount to the federal government's having a theory of the desirable structure of local government. To be fair, the Housing and Home Finance Agency has had its doubts about the present lack of coordination and has been moving gingerly towards the encouragement of metropolitan planning.

An adequate theory of the political decision-making system needs to examine the kind, range and weight of the values that are built into the relevant governmental centers of decision that determine the production and allocation of public goods and burdens as they affect cities and suburbs. The Housing and Home Finance Agency, the Bureau of Public Roads, the Department of Health, Education and Welfare, and the Pentagon, to name but four, all have major effects on local governments. The structure of powers and the controlling definitions insure that quite different values and obviously uncoordinated ones will govern their impact. What is true at the federal level is reproduced at the state. But the higher levels of government are less important in many ways in their value fragmentation than the local.

At one time the size and compositions of an ecology of local governments such as eighteenth-century Boston were probably of little importance except for religious divergences. The mix of classes was roughly the same. The difference in fiscal capability, given the modest scale of public goods, was probably of limited significance. This has radically changed. Public goods, especially for the lower income groups, are of major importance. The fragmentation and segregation of the metropolitan area have created a situation where each separate political community is in no sense a sample of people roughly similar to its neighbor. It differs in resources, in class, in ethnic and frequently in religious make-up. Thus the constituency to which each separate set of officials and civic leaders must look has built-in differences. The population mix of the metropolitan area as a whole has no political or civic leadership that must look to its total characteristics. Equally there is no way of mobilizing total metropolitan fiscal or human resources.

Two conflicting purposes are at war in American local government. First, we are more and more concerned with the consumption of public goods. This has a number of consequences. As the poor of the central city become politically aroused and competent, the old neighborhood differences in the provision of public services come under attack, and in any event more is demanded in the way of public services, with consequent increasing municipal costs. The provision of public goods becomes a municipal avenue for the redistribution of income. To escape this redistribution and to secure segregated quality public goods are major appeals of the suburb. In fact the growth of the importance of public goods in our consumption raises the serious problem of how we are to give effect to the inequality of incomes in their consumption. A range of suburbs provides a ready answer. If rents and housing costs segregate by income, it becomes possible to consume differentially public goods in accordance with one's income. The older system of neighborhood differentiation in the central city had always been vulnerable to the egalitarian norm among fellow citizens, to say nothing of legal requirements. But beyond this the higher income groups were subject to the political power to tax of their more numerous fellows.

The market array of differentiated public goods presented by central city and suburbs with their varying population mixes has seemed to some an admirable means of providing freedom and diversity in the consumption of public goods and to others a superior mode of managing conflict.

It has, however, major limitations for realizing the second great purpose that is at war with this first in American local government. If the first purpose in American local government is to promote the possibility of segregation and differentiation in the consumption of public goods, the second and contradictory purpose that is emerging is redistribution. We normally think of the federal government as the major and all-important instrument for the redistribution of wealth because of the income tax and the New Deal welfare programs. We are now beginning to appreciate the significance of education and the housing and labor market for the redistribution of roles, which is what is fundamental. Here local government and local leaderships are of enormous significance, as the civil rights struggle makes abundantly clear.

Metropolitan Toronto has been an enormous success as a public works agency to meet physical needs of near disaster proportions, acting through the common consent of the representatives of its corporate constitutents. Now that it has moved from physical public works to a consideration of redistribution, the matching of human needs with unequally distributed fiscal resources, its success is less impressive.

One should not minimize the value of Toronto's public works accomplishment and its relevance to the American metropolitan area. But when that is recognized, it must be faced that the really critical task is that of redistribution. For this task the fragmented metropolitan area has neither tools nor will. It is organized to frustrate the emergence of any sense of territorial community. It provides no means to institutionalize an effective leadership or to mobilize the ample human and fiscal resources it contains. The problems of today's cities can scarcely be dealt with seriously in areas less inclusive than the metropolitan housing market and the metropolitan labor market. Housing, jobs and education are the critical items on the municipal agenda of redistribution.

Local governments that do not embrace the resources, human and material, to handle these problems and represent the full range of the population involved with them will prove fatally anemic. The problems will not disappear. Their solution will pass to central levels of government. Centralization must make up for local incapacity. The costs in loss of local self-government and their consequences for democracy nationally will be serious.

Our present piecemeal intervention in local governments is largely designed to make viable the status quo. If a paramount need is local government capable of mobilizing the leadership, popular support and fiscal resources necessary to meet redistributive tasks that face us, then present federal policy or lack of policy toward urban change is an expensive luxury.

We must get to the serious task of examining how we can go about building local governments seriously capable of meeting our redistributory needs with as much freedom for differentiation in life styles and public goods consumption as may be compatible with meeting those needs. To do this we require some kind of minimal agreement on what we think the role of local government should be. Given our commitment to federalism and the decentralization of power, that role has to be considerable if the critical demands of present-day society are to be met. Where local leaderships are inadequate to the task of managing conflict and dealing with change, the federal government may be compelled to intervene. Where its intervention is through the blunt instrument of force, only time is bought. We are increasingly aware of the prime importance of indigenous leadership.

As presently constituted, our metropolitan areas fragment and dissipate human and material resources. The pattern of local governments implicitly and explicitly emphasizes the pursuit of certain values and the neglect or rejection of others. Specifically, no government is concerned with optimizing the use of the area-wide resources of the housing market or the labor market. This has led in the case of urban renewal to the destruction of scarce low-rent housing in the central city and its replacement with relatively abundant high-rent luxury housing. Given the powerlessness of the poor and the definition of the situation by central city officials, such a policy has seemed to make sense. Commitment to the local government status quo has made federal housing officials the abettors of policies that are designed to accentuate intermunicipal competition for scarce tax assets rather than an area-wide rational allocation of housing supply to meet the range of human needs and incomes. The pattern has built into it a balkanized competitive nationalism. Federal policy, following the lines of least resistance, tends to accept and accentuate it. Thus the poverty program conceives of poverty as being meaningfully attacked by disparate and competitive cities and towns with little or no over-all common action, and this in the face of the reality of the metropolitan housing and labor market.

In the case of the metropolitan area, the whole is considerably less than the sum of its parts. Or, more accurately, there is no whole. Yet the alternative to the creation of some meaningful, governmentally effective whole is the festering of unsolved problems and the transfer of power to those levels of government that are adequate in resources and decision-making capacity. The metropolitan area is for most people the lowest level at which an adequate sample of people and problems can be given a territorially structured government. To deal with the problems a government needs to have to deal with them in terms of its constituency and to be able to deal with them in terms of its resources. The two hundred-odd metropolitan areas that contain the bulk of us have the resources, human and material, to take on major tasks, but their lack of effective organization for these tasks paralyzes capabilities, vision and will. We are organized to avoid major local efforts rather than to undertake them. The philosophy is one of escape from rather than acceptance of governmental challenge.

The gerrymandering of the poor, the Negro, and even the rich that occurs in our metropolitan areas creates a condition of powerlessness and irresponsibility. It has been viewed by many with satisfaction as a kind of metropolitan public goods shopping center where one votes with one's feet and one's pocketbook. Consumership becomes the synonym for citizenship and all problems are solved by the workings of the political analogue of the market. This reduction of politics to economics has an escapist attraction. But it won't work. Even the democracy of the buck requires political action to insure the freedom of the market from noneconomic discrimination.

If the burden of government is not to mount inexorably to the federal level, strong local governments, strong in human and material resources with territories and constituencies embracing the full range of major problems and population resources, need to be grown. The federal government must substitute for its policy of piecemeal intervention and shoring up of the local status quo a positive, well-thought-out concern for the kind of local government that can and will bear the burdens that now concern us. Creativity was not done with once and for all with the Philadelphia Convention.

The other side of the coin of creating strong adequate local areal governments is the maintenance of variety, diversity and local creativity. While lack of human and material resources creates the apathy of powerlessness, inadequately structured size may forbid participation and engender a monotonously mediocre bureaucratized uniformity. Dean Rose of the University of Toronto School of Social Work, in his case against the total amalgamation of the corporate units of Toronto Metro into the City of Toronto, makes much of New York's inability to create meaningful civic participation at the neighborhood level. Giantism creates serious problems, especially if it destroys spontaneity, involvement and creative diversity. We need to think carefully of the structure of government that can insure the essentials of redistribution, serve as an adequate protagonist for areal planning and the metropolitan housing and labor market, and still permit room enough for a vital and even competitive diversity among its municipal components. Municipalities which seek to renew themselves do so most effectively through the maintenance of their public goods: education, police and the services. Private parties will spend large sums to renew aging structures where these services excel. The most powerful antidote to locational obsolescence in the hands of a municipality is not in the brick and mortar cosmetics of urban renewal but in the continued human renewal of the quality of its public service. Encouragement of this competitive vitality is needed to avoid the bureaucratic lethargy of giantism.

In a society devoted to the conflicting goals of freedom and equality we have to strike an uneasy and constantly shifting balance. Committed to equality of opportunity, we are equally committed to the recognition of unequal achievement. As public goods become an ever greater part of our consumption, we must re-examine the structure of their production and distribution for its consequences, intended and unintended, on the implementation of our ideals.

24

Federal Aid to Cities: Patterns of City Participation and Funding Distributions, 1950–1986*

Michael J. Rich

One of the more important changes in American federalism during the post-World War II era was the emergence of a direct federal-local partnership. In 1950, all but a small percentage of federal aid was allocated to state governments. As the amount and number of grant programs increased in the 1960s and 1970s, much of this aid was channeled directly to local governments.[1] One report estimated that by 1978 almost half of all federal aid was allocated to local governments — 25 percent directly and another 20 percent that was "passed through."[2] Formula entitlement programs such as general revenue sharing and community development block grants also broadened the scope of city participation to the extent that almost 80 percent of the 80,000-plus units of local government received some type of direct assistance from the federal treasury.[3] In 1950 federal grants were an important component of municipal expenditures in only a few big cities for a few selected functions, most notably public assistance. Twenty-five years later, federal grants had become "big ticket" items in the budgets of cities of all sizes, regions, and categories of need, and they financed activities that touched nearly every municipal department and agency. Community and economic development is an appropriate policy area for studying the impacts of changes in fiscal federalism because it mirrors many of the overall changes

*Rich, Michael J. 1989. "Federal Aid to Cities: Patterns of City Participation and Funding Distributions, 1950–1986." *Urban Resources* 5, no. 2 (Winter 1989): 7–32. Copyright © 1989 by University of Cincinnati. Reprinted by permission of Dr. Leslie Chard, ed., University of Cincinnati, Cincinnati, OH.

taking place during this period.[4] Allocations for community and economic development increased substantially. Between 1960 and 1980 such federal outlays increased by more than 1700 percent in real terms, a rate of growth about five times greater than that for total federal grant-in-aid outlays during this period.[5] All but a small percentage of this aid was allocated directly to local governments. In 1950, only a few cities were participants in the urban renewal program. In 1986, there were more than 700 entitlement cities in the CDBG program, and more than 1,000 additional cities, towns, and counties were assisted through the state-administered small cities CDBG program.[6]

This paper examines the federal program experience for the 383 cities with populations of 50,000 or more during the period 1950–1986, that is, from the beginning of the urban renewal program through most of the Reagan administration.[7] The programs and funding years examined are as follows: Urban Renewal (1949–1974), Model Cities (1967–1974), Community Development Block Grants (1974–1986), Urban Development Action Grants (1978–1986), all administered by the department of Housing and Urban Development, and the Title I Public Works (1966–1986), and Local Public Works (1976–1977) programs run by the Economic Development Administration. In particular, the paper analyzes the impacts of the shift from categorical to block grants on city participation and its attendant impacts on the distribution of federal aid. The overall study design thus involves both comparative and longitudinal features. It is comparative in that it examines city participation and funding distributions for six community development programs administered by two federal agencies and includes both project and broad-based formula grant programs within each agency. It is longitudinal in its analysis of city participation rates and funding allocations over time.

City Participation in Federal Grant Programs

Participation in the Urban Renewal program started slowly, grew very rapidly, and then leveled off in its latter years. In the program's first seven years the total number of participating cities remained fairly stable, although the composition of that pool changed as many cities dropped out because of local controversy or opposition.[8] For example, several cities were forced to suspend or terminate their urban renewal activities when their states' enabling legislation was declared unconstitutional. In the program's next seven years, the number of participant cities more than doubled, rising from 96 in 1955 to 195 to 1962. Although new cities subsequently continued to enter the program, the rate of growth slowed considerably by the late 1960s; only 26 cities entered the program between 1968 and its termination in 1974.

EDA's Title I Public Works program shows a similar pattern of development, although its funding was on a much smaller scale. The number of cities participating in the Model Cities program doubled between 1967 and 1968; this was due largely to the Johnson administration's decision to add a "second round" of competition to increase the number of participant cities, a move designed to help insure Congress' appropriation of supplemental funds to enable the first-round model cities to carry out their programs.[9] Unlike the other categorical programs, the number of cities participating in the UDAG program increased rapidly from the program's start; the number doubled within four years, from 90 in 1978 to 191 in 1981. By contrast, the number of participant cities in the CDBG program has been high and constant throughout the program's history. While there was no change in the number of *sample* cities participating in the program, the number of entitlement jurisdictions increased by nearly 40 percent between 1975 and 1986, with most of the gains taking place within the last six years. Between 1980 and 1986 the number of entitlement jurisdictions (central cities, suburban cities with populations of 50,000 or more, and urban counties with populations of at least 200,000) increased from 658 to 827.[10]

A substantial increase in city participation that occurred during the second round of the Local Public Works program can be attributed to three factors: first, EDA made a conscious outreach effort to encourage more cities to participate in the second round of the LPW program; second, cities had more time to prepare their applications than in the first round; and third, cities that were hesitant to file under round I found it difficult to resist applying under round II when the amount of funds doubled from $2.0 to $4.0 billion.[11]

Characteristics of Participant Cities.   Table 1 reports city participation rates for each of the six federal programs by population size, region, level of distress,[12] and type of jurisdiction. CDBG has the highest participation rate, with all 383 sample cities choosing to participate in this program, followed by EDA's Local Public Works program; nearly 90 percent had at least one public works project funded. Nearly three-fourths of the sample cities were active in the Urban Renewal program, and slightly more than half participated in the UDAG and EDA Title I Public Works programs. The Model Cities program showed the lowest participation rate, with only about one-fourth of the sample cities funded. Unlike the other programs, however, model cities was conceived of as a demonstration or experimental program with "limited" participation.

Population Size.   With the exception of the two formula grant programs (CDBG and LPW) in which nearly all cities participated, a relatively strong relationship exists between population size and city participation in each of the four categorical grant programs, particularly the Model Cities program. More than 80 percent of the cities with populations of 500,000 or more were participants in this program, but fewer than one-fifth of those cities with populations between 50,000 and 100,000 were designated as model cities. Among the very largest cities (populations of one million or more), Houston is the only city that did not participate in either the Urban Renewal or UDAG programs. Among the very smallest cities (populations between 50,000 and 100,000), the Urban Renewal program was the only categorical program that showed a participation rate of 50 percent or more.

TABLE 1. Percent of Cities Participating in Federal Community and Economic Development Programs by Population Size, Region, Level of Distress, and Type of Jurisdiction

	N	Urban Renewal	Model Cities	CDBG	UDAG	EDA Title I	EDA LPW
Population Size, 1970							
50,000–99,999	227	61.2	11.9	100.0	48.0	41.4	85.0
100,000–249,999	98	84.7	36.7	100.0	72.4	66.3	94.9
250,000–499,999	31	96.8	677	100.0	96.8	93.5	100.0
500,000–1 Million	21	100.0	81.0	100.0	95.2	95.2	95.2
Greater than 1 Million	6	83.3	100.0	100.0	83.3	100.0	100.0
Region							
Northeast	78	98.7	44.9	100.0	92.3	57.6	98.7
Midwest	107	69.2	27.1	100.0	55.1	49.5	81.3
South	102	74.5	24.5	100,0	66.7	58.8	92.2
West	96	53.1	18.8	100.0	37.5	58.3	88.5
Needs Index Quartiles*							
First <Worst Off>	96	93.8	54.2	100.0	94.8	77.1	96.9
Second	96	83.3	37.5	100.0	87.5	68.8	94.8
Third	95	70.5	13.7	100.0	51.6	51.6	89.5
Fourth <Best Off>	96	42.7	6.3	100.0	11.5	26.0	77.1
Type of Jurisdiction							
Central Cities	259	85.7	37.5	100.0	77.2	71.4	94.6
Suburban Cities	124	45.2	8.1	100,0	28.2	11.2	79.0
Cities Funded							
Number	383	278.0	107.0	383	235.0	214	343
Percent	100	72.6	27.9	100.0	61.4	55.9	89.6

*Distributions for Urban Renewal and Model Cities program based on 1970 needs index quartiles; distributions for remaining four programs based on 1980 needs index quartiles.

Region.   Northeastern cities were much more likely to participate in federal urban programs than were cities in other parts of the country. With the exception of EDA's Title I Public Works program, where participation rates were similar across all regions but the Midwest, Northeastern cities had the highest participation rate for each program examined. For some programs, differences in participation rates between northeastern cities and those in other regions were dramatic. In the Urban Renewal program, all cities but one (Cranston, RI) from the northeast were participants, whereas only about one-half of the western cities participated. In the Model Cities program, northeastern cities participated at a rate nearly twice as great as that for cities from any of the other three regions. Northeastern cities also show a much greater participation rate for the UDAG program; more than 90 percent received funding for at least one project through the end of Fiscal Year 1986, compared to less than 40 percent of western cities.

Need. Each of the four categorical programs examined was fairly effective at targeting participation to the neediest cities, although all six programs funded cities that ranked in each of the four needs index quartiles. The data show that those programs that included some type of needs-based eligibility requirements (e.g., EDA Title I Public Works, UDAG) were more effective at limiting participation to the neediest cities.

Among the categorical programs, the Urban Renewal and EDA Title I Public Works programs show the greatest rates of participation among those cities that rank in the least distressed quartile; more than 40 percent of the cities in the best-off quartile were funded under the Urban Renewal program and about one-fourth of the cities in this group received funding under EDA's Title I program. The data for the UDAG program, which many consider to be highly targeted, show that more than half of the cities in the third quartile received at least one UDAG grant. Participation rates are substantially lower for each of the four needs index quartiles for the Model Cities program due to the smaller number of cities funded, but the pattern does suggest that this program was fairly well targeted in terms of the types of cities selected to participate in it. The two formula entitlement programs, CDBG and LPW, show the greatest participation rates for the least distressed communities.

Prior Program Experience. The extent of prior program experience can serve as a useful proxy for the demand and capacity of local governments for federal aid. Prior program experience provides some evidence that a city is interested in participating in federal aid programs. Friedland and Wong's analysis of the urban renewal program supports this notion: "a city's previous success in obtaining HUD monies conditions its current willingness and ability to seek further funds."[13] Prior experience is also a useful indicator of local capacity. Participation in one program (or an earlier phase of the same program) suggests that a city has mastered the front-end costs of the application process, found its way through the bureaucracy, and developed some degree of capacity to put together at least one successful grant application.

Participation in one or more of the federal low-rent public housing programs was an especially important predictor of initial urban renewal participation. Only 14 percent of those cities without any previous experience with low-rent public housing programs received an initial urban renewal allocation, less than half the rate for all sample cities. When local experience with public housing programs increased, measured by the number of programs in which the city was an active participant, so did the proportion of cities with initial urban renewal allocations. Nearly three-fourths of all those cities participating in three of the four low-rent public housing programs received funding, and all five cities (Boston, Chicago, Detroit, Montgomery, and Washington) that were participants in all four public housing programs received an initial urban renewal grant reservation.[14]

In the initial years, the Urban Renewal program was predominantly focused on responding to housing needs. While program activity could take place just about anywhere within a city, the new use to which the land was to be put had to be "predominantly residential in nature." Beginning in 1954, amendments were enacted to allow an increasingly larger share of funds to be expended for nonresidential activities. Those cities that already had existing bureaucracies active in this policy area had an advantage over those communities that were just beginning to get organized to deal with urban redevelopment. As one observer noted at the time, *to apply prior expertise obtained with publicly financed low-rent housing, many states assigned redevelopment to local housing authorities as an additional duty and sometimes formally redesignated them housing and redevelopment authorities.*[15]

The importance of prior program experience was also evident in the Model Cities program. HUD officials developed an elaborate mechanism for gauging the extent of local capacity among those cities applying for model cities planning funds. As Gilbert and Specht reported, when HUD and other federal agencies involved in funding model cities program activities reviewed each city's application, they gave special attention to assessing the city's ability to plan and carry out a comprehensive program. The authors concluded that HUD would have done just as well had they considered whether or not a city participated in the urban renewal program.[16] For each of the six programs examined here, cities that had participated in prior comparable programs were more likely to be funded during the initial year of the new program than were cities without such experience. The same held true with regard to participation in subsequent programs. (See Table 2.)

Formula Grants and Local Capacity. To what extent have the formula grant programs (CDBG, LPW) that universalized city participation enhanced the capacity of previously nonparticipant cities? For example, how successful have those cities without any previous HUD categorical experience been in the competition for UDAG funds? Table 3 presents the distribution of cities by population size, region, level of distress, and type of jurisdiction for the two groups of newly participant cities: those with no prior urban renewal or model cities experience that participated in the UDAG program following receipt of CDBG funds, and those with no previous experience under EDA's Title I public works program that received funding under that program following their participation in EDA's Local Public Works program. Overall, the table shows that about 40 percent of the previously non-funded eligible EDA cities received funding for at least one project following their participation in EDA's formula entitlement program. Similarly, almost half of all eligible cities without any prior HUD categorical experience received funding for at least one UDAG project following their

TABLE 2. Importance of Prior Program Experience on Subsequent Program Participation

	Percent of Cities Funded During First Year Program			Percent of Cities Funding During Life of Program		
	Prior Experience			Prior Experience		
	Yes	No	Total	Yes	No	Total
Urban Renewal						
Public Housing	53	11	26	93	61	73
Model Cities						
Urban Renewal	23	1	14	38	22	8
Community Development Block Grants						
Urban Renewal	100	100	100	100	100	100
Model Cities	100	100	100	100	100	100
EDA Title I Public Works	100	100	100	100	100	100
Urban Development Action Grants						
Urban Renewal	30	6	24	76	20	60
Model Cities	48	14	24	90	49	60
EDA Title I	36	16	24	79	49	60
EDA LPW	25	10	24	64	25	60
EDA Title I Public Works						
Urban Renewal	6	5	6	65	31	56
Model Cities	9	4	6	84	45	56
EDA Local Pubic Works	—	—	—	60	18	56
EDA Local Public Works						
Urban Renewal	37	34	36	95	75	90
Model Cities	58	28	36	96	87	90
EDA Title I Public Works	48	30	36	95	87	90

participation in HUD's block grant program. The profile of newly funded cities under the HUD program system differs rather dramatically from that reported for EDA. Newly funded HUD cities were much more likely to be small cities (nearly 80 percent of the cities without previous HUD experience that received UDAG funding subsequent to their CDBG participation have populations less than 100,000), almost half were from the West, and more than half (13 of 22) ranked among the two least distressed quartiles, as opposed to about forty percent for the new EDA cities.

310

TABLE 3. Number and Percent of Cities with No Prior Categorical Experience Participating in Categorical Programs Following Formula Grant Participation by Population, Level of Distress, and Type of Jurisdiction

	N	None/LPW/EDA Title I						None/DCBG/UDAG					
		No Prior Experience		Post Eligible		Post Funded		No Prior Experience		Post Eligible		Post Funded	
		n	%	n	%	n	%	n	%	n	%	n	%
Population Size, 1970													
50,000–99,999	227	161	71	120	75	28	23	87	38	41	47	16	38
100,000–249,999	98	60	61	49	82	27	55	15	15	5	27	5	100
250,000–499,999	31	14	45	14	100	12	86	1	3	1	100	1	100
500,000–1 Million	27	5	24	4	80	4	100	—	—	—	—	—	—
Region													
Northeast	78	48	62	38	79	15	39	1	1	1	100	1	100
Midwest	107	74	69	56	76	20	36	33	31	16	49	5	31
South	102	63	62	45	71	21	47	24	24	11	46	6	55
West	96	55	57	48	87	15	31	45	47	18	40	10	56
Needs Index Quartiles													
First <Worst Off>	95	49	51	45	92	22	49	3	3	3	100	1	33
Second	96	51	53	48	94	21	44	13	14	13	100	8	62
Third	97	66	69	48	73	18	38	32	34	22	69	10	45
Fourth <Best Off>	95	74	77	46	62	10	22	55	57	8	15	3	38
Type of Jurisdiction													
Central Cities	259	132	51	101	77	58	57	35	14	20	57	15	75
Suburban Cities	124	108	87	86	80	13	15	68	55	26	38	7	27
Total	383	240	63	187	78	71	38	103	27	46	45	22	48

These findings illustrate different patterns of program development among the HUD and EDA funding systems. The data suggest that the earlier HUD programs had been fairly successful in reaching nearly all of the most distressed cities, as only sixteen of 103 cities without previous urban renewal or model cities experience were cities that rank within the two most distressed quartiles. By contrast, about three times as many cities entered the funding system following participation in EDA's formula grant program, and a larger portion of these newly funded cities ranked among the most distressed cities. It is important to point out, however, that the post-LPW years were also those years in which EDA categorical funding increased most dramatically, rising from $53.1 million in 1978 to $108.8 million in 1980. Thus, EDA had more funds available to distribute to more cities in the post-LPW years than in those years prior to LPW.

Despite the data reported above, evidence suggests that barriers to city participation in federal community development programs still exist in the 1980s, since fewer than half of the eligible EDA Title I and UDAG cities without prior categorical experience have participated in these programs through the end of Fiscal Year 1986. For some cities, particularly those in the least distressed needs index quartiles, the lack of participation may reflect a decision not to participate. For other communities, notably those in the more distressed quartiles, the lack of participation may reflect an inability to prepare a competitive grant application.

Distributional Impacts of Federal Funding

In examining the distributional impacts of federal grants-in-aid to cities, it is important to distinguish between two different distributional characteristics of federal programs: the distribution of participant cities and the distribution of program funds. All federal programs have both eligibility (who participates) and distributional (how funds are allocated) parameters, and each affects the ability of federal programs to target aid to the neediest communities. In this section we turn our attention to an analysis of the distribution of program funds. Table 4 summarizes the distributional impacts of total program allocations for each of the six programs by population size, region, level of distress, and type of jurisdiction.

Population Size. Of the six programs examined, Model Cities was by far the program most focused on big cities. Overall, more than half of all funds allocated during the six years of supplemental funding were directed to cities with populations of 500,000 or more. The program had a decidedly big-city orientation initially; during six of the program's first eight years, more than half of all funds reserved were allocated to cities with populations of 500,000 or more. During the next seventeen years, however, the proportion of funds allocated to big cities reached 40 percent or more in only four years: 1960, 1961, 1969, and 1971. Several factors may explain this pattern. First, as reported earlier, the data show that large cities were more likely to participate

TABLE 4. Percentage Share of Total Program Funds by Population Size, Region, Level of Distress, and Type of Jurisdiction

	Urban Renewal 1949–74	Model Cities 1969–79	CDBG 1975–86	UDAG 1978–86	EDA Title I 1966–86	EDA LPW 1976–77
Population Size, 1970						
50,000–99,999	16.8	9.2	18.0	16.1	24.5	21.9
100,000–249,999	22.7	16.3	18.2	21.9	20.8	18.4
250,000–499,999	21.8	18.2	16.0	19.9	18.3	13.9
500,000–1 Million	21.8	24.2	20.5	21.7	22.1	16.9
Greater than 1 Million	16.9	32.2	27.3	20.4	14.2	29.0
Region						
Northeast	40.3	31.8	31.7	35.6	26.5	41.1
Midwest	22.4	30.8	27.0	35.0	27.0	23.3
South	24.6	22.0	24.6	21.8	25.6	16.1
West	12.7	15.4	16.7	7.6	20.9	19.5
Needs Index Quartiles*						
First <Worst>	51.1	45.4	55.1	68.0	52.4	55.6
Second	32.4	40.9	23.4	24.3	29.7	21.6
Third	10.5	10.8	11.9	6.9	12.6	12.1
Fourth <Best>	6.1	2.9	9.7	0.8	5.3	10.6
Type of Jurisdiction						
Central Cities	93.4	96.9	90.9	94.2	94.0	88.2
Suburban Cities	6.5	3.1	9.1	5.7	6.0	11.8
Cities Funded						
Number	278	107	383	235	214	343
Percent	72.6	27.9	100.0	61.4	55.9	89.6

*Distributions for UrbanRenewal and Model Cities Program based on 1970 needs index quartiles; distributions for remaining four programs based on 1980 needs index quartiles.

in federal grant programs. In the initial years, big cities were among the first to participate in the Urban Renewal program and consequently received a larger share of the funds. Second, as the character of the Urban Renewal program changed to include a greater focus on housing rehabilitation and border geographic project areas, many smaller and medium-sized cities began to participate. Finally, total dollars allocated for urban renewal increased substantially during the 1960s; thus, while the share of funds allocated to the largest cities was declining, the amount of funds these cities received continued to increase.

EDA's Title I Public Works program shows a distributional pattern similar to that for the Urban Renewal program; it also allocated more than one-third of its total funds to large cities and showed a greater emphasis on big cities in the program's early years. Paradoxically, of the six programs examined, EDA's Title I Public Works program allocated the largest share of funds to the smallest sample cities.

Among the current programs, the CDBG program has allocated the largest share of funds to big cities. Overall, almost half of the block grant funds allocated to sample cities were distributed to those with populations of 500,000 or more. As the holdharmless provisions were phased out and the full formula funding provisions phased in, large cities increased their share of CDBG funds. Adoption of the dual formula in 1978 also contributed to the increased share of funds allocated to big cities. The share of funds allocated to large cities increased from about 40 percent in 1977 to nearly 50 percent in 1979. That share declined slightly in 1980, following the release of 1980 census data, and has remained fairly stable in subsequent years.

Region. Despite the emphasis on frostbelt cities in the funding patterns under all six programs, only the CDBG and UDAG programs show any consistent pattern or trend in allocations to them. In the initial years of the CDBG program, the share of funds allocated to frostbelt cities declined as holdharmless funding was phased out and full formula funding was phased in. This decline was evidence of the greater participation of these cities in the prior categorical programs and illustrated the advantage given southern and western cities by a formula that included population (which benefited both southern and western cities) and poverty (which principally benefited southern cities). Adoption of the dual formula, which added formula elements (aged housing, growth lag) that directed a larger share of funds to northeastern and midwestern cities, accounts for the increased share allocated to frostbelt cities between 1977 and 1978.[17]

The proportion of funds allocated to frostbelt cities has increased substantially in the UDAG program, rising from about 60 percent in 1978 to 78 percent in 1985 and 1986. Overall, more than 70 percent of the UDAG funds allocated to sample cities during the program's first eight years have been distributed to northeastern and midwestern cities. As shown in Table 5, however, although a much greater proportion of frostbelt cities was eligible for UDAG grants, the proportion of applicant and funded cities was relatively similar across all regions but the Northeast. These findings suggest that the greater share of funding awarded to frostbelt cities was the result of a greater number of eligible cities and a somewhat greater applicant rate among cities in the Northeast and Midwest, rather than an overall disproportionately greater rate of funding for frostbelt cities.

EDA's Title I Public Works program is the only program that shows a

TABLE 5. Urban Development Action Grants, 1978–1986

		Eligible Cities		Applicant Cities		Funded Cities	
	N	Number	Percent	Number	Percent	Number	Percent
Northeast	78	74	94.9	74	100.0	70	94.6
Midwest	107	72	67.3	66	91.7	57	86.4
South	102	69	67.6	61	88.4	52	85.2
West	96	42	43.8	33	78.6	28	84.8
Total	383	257	67.1	234	91.0	207	88.5

relatively balanced distributional pattern across regions, a reflection of the greater role given EDA regional and area officials in the development and review of grant applications.[18]

Need. Among the six programs examined, the UDAG program clearly stands out as the most targeted program: more than two-thirds of total UDAG funds allocated during the period 1978–1986 were awarded to sample cities ranking in the most distressed quartile. Less than one percent of total program funds was awarded to cities in the least distressed quartile during this same period. The UDAG program's success at targeting can be attributed to the structural features of the grant program, which incorporate both needs-based eligibility requirements and a needs-based allocation mechanism. To qualify and to participate in the UDAG program, cities must meet or surpass threshold levels for selected indicators of community need set at the median value for all cities with populations over 50,000.[19] Funds are awarded on a competitive basis through a project selection ranking system in which each application is rated and assigned a score, weighted 70 percent according to the level of distress of the applicant community and 30 percent on project merits. For each funding round, applications are rank-ordered and projects are selected for funding in descending order until the funds are exhausted.[20]

The two formula grant programs, which each include needs-based elements for allocating program funds, have allocated about 55 percent of total program funds to cities in the most distressed quartiles. However, because these programs do not *limit* participation on the basis of community needs, they also report the largest shares of funding for cities in the least distressed quartiles.

Formula Grants and City Need. According to Robert Stein, one of the benefits of the shift to the New Federalism was that many cities that were previously nonparticipants in the federal categorical aid system became participants through their entitlement status in the general revenue sharing and block grant programs enacted in 1970s. Stein notes that participation in the New Federalism programs stimulated many cities to seek funding under the more numerous categorical programs and that one of the principal benefits was a greater equalization of federal aid distributions as these newly funded cities tended to be those most in need. He adds that *the relationship between need and fiscal capacity is significantly strengthened by the added participation of these new beneficiaries of the federal largess.*[21]

Stein's analysis is based on total per capita direct federal aid allocations to municipalities with populations of 250,000 or more. However, if one confines the analysis to a specific functional area, such as community development, and examines the patterns there, a strikingly different picture emerges. As reported earlier in Table 3, those cities that had no prior experience with the Urban Renewal or Model Cities programs but received CDBG funds were predominantly small, suburban, and relatively well-off cities. Of the 103 cities with no previous urban renewal or model cities experience, nearly 90 percent were cities with populations between 50,000 and 100,000. Two-thirds were suburbs, and more than half ranked among the best-off cities as measured by the composite city needs index. These percentages increase further if one examines the characteristics of those cities without any previous HUD categorical experience. Table 6 reports the re-

TABLE 6. Difference of Means Test Between Cities With and Without Previous Experience with Urban Renewal or Model Cities Programs for Selected Community Development Need Indicators

Need Indicator	Cities without Previous Urban Renewal or Model Cities Experience [n = 103]	Cities with Previous Urban Renewal or Model Cities Experience [n = 280]
Community Needs Index, 1970[1]	−79.2	29.1**
Percent Population Change, 1960–70	50.1	16.8**
Percent Poverty, 1979		
Families	6.5	10.1**
Persons	8.4	13.1**
Median Family Income, 1969	11,289	9,659**
Net Changes in Median Family Income, 1959–69	4,366	3,699**
Unemployment Rate, 1970	4.4	4.7*
Percent Aged Housing, 1970	21.4	45.1**
Percent Change, Retail and Manufacturing Employment, 1967–1977	47.6	13.2**

*$p < .05$

**$p < .01$

[1]Community needs index is based on the following indicators: percent population change, 1960–70; percent employment change, 1958–67; net change in median family income, 1959–69; unemployment rate, 1970; percent poverty, 1969; and percent of housing units in 1970 built before 1940. The index is standardized at zero with cities scoring less than zero relatively better off and cities scoring above zero relatively worse off.

sults of a difference of means test for selected community development need indicators for two groups of cities, those with no prior experience with the Urban Renewal or Model Cities programs and those with previous experience with one or both programs. The data show that for every measure, cities with no previous experience were substantially better off. Thus, contrary to Stein's findings for the federal aid system as a whole, the data presented in Table 6 show that the CDBG program resulted in a spreading of federal funds to many relatively well-off places.

Conclusion

This brief review of the evolution of city participation and funding distributions in six federal community development programs provides a number of lessons for policymakers designing the next generation of federal urban programs.

First, the data show a dramatic expansion in the number and type of cities participating. In the 1950s, only a relatively few cities—large distressed cities from the northeast and midwest—were active. Today, cities of all sizes, regions, and levels of distress receive annual entitlements through HUD's community development block grant program. Concomitant with this expansion has been a contraction of funding opportunities during the 1980s. Although the number of entitlement communities in the CDBG program increased by 26 percent between 1980 and 1986, entitlement funds decreased by 26 percent during the same period. Furthermore, the effects of these funding reductions were most seriously felt by the nation's most distressed cities, as they experienced disproportionately larger funding reductions than less distressed cities.[22] Funding cutbacks have also reduced opportunities through EDA's Title I Public Works and UDAG programs. In 1980, EDA awarded $109 million for economic development projects in 79 sample cities. By 1986, EDA was only able to award $16 million to twenty cities. Similarly, in 1980 HUD awarded $573 million in UDAG funds to 102 sample cities; by 1986 the number of cities funded had dropped to sixty and the amount awarded declined to $239 million.

This analysis of city experiences with federal community development programs points out the importance of local capacity and prior program experience. For each program examined, those cities which had previous experience with comparable programs were more likely to participate in subsequent programs. More important, the data showed that cities with no prior categorical experience that were brought into the federal funding system through the formula entitlement programs of the 1970s were only moderately successful in obtaining subsequent categorical experience. This finding suggests the importance of capacity building, particularly among more distressed communities.[23]

Finally, the paper shows the need for federal policymakers to fine-tune their policy instruments. Programs enacted in the late 1970s, when targeting federal grants was in fashion, have lost much of their effectiveness due to funding cutbacks and the increasing number of recipient cities. To date, policymakers have sought to reduce domestic spending by eliminating programs altogether or reducing funding across the board. An alternative strategy, and one that merits further investigation, is the elimination of less needy jurisdictions. For instance, restricting the CDBG program to the most needy communities could achieve a savings of more than $300 million per year, more than enough to fund the UDAG program at a level greater than current efforts. In the late 1970s, targeting was generally enhanced by increasing the funds available for distribution, with the most distressed communities receiving a disproportionate share of the new revenues. In the late 1980s, significant gains in targeting are likely only if politicians and policymakers can agree to restrict program eligibility to the neediest places.

NOTES

1. David B. Walker, "The Changing Dynamics of Federal Aid to Cities," Paper presented at the 1981 annual meeting of the American Political Science Association, and Richard P. Nathan, "The Outlook for Federal Grants to Cities," in Roy Bahl, ed., *The Fiscal Outlook for Cities* (Syracuse, NY: University Press, 1978).

2. U.S. Advisory Commission on Intergovernmental Relations, *Recent Trends in Federal and State Aid to Local Governments* (July 1980), Table 5, 8.

3. U.S. Advisory Commission on Intergovernmental Relations, *An Agenda for American Federalism: Restoring Confidence and Competence* (Washington, D.C.: U.S. Government Printing Office, 1981).

4. See Nathan, "The Outlook for Federal Grants to Cities," and Thomas J. Anton, "Decay and Reconstruction in the Study of American Intergovernmental Relations," *Publius,* 15 (Winter 1985), 65–97, for a review of these developments.

5. CBO, *The Federal Government in a Federal System,* xiii.

6. U.S. Department of Housing and Urban Development, *Consolidated Annual Report to Congress on Community Development Programs, 1987* (HUD-1090-CPD, March, 1987).

7. The sample consists of the 383 cities with 1950, 1960, or 1970 populations of 50,000 or more.

8. However, of the 77 cities that dropped from the program in its early years, only thirteen failed to re-enter the program at a later date.

9. For a detailed account of the Model Cities program's legislative history see Randall B. Ripley, *The Politics of Economic and Human Resource Development* (Indianapolis, IN: Bobbs-Merrill, 1972); Charles M. Haar, *Between the Idea and the Reality* (Boston, MA: Little, Brown, 1975); Bernard J. Frieden and Marshall Kaplan, *The Politics of Neglect* (Cambridge, MA: MIT Press, 1975); and Edward C. Banfield, "Making A New Federal Program: Model Cities, 1964–68," in Walter Williams and Richard Elmore, eds., *Social Program Implementation* (New York, NY: Academic Press, 1976).

10. A substantial number of these entitlement communities were small central cities. Between 1980 and 1987 the number of entitlement cities with populations below 25,000 doubled (from 22 to 43), and those populations between 25,000 and 50,000 increased by nearly 80 percent from 87 to 172. In 1987, more than one in four entitlement cities had populations less than 50,000. See Michael J. Rich, "Community Development or General Revenue Sharing? An Assessment of the CDBG Program Under Reagan," Paper presented at the 1988 annual meeting of the Midwest Political Science Association, Chicago, IL.

11. For further discussion see U.S. Department of Commerce, *Local Public Works Program: Final Report* (Economic Development Administration, 1980).

12. The measure of city need used in this study is a composite needs index based on six indicators: population change, employment change, per capita income change, unemployment, poverty, and aged housing. In order to provide a comparable measure of need throughout the study period, four separate indices were constructed, each calculated from data centered around the decennial census years (1950 to 1980). Index scores were standardized at zero with cities scoring above zero being relatively worse off and cities below zero relatively better off.

13. Roger Friedland and Herbert Wong, "Congressional Politics, Federal Grants, and Local Needs: Who Gets What and Why?," in Alberta M. Sbragia, ed., *The Municipal Money Chase: The Politics of Local Government Finance* (Boulder, CO: Westview Press, 1983), 243.

14. See Michael J. Rich, *Congress, the Bureaucracy, and the Cities: Distributive Politics and the Allocation of Federal Grants for Community and Economic Development, 1950–1984* (Ph.D. dissertation, Northwestern University, 1985), Chap. 3, for a more detailed analysis.

15. George S. Duggar, "The Relation of Local Government Structure to Urban Renewal," *Law and Contemporary Problems,* 26 (1961), 54.

16. Neil Gilbert and Harry Specht, "Picking Winners: Federal Discretion and Local Experience as Bases for Planning Grant Allocation," *Public Administration Review,* 34 (1974), 571.

17. See Paul R. Dommel, Richard P. Nathan, Sarah F. Liebschutz, Margaret T. Wrightson and Associates, *Decentralizing Community Development* (U.S. Government Printing Office, 1978) and Harold L. Bunce and Robert L. Goldberg, *City Need and Community Development Funding* (Washington, D.C.: U.S. Department of Housing and Urban Development, April, 1979), for more detailed assessments of the distributional impacts of the dual formula.

18. See Theodore J. Anagnoson, "Federal Grant Agencies and Congressional Election Campaigns," *American Journal of Political Science,* 26 (1982), 547–61 for a discussion of EDA grant decision making.

19. These measures are population change, employment change, per capita income change, unemployment, poverty, and pre-1940 housing.

20. One of the ironic developments of funding cutbacks in the UDAG program is that only projects from the most distressed communities can score high enough to reach the funding threshold. This led to efforts that were incorporated in the 1987 housing bill to alter the project selection system to give greater weight to project merits.

21. Robert M. Stein, "The Allocation of Federal Aid Monies: The Synthesis of De-

mand-Side and Supply-Side Explanations," *American Political Science Review,* 75 (1981), 341.

23. Paul R. Dommel and Michael J. Rich, "The Rich Get Richer: The Attenuation of Targeting Effects of the Community Development Block Grant Programs," *Urban Affairs Quarterly,* 22 (June 1987) 552-79.

23. For a recent review of efforts to build local capacity see Beth Walter Honadle and Arnold M. Howitt, *Perspectives on Management Capacity Building* (Albany, NY: State University of New York Press, 1986).

25
Urban Response to Federal Program Flexibility: Politics of Community Development Block Grant*

Kenneth K. Wong and Paul E. Peterson

Categorical programs, considered the backbone of "creative federalism" in the 1960s, are no longer in vogue in the 1980s. Replacement of categoricals with block grants in the 1970s was seen by many policymakers as an effective means to eliminate bureaucratic red tape, restrain the federal role, enhance local discretion, and encourage private-sector incentives. In addition to the consolidation of 57 categorical programs into 9 block grants, as authorized in the 1981 Omnibus Budget Reconciliation Act, the Reagan administration proposed a $47 billion "swap" of federal and state services, which would have further reduced federal direction of intergovernmental programs. If the Reagan "new federalism" proposal were fully enacted, categorical programs' portion in the federal grant-in-aid system would drop from 79% in 1980 to a mere 34% in 1986 (Pechman, 1982).

The increasing prominence of block grants in our federal grant system merits a closer look at the likely policy consequences following program consolidation. The new flexibility has shifted many policy decisions from federal administrative agencies to local institutions. In the absence of tight

*Wong, Kenneth K., and Paul E. Peterson. 1986. "Urban Response to Federal Program Flexibility: Politics of Community Development Block Grant." *Urban Affairs Quarterly* 21, no. 3 (March 1986): 293–309. Copyright © 1986 Sage Publications, Inc. Reprinted by permission of Sage Publications, Inc.

local economic and political interests. Our longitudinal study of one major block grant in two big cities suggests that the increased level of local discretion resulted in less emphasis on the redistributive needs of low-income residents. Moreover, decisions with respect to the block grant inevitably became part of the local political process and, in these two cities, were influenced by mayoral preferences. The mayors, with the help of their key political advisers, allocated block grant resources in such a manner as to benefit themselves politically without sacrificing the communities' long-term economic interests. Before documenting these findings on the management of the Community Development Block Grant programs in Milwaukee and Baltimore, an elaboration on our basic arguments is needed.

DEFINING URBAN FISCAL CONCERNS AND POLITICAL LEADERSHIP

Both local economic constraints and political leaders influence block grant policy decisions. In reaching these conclusions, we differ from recent studies of federal program management. In much of this literature, the emphasis is on the pluralism of the urban political system, and the city's economic constraints are largely overlooked. Political leadership is also seen as having only modest importance (one exception is Mollenkopf, 1983). According to many analysts, given the pluralistic political environment, differences must be resolved through compromise, plans must be delayed, policies must be modified to satisfy diverse participants, and allocative benefits must be secured through coalitional resources (Pressman and Wildavsky, 1973; Derthick, 1972; Browning et al., 1984). Political leaders are mere brokers who resolve the issues others place before them.

Although the pluralistic approach has been well developed and has enriched much of our understanding of the ways federal programs are carried out, it is not by itself an adequate explanation for policy decisions taken at the local level, particularly in the period of fiscal austerity that began in the mid-1970s. Although political realities may have consequences, they do so in a context in which the economic needs and fiscal interests of local communities place important limitations on the choices made. Organized demands become effective only when they do not contradict the economic interest of the community.

Local discretion under the block grant arrangement is likely to mean less attention to redistributive needs. Regardless of their internal power alignment, local communities attempt to maximize their economic prosperity. Local communities are more constrained than the federal government by the environmental context in which they operate, because they have to compete with one another in exporting their goods (Peterson, 1981). Local jurisdictions cannot regulate the flow of productive resources — labor and capital. Without economic growth, the local government faces a stable or shrinking fiscal base. Accordingly, local communities are most likely to promote the types of policies that enhance their economic well being and to avoid policies that have negative effects on the local economy.

Because of the competitive context in which local communities operate, one can usefully distinguish between "developmental" and "redistributive" policies. *Developmental* policies are those public programs that enhance the economic position of the city in its competition with other areas. These policies strengthen the local economy, enhance the local tax base, and generate additional resources. By contrast, *redistributive* policies are those programs that benefit low-income residents but, at the same time, may negatively affect the local economy by attracting the needy and discouraging entry of productive resources. One can roughly calculate whether a policy is redistributive by estimating whether those who pay for services in local taxes are those who are receiving the services. If there is no overlap at all, such as in welfare assistance to nontaxpayers, it is a case of pure redistribution. Thus, in order to preserve the city's fiscal base, local administrations are constrained to place economic development objectives ahead of any concern they might have for social equality. With ambiguous federal objectives and an emphasis on local discretion, block grants allow leaders of local communities to pursue their own (very likely developmental) goals with the monies that block grants made available. We hypothesize that the federal government's redistributive intent, as often embedded and enforced in the categorical structuring of the grant-in-aid system, will be increasingly difficult to realize under the decentralized mechanism.

Categorical grants not only restricted local flexibility, they also were carried out within an intergovernmental system in which professional identifications and expertise become valuable political resources (Nathan et al., 1977). As the move to the block grant takes place, we expect the value of these resources to diminish. Instead, we expect to find the influence of elected politicians and their political allies to be more salient. First, political leadership is required for the effective pursuit of the development goals. Often, institutions dominated by policy professionals tend toward insularity and isolation from other institutions and sources of political support (Weidner, 1967). These professionals have fewer incentives to mobilize outsiders or to relinquish standard operating procedures. In contrast, political leaders are capable of mobilizing the private sector and of soliciting support for their policies from the electorate and various community groups.

As elected leaders become involved, they turn federal programs in a developmental direction not only because they are economically beneficial to the local economy but also because they are politically beneficial to the city leadership. The benefits of a developmental policy are widely enough distributed that policymakers are not likely to suffer much criticism for their efforts. Mayor Richard Daley, for example, was remembered as the prime figure in coordinating the interests of his political machine, the professional bureaucrats, and the downtown business for Chicago's development (Gove and Masotti, 1982). Richard Lee of New Haven, an equally consummate politician, was able to turn his widely publicized achievement in urban renewal into continued electoral support (Dahl, 1961; Wolfinger, 1974). Likewise, Boston's popular mayor, John Collins, was responsible for the ambitious use of federal funds to improve the rapid transit system (McQuade, 1966). As past chairman of San Francisco's redevelopment agency, Mayor Joseph Alioto successfully put together a political coalition of labor, real estate, and corporations as the organizational basis for his urban renewal programs (Hartman, 1974; Brugmann and Sletteland, 1971).

Finally, block grants allow local leadership to employ portions of the federal resources in ways that are even more directly related to their own political needs. Studies of political machines have long explained public resource allocation in terms of partisan calculations (Banfield and Wilson, 1963). Machine bosses were characterized by their effective delivery of a wide variety of material incentives in return for their votes. While categorical program distributions are governed in part by regulations, block grants can not be used in a less restrictive manner to recruit new supporters, consolidate existing loyalties, and suppress dissidents. What once may have been the exclusive practice of the political machine can now become the general norm for many city leaders.

THE COMMUNITY DEVELOPMENT BLOCK GRANT

These analyses are substantiated in our study of the implementation of the Community Development Block Grant (CDBG) in Baltimore and Milwaukee during the first seven program years, 1975–1981. As a major pillar of the Nixon administration's "new federalism," the 1974 Community Development Block Grant consolidated seven categorical programs and allowed for extensive local discretion in federally funded community development programs. Unlike its categorical predecessors, the block grant was governed by loosely defined requirements with respect to application, evaluation, and audit procedures. For example, the 1974 program consolidation reduced grant regulations from 2,600 pages to 120 pages, the number of annual applications from 5 to 1, and the average application size from 1,400 pages to 50 pages (GAO, 1977). Local jurisdictions were not required to create specialized administrative agencies.

Although the emphasis on local discretion remained intact, the CDBG legislation also encouraged local attention to the needs of the low-income population. The original legislation represented a compromise between those senators who wanted a greater federal presence at the local level and the Nixon administration's proposals for a more restrained federal role. As a result, the 1974 law allowed for a substantial degree of local flexibility but, at the same time, required the local use of federal dollars to provide "decent housing and suitable living environment and expanding economic opportunities, principally for persons of low and moderate income" (Section 101 (c) of Title I of the 1974 Housing and Community Development Act). Indeed, among the seven areas of eligible activities were some highly redistributive services, such as the "reduction of the isolation of law income group and the promotion of neighborhood diversity." Subsequent legislative amendments in 1977 and 1978 tightened the provisions related to citizen participation from low-income neighborhoods, housing assistance plans, and the more "targeted" use of federal resources for the inner-city poor. In these Carter years of "creeping recategorization," the HUD monitoring role became more vigorous. Although these redistributive emphases have been substantially relaxed under the Reagan administration, the CDBG legislation (particularly during the 1978–1980 period) did encourage the localities to pursue certain redistributive goals.

To examine how the CDBG was being implemented, intensive research was carried out in Baltimore and Milwaukee. The two cities were selected for their differences (on contextual details of the two cities, see Wong, 1983; Peterson and Wong, 1985). While both were hardpressed, declining central cities, Milwaukee, with its more diversified industries, had proven more capable of maintaining its economic base. Since the 1960s, Baltimore has experienced severe population loss and industrial out-migration, falling retail sales, and widespread neighborhood decay. Although the two cities have been governed under strong mayoral leadership, local political culture also differed. Whereas "machine-style" politics prevailed in Baltimore, Milwaukee inherited strong reform tradition. Because of these differences in fiscal needs, as well as local norms and practices, we were able to see how different local administrations responded to the federal block grant arrangement.

To supplement documentary sources, interviews were conducted with federal and local officials and with informed observers of the block grants in these two cities during 1981–1982. Interviews with local housing officials included top-level administrators in city hall, members of the staff responsible for the CDBG programs, and representatives of community groups. News reporters, academics, and other informed observers were also consulted. Together with documentary sources, these interviews provided us with the information that formed the basis of our analysis. Quotations in this article are taken directly from these interviews.

CITIES' FISCAL INTEREST AND BLOCK GRANT IMPLEMENTATION

Despite significant differences in political culture between Milwaukee and Baltimore, local leaders' responses toward the greater degree of flexibility in community development were strikingly similar. Recognizing their weakened economic capacity, local political leaders focused their CDBG programs on developmental goals, even though this meant that CDBG only modestly addressed the communities' redistributive needs. Specific development strategies were found to be varied. Although both administrations concentrated a significant amount of federal resources on housing preservation, Baltimore was more anxious to revitalize its downtown and commercial base. In both cases, these policy choices proved to be electorally rewarding to leadership. In this section, we will look at how the economic needs of each of the two cities had an impact on community development strategies. The next section will focus on the extent to which political considerations had their own impact.

In the absence of tight federal guidelines, local officials saw CDBG federal allocation as another lump sum available to the city that was flexible enough to be allocated in whatever ways they preferred. In Milwaukee, community development resources were used to preserve the property-owner neighborhoods at the city's outer rings. In Baltimore, the administration had directed CDBG projects to support the city's ambitious and glamorous revitalization plan in the very heart of the city's downtown commercial area. CDBG resources were seldom used to ameliorate the housing needs of the inner-city poor, which were estimated to be as many as one-third of the renter-households in both cities.

Increasing Prominence of Developmental Projects in Milwaukee

The Community Development Block Grant has played a vital role in Milwaukee's revitalization strategy, the primary objective of which was to sustain property value and neighborhood stability in the city's outlying communities. Consistent with this broad community development goal, Milwaukee's neighborhoods were categorized into three distinct types, according to their economic vitality (City of Milwaukee, 1977). Geographically, the "inner core" overlapped with the inner city, while the "stable neighborhoods" were predominantly outlying areas adjacent to the suburbs. The "transitional areas" lay between these two rings. This pattern was often referred to as the "doughnut and the doughnut hole" among local officials, with the "doughnut" being the transition area, and the "hole" the inner-city slums too deteriorated to be worth preservation efforts. Needless to say, the three areas had very different economic characteristics. The further an area was from the inner city, the more stable was its property value. The outlying stable areas, consisting of 64% of the city's housing stocks, had the healthiest investment environment with high and increasing homeownership, active market sales, and rising prices. By contrast, the housing stock in the inner core had the "lowest assessed values, the lowest rate of owner occupancy, and the highest vacancy rate relative to the other areas."

To curb the deteriorating trend from proliferating beyond the inner core, elected leaders in Milwaukee decided to focus on the preservation of transition neighborhoods. Since 1979, the emphasis on housing preservation and rehabilitation has become the leading CDBG priority (City of Milwaukee, 1979). Significantly, these CDBG programs were seen as vital in the maintenance of a stable property-owner base in Milwaukee. As one official proudly pointed out, "Blighted areas have not expanded as a result of our many CDBG rehabilitation loan programs." Another administrator concurred: "Because CDBG helped to preserve the housing stock and stabilize the living environment in transitional areas, new families were more willing to buy their houses in the city." Consequently, as suggested in Table 1,

TABLE 1. Expenditure Pattern of CDBG Funds in Milwaukee and Baltimore, 1975–1981

	1975–76	1976–77	1977–78	1978–79	1979–80	1980–81	1981–82
Milwaukee							
Developmental	35.9%	41.7%	54.7%	44.8%	50.3%	54.3%	58.5%
Redistributive	0.6	0.6	0.2	6.3	2.3	5.0	3.8
Allocational	63.5	57.8	45.0	48.9	47.4	40.7	37.7
Total Percent	100.0	100.1	99.9	100.0	100.0	100.0	100.0
Total Allocation (in $million)	13.4	13.4	12.6	20.0	21.4	22.8	22.5
Baltimore							
Developmental	71.2	49.2	59.3	56.7	60.2	54.0	55.6
Redistributive	0.6	2.3	4.0	3.7	3.1	5.2	8.3
Allocational	28.2	48.5	36.7	39.6	36.7	40.7	36.0
Total Percent	100.0	100.0	100.0	100.0	100.0	99.9	99.9
Total Allocation (in $million)	30.6	30.9	47.4[a]	35.3[b]	49.0[c]	36.8[d]	35.7[e]

SOURCES: Milwaukee, Community Development Agency, *CDBG Program: Project Summary*, from 1975–76 to 1981–82. Baltimore, Department of Housing and Community Development, *CDBG Program: Project Summary*, from 1974–75 to 1981–82. Categorization and percentage calculations are our own. In some cases, total percentages exceed 100 or are less than 100 due to rounding off figures.

Note: Definitions of the three expenditure categories are found in Peterson (1981). We have been highly selective with regard to what is classified as developmental. Preventing the further spread of "slums and blighted" influences from deteriorated areas through urban renewal projects, reinforcing the quality of housing stocks in transitional areas largely through joint endeavors with loan institutions in the private sector, and encouraging further private sector involvement in downtown/commercial projects are clearly developmental activities and are so classified. On the other hand, all services delivered to the handicapped and the elderly (regardless of their income brackets), and those projects for which only low-income residents were eligible are classified as redistributive. Finally, allocational programs included those additional services that reinforce routine municipal responsibilities. These projects varied from water and sewage works, community cultural and recreational activities, instructional and library services to the maintenance of planning and administrative staffs. Although in many cases these projects reinforce developmental activities, because their purpose remains somewhat ambiguous the middle classification is more appropriate.

[a]This total included $13,621,102 Urban Renewal Surplus fund and $4,735,000 anticipated "Program Income," in addition to the $29,042,000 federal CDBG allocation. The city did not provide data on the use of only the federal CDBG allocation from 1977 to 1981.

[b]This total included $7,108,100 anticipated "Program Income" in addition to the $28.24 million federal allocation.

[c]This grand total included $17,818,800 anticipated "Program Income" in addition to the $31,185,000 federal allocation.

[d]This grand total included $521,000 anticipated "Program Income" and $2,463,900 "city bond" funds, in addition to the $32,579,744 federal allocation.

[e]This grand total included $660,000 anticipated "Program Income" and $2.3 million "city bond" funds, in addition to the $32.58 million federal CDGB allocation.

CDBG resources being spent for developmental housing purposes increased steadily from 36% of the total entitlement to almost 60% over the first seven program years. By contrast, other (mostly allocational) expenditures have steadily declined. Capital improvement projects, such as sewerage and waterworks, which lacked a clear policy focus, were rated as less favorable. By 1982, capital improvement projects were receiving merely half of what they used to get in the initial program period, while the total sum allotted for "house-keeping purposes" shrank considerably.

Baltimore's Renaissance

Encountering economic problems more severe than those in Milwaukee, officials in Baltimore had, for some years, initiated more comprehensive community development policies to combat against any further deterioration of the city's fiscal base. Since the early 1970s, city officials have underscored both the preservation of existing housing stocks and the revitalization of those deteriorating neighborhoods in which massive demolition and relocation projects had previously been carried out. These housing policies were further reinforced by numerous joint city-business endeavors to revitalize the downtown and the central business district. Unless such a grand development scheme was undertaken, city officials were concerned that consumers would stay away from the city's downtown, and homeowners would choose to move out of the city altogether.

Deeply concerned with the much weakened city fiscal base, the William Schaefer administration called for the city's "renaissance," through which Baltimore would be recognized and praised "as a vital, full-blown, modern metropolis." What was emerging was opulence alongside adversity. In a flamboyant manner, Mayor Schaefer used a combination of CDBG funds, private sources, and other federal grants and loans to engage in an extensive variety of revitalization projects in the central financial district and its surrounding areas, as well as in various designated transitional neighborhoods. The well-known Harbor Place, Convention Center, World Trade Center, the Hyatt, and the $12 million Walbrook Shopping Center were some of the projects that made up the city's "renaissance." To attract new homeowners, particularly young, professional couples, local officials promoted the Coldspring "New Town In-Town" project, which was subsidized with over $15 million in CD funds. Federal block grant resources also helped to maintain residential rehabilitation in its many decaying areas, improve the living environment in deteriorating neighborhoods, and demolish slums and blighted areas throughout the city. CDBG-funded projects were said to have brought about the revitalization of Upton, Union Square, Reservoir Hill, South Baltimore, Fells Point, Barley Circle, and a number of transitional communities throughout Baltimore. In light of these highly visible developmental activities, city officials firmly believed these projects could "bolster the city's real estate tax base as well as providing additional jobs." As shown in Table 1, these developmental activities consistently consumed well over half of Baltimore's block grant funds over time. At the same time, neighborhood revitalization has been further supported by a variety of capital improvement undertakings, which constituted a significant portion of the stable allocational expenditure.

Modest Redistributive Activities in the Two Cities

Unlike developmental programs, redistributive concern was far from a central feature on the two cities' community development agenda. As shown in Table 1, neither city has spent more than one-tenth of its block grant resources on housing services for the poor in any single year between 1975 and 1981. While Milwaukee fluctuated in its services for the poor, Baltimore has consistently expanded its redistributive activities from less than 1% to more than 8% of its block grant budget in the seven-year period. Although both cities have steadily increased their redistributive spending, in part due to the Carter administration's "creeping recategorization," the redistributive realm remained modest throughout the years. Since the CDBG started in 1975, Milwaukee officials have only initiated one major project of a purely redistributive character, which improved the physical conditions of public housing units during 1978–1979. Most of the very few redistributive undertakings were related either to the elderly (such as providing them with transportation) or to the handicapped (mostly on accessibility to buildings). Other services were provided to certain disadvantaged groups, such as counseling service to delinquents and hot-line service for the mentally disturbed. There was also a medical check-up program for all city residents. In Baltimore, the few redistributive projects included services for the elderly, legal aid, public housing security, and a number of Model Cities-type activities. In short, despite the impact of the Carter years, our two cases suggest that only a small portion of the CD fund was used to meet housing-related needs of the aged and the low-income groups.

Despite their modest efforts in providing housing services to the needy, city officials had virtually no difficulty in complying with federal regulations, which required that 75% of the CDBG funds be spent on "low and moderate income" residents in a three-year period. Given the fact that relatively large areas of the two cities fell below the median income level, city officials enjoyed a considerable amount of discretion in targeting block grant resources to those neighborhoods in which the most critical developmental efforts were needed. CDBG-funded projects in poor areas, moreover, did not need to be redistributive. Constructing new shopping centers and improving the quality of housing stock in transitional neighborhoods provided typical examples of projects that were located in less well-off communities but were largely designed to strengthen the local tax capacity. Other undertakings, such as the pulling down of blighted structures in deteriorating neighborhoods, often improve the living environment of the affected communities but, at the same time, substantially displace poor families who can no longer afford the higher rent. These are the kinds of policy consequences that one expects to find in central cities such as Baltimore and Milwaukee. In other words, our analyses differentiated between, on one hand, those CDBG projects that were located in deteriorating neighborhoods but constituted an important component of the city's overall redevelopment strategy and, on the other, those programs that primarily delivered services to the low-income population without generating remunerative returns. In short, the use of CDBG funds in low- and moderate-income neighborhoods notwithstanding, officials in both Milwaukee and Baltimore had designed their CDBG projects in ways that were consistent with the citywide revitalization programs.

POLITICAL INFLUENCE AND THE BLOCK GRANT

The decentralized character of the block grant not only allows the local administration to focus on the city's economic concerns, it also enables political elites to exercise more complete influence over program resources. Studies of the early years of the CDBG have recognized the exercise of program control by local "generalists," the declining importance of administrative expertise in prior categorical programs, and the rising significance of electoral concerns (Nathan et al., 1977a, 1977b; Dommel et al., 1978, 1980, 1982). Our study not only confirms these findings, but further suggests that the prominent role of local political elites has continued to expand beyond the initial program years. Even more important, political power seems to have emanated from the federally endorsed local discretion over CDBG funds. Indeed, an effective exercise of political leadership is evident in the programs in the two cities. While Baltimore and Milwaukee were readily distinguished in their local norms and administrative practices, their elected leadership seemed to have accrued considerable political gains from their block grants, particularly through their active involvement in a number of highly visible, communitywide, developmental projects. In neither case did professional administrators play a predominant role in major decisions.

Political Leadership in Milwaukee

Milwaukee's socialist-progressive tradition has not precluded Henry Maier from becoming a powerful mayor over his two-and-a-half-decade tenure. The mayor not only won an unprecedented electoral victory following his handling of the 1967 racial disturbances, his cautious fiscal policy has proven to be popular throughout the 1970s. Mayor Maier's influence was expanded because of the community development block grant. The administration's emphasis on housing preservation in transitional neighborhoods was said to have particularly pleased the southside residents, who backed the mayor during the unusually close race in 1980. Although there had been numerous well-publicized incidents of disagreement during the initial program period, the mayor and powerful members of the city council reportedly came to terms on most of the CDBG issues. Neighborhood preservation as the leading program priority was widely endorsed by city council members, who were anxious to maintain a healthy environment in their respective communities. To make sure that block grant policies were politically beneficial to them, influential council members actively participated in the decision-making process. Indeed, program priorities and allocative guidelines were worked out between the political elites and were found to be the most important determinants on CDBG spending (Steger, 1984).

As the block grant became more institutionalized with well-defined priorities, about the only controversy among political leaders was over financing their pet projects. Political allies and supporters of the mayor were often hired as consultants, rewarded CDBG projects, and appointed as citizen representatives to the CDBG advisory bodies. As one neighborhood worker summarized, "Neighborhood groups are seen as either pro- or anti-mayor." CDBG resources also reinforced the mayor's "patronage" base in the city administration. Administrative expense in the CDBG, although slightly lessened in recent years, remained high enough to support a staff of some 20 people as well as a disproportionately large planning body. Given that the block grant did not encourage any "island of functional power" but, instead, consolidated the mayoral influence, it was no surprise that informed observers concluded, "The biggest winner of the CDBG is the Maier administration."

Political Leadership in Baltimore

Unlike Milwaukee, Baltimore has all the characteristics of a machine-like city with a tradition of patronage practices. With no exception, Mayor Schaefer was the prime figure in the community development block grant. The mayor was "entirely committed, and has an obsession with Baltimore," said an official. "He is not ruthless, but allows nothing to get in his way." The mayor was particularly concerned with the block grant because it played an essential role in his "renaissance" to revitalize the city's declining commercial and residential bases. Equally important was the fact that the Schaefer administration had so far been judged by the extent to which the mayor was able to realize his renaissance. As a result, the Schaefer administration used the community development resources to demonstrate its commitment to the revitalization plan, thereby sending a clear signal to the private sector that downtown interests were regarded as paramount. Often, millions of CD dollars were allocated to the mayor's renaissance projects without much discussion outside the mayor's inner circle and without properly informing the federal agency (Smith, 1980).

In order to mobilize community support for his renaissance, Mayor Schaefer allocated portions of the CDBG funds to coopt neighborhood groups. Community groups that supported the administration's renaissance have been getting the lion's share of the many CDBG-funded rehabilitation and Model Cities-type services. Outspoken dissenting groups were said to have disturbed the mayor, who seemed to want to avoid public controversy. These organizations received hardly any CDBG projects. For example, the

Coalition of Peninsula Organizations (COPO), which represented the area south of the Inner Harbor, was not allocated any CDBG dollars for two years because its leaders had criticized the mayor's community development policies. Significantly, the mayor's tactics seemed to be working. Some previously dissenting leaders joined the administration, the others were more willing to moderate their opposition in exchange for city grants. As a result, under Schaefer's leadership, the city's renaissance came alive and neighborhood revitalization was vigorously pursued. Because of these diversified CDBG-funded, land-use policies, the mayor claimed that the city had gone through a phase in which "its residents, disheartened by the exodus to the suburbs and the racial strife of the 1960s, began to see that Baltimore had potential." "We were dying on the vine," the mayor reflected, " I had to convince my own people first that the city had a future" (Baltimore Sun, December 31, 1980). And the mayor seemed to have done it and, indeed, was rewarded by an overwhelming victory for a fourth term in 1983.

CONCLUSIONS

Our study on the community development block grant indicates that the cities' economic needs predominantly shaped program priorities, once the federal government replaced well-defined program objectives and regulations with an emphasis on local discretion and flexibility. Responding to fiscal necessity, political leadership in Milwaukee and Baltimore effectively directed block grant resources toward fiscally beneficial developmental goals, while paying modest attention to the housing needs of the poor.

The pervasiveness of economic constraints, however, cannot displace the importance of political factors. Instead, politics operates within these economically shaped limits. Specifically, the adoption of different developmental projects in Milwaukee and Baltimore is in part due to the political elites' electoral concerns. In Milwaukee, Mayor Maier and influential city council members supported the preservation policy, which focused on neighborhoods in transition, because such a development strategy was both economically and electorally sound. In Baltimore, the more comprehensive strategy that revitalized the city center was believed to be necessary to encourage further business involvement, so vital to the city's economic recovery. Undoubtedly, through their direct participation in major revitalization projects, local leaders were able to serve both the communities' economic interest and their own electoral ambitions.

Given the CDBG experiences in Milwaukee and Baltimore, it is likely that central cities in the 1980s will adopt a developmental strategy in their use of federal block grants. Redistributive needs are not likely to gain recognition under the more politicized block grant arrangement. Also, the few redistributive activities will become even more confined to the few deteriorating neighborhoods. For example, the urban leadership is unlikely to channel resources for low-income housing projects outside of these decaying areas. Given the extent of fiscal constraints, localities will be extremely reluctant to use block grant dollars to provide for citywide redistributive services. The Reagan administration's spending cuts and policy on program consolidation will only reinforce these local preferences. In short, the federal block grant approach seems likely to render an intergovernmental grant system that is less capable of promoting redistributive objectives. Finally, although developmental choices are both economically and politically attractive, limited federal resources preclude a uniform distribution of developmental programs throughout the city. Instead, local officials are expected to target their developmental undertakings in those designated transitional neighborhoods, where the more critical battle against further urban decay is being fought.

Central cities, facing enormous economic challenges since the mid-1970s, often require political leadership to bring about neighborhood stability and a revitalized local economy. Our study of the CDBG in two big cities suggests the kinds of urban responses that are likely to occur when the federal government relaxes its regulatory presence. Program flexibility, although ill-suited for redistributive purpose, seems effective in promoting community revitalization. The current federal policy emphasis on local discretion is likely to encourage an even greater degree of local innovation in dealing with each city's own specific set of social and economic problems. But given the cities' fiscal priorities and the limited pool of available resources, it is unlikely that urban leaders, at least for some time, will be capable of addressing the needs of their impoverished residents.

REFERENCES

Banfield, F., and J. Q. Wilson (1963) City Politics. New York: Vintage Books.

Browning, R. P., D. R. Marshall, and D. H. Tabb (1984) Protest Is Not Enough. Berkeley: Univ. of California Press.

Brugmann, B. and G. Sletteland [eds.] (1971) The Ultimate Highrise. San Francisco: Bay Guardian.

City of Milwaukee, Community Development Task Force (1979) Funding Allocation Guide for Community Development Block Grant Funds. Milwaukee: Author.

City of Milwaukee, Department of City Development (1977) Toward a Comprehensive Plan: A Preservation Policy for Milwaukee. Milwaukee: Author.

Dahl, R. (1961) Who Governs? New Haven, CT: Yale Univ. Press.

Derthick, M. (1972) New Towns in Town: Why a Federal Program Failed. Washington, DC: Urban Institute.

Dommel, P. and Associates (1978) Decentralizing Community Development. Washington, DC: U.S. Department of Housing and Urban Development.

——— (1980) Targeting Community Development. Washington, DC: U.S. Department of Housing and Urban Development.

——— (1982) Decentralizing Urban Policy: Case Studies in Community Development. Washington, DC: Brookings Institution.

General Accounting Office (1977) The Federal Government Should but Doesn't Know the Costs of Administering Its Assistance Programs. Washington, DC: Author.

Gove, S. and L. Masotti [eds.] (1982) After Daley: Chicago Politics in Transition. Urbana: Univ. of Illinois Press.

Hartman, C. (1974) Yerba Buena: Land Grab and Community Resistance in San Francisco. San Francisco: Glide.

McQuade, W. (1966) "Urban renewal in Boston," pp. 259–277 in J. Q. Wilson (ed.) Urban Renewal: The Record and the Controversy. Cambridge, MA: M.I.T. Press.

Mollenkopf, J. (1983) The Contested City. Princeton, NJ: Princeton Univ. Press.

Nathan, R., P. Dommel, S. Liebschutz, and M. Morris (1977a) "Monitoring the block grant program for community development." Pol. Sci. Q. 92, 2.

Nathan, R. and Associates (1977b) Block Grants for Community Development. Washington, DC: U.S. Department of Housing and Urban Development.

Pechman, J. [ed.] (1982) Setting National Priorities: The 1983 Budget. Washington, DC: Brookings Institution.

Peterson, P. E. (1981) City Limits. Chicago: Univ. of Chicago Press.

——— and K. Wong (1985) "Toward a differentiated theory of federalism: education and housing policy in the 1980s." Research in Urban Policy 1: 301–324.

Pressman, J. and A. Wildavsky (1973) Implementation. Berkeley: Univ. of California Press.

Smith, F. C. (1980) "A special investigative report." Baltimore Sun (July).

Steger, M. A. (1984) "Group influence versus decision-making rules: an analysis of local CDBG allocational decision." Urban Affairs Q. 19, 3.

Weidner, E. W. (1967) "Decision-making in a federal system," pp. 229–256 in A. Wildavsky (ed.) American Federalism in Perspective. Boston: Little, Brown.

Wolfinger, R. E. (1974) The Politics of Progress. Englewood Cliffs, NJ: Prentice-Hall.

Wong, K. (1983) "Federalism and public policy implementation." Ph. D. dissertation, University of Chicago.

26
The Ambivalent State: Economic Development Policy in the U.S. Federal System under the Reagan Administration*

Susan S. Fainstein and Norman Fainstein

The tripartite federal system of the United States historically has resulted in functional fragmentation and divided accountability in the implementation of governmental programs. Responsibilities of the different levels of government and the relations among them have changed over time, however, with the national government throughout this century increasingly ascendant, at least until recently. The Reagan administration, which took office in 1981, ostensibly sought to reverse the trend and devolve authority "closer to the people." Its effort, however, was not associated with increased decentralization of federally collected resources; rather devolution was supposed to result from deregulation and reduced domestic spending by the national government.

Retrenchment by the federal government during the Reagan years took place within the context of, and in response to, the structural transformation of the American economy. It was legitimized as an antidote to an economic malaise allegedly caused by bureaucratic regulation and nonproductive domestic spending. The source of domestic waste was found in a bloated welfare state that diverted resources from capital accumulation by investors to consumption by the lower classes. Many liberal economists and business leaders had advanced proposals for a national industrial policy involving both central planning and financing (see, for example, Rohatyn, 1980; Magaziner and Reich, 1982; Thurow, 1980). But the Reagan administration successfully imposed its claim that economic problems were not to be addressed through governmental planning because planning was itself a cause of economic inefficiency.

In such a programmatic climate, regions and localities that lost jobs and revenues because of economic restructuring could no longer turn to the federal government for programs that would put people back to work.

*Fainstein, Susan S., and Norman Fainstein. 1989. "The Ambivalent State: Economic Development Policy in the U.S. Federal System under the Reagan Administration." *Urban Affairs Quarterly* 25, no. 1, (September 1989): 41–62. Copyright © 1989 Sage Publications, Inc. Reprinted by permission of Sage Publications, Inc.

Conservative strategists had assumed that federal retrenchment would result inevitably in an overall contraction of domestic governmental activity because legislatures and city councils would be unwilling to raise the necessary taxes for new programs. Strong forces, however, acted on subnational governments to push them into development policy. Local public opinion pressed them to compete with their counterparts in the rest of the country. Business executives made demands for financial and regulatory relief that in other nations would have been directed at central governments. In response, many subnational political leaders felt compelled to promote employment-creation programs. The goal of these programs (mainly initiated at the state government level[1]) was to stimulate private sector employment through subsidies to business, and they were implemented by institutions insulated from popular demands for redistributive policies.

The de facto national policy for the spatial planning of economic restructuring therefore evolved into subnational mercantilism, the establishment of a market of competing local and state governments selling their various economic development programs to American and foreign businesses. In this way, the Reagan administration helped to create a policy approach highly compatible with its political objective of empowering business, weakening labor, and reducing the penetration of governmental regulation into business decision making. Although active subnational state and local governments may not have been part of the Reagan design, they were the direct outcome of the withdrawal of federal responsibility for the consequences of economic restructuring.

In this article we discuss the recent history of intergovernmental relations in the United States and the political-economic forces that have affected them. We then examine the strategies used by state and municipal governments to foster economic development in the current period of federal spending cutbacks and deindustrialization. Finally, we interpret the contemporary response, particularly the increasing prominence of state governments, in the light of business influence and ideological resistance to governmental economic planning.

FEDERALISM AND POLITICAL FORCES

The New Deal (1932–1940) marked the beginning of federal involvement in local welfare activities and a new sponsorship of economic development schemes. Pressure on the Roosevelt administration to mitigate the Depression resulted in an array of federally funded programs. These included most importantly the Public Works Administration, aimed at transportation infrastructure, the Works Progress Administration, devoted mainly to public employment for construction of public facilities, the Tennessee Valley Authority and similar agencies involved in electrification, as well as the establishment of the first elements of a modern welfare state (old age and unemployment insurance, family assistance, public housing).

The preexistence of relatively autonomous state and local governments vested with important economic interests, combined with the long American tradition of resistance to centralized rule, meant that subnational governments rather than federal agencies became the principal administrators of public works and relief programs.[2] The admixture of different governmental entities that was the consequence of the grant-in-aid system, whereby the federal government granted funds to independently elected subnational governments but retained the right to regulate the use of these funds, led to the metaphor of the "marble cake" (Grodzins, 1960). This, in contrast to the separation of functions formally described in the Constitution, symbolized the lack of clear-cut differentiation between the responsibilities of the levels of government. The political impetus for these locally administered New Deal programs resulted from a national current that found expression in the Democratic party rather than from territorially based popular movements.

Despite the legal status of municipalities as instruments of state governments, federal legislation made cities the direct recipients of funding.[3] This model for urban grants-in-aid was repeated in the Housing Act of 1949 and continued through the Economic Opportunity Act of 1964, Model Cities Act of 1966, and Comprehensive Employment and Training Act of 1973. Under many of these later schemes the only role of citywide elected officials was to establish enabling legislation; program implementation was negotiated directly between federal and local bureaucrats. The latter were often employees of quasi-independent authorities largely free from electoral control.

Whereas the political force underlying the New Deal involved a broad coalition of labor and ethnic groups, the urban-oriented legislation of the 1960s rested on an alliance of nonwhite minorities and elements of the Democratic party elite. The impetus was the urban political movements and civil disorders that threatened political stability, as well as demographic change that forced central city officials to incorporate minorities into their electoral base (Piven and Cloward, 1971; Mollenkopf, 1983; Fainstein and Fainstein, 1974). The effort to assuage minority wrath led both to the recruitment of nonwhite elected and appointed city officials and to the development of mechanisms for citizen participation whereby community residents could have a voice in the administration of federally funded programs.

The programs of liberal Democrats, however, were under heavy attack by the late 1960s and were substantially reduced and reoriented during the following decade. When Richard Nixon came into office in 1969 with his program of "New Federalism," he sought to disassemble the aid system that contributed to urban unrest. The war against poverty was steered away from providing resources for political mobilization. Cash allowances to individuals were favored over programs that gave jobs to liberal bureaucrats who then lobbied on behalf of the poor. The autonomy of legal-services agencies was greatly restricted. In addition, Nixon substantially reduced the role of the national government in providing public housing. President Ford continued these policies. His administration ended the Model Cities and Urban Renewal programs and replaced them with Community Development Block Grants (CDBG) under the direction of elected local officials. Although President Carter, a conservative Democrat pressured by a liberal Congress, attempted to target CDBG to benefit the poor, his efforts were halfhearted and inconsistent. Carter also initiated the Urban Development Action Grant (UDAG) program, a private-sector-led version of urban renewal that won strong support from big-city mayors and downtown business interests.

By the mid-1970s, programs to assist low-income city residents were operating within a context of a shrinking national economy, burgeoning federal social welfare expenditures, and fiscal stress. The combined effects of oil price hikes, offshore production by American firms, and loss of competitiveness of domestic industry resulted in a lowered standard of living. Simultaneously both municipal and national levels of government, which had been enlarging expenditures for infrastructural development as well as for income maintenance faster than revenues, began to enter a period of fiscal crisis (O'Connor, 1973). Although popular interpretations blamed fiscal difficulties on programs to assist low-income, primarily minority, groups, antipoverty expenditures constituted relatively small items within the national budget compared to health, old age, and agricultural programs (Smith and Judd, 1984). At the municipal level, the primary cause of increased expenditures was growth in the number and salaries of civil servants. Nonetheless, the subsidence of black militancy meant that programs aimed at improving the condition of the inner-city poor could be reduced in the name of fiscal soundness without provoking a politically destabilizing reaction.

TRENDS IN PUBLIC EXPENDITURES
UNDER REAGAN

The budgetary outcomes of the Reagan regime reflected the interplay of three factors: the administration's more or less conscious strategy, the power of Congress, and the institutional structure of a federal system that gives considerable autonomy to the state governments. Reagan's strategy involved major tax cuts combined with substantial expansion of military expenditures, which increased from 5.0% to 6.6% of GNP between 1980 and 1985, a relative growth of 32%. The resulting deficits were used to justify reductions in "unnecessary" social expenditures in order to balance the budget.[4] But Reagan never was able to achieve the reductions he sought. Consequently, federal outlays as a share of GNP reached peacetime highs of nearly 25% under his regime (Table 1), exceeded in American history only during the years of World War II. Because the revenue payoffs of supply-side economics proved to be chimerical, national debt mushroomed, with net interest payments expanding 55% in terms of GNP between 1980 and 1987 (Table 1).

As part of its strategy of contracting the public sector, the administration reallocated functional responsibilities from Washington to lower levels of government. Whereas federal aid accounted for 3.6% and 3.4% of GNP in the last Carter years, it dropped to 2.2% by 1987 (Table 1). The extent to which local governments, particularly cities, felt the pinch can be seen by calculating intergovernmental aid as a percentage of own-source revenues

TABLE 1. Federal Government Expenditures as a Percentage of GNP

	Total	Net Interest	National Defense	Old-Age Pensions & Healthh Care (Medicare)	Other Federal Progams	Federal Aid to State and Local Gov'ts
1969	20.0	1.3	8.1	3.6	4.8	2.2
1976	22.4	1.6	5.0	5.5	6.7	3.6
1978	21.3	1.6	4.6	5.5	6.0	3.6
1980	22.9	2.0	5.0	6.0	6.5	3.4
1981	23.3	2.5	5.2	6.3	6.4	2.9
1982	24.9	2.7	5.9	6.8	6.8	2.7
1983	24.8	2.9	6.1	6.8	6.5	2.6
1984	23.7	3.1	6.2	6.4	5.6	2.4
1985	24.6	3.2	6.5	6.4	5.9	2.4
1986	24.4	3.2	6.6	6.5	5.6	2.5
1987 (est.)	23.7	3.1	6.6	6.5	5.2	2.2

SOURCE: U.S. Advisory Commission on Intergovernmental Relations, *Significant Features of Fiscal Federalism, 1985-86*, and *1988* (for 1984, 1985, 1986, 1987), Table 6.

(Table 2). Federal aid decreased from 23% to 15% of municipal own-source revenue between 1980 and 1984, and state aid (in turn dependent on federal transfers) declined similarly. Put another way, for every dollar the average city government raised in 1980, it was able to spend $1.56, and for every dollar it raised in 1984, it could spend $1.44. Subnational governments outside the Sunbelt, however, established on balance a liberal inertial force, substituting their own revenues to mitigate curtailed federal expenditures. After 1981, state and local governments responded by increasing their expenditures from own-source revenue to a level exceeding the 11% of GNP they had accounted for in 1974 (Table 3).[5]

The Reagan attack against the welfare state had mixed results. Numerous domestic programs, including some welfare programs, public infrastructure, and intergovernmental aid, suffered sharp contractions. Thus categories that had accounted for 9.9% of GNP during Carter's last year in office (1980) commanded 7.4% in 1987 (Table 1, last two columns). But expenditures per recipient for most income maintenance categories generally remained level, at least through the first half of Reagan's second term (Table 5). In fact, per capita expenditures increased for the broad-based entitlement programs of Social Security and Medicare as well as for means-tested health care (Medicaid). With strong liberal congressional backing, the food subsidy program, which served more than 20 million people (Food Stamps), was maintained at previous benefit levels. Moreover, it was during the Carter, not Reagan, years that real payment levels were eroded most sharply for Aid

TABLE 2. Intergovernmental Aid as a Percentage of Local Governments' Own-Source Revenue

	Federal Aid	State Government Aid
All Local Governments		
1975	13	60
1978	18	58
1980	16	63
1981	15	61
1982	13	58
1983	12	55
1984	11	54
Cities		
1975	19	42
1978	26	37
1980	23	33
1981	21	32
1982	18	32
1983	15	31
1984	15	29

SOURCE: U.S. Advisory Commission on Intergovernmental Relations, *Significant Features of Fiscal Federalism, 1985-86*, Table 46.

TABLE 3. Government Expenditures from Own-Source Revenue as a Percentage of GNP by Level of Government

	Total Public Sector	Federal Government	State Governments	Local Governments	State/Local Governments
1969	30.4	20.0	5.5	4.9	10.4
1976	33.5	22.4	6.2	4.8	11.0
1978	31.5	21.3	5.9	4.3	10.2
1980	33.0	22.9	6.0	4.1	10.1
1981	33.3	23.3	5.9	4.0	9.9
1982	35.5	24.9	6.3	4.3	10.6
1983	35.3	24.8	6.1	4.4	10.5
1984	33.9	23.7	6.0	4.2	10.1
1985	34.9	24.6	6.2	4.2	10.4
1986	35.1	24.4	6.3	4.5	10.7
1987 (est.)	34.9	23.7	n.a.	n.a.	11.3

SOURCE: U.S. Advisory Commission on Intergovernmental Relations, *Significant Features of Fiscal Federalism, 1985-86*, and *1988* (for 1984, 1985, 1986, 1987), Table 1.

TABLE 4. Government Expenditures After Intergovernmental Transfers as a Percentage of GNP by Level of Government

	Total Public Sector	Federal Government	State Governments	Local Governments	State/Local Governments
1969	30.4	17.8	4.5	8.0	12.5
1974	32.1	17.8	5.3	9.0	14.3
1976	33.5	18.8	5.4	9.2	14.6
1978	31.5	17.7	5.1	8.6	13.7
1980	33.0	19.5	5.2	8.3	13.5
1981	33.3	20.3	5.0	7.9	12.9
1982	35.5	22.2	5.2	8.1	13.3
1983	35.3	22.2	5.1	8.0	13.1
1984	33.9	21.3	5.1	7.5	12.6
1985	34.9	22.1	5.2	7.7	12.8
1986	35.1	21.9	5.4	7.9	13.2
1987 (est.)	34.9	21.4	n.a.	n.a.	13.5

Source: U.S. Advisory Commission on Intergovernmental Relations, *Significant Features of Fiscal Federalism, 1985-86*, and *1988* (for 1984, 1985, 1986, 1987), Table 2.

to Families with Dependent Children (AFDC), the least popular of all welfare programs.[6] As indicated in Table 6, aggregate federal expenditures for all means-tested programs remained unchanged between 1980 and 1986.

If Reagan left standing the component structures of the welfare state, he did manage to weaken them by severely restricting eligibility for means-tested programs like Food Stamps and AFDC, as well as for programs with special entry qualifications, such as payments to disabled workers (Bawden and Palmer, 1984). He also abolished federal support for organizations at the

TABLE 5. Support Levels, Selected Social Expenditures by All Levels of Government, in Constant (1986) Dollars

	1975	1980	1982	1984	1986
Social Security retired workers, average monthly payment	412	437	474	484	488
Medicare average benefit payment for enrolled population	1,259	1,663	1,958	2,163	2,390
Medicaid average payment per recipient	1,117	1,423	1,537	1,638	1,820
Food stamps expenditure per participant	520	549	531	538	547
AFDC[a] payment for families	465	383	350	352	358

Source: Calculated from U.S. Bureau of the Census (1987: Tables 565, 580, 588, 591, 729).

[a] Aid to Families with Dependent Children.

TABLE 6. Social Expenditure by the Federal
Government for Persons with Limited Income— 1986
Amount as Percentage of 1980 Amount

TOTAL[a]	101
Medical Care	121
Medicaid	130
Cash aid	103
AFDC	103
Food benefits	109
Food stamps	102
Housing benefits	103
Education aid	155
Jobs and Training	31
Social Services	69

SOURCE: Calculated from U.S. Bureau of the Census (1987:
Tables 557 and 729).

[a] Includes all social expenditures, of which the federal government paid about 74% in 1986 and 77% in 1980.

urban level that provided community-based social programs and acted as
advocates for the poor. Perhaps the single most devastating action of the
Reagan administration was the elimination of new commitments for the
construction of subsidized housing, a federal responsibility for almost a half
century.[7]

The Reagan attack against social expenditures should be viewed against
a background of an increasingly segmented economy, with a grossly disproportionate amount of the gain in national incomes accruing to the best-off
segment of the population (Table 7), an official unemployment rate that
continuously exceeded 5%, and a severe shortage of low-rent housing. Therefore, despite the apparent stability of social welfare expenditures, the effectiveness of public programs in meeting the needs of the low-income population was eroded substantially.

As in the case of social welfare programs, the administration's policies
for economic development reflected a series of compromises between its
ideological goals and its political capacity. President Reagan was especially
successful in curtailing those employment and training programs particularly detested by conservatives because they made the public sector the
employer of last resort. In this area, the activities of the Carter administration were replaced with a sharply scaled-down federal employment and
training program, the Job Training Partnership Act (JTPA). Federal outlays
were cut 69% between 1980 and 1986 (Table 6). In keeping with administration objectives, JTPA eliminated public employment altogether and was
dominated by business leaders at both the state and municipal government
levels (Schwartz and Poole, 1985).

The administration implemented equally substantial expenditure reductions for capital-oriented economic development programs,[8] even

TABLE 7. Distribution of Adjusted Family Income by Family Type, 1970–1986

Income Percentile	1970	1975	1980	1986	Change 1980–1986
All Families					
20th	127	132	137	139	02
40th	215	226	239	252	13
Median	260	274	291	313	22
60th	311	326	347	381	34
80th	344	471	506	571	65
Married Couples with Children					
20th	168	174	184	187	03
40th	235	251	270	287	17
Median	266	287	312	336	24
60th	303	325	354	389	35
80th	401	435	476	540	64
Non-elderly Childless Families					
20th	240	246	272	268	−04
40th	356	362	401	420	19
Median	407	426	461	491	30
60th	461	484	527	570	43
80th	612	645	700	779	79

SOURCE: U.S. Congressional Budget Office (1988).

Note: Adjusted income is cash family income before taxes measured as a percentage of the appropriate poverty threshold adjusted for inflation.

though public investment was more attractive to business leaders than were employment and training. In fact, had attainment of its budget goals not been blunted substantially by Congress, the administration would have gone far in destroying the capacity of the central government to subsidize business or to conduct even the weak regional planning efforts that characterize the U.S. system. For example, Reagan wanted to eliminate small business assistance entirely, but was forced to settle for a reduction of 27% in constant dollars between 1980 and 1985 (Mead, 1986: Table 2). He sought to reduce mass transit programs from $4.7 billion in 1981 to $1.4 billion in 1986, whereas Congress appropriated $3.3 billion in that year (Mead, 1986: Table 2).

Despite strong congressional support for the programs that most involved the federal government in urban planning (UDAG and the Economic Development Administration [EDA]), overall real expenditures for area and regional development dropped by about 53% under Reagan through 1986 (Table 8). Even the very popular CDBG program, which provided funds for

TABLE 8. Federal Program and Tax Expenditures for Economic Development in Billions of Constant (1986) Dollars

	1970	1975	1980	1982	1984	1986
Community Development	3.9	4.7	6.5	5.2	4.7	4.1
Area & Regional Devel.	2.0	3.2	5.7	4.3	3.2	2.7
UDAG	—	—	0.3	0.4	0.5	0.5
EDA	0.4	0.4	0.6	0.4	0.3	0.3
Training & Employment	4.5	8.3	13.7	6.2	4.8	5.3
Tax expenditures for interest on industrial revenue bonds issued by state & local governments	—	0.4	1.2	1.8	2.9	2.1
Increment from previous date	—	0.4	0.8	0.6	1.1	−0.8
Estimated new capital investment leveraged[a]	—	10.0	20.0	15.0	27.5	−20.0

SOURCE: U.S. Bureau of the Census, *Statistical Abstract of the United States*, 1987, Table 482, 1988, Table 471 (and comparable tables, 1977–1985); U.S. Office of Management and Budget, *Historical Tables, Budget of the United States, Fiscal Year 1988*, Table 12.3.

[a] Leveraged new investment is calculated by multiplying the increment in tax expenditures by 225 (assumes an annual tax-exempt interest of 8% with recipient in the 50% tax bracket).

local development projects, contracted more than 20% in constant dollar expenditures between 1980 and 1986. By the mid-1980s, the most important federal strategy for economic development was a pure market subsidy produced by allowing federal tax exemptions on industrial revenue bonds that financed public projects of subnational governments (like sports arenas and convention centers) and on "job-creating" investment by private firms (Table 8). Yet even here, Reagan sought to curtail outlays; the 1986 revisions of the Federal Income Tax Act sharply restricted all "tax expenditure" programs for economic development and lower-income housing.

ROLES OF CITIES AND STATES
IN ECONOMIC DEVELOPMENT

At the same time as the Reagan administration implemented its strategy of contracting federal social expenditures and aid to localities, market forces in the capitalist world were causing sharp restructuring of the American economy. The decline of the Snowbelt experienced during the 1970s became a more general process of deindustrialization in the 1980s. Economic reorganization played itself out in important ways spatially: through the redeployment of land from manufacturing to office uses, the rapid expansion of the built environment in places where rising industries were located, the recycling of ports and harbors no longer central to the flows of goods in the world economy, and the wholesale abandonment of territories that had become obsolete along with their leading industries (for example, the mining and steel mill towns of western Pennsylvania). The consequence of this process was unemployment and high levels of migration.

Cities and regions that suffered from these transformations defined their central political problem as economic decline, with the antidote being economic development. Whereas 20 years earlier the great domestic pressure on the American political system had been for the political incorporation of the black population and for the redevelopment of obsolete central cities, now it was for programs to facilitate economic investment wherever the old manufacturing economy was in trouble.

The Municipal Level

The reduction in federal assistance caused city governments to increase the incentives for private investment in new construction (Fainstein et al., 1986: Epilogue). Municipal administrations enlarged their use of revenue bonds, tax abatement, tax increment financing, and lease financing, thereby restraining future fiscal capacity. Even when city governments continued to rely on the federal CDBG program, funds were increasingly used as a lure for private investment, rather than as a vehicle for redistribution or for construction of public facilities (Wong and Peterson, 1986), as had been the case in the program's early years.[9]

Federal oversight of local programs diminished both because the Reagan administration favored a "hands-off" policy and because the federal contribution became a very small proportion of the total funding for urban redevelopment programs, as subsidies were derived increasingly from tax expenditures. One consequence of the federal withdrawal was undoubtedly a growing intercity variation in the allocation of redevelopment funding as between downtown and neighborhoods, rehabilitation and new construction, poor versus middle-income people, and industry versus housing. The mix depended on the balance of political forces in any particular city (Nathan and Doolittle, 1983: 198–200).[10]

Although program spending apparently tilted further toward subsidies to business, local regimes nevertheless continued to support housing and social service programs spawned during more generous times. The behavior of municipal governments reflected the continuity and even liberalization of municipal politics contemporaneously with the sharp turn to the right at the federal level. In three of five cities (New Haven, Detroit, and New Orleans) that we studied in an earlier work (Fainstein et al., 1986), voters reelected the same relatively liberal mayors, who changed little in their policy directions. After Mayor Feinstein of San Francisco, herself a liberal Democrat, sponsored an ordinance drastically limiting new commercial construction, Mayor John Agnos won office with a populist platform of neighborhood preservation and revitalization. In the fifth city (Denver) voters chose a Latino candidate over the incumbent in its recent election.

Similarly voters in Philadelphia replaced a white, "law and order" chief executive with a black man; Chicago residents chose a black over a white, machine-affiliated chief executive; and Boston voters selected a mayor with overtly progressive leanings who campaigned on his commitment to residential neighborhoods. In two old New Jersey cities, Hoboken and Jersey City, where intense commercial development activity had been occurring with lavish assistance from the municipal government, mayors were elected who pledged to regulate these efforts more strongly and who were committed to diverting some of their revenues to low-income housing. Only New York, of the country's major cities, continued to be led by a mayor who did not rely on minority groups as a major element of his electoral coalition. Edward Koch presided, nevertheless, over a governmental system with a heavy commitment to public expenditures, active redevelopment and rehabilitation programs, and a tax foreclosure program (the *in rem* housing program) that continually added housing units to the publicly owned stock.

This listing does not imply that American municipal governments became islands of socialism in the conservative sea of national politics during the Reagan years. All of them subsidized business as part of their efforts to "leverage" private investment. But it does indicate more concern at the local than the federal level over responding to the interests of relatively deprived population groups and over maintaining some of the institutional bases for their participation in redevelopment programs established in an earlier era. However compelling was the claim of a new conservative majority in national politics, the Democratic party prospered locally and continued to serve at least some of the interests of its traditional municipal constituencies.[11]

The State Government Level

During the 1980s, state governments moved strongly from their earlier role as mainly passive conduits of revenues to municipalities (Smith et al., 1985). They undertook a broad range of activities to foster economic growth and increasingly became the main source of urban redevelopment funding (Hall and Mushkatel, 1985; Nathan and Doolittle, 1983). The kinds of efforts they implemented included personal tax reductions designed to make their territories appealing residences for business executives, discretionary business tax incentives, bank and corporate regulatory changes, special capital funds, enterprise zones that targeted distressed areas for regulatory and tax relief, educational and training programs, and technology development (McGahey, 1986: 66). These programs represented a qualitative leap from the public works projects (mostly roads and bridges) that previously constituted the contribution of the states to economic development.[12]

The states adopted two functions that the federal government largely has forgone and that typically have formed the linchpin of national economic policy: acting as a development bank and directly sponsoring research complexes likely to spin off high-technology industry. The development bank function involved the use of both regular capital budget funds and industrial revenue bonds (IRBs). Recipient firms received loans at below-

Susan S. Fainstein and Norman Fainstein **345**

market interest rates, either because of direct state subsidy or because the tax-free character of IRBs meant that they were financed at a lower rate. IRBs, which were marketed by both states and localities, offered a number of advantages to the issuer: They were backed only by the revenues of the project itself rather than the full faith and credit of the government; they were exempt from limits on general indebtedness; and they were not subject to voter referenda (Mead, 1986: 40; Smith et al., 1985).[13]

State economic development authorities frequently financed projects considered too risky by private investors. More than a dozen state governments set up venture capital funds; authorities in Michigan, New York, and New Jersey allocated portions of their state employees' pensions funds for financing new business. Michigan's program was one of the most active in the nation. In four years $48 million was invested in 23 companies as part of the attempt to diversify the area's depressed, automobile-dependent economy (Barron, 1986).

In every state California's Silicon Valley and Massachusetts's Route 128 high-technology complexes were used as models for a restructured economy (Saxenian, 1985). Each government set up some form of university-industry-government interaction aimed at building on "centers of excellence" at its universities (Jaschik, 1986). The goal was to reduce dependence on heavy manufacturing and to move into information processing, biotechnology, electronics, and defense production.

Frequent reference was made to the example of North Carolina's Research Triangle, where a consortium of government and business interests joined with the state university to establish a research park. Although the Research Triangle did not generate many new indigenous businesses, it did attract a number of outside firms and government labs that previously would have shunned North Carolina. By the early 1980s, 25 years after inception, the park boasted 20,000 employees and had transformed the backward image of the state (Vogel, 1985: 260). Not all its imitators, however, were as successful in filling their buildings. Moreover, the desire to find a panacea for economic difficulty in high technology ran into the strategic deficiencies of this sector: a low employment multiplier, a tendency to create a bifurcated labor force, and a comparatively small share of the national economy, meaning that there was not enough total employment to have much effect except in a small number of places (Castells, 1985: 20–24).

Although state government economic initiatives were notable in the context of federal laissez-faire, they nevertheless operated with little overall rationale and often at cross purposes (Mead, 1986; Smith et al., 1985). State governments pioneered in establishing a degree of policy coordination within their own boundaries, but the one major attempt to adopt a full-fledged corporatist planning model, the Greenhouse Compact that was proposed in Rhode Island, was soundly defeated in a 1984 referendum (Silver and Burton, 1986). In summing up their study of state industrial policy efforts, Goldstein and Bergman (1986: 274–275) concluded that state governments generally were incapable of adopting "the consensual form of decision making associated with full-fledged corporatist models." Therefore, not only did subnational economic development programs fail to constitute an integrated whole at the national level, but even within state boundaries, they represented economic planning in a limited sense.

Yet it was the relative weakness of the planning component in state programs that made them politically feasible in the state legislatures. The objects of state development programs were, in effect, specific firms or regions rather than broad and spatially diffuse sectors. Policies that targeted individual firms rationalized long-accepted practices of government assistance through grants and loans and government provision of public goods (for example, infrastructure and education). Essentially, state-sponsored economic development policies permitted businesses to draw on public revenues for capital accumulation without enduring much intervention in their decision making. Whether state programs, haphazard as they were, influenced the allocation of investment between sectors or even caused firms to locate in places they would otherwise have avoided remained an open question (Netzer, 1986).

STATE ECONOMIC DEVELOPMENT PROGRAMS WITHIN THE AMERICAN POLITICAL ECONOMY

A severe recession early in the decade and continued rapid restructuring of the U.S. economy resulted in both high unemployment and growing poverty during most of the Reagan years. In such circumstances, national governments usually choose some combination of measures aimed at providing direct relief and at encouraging economic growth. The Reagan administration avoided the formulation of new welfare measures altogether, in part because of the automatic operation of the welfare state that it so disliked. Instead, energy was focused on spurring entrepreneurship, investment, and economic expansion, mainly through tax reduction. The administration was left free to follow this course by the relative absence of popular political mobilization aimed at welfare entitlements or economic redistribution.

Whereas shifts in the economy produced new action groups, several factors prevented them from identifying, and acting on, their common interests (see S. S. Fainstein and N. I. Fainstein, 1985).

1. The massive entry of women into the labor force masked male unemployment and reduced wages by maintaining a constant average family income. Moreover, the reduction of male blue-collar employment and the increase in female white-collar work placed an increasing proportion of the work force in job categories traditionally hard to mobilize.
2. As has been the case throughout the century, ethnic and racial divisions restricted working-class solidarity. New immigration, and particularly the recruitment of illegal immigrants into the worst jobs, exacerbated the difficulty of mobilizing low-income people.
3. Conservatives succeeded in developing a coherent ideology that explained individual deprivation as the result of misguided and clumsy governmen-

tal programs and promised salvation through the natural growth and efficiency produced by the free market (see Lane, 1986). Their opponents were not able to generate a counter ideology that specified a villain and offered a path of redemption.

Ronald Reagan's effectiveness and mass appeal, of course, muted popular opposition. His personal ideology also helped explain why, in pursuing economic growth, the American national government eschewed the many proposals from business interests for an industrial policy and interventionist programs. However, a more adequate explanation of the particular role of federal and state governments during the 1980s requires attention to aspects of the American political system that discouraged national economic planning while facilitating activities by state governments.

First, American business leaders were more fearful than similar groups elsewhere of penetration by the national government into their control over investment, production, and labor (see N. I. Fainstein and S. S. Fainstein, 1985). Business elites historically have viewed the federal government as potentially harming their interests through bureaucratic regulations that, at a minimum, cost money and produce inefficiency and, at worst, hand power over to either workers or consumers. From their perspective, the net benefits of deregulation outweighed those of federal planning intended to facilitate privately directed economic growth.

Second, the constellation of business interests that supported Reagan tended to be drawn from regions of the country and industries historically antagonistic to the liberal, and increasingly corporatist, wing of the Republican party personified by the Rockefellers. These entrepreneurial types from growing regions saw greater advantage for themselves in laissez-faire (with a heavy dose of tax benefits) than in planned national investment. Finally, long-standing regional identities and conflicts institutionalized in the party system and Congress made it difficult for any central regime to allocate economic resources explicitly among regions through a national planning process, investment bank, or similar mechanism. To overcome such obstacles, an incumbent president would need a strong popular mandate of a very different kind from that claimed by Reagan.

Whatever the reasons for the vacuum of national planning, the result was that economic development functions had to be conducted at a subnational level. State governments during the 1980s were under pressure to expand their own fiscal bases in the face of cuts in aid from Washington; economic growth was the only solution. In states dependent on old manufacturing industries, governments also were forced to respond to the economic dislocation of their work forces and to aggressive competition from the Sunbelt. Thus situational logic helped account, in part, for the mercantilist behavior of state governments. Nonetheless, in itself this logic was insufficient to explain why state governments were able to construct economic development programs that were apparently infeasible for the central government.

The answer is that some of the obstacles to economic development policy in Washington were mitigated in the state capitals. A de factor national program that amounted to the sum of competitive state programs was palatable to business leaders and consistent with American political institutions and traditions for a number of reasons (see Worthington, 1986). First, the program of each state could reflect the particular set of dominant business interests in that state, thereby reducing the problem of intersectoral and spatial resource allocation unavoidable in national economic planning. Second, business leaders have typically been less fearful of state governments than of the national government. Conservative interests more effectively dominated the state level of the American system than either the federal or the urban level.[14] Moreover, state governments had to balance their budgets and therefore could not engage in the deficit spending that business conservatives feared. Third, in a mercantilist system of competing states, a standard level of subsidy to business everywhere was effectively established, yet the geographical mobility of capital within the national economy was permitted —in fact, encouraged. Therefore, although business never organized a national program of state-level mercantilism, individual firms could exploit its benefits.

We should reemphasize in conclusion that the relative abundance of economic development programs at the level of the states did not produce coherent policy in any one state. Antipathy to economic planning may have been reduced at the state government level, but it certainly was not eliminated. For this reason, state governors and bureaucracies never admitted they were engaged in economic planning. Indeed, their ambivalence about the whole subject helped account for the piecemeal and sometimes contradictory character of the programs in each of the states. Moreover, although the system of subnational activity made sense politically, it was doubtful whether the aggregate efforts of the 50 states had much effect on the competitive position of the United States in the world capitalist economy.

NOTES

1. To avoid confusion we shall throughout this article consistently use the term *state* to denote a regional government like New Jersey or California. We shall use the term *government* to refer to legitimately constituted authority even where *state* in the generic sense would be more appropriate usage. *Federal* may refer either to the overall system of division of authority among various levels of government or to the national level itself.

2. Efforts at national economic planning (notably the National Recovery Administration) quickly were mired in political and legal conflict and never became permanently institutionalized.

3. Many of the New Deal programs, especially those involving large grants to localities for construction of infrastructure, were dissolved by the end of World War II (N. I. Fainstein and S. S. Fainstein, 1985). By then, however, the pattern of a direct relationship between federal agencies and municipal governments bypassing the states had been established.

4. Throughout its years in office, and despite overseeing enormous expansion in federal government deficits, the Reagan administration sought a constitutional amendment requiring a balanced budget.

5. Final expenditures by lower levels of government after transfers nonetheless remained 1.1% of GNP below their peak levels in the mid-1970s (Table 4), not because of their own tax effort, but because of the substantial contraction of federal aid.

6. AFDC, unlike social security, was not indexed for inflation, and benefit levels were not increased to compensate for the rapid price rises of the 1970s.

7. When Reagan came into office the only significant national initiative for low-income housing was the Section 8 new construction program, in which developers were guaranteed rents through vouchers provided to eligible tenants. Traditional public housing had already ended under Carter. Reagan now eliminated new commitments to Section 8. Although a long pipeline continued expenditures over the Reagan years for housing previously constructed or under way as of 1981, federally supported low-income housing construction was ended completely by the time Reagan left office. In effect this meant that for the first time in 50 years, low-income housing was no longer built in the United States. The only exceptions were in a few cities like New York where local support still existed, though on a greatly curtailed level.

8. Economic development activities included urban and regional development, city planning, employment and training, business formation or investment, and infrastructure programs (transportation, environmental protection, energy).

9. During the mid-1970s, few CDBG funds were expended for economic development. After the Reagan administration dropped the requirement that jobs created by economic development projects should go to lower-income people, the share allocated to this function grew significantly (Dommel, 1984). The bulk of CDBG funds, however, continued to be spent for land clearance and housing rehabilitation in lower- and middle-income neighborhoods.

10. The elimination of federal reporting requirements by the Reagan administration, however, meant that the data necessary to map these variations largely were lacking.

11. Although many city governments are formally nonpartisan, candidates typically are identified with either the Democratic or the Republican state party organizations.

12. State governments also increased their organizational capacity. Whereas municipalities have always been treated legally as creatures of state governments, states typically have allowed them a great deal of authority under various "home rule" statutes. Under the federal urban redevelopment programs, national administrators dealt directly with city officials, bypassing the state governments altogether so as to ensure that depressed central cities would be the program beneficiaries. In the new economic development programs, however, considerable power was invested within state economic development authorities to determine the locations and conditions of assistance. As a result, despite some programs in which distressed urban areas were targeted, much of the state effort assisted suburbs and university communities and placed central cities at a comparative disadvantage (Wood and Klimkowsky, 1985).

13. As we noted earlier, use of IRBs was restricted under the 1986 Tax Reform Act. The federal government offered the states nothing in return. The implications for state

economic development programs seemed to play little or no part in the considerations of the Treasury Department.

14. Many Southern and Southwestern states long have had conservative political cultures; in some other states conservative rural or suburban interests hold power disproportionately.

REFERENCES

Barron, J. (1986) "States back risky ventures in effort to create new jobs." New York Times (June 23).

Bawden, D. L. and J. L. Palmer (1984) "Social policy: challenging the welfare state," pp. 177–216 in J. L. Palmer and I. V. Sawhill (eds.) The Reagan Record. Cambridge, MA: Ballinger.

Castells, M. (1985) "High technology, economic restructuring and the urban-regional process in the United States," pp. 11–40 in M. Castells (ed.) High Technology, Space, and Society. Beverly Hills, CA: Sage.

Dommel, P. (1984) "Local discretion: the CDBG approach," pp. 101–114 in R. D. Bingham and J. P. Blair (eds.) Urban Economic Development. Beverly Hills, CA: Sage.

Fainstein, N. I. and S. S. Fainstein (1974) Urban Political Movements. Englewood Cliffs, NJ: Prentice-Hall.

Fainstein, N. I. and S. S. Fainstein (1985) "Is state planning necessary for capital?" International J. of Urban and Regional Research, 9 (December): 485–507.

Fainstein, S. S. and N. I. Fainstein (1985) "Economic restructuring and the rise of urban social movements." Urban Affairs Q. 21 (December): 187–206.

Fainstein, S. S., N. I. Fainstein, R. C. Hill, D. Judd, and M. Smith (1986) Restructuring the City (2nd ed.). New York: Longman.

Goldstein, H. A. and E. M. Bergman (1986) "Institutional arrangements for state and local industrial policy." J. of the Amer. Planning Assn. 52 (Summer): 265–276.

Grodzins, M. (1960) "The federal system," pp. 265–284 in President's Commission on National Goals, Goals for Americans. Englewood Cliffs, NJ: Prentice-Hall.

Hall, J. S. and A. H. Mushkatel (1985) "Local influence over national policy: the case of community development," pp. 75–90 in D. R. Judd (ed.) Public Policy Across States and Communities. Greenwich, CT: JAI Press.

Jaschik, S. (1986) "University-industry-government projects: promising too much too soon?" Chronicle of Higher Education 31 (January 29): 1, 12.

Lane, R. E. (1986) "Market justice, political justice." Amer. Pol. Sci. Rev. 80 (June): 383–402.

Magaziner, I. C. and R. B. Reich (1982) Minding America's Business: The Decline and Rise of the American Economy. New York: Random House.

McGahey, R. M. (1986) "State economic development in a changing world economy: strategic planning and economic extension services." New York Affairs 9(3): 63–80.

Mead, L. M. (1986) "Resources for state development: the reform of federal-state development programs." New York Affairs 9(3): 37–62.

Mollenkopf, J. H. (1983) The Contested City, Beverly Hills, CA: Sage.

Nathan, R. P. and F. C. Doolittle (1983) The Consequences of Cuts. Princeton, NJ: Princeton Urban and Regional Research Center.

Netzer, D. (1986) "State tax policy and economic development: what should governors do when economists tell them nothing works?" New York Affairs 9(3): 19–36.

O'Connor, J. (1973) The Fiscal Crisis of the State. New York: St. Martin's Press.

Piven, F. F. and R. A. Cloward (1971) Regulating the Poor. New York: Pantheon.

Rohatyn, F. (1980) "The coming emergency and what can be done about it." New York Rev. of Books 27: 20–25.

Saxenian, A. (1985) "Silicon Valley and Route 128: regional prototypes or historic exceptions?" pp. 81–105 in M. Castells (ed.) High Technology, Space, and Society. Beverly Hills, CA: Sage.

Schwartz, G. G. and K. E. Poole (1985) "The significance of the Job Training Partnership Act for federal-state-local relationships," pp. 184–201 in C. R. Warren (ed.) Urban Policy in a Changing Federal System. Washington, DC: National Press.

Silver, H. and D. Burton (1986) "The politics of state-level industrial policy: lessons from Rhode Island's Greenhouse Compact." J. of the Amer. Planning Assn. 52 (Summer): 227–289.

Smith, M. P. and D. R. Judd (1984) "American cities: the production of ideology," pp. 173–196 in M. P. Smith (ed.) Cities in Transformation. Beverly Hills, CA: Sage.

Smith, M. P., R. L. Ready, and D. R. Judd (1985) "Capital flight, tax incentives and the marginalization of American states and localities," pp. 181–202 in D. R. Judd (ed.) Public Policy Across States and Communities. Greenwich, CT: JAI Press.

Thurow, L. C. (1980) The Zero-Sum Society. New York: Basic Books.

U.S. Advisory Commission on Intergovernmental Relations (1988) Significant Features of Fiscal Federalism. Washington, DC: Author.

U.S. Bureau of the Census (1987) Statistical Abstract of the United States, 1988. Washington, DC: Author.

U.S. Congressional Budget Office (1988) Trends in Family Income, 1970–1986. Washington, DC: Author.

U.S. Office of Management of Budget (1988) Historical Tables, Budget of the United States Government, Fiscal Year 1988. Washington, DC: Author.

Vogel, E. (1985) Comeback. New York: Simon & Schuster.

Wong, K. K. and P. E. Peterson (1986) "Urban response to federal program flexibility: politics of Community Development Block Grant." Urban Affairs Q. 21 (March): 293–310.

Wood, R. C. and B. Klimkowsky (1985) "Cities in the new federalism," pp. 228–253 in C. R. Warren (ed.) Urban Policy in a Changing Federal System. Washington, DC: National Academy Press.

Worthington, R. (1986) "Industrial policy in the American states: a critical perspective on public administration and democracy." Presented at the annual meeting of the New York State Political Science Association.

27
Urban Policies and Urban Impacts after Reagan*

William R. Barnes

The years since 1978 have not been an encouraging time for advocates of federal urban policy. From the announcement and subsequent dissipation of the Carter urban policy to the public disclosures of scandals at the Department of Housing and Urban Development, the federal government has not been an important urban policymaker. Similarly, the urban impacts of federal actions have not been an important criterion in policy development or program evaluation. The federal government nonetheless has importantly affected the shape and condition of urban America throughout these years.

Regarding urban policy and urban impacts in the Bush administration, the past is the best indicator of the near future. Continuity with the Reagan era seems more likely than major change because key determinants are aligned: the interests of electoral constituencies, urban policy ideas, ideology, and the actual effects of relevant federal actions. The continuity and alignment are barriers to urban policy development and to achievement of the more important goal: a domestic policy with an urban consciousness.

CONTINUITY IN POLICY IDEAS

In its first urban policy report, the Reagan administration declared that it sought to "reduce the influence of the federal government in domestic affairs so that other more effective centers of decision-making can flourish" (U.S. Department of Housing and Urban Development, 1982: 57). That same report declared that "the foundation for the administration's urban policy is the Economic Recovery Program," the title given to Reagan's overall economic policy effort (p. 1).

The Bush administration begins with basically the same commitments. A compilation of Bush campaign statements reveals little by way of goals regarding urban America directly and few program promises that reflect urban concerns. In response to a candidate questionnaire during the campaign, Bush (National League of Cities Institute, 1987: 50) declared that "the state of American cities reflects the state of the economy." Furthermore, he said that

*Barnes, William R. 1990. "Urban Policies and Urban Impacts after Reagan." *Urban Affairs Quarterly* 25, no. 4 (June 1990): 562–573. Copyright © Sage Publications, Inc. Reprinted by permission of Sage Publications, Inc.

President Reagan's "New Federalism," his effort to shift much of the responsibility for local needs from Washington to our states and cities, has started a process with potentially far reaching results. I'm confident that we are laying a good foundation, not only to return to the proper roles of state and local governments under the constitution, but also to deal effectively with local problems.

If one takes these ideas seriously — and one should — then the combination of the New Federalism and an economic focus on the national rising tide renders urban policy a noncategory. When urban policy is a noncategory, a concern with urban impacts is unlikely to flourish.

The second major legacy that Bush seems likely to carry forward from the Reagan years is the politics of deficit budgets and deficit policy making. Bush's campaign pledge of "no new taxes" and his apparent desire, at least in 1989, to fulfill that commitment ensure that the federal government will continue to function deep in the red. Reductions in projected defense spending are unlikely to alter this situation significantly in the short run.

To date, the major demonstrable effect of these immense federal deficits has not been economic. The major visible result has been to hinder or derail policy making.

Urban programs were particularly hard hit in the budget cutting of the 1980s, and there is no reason to predict that this will change. Indeed, in the Reagan years, budget cuts were the primary means by which the New Federalism was implemented. Aside from a few programs, there was never a substantial devolution of functions from the federal government to states or local governments. Instead, the federal government simply stopped or decreased doing certain things. The possibility that state and/or local governments would pick up the functions or fill the funding gaps was sufficient for the rhetorical and budgetary purposes of the New Federalism effort. The original Bush budget, offered in February 1989, would have been even more devastating to urban programs than the budget that Reagan left when he departed office.

CHANGE

The Bush administration, however, is not simply, nor only, a continuation of the Reagan administration. There is change as well as continuity. Among these changes are (1) Bush's sense of seriousness about government rather than hostility to it, (2) a few initiatives emerging from the campaign that clearly are relevant to the urban agenda, and (3) the appointment of a highly visible Secretary of the Department of Housing and Urban Development (HUD).

Bush arrived in the White House with a reputation as a government man and specifically as a man of the federal government. This is a distinct contrast with Reagan, who ran his election campaigns essentially against the federal government, even in 1984 when he already held the White House. It also distinguishes Bush from Carter, who similarly ran against inefficiencies and unethical behavior inside the Beltway. This reputation seems based not on a tendency to public sector activism but rather on an attitude toward the institutions of government. In 1989 that attitude appeared to be composed of respect for the institutions of government and an emphasis on prudence in policy making. Thus columnist Broder (1989) speculated that the Bush era will be a period of consolidation and that Bush will, in this respect, be like Eisenhower. These attitudes need not but could translate into a problem-solving posture that would be conducive to program development.

In appointing Jack Kemp, congressman from Buffalo, New York, to be Secretary of the Department of Housing and Urban Development, Bush not only co-opted a former rival for the Republican nomination for president but also automatically gave HUD and HUD programs more access to public attention than has been true for eight years under Secretary Samuel Pierce. Kemp immediately declared that a "war on poverty" would be an important focus of his tenure (Shafroth, 1988: 1). His avowed priorities are home ownership and affordable housing, economic development through enter-prise zones, ending homelessness, resident management and homesteading, fair housing, and drug-free public housing. Kemp has been demonstrably delayed in pursuing his intentions and ambitions by the revelation of various scandals at HUD under the previous administration (*Housing and Develop-ment Reporter*, 1989: 390). Budget and policy constraints plus the need for Kemp to attend to and resolve the program issues that underlay these scandals leave the extent to which Kemp will be able to carry out new urban policy development in question as of this writing.

Kemp will probably get (at last) an enterprise zones (EZ) program, a proposal he has advocated for a decade. This may be useful, but of course that depends on the specific incentives that are provided and the targeting that is used. A Bush urban policy with an EZ program as the centerpiece will have more effect on symbolic politics than on urban conditions.

During 1989, the Bush administration also made several initiatives that clearly are relevant to urban policy concerns, including

1. Bush announced in September 1989 a national program related to illegal drugs. Much of the money involved simply rearranged existing programs, and much else was based on assumptions about additional state and local expenditures.
2. He offered a major proposal with regard to clean air. Conflicts within the administration resulted in important shifts in the stringency of the pro-gram that Bush originally had announced.
3. Bush followed through on his campaign promise to support child care. Conflict between Bush's interest in a tax program versus the Democratic Congress's interest in an expenditure program reflects some difference in targeting.
4. Working toward a "clean bill" for the savings and loan bail-out legisla-tion, the White House opposed efforts to add requirements that savings and loans provide stable funds for low-income housing. Those require-

ments were written into the laws, and it remains to be seen how effectively the executive branch will enforce these requirements.

5. Seeking to be the "education president," Bush convened an education summit with governors in September. It seems unlikely that this summit will result in additional federal monies for education or in any substantial change in the balance of intergovernmental responsibilities.

All of these issues are before the Congress and/or unresolved at the time this is written.

Some of these initiatives are not the traditional stuff of urban policy. But, for example, *drugs* was rated most frequently as an important community problem in a survey of city officials in December 1988 (Peterson, 1989). A survey of city hall officials showed that child care tops their concerns about the needs of children in cities; low-income housing is first in their concerns about the needs of families (Born, 1989: vi). The view of these kinds of programs as nonurban may reflect a lag in the perception of analysts behind the evolving urban policy agenda.

A decade of inaction at the federal level may indeed have caused the politics of these issues to crystallize at state and local levels. Those local officials now must act as spokespersons for the needs of their citizens rather than as directors of institutions who are mainly concerned with programs for which monies flow through their corporation. This is surely an optimistic assessment, but the beginnings of some such transformation occurred during the 1980s. If that transformation continues, local support for a new urban policy agenda could evolve.

URBAN IMPACTS: CONSTITUENCY AND IDEOLOGY

The balance of continuities and changes from the Reagan years into the Bush administration provides good reason to expect little interest on the part of the Bush administration in urban policy per se and, consequently, little interest in the issue of the urban impacts of nonurban policies. In addition, there is no reason to expect any substantial change in the general nature of urban effects under the Bush administration as compared to those during the Reagan years.

Two researchers who searched for "Reagan's real urban policy" and for the effects of "nonurban policies as urban policies" described the direction and nature that probably can be expected of urban effects of the activities of the Bush administration. Glickman (1984) found that

> Reagan's *real* urban policies have remarkably consistent effects. . . . First, changes in the tax laws directly aid firms and taxpayers in growing areas and the suburbs. . . . Second, changes in the composition of the budget reduced social programs that most affect declining areas.
>
> Therefore, the real urban policy rewarded key Reagan constituencies in important ways. Voters in growth areas (such as the South, Southwest and the suburbs)

that backed the President have benefited from the Reagan economic program in two ways: first, because of Reaganomics class bias and second, because their regions have been aided in the interregional battle for federal funds and new jobs. Although rewarding the wealthy was an unabashed goal of the administration, the urban effects were basically incidental and unplanned [p. 476].

Mills (1987) concluded that the "clearest effect" of the range of programs and policies he analyzed was "that most have favored high income residents." He concluded further that "it seems almost certain that the net effect of government programs has been to induce excessive suburbanization" (p. 568).

One can read these two assessments either in terms of the implicit analyses about political constituencies being served or in terms of program assessments. Either way, one has little reason to expect substantial positive impacts, for example, around redistributive concerns or around the central-city revitalization concerns of President Carter's urban policy. Policies, programs and indirect effects seem well shaped to constituencies; outcomes will benefit middle- to upper-income groups, the suburbs, and the Sunbelt.

The Reagan-Bush orientation also can be understood as an effort to ensure or to establish the smooth workings of economic and political marketplaces in metropolitan areas. This view pretty much takes them at their word. On the one hand, they would prefer to leave decisions to the private market, which they see as autonomous and smoothly operating only if it can be protected from public tinkering and intervention. They believe in the beneficial functioning of the "invisible hand." In addition, they want to remove federal intervention from a similarly autonomous mechanism at the local level in which people "vote with their feet" to determine the mode of governance and the mix of services provided by state and local governments. They believe in the beneficial functioning of "the invisible foot."[1] But of course the current functioning of the invisible hand and the invisible foot precisely benefits the constituencies of the Reagan-Bush coalition. Thus there is a happy confluence of political interests with the allegedly natural functioning of these economic and political systems.

If these systems fail to function in substantial ways or if they begin to function to the benefit of other interests to the detriment of the coalition's interests, these ideological beliefs would be shelved and the Bush administration would likely respond in various ways, perhaps including an urban policy. That policy would speak to the concerns of these interests, not necessarily at all to the concerns of central cities or the poor or older cities that were the basis of Carter's urban policy coalition.

There is likewise little political basis for expecting this alignment to change. A recent *National Journal* article summed up the situation as "more problems, less clout" for big cities (Kirschten, 1989: 2026). A similar report in *Governing* leads with a headline declaring that "a shrinking urban bloc in Congress plays defense" (Ehrenhalt, 1989: 21) These analyses identify urban policy with the interests of older central cities. They overlook the changing nature of urban America, which includes suburbs that contain more population and more jobs than their central cities and new kinds of urban communities in Austin, Phoenix, and San Jose as well as the older urban centers such as Detroit, Cleveland, and Newark. The new "technocities" and "technoburbs" (Fishman, 1987: 184) have turned their backs on central cities locally and at the state level just as the federal government has turned away nationally.

This alignment of constituencies, ideology, and policy effects also reflects the pattern of Democratic and Republican voting in the presidential election. In 1988 the total presidential vote split 53.4% for the Republican ticket and 45.6% for the Democratic. The central areas that contain the 32 largest cities, in contrast, reversed that split: 45.5% Republican and 53.5% Democratic. (These data probably understate the Democratic preference in the central cities because the votes are mostly reported by county and thus do include some suburbs.) Table 1 illustrates George Bush's lack of electoral obligation to some of the nation's largest central cities and their disproportionately minority populations. Vote counts do not necessarily mirror what Ferguson and Rogers (1981: 6) call the "hidden" election involving conflict and coalitions among "pivotal interest groups." The patterns of such groups as well as the political constellations of the Congress may be different and even countervailing but are beyond my scope and capacity here.[2]

The loosening grip of older central cities on our intellectual and political frameworks may also be seen as both cause and effect of the emphasis on

TABLE 1. 1988 Presidential Voting Patterns by Selected Cities

City[a]	% 1988 Total Vote[b]		% Black and Hispanic[c]	
	Republican	Democrat	Black	Hispanic
New York City, NY	32.8	66.2	25.23	19.88
Chicago, IL	29.8	69.2	39.83	14.05
Philadelphia, PA	32.5	66.6	37.84	3.77
Baltimore, MD	25.4	73.5	54.80	.97
San Francisco, CA	26.1	72.8	12.73	12.28
Washington, DC	14.3	82.6	70.32	2.77
Boston, MA	33.2	65.2	22.42	6.41
New Orleans, LA	35.2	63.6	41.12	1.34
Denver, CO	37.1	60.7	12.03	18.76
St. Louis, MO	27.0	72.5	45.55	1.22
United States	53.4	45.6	12.2[d]	6.45

[a] Large cities for which vote totals are reported by municipal jurisdiction.

[b] Data furnished by Alice McGillivary, Election Research Center.

[c] Data furnished by U.S. Bureau of the Census.

[d] Unpublished data from the Bureau of the Census.

federal programs that help people rather than places. This distinction was crystallized in the urban policy report of the President's Commission on a National Agenda for the Eighties (1980). Recently, Dearborn (1989) argued that as the federal government turns its back on large cities but problems accumulate and demand attention, "urban problems ultimately are likely to land on the state's doorsteps." He predicted that "additional assistance may come in the form of new and enlarged state programs directed at people with problems not at city governments" and this will "mean an expansion of state governments and diminishment of city governments."[3]

Urban historians[4] are reinterpreting the development of metropolitan America with a focus on the development of suburbs and the suburban ideal. In this view, it is precisely the extraction of the suburb and its goals from the complex web of the urban system that has created the class- and race-segregated metropolitan areas of twentieth-century America. As the black middle class moves out from central cities, race is meshed with class and with images of physical decay in the central area to form the antithesis of the suburban ideal. A similar phenomenon is occurring with regard to Hispanics in some cities, especially in the Southwest.

Those suburbs and the new cities created in the image of the suburban ideal are the main constituency of the Reagan-Bush coalition. Their lack of interest in urban policy is essential to their definition. Here is President Bush on August 8, 1989, in remarks to the National Urban League: "In many respects—let's face it—urban America offers a bleak picture—an inner city in crisis. And there is too much crime, too much crack. Too many dropouts, too much despair, too little economic success, too little advancement—and the bottom line, too little hope" (The White House, 1989: 1). Here is urban America as poor, black, isolated, without power. In this formulation, urban policy is about what George Bush and his constituency are not. . . .

THE SEARCH FOR THE REAL *URBAN*

The search for the real urban policy of Reagan or Bush reveals the ultimate fruitlessness of arbitrary distinctions between urban and nonurban federal actions. A recitation of the categories used by Glickman (1984) and Mills (1987) illustrate this point. Mills noted that his selection of programs to analyze is "inevitably somewhat arbitrary." His selection included the following: government procurement, the U.S. system of local government, national transportation policies, housing programs, urban development programs, antipoverty programs, capital taxation, and the 1986 tax reform act (p. 562).

Glickman suggested that the "real urban policy" of any administration consists of four parts. The first three are what he called "explicit" or "nominal" urban policy: place-targeted urban programs in functional areas, the federal system of intergovernmental grants, and people-oriented social programs, particularly income transfers that serve urbanites. "The fourth element consists of the urban effects of economic and other non-urban policies." The fourth element "dominates the others" and "any comprehensive analyses of the real urban policy must centrally consider economic programs as well as nominal urban policies" (pp. 471–472). Wolman, in a separate effort to assess the impacts of the Reagan urban policy, stated that "it is likely that in aggregate the effects of implicit urban policy on urban areas far outweigh those of explicit urban policy" (1986: 317).

Thus the interest here is in the entire array of domestic policies and indeed other policies such as trade. "Urban policy" may be a useful basket for carrying a jumble of program initiatives. More important, however, the goal is probably more aptly stated as a domestic policy with an urban consciousness.

The politics of disengagement and polarization described earlier work against such an approach and go far beyond the capacities of policy analysis to overcome. Nonetheless, policy analysis has a chore in the eventual bridging of the disengagement. That chore is to create frameworks for understanding the connections between ghetto and suburb and between old and new cities. In short, the task—which needs to be undertaken politically as well as analytically—is to reconstitute the whole urban community that encompasses these dangerously and increasingly distant parts.

This chore shifts the focus from urban policy to urban reality. Markusen (1980: 103) noted critically that the urban impact analysis "heralds a historical shift of presumed culpability for urban problems from the private sector toward the public sector." Her comment foreshadowed Ronald Reagan saying that government is part of the problem rather than part of the solution. There is, of course, enough "culpability" to go around: hand and foot, visible and invisible. We need usable analytic and political frameworks that encompass both federalism and capitalism, both public and private sector factors at work in creating and sustaining urban problems.

The short-run outlook is that the nation's communities will continue to be affected by federal actions that are and are not labeled urban and that most frequently have not been examined in terms of their urban impacts. Some of these effects will be substantial and significant; some will be negative. The current pattern of urban impacts will likely persist. Although some new federal programs may be undertaken and the urban policy agenda may broaden at the local level, it is hard to find the political or policy source for a full-fledged federal urban policy in the early 1990s.

NOTES

1. This provocative and insightful phrase was used by Burton (1970: 146) in testimony to a Congressional committee. The context for the remark was a critique of the Tiebout model for understanding public finance.

2. Alice McGillivary from the Election Research Center provided these data upon my request. I very much appreciate her assistance.

3. Dearborn (1989) predicts that "urban fiscal crises are only a recession away from happening."

4. See especially the studies by Fishman (1987) and Stilgoe (1988). See also Jackson (1985) and Keating (1988).

REFERENCES

Born, C. E. (1989) Our Future and Our Only Hope: A Survey of City Halls Regarding Children and Families. Washington, DC: National League of Cities.

Broder, D. S. (1989) "Eisenhower lives." Washington Post (September 13): A25.

Burton, R. N. (1970) "The metropolitan state: a prescription for the urban crisis and the preservation of polycentrism in metropolitan society." U.S. Congress Subcommittee on Urban Affairs of the Joint Economic Committee. 91st Congress, 2nd session, October 13–15.

Dearborn, P. M. (1989) "Hard times ahead for cities." Washington Post (May 10): A21.

Ehrenhalt, A. (1989) "As interest in its agenda wanes, a shrinking urban bloc in Congress plays defense." Governing 10 (July): 21–25.

Ferguson, T. and J. Rogers [eds.] (1981) The Hidden Election: Politics and Economies in the 1980 Presidential Campaign. New York: Random House.

Fishman, R. (1987) Bourgeois Utopias: The Rise and Fall of Suburbia. New York: Basic Books.

Glickman, N. J. (1984) "Economic policy and the cities." J. Amer. Planning Assn. 50 (Autumn): 471–569.

Housing and Development Reporter (1989) "Kemp, Cranston unveil wide-ranging proposals for reform, new programs." Vol. 17 (October): 390.

Jackson, K. T. (1985) Crabgrass Frontier: The Suburbanization of the United States. New York: Oxford Univ. Press.

Keating, A. D. (1988) Building Chicago: Suburban Developers and the Creation of a Divided Metropolis. Columbus: Ohio State Univ. Press.

Kirschten, D. (1989) "More problems, less clout." National J. 21 (August): 2026–2030.

Markusen, A. R. (1980) "Urban impact analysis: a critical forecast," pp. 103–118 in N. J. Glickman (ed.) The Urban Impacts of Federal Policies. Baltimore, MD: Johns Hopkins Univ. Press.

Mills, E. S. (1987) "Non-urban policies as urban policies." Urban Studies 24: 561–569.

National League of Cities Institute (1987) "Election '88: presidential candidate questionnaire responses." Washington, DC: Author.

Peterson, D. (1989) "Municipal officials worry, but are optimistic on future." Nation's Cities Weekly 12 (January 16): 7–10.

President's Commission on a National Agenda for the Eighties (1980) Urban America in the Eighties: Perspectives and Prospects. Washington, DC: Government Printing Office.

Shafroth, F. (1988) "Kemp tapped to lead Bush housing initiative." Nation's Cities Weekly 11 (December 19): 1, 11.

Stilgoe, J. R. (1988) Borderland: Origins of the American Suburb; 1820–1939. New Haven, CT: Yale Univ. Press.

U.S. Department of Housing and Urban Development (1982) The President's National Urban Policy Report. Washington, DC: Government Printing Office.

The White House (1989) Remarks by the President to the National Urban League conference. Washington, DC: Office of the Press Secretary (August 8).

Wolman, H. (1986) "The Reagan urban policy and its impacts." Urban Affairs Q. 21 (March): 311–335.

Suburban Regimes

28

The Planners of Levittown*

Herbert J. Gans

In order to describe Levittown's origin, one must begin with its planners: who made the critical decisions for the conception of the community, with what goals in mind, and for what kinds of residents and aspirations? The most important role was, of course, played by the builder, Levitt and Sons. The firm was founded during the Depression by the late Abraham Levitt, a "self-made" son of Russian-Jewish immigrants who had practiced real estate law for a quarter of a century before going into the building business, and by his two sons, William and the late Alfred. Until the beginning of World War II, the firm built a number of small suburban subdivisions on Long Island, priced to appeal to the upper middle class then streaming to the Island. After World War II, as a result of experience gained in building Navy housing, the Levitts developed a mass production scheme that allowed them to build inexpensive housing for the postwar flood of veterans and their families.[1]

Most of the concepts that went into planning Levittown, New Jersey, were evolved in the two earlier Levittowns, in New York and Pennsylvania. Levittown, Long Island, begun in 1947, was built in traditional subdivision style, with the builder buying a piece of land — much larger than most others, to be sure — and then acquiring further acreage as sales continued to go well. The houses in Levittown were smaller versions of the expensive suburban ones the Levitt firm had built previously, but included an array of home appliances and were located around Village Greens that consisted of neighborhood shops, a playground, and a swimming pool.[2] Perhaps these additional items were provided because of the builder's uncertainty that the

*Gans, Herbert J. 1967. "The Planners of Levittown." Pp. 3–14 and 20–21 in *The Levittowners: Ways of Life and Politics in a New Suburban Community*. New York: Pantheon Books. Copyright © 1967 by Herbert J. Gans. Reprinted by permission of Pantheon Books, a division of Random House, Inc.

house alone was salable. Levittown was, after all, an experiment, begun when the housing industry as a whole had known only lack of demand and when fears of a postwar depression were still prevalent. But the firm also had an additional goal: to create a community. This emerged more clearly when Alfred Levitt, who was trained in architecture, proposed his scheme for Landia, a 675-acre community elsewhere on Long Island.[3] It was planned to provide separate residential neighborhoods without through streets, a town center, and a complete set of community facilities, including parks.

Landia was never built, partly because of the moratorium on housing at the start of the Korean War, but some of its ideas were incorporated in the building of the second Levittown, in Bucks County, Pennsylvania, in 1951. Although the Levitt firm was secure enough by this time to buy a much larger amount of land at the start, the community was still not totally planned in advance, the individual neighborhoods being laid out just before their construction. The plan for this second Levittown called for about 17,000 homes, and neighborhoods free from through traffic, with elementary schools, playgrounds, and pools at their center. The local shopping centers were almost entirely eliminated after the firm learned to its dismay that a large shopping center in the Long Island Levittown — not built by the firm —was drawing most of the sales away from shops on the Village Greens. Instead, the Levitts built a huge "regional" shopping center on the edge of their new Levittown, hoping to attract not only their house buyers but people from other communities as well. The firm also gave land to a number of churches, institutionalizing a practice that had begun on an ad hoc basis in the initial Levittown when a church came to the builder with a request for free land.

But Levittown, Pennsylvania, like Levittown, Long Island, had one major drawback. Because of the way land had been purchased, the final community was spread out over four townships and many other governmental units, and in developing the land the builder had to negotiate separately with each unit. This not only took considerable time and energy, but required changes in the initial plan, particularly in the design of neighborhoods and locations of schools, and also forced the firm to administer recreation areas so as to limit their use to purchasers of Levitt houses. As a result, the firm's executives were frequently diverted from the business of building and even became embroiled in community conflicts.

Not long after the Bucks County development had gotten off to a successful start, the firm began to consider yet a third Levittown, and this time it sought to eliminate the difficulties it had encountered previously by purchasing land within a single township. Ultimately, the choice fell on Willingboro township in New Jersey. Willingboro township was an area of small farms, producing peaches, plums, and tomatoes on the region's sandy soil. Just outside the ring of postwar suburbs that had sprung up around Philadelphia, and only about ten miles from Levittown, Pennsylvania, it was eminently "ripe" for residential development. It was particularly suitable for

Levitt and Sons because it was inhabited only by individual farmers, a few owners of what had once been a summer home colony, and the village of Rancocas, a nineteenth century Quaker settlement of less than 500 people. Soon after the firm bought the land, it had the township boundaries changed so that Rancocas was incorporated into the neighboring township of Westampton. Thus it had obtained a large acreage, located entirely within one township and occupying most of it. Once Rancocas had been moved out, only about 600 people were left in the township, and they, the builder felt, could be persuaded to give him a free hand to build as he wished. Willingboro would provide a virtual *tabula rasa* for realizing William Levitt's goals and plans.

THE PLANNING PROCESS

By the time the planning for Levittown, New Jersey, began, control of the firm was entirely in the hands of William Levitt. Abraham Levitt had retired because of increasing age, and Alfred Levitt had left the firm, selling his share of the stock to his brother, reputedly because they could not develop a method for making decisions jointly. Working with William Levitt were half a dozen executives, many of whom had been with the firm since the late 1940s, but the final decisions were his.[4] Like his brother, he was open to advice, but he was known as a man who rarely changed his mind once he had made it up.[5] William Levitt's goals were to build another profitable development and a better community, more comprehensively planned in advance and more completely stocked with public facilities. He also sought to end the attacks by planners, architects, and social critics against the firm and the past Levittowns. Known for his low opinion of the city planning profession, however, and lacking Alfred's interest in its concepts and schemes, he had no intention of building the community to please the planners. Nor was he especially concerned about how to satisfy the buyers and meet their aspirations. As the most successful home builder in the East, with a decade's reputation for providing "the best house for the money," he felt he knew what they wanted. Unlike his father, he had no desire to involve the firm in the life of the community or to uplift the cultural level and civic performance of the residents. He wanted only to build what he deemed to be a better Levittown, what he often called a "showplace."

Because of the success of the Bucks County community, Levitt felt secure enough to buy 80 per cent of the land he would need for the entire community, with options on the remaining portion. A fairly complete plan of the eventual community was developed, including an overall road system, a community-wide sewage and water supply system to be built before the community was occupied, and a generalized scheme for shopping, including both a regional retail center and a series of local ones, and for locating schools and churches. The plan was generalized in that preliminary locations for these facilities were included in the site maps with which the firm worked, but final locations and facility designs were not made until just before actual construction. No longer needing to accommodate his ideas to several township boundaries, the builder could plan the community as a set of residential "parks," with school, playground, and pool located at the center in true neighborhood planning tradition.

There were other innovations in the plan for the third Levittown. The elementary schools would be provided by the firm and their cost incorporated into the house price. They could be "donated" to the community, thus keeping taxes down, and would be open when people moved in. The previous pattern of neighborhoods with only one house type was dropped. From now on, the three types of houses were to be mixed on each street: a four-bedroom "Cape Cod" initially selling for $11,500; a three-bedroom, one-story "Rancher" for $13,000; and a two-story "Colonial," one with three, another with four bedrooms and costing $14,000 and $14,500 respectively. Each house type was built in two elevations, but with the same floor plan, and was varied in external color to effect yet more visual heterogeneity. Whereas the houses in Levittown, Pennsylvania, were of a fairly severe modern style, those in New Jersey would be in the pseudo-Colonial style popular all over the Eastern seaboard. The shopping center, again located at the edge of the community, was designed by a nationally known architect who had built a prizewinning center in the Middle West, providing a considerably more attractive shopping area than in the Pennsylvania Levittown.

During the initial planning phase, Levitt employed an engineer with city planning experience to develop the overall plan, and also brought in a number of nationally known consultants to design detailed plans for educational and recreational facilities; but no city planners were included among the consultants. Subsequently, he did work with the planner hired by Willingboro township, and in 1964, when the firm was building developments of varying size in a number of locations all over the world, it finally hired a city planner to help select sites and make preliminary master plans.

The executives themselves were divided into two relatively stable factions, the self-styled "idealists" who wanted to build what they considered the best possible community, and the "realists," concentrated mainly in the comptroller's office, who were concerned with economy and sometimes questioned innovations that might increase costs or affect sales. Levitt himself seems to have mediated between the two groups. In the initial phases of planning he sided with the idealists, but later, when plans were about to be implemented, he became more conscious of cost and market considerations and often supported the realists. Generally speaking, the plans put forth by the idealists and their consultants were accepted when they contributed to the development of the best community at the lowest cost, and rejected when they were too expensive or added "frills" that would not help sales. Although Levitt had been traditionally hostile to outsiders, he accepted many of the consultants' proposals — often because they agreed with his own ideas. The consultants had been chosen initially because of their national reputations, and the agreement between them and Levitt was often fortuitous. For example, the concept of the school at the center of the neighborhood, originally brought into the firm by Alfred Levitt, was also part of traditional planning ideology and was favored by the school consultants as well. Similarly, because the firm wanted to divest itself of control of the recreation facilities and believed that the school and playground would be used by the same people and should therefore be administered jointly, it proposed a combined school-playground-pool area. When the firm asked the National Recreation Association for technical help, it did not know that that organization had advocated such a combination for almost forty years.

But some plans were rejected. One Levitt official wanted a new and comprehensively planned educational system to be designed under the aegis of the Ford Foundation, but when Foundation funds for this scheme were not available, a more conventional school system, more akin to existing county and township values and practices, was developed instead. The ambitious recreation plan of another firm member, providing for a large park and playground system around the school and more than one swimming pool for each neighborhood, was similarly cut down to make more land available for houses. As the time for building drew closer, both of these officials who stood for a maximum investment in community facilities could not agree with the emphasis on housing, and eventually they were fired, although not for this reason alone.

Perhaps the principal innovation in the new Levittown was the mixing of house types. This idea, originally suggested by Mrs. Levitt, debated within the firm for several months, and finally carried out by Levitt over the strong objections of all his executives, stemmed indirectly from the criticisms of the city planners, particularly Lewis Mumford. During the 1950s, when attacks on the physical and demographic homogeneity of the postwar suburban subdivisions began, Levittown was frequently mentioned as the prototype. At first, the firm shrugged off this criticism. As it continued to mount, however, and spread into the mass media, Levitt became concerned that Levittown's image would be impaired and even that sales might be affected, particularly when, later in the decade, the sellers' market was starting to become a buyers' market. By the time he was ready to start the third Levittown, Levitt also wanted a reputation for building the best possible communities.

In addition, the firm was beginning to upgrade the image of the purchaser it was seeking. In Long Island it had built for veterans and had attracted predominantly lower middle class buyers. In Pennsylvania, however, Levittown also drew a number of blue collar workers and what Levitt officials worriedly called "marginal" buyers, people who could not really afford the house but were able to take it because no down payment had been required under Veterans Administration mortgage insurance regulations. The firm did not want marginal buyers in the new Levittown, and, in fact, hoped to build somewhat more expensive houses which would increase its profit margin. If it was to do so, and bring in middle and upper middle class home buyers, Levitt wanted to prove incorrect the critical magazine articles on suburbia read by this population. When the idea of mixed house types was approved, one of the Levitt executives pointed out, "Now Lewis Mumford can't criticize us any more"; later, the firm promoted the innovation as a sales device. In the press release announcing the opening of the new Levittown, Levitt said, "We are ending once and for all the old bugaboo of uniformity. . . . In the new Levittown, we build all the different houses . . . right next to each other within the same section."

The struggle against criticism affected other features of the plan. Although the Levitts personally identified so much with their developments as to give them the family name, William Levitt was quite aware that some people considered "Levittown" a symbol of the worst in suburban development, even if others saw it as a brand name for good and inexpensive houses.[6] Several executives urged strongly that the name be dropped, but Levitt rejected the idea. As a compromise, the merchandising was to stress the individual parks into which people would buy. A Levitt official pointed out, "One of the major reasons for the neighborhood plan was to answer the critics of Levittown who say that it is one huge mass of homogeneous mass-produced housing, all preplanned to standardization and mass production."

Shortly before Levittown, New Jersey, opened for occupancy, an article by William Levitt entitled "What! *Live* in a Levittown?" appeared in *Good Housekeeping*.[7] In it, the builder argued—and quite rightly so—that mass-produced housing did not lead to conformity or homogeneity among the population. After Levittown opened, many tongue-in-cheek advertisements appeared in the Philadelphia papers which sought to give the impression that Levittowners were diverse, respectably middle class, but not overly sophisticated. One ad, headed "Wanted: Zoologist for a Neighbor," indicated that all occupations were represented in Levittown but listed mostly professional ones. Another, entitled "Hi and Middle Fi," suggested that the Levitt house could be rigged up for hi-fi enthusiasts, but poked fun at such sophisticated taste and concluded, "You'll find all kinds of music lovers in Levittown, but we've discovered that most of them are middle-fi, like ourselves."[8]

When it came to planning the houses, however, there was less concern with status than with livability and effective use of space. The houses built in the third Levittown were radically improved versions of the models built in the earlier ones, altered frequently and sometimes annually in a process of trial and error that responded partly to market reactions, party to technological innovation and cost-cutting opportunities, and partly to a desire for change within the Levitt firm. The basic construction concepts and layouts have remained remarkably stable, however. The Levitt house is built on a concrete slab with precut materials and is put together on an assembly line basis.[9] The layout provides a relatively open house plan, with maximum space for rooms and for storage, and a minimum for circulation or symbolic, nonutilitarian space such as a foyer.

In the initial planning phase, Levitt considered a total revision of the basic house types, and asked two world-famous architects to submit sketch plans. When their houses turned out to cost about $50,000, they had to be dropped, and the firm's own small architectural department, with assistance from Levitt executives, was given the job of revamping the designs used in

Levittown, Pennsylvania. When models of the houses were erected, Levitt himself looked them over and suggested changes. After the model was opened to the public, criticisms and suggestions for it were recorded at the sales desk. If a model did not sell, it was redesigned at once. Usually the models were not altered until the annual model change or until sales dropped to a point where alteration was considered necessary.[10]

The improvements made in the houses over time have increased their spaciousness and efficiency, with little concern for fashion except in inexpensive externals. Despite the popularity of basement or split-level designs, the firm refused to consider them until 1965, when it built some basement houses in a new Long Island project. Likewise, Levitt officials chose the pseudo-Colonial design for New Jersey, not because of its popularity, but because they felt it would help them attract higher-income purchasers, and because they themselves disliked the starkly modern designs they had initially built in Levittown, Pennsylvania. The design of the Levittown houses proceeded, then, on an ad hoc basis, with periodic improvements based on what the firm thought best and with recognition of the vetoes expressed in the market. Beyond this point, there was no catering to the customers.

For this reason, no market research of any kind went into the planning of Levittown, New Jersey, although just before the community opened some of the less optimistic Levitt officials commissioned a prominent land economist to estimate the market for the community. His report was extremely pessimistic, noting that the metropolitan area market for low-priced, single-family housing was almost saturated, and that the new Levittown was located outside of what were then considered the boundaries of Philadelphia's suburban commuting zone. As it turned out, the consultant's prediction was accurate, for by 1960 the soft market conditions he had forecast began to appear, forcing a slowdown in the construction schedule that has continued until the present. Although the firm expected to build 12,000 houses by 1965, it had only put up about 6000 by that date—and it had also established a market research department.

In planning for the new Levittown, however, Levitt had no inkling of what was to come. His mass production techniques had previously enabled the firm to undersell its competitors in the area, and in a seller's market it did not need to think about the buyers. The Levitt officials' ability to make decisions without consulting them was aided considerably by their consensus with and similarity to their customers. Most of the Levitt executives were born and raised in the suburbs, and had little or no use for the city, other than as a place for occasional recreational and shopping trips. They favored single-family housing and could not understand why anyone would want to live either in apartments or in the row houses that had been Philadelphia's dominant building type. They believed that the utility of the house for family living came first and that style was secondary. Their taste was not much different from that of their customers; both rejected the abstract and severe contemporary design that dominated the architectural magazines of the late 1950s.

If anything, the firm's official style was a more exuberant version of its customers', in much the same way as movie stars are often exaggerated versions of what their fans would like to be. Indeed, a decade earlier, Eric Larrabee had described the first Levitt office building as "Selznick Colonial."[11] The new headquarters building the firm put up in Levittown, New Jersey, was furnished in what one might call Dionysian-Modern, a vivid and often garish mixture of bright colors, strong textures, and antique as well as modern knicknacks. Levitt's office had white rugs and gold-plated bathroom fixtures, and the model homes, furnished to entice purchasers, displayed a similar, if less expensive, Dionysian motif.

About their purchasers' aspirations for life in Levittown, the Levitt officials thought only rarely. Some looked down on them as being of a lesser status, but others saw them as smart, young, socially mobile couples who really wanted to live in high-status suburbs but could not afford to do so. Mostly, the firm viewed them as people who needed a new house and were obviously sensible in their choice of Levittown, because they realized that Levitt's houses were the best value for the money. It also felt that most of their buyers were moving to Levittown only because of the house and had little interest in the wider community. As a result, whenever Levittowners objected to conditions in the community, firm officials were quick to argue —whether the firm was responsible or not—that the objections were those of a minority, "self-seeking politicians," or "sick" people who just wanted to show off for psychological reasons. Suspicion of community participation was a tradition of the Levitt organization, even though there had been much less builder-buyer conflict in the Levittowns than in most other new housing developments.[12]

Marketing the House

The only deliberate planning vis-à-vis the eventual purchasers took place in marketing the house. That process was aimed at attracting the young family buying its first home, a group to which the builder had appealed ever since he began to build the first Levittown. The houses were designed with young children in mind, with bedrooms just large enough to serve as playrooms as well, an extra bathroom for them, and the kitchen located so mothers could watch their children play outside.[13] In addition, Levitt provided all the necessary kitchen appliances, eliminating extra initial expenditures. He absorbed settlement costs, which often come to 5 per cent or more of the house price, and he simplified the sales procedure so that buying a house was almost as easy as buying a washing machine. His advertising stressed that there were "no hidden extras, and the price you pay is the price we say." Unlike builders of higher-priced houses, he emphasized the size of the down payment—which thanks to FHA insurance was low—and the monthly payments, so that prospective purchasers could readily figure exactly how much the house would take out of the paycheck.

The firm went to a considerable effort to keep the monthly payment figure as low as possible. As already noted, the builder "donated" the schools to the community. During the first years, he subsidized the schools' operating costs as well, holding taxes, which were added to the monthly payment, at a level that would not frighten away the family earning $6000 to $7000 a year. Thanks to the scale on which the firm was operating, the cost of schools, utilities, and road system could be added to the house price without raising it beyond what other builders in the area were charging.

While all the ads mentioned the schools, churches, and pools, the major emphasis was on the size and value of the house, presented in a confident yet catchy style as if to dare skeptics to come to see whether Levittown's values were real. Many ads were written by William Levitt himself. When the prospective purchaser came out to the model homes area, his attention was focused on the house, and the sales process itself was muted as much as possible. The salesmen were carefully selected and trained to contradict the image of the fast-buck, easy-talking salesmen traditionally associated with real estate. "Courteous representatives are on hand to answer your questions," the ads read. They were dressed in conservative dark clothes—to look like bankers, as one Levitt official put it—and they were instructed by a professional speech teacher to talk in a sedate but friendly manner.

While everyone was welcome to buy in Levittown, the firm did try to screen out two types of people: the marginal buyers and the socially undesirable or emotionally disturbed. Partly because of FHA regulations, the firm had set an income floor for purchasers: people who wanted to buy had to have a weekly income 10 per cent above the monthly carrying charge—more if they had many children or large outstanding debts. Those who could not meet this figure were asked for a larger down payment or were advised against putting down the deposit, and some were excluded by the subsequent credit check. The salesmen were not to sell to disreputable or especially unkept people, and the credit check excluded people with a record of job instability or legal difficulties.[14] The "social filtering" process was, however, less effective than the income check, for some people with serious—but not visible—problems were able to buy into the community.

Until the state enforced a nondiscrimination law, salesmen refused to sell to Negroes and assured whites who asked about Negroes that the community would be as lily-white as the other Levittowns. After the law was enforced, the salemen protected themselves by citing the law, and promised to locate people who did not like to be near Negroes away from them, but also discouraged those who were strongly biased against Negroes from buying in Levittown. . . .

NOTES

1. For an early history of the Levitt organization, see Larrabee, Eric. "The Six Thousand Houses that Levitt Built," *Harper's Magazine*, Vol. 197, September 1948, pp. 79–88.

2. Larrabee. For a more detailed description of Levittown, New York, see Liell, John T. *Levittown: A Study in Community Development and Planning.* Unpublished Ph.D. dissertation, Department of Sociology, Yale University, 1952, Wattel, Har-

old. "Levittown: A Suburban Community," in William M. Dobriner, ed., *The Suburban Community.* New York: Putnam, 1958, pp. 287–313, and Dobriner, William M. *Class in Suburbia.* Englewood Cliffs: Prentice-Hall, 1963, Chap. 4.

3. See Alfred S. Levitt. "A Community Builder Looks at Community Planning," *Journal of the American Institute of Planners*, Vol. 17, Spring 1951, pp. 80–88.

4. In the pages that follow, I will for this reason use Levitt, meaning William Levitt, as a synonym for the firm, although he did not always make personally all the decisions thus ascribed to him.

5. The material in the following section is based on interviews with a number of Levitt executives. Unfortunately, I was never able to obtain interviews with either William or Alfred Levitt.

6. Early in the building of Levittown, Long Island, a group of Levittowners tried to get their post office address changed to Hicksville. Later, in Levittown, Pennsylvania, the people who had bought the high-priced houses also wanted to detach themselves from Levittown, and at one point tried to buy the neighborhood pool for their own use.

7. William J. Levitt, "What! *Live* in a Levittown?" *Good Housekeeping*, Vol. 147, July 1958, pp. 47, 175–176.

8. *Philadelphia Evening Bulletin*, March 1, 1959, and February 26, 1959, respectively.

9. The firm's building methods are described in Levitt and Sons, "Levitt's Progress" and "Most House for the Money," *Fortune*, Vol. 46, October 1952, pp. 151–169, and in *Practical Builder*. "P.B. Reveals Levitt's Building Methods," Vol. 23, August 1959, pp. 80–91.

10. Often, the saving is passed on to the purchaser, for the cost of the house on a square-foot basis has not increased significantly since the first Levittown. The houses themselves have grown in size; the Levittown, Long Island homes had only two bedrooms and an unfinished attic; in Levittown, New Jersey, they initially had three or four bedrooms, and a minimum square footage of over 1200 square feet even in the smallest one. In 1963, the firm began to experiment with five-bedroom houses, and in 1964, to build them.

11. Larrabee, p. 81.

12. On earlier manifestations of this suspicion, see Larrabee, p. 84, and Liell (1952).

13. Conversely, the house was less suited to families with teenage children, for the bedrooms were not large enough to serve their needs, and the compact design of the house and its lack of soundproofing made it difficult for teenagers and adults to have privacy from each other.

14. One Levittowner tested this by coming in shabby clothes and several days' beard to buy a house, only to be refused. The next week, he came back clean and clean-shaven and was sold a house.

29
Suburban Autonomy*

Michael N. Danielson

Suburbia is essentially a political phenomenon. Political independence is the one thing the increasingly diversified settlements beyond the city limits have in common. Local autonomy means that suburban communities seek to control their own destiny largely free from the need to adjust their interests to those of other local jurisdictions and residents of the metropolis. Since local governments in the United States bear the primary responsibility for the provision of basic public services such as education, police and fire protection, as well as the regulation of housing and land use, independence provides suburbs with considerable control over the vital parameters of community life, including the power to exclude unwanted neighbors. In the differentiated and fragmented metropolis, these powers are exercised by suburban governments which are usually responsive to the interests of their relatively homogeneous constituencies. The result, as Robert C. Wood notes, is the division of the metropolitan population into "clusters homogeneous in their skills and outlook which have achieved municipal status and erected social and political barriers against invasion."[1]

With few exceptions, political autonomy affords suburbanites a potential for exclusion which exceeds that usually available to the resident of the central city. Through zoning, building codes, and other planning powers, suburban communities to a far greater degree than city neighborhoods are able to protect the local turf from undesirable housing and residents. Independence also means that the formal consent of local government must be obtained before most state or federal housing programs for the poor can be initiated, a power rarely delegated by city hall to its neighborhoods. In addition, exclusionary policies are more easily pursued in small and relatively cohesive political systems than in large ones with diverse constituency interests. To protect itself from unwanted developments, a city neighborhood must keep an eye on a variety of agencies and possess substantial clout in complex political arenas.

By living in a smaller, more homogeneous, and less complex polity, the resident of an autonomous suburb tends to be insulated from unwanted change. Local actions are far less likely to threaten him with lower-income neighbors or other disturbing developments in a jurisdiction where both fellow citizens and public officials share his frame of reference. As a consequence, political independence reduces the chances that suburban dwellers

*Danielson, Michael N. 1976. "Suburban Autonomy." Pp. 27–49 and 363–367 in *The Politics of Exclusion*. New York: Columbia University Press. Copyright © 1976. Reprinted by permission of Columbia University Press.

will face the sorts of issues concerning race, status, property values, and community character that frequently confront blue-collar and middle-class neighborhoods in the central city. When suburbanites cannot avoid such challenges, they are more likely to enlist the support of a local government that is closely tuned to their interests and values than is commonly the case in the large and heterogeneous central city.

Because of these considerations, the use of local powers over land, housing, and urban development to promote local social values and protect community character are widely viewed as the most important functions of local governments in suburbia. Residents of upper- and middle-class suburbs in the Philadelphia area ranked maintenance of their community's social characteristics—defined in terms of keeping out "undesirables" and maintaining the "quality" of residents—as a more important objective for local government than either the provision of public services or maintenance of low tax rates. In suburbs of lower social rank, maintenance of social characteristics was considered more important than the provision of local services and amenities, and almost as important as keeping down local tax rates.[2]

Exclusionary considerations, of course, are neither the sole nor the most important factor underlying the exodus to the suburbs. Most urban Americans have moved outward in search of better housing, nicer surroundings, social status, and separation from the inner city and its inhabitants. Increasingly, however, political separation has come to be an essential element of the appeal of the suburbs. In the words of a local leader in a blue-collar suburb in the Detroit area, "the most important thing to many people in Warren is just the simple fact that it isn't Detroit."[3] Speaking of the blacks who flocked to East Cleveland during the 1960s, the suburb's black city manager notes that "they feel that at least they are not living in the inner city."[4] Regardless of their reasons for moving outward, most suburbanites quickly discover the utility of local autonomy as a means of protecting their neighborhood, their social standing, their property values, and the racial integrity of the local schools from outside threats. As Daniel J. Elazar notes: "People sought *suburbanization* for essentially private purposes, revolving around better living conditions. The same people sought *suburbs* with independent local governments of their own for essentially public ones, namely the ability to maintain these conditions by joining with like-minded neighbors to preserve those life styles which they sought in suburbanization."[5] In the process, local autonomy and exclusion have become closely intertwined. Political independence greatly strengthens the suburban community's ability to exclude, while the desire to exclude both enhances the attractions of local autonomy and reinforces the suburban commitment to the preservation of local control over the vital parameters of community life. . . .

Incorporation . . . provides suburbanites with a local government more responsive to community desires than is the case with unincorporated areas. Responsiveness results primarily from size and spatial differentiation. Most suburban municipalities are quite small. In 1967, two-thirds of all incorporated local jurisdictions in metropolitan areas had fewer than 5,000 inhabitants. And half of all suburban municipalities encompassed less than a square mile of land area.[6] Superimposing these small governmental units on the spatially differentiated population of the metropolis commonly results in relatively homogeneous local constituencies. Within these jurisdictions, local government tends to be highly responsive to the wishes of residents, particularly on sensitive issues such as housing and community development. By contrast, constituencies are larger and more diverse in most unincorporated areas in suburbia. In these larger local units, governments generally are less concerned about particular neighborhoods than is the typical small-scale incorporated suburban government.

The desire to secure local control over land use, housing, and urban development has been a common motivation for the incorporation of suburban municipalities. Local land owners, builders, and developers have employed incorporation to secure control over planning and zoning in order to advance or protect their economic interests. On the other hand, residents, particularly in newly suburbanizing areas, have frequently sought to incorporate their communities in order to transfer planning responsibilities and land-use controls from the hands of county and township officials to those of local residents, elected to office by their neighbors. Often with good reason, these larger units of suburban local government are considered to be too sympathetic to development interests and insufficiently concerned with the interests of individual communities. As the leader of a homeowner's group seeking to incorporate a suburban neighborhood in the Chicago area explains: "Our main goal in trying to incorporate is to protect our residents from improper zoning. Present restrictions by the county, which . . . controls zoning within our boundaries, is rather loose."[7]

Another common but usually unvoiced concern which has stimulated incorporation efforts is the desire to exclude blacks and subsidized housing. In the San Francisco area, John H. Denton believes "that one of the principal purposes (if not the entire purpose) of suburban incorporations is to give their populations control of the racial composition of their communities."[8] Municipal status substantially enhances the capability of a suburban community to exclude subsidized housing, and the blacks who might live in such units. Incorporation permits local officials to decide whether the community will participate in subsidized housing programs. It also provides local residents with control over zoning and other powers which can prevent the construction of subsidized housing.

An illustration of the creation of a suburban municipality to foreclose the construction of subsidized housing is provided by the incorporation of Black Jack, a community of 2,900 in the St. Louis area.[9] Late in 1969, a nonprofit group organized by church organizations in the St. Louis area took an option on a twelve-acre site in an unincorporated section of St. Louis County known as Black Jack. The land in question was part of 67 acres which had been zoned by the county government for multiple-family dwellings; and over 300 apartments already had been constructed by private developers on fifteen of the acres. The church group planned to construct

210 apartments for rental to families earning between $5,700 and $10,200 under the federal government's Section 236 program for moderate-income housing. The site was chosen by the church groups because they "wanted to determine the feasibility of providing subsidized housing for people—black and white—just beginning to climb above the poverty line but still too poor to move to the suburbs."[10]

For residents of the area, almost all of whom were white, middle-income, and living in single-family homes costing between $25,000 and $45,000, the notion of subsidized and integrated housing for lower-income families in their community was not at all feasible. Their reaction was vehement and their actions swift. With local neighborhood associations leading the opposition, circulars were distributed, mass meetings held, and public officials contacted. In addition, a delegation was dispatched to Washington to present petitions to top officials of the Department of Housing and Urban Development. In opposing the project, residents emphasized the lack of public services, overcrowded local schools, poor transportation links with the rest of the metropolis, and the absence of jobs in Black Jack's portion of St. Louis County. Concern also was expressed over the impact on property values and community character if lower-income families, and particularly poor blacks, were to live in Black Jack.

Dissatisfaction with county housing and land-use policies in the Black Jack area had stirred thoughts of incorporation before the subsidized housing project materialized. With the announcement of the project, local residents moved quickly to seek incorporation in order to deny the development of the site for apartments. Two weeks after the federal government agreed to finance the project, over 1,400 residents of the area petitioned the St. Louis County Council for incorporation of 2.65 square miles encompassing the proposed housing. At the request of the county council, the incorporation proposal was evaluated by the county planning department, which opposed the creation of a new municipality "on fiscal, planning, and legal grounds."[11] Far more influential with the county council, however, was the strong local support for incorporation. Black Jack's advocates successfully linked opposition to incorporation with support for subsidized housing. Suburbanites throughout the northern portion of the county were warned by the Black Jack Improvement Association that approval of the project "could open the door to similar projects being located almost anywhere in the North County area. By stopping this project, you would lessen the chance of one perhaps appearing in your neighborhood."[12] Obviously, the way to stop the project was to permit incorporation. Framing the issue in these terms, as one observer notes, rendered the council members "powerless. The housing issue which precipitated the incorporation was too politically sensitive to allow the council to turn down the petition, and thus indirectly sanction" the construction of subsidized housing.[13]

The result was approval by the county council of the creation of the city of Black Jack, the first new municipality in St. Louis County in over a decade. With incorporation, control over land use within Black Jack was transferred from the county to the new municipality. Less than three months after incorporation, Black Jack's City Council enacted a zoning ordinance which prohibited the construction of apartments within the municipality, thus blocking the proposed subsidized housing.[14]

While the powers available to independent local governments provide suburban communities such as Black Jack with the capability to exclude, local autonomy is relative rather than absolute. Local control over land use, housing, and related matters, like all local powers in the United States, is derived from state governments. Autonomy of suburban governments is limited by municipal charters which are granted by the state and by delegation of responsibilities to other units of local government, such as townships and counties by the state constitution or legislature. The states oversee a wide range of local activities and provide local governments with substantial financial assistance, particularly for public education. They also construct most of the major roads and regulate sewer development, a pair of activities which greatly influence the accessibility of land for development. State actions may constrain suburban autonomy, as in the establishment of public agencies empowered to supersede local land-use controls, such as New Jersey's Hackensack Meadowlands Development Commission or New York's Urban Development Corporation.[15] On the other hand, the state may expand the powers of residents of independent suburbs, as have those states which require that public housing proposals be approved by local voters in a referendum.

Local autonomy in the suburbs also is affected by activities of metropolitan and federal agencies, as well as by intervention from the courts. A wide variety of metropolitan agencies exercise responsibility for area-wide planning, major public works, and other activities which affect housing and development patterns within local jurisdictions in the metropolis. The federal government supports housing, highway, water, sewer, planning, and other programs which influence the ability of suburban governments to shape the nature and timing of development within their boundaries. The federal government also has substantial powers to prevent local governments from discriminating against minorities in the development, sale, and rental of housing. In addition, all local authority is subject to review in state courts, and the exercise of many local powers raise issues which fall within the jurisdiction of federal courts.

In the policy areas of greatest importance for exclusion, however, local autonomy tends to be particularly broad. As Richard F. Babcock notes: "Local control over use of private land has withstood with incredible resilience the centripetal political forces of the last generation."[16] State governments typically have delegated virtually all responsibility for planning, zoning, building codes, and related activities to local governments. Few states even maintain an administrative machinery to oversee local land-use and housing controls. Only in response to environmental problems and pressures have states begun to develop plans and regulatory mechanisms which seek to guide or supercede the land-use activities of local governments. Almost all of these state efforts, however, are limited to areas of critical ecological concern, such as coastal zones and floodplains.[17]

Most states also have done little to enlarge the scale of land-use control in suburbia. County governments usually are limited to regulating unincorporated areas, with few states providing counties with a significant land-use role within suburban municipalities. When states provide for county agencies or regional bodies to review local zoning actions, the review power typically, as Coke and Gargan note, "is advisory only; the reviewing agency has no authority unilaterally to overrun the zoning action."[18] Nor have states necessarily permitted metropolitan governments, in the few areas where they have been created, to exercise land-use controls throughout their jurisdiction. In Miami, as the National Commission on Urban Problems pointed out, "the metropolitan government has zoning authority only in unincorporated territory. In Nashville-Davidson County, several small suburban municipalities continued in existence after the creation of the metropolitan government and retained their zoning powers."[19] The state law creating Unigov in the Indianapolis area also permitted suburban municipalities to continue to control land use.

Local autonomy over housing and land use is bolstered further by the absence of a direct federal role in zoning and other development controls. Moreover, local rather than federal officials determine the location of housing units supported by national subsidy programs.[20] A final factor enhancing the ability of suburban governments to use their autonomy to foster exclusion has been the reluctance of most courts to impose significant constraints on the exercise of local land-use powers.[21]

As a result of these developments, suburban governments have been able to use their autonomy to influence housing opportunities with relatively little outside interference. And because land-use patterns strongly affect local taxes and public services, community character, and the quality of local schools, zoning has become the essence of local autonomy for most suburbanites. . . .

MAXIMIZING INTERNAL BENEFITS

Local autonomy combines with limited size, a fairly homogeneous population, and the mobilization of residential interests to provide most suburbanites with a highly parochial perspective on the metropolis. The community tends to be perceived solely in terms of the interests of its current residents, who claim "a right to decide how their town develops."[22] Residents of the suburbs and their local governments rarely take the interests of nonresidents into account. Nor do they consider housing, land use, and other issues in an areawide perspective. Within this narrow frame of reference, the overriding purpose of government in suburbia becomes the protection and promotion of local interests. In defense of "the fact that the poor and middle income people cannot afford to move into Mount Laurel" because of local land use controls, a suburban attorney contends that "the Mount Laurel fathers are trying to do their best for the people of Mount Laurel."[23] Doing their best for constituents usually means that local officials ignore broader issues. For example, when deciding whether to permit the construction of apartment units, suburbanites rarely consider metropolitan housing needs or the growing demand of a diversifying suburban population for multiple-family dwellings. Instead, local debate centers on the costs and benefits of apartments to the community and its residents, and construction commonly is permitted only when the local jurisdiction is convinced that the development will make a net contribution to local revenues. "We must be selective as possible—approving only those applications which are sound in all respects" argues a local committeeman in Mount Laurel. "We can approve only those development plans which will provide direct and substantial benefits to our taxpayers."[24]

Suburban indifference to broader needs, including those created by their own land-use policies, is illustrated by the frequent refusal of jurisdictions which have been successful in attracting industry and commerce to permit the construction of housing within the means of local workers. The presence of the Grumman Corporation with 30,000 workers and the arrival of forty-five new industries during the late 1960s produced no changes in zoning and housing policies in Oyster Bay. This Long Island suburb prohibited apartments except by special exception, required one- and two-acre lots for single-family homes, and had less than 350 units of subsidized housing, most of which had been reserved for the elderly. In New Jersey, Mahwah steadfastly refused to alter its zoning codes to permit the United Automobile Workers Housing Corporation to build subsidized housing within the price range of workers at a Ford Motor Company plant which employed 5,200 in Mahwah. The presence of the automobile factory and other industries gives Mahwah a substantially lower tax rate than neighboring suburbs. Yet the town has been no more willing to open its doors to Ford workers—40 percent of whom are black—than are adjacent suburbs with less industry and higher tax rates. In Mahwah, as in nearby Franklin Lakes, which welcomed a large IBM installation but not garden apartments, the local beneficiaries of nonresidential development see no obligation to provide housing for workers: "There is lots of empty land and cheap housing further out—there's no reason why people should feel that they have to live in Franklin Lakes just because they work here."[25] A member of the planning commission in Oak Brook, an affluent suburb of 4,000 in the Chicago area which attracted $350 million in offices, hotels, research facilities, and shopping centers without providing any low-cost housing, insists that "we are sympathetic to the achievers and the underprivileged," but adds: "We have provided for the achievers, however."[26]

Cooperation among neighboring suburbs to secure adequate housing for the local work force also is rare. In 1970, the zoning ordinances of twenty suburbs in central New Jersey set aside sufficient land for industrial and research purposes to support 1.17 million jobs, but would allow residential development to house only 144,000 families, for an imbalance between new jobs and residences of eight to one.[27] Less than one in five mayors surveyed in a New Jersey study indicated that their communities were willing to cooperate with neighboring jurisdictions on zoning. Even fewer suburbs actually consulted adjacent municipalities in setting land-use policies, leading the study to conclude that "cooperation is almost non-existent" in planning and zoning matters in New Jersey.[28]

Exclusion is a natural concomitant to suburban insularity. Since the community's resources are perceived as belonging to its residents, outsiders cannot share in these resources without local consent. Suburbs commonly employ the local police power to exclude nonresidents from parks, beaches, and other public recreational facilities. In suburban Westchester and Nassau Counties in New York, local governments ban nonresidents from parking lots adjacent to commuter railroad stations, or set parking fees for nonresidents many times higher than those for residents. These policies are justified on the grounds that community facilities belong to local taxpayers, that restrictions are essential to insure enjoyment of public facilities by local residents, and that the locality must be able to protect itself from the crowds, traffic, and other burdens that large numbers of nonresident swimmers, picnickers, or parkers would impose on the limited capabilities of the typical suburb. As a suburban official on Long Island explains, "our town has grown so large there is barely enough beach room for our own people."[29] The same rationale is commonly applied to other facilities by suburbanites. River Hills, an affluent suburb in the Milwaukee area, sought to block the construction of a church, arguing that no need existed because only three members of the congregation were residents of the community. "We are not trying to keep outsiders out," explained the suburb's planning commissioner, "but it is not feasible to have people come in here with things which [serve] no residents from the village."[30] In northern New Jersey, Saddle River sought to block construction of a college because the community was "not the type of town for any large school." According to the suburb's mayor: "This is a residential community, there are no public transportation facilities, and we have no sewage disposal system. We haven't even got a full-time police department and 90 per cent of our roads are private."[31]

Local considerations are of paramount importance in the case of housing and land-use policies which determine who "our own people" are in a particular suburb. Exclusion of those who threaten to change a community's character, lower the status of its residents, jeopardize local property values, or burden public services is widely perceived by suburbanites as an inherent aspect of local autonomy. As Anthony Downs notes, "defenders of residential exclusion argue that any group of citizens ought to be able to establish a physical enclave where certain standards of environmental quality and behavior are required for all residents. The resulting exclusion of those too poor to meet the standards is considered essential to protect the rights of those who established the standards."[32] The more homogeneous a suburb, the more easily it can seek to maximize internal benefits through exclusionary housing policies. And the more successful these policies, the less likely becomes the presence of dissenting voices within the local constituency.

Efforts to maximize internal benefits often go beyond using local autonomy to exclude outsiders. Suburban jurisdictions also have sought, with considerable success, to get rid of residents deemed undesirable by the local community. Zoning changes, code enforcement, urban renewal, road building, and other governmental actions have eliminated substandard and lower-income housing in many communities. Rarely is adequate housing provided for the displaced. The urban renewal plans of thirteen suburbs in Westchester County in the New York region called for the demolition of over 4200 housing units in 1967, most of which were occupied by lower-income and minority families, and their replacement by less than 700 subsidized units.[33] Displacement without replacement, as in one New Jersey suburb, often reflects the widespread local desire "to clear out substandard housing . . . and thereby get better citizens."[34] Facilitating these efforts in most suburban jurisdictions is the meager political influence of lower-income residents, who usually are outnumbered and almost always lack political resources in contrast with their more affluent neighbors.[35]

Black suburbanites are the most common targets of suburban efforts to displace "undesirables." A study conducted for the U.S. Commission on Civil Rights concluded that "development control activities in Baltimore County over the past ten years have functioned to substantially reduce housing opportunities in the county for low-income, predominantly (but not exclusively) black households."[36] One black residential area was eliminated by rezoning for commercial purposes, another was destroyed by zoning the area for industrial uses. In the St. Louis area, federal urban-renewal funds were used by suburban Olivette to redevelop a black neighborhood for industrial purposes. In the process, all but six of the thirty black families in the community of 10,000 were forced to move away.[37]

Reinforcing suburbia's exclusionary tendencies is the dependence of most local governments on tax sources located within their boundaries. Defending his community's ban on nonresident commuter parking, a suburban mayor in the New York area contends that "there is no way I can morally justify spending the tax revenue of my little village on nonresidents."[38] Speaking of restrictions on the use of Nassau County's recreational facilities, County Executive Ralph G. Caso emphasizes that "it is our residents who pay for them and maintain them through taxes."[39]

Local property taxes, and their relationship to public-school costs and land-use patterns, have an especially important influence on suburban policies affecting housing and urban development. Over 80 percent of all local revenues in the suburbs are derived from property taxes, while 60 percent or more of all public expenditures are for education. Yields from the property tax depend primarily on the extent and value of development within a jurisdiction. School costs are directly related to the density of residential settlement. The logic of these relationships leads suburbs to judge development increasingly in fiscal terms. Speaking of Westchester County, New York's Regional Plan Association notes that in "municipality after municipality, planning to achieve a satisfying local environment has been replaced by planning to meet the school tax bills."[40]

From the perspective of the individual suburb, desirable development generates a profit for the local government and its residents, hopefully at not too high a cost to other things valued by the community, while undesirable development creates a net deficit of tax revenues to local costs. As a result of tax considerations, suburbs both compete for desirable development and are attracted to exclusionary policies designed to foreclose undesirable development. In the words of the U.S. Advisory Commission on Intergovernmental Relations, "the name of the game is cutthroat intergovernmental competition, and the object of the game is to 'zone in' urban resources and to 'zone out' urban problems."[41]

The desire to "zone in" tax resources and "zone out" problems for fiscal reasons influences land-use and housing policies to some degree in most suburban jurisdictions. Few suburbs, and particularly bedroom communities whose tax base is wholly or largely residential, can afford to ignore the fact that most residential development costs local government more than it contributes in taxes. . . . A typical four-bedroom house in a Chicago suburb generated approximately $1,200 in school taxes in 1968, but the costs of educating the two school-age children likely to live in the house exceeded $1,600. With more school-age children in the family, or in the case of a cheaper house which would generate less tax revenues, the local deficit would be even greater. In general, the gap between local costs and revenues is greater for subsidized housing occupied by families with children. Such housing typically involves higher residential densities than is the case with conventional single-family housing, as well as lower per capita property tax receipts and greater demands on local public services. Local taxes on subsidized housing financed by the New Jersey Housing Finance Agency, for example, cover 20 percent or less of the public service costs imposed on local governments and school districts by the residents of the projects.

In New Jersey, where local property taxes provide a particularly large share of all local revenues, a state planner believes that most local land-use controls are "designed for the . . . purpose of trying to avoid the costs implied in residential growth and its effect on public school growth."[42] Even in New Jersey, however, relatively few suburbs base their housing and land-use policies solely on tax calculations. Instead, concern over the implications of housing development for local taxes tends to reinforce, and to be reinforced by, exclusionary behavior rooted in community, property-value, class, and racial considerations. Equally important, the workings of the property tax provide suburbanites with a respectable rationale to justify the exclusion of lower-income groups, subsidized housing, and blacks, regardless of the actual mix of motives which underlie a particular local policy.

The same fiscal considerations which lead suburban governments to exclude lower-income families and higher-density residential development induce them to seek commercial and industrial tax ratables as a means of easing the burdens of financing local services. Some affluent suburbs prefer to remain exclusively residential, although their ranks have been thinned in recent years with rapid rises in the costs of local services. Others can afford to be selective, accepting only research or office activities in campus-like settings. Many suburban jurisdictions, however, are sufficiently hardpressed financially that they are willing to take any nonresidential tax ratable they can get, even at considerable cost to local amenities and community character.

Suburbs frequently attempt to reduce the impact of these developments on local residents by restricting large-scale commercial and industrial facilities to areas that are separated from residential neighborhoods within the community by highways or natural features. In the process, costs often are displaced to adjacent communities, which receive no tax benefits from the development. A study by the League of Women Voters in Bergen County, New Jersey, indicated that one "community proposed to zone for heavy industry in an area adjacent to one of the most expensive residential areas of a neighboring town." In another instance, access roads "to a new plant were placed so that the traffic moved along roads in an adjacent community."[43] The principle of beggar-thy-neighbor embodied in the common suburban conception of local autonomy and maximization of internal benefits was succinctly expressed by the former mayor of Wayne in northern New Jersey in explaining the impact of Willowbrook shopping center on residents of his community. "Willowbrook doesn't bother anyone here because it's way on the south border, next to Little Falls Township. It bothers them; they get all the traffic and harassment. We get all the taxes."[44]

Residents of both rich and poor suburbs frequently rue the necessity for local efforts to bolster the tax base with nonresidential development. "Our town is slipping away from us," complains a resident of affluent Greenwich, where 150 companies located during the 1960s.[45] The spread of such feelings, along with the rising influence of residential interests in suburban politics, has increased resistance to the location of commercial and industrial facilities in suburbs across the nation. For example, Greenwich's Planning and Zoning Commission responded to widespread local opposition late in 1973 by rejecting the application of Xerox for a zoning change needed to construct a $20 million corporate headquarters on a 104-acre site in an area reserved for single-family homes. Reinforcing these concerns over community character and status is the fear that offices and factories will lead to requirements that housing be provided locally for employees and other lower-income families. As an official in New Canaan, another Connecticut suburb, explains, "we would welcome RCA's contribution to the tax base, but not if we have to take the caboose of low income housing as well."[46]

Businessmen too seek to maximize internal advantages in the suburbs. From the perspective of many, the most attractive suburban location is within a jurisdiction with as few residents as possible. As a result, people have been zoned out of a number of municipalities in order to create a favorable tax situation for commerce and industry. With fewer than a dozen residents, Teterboro in northern New Jersey offers its fifty industries an extremely low tax rate, with almost all local revenues devoted to public services needed by industry. Similar considerations led to the incorporation of Emeryville, Vernon, Union City, Industry and Commerce, all in southern California. In 1960, Vernon had fewer than 300 residents, but over 70,000 worked in industries located there, insuring highly attractive tax rates.[47] Low rates give these enclaves substantial competitive advantages over other suburbs and the central city in the quest for desirable tax ratables. Moreover, by separating the taxable wealth of commercial and industrial development from the needs of employees and the metropolitan community more generally, these single-purpose suburbs intensify disparities among local governments in the politically fragmented metropolis, and thus enhance competition and exclusion.

Environmental considerations also reinforce the suburban desire to maximize internal benefits through exclusionary local policies. Rapid and usually unplanned growth has exacted a heavy environmental price in many suburban areas. In the scramble for private profit and desirable tax ratables, environmental costs commonly have been ignored by developers and local officials. As a result, suburban growth has left in its wake bulldozed hills, treeless and tasteless subdivisions and apartment complexes, garish highway strip development, acres and acres of parking lots, overtaxed sewerage and water systems, polluted and silted streams, and a general lack of the open space that was the original attraction of suburbia to so many of its inhabitants. Political fragmentation has exacerbated these problems. In most metropolitan areas, the mosaic of small and independent suburban jurisdictions has foreclosed comprehensive planning, areawide controls on development, and regional instrumentalities empowered to regulate and conserve land, water, and other natural resources. The ability of developmental interests to dominate many of the local governments in newer areas has negated the role of local land-use controls in guiding growth and protecting the environment along the metropolitan rim. Further contributing to haphazard and short-sighted development is competition for attractive tax ratables among suburban governments heavily dependent on local property taxes.

With the movement of ecological concerns to the forefront of the American political consciousness in the late 1960s, most suburbanites responded in typically parochial fashion. Relatively few recognized the role of the decentralized suburban political system in fostering the erosion of environmental amenities in their communities and surrounding areas. Instead, residents of the suburbs commonly emphasized the need to employ local autonomy to preserve and protect their local turf. To maintain the quality of life for residents of the particular suburban community, the power of local governments over land use and housing have been widely employed to prevent outsiders from sharing the local environment with those who already live there. As in the case of the local property tax, ecological concerns tend to be mixed with other exclusionary motivations as the typical suburb seeks to maximize internal benefits. For example, the desire to exclude "unprofit-able" residential development bolsters the case for "no growth" policies and other environmental controls on housing. And, as Ernest Erber of the National Committee Against Discrimination in Housing emphasizes: "'No Growth's' pervasive spread provides an insidious rationale . . . to perpetu-ate racial and economic segregation. It serves to remove the stigma of local, selfish motivations from exclusionary acts and cloaks them with broad national purposes."[48]

THE CHANGING SUBURBS

Growing suburban concern with environmental issues is one manifestation of the physical, economic, social, and political changes which constantly increase the scale and complexity of life in the suburbs, and in the process alter the nature and autonomy of local governments in suburbia. With growth and diversification of the suburban population and economy have come expanding pressures on local governments to provide services, deal with a widening range of problems, and resolve conflicts which multiply in suburban jurisdictions with increasingly diverse constituencies. In response, the tasks, budgets, and staffs of local governments have steadily expanded. Independent functional agencies have proliferated to provide water, sewer-age, and a host of other local services. And perhaps most significant, "big" government, with its professional politicians and specialized bureaucracies, has become increasingly common in the land of small scale, amateur, neigh-borhood government. A growing proportion of the suburban population lives in larger local jurisdictions such as Oyster Bay in the New York area which had 330,000 residents in 1970, Warren in the Detroit area with 179,000, Woodbridge in New Jersey with 99,000, and Bloomington in the Twin Cities area with 82,000. County governments also have expanded significantly in many metropolitan areas, both to serve burgeoning unincor-porated areas and to provide a variety of services for the residents of subur-ban municipalities located within county boundaries. As a result of these changes, a declining proportion of suburbanites live in the prototypical small and homogeneous local jurisdiction.

Despite this general increase in the scale of local government in the suburbs, political fragmentation and spatial differentiation mean that few suburban jurisdictions reflect the increasing heterogeneity of suburbia. Even the larger suburban units tend to encompass considerably less diverse socio-economic development than the central cities of most metropolitan areas. And the smaller local units, which continue to be the most common type of suburban government, typically retain both their relatively homogeneous constituency and their extremely narrow perspective on issues such as hous-ing and land use.

With respect to local governmental efforts to influence settlement pat-terns, growth and heterogeneity have produced changes in the tone and style of suburban politics rather than its basic exclusionary aims. Increasing scale and diversity have made many suburban units less responsive to particular neighborhood interests. Consensus on particular development policies is also more difficult to reach in larger suburban jurisdictions which encompass a variety of interests on such issues as construction of apartment houses, large-scale industrial or commercial development, or local participation in subsidized housing programs.

At the same time, apartment houses, shopping centers, industrial and research parks, office clusters, sports complexes, and other harbingers of change in the suburbs reinforce the desire of suburbanites to maintain local autonomy and to use the powers of local government to control the local turf. Growth and change in the suburbs also bolster the fears of the inner city, of lower-income and minority groups, of crime and drugs, of housing projects and integrated schools. As a result, in suburbs of every size and type, the common response to diversification and heterogeneity are efforts to protect and preserve the local community, its residents, and their environment from external threats. Increasingly, suburban officials are confronted by aroused constituents who want their local government to find a means of shielding them from change. In DeKalb County outside Atlanta, as in suburbs across the nation, activists "raise hell twenty-four hours a day." In the words of a suburban state legislator: "It's enough to drive a normal person insane."[49]

NOTES

1. *Suburbia: Its People and Their Politics* (Boston: Houghton Mifflin, 1958), p. 128.
2. See Oliver P. Williams et al., *Suburban Differences and Metropolitan Policies: A Philadelphia Story* (Philadelphia: Univ. Of Pa. Press, 1965), pp. 217–19.
3. See Walter S. Mossberg, "A Blue Collar Town Fears Urban Renewal Perils Its Way of Life," *Wall Street Journal*, Nov. 2, 1970.
4. Gladstone L. Chandler, Jr., city manager, East Cleveland, O., quoted in Paul Delaney, "The Outer City: Negroes Find Few Tangible Gains," *New York Times*, June 1, 1971; reprinted as "Negroes Find Few Tangible Gains," in Louis H. Masotti and Jeffrey K. Hadden, eds., *Suburbia in Transition* (New York: Franklin Watts, 1974), p. 278. East Cleveland had no black residents in the mid-1950s; by 1970, 60 percent of its population was black.
5. "Suburbanization: Reviving the Town on the Metropolitan Frontier," *Publius* 5 (Winter, 1975), p. 59.
6. See Allen D. Manvel, "Metropolitan Growth and Governmental Fragmentation," in A. F. Kier Nash, ed., *Governance and Population: The Governmental Implications of Population Change*, Vol. 4, Research Reports, U.S. Commission on Population Growth and the American Future (Washington: U.S. Government Printing Office, 1972), p. 181.
7. Robert Poltzer, Prospect Heights Improvement Association, quoted in Dan Egler, "Prospect Heights Seeks to Incorporate," *Chicago Tribune*, Oct. 1, 1972.
8. "Phase I Report" to the National Committee Against Discrimination in Housing,

U.S. Department of Housing and Urban Development Project, No. Cal. D-8 (n.d.), pt 3, p. Jc-11.

9. For a summary of the events leading to the incorporation of Black Jack, see Ronald F. Kirby, Frank de Leeuw, and William Silverman, *Residential Zoning and Equal Housing Opportunities: A Case Study in Black Jack, Missouri* (Washington: Urban Inst., 1972), pp. 17–27.

10. See B. Drummond Ayres, "Bulldozers Turn Up Soil and Ill Will in a Suburb of St. Louis," *New York Times*, Jan. 18, 1971.

11. See *Park View Heights Corporation v. City of Black Jack*, 467 F.2d 1208 (1972) at 1211.

12. See William K. Reilly, ed., *The Use of Land: A Citizens' Policy Guide to Urban Growth*, A Task Force Report Sponsored by The Rockefeller Brothers Fund (New York: Thomas Y. Crowell Company, 1973), p. 90.

13. Jerome Pratter, "Dispersed Subsidized Housing and Suburbia: Confrontation in Black Jack," *Land-Use Controls Annual* (Chicago: American Society of Planning Officials, 1972), p. 152.

14. Black Jack's actions were challenged in court by the sponsors of the project, other organizations, and the federal government; see *United States* v. *City of Black Jack, Missouri*, 372 F.Supp. 319 (1974); *United States* v. *City of Black Jack, Missouri*, 508 F.2d 1179 (1974); *Park View Heights Corporation* v. *City of Black Jack*, 467 F.2d 1208; and the discussion of the Black Jack litigation in chapter 7.

15. Suburban opposition to this grant of power to the Urban Development Corporation led the New York legislature to rescind it in 1973; see chapter 10 for a discussion of the New York Urban Development Corporation's turbulent efforts to open the suburbs.

16. *The Zoning Game: Municipal Practices and Policies* (Madison: Univ. of Wis. Press, 1966), p. 19.

17. State land-use activities and their impact on suburban exclusion are discussed in detail in chapter 10.

18. James G. Coke and John J. Gargan, *Fragmentation in Land-Use Planning and Control*, Prepared for the consideration of the National Commission on Urban Problems, Research Report No. 18 (Washington: U.S. Government Printing Office, 1969), p. 6.

19. *Building the American City*, Report of the National Commission on Urban Problems to the Congress and President of the United States, 91st Cong., 1st sess., House Doc. No. 91–34 (Washington: U.S Government Printing Office, 1968), p. 209.

20. The federal role in suburban exclusion is examined in chapter 8.

21. Judicial attitudes concerning exclusionary zoning and housing policies began to shift in the late 1960s; see chapter 7 for an analysis of the role of the courts in opening the suburbs.

22. James Walsh, chairman, Committee to Aid Lake Mohegan, Yorktown, N.Y., quoted in Paula R. Bernstein, "Suburbia Learning to Fight Town Hall," *New York Times*, July 15, 1973.

23. John W. Trimble, quoted in Walter H. Waggoner, "State High Court Weighs Attacks by Poor on Zoning," *New York Times*, Mar. 6, 1973. Mount Laurel is in Burlington County, N.J., and lies within the Philadelphia metropolitan area. The

comment was made during oral arguments before the New Jersey Supreme Court in litigation which is discussed in chapter 7.

24. See *Southern Burlington County NAACP v. Township of Mt. Laurel*, 119 N.J.Super. 164, 290 A.2d 465 (1972) at 468.

25. See National Committee Against Discrimination in Housing. *Jobs and Housing: A Study of Employment and Housing Opportunities for Racial Minorities of the New York Metropolitan Region*, Interim Report, Mar., 1970 (New York, 1970), p. 116.

26. See Robert Cassidy, "Planning for Polo, not People," *Planning* 40 (Apr.–May, 1974), pp. 34–37.

27. See Middlesex-Mercer-Somerset Regional Study Council, *Housing and the Quality of Our Environment*, Research Report (Princeton, N.J., 1970), p. 1.

28. State of New Jersey, County and Municipal Government Study Commission, *Joint Services—A Local Response to Area-wide Problems*, Third Report, Sept., 1970 (Trenton: 1970), p. 26.

29. See John Darnton, "Suburbs Stiffening Beach Curbs," *New York Times*, July 10, 1972.

30. See "Next Thing You Know They'll Build a Church," *Planning* 37 (Aug., 1971), p. 126. The suburban effort to block construction of the church did not survive a challenge in the courts.

31. Mayor G. Tapley Taylor, Saddle River, N.J., quoted in Richard Johnston, "Act to Ban College," *Newark Evening News*, Mar. 23, 1961.

32. *Opening Up the Suburbs: An Urban Strategy for America* (New Haven: Yale Univ. Press, 1973), p. 65.

33. See Urban League of Westchester County, Housing Council, *Urban Renewal in Westchester County: Its Effect on the General Housing Supply and on the Housing Occupied by Negroes* (White Plains, N.Y., 1967), p. 3.

34. See *Southern Burlington County NAACP v. Township of Mt. Laurel*, 119 N.J.Super. 164, 290 A.2d 465 (1972) at 468.

35. The political weaknesses of lower-income and minority suburbanites are discussed in chapter 5.

36. Yale Rabin, "The Effects of Development Control on Housing Opportunities for Black Households in Baltimore County, Maryland," A Report to the U.S. Commission on Civil Rights, Aug. 1970, p. 2; reprinted in U.S. Commission on Civil Rights, *Hearing Held in Baltimore, Maryland, August 17–19, 1970* (Washington: U.S. Government Printing Office, 1970), p. 701.

37. See Simpson F. Lawson, *Above Property Rights*, U.S. Commission on Civil Rights, Clearinghouse publication #38, Dec., 1972 (Washington: U.S. Government Printing Office, 1972), pp. 21–22.; and U.S. Commission on Civil Rights, *Hearing Held in St. Louis, Missouri, January 14–17, 1970* (Washington: U.S. Government Printing Office, 1970), pp. 384–410.

38. Mayor Kevin O'Neill, Irvington, N.Y., quoted in Linda Greenhouse, "Nonresident Autoists Seek Equal Parking Privileges," *New York Times*, Feb. 5, 1973.

39. Quoted in Darnton, "Suburbs Stiffening Beach Curbs."

40. *The Future of Westchester County*, A Supplement to the Second Regional Plan, Bulletin 117, Mar., 1971 (New York, 1971), p. 45.

41. *Urban America and the Federal System*, Commission Findings and Proposals, Oct., 1969 (Washington: U.S. Government Printing Office, 1969), p. 12.

42. Sidney Willis, director, Division of State and Regional Planning, N.J. Department of Community Affairs, quoted in Sharon Rosenhause and Edward J. Flynn, "The What, Why, How of Zoning," *Bergen Record*, Aug. 3, 1970.

43. League of Women Voters of Bergen County, *Where Can I Live in Bergen County? Factors Affecting Housing Supply* (Closter, N.J., 1972), p. 10.

44. Harry J. Butler, Wayne, N.J., quoted in Jack Rosenthal, "Suburbs Abandoning Dependence on City," *New York Times*, Aug. 16, 1971; reprinted as "Toward Suburban Independence," in Masotti and Hadden, *Suburbia in Transition*, p. 295.

45. See "The Battle of Greenwich," *Newsweek* 79 (June 5, 1972), p. 82.

46. See Marc Charney, "RCA's Move to New Canaan Raises Issue of Biased Zoning," *Hartford Times*, July 7, 1971.

47. See Samuel E. Wood and Alfred E. Heller, *The Phantom Cities of California* (Sacramento: California Tomorrow, 1963), pp. 47–48.

48. "Housing and Environment," Paper presented at the National Committee Against Discrimination in Housing Conference, Washington, D.C., Jan. 1973, p. 5.

49. Representative Howard Atherton, Marietta, Ga., quoted in John Herbers, "The Outer City: Uneasiness Over Future," *New York Times*, June 2, 1971; reprinted as "A Deep Uneasiness About the Future," in Masotti and Hadden, *Suburbia in Transition*, p. 283.

30

The Roots of Segregation in the Eighties: The Role of Local Government Actions*

Yale Rabin

One of the most persistent and pervasive characteristics of U.S. metropolitan areas is residential segregation by race. While gross national data on suburbanization of blacks during the 1970s may, at first glance, appear to suggest some improvement, this optimistic view is readily dispelled by closer scrutiny. Although the black population outside the central cities of metropolitan areas increased by 2.8 million between 1970 and 1980, a 43% gain, black suburban residents are disproportionately concentrated outside the central cities of a small number of large SMSAs. Over half of all suburban blacks are in the outer rings of seven SMSAs, and their developing spatial distribution there exhibits familiar patterns of racial segregation (Rabin, 1983). And while large-scale suburbanization of blacks has occurred in these few places, the continuing increase of blacks as a proportion of central city population has been widespread (Long & DeAre, 1981). Contributing to this concentration has been a concurrent out-migration of blacks from suburbs to central cities that continued at significant levels during the 1970s (Nelson, 1979).

Kain's observation in 1974 that this process of racial segregation "has created major distortions in the patterns of metropolitan growth, and bears a major responsibility for a surprisingly long list of ills" (p. 16) is as accurate in the mid-1980s as it was then; and among these ills, segregated schools and isolation from decentralized employment opportunities remain as chronic disorders. Governments at all levels have failed to provide adequate or appropriate remedies.

This failure is attributable, in part, to unreasonably constricted views of the causes of segregation. These views ignore the critical effects of public intervention in land development in general and in housing markets in particular. A substantial body of research, focused almost exclusively on housing market behavior, supports the notion that certain demographic characteristics and racial attitudes primarily influence the behavior of buyers and sellers as they participate in the operation of housing markets. Data for these many studies have generally been derived from the census and from public opinion surveys (Streitweiser & Goodman, 1983).

*Rabin, Yale. 1987. "The Roots of Segregation in the Eighties: The Role of Local Government Actions." Pp. 208–226 in *Divided Neighborhoods*, ed. Gary Tobin. Newbury Park, CA: Sage Publications. Copyright © 1987. Reprinted by permission of Sage Publications, Inc.

But other studies show compelling evidence that disparities in income are not sufficient to explain the extent to which blacks are segregated from whites (Tauber & Tauber, 1965). This conclusion has been reinforced by more recent findings that increases in income for blacks yield increases in integration, while increases in income for whites result in increase in segregation (Jones, 1982).

In reviewing a series of attitude surveys, Pettigrew (1973) found a steady decline in expressions of resistance by whites to integrated living, but concluded, based on his own study, that "there remains an enormous degree of fear, reluctance and downright opposition" (pp. 32–33). More recently, Farley et al. (1983), in a more probing analysis, concluded that earlier studies have tended to understate the extent and degree of white opposition to integration. Another review in a position paper on the relationship between school segregation and housing segregation, which was signed by 37 social scientists, noted emphatically that "every major study of the housing of Blacks and Whites has identified racial discrimination as a major explanation of the observed segregation" (Orfield et al., 1980). Evidence that "white flight" is motivated more by hostility to blacks than opposition to busing (Cusick, Gerbing, & Rossel, 1979) serves to further corroborate these findings.

A concise, but cogent overview of this discrimination-segregation relationship is provided by Yinger (1979, p. 459) who found that the evidence

> overwhelmingly supports the proposition that racial discrimination is a powerful force in urban housing markets. Only a theory that involves discrimination can explain why blacks are concentrated in a central ghetto, why blacks pay more for comparable housing than whites in the same submarkets, why prices of equivalent housing are higher in the ghetto than in the white interior, and why blacks consume less housing and are much less likely to be home owners than whites with the same characteristics. This evidence of discrimination, based on recent data, makes a convincing case for government intervention in the housing market.

Given the persistent transformation of old patterns of segregation into new ones, the repeated finding that these conditions are attributable to racial discrimination by whites is hardly surprising. Nor is it surprising, since the vast majority of these studies have focused on the influence of discrimination on market behavior, that the inference is readily and widely drawn that racial discrimination in the private housing market is the only significant cause of housing segregation. However, since whites make up the overwhelming majority of those who govern, legislate, judge, administer, and enforce in this society, it does seem remarkable that little attention has been devoted to the ways in which this widespread racial prejudice may have influenced the nature and implementation of housing-related public policies and programs, and the behavior of public officials in those government agencies whose activities affect housing patterns.

To be sure, several studies have acknowledged the segregative effects of

some, mainly discontinued, government practices, including the enforcement of racially restrictive covenants, racially discriminatory FHA policies,
the segregative site selection and tenant assignment practices of local public
housing authorities, the implementation of urban renewal programs, and the
ongoing practice of exclusionary zoning (for example, Feagin & Feagin,
1978; Foley, 1973; Orfield et al., 1980). Generally, however, these government actions are seen as peripheral to the central issue of housing market
discrimination; and no study was found that dealt, even in relative terms,
with the extent of the impact of these government practices on existing
segregation or attached any importance to their influence on emerging patterns of segregation.

My findings, derived from empirical case studies conducted over the
past twenty years in over fifty cities, towns, and counties,[1] reveal that while
widespread hostility to blacks may be a major influence on the kinds of
locational decisions made in private housing transactions, the actual spatial
distributions that result are strongly influenced by public actions. *Indeed, the
land use-related policies and practices of government, at all levels, have been,
and in many cases continue to be, important influences on both the creation
and the perpetuation of racially segregated housing patterns.*

These relationships are most clearly evident in metropolitan areas
where, since World War II, massive federal investments in highways have
created new patterns of access and spawned millions of acres of new suburban development, providing new housing and job opportunities for millions
of young, white, middle-income families. These new communities excluded
blacks first by state-enforced racially restrictive convenants and the official
segregation policies of the Federal Housing Administration, and then by
locally enacted exclusionary zoning. These mutually reinforcing actions,
either concurrently or successively, have provided both impetus and guidance to the dynamic process from which the landscape of metropolitan racial
polarization continues to develop.

The pervasive influence of racist attitudes on the implementation of
public programs is vividly illustrated by the failure of government agencies at
all levels to implement the Congressionally enacted response to these metropolitan developments. The racially and economically polarizing consequences of the highway-stimulated process of metropolitan decentralization
were recognized relatively early. Beginning in 1962, Congress responded
with a remarkably consistent series of acts clearly expressing its concern
about the decline of central cities and public transportation, and the plight of
inner-city minority residents. Determination was also expressed to prevent
or minimize the further adverse social, economic, and environmental impacts of highways and other federally funded programs.[2] These laws required
the establishment of regional planning agencies, the formulation of regional
plans, and the evaluation of local applications for federal funds for their
compliance with regional plans and federal goals. They prohibited racial
discrimination in the benefits of federally supported programs, and required
the identification and public disclosure of the probable adverse impacts of

such programs at public hearings and in environmental impact statements. However, these requirements, at least to the extent that they might have protected the welfare and expanded the housing opportunities of inner-city blacks, have been largely ignored, a response implicitly endorsed by token compliance reviews and encouraged by negligible enforcement (Rabin, 1980).

SEGREGATIVE LOCAL GOVERNMENT ACTIONS

In the dynamic interplay of public actions and private attitudes on racial segregation, federal funds and state-enabling legislation often combined to provide incentive and authority for local action. However, while the delegated powers of the states continue to provide an underlying basis for local action, severe reductions in the availability of federal funds for local land use-related purposes have significantly reduced direct federal involvement. While these intergovernmental relationships are of fundamental importance, an adequate examination of the complex web of federal-state-municipal influences on residential segregation is beyond the scope and intention of this chapter. In addition, with the probable exception of highway planning, the particular spatial outcomes of public segregative actions are most directly shaped by the decisions and initiatives of local government. Finally, some segregative actions such as exclusionary and expulsive development controls continue to be instruments of public policy at the local level. For these reasons, and to promote organizational clarity, the focus of what follows is on the segregative actions of local government.

Nevertheless, this limitation is not intended to suggest that past discriminatory policies and practices of the federal government have not been important and lasting influences on the establishment of present patterns of racial segregation, or that the recent (since 1980) shift of federal policy from inadequate civil rights enforcement to open opposition to civil rights enforcement has not substantially encouraged the current resurgence of public and private discrimination.

The principal local government actions and practices that have influenced residential location by race and that are segregative in their effect include:

- clearance and elimination of minority residential areas
- creation of physical barriers to expansion of minority areas
- exclusion of public and/or subsidized housing
- segregative relocation practices
- segregative site selection and/or tenant assignment for public and subsidized housing and schools
- exclusionary zoning
- discrimination in the provision of municipal facilities and services
- *de jure* segregation of housing or schools
- court-enforced racially restrictive covenants

- expulsive zoning
- changing or failing to change municipal or school district boundaries
- use of racial criteria identifying and planning neighborhoods
- public pronouncements by government officials that serve to reinfoce racially discriminatory attitudes and practices

These actions and practices can be grouped into three general categories based on the nature of their effects on locational patterns. Some fall into more than one category:

1. Those that eliminate areas of minority residences.
2. Those that create barriers to the direction in which or the extent to which a minority area may expand.
3. Those that foster the movement of minorities into minority areas or promote the transition of majority to minority areas.

The examples cited here are necessarily limited in number and descriptive detail. Those cited are not isolated or unique phenomena; they are typical of widespread practices, and have been selected because they strikingly illustrate the segregative nature of common public actions. However, in selecting examples from a large number of settings, attempting to emphasize more recent practices and grouping them by category of impact, the mutually reinforcing effects of other concurrent or sequential discriminatory and segregative actions, both public and private, is substantially understated.

BACKGROUND AND METHODOLOGY

The case studies that provided evidence of segregative public action were conducted in many regions of the country in towns as small as Osage, West Virginia and cities as large as Kansas City, Missouri and Philadelphia, Pennsylvania. Most, but not all, were undertaken in response to allegations that in the conduct of some land use-related activity, a government agency had illegally discriminated, usually against blacks but often against Hispanics and sometimes against Native Americans. These land use-related activities included locational decisions for assisted housing and schools, the planning and construction of transportation facilities, urban renewal, the relocation of displacees, the exercise of development controls, the provision of municipal facilities and services, and similar activities funded under the Community Development Block Grant Program. The studies were often, but not always, carried out in support of class action civil rights litigation and were commissioned by both public interest legal assistance organizations and government agencies at the federal, state, and municipal levels.

The information base for these empirical studies was derived from examinations of change in the size, location, concentration, housing conditions, and other relevant demographic characteristics of the affected minority group, comparisons of these to characteristics of the majority white population, and historical reviews of relevant government actions. Data from the census and other available surveys and studies were collected, analyzed, and mapped at a fine level of geographic detail, whenever feasible, at block level. Changes over time were then evaluated in the context of actions and events recorded in public documents, and newspapers and library archives.[3]

DISPLACEMENT OF MINORITY AREAS

The term *displacement* is used to describe those public actions that contribute to the removal of minorities from an area. The result is an area that is subsequently redeveloped for majority residential occupancy or for some nonresidential use. The early role of clearance for highway construction and urban renewal has been widely recognized. Less well recognized, and as yet untested in the courts, is the use of zoning as an expulsive mechanism—that is, to create or facilitate market conditions that cause minority displacement. This practice, as will be shown below, is not new, and in the current absence of resources or political support for clearance, it provides an expedient, effective, and inexpensive means of pursuing the same ends. It is often a factor in gentrification that has become a significant cause of minority displacement (LeGates & Hartman, 1982).

The displacement of minority areas by public action has been observed to have one of three general spatial characteristics, each of which has perceptibly different consequences.

1. Clearance of minority housing on the edge of a large area of minority concentration.
2. Clearance of an entire enclave of minority housing from a majority area.
3. Clearance within a large area of minority concentration for some nonresidential uses, either within a contained site as for a recreation area or along a linear path as for a highway.

The effect of clearance on the edge of an area of minority concentration has most often been to direct the expansion of the minority area in a direction away from the cleared area. This was observed in Kansas City, Missouri; Charlotte, North Carolina; Nashville, Tennessee; Jackson, Tennessee; Charlottesville, Virginia; and Norfolk, Virginia. In each case, the area cleared was immediately adjacent to the central business district (CBD) or government center. In each, the direction of black residential area expansion was established and continues today.

In Charlottesville, an interview was conducted with an elderly former superintendent of schools. He had been influential in 1936 in selecting a site at the edge of a black neighborhood for the construction of a large new high school for whites only. He frankly acknowledged that the determining factor was the view of the school board that "those people didn't belong there so close to our nice downtown." Less than twenty years later, the remainder of the black neighborhood was cleared by urban renewal. In Norfolk, the plan for the CBD explained that nearby housing of low-income blacks, which was subsequently cleared through renewal, placed the downtown center "in a setting inappropriate to its intended character." Clearance activities in Norfolk during the 1950s were so extensive that one out of every four black families was displaced to make way for highways or urban renewal (*Riddick v. School Board of the City of Norfolk*, 1984).

The elimination of minority enclaves appears to be among the most persistent in its impact on present neighborhood patterns. The term *minority enclave* is used to describe relatively small concentrations of minority housing ranging in size from one to perhaps ten city blocks and spatially separated from the principal minority housing area. Several such enclaves were to be commonly found in the central cities of many metropolitan areas as recently as the early 1960s, and many still exist in the outer rings. In most cities that were studied, areas from which blacks were removed thirty years ago and more recently, have no black residents in them today. The elimination of minority enclaves has been brought about by several common types of government activities, primarily clearance and displacement, but sometimes discriminatory pressure. Sometimes the results are extreme. In Osage, West Virginia, blacks made up about one-third of the population in 1960. Acquisition of the right-of-way for Interstate 79, running north-south through the town, eliminated every black-occupied dwelling in the town.

In Kansas City, three radial elements of the Interstate Highway System entering the city from the east, north, and west followed curiously winding routes, each of which eliminated a black neighborhood enclave. The effect of this clearance during the 1950s and 1960s and concurrent urban renewal displacements was to increase the proportion of the city's black population living in the principal ghetto area from 81% to 94%.

The black residents of a six-block enclave in the Whitman neighborhood in southeast Philadelphia, which was cleared in 1959 to provide a site for a public housing project, moved into available housing nearby in the predominantly white area adjacent to the cleared site. The city then sought and obtained federal approval for the designation of the entire Whitman neighborhood as a spot clearance and rehabilitation urban renewal project. This project involved the clearance of about 3% of the Whitman area housing units (about 100 dwelling units), and removed every house occupied by a black household in the blocks surrounding the public housing site (*Residents Advisory Board v. Rizzo*, 1976).

Following completion of the urban renewal project, the Whitman neighborhood association, encouraged by then mayoral candidate and later Mayor Frank Rizzo, mounted a vociferous and often violent campaign of opposition to the planned construction of the public housing project on the grounds that it would bring blacks into an all-white neighborhood. After more than 20 years of conflict, the project was ordered built by the federal courts and has now restored some integration to the Whitman neighborhood. As was the case in Kansas City and Norfolk, this period of renewal activity was characterized by the extensive growth of the major ghetto areas in north and west Philadelphia.

During the mid-1960s in Easton, Pennsylvania, there were three predominantly black enclaves north of the Lehigh River and a somewhat larger black community south of the Lehigh River. A series of urban renewal projects, which cleared the three northern enclaves, and the timely construction of subsidized housing in the majority black area south of the river combined to form the more rigid pattern of a single ghetto.

Sometimes housing available to blacks was so limited that local actions forced minority displacees to move to another municipality. In Hamtramck, Michigan during the late 1960s, the city carried out several urban renewal projects in black enclaves in order to provide land for the expansion of adjacent automobile plants. Nearly a third of the city's black population was displaced. Since the cleared areas were converted to nonresidential use, and because no relocation housing was provided, most were forced to move to adjacent Detroit.

In sections of the country that once imposed *de jure* school segregation, a powerful influence on the disappearance of minority enclaves has been the closing of the minority schools that served them. In Austin, Texas the school board closed black schools serving five black enclaves in north and west Austin, leaving black parents with the burden of transporting their children to black schools in the principal black area in southeast Austin. Within ten years four of the enclaves had disappeared.

In Mt. Laurel, New Jersey the homesites in an existing low-income black community have been designated by the zoning ordinance as nonconforming uses, thereby providing the local government with a rationale for the refusal of permits for the replacement or renovation of the housing there. A systematic process of inspections, condemnations, and demolitions is slowly but steadily eliminating the minority community there. Between 1971 and 1974, nearly a third of the households in that community were displaced; and since no affordable relocation housing was available in Mt. Laurel, they have been forced to move to other jurisdictions (*Burlington County NAACP v. Mt. Laurel*, 1974).

This form of development control, which I have termed *expulsive zoning*, has been widespread and has frequently resulted in the destabilization and elimination of minority enclaves by promoting private conversion to other uses or by creating a convenient rationale for redevelopment. The first zoning ordinances adopted during the late 1920s and early 1930s in Charlotte, Charlottesville, Kansas City, Norfolk, Jackson, Tennessee, and Selma (early zoning maps were not always available in other places) zoned only the major black areas for residential use. Separate enclaves and sometimes sections on the edge of the main black residential area were zoned for industrial or commercial uses. Although the black residential use predated the adoption of zoning, the nonconforming status of these areas formed part of the basis for later clearance through renewal in Kansas City, Jackson, and Norfolk.

In Baltimore County, Maryland, some suburban black enclaves were zoned for nonresidential uses even though adjacent white areas were zoned residential (Rabin, 1970). A recent report on displacement from El Paso's barrio revealed that population there had declined by over half in the last fifteen years, and that expulsive zoning had played a significant role. "For decades, the M-1 (light manufacturing) zoning has inflated land values, promoted commercial encroachment, and allowed chaotic land-use leaving the predominantly residential community in non-conforming status" (National Low-Income Housing Information Service, 1986).

Since the displacement through urban renewal of over 300 black families from the Old Town historic district of Alexandria in the 1970s, market pressures have increased steadily there for nineteenth-century row-houses and twentieth-century imitations. For over fifteen years, those pressures have focused on the Parker-Gray district, a long-established low- and moderate-income black residential neighborhood adjacent to Old Town whose residents fought repeated attempts by the City Council to extend the boundaries of the historic district to include their neighborhood.

In 1984, the neighborhood residents lost. In spite of an earlier finding by the Virginia Historic Landmarks Commission that the neighborhood did not merit designation as a historic area, the City designated most of the neighborhood as the Parker-Gray Old and Historic District, thus accelerating the displacement of blacks and the transformation of the neighborhood into a white upper middle-income facsimile of Old Town.

CREATION OF RACIAL BARRIERS

Public action has helped to create physical barriers that restrict minority geographic movement. The construction of highways between minority and majority residential areas in an example. Other actions influence development in ways which tend to exclude minorities. The most common physical barrier has been the limited access highway, which in numerous instances has been aligned, or was proposed to be aligned, along a route that separated minority and majority residential areas.

In Philadelphia, the initially proposed route of the Crosstown Expressway ran east-west along a line between an affluent white area adjacent to the CBD and a low-income black area to the south. After the initial proposal was made, several years elapsed during which the process of gentrification extended the white area more than a block further to the south. It was then proposed, ostensibly on traffic grounds, that the route of the highway be shifted to the south along a line that coincidentally corresponded to the new boundary between the black and white neighborhoods. After much public opposition, the road proposal was withdrawn entirely.

In the northwestern corner of Hamtramck, the route of a highway was diverted to isolate a black enclave between the highway and an automobile plant, and the isolated area then rezoned from residential to industrial use, thereby reinforcing the barrier effect by expulsive zoning. Among other cities studied, it was observed that highways were built that formed barriers between white and minority residential areas in Charlotte, Charleston, West ginia, El Paso, Texas, Flint, Michigan, Indianapolis, Indiana, Kansas City, and Ossining, New York. Some divisive highways did not remain effective as barriers to racial movement for more than a few years, but other publicly erected physical barriers have been more enduring.

In Jackson, Kansas City, Alexandria, and Norfolk extensive redevelopment for government and commercial uses, which displaced black residential areas, has forced the growth of the black residential areas away from central business districts. In Nashville, urban renewal land was provided to create an extension of the Music City area, which would serve as both a buffer and a barrier between the Vanderbilt University campus area to the west and the all black Edgehill neighborhood to the east. Physical barriers can result from discontinuous street systems between white and adjacent to black areas. Access to such black enclaves is usually via a single street connecting to a major artery or nonresidential street. The Catonsville area of Baltimore County provided a striking example of this isolating condition. There one could look from streets in the black neighborhood across a fifty foot wide patch of trees and underbrush to the continuation of the same streets in the adjacent white neighborhood. Interestingly, these streets were shown as continuous on the county's maps.

Lack of municipal facilities in black areas constituted barriers that kept blacks segregated. In Shaw, Mississippi, the town failed to provide the segregated section in which blacks lived with basic municipal facilities such as paved streets, sidewalks, street lights, water supply, and sewers. In appealing the ruling by the district court that the town had violated the rights of its black residents, the attorney for the town argued that it was necessary to withhold these public improvements in order to ensure that there would be an area of town in which blacks could afford to live. In Alexandria, Virginia, complaints by blacks that the city had failed to make promised neighborhood improvements under a Community Renewal Program were met with a similar response (Hammer, Siler, & George, 1976). The provision of inferior municipal facilities and services to black residential areas was also documented in Mt. Laurel and in seventeen other cities, towns, and counties in Alabama, Arkansas, Florida, Georgia, Louisiana, Mississippi, Nevada, Tennessee, and Virginia.[4]

Exclusionary zoning also forms barriers around some black enclaves in the suburbs that predate post-World War II suburbanization. The expansion of these areas is often prevented and their declines accelerated by zoning the immediately surrounding area for nonresidential use or for large-lot, low-density residential use. Several such zoning-bound communities were found in Baltimore County, Maryland (Rabin, 1970).

ACTIONS THAT PROMOTE RACIAL CONCENTRATION OR TRANSITION

The public actions that fall into this category are the most varied and have also produced some of the most persistent segregative effects. The widespread practice of concentrating public and other assisted housing in the principal minority area is prominent. Early official city planning studies carried out in Kansas City, Norfolk, and Selma used explicitly racial criteria in identifying and delineating neighborhoods. In Norfolk and Kansas City these neighborhoods continue to form the basis for current plans.

Out of a total of twenty-two family public housing projects in Norfolk, twenty-one were located in all-black residential areas and were all-black occupied. Close cooperation between the school board and the housing authority led to the practice of locating elementary schools adjacent to these all-black projects thus assuring a mutually reinforcing pattern of segregated housing and schools that persists in the 1980s. These housing projects, in 1983, accommodated one out of every four black families in Norfolk. When Philadelphia, during the late 1960s, received authorization from HUD for the acquisition of over 4,300 single-family houses under the Used House Program, the city council passed an ordinance restricting the area within which the houses could be purchased to the North Philadelphia ghetto. Philadelphia is one of the few major cities in which the Index of Segregation increased between 1970 and 1980 (Tauber & Tauber, 1983).

In Nashville, three public housing projects and one rent subsidy project, all black occupied and totaling nearly 900 units, were concentrated in a single urban renewal project within an already black residential area, thereby intensifying the levels of both racial and economic segregation. In Cuyahoga County, Ohio, the housing authority, whose jurisdiction extends over 67 municipalities had, by 1975, built all of its projects in Cleveland because none of the other jurisdictions would permit public housing to be built. Since that time under limited cooperation agreements, housing for the elderly has been built in four suburban municipalities and a total of fewer than fifty family public housing units has been produced outside Cleveland.

In Goldsboro, North Carolina, the western section of the city and a small adjacent portion of the county just west of the city are served by a majority black school district. The larger eastern section of the city and the remainder of the surrounding county are served by a majority white school district. The county housing authority, which has jurisdiction over both areas, has built public housing projects only within the boundaries of the majority black school district within the city. Kansas City and Jackson are also characterized by gross spatial disparities in the areas included within the municipal and school district boundaries, with the result that black pupils are overwhelmingly concentrated in a single school district that serves only a portion of the city. A recent landmark ruling in a school desegregation case filed by the U.S. Department of Justice in the closing days of the Carter administration also recognized the fundamental relationship between the racial characteristics of housing occupancy and school enrollment, and found that a long history of housing-related actions by the City of Yonkers, New York has contributed significantly to maintaining segregation in both ("Judge finds," 1985). Pearce (1981) has demonstrated that racially identifiable segregated schools in situations such as these are significant in promoting the segregated locational choices of white home buyers.

The relocation of displacees from public programs has frequently had the effect of increasing the concentration in existing minority areas, as was the case in the examples from Kansas City and Easton cited above; at other times, relocation has served to bring about the transition of majority area to a minority area. In another Kansas City example, over 1,400 black households displaced by right-of-way acquisition for a contested freeway have been relocated into a single highway department designated zone in southeast Kansas City along the path of the freeway, a process that has greatly accelerated and reinforced the ongoing transition of that zone from white to black.

In Norfolk during the 1960s, black displacees from urban renewal were referred by the redevelopment authority to two real estate firms whose offices and areas of operation were in the all-white Park Place neighborhood adjacent to the northwestern edge of the downtown ghetto. By 1970 this neighborhood was entirely black. In Jackson, Tennessee, the ongoing clearance of black residential areas west of the downtown continues to increase the concentration of blacks in east Jackson.

SUMMARY AND CONCLUSIONS

Varied and widespread actions by local government, often in the implementation of federal or state programs, have been instrumental in shaping patterns of racial segregation. Many, if not most, of these activities have resulted from the implementation of ostensibly beneficial plans and proposals by agencies such as planning departments, redevelopment authorities, housing authorities, and highway departments. These agencies, rarely, if ever, attempt to avoid segregation or actively pursue integration. While it is not possible to quantify precisely the individual or collective impacts of these actions, it is certainly reasonable to generalize about their relative effects, based in part on the numbers of households affected, the size of the areas involved, and the observable evidence of the duration of their impacts.

In some cities, such as Norfolk and Easton, the scale and scope of these segregative activities have been so great that they might reasonably be characterized as the principal determinants of racial patterns in those places. In other cities, where the scale of government segregative activity may have been smaller, the momentum and direction established by activities, such as clearance and relocation, have nevertheless had an influence far out of proportion to the numbers displaced. Displacements of large numbers of households were generally carried out over relatively short periods of time and had the effect of concentrating relocatees in a single direction or a circumscribed area. This resulted in a rapid process of racial transition, with a momentum that continues for many years. The trends thus established were then reinforced by the sites selected for assisted housing and schools, and by the erection of physical and regulatory barriers, all the while providing implicit sanction and tangible support for private discriminatory practices.

As a consequence of these actions, racial segregation continues to be one of the most deplorable conditions in urban America. The actions of the

1950s, 1960s, and 1970s, and before, have established patterns that persist today. Without active remedy, these patterns will remain. *The need for an understanding of government's role in creating and perpetuating these segregated conditions is of fundamental importance.* To suggest, as the demographic literature generally does, that preference and income levels are the only significant causes of present patterns of segregation is to reinforce a distorted view of the past, and provide a convenient rationale for the denial of public accountability and action, an excuse for the reduction of government's role in protecting civil rights, and a basis for subverting equitable outcomes in the courts.

Employing this self-serving rationale, the Reagan administration has not only reduced government's efforts on behalf of civil rights but has reversed policies that have been effective in promoting opportunities for minorities (Palmer & Sawhill, 1984), even eliminating previously required certifications that recipients of federal funds comply with civil rights laws (Palmer & Sawhill, 1984). In further pursuit of these policies, the Justice Department is seeking to dismantle ongoing efforts toward school desegregation by its intervention in a number of lawsuits on behalf of local government or public agency defendants who are seeking to relieve themselves of obligations under court-imposed desegregation plans. In some instances, the department has initiated litigation to halt the implementation of desegregation plans that had been voluntarily entered into by their participants. In the presence of well-documented, widespread racial prejudice, these policies and their racially isolating consequences can only serve to consign a significant portion of the minority population to the status of a permanent underclass, living in racially segregated areas.

As a first step, past efforts to reduce segregation and achieve a more equitable distribution of opportunities must be understood not as futile and inappropriate interference with market processes but as an unfinished task —unfinished because government's commitment and effort have been grossly inadequate. Myths and misconceptions, whether promulgated by partisan politicians, or inferred from narrowly focused academic research, are fundamental obstacles to this understanding.

Segregation in the 1980s is the legacy of many decades of government complicity in the process of racial isolation. To begin to undo this systemic pattern of racial segregation will require a commitment of resources and effort on a scale that seems inconceivable in the current political climate.

At current (1986) levels, $290 billion is being spent annually—$33 million an hour—for increasingly hostile activities characterized as national defense. The diversion of just two hours per day of this expenditure would provide $24 billion per year, a sum that might conceivably fund the undertaking of a serious national effort to redress past injustices. It might be enough to initiate the long overdue process of change from institutionalized separation and inequality based on race to some approximation of the equal opportunity that the society's rhetoric proclaims. While this is not likely to happen in the near future, it will never happen unless, and until, there is widespread recognition of the role of government in creating and perpetuating the racial disparities which exist.

NOTES

1. Studies of one or more racially discriminatory practices by government agencies were carried out in Birmingham, Lowndes County, and Selma, Alabama; Pine Bluff, Arkansas; Irvine, California; Denver, Colorado; Washington, D.C.; Sanford, Florida; Ocilla, Georgia; Indianapolis, Indiana; Shreveport, Louisiana; Baltimore County, Maryland; Detroit, Flint, Hamtramck, Inkster, and Livonia, Michigan; Minneapolis and St. Paul, Minnesota; Drew, Gulfport, Itta Bena, Senatobia, Shaw, and West Point, Mississippi; Kansas City, Missouri; Las Vegas, Nevada; Camden, Mt. Laurel, and Newark, New Jersey; Huntington and Ossining, New York: Charlotte, Goldsboro, and Wilmington, North Carolina; Cuyahoga County and Defiance, Ohio; Easton and Philadelphia, Pennsylvania; Columbia, South Carolina; Chattanooga, Jackson, Knoxville, Nashville, and Pulaski, Tennessee; Austin and El Paso, Texas; Alexandria, Charlottesville, Fairfax County, Greenville County, and Norfolk, Virginia; Charleston and Osage, West Virginia.

2. This legislation included the 1962 Highway Act, 1964 Civil Rights Act, 1965 Department of Housing and Urban Development Act, 1966 Demonstration Cities and Metropolitan Development Act, 1966 Department of Transportation Act, 1968 Intergovernmental Cooperation Act, 1968 Civil Rights Act, 1969 Environmental Policy Act, and the 1974 Housing and Community Development Act.

3. Additional resources included historical photographs and maps, visual and questionnaire surveys, and numerous interviews, both informal and by formal deposition. Examples from the most recent studies, in Norfolk, Alexandria, and Kansas City, are more frequently cited here.

4. The places where discriminatory disparities were found in the provision of municipal facilities to black residential areas included Lowndes County and Selma, Alabama; Pine Bluff, Arkansas; Sanford, Florida; Ocilla, Georgia; Shreveport, Louisiana; Baltimore County, Maryland; Drew, Gulfport, Itta Bena, Senatobia, Shaw, and West Point, Mississippi; Las Vegas, Nevada; Mt. Laurel, New Jersey; Jackson, Tennessee; Fairfax County and Greenville County, Virginia.

REFERENCES

Bowden, D. L., & Palmer, J. L. (1984). Social policy: Challenging the welfare state. In J. L. Palmer & I. V. Sawhill (Eds.), *The Reagan record: An assessment of America's changing domestic priorities* (pp. 177–215). Cambridge: Ballinger.

Cusick, P. A., Gerbing, D. W., & Rossel, E. L. (1979). The effects of school desegregation and other factors on white flight from an urban area. *Educational Administration Quarterly, 15*(2), 35–49.

Farley, R., Schuman, H., Biachi, S., Colosanto, D., & Hatchett, S. (1983). Chocolate city, vanilla suburbs: Will the trend toward racially separated communities continue? In M. Baldassare (Ed.), *Cities and urban living* (pp. 292–315). New York: Columbia University Press.

Farley, R., & Tauber, K. E. (1968). Population trends and residential segregation since 1960. *Science, 159*(3818), 952–956.

Feagin, J. R., & Feagin, C. B. (1978). *Discrimination American style: Institutional racism and sexism.* Englewood Cliffs, NJ: Prentice-Hall.

Foley, D. L. (1973). Institutional and contextual factors affecting the housing choices of minority residents. In A. H. Hawley & V. P. Rock (Eds.), *Segregation in residential areas* (pp. 85–147). Washington, DC: National Academy of Sciences.

Hammer, Siler, George. (1976). *Final NEA study report to the city of Alexandria, Virginia.* Washington, DC: Government Printing Office.

Jones, E. R. (1982). *The differential impact of income and preference on residential segregation* (Planning paper 82-002). Urbana-Champaign: University of Illinois Bureau of Urban and Regional Planning.

Judge finds Yonkers segregates schools. (1985, November 21). *New York Times,* p. 1.

Kain, J. F. (1974). Housing segregation, black employment and metropolitan decentralization: A retrospective view. In G. M. von Furstenberg, B. Harrison, & A. R. Horowitz (Eds.), *Patterns of racial discrimination: Vol. 1 Housing* (pp. 5–18). Lexington: Heath.

LeGates, R., & Hartmann, C. (1982). Chapter 14. In *Displacement: How to fight it.* Berkeley, CA: National Housing Law Project.

Long, L., & DeAre, D. (1981, September). The suburbanization of blacks. *American Demographics,* pp. 17–21, 44.

National Low Income Housing Information Service. (1986). *Displacement Forum, 1*(1), 2.

Nelson, K. P. (1979). *Recent suburbanization of blacks: How much, who, and where.* Washington, DC: HUD.

Orfield, G. et al. (1980). A social science statement: School segregation and residential segregation. In W. G. Stephen & J. R. Feagin (Eds.), *School desegregation past, present, and future* (pp. 231–247). New York: Plenum.

Palmer, J. L., & Sawhill, I. V. (Eds.). (1984). Overview. In J. L. Palmer & I. V. Sawhill (Eds.), *The Reagan record: An assessment of America's changing domestic practices* (pp. 1–30, 206). Cambridge: Ballinger.

Pearce, D. M. (1981). Deciphering the dynamics of segregation: The role of schools in the housing choice process. *Urban Review, 13*(2), 85–102.

Pettigrew, T. F. (1973). Attitudes on race and housing: A social-psychological view. In A. H. Hawley & V. P. Rock (Eds), *Segregation in residential areas* (pp. 21–84). Washington, DC: National Academy of Services.

Rabin, Y. (1970, August). *The effects of development control on housing opportunities for black households in Baltimore County, Maryland* (Report to the U.S. Commission on Civil rights).

Rabin, Y. (1975). *Housing segregation in Philadelphia and the Whitman Park Housing Project: The role of city and federal actions* (Report to Community Legal Services of Philadelphia).

Rabin, Y. (1980). Federal urban transportation policy and the highway planning process in metropolitan areas. *Annals of the American Academy of Political and Social Science, 451,* 21–35.

Rabin, Y. (1983). The final question: Who benefits? *Planning, 49*(10).

Rabin, Y. (1984). Suburban racial segregation and the segregative actions of government: Two aspects of metropolitan population distribution. In *A sheltered crisis: The state of fair housing in the eighties* (pp. 31–53). Washington, DC: G.O.P.

Streitweiser, M. L., & Goodman, J. L., Jr. (1983). A survey of recent research on race and residential location. In *Population Research and Policy Review, 2* (pp. 253–283). Amsterdam: Elsevier.

Tauber, K. E. (1984). *Racial residential segregation, 28 cities, 1970–1980* (CDE Working Paper 87-12). Madison: University of Wisconsin.

Tauber, K. E., & Tauber, A. E. (1965). *Negroes in cities.* Chicago: Aldine.

Yinger, J. (1979). Prejudice and discrimination in urban housing. In P. Mieszkowski & M. Straszheim (Eds.), *Current issues in urban economics* (pp. 430–468). Baltimore: Johns Hopkins.

31
The No Party Politics of Suburbia*

Robert C. Wood

. . . Especially at the municipal level, suburban politics appear to differ, at least in degree, and probably in substance, from those of other American communities, both urban and rural. In the end, this difference has important implications for the state and national pattern.

One indication of this difference, which Harris has described, is the relative respectability and restraint of suburban politics at the local level—the yearning to shed the disreputable political habits of the big city. Another bit of evidence, which Whyte and Henderson have discovered on a sample basis, is the strong sense of community consciousness and civic responsibility that impels active participation in local affairs. Deeply concerned with the quality of schools, conscious of their new status, suburbanites are inclined to "care" about local affairs—zoning regulation, recreational plans, garbage collection, school curricula, street paving—in an especially intense way. As the logical converse of their apathy toward strong party affiliations, suburbanites approach the politics of the community on the basis of individual preferences; they are, more and more frequently, nonpartisan, sharply distinguishing their local public preferences from their views of national and state affairs.

Suburban nonpartisanship takes several forms. Sometimes, as in the Washington environs, it is simply a way of interjecting another party on the local scene, an organization closely identified in attitude and outlook with a national party but separately organized to overcome the minority status of its big brother in the area. In these cases nonpartisan groups parallel the earlier efforts of municipal reformers in the large cities to overthrow an established—and in their eyes—unpalatable party machine. Sometimes, as is customary in New York and Connecticut suburbs, nonpartisanship takes the form of the inclusion of members of the minority party in local councils in a ratio that preserves the majority party's control but that the minority could never achieve on its own. Finally, and apparently most frequently, local politics have no association, open or covert, with the established parties at all. Public affairs are the province of essentially political organizations—civic clubs, social leagues, or improvement organizations—whose members are loosely tied together and whose announced goals are "what is best for the community." There are exceptions amid the variety of suburbs, of course;

*Wood, Robert C. 1958. "The No Party Politics of Suburbia." Pp. 153–166 in *Suburbia: Its People and Their Politics*. Boston: Houghton Mifflin. Copyright © 1958 by Houghton Mifflin Company. Used with permission.

some remain staunchly and overwhelming partisan in outlook. But the general trend is in the other direction — nonpartisanship is legally recognized in 61 per cent of the suburban governments reporting in the *Municipal Yearbook*, and for those under 10,000 population, the percentage is probably even higher.

This emphasis on nonpartisanship is, of course, a familiar element in the local politics of many communities which are not suburban. As the authors of the Federalist Papers early noted and as V. O. Key has more recently pointed out, nonpartisanship reflects highly integrated community life with a powerful capacity to induce conformity. "Party, as such, often has no meaning except as a combination to fight the opposition. It is rather an expression continued from generation to generation of the consensus of a more or less individual community or at least of a majority in such over- whelming command that it is unaware of any challenge to its position. The politics of the locality is a politics of personality and of administration rather than a politics of issues." In this broad sense, suburban nonpartisanship does resemble the politics of all localities, stressing the candidate and not the platform, and exhibiting a high degree of disorganization.

Yet there is a significant distinction between the no-party pattern com- mon to suburbia and the one-party localism that Key identifies, just as there is a distinction between the structured homogeneity of a relatively isolated town, with its banker, lawyer, merchant, farmer, clerk, and workingman, and the more unified composition of an individual suburb. In traditional one-party politics, intramural competition among factions, interest groups, and cliques within the same organization is accepted as normal at the local level, disruptive as it may sometimes be for party leadership. This kind of factionalism, prevalent in one-party states and large cities, is not antagonistic to the idea of partisanship as such and does not preclude organized group action at higher levels. On the contrary, party regularity beyond primary or convention fights is expected and encouraged; the existence of the party structure, tightly or loosely organized, is taken as natural, and the politically minded work within it.

The no-party politics of so many suburban governments, however, often exhibits quite different characteristics. There is, first of all, an outright reaction against partisan activity, a refusal to recognize that there may be persistent cleavages in the electorate, and an ethical disapproval of perma- nent group collaboration as an appropriate means for settling public dis- putes. "No-partyism" eats away at the idea of partisanship by outlawing party influence to "outside" elections and by discouraging outright displays of party allegiance in the community as indicative of bad taste. The political animal is tamed; as the suburbanite approaches the ballot box in local elections, he is expected to strive for a consensus with his friends and neighbors, to seek "the right solution" as distinct from favoring one or another faction of his party.

One explanation for this rise in the number of independents is that this view of citizenship spills over into national and state campaigns. The "local political man" dampens proclivities of the party political man, restrains his condemnation of the Man in the White House or his suspicion of big business or his conviction that labor racketeers spell the downfall of the nation. Instead, the nonpartisan is more likely to believe that the good citizen seeks the best man and the right answer in every campaign, so that the almost inarticulate loyalties common in one-party localities are consciously rejected.

Thus, Edward Janosik, after an investigation of politics in 57 suburban counties around the 20 largest metropolitan areas, concluded: "Many suburbanites in the United States seem to take pleasure in cultivating a politically independent state of mind. Some counties normally designated as suburban have population densities as high, if not higher, than sections of the core city. Even so, the pattern of political favors and resultant political obligations characteristic of older urban areas has never been strongly established in suburban communities."

A second feature of nonpartisanship is the suburbanite's acceptance of an obligation for extensive civic participation on the part of the lay constituency. So far as general political activity is concerned, this proclivity shows up in the large proportion of eligible voters who actually get to the polls in national elections. Janosik estimates that for these elections the chances are nine to one that the eligible suburban voter will cast his ballot. On the local level civic interest may express itself in the citizens' inclination to undertake the supervision of the local bureaucracy directly, or in his suspicion of the role of the professional political leader. Here the image of resurrected grassroots democracy commits the citizen, theoretically at least, to a do-it-yourself brand of politics, in which as many issues as possible, simple and complex, require his personal sanction, and the acceptable elected official is the part-time amateur, taking his term in office just as he once led the community chest drive.

Finally, and most fundamentally, no-party politics implies some positive assumptions about political behavior that go beyond simple antagonism to partisanship. Inescapably, there is a belief that the individual can and should arrive at his political convictions untutored and unled; an expectation that in the formal process of election and decision-making a consensus will emerge through the process of right reason and by the higher call to the common good. Gone is the notion of partisan groups, leaders and followers, and in its place is the conscious or unconscious assumption that the citizen, on his own, knows best.

This set of convictions, of course, marks the basic distinction between one-party and no-party politics, for it establishes a standard for acceptable political behavior that antedates the party system. As a theory, nonpartisanship harks back to the traditional concept of local government, to Jefferson's high expectations for the rational capacity of the yeoman, and to that strand in American political reasoning that relies on unfettered individualism, and that manifests itself in the agitation for primaries, referendums and recalls. It is in these assumptions that the suburbanite is linked most directly with his small town ancestors, and not in a coincidence in political attitude, which the theory of conversion tried to establish between the two.

This resurrection of conscious nonpartisanship so evident in the suburban brand of politics — as distinct from big city and rural patterns — has some quite specific consequences in the modern world. The antagonism toward party, the obligation for extensive citizen participation, and the expectation that there is likely to be a single right answer to a political problem results in an unwavering commitment to political forms in which direct democracy can be applied. This commitment, in turn, leads to an important redefinition of the relationship between the citizen and the bureaucrat, and an equally important de-emphasis on the role of the politician. Most important, under the cloak of local nonpartisanship, specific patterns of small, informally organized cliques develop which interact against the doctrine of nonpartisanship itself.

As we shall see, in the context of the modern service state, rather bizarre methods of conducting public business result. They are not evident in all suburbs at all times, and sometimes they are indistinguishable from practices in medium-sized independent cities and other localities that have adopted municipal reform's reinterpretation of the republic in miniature. But essentially they resemble more closely American political practice of two hundred years ago, as it grappled with contemporary public problems, than they do the more typical political process of twentieth century America.

INSTITUTIONS FOR NONPARTISANSHIP

The most obvious consequence of the suburbanite's insistence on the management of local affairs uncontaminated by partisan considerations is his preference for small governments which permit the greatest degree of individual participation. The most perfect institutional expression of this preference is found today, as it was found originally, in New England. Here, nonpartisanship relies on the same governmental structure which existed when the American theory of localism began — the Town Meeting — and here the principle of the enlightened, unselfish citizen dedicated to the general advancement of his community can be applied in undiluted form.

In the environs of Boston, Portsmouth, and New Haven, every citizen who wishes to crowd into the town hall, studies with care the town warrant, judiciously considers the recommendations of the selectmen and the finance committee. He deliberates the advisability of replacing the pump on fire engine Number 52, and delivers, in consort with his neighbors, his decision. As the evening wears on, he listens to the careful pros and cons of the School Committee as to the site and construction of the new high school or the recommendation of the Planning Commission for a new building code. He examines the details of gymnasium construction, the efficacy of outdoor exits for each classroom, and studies the implications of the load factor for four-inch joists. If he detects a flaw in the expert's judgment or discovers a better method for achieving the common objective, he rises to his feet, and walks thirty yards to the nearest microphone. There, succinctly and with good-humored wit, he exposes the error or suggests the improvement before five hundred of his neighbors. By such a process of debate, forethought on the part of each citizen, and the leisurely development of a consensus—not infrequently crystallizing at two o'clock in the morning—the affairs of the town are popularly ordered.

Only the suburbs of New England are blessed today with these institutional arrangements to ensure that the collective knowledge of the town is brought to bear on all major problems and to guarantee the airing of grievances. In the other sections of the country, the form of government is a municipality, a borough, a village, a township, or even a county. But the principle of maximum participation remains the same throughout the country. When suburbanites cannot congregate physically they prefer to choose directly their mayor, their councilmen, aldermen, supervisors, board members, and to ensure that each citizen has free and easy access to his government. Elaborate appeal systems before the zoning board are established; open hearings on all important actions are required; the proposed budget is published in advance; volunteer advisory committees flourish at every turn.

Almost always, the governing body has several members, and rarely is the executive equipped with decisive powers. Every effort is made to "bring in" the minority in local decisions, by identifying their cooperative and responsible members and thereby ensuring that they have the chance to work as good citizens too. Should individual problems arise—a broken water pipe, a problem with the building inspector, an inconvenient new schedule for rubbish collection—the citizen goes straight to the top and expects to have his problem handled on a rational, objective basis. If direct participation by all members of the constituency is not possible, public affairs can still be carried on with the reassuring conviction that the government is readily accessible. The always difficult relationship of individual to state, so the theory runs, is eased by the sure conviction that there is no party hierarchy, no structure of leadership to stand between the man and his government.

To be sure, there is the additional problem of identifying which government is in fact appropriate for given problems. The metropolitan reformers were quite right in emphasizing the scatteration of governments, for the good citizen may have trouble knowing who is responsible for what in the provision of local services. Typically a separate school district or system exists with its own elected officials, to oversee public education quite independently of the municipality or town or borough. Quite frequently special water districts, fire districts, garbage districts, and highway districts, each independently organized and financed, appear on the scene. When a resident of Hempstead, Long Island, receives a tax bill composed of the levies of a half dozen separate taxing jurisdictions, conceivably he may have difficulty in determining the drift of local financial affairs. When he is called on to elect five or six different boards and commissions he may be excused for not being intimately familiar with the qualifications of all the candidates. Yet if these are unfortunate departures from the town-meeting model, they at least generally continue faithful to the principle of direct participation. The thousand-odd separate suburban jurisdictions around New York City may be difficult to fit together, and they erect additional obstacles to the exercise of prudent enlightened citizenship, but they are nonetheless of limited size and they offer an abundance of elected officials.

This insistence on easily accessible avenues into the decision-making arena, this passion for being able to participate without formal organization or selection, are the first fruits of suburban non-partisanship. Because local politics is viewed as a thing in itself more clearly than in one-party localities, it is no mere stepping stone to higher office. On this point suburbanites differ sharply from big city dwellers or rural folk; their political action expresses the conviction that a man *can* beat city hall, or that it is undemocratic to let the sheriff or the county judge "run things around here." So the suburbanite resists the lure of the larger, more efficient units, even as he becomes bewildered by the number of public decisions he is called upon to make, secure in the conviction that his preferences can make a difference in the way his government is run.

THE MANAGEMENT OF ISSUES

The second consequence of no-party suburban politics follows from the first; given a structure designed to encourage as much participation as possible, the citizen is expected to handle, on his own, the hot issues of the day. No barrier stands between him and his government; he takes pride in calling the police chief by his first name. As a consequence, the quality of the police force is the citizen's responsibility. Ideally, he is always in charge; and, ideally, he is committed to the tasks of constant surveillance of the public's business.

The reality of this energetic, civic-minded model citizen is frequently questioned by observers. As the activities of suburban government grow more complex, the town meeting or the public sessions of the borough council are sometimes described as "government by wisecrack" and written off as mechanisms too cumbersome to make real decisions. It is pointed out that even the most earnest voter is not able to give sensible decisions about water mains, fire engines, school curricula, and zoning patterns. It is suggested that while his present political institutions may serve a useful purpose in creating a sense of community, they rarely serve as effective instruments of popular government.

This less romantic interpretation of the actual results of nonpartisanship suggests that it is not the citizen but the local bureaucrat who is most influential. As the citizen finds the substance of public affairs growing increasingly intricate he finds ways to whittle down the size of his civic job. This feat is accomplished by a redefinition of what falls within the province of popular decision-making and what does not. Because nonpartisanship is built on the assumption of a like-minded constituency, contemplating no fundamental disagreements, it is a short, logical step to classify a whole range of public activities as entirely nonpolitical.

Thus, by making budget preparation the province of the professional finance director, zoning decisions the responsibility of the professional planning director, and supervision of the local bureaucracy the duty of the professional city manager, the burden on the citizen is mercifully lightened. Street repair and traffic control, it is argued, are no longer matters of each resident filling in the potholes in the public ways adjacent to his own property and warning the teamster that the bridge down the road will not bear his wagon's weight. They are properly the province of the highway department and the traffic engineer. Issues of public health can no longer be decided by public debate, or even by general practitioners in medicine; their resolution requires the scientific investigation of public health specialists. It is not enough to maintain a jail for the unruly. Criminology and penology are complex subjects, and sentences and prison routines need to be guided by the latest findings on juvenile delinquency. A modern welfare program is not a matter of Thanksgiving baskets for the poor, but a complicated process of interview, determination of need, case investigations and evaluations in which many specialists may take part.

So, function by function, more and more public activities in suburbia are called administrative and professional, removed from the list of subjects to be discussed and decided by public action, and routinized in budgets too large for scrutiny, let alone understanding. Since the average citizen cannot in fairness be asked to comment upon building codes, methods of water treatment and the relative merits of various types of police equipment, no citizen should have to comment at all. The exercise of popular control is restricted to only the most important of local issues, carefully culled to ensure that the citizen will have the time, energy and capacity to deal with them, and the arena of popular debate is kept small.

But exactly what are the issues that remain? With so many of the activities of local government the special province of the expert, acceptable matters for debate, so far as the general suburban government is concerned, are usually reduced to three: honesty, the tax bill, and land development. The question of outright corruption and wrongdoing on the part of public officials, by its nature, arises only sporadically, and, in a nonparty suburb, usually as a result of the suspicions and energy of the local press. It is likely never to be a major problem, if only because of the growing professionalization of the administrative side of local government. Even when skulduggery is detected, the average citizen can be expected to be indignant but not especially useful in either investigating or punishing it. Public action can express itself only by locking the barn door after the horse is stolen.

Nor does the issue of taxes offer the public much more opportunity to make rational policy. A higher tax rate can call forth cries of anguish and protest, but without familiarity with the budget and adequate information about the relative priorities among the locality's public needs, citizen action is not likely to be effective, and it can quite easily be harmful. Organized legislatures on the state and national level, equipped with committees and featuring an opposition party primed for attack, have difficulty enough in establishing a reasonable budget process. Town meetings, city councils, and commissions run into more trouble; and the voter's role, in a nonpartisan atmosphere, is usually reduced to accepting or rejecting bond issues at election time. Conflicts between the professional administrators and the elected officers quite frequently arise, but the lay citizen rarely finds an effective channel for participation.

Roughly the same situation exists so far as the control of land use and zoning is concerned. In suburbia, most residents reserve their strong opinions for the topic of the community's future development. Home ownership is, after all, a distinguishing characteristic of the residential suburb, and the instinct to protect property values is strong and widespread. Yet once again the effectiveness of citizen action is questionable. Planning has become the preserve of the specialists, and if the planner goes unheeded, a vast range of alternatives faces any locality. Shall developments be permitted or excluded? Shall the design of residences be regulated, to make sure that ultra-modern or ultra-conservative homes are kept out? Shall architects be permitted to experiment with newfangled construction materials and techniques? Is there to be a commercial sector or an industrial zone to relieve pressures on the tax rate, and if so, where and how big? What reservations are proper for recreational purposes? What attitude should be taken toward the location of the new express highway, other than the obvious position that it should not be allowed to come through the town?

Even assuming a collective, public, nonpartisan answer to these questions and a consensus about what the suburb wishes to become, stubborn technical problems of law and zoning remain. Private property rights still have sizable defenses, and the complicated procedures of zoning, regulations, appeals, and exceptions permit many modifications of any suburb's master plan. If the citizen were truly to fulfill his obligation with respect to land use, he would spend evening after evening listening to individual pleas for extending the building line in this instance or that, constructing a "nonconforming" garage, or putting a commercial building, by spot zoning, in an established residential area.

It is quite true that citizens of the metropolis as well as of more isolated cities face the same problem of understanding the technicalities of modern government and of controlling the burgeoning ranks of bureaucrats. Where nonpartisanship holds sway, all these municipalities may be in the same boat with the suburbs. Where party politics exist, however, even if predominantly one-party politics, there are professional politicians who make it their business to know developments and there are party organizations which, in the end, and, if the situation becomes too outrageous, may be held accountable.

Suburban municipalities, committed for the most part to part-time mayors and selectmen, resentful of open claims to political leadership, dependent upon the energy and zeal of the individual citizen, do not often possess this intervening layer of surveillance. Despite the classification of more and more problems as administrative, and the most energetic displays of public spirit, the average suburban citizen's capacity to deal effectively even with the issues which remain in his province grows more questionable. Nonpartisanship may faithfully preserve the image of Emerson's restless, prying conscious man, and the resort to professional expertness may limit the range of issues into which he is expected to inquire. More and more frequently, however, the reality of control seems to rest on the shoulders of relatively few, either elected officials or informal leaders, who stand between bureaucracy and the nonpartisan public.

32
Morning in Privatopia*

Evan McKenzie

From Plato's *Republic* to Sir Thomas More's *Utopia* to B. F. Skinner's *Walden Two* and beyond, many social theorists have tried to design, even to build, an ideal human community. It is a prospect that many view with ambivalence. As Louis Mumford wrote, "The word UTOPIA stands in common usage for the ultimate in human folly or human hope. . . ."

Recently, a new form of urban and suburban housing known as the "common interest development" (CID) has risen to prominence in most rapidly growing areas of America. CIDs include condominiums, community apartments, co-ops, and planned unit developments (PUDs) of detached, single-family housing. These types of housing have one thing in common: Residents own or exclusively occupy their own units, but they share ownership of the "common areas" used by all.

Although this seems an innocuous concept, CIDs may be taking urban and suburban America on a purposeful course toward a vision of utopia where the twin values of private property and private government reign—a sort of "privatopia," in which the residents are essentially citizens of a separate polity.

Some forty million Americans now live in common-interest housing developments where the residents privately support—and exclusively enjoy—a variety of services, ranging from police protection to swimming pools to local self-government, that were once the province of cities. The spread of CIDs could potentially accelerate the decline of cities, affect the political balance of power in urban and suburban America, and put more formerly public services into the private sector on a "pay-for-your-own" basis. It could also accustom many Americans to a form of local government free from constitutional limitations. In the words of Richard Louv, author of *America II*, "We have a generation of kids growing up in this country who don't know you should be able to paint your house any color you want."

Common property ownership requires organization, usually an incorporated "homeowners association," and a private residential government, usually in the form of a corporate board of directors. The board collects monthly dues and special assessments from all owners to maintain the development and enforces rules designed to protect property values. These elements—organization and self-government—distinguish CIDs from other housing developments.

There were only a few hundred CIDs in 1960. Today there are over 125,000, and collectively they rival—and may soon surpass—the fewer than 50,000 elected local governments in numbers, income, and potential political power. The Department of Housing and Urban Development (HUD) estimates that by 1990 the annual income of CIDs will top $20 billion. These bastions of the white middle class are competing with cities for residents, offering homogeneous population, physical security, stable housing values, local control, and freedom from exposure to the social ills of the cities.

In exchange for these material benefits, however, the residents subject themselves to government by their neighbors—a kind of government that is not restricted by the Constitution because it is private and, in the eyes of the law, no more capable of "state action" than the Kiwanis Club. Yet these private governments do much more than organize backyard barbecues. They are capable of regulating and restricting political, religious, and social activity. Perhaps most important, they have enormous economic and political resources that they are only beginning to tap.

THE RISE OF PRIVATOPIA

Even suburbia started as a utopian vision. Historian Robert Fishman, in *Bourgeois Utopias*, shows how modern suburbia was born in eighteenth-century England as a middle-class utopia and how it was exported to the United States in the nineteenth century. These first bourgeois utopias saw suburbia as a place where their most cherished values—the nuclear family, religious faith, private property, contact with nature—could be fully realized, free from the corrupting influence of the cities and the lower classes.

Common-interest housing had its genesis in the transformation of housing into a mass-produced commodity—the development—after World War II.

The CID revolution itself began in about 1960, when the federally assisted "New Town" movement spawned such heavily planned, privately governed, and eerily self-contained communities as Reston, Virginia; Columbia, Maryland; and Irvine, California. With populations of up to six hundred thousand, they were heirs to the European "Garden City" concept espoused by Ebenezer Howard in the late nineteenth century. The sponsors of these "instant cities," as Theodore Roszak called them in the *Nation* in 1967, included Gulf Oil, Humble Oil, Goodyear Tire and Rubber, Westinghouse, and General Electric.

However, in contrast to the European experience, the American national government pulled out of this planned housing partnership in the 1970s, which made city-sized developments too big and risky an undertaking for private industry. This led to smaller developments and promoted the takeover of housing construction by large corporations, including insurance companies, pension funds, large-scale joint ventures, and building corporations that went public and tapped the stock market for equity capital.

These large-scale developers fell in love with the common-interest ownership concept because it enabled them to satisfy consumer preferences for amenities such as swimming pools, golf courses, parks, private beaches, recreation rooms, security gates and guards, and so forth, which would be prohibitively expensive for individual owners.

Cities and counties are more likely to permit construction of a new development if it promises a level of self-sufficiency that will add property tax revenue without a concomitant burden on public services. Consequently, if the large corporate developer can equip the development with a new highway off-ramp, a private sewer system, a park, and a school building — things many cities just can't afford on their own anyway — local government authorities are more easily mollified.

LOCKE IN A CONDOMINIUM?

The millions of Americans who live in these places, including — and perhaps especially — those who govern them, are undergoing a subtle indoctrination process, courtesy of the developers who wrote the rules they live by. The community structure combines direct rule enforcement, subtle conformist pressures, and the rational self-interest in preserving property values into a powerful formula that all but guarantees obedience. People are led without feeling led, for the most part, and they do not resent anything except the most overt examples of oppression.

When the developer subdivides the property into individual lots, he sets up a system of restrictive covenants in all the deeds — colloquially called the "CC&Rs," short for covenants, conditions, and restrictions — that mutually bind all purchasers and require them to live by the dictates of the homeowners' association. Anyone who buys a unit is automatically subject to this regime, but it is considered a "voluntary association" by the law because nobody forced anyone to buy. This ignores the economic realities that force many people into this kind of housing against their will. In addition, this kind of logic turns social contract theory on its head. Instead of a group of individuals in a state of nature banding together and consenting to live by a set of rules of their choosing, we have the reverse: first the rules, then the houses, then the people.

CID residents are in a box, but they don't see it that way. After all, everybody else obeys the rules. All the lawns are mowed, all the cars are parked in the driveways after 8:00 p.m., all the houses are the same color, and all the dogs weigh less than thirty pounds. Rational self-interest supports this sort of conformity. A clean, well-kept development with no signs of human wear-and-tear will attract buyers, who see property values being protected.

If these informal pressures fail, formal procedures will pick up the slack. Paint your house a different color than everybody else's and see what happens. First, one of your neighbors, a representative of the architectural committee, politely asks you to repaint it in accordance with the CC&Rs. You refuse. Next, you receive a letter from the board of directors ordering you to repaint it. You ignore it. Then, you receive a notice that the association has assessed a fine of $50 per day until you repaint the house. You ignore that. A month later you receive legal documents informing you that the association is preparing to sell your house to pay the fine. If you ignore that, you may discover in short order that this is not just a neighborhood tiff—CIDs are suburbia with teeth.

Yet they defy definition. Do they amount to Locke's social contract reduced to writing, with community membership and voting based upon property ownership? Or, with their shared property interests, do they represent socialism-by-contract for the affluent? Are they libertarian "private protective associations," as in Robert Nozick's *Anarchy, State and Utopia*? What about the cultlike isolation some CIDs cultivate? Should we look at them as communes? Is there a communalist strain under all this privatization? Or do they represent the corporation of the home, with each family a shareholder?

WHO GOVERNS?

The exterior look and feel of these developments often echo America's mythical idyllic past and attempt to project at least the illusion of community and town meeting government. Yet the residents who run for places on the board of directors—unpaid positions—are often controlling, autocratic types who see their role as enforcing their way of life on everybody else. Their power is very real and substantial and often dwarfs their ability to exercise it. As a result, some odd political decisions emerge from privatopia. Here are some examples of CID private government in action across America, all reported in the press:

- In Ashland, Massachusetts, a Vietnam veteran was told that he could not fly the American flag on Flag Day. The board backed down only after he called the press and the story hit the front page.
- In Monroe, New Jersey, a homeowners' association took a married couple

to court because the wife, at age forty-five, was three years younger than the association's age-forty-eight minimum for residency. The association won. The judge ordered the sixty-year-old husband to sell, rent the unit, or live without his wife.

- In Houston, Texas, a homeowners' association took a woman to court for keeping a dog in violation of her CID rules. The association won. She kept the dog anyway. The judge sent her to jail for contempt of court.
- In Fairbanks Ranch, an affluent CID in southern California, behind six locked gates there are forty-five private streets patrolled by private security officers who enforce a private speed limit. First-time speeders get a warning; the second offense brings a hearing before the board and a reprimand; a third offense means a $500 fine, and the car and driver are banned from the private streets for a month.

AMERICA — A HOUSE DIVIDED?

It is hard to say — and maybe irrelevant, like all chicken-egg questions — whether this sort of internal behavior is the result of a particular kind of private political socialization or whether CIDs attract a large number of people who think a certain way. Whatever the reason, there are signs that homeowner associations are beginning to extend their influence outward. Privatopia may be coming into its own as a political pressure group with a distinct agenda revolving around the enhancement of property values and a kind of residential isolationism. Given their affluence, organization, connections, and potential for bloc voting. CIDs could advance their agenda quickly.

Many of Florida's CID residents are politically organized. They have become known in the press as the "Condo Commandos," and former President Jimmy Carter tapped their support.

Three thousand miles away is Indian Wells, California, a desert community made up primarily of CIDs, whose residents enjoy the state's highest per capita income behind their walls and gates. The city declared itself "blighted" in order to take advantage of a state law intended to permit truly afflicted communities to retain tax money for community redevelopment.

This might seem offensive enough, but there's more. The law required that 20 percent of the tax windfall be used to build low-income housing. Indian Wells took the tax money, used it to build a luxury gold course and attract several resorts catering to the super-rich, and then went to the state legislature for special legislation exempting it from the housing requirement so it could build the low-income housing somewhere else, outside of Indian Wells. The California legislature passed the bill, after receiving $400,000 in political campaign contributions from private developers who had more lucrative plans for the land. However, after the measure received bad press, the governor vetoed it.

This atrophied sense of social responsibility has led to a logical conclusion — the demand for special tax breaks. The Community Associations

Institute (CAI) is a nationwide organization of CIDs. Recent newsletters and published articles by its current president have suggested that CID residents are paying a "double tax." That is, they pay property tax, which goes to support public services, but they also pay dues and assessments to maintain their own, sometimes duplicative, private services. They consider this unfair, and they want a tax deduction for all or part of their homeowner dues.

Since annual CID revenues are approaching equivalency with total local government income, this could potentially bankrupt many cities and counties. However, we can safely anticipate that some aspiring politician will make this proposal the centerpiece of a campaign and, in the right area, ascend to statewide office and try to implement it.

The framework for such campaigns is taking shape. Through the activities of CAI and other organizations, we are now seeing the emergence of a "CID vote." While the nonprofit homeowners' association is ordinarily not allowed to get involved in partisan politics, there is nothing to prevent a CID from organizing or belonging to a political action committee, and such CID PACs already exist.

It seems inescapable that this development will have major impact on the shape of state and local politics. CIDs, with their unique brand of internal politics, have the potential to exacerbate the real conflict that is developing in many metropolitan areas between urban centers and their surrounding suburbs. Unemployment, inequality, crime, drug abuse — these are all easily seen as city problems for which the CID resident has no responsibility — social, financial, political or otherwise — except the responsibility for escaping them.

33

The Mallennium Factors: Mallcondo Continuum, Fortress of the Future, or, Where No Mall Has Gone Before*

William Severini Kowinski

All we know about the future is fiction. The generations after the marking of the millennium—the post-2001 world—are best dealt with in terms of scenarios and fictional but possible contexts. That the mall or its progeny will have a large part in a number of likely futures is my premise, and the conclusion I came to in my mall journeys and musings: One way or another, the millennium will be the mallennium.

The first and most often proffered fiction about the future is usually called "If Present Trends Continue," which is a scenario based on the assumption that certain elements of the present will predominate to form the character of the coming years. Right now the mall is in excellent position to be a major and defining part of such a pattern, since it is already interlocking with forms of housing, business, entertainment, and living that use its basic system of organization, as well as being compatible with its economic and cultural premises and implications.

Even now, the evidence is visible almost everywhere, in small towns, big cities, the wide swaths of suburbia and the fast-growing concentrations of the Sun Belt—all of them filling up with the same kinds of new enclosures, all connected by the same new electronic information and communications systems. It's the Mallcondo Continuum, and by 2001 it could be where America lives.

What so many of these new objects on the physical and social landscape have in common is their nature as controlled environments that separate themselves from the outside world in order to create an artificial internal world that is as self-sustaining and self-referential as possible. Sometimes it's the sense of total enclosure that's most obvious, as in the domed stadium (with artificial weather and artificial grass) that can be converted from a venue for one sport or amusement to another overnight. Sometimes it's the sense of variety under one roof, as in the multi-arts complexes found in cities and suburbs, which offer a shopping mall of culture. Or sometimes the combination of control and entertainment makes the resemblance to the

*Kowinski, William Severini. 1985. "The Mallennium Factors: Mallcondo Continuum, Fortress of the Future, or, Where No Mall Has Gone Before." Pp. 383–385 and 391–394 in *The Malling of America*. New York: William Morrow. Copyright © 1985 by William Severini Kowinski. Reprinted by permission of William Morrow and Company, Inc.

mall clearer, as in the new generation of theme amusement parks like Sea World, or their adult counterparts, like the Condado Beach Hotel In Puerto Rico, which advertises itself as a "self-contained resort world of beach, pool, nightclub, disco, cocktail lounges, casinos, shops and gardens," all with a Roaring Twenties theme.

The same basic mode of organization is also used in the form of housing known as the condominium, which provides living units within a unified, centrally managed complex. Like the mall, it exacts from its tenants a fee above the purchase price for providing common services and facilities—for security, landscaping, recreation, and community events. Like some malls, some condos have "themes," as senior-citizen or singles-only enclaves. Condo complexes not only seem to sprout naturally near malls, some malls build their own.

The next step in the theoretical and actual expansion of the mall/condo concept is the "new town" or planned community. In such communities the homeowner or renter is subject to rules set forth by central management under the supervision of a private corporation that controls the community's growth and common environment. In exchange for the generally high prices of the homes and these restraints (and the fees exacted for their administration), the town's ownership provides stability, safety, and amenities. New towns guarantee the living fantasy of a peaceful, steady-state small town, enclosed by walls of rules and money.

The planned community is the logical extension of the mall concept. Not altogether incidentally, then, some of them have been built or owned by mall developers, and many—including Irvine, California (the largest)— have a major shopping mall as their centerpiece.

These environments, from mall and condo to theme park and planned town, are popular because they are economical castles that protect against the unwanted outside of soot and strife and uncertainty while providing efficient fantasy worlds inside. . . .

In an era of unparalleled prosperity and enlightenment, our society has still failed to eradicate poverty and racism, and America's cities still contain tinderboxes of wasted lives, nurseries of violence, breeding grounds for a subculture of potential killers whose survival depends on their remorselessness. Vast numbers of the world's people are starving; the only access to the modern age some of them have is to modern weapons.

The end of the first millennium—the year 1000—saw the dawn of the Dark Ages in Europe, a long period of widening disorganization after the Roman Empire collapsed and the waves of Germanic and Moslem conquests destroyed the patterns of European culture. Cities, towns, and villages fell into ruin and disappeared; fields went uncultivated, famine spread, and wolves and other wild animals roamed freely, as did the highwaymen who preyed upon travelers. Violence, from organized warfare to frequent random murder, ruled the bleak landscape. Government was nearly nonexistent and the monetary system disintegrated. For a while, even the measuring of time was lost.

The year 1000 began with portents and terrors: a comet hanging in the sky for months, and then earthquakes that set off widespread hysteria and panic. The millennial sense we have as the year 2000 approaches could find even more justification: global terrorism, nuclear blackmail, the vengeance of the Greenhouse Effect, the awful start of the Nuclear Winter, or simply another earthquake—the giant quake overdue in California along the San Andreas fault and in the Midwest and part of the East affected by the even larger New Madrid fault. If centered in a major city, a world information and financial center like Chicago or especially Los Angeles, such a major quake would send shock waves through the American and world economy that could cause incalculable changes in our way of life, as well as possibly devastating our national psyche. Or catastrophe could begin more quietly, with financial crisis and the collapse of an aging infrastructure and damaged ecology we can no longer afford to fix.

Once disorganization begins, history shows, it can feed on itself until it becomes chaos. Then it is a long way back to organization again. When this happened in the eleventh century, there arose a new system—feudalism— and a new institution, the feudal castles, fortresses against the wilderness which created small societies within themselves. Similarly protected enclosures, such as the monasteries and later the walled towns, became the only continuity; they saved the remnants of the old culture and served as the incubator of the new.

In such an apocalyptic future, the dour role of the mall might well be the same as that of those castles. For the malls are already becoming the citadels of our time, fortresses protecting the dream worlds of our culture. The vicissitudes of nature and urban life have already driven some malls underground. Huge multilevel shopping centers have been built underneath several earthquake-endangered cities in Japan. Toronto has several large underground malls connected by almost two miles of passage ways. Toronto's planning and development commissioner worried that citizens might forsake the aboveground streets altogether, "except for a few brave souls dashing between buildings from urban fort to urban fort under the eye of skyscraper security guards."

Although most malls, including those underground, are obviously fortresslike, the resemblance is strongest in Southern California, where the malls along the freeways are very similar to the castle complexes of the Carolingian period, complete with walls and defensible perimeters as well as their own flags and coat-of-arms insignia. Even the mall's organizational system is similar to the feudal model: Instead of lords' distributing land among vassals who paid the lord in food, service, and loyalty in exchange for the castle's protection, the mall distributes space among tenants who pay the manager with money and obedience to the mall rules for the privilege of being inside the mall and not out in the unprofitable wilderness. Like the feudal tenants who bore the cost of the castle's court and the lord's army, the mall tenants pay for the mall's courts, the officers of marketing, and the foot soldiers of maintenance and security.

Whether or not apocalypse accompanies the millennium, it's clear that malls are the castles of our own prosperous but anxious times. As fortresses against a perilous present and the prospect of a disintegrating future, the malls expressed our fears in feudal images. Many of our fictions posit the aftermath of apocalypse in feudal terms, from the futuristic highwaymen in such films as *Road Warrior* to the industrial lord ensconced in his impregnable high-rise castle amid the bleak high-tech slum that Los Angeles has become in *Blade Runner*; and the Duke of New York, who rules a domain of broken streets and demented subjects from his fortress in the public library in *Escape from New York.*

But no fiction so far has taken into account the ready-made qualities of the mall as the model for the new feudalism. Such a text might not appear until the language has been slightly transformed by the heirs of James Joyce, John Lennon, and Russell Hoban's *Riddley Walker*, and discovered in a surviving cassette from a seminar conducted by a traveling video minstrel in the post-apocalyptic future. . . .

To the Mallgather I'm telling to you, this is my learnings with respect to the Lurd of this Mall. In the Beforetimes, in the High Dollar Deis, malls was places of cargathers and hot kultourism, and all was shopping to the muzak sinfunnies of GasHave Maller.

Then come the Betweentimes, the Final Dollar Deis, when affinity gropes attacked with Big Bucks to take over Malls for theirsown. Some of these Great Malls were called Secular Humanism Esplanade, Moral Majorette Phamly Plaza, Big Survivorist Center, and oft in the Holy Wood Hills was the Gestalt Mall. Them was the days of the first Panic Wars that brut down the great Amerry-cannan empyre.

Now we who owe feelty to the Duke of Orange and are under his portection here at the Great Mall of Orange soon will be in wretchous battle with the forces of the Archbiship of Westminster Mall, fighting for free ways and just us.

Our lifes is hard, scrapping by and struggles to put mcdonalds on the table. In the Beforetimes people like us owned their own hojoinns, one per phamly. Now we lifes togather in the one holy Mall, but we are the lucky ones. At least we life in the End 'O Sungo Land (called Californica in the Beforetimes) in the ferdle feels of jolly green, the Beach and the Whether. We still Have a Good Day. Not like the terrorble Panic Wars of the High Walls in the big sities, all acros the Sunbolt and worst of all in the sities of the East Cost, wherre as our minstrel cassetters tell us, men and beest cannot be told apart as they forage in the avanews and undergrind, and horrorble Genesters from demento labs roam the broken ramps and cleverleaves.

Fer sure, we have the wolfpacks and kyotes comin down from the hills, and the freewaymen robbin us, but we are lucky because we live in the Great Mall, where the Wall portect us, and we have the Warmth and Stuff inside. After the fal de rol, isn't the Mall the winner of our disconnect?

Central City Regimes

34
The New Machine

Theodore J. Lowi

. . . New York city government, like government in almost all large American cities except Chicago, is a product of Reform. It is difficult to understand these cities without understanding the two strains of ideology that guided local Reform movements throughout the past three-quarters of a century. *Populism* and *efficiency*, once the foundations of most local insurgency, are now, except in rare holdout cases like Chicago, triumphant. These two tenets are now the orthodoxy in local practice.

Populism was originally a statement of the evils of every form of bigness and scale in the city, including big business, big churches, and big labor as well as big political organizations. Decentralization was an ultimate goal. In modern form it has tended to come down to the charge to eliminate political parties, partisanship, and, if possible, politics itself.

Efficiency provided the positive program to replace what populist surgery excised. The doctrine calls essentially for a new form of centralization; that is, centralization and rationalization of government activities and services to accompany the decentralization of power. Some assumed that services do not constitute power. Others assumed the problem away altogether by defining a neutral civil servant who would not abuse centralized government but could use it professionally to reap the economies of scale and specialization. That was the secret of the business system; and, after all, the city is rather like a business. ("There is no Republican or Democratic way to clean a street.")

While there are many inconsistent assumptions and goals between these

*Lowi, Theodore J. 1968. "Gosnell's Chicago Revisited via Lindsay's New York." Pp. 7–16 in *Machine Politics: Chicago Model*, ed. Harold F. Gosnell. Chicago: The University of Chicago Press. Copyright © 1968 by The University of Chicago Press. Reprinted by permission of Theodore J. Lowi and The University of Chicago Press.

two doctrines, they lived well together. Their coexistence was supported by the fact that different wings of this large, progressive movement were responsible for each. Populism was largely the province of the working-class, "progressive" wing. Doctrines of efficiency were very much the responsibility of the upper-class wing. Populism resided with the politician-activists. Efficiency was developed by the intellectuals, including several distinguished university presidents, such as Seth Low, Andrew Dickson White, Harold Dodd, and, preeminently, Woodrow Wilson, who wrote a classic essay while still a professor of political science proclaiming the virtues of applying Prussian principles of administration in the United States.

These two great ideas were, by a strange and wonderful chemistry, combined into a movement whose influence is a major chapter of American history. Charters and laws have consistently insulated government from politics (meaning party politics). It became increasingly necessary with each passing decade to grant each bureaucratic agency autonomy to do the job as its professional commissioner saw fit.

On into the 1960's the merit system extends itself "upward, outward and downward," to use the Reformers' own dialectic. Recruitment to the top posts comes more and more often from the ranks of lifetime careerists in the agencies, party backgrounds increasingly signifying automatic disqualification. Reform has succeeded in raising the level of public morality and in making politics a dirty word. "Good press" for mayors consists of a determination to avoid intervening in the affairs of one department after another. The typical modern mayor is probably eager to cooperate, because this is a release from responsibility. Absolution-before-the-fact has become part of the swearing-in ceremony.

Reform has triumphed, and the cities are better run than ever before. But that, unfortunately, is not the end of the story, nor would it have been even without a Negro revolution. The triumph of Reform really ends in paradox: Cities like New York are now *well run but ungoverned.*

Politics under Reform is not abolished. Only its form is altered. *The legacy of Reform is the bureaucratic state.* Destruction of the party foundation of the mayoralty cleaned up many cities but also destroyed the basis for sustained, central, popularly based action. This capacity, with all its faults, was replaced by professionalized agencies. But this has meant creation of new bases of power. Bureaucratic agencies are not neutral, they are only independent. The bureaucrat may be more efficient and rational and honest than the old amateur. But he is no less political. If anything, he is more political because of the enormously important decisions so willingly entrusted to his making.

Modernization in New York and other modern cities has meant replacement of Old Machines with New Machines. The bureaucracies—that is, the professionally organized, autonomous career agencies—are the New Machines.

Sociologically, the Old Machine was a combination of rational goals and fraternal loyalty. The cement of the organization was trust and discipline created out of long years of service, probation and testing, slow promotion through the ranks, and centralized control over the means of reward. Its power in the community was based upon services rendered.

Sociologically, the New Machine is almost exactly the same sort of organization. There are more New Machines in any given city. They are functional rather than geographic in their scope. They rely on formal authority rather than upon majority acquiescence. And they probably work with a minimum of graft and corruption. But these differences do not alter their definition; they only help to explain why the New Machine is such a successful form of organization.

The New Machines are machines because they are relatively irresponsible structures of power. That is, each agency shapes important public policies, yet the leadership of each is relatively self-perpetuating and not readily subject to the controls of any higher authority.

The New Machines are machines in that the power of each, while resting ultimately upon services rendered to the community, depends upon its cohesiveness as a small minority in the midst of the vast dispersion of the multitude.

The modern city is now well run but ungoverned because it now comprises islands of functional power before which the modern mayor stands impoverished.[1] No mayor of a modern city has predictable means of determining whether the bosses of the New Machines—the bureau chiefs and the career commissioners—will be loyal to anything but their agency, its work, and related professional norms. Our modern mayor has been turned into the likeness of a French Fourth Republic premier facing an array of intransigent parties in the National Assembly. The plight of the mayor, however, is worse: at least the premier could resign. These modern machines, more monolithic by far than their ancient brethren, are entrenched by law and are supported by tradition, the slavish loyalty of the newspapers, the educated masses, the dedicated civic groups, and, most of all, by the organized clientele groups enjoying access under existing arrangements.

The Reform response to the possibility of an inconsistency between running a city and governing it would be based upon the assumption of the Neutral Specialist, the bureaucratic equivalent to law's Rational Man. The assumption is that if men know their own specialties well enough they are capable of reasoning out solutions to problems they share with men of equal but different technical competencies. That is a very shaky assumption indeed. Charles Frankel's analysis of such an assumption in Europe provides an appropriate setting for a closer look at it in modern New York: "[D]ifferent [technical] elites disagree with each other; the questions with which specialists deal spill over into areas where they are *not* specialists, and they must either hazard amateur opinions or ignore such larger issues, which is no better. . . ."[2]

During the 1950's government experts began to recognize that, despite vast increases in efficiency flowing from defeat of the machine, New York City government was somehow lacking. These concerns culminated in the

1961 Charter, in which the Office of Mayor was strengthened in many impressive ways. But it was quickly discovered that no amount of formal centralization could definitively overcome the real decentralization around the mayor. It was an organized decentralization, and it was making a mockery of the new Charter. The following examples, although drawn from New York, are virtually universal in their applicability:

1. Welfare problems always involve several of any city's largest agencies, including Health, Welfare, Hospitals, etc. Yet, for more than forty years, successive mayors of New York failed to reorient the Department of Health away from a regulative toward more of a service concept of organization.[3] And many new aspects of welfare must be set up in new agencies if they are to be set up at all. The new poverty programs were very slowly organized in all the big cities—except Chicago.[4]

2. Water pollution control has been "shared" by such city agencies as the Departments of Health, Parks, Public Works, Sanitation, Water Supply, and so on. No large city, least of all New York, has an effective program to combat even the local contributions to pollution. The same is true of air pollution control, although for some years New York has had a separate department for such purposes.

3. Land-use patterns are influenced in one way or another by a large variety of highly professional agencies. It has proved virtually impossible in any city for any one of these agencies to impose its criteria on the others. In New York the opening of Staten Island by the Narrows Bridge, in what may be the last large urban frontier, found the city with no plan for the revolution of property values and land uses in that Borough.

4. Transportation is also the province of agencies too numerous to list. Strong mayors throughout the country have been unable to prevent each agency from going its separate way. For just one example, New York pursued a vast off-street parking program, at a cost of nearly $4,000 per parking space, at the very moment when local rail lines were going bankrupt.

5. Enforcement of civil rights is imposed upon almost all city agencies by virtue of federal, state, and local legislation. Efforts to set up public, then City Council review of police processes in New York have been successfully opposed by professional police officials. Efforts to try pairing and busing of school children on a very marginal, experimental basis have failed. The police commissioner resigned at the very suggestion that values other than professional police values be imposed upon the Department, even when the imposition came via the respect tradition of "legislative oversight." The superintendent of education, an outsider, was forced out. He was replaced by a career administrator. One education journalist at that time said: "Often . . . a policy proclaimed by the Board [of Education], without the advice and consent of the professionals, is quickly turned into mere paper policy. . . . The veto power through

passive resistance by professional administrators is virtually unbeatable. . . ."

The decentralization of city government toward its career bureaucracies has resulted in great efficiency for the activities around which each bureaucracy was organized. The city is indeed well run. But what of those activities around which bureaucracies are not organized, or those which fall between or among agencies' jurisdictions? For these, as suggested by the cases above, the cities are suffering either stalemate or elephantitis—an affliction whereby a particular activity, say urban renewal or parkways, gets pushed to its ultimate success totally without regard to its balance against the missions of other agencies. In these as well as in other senses, the cities are ungoverned.

Mayors have tried a variety of strategies to cope with these situations. But the 1961 mayoral election in New York is the ultimate dramatization of their plight. This election was confirmation of the New York system in the same way the 1936 election was confirmation of Gosnell's Chicago. The 1961 New York election will some day be seen as one of the most significant elections in American urban history. For New York it was the culmination of many long-run developments. For the country it may be the first of many to usher in the bureaucratic state.

The primary significance of the election can be found in the spectacle of a mayor attempting to establish a base of power for himself in the bureaucracies. The mayor's "organization" included the following persons: his running mate for president of the City Council had been commissioner of sanitation, a position which culminated virtually a lifetime career in the Department of Sanitation. He had an impressive following among the sanitation workers, who, it should be added, are organized along precinct lines. The mayor's running mate for comptroller had been for many years the city budget director. As a budget official he had survived several administrations and two vicious primaries pitting factions of the Democratic Party against one another. Before becoming director he had served a number of years as a professional employee in the Bureau. The leaders of the campaign organization included a former, very popular fire commissioner who retired from his commissionership to accept campaign leadership and later to serve as deputy mayor; it also included a former police commissioner who had enjoyed a strong following among professional cops as well as in the local Reform movement. Added to this was a new and vigorous party, the Brotherhood Party, which was composed in large part of unions with broad bases of membership among city employees. Before the end of the election most of the larger city bureaucracies had political representation in the inner core of the new Administration.

For the 1961 election Mayor Wagner had put his ticket and his organization together just as the bosses of old had put theirs together. In the old days the problem was to mobilize all the clubhouses, districts, and counties in the city by putting together a balanced ticket about which all adherents could be enthusiastic. The same seems true for 1961, except that by then the clubhouses and districts had been replaced almost altogether by new types of units.

The main point is that destruction of the machine did not, in New York or elsewhere, elevate the city into some sort of political heaven. Reform did not eliminate the need for political power. It simply altered what one had to do to get it. In the aftermath of twenty or more years of modern government it is beginning to appear that the lack of power can corrupt city hall almost as much as the possession of power. Bureaucracy is, in the United States, a relatively new basis of collective action. As yet none of us knows quite what to do about it.

These observations and cases are not supposed to indict Reform cities and acquit Chicago. They are intended only to put Chicago in a proper light and to provide some experimental means of assessing the functions of the machine form of collective action. Review of Reform government shows simply and unfortunately that the problems of cities, and the irrational and ineffectual ways city fathers go about their business, seem to be universally distributed without regard to form of government or type of power base.

All cities have traffic congestion, crime, juvenile delinquency, galloping pollution, ghettos, ugliness, deterioration, and degeneracy. All cities seem to be suffering about equally with the quite recent problems of the weakening legitimacy of public objects, resulting in collective violence and pressures for direct solution to problems. All cities seem equally hemmed in by their suburbs and equally prevented from getting at the roots of many of their most fundamental problems. Nonpartisan approaches, even approaches of New York's Republican mayor to Republican suburbs and a Republican governor, have failed to prevent rail bankruptcy in the vast Eastern megalopolis, to abate air or water pollution, to reduce automobile pressure, or to ease the pain of the middle-class Negro in search of escape.

The problems of the city seem to go beyond any of the known arrangements for self-government. However, low morality and lack of what Banfield and Wilson call "public-regardingness" may be a function simply of mass pressure, poor education, and ethnic maladjustment. The old machine and its abuses may have been just another reflection of the same phenomena. If that is so, then the passage of more time and the mounting of one sociocultural improvement after another might have reformed the machines into public-regarding organs, if they had not been first too much weakened to be repaired.

NOTES

1. Compare Wallace Sayre and Herbert Kaufman, *Governing New York City* (New York: Russell Sage, 1960), pp. 710 ff.

2. Charles Frankel, "Bureaucracy and Democracy in the New Europe," *Daedalus* (Winter, 1964), p. 487.

3. Sayre and Kaufman, *op. cit.*, p. 274.

4. Compare Paul Peterson, unpublished doctoral dissertation, University of Chicago, 1967.

35
Political Interests and Urban Economic Growth*

John R. Logan and Harvey L. Molotch

THE ORGANIZATION OF THE GROWTH COALITION

The people who use their time and money to participate in local affairs are the ones who—in vast disproportion to their representation in the population—have the most to gain or lose in land-use decisions. Local business people are the major participants in urban politics (Walton, 1970), particularly business people in property investing, development, and real estate financing (Spaulding, 1951; Mumford, 1961). Peterson (1981:132), who applauds growth boosterism, acknowledges that "such policies are often promulgated through a highly centralized decision-making process involving prestigious businessmen and professionals. Conflict within the city tends to be minimal, decision-making processes tend to be closed." Elected officials, says Stone (1984:292), find themselves confronted by "a business community that is well-organized, amply supplied with a number of deployable resources, and inclined to act on behalf of tangible and ambitious plans that are mutually beneficial to its own members."

Business people's continuous interaction with public officials (including supporting them through substantial campaign contributions) gives them *systemic* power (Alford and Friedland, 1975; Stone, 1981, 1982). Once organized they stay organized. They are "mobilized interests" (Fainstein, Fainstein, and Armistead, 1983:214). Rentiers need local government in their daily moneymaking routines, especially when structural speculations are involved. They are assisted by lawyers, syndicators, and property brokers (Bouma, 1962), who prosper as long as they can win decisions favoring their

*Logan, John R., and Harvey L. Molotch. 1987. "Political Interests and Urban Economic Growth." Pp. 62–82 in *Urban Fortunes: The Political Economy of Place.* Berkeley: The University of California Press. Copyright © 1987 by The Regents of The University of California. Reprinted by permission of The University of California Press.

clients. Finally, there are monopolistic business enterprises (such as the local newspaper) whose futures are tied to the growth of the metropolis as a whole, although they are not directly involved in land use. When the local market is saturated with their product, they have few ways to increase profits, beyond expansion of their surrounding area. As in the proverbial Springdale, site of the classic Vidich and Bensman (1960:216) ethnography of a generation ago, there is a strong tendency in most cities for "the professionals (doctors, teachers, dentists, etc.), the industrial workers, the shack people and the lower middle-class groups [to be] for all intents and purposes disenfranchised except in terms of temporary issues."

Because so much of the growth mobilization effort involves government, local growth elites play a major role in electing local politicians, "watchdogging" their activities, and scrutinizing administrative detail. Whether in generating infrastructural resources, keeping peace on the home front, or using the city mayor as an "ambassador to industry" (Wyner, 1967), local government is primarily concerned with increasing growth. Again, it is not the only function of local government, but it is the key one.

In contrast to our position, urban social scientists have often ignored the politics of growth in their work, even when debates over growth infrastructures were the topic of their analyses (see Banfield, 1961; Dahl, 1961). Williams and Adrian (1963) at least treat growth as an important part of the local political process, but give it no priority over other government issues. There are a number of reasons why growth politics is consistently undervalued. The clue can be found in Edelman's (1964) distinction between two kinds of politics.

The first is the "symbolic" politics of public morality and most of the other "big issues" featured in the headlines and editorials of the daily press: school prayer, wars on crime, standing up to communism, and child pornography, for example. News coverage of these issues may have little to do with any underlying reality, much less a reality in which significant local actors have major stakes. Fishman (1978) shows, for example, that reports of a major crime wave against the elderly in New York City appeared just at a time when most crimes against the elderly were actually on the decline. The public "crime wave" was created by police officials who, in responding to reporters' interest in the topic, provided "juicy" instances that would make good copy. The "crime wave" was sustained by politicians eager to denounce the perpetrators, and these politicians' pronouncements became the basis for still more coverage and expressions of authoritative police concern. Once this symbiotic "dance" (Molotch, 1980) is in motion, the story takes on a life of its own, and fills the pages and airwaves of news media. Such symbolic crusades provide the "easy news" (Gordon, Heath, and leBailly, 1979) needed by reporters pressed for time, just these crusades satisfy the "news needs" (Molotch and Lester, 1974) of politicians happy to stay away from issues that might offend growth machine interests. The resulting hubbubs often mislead the general public as well as the academic investigator about what the real stuff of community cleavage and political process might be. To the degree that rentier elites keep growth issues on a symbolic level (for example, urban "greatness"), they prevail as the "second face of power" (Bachrach and Baratz, 1962), the face that determines the public agenda (McCombs and Shaw, 1972).

Edelman's second kind of politics, which does not provide easy news, involves the government actions that affect the distribution of important goods and services. Much less visible to publics, often relegated to back rooms or negotiations within insulated authorities and agencies (Caro, 1974; Friedland, Piven, and Alford, 1978), this is the politics that determines who, in material terms, gets what, where, and how (cf. Lasswell, 1936). The media tend to cover it as the dull round of meetings of water and sewer districts, bridge authorities, and industrial development bonding agencies. The media attitude serves to keep interesting issues away from the public and blunt widespread interest in local politics generally. As Vidich and Bensman (1960:217) remark about Springdale, "business control rests upon a dull but unanimous political facade," at least on certain key issues.

Although there are certainly elite organizational mechanisms to inhibit them (Domhoff, 1971, 1983; Whitt, 1982), cleavages within the growth machine can nevertheless develop, and internal disagreements sometimes break into the open. But even then, because of the hegemony of the growth machine, *its* disagreements are allowable and do not challenge the belief in growth itself. Unacceptable are public attacks on the pursuit of exchange values over citizens' search for use value. An internal quarrel over where a convention center is to be built, Banfield (1961) shows us, becomes the public issue for Chicago; but Banfield didn't notice that there was no question about whether there should be a convention center at all.

When elites come to see, for example, that inadequate public services are repelling capital investment, they can put the issue of raising taxes on the public agenda. Trillin (1976:154) reports on Rockford, Illinois, a city whose school system was bankrupted by an antitax ideology. Initially, local elites opposed taxes as part of their efforts to lure industry through a low tax rate. As a result, taxes and therefore tax money for schools, declined. Eventually, the growth coalition saw the educational decline, not the tax rate, as the greatest danger to the "economic vitality of the community." But ironically, elites are not able to change overnight the ideologies they have put in place over decades, even when it is in their best interests to do so.[1] Unfortunately, neither can the potential *opponents* of growth. As the example of Rockford shows, even such issues as public school spending can become subject to the growth maximization needs of locality. The appropriate level of a social service often depends, not on an abstract model of efficiency or on "public demand" (cf. Tiebout, 1956), but on whether the cost of that service fits the local growth strategy (past and present).

By now it should be clear how political structures are mobilized to intensity land uses for private gain of many sorts. Let us look more closely, therefore, at the various local actors, besides those directly involved in generating rents, who participate in the growth machine.

Politicians

The growth machine will sustain only certain persons as politicians. The campaign contributions and public celebrations that build political careers do not ordinarily come about because of a person's desire to save or destroy the environment, to repress or liberate the blacks or other disadvantaged groups, to eliminate civil liberties or enhance them. Given their legislative power, politicians may end up doing any of these things. But the underlying politics that gives rise to such opportunities is a person's participation in the growth consensus. That is why we so often see politicians springing into action to attract new capital and to sustain old investments. Even the pluralist scholar Robert Dahl observed in his New Haven study that if an employer seriously threatened to leave the community, "political leaders are likely to make frantic attempts to make the local situation more attractive" (quoted in Swanstrom, 1981:50).

Certainly, politicians differ in a number of ways. Like Mayor Ogden of Chicago, some are trying to create vast fortunes for themselves as they go about their civic duties on behalf of the growth machine. Robert Folson, the mayor of Dallas, has direct interests in over fifty local businesses, many of which have stakes in local growth outcomes. When the annexation of an adjacent town came up for a vote, he had to abstain because he owned 20 percent of it (Fullinwider, 1980). Another Texan, former governor, John Connally, has among his holdings more than $50 million in Austin-area real estate, property slated to become its county's largest residential and commercial development ("Austin Boom," *Santa Barbara News Press*, June 24, 1984, p. B-8). According to Robert Caro (1974), Commissioner Robert Moses was able to overcome opposition to his vast highway and bridge building in the New York City area in part because the region's politicians were themselves buying up land adjacent to parkway exits, setting themselves up for huge rent gains. Most of Hawaii's major Democrat politicians, after winning election on a reform platform in 1954, directly profited as developers, lawyers, contractors, and investors through the zoning and related land-use decisions they and their colleagues were to make over the next thirty years of intensive growth and speculation (Daws and Cooper, 1984). Machine politics never insulated candidates from the development process; builders, railroaders, and other growth activists have long played crucial roles in boss politics, both in immigrant wards (Bell, 1961) and in WASP suburbs (Fogelson, 1967:207). All this is, as George Washington Plunkitt said in 1905, "honest graft" as opposed to "dishonest graft" (quoted in Swanstrom, 1985:25).[2]

Although a little grease always helps a wheel to turn, a system can run well with no graft at all—unless using campaign contributions to influence elections is considered graft. Virtually all politicians are dependent on private campaign financing (Alexander, 1972, 1980, 1983; Boyarsky and Gillam, 1982; Smith, 1984), and it is the real estate entrepreneurs—particularly the large-scale structural speculators—who are particularly active in supporting candidates (see chapter 6 for additional documentation). The result is that candidates of both parties, of whatever ideological stripe, have to garner the favor of such persons, and this puts them squarely into the hands of growth machine coalitions. Thus many officeholders use their authority, not to enrich themselves, but to benefit the "whole community" — that is, to increase aggregate rents. Again, this does not preclude politicians' direct participation in property dealing on occasion and it certainly does not preclude giving a special hand to particular place entrepreneurs with whom a politician has a special relationship.

Elected officials also vary in their perception of how their authority can best be used to maximize growth. After his thorough study of the Cleveland growth machine, Swanstrom (1985) concluded that there are two types of growth strategists: the "conservative" and the "liberal." The former, paramount during the city's age of steel, favor unbridled exploitation of the city and its labor force, generally following the "free economy" political model. Programs of overt government intervention, for purposes of planning, public education, or employee welfare, are all highly suspect. The liberal growth machine strategy, in contrast, acknowledges that longer-term growth can be facilitated by overt government planning and by programs that pacify, coopt, and placate oppositions. This is a more modern form of growth ideology. Some politicians, depending on place and time, tend to favor the hard-line "unfettered capitalism" (Wolfe, 1981); others prefer the liberal version, analogous to what is called, in a broader context, "pragmatic state capitalism" (Wolfe, 1981; see also Weinstein, 1968). These positions became more obvious in many regions when urban renewal and other federal programs began penetrating cities in the postwar period. Especially in conservative areas such as Texas (Melosi, 1983:185), elites long debated among themselves whether or not the newfangled growth schemes would do more harm than good.

On the symbolic issues, politicians may also differ, on both the content of their positions and the degree to which they actually care about the issues. Some are no doubt sincere in pushing their "causes"; others may cynically manipulate them to obscure the distributional consequences of their own actions in other matters. Sometimes the results are positive, for example, when Oklahoma City and Dallas leaders made deliberate efforts to prevent racist elements from scaring off development with "another Little Rock." Liberal growth machine goals may thus help reform reactionary social patterns (Bernard, 1983:225; Melosi, 1983:188). But despite these variations, there appears to be a "tilt" to the whole system, regardless of time and place. Growth coalition activists and campaign contributors are not a culturally, racially, or economically diverse cross section of the urban population. They tend to give a reactionary texture to local government, in which the cultural crusades, like the material ones, are chosen for their acceptability to the rentier groups. Politicians adept in both spheres (material and symbolic) are the most valued, and most likely to have successful careers. A skilled politician delivers growth while giving a good circus.

The symbolic political skills are particularly crucial when unforeseen circumstances create use value crises, which can potentially stymie a locality's basic growth strategy. The 1978 Love Canal toxic waste emergency at Niagara Falls, New York, reveals how local officials use their positions to reassure the citizens and mold local agendas to handle disruptive "emotional" issues. In her detailed ethnographic account, Levine (1982:59) reports that "the city's chief executives, led by the mayor, minimized the Love Canal problem in all public statements for two years no matter how much personal sympathy they felt for the affected people whose health was threatened by the poisons leaking into their homes" (see also Fowlkes and Miller, 1985). Lester (1971) reports a similar stance taken by the Utah civic leadership in response to the escape of nerve gas from the U.S. military's Dugway Proving Grounds in 1969 (see also Hirsch, 1969). The conduct of politicians in the face of accidents like the leakage of poison into schoolyards and homes in Niagara Falls or the sheep deaths in Utah reveal this "backup" function of local leaders (Molotch and Lester, 1974, 1975).

Still another critical use of local politicians is their ability to influence higher-level political actors in their growth distribution decisions. Although capital has direct links to national politicians (particularly in the executive office and Senate, see Domhoff [1967, 1970, 1983]), rentier groups are more parochial in their ties, although they may have contact with congressional representatives. Hence, rentiers need local politicians to lobby national officials. The national politicians, in turn, are responsive because they depend on local political operators (including party figures) for their own power base. The local politicians symbiotically need their national counterparts to generate the goods that keep them viable at home.

The goods that benefit the local leaders and growth interests are not trivial. The development of the Midwest was, as the historical anecdotes make clear, dependent on national decisions affecting canal and railroad lines. The Southwest and most of California could be developed only with federal subsidies and capital investments in water projects. The profound significance of government capital spending can be grasped by considering one statistic: Direct government outlays (at all levels) in 1983 accounted for nearly 27 percent of all construction in the United States (Mollenkopf, 1983:43). The figure was even higher, of course, during World War II, when federal construction expenditures laid the basis for much of the infrastructural and defense spending that was to follow.

Local Media

One local business takes a broad responsibility for general growth machine goals—the metropolitan newspaper. Most newspapers (small, suburban papers are occasionally an exception) profit primarily from increasing their circulation and therefore have a direct interest in growth.[3] As the metropolis expands, the newspaper can sell a larger number of ad lines (at higher per line cost), on the basis of a rising circulation base; TV and radio stations are in a similar situation. In explaining why this newspaper had supported the urbanization of orchards that used to cover what is now the city of San Jose, the publisher of the *San Jose Mercury News* said, "Trees do not read newspapers" (Downie, 1974:112, as cited in Domhoff, 1983:168). Just as newspaper boosterism was important in building the frontier towns (Dagenais, 1967), so today "the hallmark of media content has been peerless boosterism: congratulate growth rather than calculate consequences; compliment development rather than criticize its impact" (Burd, 1977:129; see also Devereux, 1976; Freidel, 1963). The media "must present a favorable image to outsiders" (Cox and Morgan, 1973:136),[4] and only "sparingly use their issue-raising capacities" (Peterson, 1981:124).

American cities tend to be one-newspaper (or one-newspaper company) towns. The newspaper's assets in physical plant, in "good will," and in advertising clients are, for the most part, immobile. The local newspaper thus tends to occupy a unique position: like many other local businesses, it has an interest in growth, but unlike most others, its critical interest is not in the specific spatial pattern of that growth. The paper may occasionally help forge a specific strategy of growth, but ordinarily it makes little difference to a newspaper whether the additional population comes to reside on the north side or the south side, or whether the new business comes through a new convention center or a new olive factory. The newspaper has no ax to grind except the one that holds the community elite together: growth.

This disinterest in the specific form of growth, but avid commitment to development generally, enables the newspaper to achieve a statesmanlike position in the community. It is often deferred to as a neutral party by the special interests. In his pioneering study of the creation of zoning laws in New York City in the 1920s, Makielski (1966:149) remarks, "While the newspapers in the city are large landholders, the role of the press was not quite like that of any of the other nongovernmental actors. The press was in part one of the referees of the rules of the game, especially the informal rules, calling attention to what it considered violations." The publisher or editor is often the arbiter of internal growth machine bickering, restraining the short-term profiteers in the interest of more stable, long-term, and properly planned growth.

The publishing families are often ensconced as the most important city builders within the town or city; this is the appropriate designation for such prominent families as Otis and Chandler of the *Los Angeles Times* (see Clark, 1983:271; Halberstam, 1979); Pulliam of the *Arizona Republic* and *Phoenix Sun* (see Luckingham, 1983:318); and Gaylord of the *Daily Oklahoman* (see Bernard, 1983:216). Sometimes these publishers are directly active in politics, "kingmaking" behind the scenes by screening candidates for political office, lobbying for federal contracts and grants, and striving to build growth infrastructure in their region (Fainstein, Fainstein, and Armistead, 1983:217; Judd, 1983:178). In the booming Contra Costa County suburbs of the San Francisco Bay Area, the president of the countywide organization of builders, real estate investors, and property financiers was the owner of the regional paper. In his home county, as well as in the jurisdictions of his eleven other suburban papers, owner Dean Lesher ("Citizen Lesher") acts as "a cheerleader for development" who simply kills stories damaging to growth interests and reassigns unsympathetic reporters to less controversial beats (Steidtmann, 1985). The local newspaper editor was one of the three "bosses" in Springdale's "invisible government" (Vidich and Bensman, 1960:217). Sometimes, the publisher is among the largest urban landholders and openly fights for benefits tied to growth in land: The owners of the *Los Angeles Times* fought for the water that developed their vast properties for both urban and agricultural uses. The editorial stance is usually reformist, invoking the common good (and technical planning expertise) as the rationale for the land-use decisions the owners favor. This sustains the legitimacy and the paper itself among all literate sectors of society and helps mask the distributive effects of many growth developments.

The media attempt to attain their goals not only through news articles and editorials but also through informal talks between owners and editors and the local leaders. Because newspaper interests are tied to growth, media executives are sympathetic to business leaders' complaints that a particular journalistic investigation or angle may be bad for the local business climate, and should it nevertheless become necessary, direct threats of advertising cancellation can modify journalistic coverage (Bernard, 1983:220). This does not mean that newspaper (or advertisers) control the politics of a city or region, but that the media have a special influence simply because they are committed to growth per se, and can play an invaluable role in coordinating strategy and selling growth to the public.

This institutional legitimacy is especially useful in crises. In the controversy surrounding the army's accidental release of nerve gas at the Dugway Proving Grounds, Lester found that the Utah media were far more sympathetic to the military's explanations than were media outside Utah (Lester, 1971). The economic utility of the Dugway Proving Grounds (and related government facilities) was valued by the local establishment. Similarly, insiders report that publicizing toxic waste problems at Love Canal was hindered by an "unwritten law" in the newsroom that "a reporter did not attack or otherwise fluster the Hooker [Chemical Company] executives" (Brown, 1979, cited in Levine, 1982:190).

As these examples indicate, a newspaper's essential role is not to protect a given firm or industry (an issue more likely to arise in a small city than a large one) but to bolster and maintain the predisposition for general growth. Although newspaper editorialists may express concern for "the ecology," this does not prevent them from supporting growth-inducing investments for their regions. The *New York Times* likes office towers and additional industrial installations in the city even more than it loves "the environment." Even when historically significant districts are threatened, the *Times* editorializes in favor of intensification. Thus the *Times* recently admonished opponents to "get out of the way" of the Times Square renewal, which would replace landmark structures (including its own former headquarters at 1

Times Square) with huge office structures (*New York Times*, May 24, 1984, p. 18). Similarly, the *Los Angeles Times* editorializes against narrow-minded profiteering that increases pollution or aesthetic blight—in other cities. The newspaper features criticism, for example, of the Times Square renewal plan (Kaplan, 1984:1), but had enthusiastically supported development of the environmentally devastating supersonic transport (SST) for the jobs it would presumably lure to Southern California. In an unexpected regional parallel, the *Los Angeles Times* fired celebrated architectural critic John Pastier for his incessant criticisms of Los Angeles's downtown renewal projects (Clark, 1983:298), and the *New York Times* dismissed Pulitzer Prize winner Sydney Schanberg as a columnist apparently because he "opposed civic projects supported by some of New York's most powerful interests, particularly those in the real estate industry" (Rosenstiel, 1985:21).

Although newspapers may openly support "good planning principles" of a certain sort, the acceptable form of "good planning" does not often extend to limiting growth or authentic conservation in a newspaper's home ground. "Good planning principles" can easily represent the opposite goals.

Utilities

Leaders of "independent" public or quasi-public agencies, such as utilities, may play a role similar to that of the newspaper publisher: tied to a single locale, they become growth "statesmen" rather than advocates for a certain type of growth or intralocal distribution of growth.

For example, a water-supplying agency (whether public or private) can expand only by acquiring more users. This causes utilities to penetrate deep into the hinterlands, inefficiently extending lines to areas that are extremely costly to service (Gaffney, 1961; Walker and Williams, 1982). The same growth goals exist within central cities. Brooklyn Gas was an avid supporter of the movement of young professionals into abandoned areas of Brooklyn, New York, in the 1970s, and even went so far as to help finance housing rehabilitation and sponsor a traveling slide show and open houses displaying the pleasant life styles in the area. All utilities seem bent on acquiring more customers to pay off past investments, and on proving they have the good growth prospects that lenders use as a criterion for financing additional investments. Overall efficiencies are often sacrificed as a result.

Transportation officials, whether of public or private organizations, have a special interest in growth: they tend to favor growth along their specific transit routes. But transportation doesn't just serve growth, it creates it. From the beginning, the laying-out of mass transit lines was a method of stimulating development; indeed, the land speculators and the executives of the transportation firms were often the same people. In part because of the salience of land development, "public service was largely incidental to the operation of the street railways" (Wilcox, quoted in Yago, 1983:44). Henry Huntington's Pacific Electric, the primary commuting system of Los Angeles, "was built not to provide transportation but to sell real estate" (Clark,

1983:272; see also Binford, 1985; Fogelson, 1967; Yago, 1983). And because the goal of profitable transportation did not guide the design and routing of the system, it was destined to lose money, leaving Los Angeles without a viable transit system in the end (Fogelson, 1967).

Transit bureaucrats today, although not typically in the land business, function as active development boosters; only in that way can more riders be found to support their systems and help pay off the sometimes enormous debts incurred to construct or expand the systems. On the national level, major airlines develop a strong growth interest in the development of their "hub" city and the network it serves. Eastern Airlines must have growth in Miami, Northwest Airlines needs development in Minneapolis, and American Airlines rises or falls with the fortunes of Dallas-Fort Worth.

AUXILIARY PLAYERS

Although they may have less of a stake in the growth process than the actors described above, certain institutions play an auxiliary role in promoting and maintaining growth. Key among these auxiliary players are the cultural institutions in an area: museums, theaters, universities, symphonies, and professional sports teams. An increase in the local population may help sustain these institutions by increasing the number of clients and support groups. More important, perhaps, is that such institutions often need the favor of those who are at the heart of local growth machines—the rentiers, media owners, and politicians, who can make or break their institutional goals. And indeed, cultural institutions do have something to offer in return.

Universities

The construction and expansion of university campuses can stimulate development in otherwise rural landscapes; the land for the University of California at Los Angeles (UCLA) was originally donated for a state normal school in 1881 "in order to increase the value of the surrounding real estate" (Clark, 1983:286). Other educational institutions, particularly the University of California campuses at Irvine and Santa Barbara, had similar origins, as did the State University of New York at Stony Brook and the University of Texas at San Antonio (Johnson, 1983), Building a university campus can be the first step in rejuvenating a deteriorated inner-city area; that was the case with the Chicago branch of the University of Illinois (Banfield, 1961), the expansions of Yale University in New Haven (Dahl, 1961; Domhoff, 1978), and the University of Chicago (Rossi and Dentler, 1961). The use of universities and colleges as a stimulus to growth is often made explicit by both the institution involved and the local civic boosters.

The symbiotic relationship between universities and local development intensified in the 1980s. Drawing on the precedent of Silicon Valley (with Stanford University as its intellectual center) and Route 128, the high-tech highway, in the Boston area (with MIT as its intellectual center), many localities have come to view universities as an infrastructure for cutting edge industrial growth. Universities, in turn, have been quick to exploit this opportunity to strengthen their local constituency. A clear illustration is the Microelectronics and Computer Technology Corporation (MCTC), a newly created private firm with the mission of keeping the United States ahead of Japan in the microelectronics field. Jointly funded by twelve of the most important American firms in advanced technology, the new company had to build, at its founding, a $100 million installation. Austin, Texas, won the project, but only after the local and state governments agreed to a list of concessions, including subsidized land, mortgage assistance for employees, and a score of faculty chairs and other positions at the University of Texas for personnel relevant to the company mission (Rivera, 1983a).

The Austin victory reverberated especially through California, the location of the runner-up site. A consensus emerged, bolstered by an MCTC official's explicit statement, that faltering support for California higher education had made Texas the preferred choice. The view that a decline in the quality of higher education could drive away business may have been important in the fiscally conservative governor's decision to substantially increase allocations to the University of California in the following year. Budget increases for the less research-oriented state college system were at a much lower level; the community college system received a decrease in real dollar funding. The second and third groups of institutions play a less important role in growth machine strategies. As the president of the University of Texas said after his institution's victory. "The battle for national leadership among states is being fought on the campuses of the great research universities of the nation" (King, 1985:12).

Museums, Theaters, Expositions

Art and the physical structures that house artworks also play a role in growth strategies. In New York City, the art capital of the country, the arts generate about $1.3 billion in annual economic activity, a sum larger than that contributed by either advertising or computer services (Pittas, 1984). In Los Angeles, another major art center, urban redevelopment funds are paying for the new Museum of Contemporary Art, explicitly conceived as a means of enhancing commercial success for adjacent downtown residential, hotel, and office construction. Major art centers are also being used as development leverage in downtown Miami, Tampa (Mormino, 1983:152), and Dallas. The new Dallas Museum of Art will be the central focus of "the largest downtown development ever undertaken in the United States" (Tomkins, 1983:92). Whatever it may do to advance the cause of artists in Texas, the museum will do much for nearby rents. According to a Dallas newspaper report, "The feeling persists that the arts have been appropriated here primarily to see massive real estate development" (quoted in Tomkins, 1983:97).

Other sorts of museums can be used for the same purpose. Three Silicon

Valley cities are locked in a battle to make themselves the site for a $90 million Technology Museum that "is expected to draw one million visitors a year, boost hotel occupancy and attract new business." (Sahagun and Jalon, 1984:1). Two of the competing cities (Mountain View and San Jose), in promising millions in subsidies, would use the museum as a focal point for major commercial developments. In a not dissimilar, though perhaps less highbrow effort, the city of Flint, Michigan ("the unemployment capital of America") invested city money in a Six Flags Auto World Theme Park that displayed cars (old and new) and used the auto as a motif for its other attractions. The facility was situated so as to boost the city's crumbling downtown; unhappily, gate receipts were poor and the park was closed, and the $70 million public-private investment was lost (Risen, 1984).

Theaters are also being used as a development tool. Believing that the preservation of the legitimate theater will help maintain the "vitality" of Midtown Manhattan, city officials are considering a plan to allow theater owners to sell the "development rights" of their properties, which the dense zoning in the theater district would otherwise permit. The buyer of these rights would then be allowed bonus, or greater, densities on other nearby sites, thereby protecting the theaters' existence while not blocking the general densification of the area (*New York Times*, September 19, 1983, p. 1). In many parts of the country, various individuals and groups are encouraging (and often subsidizing) the construction and rehabilitation of theaters and concert halls as growth instruments. Downtown churches are looking to the heavens for financial returns, arranging to sell air rights over their imposing edifices to developers of nearby parcels.

These programs allow cultural institutions, in effect, to collect rents they otherwise could gain only by tearing down their structures. The arrangement heads off any conflict between developers and those oriented to the use values that theaters and historic buildings might provide and helps to maintain these "city treasures" that help sustain the economic base. But aggregate levels of development are not curtailed.

Still another kind of cultural institution involved in the growth apparatus is the blue-ribbon committee that puts together local spectaculars, like annual festivals and parades, or a one-shot World's Fair or Olympics competition. These are among the common efforts by Chambers of Commerce and Visitors Bureaus to lure tourists and stimulate development. There are industrial expositions, music festivals, and all manner of regional annual attractions. Such events are considered ways of meeting short-term goals of generating revenue, as well as ways of meeting long-term goals of attracting outside businesses. They show off the locality to outsiders who could generate additional investments in the future. Los Angeles business leaders, for example, "created the Rose Parade to draw national attention to Southern California's balmy weather by staging an outdoor event with fresh flowers in the middle of winter" (Clark, 1983:271).

The short-term results of big events can mean billions of dollars injected into the local economy, although costs to ordinary citizens (in the form of traffic congestion, higher prices, and drains on public services) are notoriously understated (Clayton, 1984; Shlay and Gilroth, 1984). To help gain the necessary public subsidies for such events, the promoters insist that "the community" will benefit, and they inflate revenue expectations in order to make trickle-down benefits at least seem plausible (Hays, 1984). The 1983 Knoxville World's Fair, one of the few World's Fairs to actually produce a profit on its own books, nevertheless left its host city with $57 million in debts (Schmidt, 1984), a debt large enough to require an 8 percent increase in property taxes in order to pay it off. The 1984 New Orleans World's Fair showed a $100 million loss (Hill, 1984). Other spectaculars, like the Los Angeles Olympics, do come out ahead, but even so, certain costs (like neighborhood, disruption) are simply not counted.

Clearly, a broad range of cultural institutions, not often thought of in terms of land development, participate closely as auxiliary players in the growth process for many reasons. Some participate because their own organizational goals depend on local growth, others because they find it diplomatic to support the local rentier patrons, others because their own properties become a valuable resource, and still others because their boards of directors are closely tied to local elites. Whatever the reasons, the growth machine cuts a wide institutional swath.

Professional Sports

Professional sports teams are a clear asset to localities for the strong image they present and tourist traffic they attract (Eitzen and Sage, 1978:184). Baseball, the American pastime, had its beginning in amusement parks; many of the team owners were real estate speculators who used the team to attract visitors to the subdivisions they offered for sale. Fans would ride to the park on trolley lines that the team owner also owned (Roderick, 1984). In more recent years, baseball and football stadia and hockey and basketball arenas have been used by local *governments* to provide a focus for urban renewal projects in Pittsburgh, Hartford, Minneapolis, and other cities (Roderick, 1984). New Orleans used the development of the Superdome "to set the stage for a tourist-based growth strategy for the future development of downtown" (Smith and Keller, 1983:134). The facility ended up costing $165 million (instead of the projected $35 million), and has had large annual operating losses—all absorbed by the state government.

St. Petersburg, Florida, seems to be following the example of New Orleans. The Florida city has agreed to invest $59.6 million in a new stadium *in the hope* that it will lure a major league franchise to a city that woefully lacks the demographic profile necessary to support major league sports. So far the project has required displacement of four hundred families (primarily black) and saddled the city with a huge debt. A city official insists it will be worth it because

> When you consider what it would mean in new business for hotels, jobs, pride, tourism—then it's a real good deal. We believe for every dollar spent inside a stadium, seven are spent outside. [Roderick, 1984:24.]

In an even more dubious effort, the city of Albany, New York, gained popular support (and some state funding) for a $40 million multipurpose downtown civic center on the grounds that it *might* attract a hockey team to the city (D'Ambrosio, 1985). Like the New Orleans project, this plan puts sports boosters behind a project that will help local business with its other events (such as conventions), regardless of its success in attracting a professional team.

Local teams are an industry in themselves. Atlanta's professional sports organizations have been estimated to be worth over $60 million annually to the local economy (Rice, 1983:38). But a local team does much more than the direct expenditures imply: It helps a city's visibility, putting it "on the map" as a "big league city," making it more noticeable to all, including those making investment decisions. It is one of "the visible badges of urban maturity" (Rice, 1983:38). Within the city, sports teams have an important ideological use, helping instill civic pride in business through jingoistic logic. Whether the setting is soccer in Brazil (Lever, 1983) or baseball in Baltimore, millions of people are mobilized to pull for the home turf. Sports that lend themselves to boosting a locality are the useful ones. Growth activists are less enthusiastic about sports that honor individual accomplishment and are less easily tied to a locality or team name (for example, tennis, track, or swimming). Only when such sports connect with rent enhancement, for example, when they are part of an Olympic competition held on home ground, do they receive major support.

The mobilization of the audience is accomplished through a number of mechanisms. Money to construct stadia or to attract or retain the home team is raised through public bond issues. About 70 percent of current facilities were built with this tool, often under conditions of large cost overruns (Eitzen, 1978). Enthusiastic corporate sponsorship of radio and TV broadcasts greatly expands public participation (and by linking products with local heroes this form of sponsorship avoids any danger of involving the corporate image with controversial topics). Finally, the news media provide avid coverage, giving sports a separate section of the newspaper and a substantial block of broadcast time during the period designated for the news (including the mention of the city name on national news). No other single news topic receives such consistent and extensive coverage in the United States.

The coverage is, of course, always supportive of sports itself and the home team in particular. There is no pretense of objectivity. It is all part of the ideological ground for other civic goals, including the successful competition of cities for growth-inducing projects. Professional teams serve many latent social functions (Brower, 1972); sustaining the growth ideology is clearly one of them.

Organized Labor

Although they are sometimes in conflict with capitalists on other issues, labor union leaders are enthusiastic partners in growth machines, with little careful consideration of the long-term consequences for the rank and file. Union leadership subscribes to value-free development because it will "bring jobs," particularly to the building trades, whose spokespersons are especially vocal in their support of development. Less likely to be openly discussed is the concern that growth may bring more union members and enhance the power and authority of local union officials.[5]

Union executives are available for ceremonial celebrations of growth (ribbon cuttings, announcements of government contracts, urban redevelopment ground breakings). Entrepreneurs frequently enlist union support when value-free development is under challenge; when growth control was threatened in the city of San Diego in 1975, three thousand labor union members paraded through downtown, protesting land-use regulations they claimed were responsible for local unemployment (Corso, 1983:339). Labor leaders are especially useful when the growth machine needs someone to claim that development opponents are "elitist" or "selfish." Thus, in a characteristic report on a growth control referendum in the city of Riverside, California, Neiman and Loveridge (1981:764–65) found that the progrowth coalition "repeated, time and again, that most of organized labor in the area opposed Measure B, firms wishing to locate in Riverside were being frightened away . . . and thousands of voters would lose their jobs if Measure B passed." Although this technique apparently worked in Riverside at the polls and in San Diego in the streets, it is doubtful that the majority of the rank and file share the disposition of their leaders on these issues (a point to be documented in chapter 6). Nevertheless, the entrepreneurs' influence over the public statements and ceremonial roles of union leaders, regardless of what their members think, helps the rentiers in achieving their aggressive growth policies.

The co-optation of labor leadership is again evident in its role in national urban policy. Labor essentially is a dependable support of growth—anywhere, anytime. Although its traditional constituency is centered in the declining areas of the country, the unions' national hierarchy supports policies little more specific than those that provide "aid to the cities." The active campaign by the United Auto Workers (UAW) for increased investment in Detroit and other sections of the country's "automotive realm" (Hill, 1984) is an exception. Although unions may be especially concerned with the future of the declining areas, they have not tried to develop an effective strategy for directing investment toward these places, at the expense of other places. Labor cannot serve the needs of its most vulnerable and best organized geographical constituency because it won't inhibit investment at any given place. The inability of labor to influence the distribution of development within the United States (much less across world regions) makes organized labor helpless in influencing the political economy of places. Labor becomes little more than one more instrument to be used by elites in competing growth machines.

NOTES

1. Trillin remarks that rejection of high taxes by the citizens of Rockford is "consistent with what the business and industrial leadership of Rockford has traditionally preached. For years, the industrialists were considered to be in complete control of the sort of local government industrialists traditionally favor—a conservative, relatively clean administration committed to the proposition that the highest principle of government is the lowest property tax rate" (Trillin, 1976: 150).

2. Local planning officials also sometimes get in on some of the corruption; they may make real estate investments of their own. Los Angeles Planning Director Calvin Hamilton was pressured to resign after twenty years on the job in part because of revelations that he accepted free rent from developers for a side business and had other conflicts of interest (Clifford, 1985d).

3. Although many suburban newspapers encourage growth, especially of tax-generating businesses, the papers of exclusive suburban towns may instead try to guard the existing land-use patterns and social base of their circulation area. Rudel (1983:104) describes just this sort of situation in Westport, Connecticut. There are a number of reasons for this occasional deviation from the rule we are proposing. When trying to attract advertising dollars, newspapers prefer a small, rich readership to a larger but poorer one. Maintaining exclusivity is itself occasionally a growth strategy for smaller communities. Opposition to growth in these cases is consistent with the desires of local elites.

4. Cox and Morgan's study of British local newspapers indicates that the booster role of the press is not unique to the United States.

5. Unions oppose growth projects that bring nonunion shops; the UAW did not welcome Japanese-owned auto plants that would exclude the union.

REFERENCES

Alexander, Herbert E. 1972. *Money in Politics.* Washington, D.C.: Public Affairs Press.

Alexander, Herbert. 1980. *Financing Politics: Money, Elections and Political Reform.* 2nd ed. Washington, D.C.: Congressional Quarterly Press.

Alexander, Herbert, 1983. *Financing the 1980 Election.* Lexington, Mass.: D. C. Heath.

Alford, Robert, and Roger Friedland. 1975. "Political Participation and Public Policy." *Annual Review of Sociology* 1:429–479.

Bachrach, Peter, and Morton Baratz. 1962. "The Two Faces of Power." *American Political Science Review* 56:947–952.

Banfield, Edward C. 1961. *Political Influence.* New York: Macmillan.

Bell, Daniel, 1961. "Crime as an American Way of Life," Pp. 127–150 in Daniel Bell, *The End of Ideology: On the Exhaustion of Political Ideas in the Fifties.* New York: Collier Books.

Bernard, Richard M. 1983. "Oklahoma City: Booming Schooner." Pp. 213–234 in Richard M. Bernard and Bradley R. Rice (eds.), *Sunbelt Cities: Politics and Growth since World War II.* Austin: University of Texas Press.

Binford, Henry C. 1985. *The First Suburbs: Residential Communities on the Boston Periphery 1815–1860.* Chicago: University of Chicago Press.

Bouma, Donald. 1962. "Analysis of the Social Power Position of a Real Estate Board." *Social Problems* 10(Fall):121–132.

Boyarsky, Bill, and Jerry Gillam. 1982. "Hard Times Don't Stem Flow of Campaign Gifts." *Los Angeles Times,* April 4, sec. I, pp. 1,3,22,23.

Brower, John. 1972. *The Black Side of Football.* Ph.D. dissertation, Department of Sociology, University of California, Santa Barbara.

Brown, Mike, 1979. *Laying Waste: The Poisoning of America by Toxic Chemicals.* New York: Pantheon.

Burd, Gene. 1977. "The Selling of the Sunbelt: Civic Bosserism in the Media." Pp. 129–150 in David Perry and Alfred Watkins (eds.), *The Rise of the Sunbelt Cities.* Beverly Hills, Calif.: Sage.

Caro, Robert A. 1974. *The Power Broker: Robert Moses and the Fall of New York.* New York: Knopf.

Clark, David L. 1983. "Improbable Los Angeles." Pp. 268–308 in Richard M. Bernard and Bradley R. Rice (eds.), *Sunbelt Cities: Politics and Growth since World War II.* Austin: University of Texas Press.

Clayton, Janet. 1984. "South-Central L.A. Fears Olympics to Disrupt Lives." *Los Angeles Times,* February 5, sec. II, p. 1.

Corso, Anthony. 1983. "San Diego: The Anti-City." Pp. 328–344 in Richard M. Bernard and Bradley R. Rice (eds.), *Sunbelt Cities: Politics and Growth since World War II.* Austin: University of Texas Press.

Cox, Harvey, and David Morgan. 1973. *City Politics and the Press: Journalists and the Governing of Merseyside.* Cambridge: Cambridge University Press.

Dagenais, Julie. 1967. "Newspaper Language as an Active Agent in the Building of a Frontier Town." *American Speech* 42(2):114–121.

Dahl, Robert Alan. 1961. *Who Governs?* New Haven: Yale University Press.

D'Ambrosio, Mary. 1985. "Coyne Slates Talks on Hockey Franchise." *Albany Times Union.* February 14, sec. B, p. 1.

Daws, Gavan, and George Cooper. 1984. *Land and Power in Hawaii: The Democratic Years.* Honolulu: Benchmark Press.

Devereux, Sean. 1976. "Boosters in the Newsroom: The Jacksonville Case." *Columbia Journalism Review* 14:38–47.

Domhoff, G. William. 1967. *Who Rules America?* Englewood Cliffs, N.J.: Prentice-Hall.

Domhoff, G. William. 1971. *The Higher Circles: The Governing Class in America.* New York: Random House.

Domhoff, G. William. 1978. *Who Really Rules: New Haven Community Power Re-Examined.* Santa Monica, Calif.: Goodyear.

Domhoff, G. William. 1983. *Who Rules America Now? A View for the 80's.* Englewood Cliffs, N.J.: Prentice-Hall.

Downie, Leonard, Jr. 1974. *Mortgage on America.* New York: Praeger.

Edelman, Murray. 1964. *The Symbolic Uses of Politics.* Urbana: University of Illinois Press.

Eitzen, D. Stanley, and George H. Sage. 1978. *Sociology of American Sport.* Dubuque, Iowa: William C. Brown.

Fainstein, Susan, Norman Fainstein, and P. Jefferson Armistead. 1983. "San Francisco: Urban Transformation and the Local State." Pp. 202–244 in Susan Fainstein (ed.), *Restructuring the City.* New York: Longman.

Fishman, Mark. 1978. "Crime Waves as Ideology." *Social Problems* 25(5):532–543.

Fowlkes, Martha R., and Patricia Miller. 1985. "Toward a Sociology of Unnatural Disaster." Paper presented at the 80th annual meeting of the American Sociological Association, Washington, D.C., August 31.

Freidel, Frank. 1963. "Boosters, Intellectuals and the American City." Pp. 115–120 in Oscar Handlin and John Burchard (eds.), *The Historian and the City.* Cambridge, Mass.: MIT Press.

Friedland, Roger, Frances Piven, and Robert Alford. 1978. "Political Conflict, Urban Structure, and the Fiscal Crisis." Pp. 175–225 in Douglas Ashford (ed.), *Comparing Urban Policies.* Beverly Hills, Calif.: Sage.

Fullinwider, John. 1980. "Dallas: The City with No Limits?" *In These Times* 5(6): 12–13.

Gaffney, M. Mason. 1961. "Land and Rent in Welfare Economics." Pp. 141–167 in *Land Economics Research* (papers presented at a symposium on land economics research, Lincoln, Nebraska, June 16–23). Washington, D.C.: Resources for the Future. Distributed by Johns Hopkins University Press, Baltimore.

Gordon, Margaret T., Linda Heath, and Robert leBailly. 1979. "Some Costs of Easy News: Crime Reports and Fear." Paper presented at the annual meeting of the American Psychological Association, New York.

Halberstam, David. 1979. *The Powers That Be.* New York: Knopf.

Hayes, Thomas C. 1984. "Shortfall Likely in Olympic Income." *New York Times.* May 9, p. 5.

Hill, Richard Child. 1984. "Economic Crisis and Political Response in the Motor City." Pp. 313–338 in Larry Sawers and William K. Tabb (eds.), *Sunbelt/Snowbelt: Urban Development and Regional Restructuring.* New York: Oxford University Press.

Hirsch, Seymour. 1969. "On Uncovering the Great Nerve Gas Coverup." *Ramparts* 3(July):12–18.

Johnson, David R. 1983. "San Antonio: The Vicissitudes of Boosterism." Pp. 235–254 in Richard M. Bernard and Bradley R. Rice (eds.), *Sunbelt Cities: Politics and Growth since World War II.* Austin: University of Texas Press.

Judd, Dennis. 1983. "From Cowtown to Sunbelt City." Pp. 167–201 in Susan Fainstein (ed.), *Restructuring the City.* New York: Longman.

Kaplan, Sam Hall. 1984. "Will Times Square Plan Destroy It?" *Los Angeles Times,* October 3, sec. I, p. 1.

King, Wayne, 1985. "U. of Texas Facing Cuts in Its Budget." *New York Times,* March 17, p. 12.

Lasswell, Harold. 1936. *Politics: Who Gets What, When, How.* New York: McGraw-Hill.

Lester, Marilyn. 1971. "Toward a Sociology of Public Events." Master's thesis, Department of Sociology, University of California, Santa Barbara.

Lever, Janet, 1983. *Soccer in Brazil: Sports' Contribution to Social Integration.* Chicago: University of Chicago Press.

Levine, Adeline Gordon. 1982. *Love Canal: Science, Politics and People.* Lexington, Mass: D. C. Heath.

Luckingham, Bradford. 1983. "Phoenix: The Desert Metropolis." Pp. 309–327 in Richard M. Bernard and Bradley R. Rice (eds.), *Sunbelt Cities: Politics and Growth since World War II.* Austin: University of Texas Press.

McCombs, Maxwell E., and Donald Shaw. 1972. "The Agenda Setting Function of Mass Media." *Public Opinion Quarterly* 36:176–187.

Makielski, Stanislaw J. 1966. *The Politics of Zoning: The New York Experience.* New York: Columbia University Press.

Melosi, Martin, 1983. "Dallas-Fort Worth: Marketing the Metroplex." Pp. 162–195 in Richard M. Bernard and Bradley R. Rice (eds.), *Sunbelt Cities: Politics and Growth since World War II.* Austin: University of Texas Press.

Mollenkopf, John. 1983. *The Contested City.* Princeton, N.J.: Princeton University Press.

Molotch, Harvey. 1980. "Media and Movements." Pp. 71–93 in Mayer Zald and John McCarthy (eds.), *The Dynamics of Social Movements.* Cambridge, Mass.: Winthrop.

Molotch, Harvey, and Marilyn Lester. 1974. "News as Purposive Behavior: On the Strategic Use of Routine Events, Accidents, and Scandals." *American Sociological Review* 39(1):101–113.

Molotch, Harvey, and Marilyn Lester. 1975. "Accidental News: The Great Oil Spill as Local Occurrence and National Event." *American Journal of Sociology* 81(2): 235–260.

Mormino, Gary R. 1983. "Tampa: From Hell Hole to the Gold Life." Pp. 138–161 in Richard M. Bernard and Bradley R. Rice (eds.), *Sunbelt Cities: Politics and Growth since World War II.* Austin: University of Texas Press.

Mumford, Lewis. 1961. *The City in History.* New York: Harcourt.

Murray, Richard. 1980. "Politics of a Boomtown." *Dissent* 27(4):500–504.

Neiman, Max, and Ronald O. Loveridge. 1981. "Environmentalism and Local Growth Control: A Probe into the Class Bias Thesis." *Environment and Behavior* 13(6):759–772.

Peterson, Paul E. 1981. *City Limits.* Chicago: University of Chicago

Pittas, Michael. 1984. "The Arts Edge: Revitalizing Economic Life in California's Cities."

Speech presented at a conference sponsored by the California Economic Development Commission Local Government Advisory Committee, Santa Barbara, July 15.

Rice, Bradley R. 1983. "If Dixie Were Atlanta." Pp. 31–57 in Richard M. Bernard and Bradley R. Rice (eds.), *Sunbelt Cities: Politics and Growth since World War II.* Austin: University of Texas Press.

Risen, James. 1984. "Auto World Theme Park to Close." *Los Angeles Times,* June 12, sec. IV, p. 1.

Rivera, Nancy. 1983a. "High Tech Firm Picks Austin over San Diego." *Los Angeles Times,* May 18, sec. IV, pp. 1,2.

Roderick, Kevin. 1984. "Cities Play Hardball to Lure Teams." *Los Angeles Times,* June 30, sec. I, pp. 1,24.

Rosenstiel, Thomas B. 1985. "'Killing Fields' Writer Loses N.Y. Times Column, to Be Reassigned." *Los Angeles Times,* August 21, sec. I, p. 21.

Rossi, Peter, and Robert Dentler. 1961. *The Politics of Urban Renewal.* New York: Free Press.

Sahagun, Louis, and Allan Jalon. 1984. "Cities Battle to House Technology Museum." *Los Angeles Times,* November 29, sec. IV, pp. 1,4.

Schmidt, William E. 1984. "Suburbs' Growth Pinches Atlanta." *New York Times,* April 24, sec. A, p. 14.

Shlay, Anne B., and Robert P. Gilroth. 1984. "Gambling on World's Fairs: Who Plays and Who Pays." *Neighborhood Works* 7(August):11–15.

Smith, Michael Peter, and Marlene Keller. 1983. "Managed Growth and the Politics of Uneven Development in New Orleans." Pp. 126–166 in Susan Fainstein (ed.), *Restructuring the City.* New York: Longman.

Smith, Reginald. 1984. "Willie Brown's Big Income Revealed in State Report." *San Francisco Chronicle,* March 7, p. 12.

Smith, Reginald. 1985. "Downtown Plan Okd on Quick 6-to-5 Vote." *San Francisco Chronicle,* September 11, pp. 1,16.

Steidtmann, Nancy. 1985. "Citizen Lesher: Newspaper Publisher." *Bay Area Business Magazine* IV(October 3):14–18.

Stone, Clarence N. 1981. "Community Power Structure—A Further Look." *Urban Affairs Quarterly* 16(4):505–515.

Stone, Clarence N. 1982. "Social Stratification, Non-Decision-Making and the Study of Community Power." *American Politics Quarterly* 10(3):275–302.

Stone, Clarence N. 1984. "City Politics and Economic Development: Political Economy Perspectives." *Journal of Politics* 46(1):286–299.

Stoneman, Colin. 1975. "Foreign Capital and Economic Growth." *World Development* 3(1):11–26.

Swanstrom, Todd. 1981. "The Crisis of Growth Politics: Cleveland, Kucinich, and the Challenge of Urban Populism." Ph.D. dissertation, Princeton University.

Swanstrom, Todd. 1985. *The Crisis of Growth Politics: Cleveland, Kucinich, and the Challenge of Urban Populism.* Philadelphia: Temple University Press.

Tiebout, Charles M. 1956. "A Pure Theory of Local Expenditures." *Journal of Political Economy* 64(October):416–424.

Tomkins, Calvin. 1983. "The Art World: Dallas." *New Yorker* 59(17):92–97.

Trillin, Calvin. 1976. "U.S. Journal: Rockford, Illinois—Schools without Money." *New Yorker* 52(38):146–154.

Vidich, Arthur J., and Joseph Bensman. 1960. *Small Town in Mass Society: Class, Power and Religion in a Rural Community.* Garden City, N.Y.: Doubleday.

Walker, Richard A., and Matthew J. Williams. 1982. "Water from Power: Water Supply and Regional Growth in the Santa Clara Valley." *Economic Geography* 58(2):95–119.

Walton, John. 1970. "A Systematic Survey of Community Power Research." Pp. 443–464 in Michael Aiken and Paul Mott (eds.), *The Structure of Community Power.* New York: Random House.

Weinstein, James. 1968. *The Corporate Ideal in the Liberal State, 1900–1918.* Boston: Beacon Press.

Whitt, J. Allen. 1982. *Urban Elites and Mass Transportation: The Dialectics of Power.* Princeton, N.J.: Princeton University Press.

Williams, Oliver, and C. R. Adrian. 1963. *Four Cities: A Study of Comparative Policy Making.* Philadelphia: Temple University Press.

Wolfe, Alan. 1981. *America's Impasse: The Rise and Fall of the Politics of Growth.* New York: Pantheon.

Wyner, Allen. 1967. "Governor-Salesman." *National Civic Review* 61(February):81–86.

Yago, Glenn. 1983. "Urban Transportation in the Eighties." *Democracy* 3(1):43–55.

36
Black Mayoral Leadership: A Twenty-Year Perspective*

William E. Nelson, Jr.

THE EMERGENCE OF BLACK MAYORAL LEADERSHIP

The search for power by blacks in the American political system over the past two decades has witnessed the emergence of black mayors as the unrivaled champions of black social, economic, and political aspirations. During this period, the black community became deeply committed to a new political consciousness, ethos, and program, one that stressed the utilization of the electoral process as a mechanism for capturing major public offices and transforming the content and the impact of public policy. The election of blacks to the mayorship of some of America's most important cities — beginning with the historic victories of Carl Stokes in Cleveland and Richard Hatcher in Gary in 1967 — symbolized in a profound and poignant way the quest by blacks to enhance their bargaining power in the political process, to control large blocks of strategic economic and political resources, and to engage in self-governance in accordance with the primordial principal of self-determination. Changing social demographics in American cities, characterized by the flight of whites to the suburbs and the concentration of black majorities in the cities, created prospects for a thorough-going and permanent transformation in the structure of local power. Blacks, whose potential for political influence had been negated by the dominant power of white-led urban machines, were now in a position to design and implement their own political revolution. Taking advantage of their superior numbers and high political consciousness, blacks could now use the electoral process to elevate black politicians to the pinnacle of power and authority in local jurisdictions.

As symbolic acts, the election of black big-city mayors represented landmark events in the political history of black America. The luster of black victories in the courts was muted by the reality that judicial policy changes could only be brought to fruition through complicated legal maneuvering and voluntary compliance. Black mayoral victories symbolized defiant acts of self-liberation. They were concrete evidence of a new consciousness, a new determination, a new political sophistication, and a wellspring of courage reminiscent of the heroic slave rebellions and abolitionist campaigns of the eighteenth and nineteenth centuries. Decades of self-doubt by blacks about their capacity to break free from machine control and change the course of public policy under their own momentum was washed away. The skeptics who counseled Richard Hatcher that he could not win—that he could not overthrow Eastern European domination in Gary—were proven wrong. The lessons of Gary and Cleveland were not lost on hundreds of black communities across the country where effective political mobilization by blacks could, possibly radically, alter the process of governance at the local level.

DEMANDS AND EXPECTATIONS

As the political significance of the civil rights movement began to wane and the electoral strength of black voters began to surge—especially in local races—in the decade of the 1970s, black mayors began to ascend to the apex of the leadership hierarchy in the black community. Enormous responsibility was placed on their shoulders to fight and win the ongoing struggle for black social justice and economic security. In the wake of a dramatic recession and rising poverty in the black community, black mayors were expected to be the premier leaders in the search for jobs. This was to be accomplished, in part, by halting the out-migration by old industries from the cities, while attracting new industries into a declining economic environment. Black mayors were also expected to be skillful political brokers. In this role, they were pressured to maintain effective relations with the media, fend off efforts by machines to build new bases of power in city politics, satisfy the continuing demand by whites for preferential treatment, and establish the kind of rapport with other local governments and Congress required to prevent cities from being shortchanged in the allocation of state and local fiscal resources (Nelson, 1978).

OUTSTANDING ACCOMPLISHMENTS

To what extent have black mayors been able to live up to these demands and expectations? The list of major accomplishments by black mayors over the past twenty years is extraordinarily impressive. Adopting the posture of activist entrepreneurs, black mayors have been frontline warriors in the struggle to avert the total collapse of the local fiscal economy. They have played prominent roles in organizations like the National League of Cities, the Urban Coalition, and the National Conference of Mayors. Their leadership roles were critical in the fight waged by mayors across the country against proposals advanced by the Reagan administration to savagely cut General Revenue Sharing, Community Development, Block Grants, and other important sources of federal fiscal assistance to the cities.

The work of black mayors has been path breaking in the vital arena of fiscal resource mobilization. During their first year in office, Carl Stokes in Cleveland and Richard Hatcher in Gary were extremely successful in bringing federal and private funds into their cities to address a multiplicity of critical problems faced by their black constituents (Nelson and Meranto, 1977). Similarly, Coleman Young of Detroit was able to convert his cordial political relations with the Republican governor, William Milliken, and the Democratic president, Jimmy Carter, into strong support for economic development in Detroit by the state and federal governments (Rich, 1989:150). Under the leadership of black mayors, the priorities of city government began to significantly change. Demonstrating extraordinary sensitivity to the needs of their black constituents, black mayors began to make issues such as increased availability of low- and moderate-income housing, expanded job-training services, and improvement in police-community relations major components of their legislative and administrative agendas. Research on the administrative performance of black mayors clearly shows that black mayors have been more responsive to the needs of low- and moderate-income citizens than their white counterparts. A quantitative study of spending patterns in American cities by Albert Karnig and Susan Welch found that cities with black mayors increased both their total expenditures and their social-welfare expenditures more than other municipalities (Karnig and Welch, 1980). Black mayors have also been more assertive in the pursuit of affirmative action goals through the employment of unprecedented numbers of minorities in significant positions in their administrations. Within two years after his election, Mayor Hatcher of Gary had managed to place fourteen blacks as head of the city's twenty-nine departments. During his four years as Mayor of Cleveland, Carl Stokes promoted 274 minority individuals to supervisory positions in Cleveland city government. The aggressive action taken by black mayors in the area of affirmative action has often produced radical change in some of the most conservative and intractable city bureaucracies. A study by Peter Eisinger of affirmative action practices in cities governed by black mayors reveals that over a ten-year period, black representation in the police force increased sixfold in Detroit, and threefold in Newark and Atlanta (Eisinger, 1984:251). Eisinger underscores the proactive nature of affirmative action programs in black mayoral cities. Personnel departments in these cities do not wait for black candidates to file applications but actively initiate searches for appropriate candidates (Eisinger, 1984:251).

Studies have also shown that black mayors have been instrumental in expanding the participation of minority-owned firms in city contracting and purchasing. In Newark, Detroit, and Atlanta, black participation in public purchasing contracts increased from nothing in the early 1970s to a substantial share by 1980 (Eisinger, 1984:253). Joint-venture policies promoted by the administration of Mayor Maynard Jackson in Atlanta in the construction of the Atlanta airport resulted in the creation of $36 million worth of contracts for minority firms in 1977 (Eisinger, 1984:254).

The outstanding record of legislative and administrative achievements compiled by black mayors over the past twenty years clearly establishes the fact that black mayoral offices are not hollow prizes. Black mayors have established new instructional mechanisms for delivering benefits to less-well-off citizens; in the process they have transformed the lives of individuals who have historically been the intended and unintended victims of non–decision making in the urban-policy process. The late Harold Washington is a shining example of what can be done by a black mayor who is committed to the progress of his people. In a few short years, Washington totally reconstructed Chicago's economic-development model. Washington designed a growth model that emphasized the inclusion of neighborhood groups and small businesses in economic planning and the use of the city's purchasing power to generate business for minority-owned firms (Judd and Ready, 1986.) Clearly, these are the kind of policy initiatives by black mayors that can make a critical difference in the social and economic status of the black community.

THE LIMITS OF LEADERSHIP

The past twenty years have not only revealed the possibilities of black mayoral leadership, they have also illuminated important limitations on the programs and powers of black mayors. Despite the heroic effort of black mayors, the urban agenda for black America remains unfinished. Twenty years of effort by black mayors has not eliminated the social, economic, and political crisis faced by blacks in America. This should come as no surprise since many of the most critical problems facing the cities are beyond the reach of local officials. Black mayors cannot be blamed for the failure of Congress to halt the piling up of deficits and the construction of supply-side economic policies that transfer funds from the cities to the military. Welfare, poverty, joblessness, and juvenile crime are the results of national and international forces; the solution to these problems cannot be found by focusing exclusively on public-policy practices at the local level. The environmental settings in which black mayors function also deeply constrain their capacity to solve many pressing issues that impact on the lives of their black constituents. Black mayors are not and cannot be dictators; they must share power with a wide variety of individuals, institutions, and associations (Nelson, 1978). It is important to observe that some of the strongest opposition to black mayoral policy initiatives has come from dissatisfied and disenchanted elements of the black community. The high-pitched, emotional campaigns run by black mayors frequently produce unrealistic expectations about what a black mayor can accomplish. Black mayors find it difficult to convince individuals with these kinds of attitudes that they remain unswervingly committed to an agenda of community progress (Nelson, 1972).

A part of the blame for the black community's difficulty in translating its electoral resources into policy benefits can be laid at the feet of black mayors. Black mayoral leadership has not always lived up to the minimum requirements of a new, progressive politics. It is distressing to find recent black mayoral candidates entering into coalitions with conservative white-led political organizations to block the election of race-oriented black candidates. This pattern suggests the possibility that a new generation of black mayors will emerge committed to the agenda of old politics that served to suppress the ascendancy of blacks in the political process in the decades before the 1960s civil rights revolution. Many of these new black leaders were not active in the civil rights movement and were not socialized into activist entrepreneurial roles. In contrast to the first generation of black urban leadership, the new black leaders appear to suffer from a poverty of vision and a poverty of analytical sophistication. They have therefore been less inclined to embrace policies that challenge the system of racial subordination in the political process.

Some black mayors have also embraced too enthusiastically corporate-center strategies for urban development. Coleman Young of Detroit has been one of the chief architects of plans to rescue the cities fiscally by encouraging corporate investment in the cities, especially in declining downtown central business districts (Rich, 1989). The stress on corporate development, while potentially beneficial in terms of the generation of new jobs and taxable revenue, creates the danger of unbalanced urban growth (promoting the interests of the affluent while neglecting the needs of the nonaffluent) and expanding private-sector control over the policy-making process (Hill, 1983; Swanstrom, 1985). The strategy of balanced growth adopted by Mayor Washington in Chicago appears to be more in keeping with the long-term economic and social interests of the black community than the corporate-center models now in place in Detroit, Atlanta, Oakland, and Philadelphia.

THE ISSUE OF POLITICAL INCORPORATION

The most serious failing of black mayors has been their unwillingness to play a major leadership role in moving the quest for black political incorporation beyond the narrow confines of elected office. Effective black political incorporation must involve the institutionalization of black influence across broad dimensions of the policy-making process, not merely the election of black politicians to public office. In this regard, it is important that we keep in mind the distinction made by James Jennings and Mel King between "access" and "power." Black office holding is not synonymous with black power; at issue in the final analysis is the extent to which the resources of public offices can be utilized to institutionalize black control in the realms of public and private decision making.

The history of the political emergence of European ethnic groups in American politics suggests that the process of political incorporation has traditionally involved strategic consideration of the transfer of a range of benefits to upwardly mobile, politically significant, demand-making interest groups. In Providence, Rhode Island, the Irish began making demands for representation on Democratic party committees as early as 1876. By 1900, 73 percent of the committee memberships of the Democratic party were in the hands of the Irish (Cornwell, 1960:205–10). Italians began making demands on the Democratic and Republican parties after World War I, in the wake of the growth of Italian electoral strength to a position of commanding influence. By 1957, Italians had gained 35 percent of the memberships in the Republican party and 22 percent of the memberships in the Democratic party (Cornwell, 1960:205–10). In New York City, the Irish began infiltrating the Democratic party via Tammany Hall in the 1850s. By 1880, the Irish had taken complete control of this organization. Building from the ward level, the Irish were successful in establishing an elaborate party bureaucracy extending from block and building captains to top party positions in the county (Glazer and Moynihan, 1963). Thus, long before they developed the clout to elect a member from their ethnic group to high public office, the Irish and Italians began to demand and receive major instrumental benefits. The election of Irish and Italian politicians to high public office did not represent the culmination of the process of political incorporation but was an interim step in that process. The process continued with the institutionalization of ethnic power through the control of the electoral organization, the domination of the city bureaucracy, and the infiltration of Irish and Italians into important private sectors of the economic order (Dahl, 1961).

In contrast to the European ethnic incorporation pattern, the election of black politicians to high public office has not led to effective black penetration of other sectors of the economic and political system. Blacks have not used their control over mayorships to substantially infiltrate existing party structures, or to build permanent independent organizations of their own. The logical focal point for such institutional development would be the mayor's office, where extensive patronage benefits could bring the personnel and the energy of the campaign into the formal arena of governmental administration. Black mayors have tended not to be receptive to the notion of building and maintaining racially cohesive, nonelectoral organizations. There appears to be a visceral fear that such organizations would be difficult to effectively manage and might inappropriately intrude into delicate day-to-day administrative matters (Nelson, 1972). In many respects, this fear is unwarranted. Mayor Carl Stokes of Cleveland demonstrated unequivocally that the advantages of an ongoing black organizational alliance far outweigh its potential liabilities. During his term as mayor, Stokes was able to build one of the most effective political organizations in urban America. In doing so, he greatly increased black political influence over the outcome of elections as well as the stock of concrete social and economic benefits the black community was able to demand (Nelson, 1982).

A look across the black political landscape reveals a paucity of stable, black-led political organizations. It is at once informative and heartbreaking to note that after more than twenty years of black control in Gary, no organization exists to lobby for black goals, and to organize black political resources on a continuous basis. The failure to build such an organization in Chicago meant that when Harold Washington died, black political momentum was lost, and the programmatic agenda of the Washington administration became the shattered victim of the machinations of a multiplicity of warring factions. In the midst of this political chaos, the white machine stepped forward to reassert its dominance over black social, economic, and political decision making in Chicago.

CRITICAL LESSONS

The failure of black leadership and organization has prevented the process of black incorporation from translating itself into major gains in the private sector. This is a critical failure, since much of the decision-making authority exercised in urban politics is exercised in the private sector (Judd, 1988). Effective black political incorporation must result in greater black involvement in and control over the politics of corporate decision making. The public-private partnership forged between Coleman Young and the business community in Detroit may be good for General Motors, but is savory benefits for Detroit's black poor (many of whom used to work for General Motors) are questionable. Clearly Mayor Wilson Goode did not have the interests of his black constituents principally in mind when he made the campaign to keep the Eagles in Philadelphia a top priority of this administration. Sky boxes and tax abatements are poor substitutes for health-care centers, family-counseling programs, job training and development programs, and head-start initiatives. Nor will coalitions between blacks and liberal whites of the kind endorsed by Browning et al. in *Protest Is Not Enough* be effective in diluting the hegemonic power of corporate interests if blacks cannot summon sufficient internal strength to design, propose, and ratify Afrocentric approaches to urban policy making (Browning et al., 1984).

The pivotal lesson to be learned from the past experience of black mayors is that black political leaders in the decades ahead must help to define and implement a new programmatic agenda for the black community. This agenda must, at least, seek to achieve a fundamental redistribution of resources, reverse the subordinate position of blacks in the political system, and establish mass-based political formations at every level of the political process that will be actively and effectively involved in setting and implementing the civic agenda.

REFERENCES

Browning, Rufus P., Dale Rogers, Marshall, Tabb, and David H. Tabb. 1984. *Protest Is Not Enough: The Struggle of Blacks and Hispanics for Equality in Urban Politics.* Berkeley, Los Angeles, London: University of California Press.

Cornwell, Elmer E., Jr. 1960. "Party Absorption of Ethnic Groups" *Social Forces,* 38 (March).

Dahl, Robert. 1961. *Who Governs?: Democracy and Power in an American City.* New Haven and London: Yale University Press.

Eisinger, Peter. 1984. "Black Mayors and the Politics of Racial Economic Advancement." In Harlan Hahn and Charles Levine, eds., *Readings in Urban Politics, Past, Present and Future.* New York, London: Longman Incorporated.

Glazer, Nathan, and Daniel Patrick Moynihan. 1963. *Beyond the Melting Pot.* Cambridge, Mass.: The M.I.T. Press.

Hill, Richard Child. 1983. "Crisis in the Motor City: The Politics of Economic Development in Detroit." In Susan S. Fainstein, Norman I. Fainstein, Richard Child Hill, Dennis Judd, and Michael Peter Smith, eds., *Restructuring the City.* London, New York: Longman Incorporated.

Judd, Dennis L. 1988. *The Politics of American Cities: Private Power and Public Policy.* Glenview, Illinois, Boston, London: Scott, Foresman Incorporated.

Judd, Dennis L., and Randy L. Ready. 1986. "Entrepreneurial Cities and the New Policies of Economic Development." In George E. Peterson and Carol W. Lewis, eds., *Reagan and the Cities.* Washington, D.C.: The Urban Institute Press.

Jennings, James, and Mel King, eds. 1986. *From Access to Power: Black Politics in Boston.* Cambridge Mass: Schenkman Books Incorporated.

Karnig, Albert, and Susan Welch. 1980. *Black Representation and Urban Policy.* Chicago, Ill.: University of Chicago Press.

Nelson, William E., Jr., 1972. *Black Politics in Gary: Problems and Prospects.* Washington, D.C.: Joint Center for Political Studies.

———. 1978. "Black Mayors as Urban Managers." In John R. Howard and Robert C. Smith, eds., *Urban Black Politics. The Annals of the American Academy of Political and Social Science,* 439 (September).

———. 1982. "Cleveland: The Rise and Fall of the New Black Politics." In Michael B. Preston, Lenneal J. Henderson, Jr., and Paul Puryear, eds., *The New Black Politics: The Search for Political Power.* New York, London: Longman Incorporated.

Nelson, William E., Jr., and Philip J. Meranto. 1977. *Electing Black Mayors: Political Action in the Black Community.* Columbus: Ohio State University Press.

Rich, Wilbur C. 1989. *Coleman Young and Detroit Politics: From Social Activist to Power Broker.* Detroit: Wayne State University Press.

Swanstrom, Todd. 1985. *The Crisis of Growth Politics: Cleveland, Kucinich, and the Challenge of Urban Populism.* Philadelphia: Temple University Press.

37
Chicago Divided: The Politics of Race*

Paul Kleppner

The mostly black crowd that gathered in Donnelley Hall at 23rd and Martin Luther King Drive on the South Side was in a joyous mood. The Sunshine Festival Band played rock music, and souvenir salesmen peddled T-shirts and beanies. The people danced and clapped, laughed and wept, and they cheered in the early reports that Harold Washington was piling up a huge lead in the black wards. At 7:01 P.M., WLS-TV (ABC) called him the winner, with an estimated 55 percent of the vote. The WBBM-TV (CBS) and WMAQ-TV (NBC) exit polls also showed Washington ahead, but those stations hedged their bets and held back their predictions.

When the returns from the white wards poured in, WLS-TV scaled back its estimate to 52 percent, and the other networks still claimed the result was too close to call. At about 11 P.M., Bernard Epton appeared before his crowd of mostly white supporters in the Grand Ballroom of the Palmer House. He told them that he was then running only about 5,000 votes behind, but "I think most of the outstanding wards are our wards." The crowd cheered. "Keep smiling, keep praying, and keep waiting. I'll be back down just as soon as we get those figures," he assured them. But Epton made no second appearance that night. He left the hotel about an hour later, after his analysts confirmed that his bid had fallen short. On the way out he told reporters that he wished Washington luck in managing the city, especially in coping with its financial problems. "Maybe he'll learn to pay his bills promptly and his taxes," he added. A few steps later, apparently referring to his almost complete lack of votes from blacks, he said, "I certainly will save a lot of money in the future on charitable causes." On of his key supporters called it a "graceless" exit, one last note of bitterness ending a divisive and racially polarizing campaign.[1]

While Epton was leaving the Palmer House, the crowd at Donnelley Hall awaited the arrival of the mayor-elect. At about 1:30 A.M., Harold Washington made his way through the throng and responded to their chants of "Harold, Harold, Harold." "You want Harold?" he asked. "Well here is Harold." Under a banner proclaiming "Washington for All Chicago," the mayor-elect spoke of the meaning of his triumph. "Out of the crucible of this city's most trying election, . . . blacks, whites, Hispanics, Jews, gentiles,

Protestants and Catholics of all stripes have joined hands to form a new Democratic coalition and to begin in this place a new Democratic movement." We have been victorious, he continued, "but I am mindful that there were many other friends and neighbors who were not a part of our campaign." But now "each of us must . . . rededicate [our] efforts to heal the divisions that have plagued us. . . . Together we will overcome our problems[.]"[2]

Later that day, Washington met with several of his former campaign foes for a symbolic "ecumenical prayer unity luncheon" at the Conrad Hilton Hotel. Saul Epton represented his brother, who was then on route to Florida, and delivered "a clear-cut good will message" from the losing candidate to the mayor-elect. Mayor Byrne and State's Attorney Daley attended the luncheon, as did eighteen of the city's religious leaders, including Joseph Cardinal Bernardin, the Roman Catholic archbishop. Speaking later to reporters, Washington said "we are now in the process of building a new city, a multi-ethnic city," and he pledged "to reach out to every area of the city."[3]

The mayoral contest opened old wounds and brought unresolved tensions and fears into public view. In a city with a long and bitter history of racial conflict, the campaign inflamed group relations and complicated the task of reconciliation. With no reservoir of mutual trust to draw on, whites and blacks were not likely to heed Washington's call to "reach out and open our arms" to each other. Too many Chicagoans silently shared the cynical outlook of Mike Royko's mythical friend Wally. "You open your arms to somebody in this town and they'll either yell for the cops or hit you in the mouth because you've left yourself wide open."[4]

The electoral war between the races changed the shape of Chicago's politics, but its importance reached beyond the city. What happened among Chicago's blacks was both part of and made its own contribution to a larger national movement, which has enormous significance for the future course of race relations and for the operation of the political system.

BEYOND APRIL 1983

On Friday, 29 April 1983, in ceremonies at Navy Pier, Harold Washington became Chicago's forty-second mayor and its first black chief executive. Addressing his inaugural remarks to the invited guests and to the citywide television audience, Mayor Washington called for a new approach to the government of the city, while offering a stunning indictment of the outgoing administration. "My transition team advises me that the city government is . . . in far worse financial condition than we thought," the mayor said, calling attention to a gap as large as $150 million in the current budget. To remedy financial problems he described as "enormous and complicated," Washington promised cuts in executive salaries, a hiring freeze, and the release of "the several hundred new city employees who were added because of political considerations" in the closing days of the Byrne Administration.[5]

The 4,000 invited guests, many of whom were Washington campaign workers, applauded his promise to heal the "racial fears and divisiveness [that] have hurt us in the past." And they cheered thunderously when he pledged to remain true to the reform spirit of his campaign, vowing a more open government and greater citizen involvement. "My election was made possible by thousands of people who demanded that the burdens of unfairness and inequity be lifted so that the city can be saved," he told them. "One of the ideas that held us together said that neighborhood involvement has to take the place of the Machine."

To the newly sworn members of the City Council, including its Machine stalwarts, the mayor issued both a challenge and an appeal. "Today, I am calling on all of you . . . to respond to a great challenge: Business as usual will not be accepted. . . . Help me institute reform and bring about a renewal of this city while we still have time."

Washington's tough words probably didn't surprise the party regulars, although several claimed publicly that the tone of his speech discouraged harmonious relations. "He came off like Attila the Hun," Alderman Thomas Cullerton (38th Ward) remarked. "That's not going to help him win the aldermen over."[6] But as Cullerton knew, the battle for control over the city was already raging behind the scenes, and nothing Washington said during his inauguration could have changed many minds or altered the balance of forces.

On 2 May, when the City Council met for the first time under the new mayor, the Democratic regulars, led by Alderman Edward Vrdolyak (10th Ward), formed a solid voting bloc of twenty-nine members. Knowing that he didn't have the votes to prevent the adoption of resolutions that created new committees, distributed their chairmanships, and adopted new rules shackling the mayor, Washington hastily adjourned the meeting, ignoring verbal demands for a roll call on the motion. As the mayor and his twenty-one allies walked out of the Council chamber, Vrdolyak seized the gavel and the Council majority adopted its resolutions. The "Council wars" had formally begun, with Vrdolyak and Alderman Edward Burke (14th Ward), his chief ally and the newly designated chairman of the powerful Finance Committee, in control of the Council.[7]

The battle had begun before the Council's initial session. "That's when I knew how it was going to be," Vrdolyak said, referring to Washington's demand on 19 April that Vrdolyak yield the chairmanship of the Building and Zoning Committee. "That's when I knew it would be war. . . . I'm not the kind of guy you can tell 'Go sit in the corner'—and I just go sit there. I never was. That's not how I got where I got. . . . Nobody can blow me off like that." He wasn't going to be a passive bystander while Washington and his allies were "trying to take my manhood away." They "read me all wrong. I'm a fighter. I don't go down easy."[8]

According to Vrdolyak, his decision to resist came on the occasion of a highly publicized unity meeting between the mayor-elect and the aldermen on 19 April. The breakfast at the Bismarck Hotel was intended as a peace-making session. Washington spoke briefly, telling the aldermen he would "not overly interfere with the council" and would cooperate and communicate with them. "I look forward to four years of hard work, but there will be controversy." The mayor-elect then made the rounds of all the tables, chatting at length with several aldermen who had opposed him in the general election. After the breakfast, in a private meeting with Alderman Wilson Frost (34th Ward) and Vrdolyak, Washington told the alderman and committeeman from the 10th Ward and the chairman of the Democratic Central Committee of Cook County that he should relinquish his post as the Council's president pro tem and take a committee chairmanship other than Building and Zoning. Vrdolyak agreed to give up the honorific position but objected to losing his control over the powerful (and profitable) committee. "You're attacking my manhood," he told Washington.[9]

Needless to say, Vrdolyak's version of the details serves his own purpose. It presents him as willing and ready to cooperate with the new mayor, while depicting Washington as ungratefully rebuffing Vrdolyak's gracious offer and pushing him out of the leadership. In this version, the responsibility for conflict falls heavily on the mayor, with Vrdolyak and his allies appearing as the aggrieved parties. "None of this would have happened if Harold had come to us the way Byrne did," Alderman Burke said.[10]

But Washington was not another Jane Byrne, willing to yield control over the city to the parochial ward barons. Vrdolyak, Burke, and the other party regulars knew that from the outset, and because they did, they worked for Epton's cause, some openly and others covertly. Vrdolyak himself played all ends against the middle, verbally backing Washington, secretly aiding Epton, and all the while organizing his own bloc among the aldermen. When Washington won the general election, Vrdolyak stepped up his organizing efforts, cleverly exploiting the racial fears of white aldermen, playing to their desire for the prestige and patronage of committee chairmanships, and taking advantage of conflicting signals and indecisive counterefforts by Washington's camp. Acting as both coach and cheerleader, Vrdolyak "created a sense among these guys [i.e., his allies] that they could win," one insider observed. He called frequent meetings, kept in touch with everyone, set up a "buddy system" to keep tabs on the freshman aldermen, and even sent flowers to the wives of the twenty-nine on Mother's Day. And the Vrdolyak group did its homework thoroughly: they checked the statutes and precedents with lawyers and were ready for any eventuality.[11]

Washington wasn't unaware of Vrdolyak's early efforts to organize his own majority on the Council. Cook County Board President George Dunne and others warned him of the behind-the-scenes maneuvering, and the unity breakfast on 19 April was a response to those warnings. In his meeting with Vrdolyak after the breakfast, Washington told him directly, "You supported Epton, bullshitted me, and you've been organizing from day one. Let's get it out front."[12] But Washington's attempt to slow the opposition's momentum was limited by his own commitment to reform, which prevented him from outbidding Vrdolyak for support, and the continuing fear of a black mayor among most white Chicagoans, which made even those white aldermen who were uncomfortable with Vrdolyak reluctant to join Washington's bloc of supporters on the Council.

Earlier and better organizing by Washington and his followers might have recruited more support on the Council. But no amount of maneuvering, no matter how skillful, could have prevented the battle, since it is simply another episode in the ongoing war for control over the city. At one level, that war involves competition between racial groups for dominance over the city's culture-transmitting institutions; at another level, it represents a contest for power, prestige, and profits between Machine and anti-Machine politicians. And in the real world of Chicago politics, these two separate threads of conflict have been closely interwoven.

While the "Council wars" are a direct continuation of the primary and general election skirmishes, their roots lie in the demographic changes the city has experienced since the 1940s, and the ways in which its political leaders responded to them. The growth and residential expansion of the black population raised integration issues and strained the bonds that tied blacks and lower-income whites to Chicago's Democratic Machine. With the civil unrest of the 1960s and the rise of a more assertive black leadership, Machine politicians came to view blacks as an undependable part of their electoral coalition and become increasingly dependent on the white ethnic neighborhoods for voting support. The Machine's responsiveness to its white constituency forestalled the type of white backlash that occurred in other northern cities, while further alienating and demobilizing black voters. But it also made the Machine vulnerable to continuing "white flight," which threatened its electoral base. Thus, pursuing policies designed to stop or slow white out-migration became linked with preserving the Machine's electoral control and its status as the city's ruling institution. This reciprocal relationship between the Machine and the white ethnic areas is the context that gives meaning to the politics of the city's culture-transmitting agencies over the past twenty years. Appointments to the police and fire departments, to the Board of Education, and to the Chicago Housing Authority have been focal points of the ongoing competition between whites and blacks for cultural dominance. Because it defended their racial interests, white voters supported the Machine and developed a high tolerance for fiscal mismanagement and outright corruption.

The relationship worked as long as the white ethnics turned out at high rates and supported the Machine's slated candidate, or when the opposing groups turned out at low rates or split their votes among competing anti-Machine candidates. Although in different ways, the formula worked in 1975 and again in 1977; it faltered in 1979, and it finally collapsed in the 1983 primary election. Then most whites simply underestimated the seriousness of Washington's challenge and split their support between the white candidates, both with Machine links and identifications. A mobilized and cohesive black community took advantage of the split and delivered the nomination to its own candidate. The result gave a new twist to the guiding adage of politics Chicago style: blacks not only got mad, they also got even.

Writing the Machine's obituary has been a routine post-election exercise for some time, but it always seems to rise again to fight another battle and discredit the news of its death. Fighting battles, however, is not the same as winning them, and since Mayor Daley's day, the regular Democratic organization has barely limped along, losing every major Democratic primary contest since 1979.[13] Thus, for some years, there has been more myth than reality to the notion of the Machine's invincibility, and there are solid reasons to suppose that its decade-long decline is not going to be reversed.

After Washington won the primary, white voters took his candidacy seriously. Faced with the prospect of a black Democrat as mayor, most of the city's white Democrats, and especially those in the ethnic neighborhoods on the Northwest and Southwest Sides, chose the "lesser evil" and voted for a Republican. Despite this breakdown of party loyalty, and despite the absence of a significant third candidate to siphon off some share of the anti-black vote, Washington won the general election, although narrowly. He won primarily because black turnout was unprecedentedly high and cohesive. Of course, Epton's defeat can be "explained away" on the grounds that he was a Republican, a weak campaigner, and so forth. The search for disingenuous explanations will no doubt continue, because it springs from an implicit disbelief that blacks could have conceived, organized, and carried out Chicago's electoral revolution. In the final analysis, however, that is the simple reality, which cannot be wished away or explained away, and to which white politicians and voters must accommodate.

Add one more ingredient to that reality: Washington's support among Hispanics, a group not yet fully mobilized politically. A black-brown coalition even now makes up a bare majority (51.5 percent) of the city's voting-age population, and it will have even greater potential in the future. Population projections point to stabilization in the size of the black population, a further slight decline in the number of whites, and a near doubling of the size of the Hispanic component.[14] Chicago's minority groups are well on their way to becoming the numerically dominant part of the city's electorate. Moreover, as the outcome of the April election showed, the Machine's formula for electoral success no longer works. High turnout and solid support among white ethnic voters no longer assures a citywide victory. The tactic of patching a variety of ethnic fragments into a majority coalition can no longer offset mobilized and cohesive support among blacks and Hispanics, whose numbers now give them the political "clout" they previously lacked.

Still, many white Chicagoans cling to the myth of the Machine, hoping somehow that it will rescue them again in four years. And regular party leaders, taking advantage of racial anxieties to secure their electoral base and assure their continued power, prestige, and access to profits, encourage that popular belief in the Machine's unique ability to restore white control over the city. The "Council wars" reflect this complex mix of conflicting racial outlooks, powerful egos, and driving personal ambitions. They involve both a struggle for power between leadership blocs and a clash of vital constituency interests.

By organizing a majority bloc, Vrdolyak and Burke tried to win what they had already lost in the primary and general elections—executive control over the city.[15] Their creed remains what it always had been—politics, patronage, and profits as usual. And their aim is to continue Machine politics, with no effective limits on the power of the parochial ward barons to channel city business to favored companies and contractors.

But the alignment on the Council also reflects the racial polarization that exists in the city. With four exceptions, the "Vrdolyak 29" represent heavily white wards, whose populations are sensitive to integration issues and gave Washington relatively little support in the general election (Table 1). The members of the "Washington 21," again with four exceptions, represent areas of strong black concentration and voting support for Washington.[16] This obvious racial division at the leadership level encourages voters of both races to view the contest as a continuation of the struggle for cultural dominance. Through their actions and statements, the leaders on both sides reinforce that perception, because it strengthens the resolve of their electorates and keeps the pressure on their aldermanic supporters. Alderman Vrdolyak, for example, spread the word through the publishers of community newspapers on the Northwest and Southwest Sides that the mayor intended to encourage "white flight" by abolishing the residency requirement for public employees and concentrating public housing in white areas. For similar reasons, Washington and his supporters haven't hesitated to portray the struggle as a "war" with distinct racial overtones.[17]

On a number of specific issues of public policy, such as tax support for the city's schools, funds for the Chicago Transit Authority, and the distribution of resources by the police and fire departments and the Chicago Park District, the tangible interests of the white and black communities diverge. And there is a clear and long-standing racial conflict over the siting of future public housing projects. Indeed, despite Washington's post-election effort to soothe fears by assuring that "no neighborhood is going to be inundated by public housing," his refusal to obstruct the Chicago Housing Authority's scattered-site program is a prime source of the distrust that persists among the city's wide ethnics. In a fund-raising letter distributed in November 1983, the Southwest Parish and Neighborhood Federation claimed that "Mayor

TABLE 1. Racial and Political Base of City Council Blocs

	Vrdolyak 29	Washington 21
Voting-age Population		
% White	68.8	21.9
% Black	10.8	71.7
% Hispanic	16.9	3.9
Support in Mayoral Election		
% Washington	25.9	86.1
% Epton	73.7	13.6

Washington is running City Hall with a vengeance. Either we build a more powerful organization with which to confront this administration or we decide it's not worth it and leave the city."[18]

Although it would be a difficult task, some of the tensions might be resolved if they could be addressed concretely rather than symbolically. But as long as both sides see specific disagreements within the larger context of a struggle for cultural dominance, their competing demands will remain indivisible and uncompromisable. Because they emphasize and strengthen that symbolic view of the racial competition, the "Council wars" complicate the task of assuaging the legitimate concerns that exist on both sides of the city's racial divide.

The struggle also encourages white voters to hunker down and await redemption by the city's Democratic Machine—their Great White Hope. By prompting whites to see black political empowerment as a transitory phase, a period to be lived through until the Machine restores white dominance, it discourages accommodation. Under that condition, whites will continue to see flight or resistance as their only viable options. Only when white voters recognize the city's changed demographic and political realities are they likely to realize that Machine politicians are jeopardizing their long-term interests by exploiting their current anxieties. That realization will not occur, however, until the actions of the Washington Administration persuade them that "it's our turn" does not have to mean "we want it all."

BEYOND CHICAGO

What happened in Chicago in April 1983 was not an isolated event. In other places, blacks have also awakened to the strength of their numbers, and in the future they are likely to do so in still more locales, especially where there are reasonably sized concentrations of black voters. Biracial contests elsewhere may not involve the open and strident racial appeals that characterized Chicago's mayoral contest. But we should not mistake tone for substance; each biracial contest will bring latent tensions and hostilities to the surface and strain intergroup relations.

Philadelphia's Democratic primary is a good example. That contest pitted a black candidate, W. Wilson Goode, the city's managing director, against its former mayor, Frank Rizzo. During the campaign and after the primary election on 17 May, Philadelphians congratulated themselves, while accepting the plaudits of the national media, because their contest was free of the open anger that marked Chicago's.[19] While the tone of Philadelphia's campaign surely was less heated than Chicago's, the difference stopped there: the voting results were quite similar in both cities. In a very high turnout election, Goode scored a relatively narrow win, although most observers (and pollsters) had originally predicted a landslide. Like Washington, he forged his victory in the black community, polling 98 percent of a high turnout among black voters. But despite having none of the personal liabilities that troubled Washington's candidacy, Goode received only 24 percent

TABLE 2. White Ethnic Voting for Black Mayoral Candidates:
Chicago and Philadelphia, 1983[a]

	Italian	German	Polish	Irish	Total
Catholics: White-collar and Professional					
Chicago	15.2	22.5	19.3	26.9	21.3
Philadelphia	14.0	38.2	31.8	22.0	22.3
Catholics: Blue-collar Occupations					
Chicago	0.0	12.9	10.2	18.9	10.2
Philadelphia	12.2	18.2	5.9	10.5	11.9

[a]Entries are the percentages for Washington in the 12 April general election and for Goode in the 17 May primary election.

SOURCE: NBC exit polls.

from Philadelphia's white voters, which was only slightly higher than the level the exit polls gave to Washington in Chicago's general election. Moreover, Philadelphia's white ethnics, especially its blue-collar Catholics, voted about as heavily against Goode as their Chicago counterparts did against Washington (Table 2).[20]

It's not surprising that Philadelphia's election results show about as much racial polarization as Chicago's.[21] Beneath the self-congratulatory hoopla, there were clear signs of its development. Goode complained throughout that "the Rizzo camp was running an 'underground campaign' that included racist slanders and personal rumors such as one accusing him of wife-beating." And Rizzo repeatedly dismissed the preelection poll results and professed a nearly mystical faith in what he called the "hidden vote," those whites who would not admit to pollsters their unwillingness to support a black candidate. The erosion of Goode's support among white voters during the final two weeks of the campaign suggests that Rizzo was on target; he simply overestimated the size of his "hidden vote" and underestimated black turnout.[22]

More so than the Washington-Epton contest, the Goode-Rizzo battle illustrates the problem black candidates confront. When even exceptionally qualified blacks run for highly visible public offices, they are less likely to win support from voters who are not their own ethnic compatriots than are candidates from most other groups. Thus, without a large-sized black voting constituency, black candidates normally have little chance of election. However, a black base heightens white fears and increases the likelihood of racially polarized voting patterns, because whites apparently presume that black officeholders will respond vigorously to black interests and ignore white concerns. In fact, where some white support is required for election, black candidates and officeholders have generally avoided postures and actions that antagonize the white component of the electorate. They have been sensitive to the requirements of building a biracial coalition, even at the expense of criticism from more militant blacks. The problem lies in communicating this record and its message of political accommodation to white voters. And the problem is magnified when entrenched white politicians seek to avoid displacement by polarizing white voters through coded (or overt) appeals to their standing suspicions and anxieties.[23]

The developments in Chicago and Philadelphia in the spring of 1983 were parts of the larger national movement that produced extraordinarily high turnout and partisan cohesiveness among blacks in November 1982. In nine states, black turnout actually exceeded the white participation rate; and the white edge nationally was only 6.9 percentage points, the smallest difference since the U.S. Census Bureau began reporting the data in 1964.[24] These turnout gains reflected the success of voter registration drives in black communities throughout the country. Between 1980 and 1982, reported registration among blacks in the United States showed a net gain of 573,000, compared with a net increase of only 93,000 among white voters and 107,000 among Hispanics.[25]

Blacks not only turned out to vote at higher rates than usual, they voted overwhelmingly for Democrats. They gave over two thirds of their vote to Democratic candidates in twelve of the twenty gubernatorial races and seventeen of the twenty-three senatorial contests surveyed by the CBS–New York Times exit poll. And cohesive black support made the difference in several key races, including the gubernatorial contests in New York and Texas and the Senate race in New Jersey.[26]

This surge in black turnout was propelled by their evaluation of the Reagan Administration. While white voters may have been ambivalent toward Reagan's policies, concerned about unemployment but willing to give the Reagan formula more time, blacks had made up their minds. On election day, whites narrowly approved Reagan's overall performance (by 50 percent to 47.3 percent), while blacks registered clear disapproval (by 87 percent to 6.3 percent); and blacks expressed even stronger dissatisfaction with Reagan's economic performance (by 89.4 percent to 5.8 percent).[27]

The off-year voter mobilization drives channelled this discontent among blacks into the political process, inaugurating a much-delayed second phase of the civil rights movement. The first phase began in the South during the 1955–1960 period, with the mobilization of the indigenous institutions of the black community, especially the campus- and church-based organizations. As the initial wave of insurgency attracted external resources, organizations formally dedicated to the movement (e.g., SCLC, SNCC, CORE) grew in size and prominence, and over the 1961–1965 period they assumed leadership. The transformation was relatively quick and successful, since these formal movement organizations incorporated the existing institutions and resources of the southern black community into their programs, and support for the movement was broadly based in the early 1960s. Its strength was further increased by the fact that its insurgent campaign was sharply focused. Between 1955 and 1965, three quarters of the actions initiated by the movement occurred in the seventeen southern and border states, and 65.2 percent of them had racial integration as their goal. Thus, through the mid-1960s, the civil rights movement rallied a broad base of support around an issue consensus focusing on exclusionary racial practices in the South.[28]

As the movement shifted its focus from the South to the North, and broadened the range of its issue concerns, this consensus rapidly dissolved. External support declined and internal conflict over goals increased and fragmented the movement. The urban riots of the mid-1960s, which completed the process of transferring racial conflict from the South to the cities of the North, mobilized a powerful political opposition in the form of a "white backlash," which made itself felt in the 1966 off-year elections. The growing importance of racial issues in northern elections polarized the Democrats' traditional urban coalition, as white ethnics abandoned the party in droves. As a result, the political strategies of both parties reestimated the value of mobilizing black voters at the cost of antagonizing large numbers of whites. Under conditions of strong racial polarization, the black vote ceased to be a political asset.[29]

The George Wallace phenomenon contributed immensely to this devaluation of the black vote. In 1968 the two major parties polled roughly equal shares of the popular vote, with Richard Nixon running slightly ahead and winning the presidency, but Wallace garnered an additional 14 percent of the total vote. Thereafter, the electoral strategies of both major parties gave priority to the perceived political interests of the Wallace voters, thus further diminishing the political influence of blacks.

In the face of these developments, a sense of pessimism and impotence regarding prospects for racial change spread among blacks. Their responses on national surveys provide unmistakable evidence of the trend in black public opinion. Beginning around 1970, blacks became more pessimistic about their future prospects and less confident of their capacity to improve conditions. For example, the proportion of blacks who said that they "usually get to carry things out the way" they planned in their personal lives dropped by half between 1964 and 1970. At the same time, the proportion of black respondents who said things were improving for them declined. Through the mid-1960s, nearly 60 percent felt that the position of blacks had improved "a lot" in the past few years, but the percentage was only about half as large in 1976. The judgment that their collective status was no longer improving led more blacks to express a sense of impatience with the pace of change on civil rights questions. Through 1968 only about a quarter of them indicated that the pace was "too slow"; in 1970 the proportion jumped to 39.6 percent, and it has remained in the mid-30s since then.[30]

As white opposition mobilized politically and impressed itself on the strategists of the major parties, an increasing proportion of blacks began to express pessimism about their future status and disillusionment with the pace of change through the political process. In turn, these developments led blacks to become increasingly negative and distrustful of government. By 1970, for the first time since 1958, more blacks (by 25 percentage points) gave cynical responses than trustful ones when queried about their confidence in government, and the gap grew thereafter to a peak of 55 percentage points by 1974. Much more so than whites, blacks also became dubious about whether they could have an impact on the political process. Among whites the difference between those who doubted their capacity to influence politics and those who felt they had impact has never been larger than 23 percentage points (in 1978), but since 1970 it has never been smaller than 37 percentage points among blacks. Finally, while most whites believe that government and public officials pay attention to popular opinion, from 1970 on, the blacks who doubted the government's responsiveness have been a larger group than those who believed in it.[31]

It was this context of pessimism, impotence, distrust of government, and lack of confidence in the responsiveness of political institutions to their interests that shaped black political participation in the late 1960s and 1970s. Of course, in the South, voting rights legislation and mobilization campaigns boosted black turnout over its pre-1960 levels, but the rate never moved much above the 59.2 percent recorded in 1968, and by 1980, black turnout was only 58 percent. Among the black electorate in the North, the decline was steeper, from a high of 75.3 percent in 1964 to only 53.2 percent in 1980.[32]

The disillusionment and fatalism that prompted northern blacks to withdraw from electoral politics also nurtured separatist inclinations. Some blacks rejected a political process that had frustrated their aspirations and denounced cooperation with whites, whose mobilization had constricted their opportunities for political gains. A few also rejected racial integration as a goal and preached instead a doctrine of black exclusiveness. Because it seemed to be only the other side of the same coin, black power became as odious a phrase to whites, including many supporters of the civil rights movement, as Jim Crow had been only a decade or so before.[33]

The developments of 1982 and 1983 provide unambiguous evidence that blacks have refocused their attention on electoral politics and have once again displayed their faith in the ballot box. Using the sole resource indisputably available to them — their sheer numbers — blacks have chosen to pursue their legitimate group goals and demands for group benefits through the traditional political process.[34]

This rising political awareness will surely bring blacks into conflict with other groups assertively defending their own prerogatives, and the ensuing struggles may become overheated at times. But like similar contests in the past, these battles for political leverage will also necessarily involve compromising group interests to build a majority coalition. That insures that no combatant will score an unconditional victory, but it also guarantees that none will suffer an unconditional defeat. Whatever the short-term pain, operating through the political process increases the likelihood of eventually reconciling conflicting demands and reducing group tensions.

NOTES

1. The quotations are in Douglas Frantz, "As Backers Wait, Epton Abruptly Leaves," *Chicago Tribune*, 14 April 1983. On Thursday, while vacationing in Palm Beach, Florida, Epton said: "It seems like the people voting left their brains at home." And he accused the Chicago media of "vicious, vile" reporting that unfairly depicted him as a racist. "I think the media should be thoroughly ashamed of itself for finding racial hatred when it was almost nonexistent." For these sentiments by Epton, see *Chicago Tribune*, 16 April 1983.

2. The text of Washington's victory speech is in *Chicago Sun-Times*, 14 April 1983; I have reversed the order of the phrases but not changed the meaning of the statement.

3. David Axelrod and Monroe Anderson, "Washington Unity Plea," *Chicago Tribune*, 14 April 1983.

4. Mike Royko, "Picking Up on New Era," *Chicago Sun-Times*, 14 April 1983. For another view, see David Axelrod, "Washington Well-Equipped to Heal the City's Wounds," *Chicago Tribune*, 17 April 1983.

5. The quotations from Washington's inaugural address in this and the following paragraphs are in David Axelrod and Mitchell Locin, "Mayor Comes in Firing," *Chicago Tribune*, 30 April 1983. For Jane Byrne's reaction, see Andy Knott, "Byrne's Poker Face Finally Fades," *Chicago Tribune*, 30 April 1983.

6. Quoted in Axelrod and Locin, "Mayor Comes in Firing," *Chicago Tribune*, 30 April 1983.

7. On 11 May, Washington vetoed the resolutions, but his action was disallowed by both the Cook County Circuit Court and the Illinois Appellate Court. See *Chicago Sun-Times*, 11 June 1983, for a convenient chronology of events.

8. Rick Soll, "Vrdolyak: 'I knew It Would Be War,'" *Chicago Sun-Times*, 8 May 1983; and Harry Golden, Jr., and Jim Merriner, "Mayor's Tough Talk Blamed for Swing to Revolt," *Chicago Sun-Times*, 4 May 1983.

9. Robert Davis, "Washington, Aldermen Talk Peace over Breakfast," *Chicago Tribune*, 20 April 1983; David Moberg, "The Man Who Wants to Break the Mold," *Chicago* 32 (October 1983): 172–77, for the meeting between Vrdolyak and Washington and its background.

10. Quoted in Moberg, "Man Who Wants to Break the Mold," p. 174.

11. The quotation is in Golden and Merriner, "Mayor's Tough Talk," *Chicago Sun-Times*, 4 May 1983. The best treatment of Vrdolyak's organizing efforts is Moberg, "Man Who Wants to Break the Mold," pp. 172–75.

12. Quoted in Moberg, "Man Who Wants to Break the Mold," p. 173.

13. David Axelrod, "'The Party's Over'—Again—for Chicago's Political Machine," *Chicago Tribune*, 17 April 1983.

14. *Chicago Sun-Times*, 24 April 1983; *Chicago Tribune*, 19 May 1983.

15. Moberg, "Man Who Wants to Break the Mold," p. 172.

16. Washington carried wards 1, 15, 22, and 37, whose aldermen have voted with the Vrdolyak bloc; and he lost wards 42, 43, 48, and 49, whose aldermen opposed the Vrdolyak group. The conviction and resignation of one of Washington's supporters

reduced the effective size of his bloc to twenty. The alignment among the mass electorate is remarkably similar to that among the aldermen. A Gallup poll conducted between 5 and 18 October 1983 showed that 30 percent of the white respondents, and 82 percent of the blacks, supported Washington in the power struggle with Vrdolyak. The level of white support represented an 8-percentage-point gain from a poll on 2 August. For both sets of poll results, see *Chicago Sun-Times*, 6 November 1983.

17. Although he later denied having said it, the Vrdolyak statement was published in the Lerner newspapers. See the report by Harry Golden, Jr., and Jim Merriner, "Council Factions May Turn Scrap into 4-Year Saga," *Chicago Sun-Times*, 26 June 1983. In a 23–25 September 1983 poll by Market Shares Corporation, 43 percent of the white respondents and 72 percent of the blacks picked racism as the main reason for opposition to Washington by the Vrdolyak bloc. The results of the poll are in *Chicago Sun-Times*, 19 October 1983.

18. The quotations are in Stanley Ziemba, "Mayor Plans No Housing 'Stampede,'" *Chicago Tribune*, 17 April 1983; and Hugh Hough, "'Ethnic Distrust' of Mayor Told," *Chicago Sun-Times*, 1 February 1984. For other indications of the sensitivity of white ethnics to the location of public housing, see the reports in *Chicago Sun-Times*, 15 April and 19 June 1983; and for their all-or-nothing attitude, see Jim Keck, "CHA's Scattered-Site Program Perils Neighborhoods near Minority Areas," *Chicago Sun-Times*, 11 July 1983, op-ed essay. Keck is the consultant to the Southwest Parish and Neighborhood Federation.

19. *New York Times*, 12 April, 6, 15, and 19 May 1983; *Washington Post*, 18 April 1983. For another view of the larger impact of Chicago's results, see Joseph Clark, "Chicago Changes the Agenda," *Dissent* (Summer 1983): 281–85.

20. *New York Times*, 19 May 1983. According to the NBC exit polls, 19 percent of the whites in Chicago and 24 percent in Philadelphia voted for the black candidate. The data from both exit polls were obtained from the Roper Center for Public Opinion Research, University of Connecticut.

21. More technically, when controlled for the effects of education, ideology, income, party identification, religion, and sex, race in Chicago had a partial standardized regression coefficient of .67, and its inclusion in the model explained an additional 26.3 percent of the variance of the vote for Washington in the general election. In the same model for Philadelphia, race had a partial standardized regression coefficient of .61, and its inclusion added 16.8 percent to the explained variance of the vote for Goode. In both cities, race was by far the best predictor of voting choice, and its standardized regression coefficient was over three times larger than the second-best predictor, education.

22. *New York Times*, 20 April, 6 and 16 May 1983; *Pittsburgh Press*, 8 May 1983; and *Chicago Sun-Times*, 27 March 1983.

23. See the discussion by Stanley Lieberson, *A Piece of the Pie: Blacks and White Immigrants since 1880* (Berkeley: University of California Press, 1980), pp. 51–76; and for the process of accommodation among white elites in Atlanta and Detroit, see Peter K. Eisinger, *The Politics of Displacement: Racial and Ethnic Transition in Three American Cities* (New York: Academic Press, 1980), pp. 147–99.

24. U.S. Bureau of the Census, News Release CB83–63 (18 April 1983). The nine states were California, Illinois, Indiana, Kentucky, Louisiana, Missouri, Ohio, South Carolina, and Tennessee. If we take into account differences in the composition of the

white and black groups in age, sex, income, and education, black turnout in 1982 was 9.3 percentage points higher than white turnout. In 1978, the same five-variable model showed black turnout to be 5.5 percentage points below white participation. These observations derive from a reanalysis of the data from the National Election Studies conducted by the Center for Political Studies, University of Michigan. The data were obtained from the Inter-University Consortium for Political and Social Research, University of Michigan.

25. U.S. Bureau of the Census, *Current Population Reports*, Series P-20, No. 370, *Voting and Registration in the Election of November 1980* (Washington, D.C.: Government Printing Office, 1982), Table 2, pp. 10–21; and U.S. Bureau of the Census, News Release, CB83–63 (18 April 1983), Table 2. For local reaction to the report on turnout in 1982, see *Chicago Defender*, 18 April 1982.

26. The observations derive from a reanalysis of the CBS–New York Times exit poll data, which were obtained from the Inter-University Consortium for Political and Social Research, University of Michigan. Also see Thomas E. Cavanagh, "The Reagan Referendum: The Black Vote in the 1982 Election" (paper presented at the annual meeting of the Midwest Political Science Association, Chicago, April 1983).

27. Whites also disapproved of Reagan's economic performance, but by only 53.1 percent to 44.4 percent. These data are from a reanalysis of the 1982 NBC exit poll, and the data were obtained from the Roper Center for Public Opinion Research, University of Connecticut. On both questions, I have treated an excellent or good rating as approval, and a fair or poor rating as disapproval. For similar pre-election results, see *The Gallup Report*, No. 207 (December 1982): 19–26; Cavanagh, "Reagan Referendum," pp. 2–5. The trend continued after the election. By April 1983 only 10 percent of the black respondents approved of Reagan's job performance; see the Gallup poll reported in *Chicago Sun-Times*, 1 May 1983. *The Gallup Report*, No. 212 (May 1983): 8, indicated a racial split on the question of whether blacks were being fairly or unfairly treated by the Reagan Administration: 77 percent of the blacks said unfairly, while 55 percent of the whites said fairly.

28. The information on the geographic and issue focus of movement actions was developed from data reported by Doug McAdam, *Political Process and the Development of Black Insurgency* (Chicago: University of Chicago Press, 1983), Tables 7.2 and 7.3, pp. 152–53; see pp. 146–80 for his insightful analysis of the movement's dynamics.

29. Between 1966 and 1970, only 34 percent of the actions initiated by the movement occurred in the southern and border states; see McAdam, *Political Process*, Table 8.3, p. 190, and pp. 181–229 for analysis of the factors underlying the decline of the movement.

30. Philip E. Converse et al., *American Social Attitudes Data Sourcebook, 1947–1978* (Cambridge, Mass.: Harvard University Press, 1980), Tables 1.11, 2.22, and 2.27, pp. 12, 79, and 83.

31. Warren E. Miller, Arthur H. Miller, and Edward J. Schneider, *American National Election Studies Data Sourcebook, 1952–1978* (Cambridge, Mass.: Harvard University Press, 1980), Tables 4.32, 4.38, and 4.41, pp. 269, 278, and 284. More whites gave cynical than trustful responses for the first time in 1974, which provides evidence of a Watergate effect, but the trend among blacks predated that by four years.

32. Paul Kleppner, *Who Voted? The Dynamics of Electoral Turnout, 1870–1980* (New York: Praeger, 1982), pp. 114–22. The off-year turnout rates were consistently lower, of course, but they display the same trend.

33. Joel D. Aberbach and Jack L. Walker, "The Meanings of Black Power: A Comparison of White and Black Interpretations of a Political Slogan," *American Political Science Review* 64 (June 1970): 367–88.

34. Vernon Jarrett, "Blacks Show Faith in the Ballot Box," *Chicago Tribune*, 9 February 1983; and Jacqueline Thomas, "Blacks Looking to New Political Horizons," *Chicago Sun-Times*, 18 April 1983.

38
The Political Transformation of Sunbelt Cities*

Carl Abbott

Two recent overviews of politics in the emerging Sunbelt confirm the importance of [the] postwar transformation. For the broadly defined Southwest from Texas to California, political scientist Amy Bridges emphasizes that the agitation and adoption of formal governmental changes in a wide range of cities constituted an effective "refounding" of city governments. Reform regimes that matched textbook models replaced factional politics and personal nonpartisan machines. Focusing on the traditional South, Richard Bernard distinguishes between the G.I. revolts, whose intent was to replace older political cliques with younger leadership, and the more systematic efforts at structural reform that followed in the late 1940s and 1950s. From Oklahoma City to New Orleans, however, the results reflected a common interest in economic growth without social change.[1]

If the immediate aim of postwar reformers was to throw the rascals out and to stencil new names on the doors at city hall, their broader goal was to define and implement a single set of policies to guide the development of the entire metropolitan area. The frequently expressed worries about the disease of decentralization arose from an early concern about possible development of intrametropolitan conflict. Ambitious mayors and planners in the optimistic years of the later forties and early fifties therefore offered programs of annexation and regional planning in order to preserve the dominant role of the central city in local decisions and to block the development of independent political influence in suburban areas. Business and political leaders in city halls and downtown clubs also expected that rapid economic growth under central city leadership would prevent the emergence of dissatisfaction in peripheral areas by bringing prosperity to individual suburbanites and an expanding tax base to suburban governments.

A decade of reform campaigns, charter review commissions, and charismatic candidates gave way in the 1950s to the urban renewal era in sunbelt cities. As postwar reformers consolidated their hold on city governments, they implemented their agenda of administrative modernization and economic development. Businesslike government meant new budgeting, purchasing, and personnel practices, the restructuring of operating departments, and the recruitment of professional workers from a national pool. It also meant the creation of businesslike housing and redevelopment agencies whose semiindependent status made it easy to provide public services without worrying about the satisfaction of specific interests. Government partnership with the private sector meant new freeways, port and airport improvements, downtown office space, and enticements to new manufacturing industries.

The men in the foreground during the 1950s and 1960s were the same people who could be found in the Chamber of Commerce board room or at the monthly meetings of the Jaycees, for the sunbelt reform movements operated with the assumption that leadership should come from certain groups within the local business community. In the Virginia of Jefferson and Washington, the gentleman freeholders who owned the large plantations took it as a matter of course that their stake in the economy entitled them to control public decisions. Two centuries later, local market businessmen in Norfolk and Richmond drew the same conclusion, stepping from private to public offices as naturally as the Lees and Randolphs had accepted the call to Williamsburg. From one ocean to the other, it was difficult to distinguish the members of the Good Government League in San Antonio, the Charter Government Committee in Phoenix, or the Myers Park clique in Charlotte from the crowd in the country club lounge.

The natural allies of the downtown businessmen were the municipal bureaucrats. Programs of economic growth promised a large tax base with which to implement new initiatives, while the promotion of administrative efficiency allowed opportunities to establish reputations among their professional peers. Along with Cincinnati and Kansas City, the showcases for ambitious city managers were large sunbelt cities like San Diego, Dallas, Fort Worth, Richmond, and Norfolk, where an organized business community offered a stable base of support. The same years were also a golden age for the planners, housing experts, public health specialists, and redevelopment officials who filled the operating bureaus and agencies. As Lester Salamon has stated, urban planning on a broad scale "has never been more effective than when it was harnessed to the goals of that powerful coalition of progressive business elements and activist chief executives that took shape in city after city following the Second World War and that exploited the potent planning tools made available by the federal urban renewal and highway programs to lay claim to the decaying urban core for the administrative activities required in an increasingly technological society."[2]

The sunbelt states in the 1950s and 1960s easily offered more than a score of examples of booster governments. The homogeneous, middle-American populations of most western cities made it easy for civic leaders to construct agreement around the related goals of population growth and a white-collar economy. New residents had moved to San Jose, Albuquerque, and Denver precisely because of their range of high-status jobs, while established businessmen enjoyed the resulting booms in retailing and real estate. The tightly guarded political systems of many southern cities achieved the same consensus by excluding dissident voices and admitting minorities on carefully defined terms. Indeed, one of the significant differences between the booming cities of the economic Sunbelt during the urban renewal era and the less successful cities of the Mid-South lies in the area of political accommodation between whites and blacks. Particularly prosperous cities such as Norfolk, Charlotte, and Atlanta developed a tacit contract that traded white backing for substantial public housing programs and expanded municipal jobs in return for black acceptance of downtown renewal and freeway programs that often disrupted black neighborhoods. San Antonio and other Texas cities also managed voluntary desegregation of public facilities with minimal white resistance. The white business communities in deep South cities like Little Rock, Memphis, New Orleans, and Birmingham, however, were unwilling or unable to offer black residents the same sort of accommodation until the end of the 1960s.[3]

Despite its importance, the postwar reform era in sunbelt cities received relatively little attention from contemporary observers. For most urban experts, references to a modern "civic renaissance" brought to mind a list of cities in the old industrial belt. The editors of *Fortune* in 1957 and 1958 defined what is still a commonly accepted list of cities that benefited from reinvigorated leadership after 1945. One article described a "new breed" of big-city mayors who were not so much politicians as public entrepreneurs interested in the promotion of economic growth. Examples included Richard Daley of Chicago, Richardson Dilworth of Philadelphia, David Lawrence of Pittsburgh, Robert Wagner of New York, Charles Taft of Cincinnati, Raymond Tucker of Saint Louis, and Frank Zeidler of Milwaukee. Another editorial called attention to the "businessman's city," with particular reference to the Greater Philadelphia Movement and Saint Louis Civic Progress. *Fortune* also cited Cincinnati, New York, Philadelphia, Milwaukee, Pittsburgh, Baltimore, Detroit, and San Francisco as evidence that large cities were among the best-run organizations in the country.[4]

Historians and political scientists who examined the civic renaissance of the 1950s tended to start with general propositions and to end with examples drawn from the Northeast and Middle West. In 1964, for instance, Robert Salisbury argued that a "new convergence of power" was reshaping American urban politics as strong mayors, professional planners, and businessmen combined their efforts to promote economic growth. His cases in point were Chicago, Saint Louis, Pittsburgh, and New Haven. Three years later, Jeanne Lowe argued that New York, New Haven, Pittsburgh, Philadelphia, and Washington were the cities that were winning their "race with time."[5] Several studies in the 1970s summarized the experience of the same sorts of cities. New Haven, Boston, Chicago, Pittsburgh, Philadelphia, Saint Louis, and New Orleans appear on every list; Wilmington, Newark, Syracuse, Baltimore, Cleveland and San Francisco appear on occasion.[6]

If the postwar decades in fact brought a "burst of civic reform activity not seen since the progressive era," the focus of change was more properly the emerging Sunbelt than the Northeast. In the first place, the spirit of civic optimism in the Northeast scarcely survived the 1960 census of population and the 1963 censuses of business and manufacturers. In combination with the high unemployment of the 1959 recession, population losses or minimal gains in the older cities were a painful shock to their activist leadership. Data on business locations similarly showed that heroic revitalization programs in cities like Pittsburgh had failed to modernize the economic base or to counteract the national tilt toward the South and West.[7]

In the second place, reform-minded businessmen in many northern cities were as much front men for regular political organizations as they were independent actors. In Chicago, Richard Daley was not a representative of a new breed of civic leaders but a canny politico who reinvigorated the Democratic party with the assistance of businessmen and establishment institutions like the University of Chicago. Mayor Lee of New Haven similarly used the local Democratic machine as a tool for urban redevelopment and as an independent power base for negotiations with business interests. In Pittsburgh and Saint Louis, the civic renaissance involved a sometimes uneasy partnership between regular party politicians and central city business interests. Pittsburgh's Mayor David Lawrence and his Democratic organization worked as senior partners with the Alleghany Conference on Community Development, which represented Richard Mellon and other major industrialists. Without the same tight central control, progressive government in Saint Louis depended on constant negotiations between the "good government" mayor and the professional politicians based in county offices and ward committees.[8]

The "renaissance coalition" in the North also involved the customary mobilization of labor unions and European ethnic groups. No matter how shiny the new buildings looked to a visitor or how new the rhetoric sounded in *Harpers* or *Fortune*, local residents viewed urban redevelopment as another manifestation of traditional city politics. Scholars generally agree that urban machines and politicians from the 1930s to the 1960s were able to use the new programs of state and federal aid to preserve their own influence.

Certainly Richard Lee and Richard Daley sold their programs to the voters not in terms of general issues but as a way of satisfying a package of specific interests. In short, the new progressivism in northern cities with strong ethnic communities and established party organizations was an effort to use new tools to assemble the same sort of investment coalition that historians associate with turn-of-the-century bosses.

The postwar reform movements in sunbelt cities as described in this study differ from those of the northern cities on each of the points described. As chapter two indicates, sunbelt cities on the average have smaller European ethnic communities and weaker unions. They are also likely to have city manager administrations and nonpartisan elections. Both characteristics helped the civic-minded businessmen who had assumed control after 1945 to make their decisions without worrying about other interests within the city. Indeed, if the editors of *Fortune* had really wanted to find the "businessman's city" in its pure form in 1957, they should have looked to Dallas, San Antonio, Norfolk, Denver, and San Jose.

The third stage in the cycle of urban reform in the postwar Sunbelt was the gradual weakening or breakup of the businessmen's coalitions between 1965 and 1980. In part, the decline stemmed from problems among the reformers themselves. The neoprogressives in many cities by the 1970s were as tired as the original progressives had been in 1920. A decade or two decades of political control had allowed the reformers to achieve many of their goals in restructuring city administrations, installing modern management practices, and rebuilding sections of downtowns. More and more of the old leaders preferred a graceful exit from the public arena to further years of strenuous effort to accomplish a dwindling list of reforms. Most of the reform efforts also failed to recruit successors as the original leaders dropped out of politics or moved to new jobs. Even the highly organized Good Government League forgot to replace sixty-year-old and seventy-year-old members with men and women in their thirties and forties. As a consequence, younger businessmen and lawyers with political ambitions tended to develop new issues and to build careers outside the reform context.

The rapid growth of suburbs relative to central cities offered a direct challenge to the business-oriented conditions in many metropolitan areas. Tentatively during the 1950s and more strongly during the 1960s, governments within the suburban ring raised the basic question of equity in the allocation of the benefits and burdens of local government. Indeed, the same rapid growth that demonstrated the success of central city reform movements also exacerbated intrametropolitan conflict by forcing quick decisions and quick action on the service needs of new suburbs. With little time for careful debate and inadequate institutions for areawide decision making, residents of each metropolis had to apportion limited public resources between the competing demands of suburban development and urban redevelopment. The result, with growing frequency, was a politics of confrontation between older and newer areas over taxes and services led by increasingly self-sufficient suburban governments. Because of the rapid sorting of metropolitan population by socioeconomic status, conflicts between older and newer areas were often conflicts as well between poorer and richer communities. Both city and suburban officials scrambled to make sure that decisions on highway construction, bus routes, sewers, and other metropolitan service networks met the specific needs of their own constituents. Suburbs looked jealously at water systems and other physical services that remained under control of city agencies at the same time that they worked to fend off annexation and the extension of city school districts. Residents on both sides of the boundary markers argued loudly that they were being gouged by the tax collectors but short-changed on the services that their taxes purchased.

The suburbanization of retailing, recreation, and construction also had a direct impact on the downtown-oriented administrations of the 1950s by opening a gap between businessmen dependent on inner-city markets and real estate values and those whose prosperity was tied to peripheral growth. In San Antonio, the split among locally oriented businesses was a major element in the collapse of the Good Government League. In Charlotte, a similar split helped to defeat a city-county consolidation proposal in 1971. The new charter was developed and supported by the Chamber of Commerce and the downtown business interests that had pushed urban renewal and economic development programs in the later fifties and sixties. It mobilized the opposition of suburban voters who feared the creation of a single school system and of suburban businessmen who saw it as a tool for maintaining downtown dominance of local growth patterns. Across the continent, the rise of San Jose's sprawling suburbanized electronics industry had similar effects. Represented through the Santa Clara Manufacturing Group, the new industrialists diluted the remaining influence of an already weak downtown elite in the 1970s. In the rebalanced political system, "downtown San Jose has simply not been a serious concern for the major corporate interests who have built their low-rise headquarters in Silicon Valley cities to the north such as Mountain View, Sunnyvale, Santa Clara, and Palo Alto."[9]

Fragmentation of the reform consensus also involved the definition and legitimation of geographically localized interests within central cities themselves, bringing the replacement of the simple city-suburb dichotomy by a complex pattern of spatial politics based on the particular interests of numerous subareas.

The unexpected defection of portions of the central city middle class was rooted in the growth histories of sunbelt cities themselves. The first members of the 1940s baby boom (which was intensified in the Sunbelt by the extraordinary wartime and postwar migration of people in their twenties and thirties) reached voting age in the 1960s. Reduction in the average age of the urban electorate brought pressures for younger leadership and changes in service demands, such as an increased emphasis on urban environmental amenities. Rapid expansion of downtown professional and managerial employment also brought in new migrants with no loyalties to the power brokers of the 1950s. These new voters supported the preservation of older centrally located neighborhoods for the middle class. One result in cities like

Seattle, Portland, and Denver was the incorporation of neighborhood interests into both political rhetoric and the bureaucratic decision process.[10]

Greater long-range impact on local politics came from the empowerment of geographically concentrated minority populations. The Voting Rights Act of 1965, which was extended to Hispanic voters in 1975 and renewed in 1982, provided an essential tool for minority representation. Richmond, Houston, San Antonio, Fort Worth, Albuquerque, Oakland, Stockton, Sacramento, San Jose, and San Francisco were a few of the cities that shifted to full or partial ward systems for city council elections during the 1970s and early 1980s. Overall, one-third of the cities in the Confederate South with significant black populations made the same shift. The result has been substantial and presumably permanent increases in minority representation within city governments.[11]

Trends in the 1980s have reflected both the changing environment of national politics and the continuing logic of political development within sunbelt cities. The most predictable extension of the trends of the 1970s has been the maturing of suburban political independence. In the 1960s and 1970s, suburbs were increasingly able to block central city growth agendas. By extension, the 1980s have brought greater prominence for suburb-focused development agendas in direct competition with central cities.[12] Metropolitan Miami provides a good example of such active promotional suburban governments. Coral Gables (42,000 population in 1980) has declared itself the "Global City of the Future." Local business interests and the city government have cooperated to make Coral Gables an international banking center for Latin American trade. A few miles to the north, Hialeah (145,000) has captured and facilitated much of the peripheral industrial growth associated with Miami International Airport. Bellevue (74,000) has planned and promoted an alternative downtown across Lake Washington from Seattle. DeKalb and Cobb counties function as full-service governments that help Atlanta's booming northern suburbs turn their back on the central city.[13] Other supersuburbs that view themselves as full peers of their regional centers include Long Beach; Arlington, Texas; and Virginia Beach.[14]

Even without the governmental support of a supersuburb, new suburban business interests have emerged in many sunbelt cities to directly challenge the redevelopment schemes of the old downtown elite with their own programs for investment in suburban services and promotion of suburban growth. In the 1980s Portland's west suburban electronics industry began to veto the central city's public service strategy and to argue effectively its own contradictory needs. In Phoenix, "Los Angeles–like urban sprawl resulted in the creation of multiple power centers throughout the Salt River Valley" from the late 1960s. Peripheral development created new, localized sets of business and investment interests different from those of the postwar city elite. New centers with their own groups of economic and civic leaders include the independent suburbs of Scottsdale and Mesa-Tempe-Chandler and the growing northwest and Camelback-Biltmore regions.[15]

The full impacts of suburban independence can be seen in Denver. The eastern suburb of Aurora (159,000) has dealt with Denver as an equal since the early 1970s. The city has invested heavily in the infrastructure for economic growth, including a joint water supply system with Colorado Springs that frees Aurora of its dependence on the transmountain pipelines of the Denver Water Board. The city markets itself intensively as an office and industrial location. It has annexed aggressively at the same time that state law has largely locked Denver within its boundaries. Arvada (85,000) and Lakewood (114,000), on the other side of Denver, have plans for major territorial expansion and employment growth. Fort Collins, the core city of a separate metropolitan area adjacent to Denver on the north, rejected a "slow-growth" regulation in 1979 and rode a high-tech boom to a population of 53,000 by 1985.

The political and economic power of suburban Colorado was sufficient during the last decade to block Governor Richard Lamm's efforts to maintain planning controls on sprawling metropolitan growth. The decision to build a modified form of Interstate 470 through the southwest suburbs, with its inevitable stimulation of population development, was an early defeat for Lamm's campaign platform of controlled growth. A set of "Human Settlement Policies," adopted by executive order in 1979 and designed to mitigate and guide urban growth, foundered within months on suburban legislative resistance. Lamm's citizen-based Front Range Project produced broad policy goals rather than specific growth controls. According to political scientist Dennis Judd, the result was inevitable, for "business and political leaders promoting controls tended to reside in or near Denver City proper: their motivation was to prevent competition with the downtown and to promote 'compatible' development outside the city. In contrast, suburban officials and developers were quite anxious to develop their own economic bases, and they cared little if this was compatible or competitive with Denver."[16]

In the face of aggressive suburban development, many central cities themselves have shown renewed interest in "businesslike," growth-oriented local government.[17] The reaction is in part a response to the shrinking of available resources. Portland and some other cities have been trying to shake off the effects of the depression of the early 1980s in the resource-extraction industries. The shifting of national priorities and cuts in federal urban programs have directly limited city budgets, increased competition for available discretionary funds, and provided support for policies and coalitions that promise local investment and jobs.[18] At the same time, the shift to the center can be seen as a logical synthesis of postwar political trends. Quality-of-life liberals have become middle-aged quality-of-life consumers and yuppies have replaced granola-eaters. More important, newly empowered minorities are pressing for a fair share of an expanding pie. The political rebalancing of the 1970s now means that there are strong pressures to assure that the benefits and burdens of growth are more equitably distributed than in the 1950s and 1960s.

Andrew Young's administration as mayor of Atlanta is representative. Elected in 1981 following a temporary downturn in local business, he cemented relations with the white business community and helped the city out of its economic doldrums. His day-to-day support and his overwhelming reelection margin in 1985 reflect an effective coalition of the white commercial-civic elite and the black middle class. Young sided with the business community on specific issues including a sales tax increase and a controversial parkway to the Carter presidential library that threatened neighborhoods reprieved from freeway construction in the 1970s. More broadly, Young has embraced the development program of Central Atlanta Progress. "A large measure of cooperation and good will" between the city administration and major business interests, argues Clarence Stone, "marks the emergence of a revamped but apparently stable urban regime, as in the past devoted mainly to promoting economic development especially in Atlanta's central business district."[19]

Other southern cities in the 1980s have shown similar biracial coalitions around economic growth. Like Andrew Young, Birmingham's Mayor Richard Arrington has built his success on a simultaneous appeal to blacks and to white professionals. The replacement of civil rights activist Henry Marsh as mayor of Richmond by Roy West in 1981 marked a sharp return to the downtown development and pro-business policies formed by that city's white establishment—an approach that West himself defines as building Richmond's "New South image." Mayor Ernest Morial of New Orleans was described in 1983 as a "new breed" executive who took an aggressive role in business recruitment and promotion of downtown development. As the city's first black mayor, however, he also seemed to the white establishment to play to racial tensions. Sidney Barthelemey, a black council member, defeated Morial in 1986 with a conciliatory racial style that won about a quarter of the black voters and nearly all of the white.[20]

Successful local politicians in western cities in the mid-1980s have tended to emphasize the importance of economic growth while retaining a commitment to values of livability. Seattle's Charles Royer placed his first emphasis on the city's economic health in contrast to the neighborhood orientation of Wes Uhlman. Harvey Kinney won the mayor's office in Albuquerque by running against his predecessor's "environmentalism," but he adopted many of the same policies without the rhetoric. Portland's Bud Clark, elected in 1985, had political roots in neighborhood organizations and an informal personal style but stressed economic development and the need to try "anything you can do to bring business to Portland." In San Francisco, Mayor Diane Feinstein has followed the factionalized neighborhood- and minority-based politics of the 1970s with an administration that promotes closer ties to major economic interests. As journalist Francis Fitzgerald has recently written, "Feinstein had urged a return to citywide elections for the Board of Supervisors, and the city supported her. Now that she had an electoral system in which the neighborhoods could not prevail over the downtown . . . she could proceed to steer the city back to a more conservative, pro business course. Though she was a liberal Democrat, she would not be out of step in the eighties."[21]

Denver and San Antonio may offer the clearest examples of administrations that have tried to bring together newly mobilized constituencies of the 1970s and the downtown establishment around programs of diversified and planned economic expansion. In each case, a young Hispanic politician has brought new ideas into city government. Henry Cisneros of San Antonio defeated a representative of the downtown establishment in 1981. Federico Peña ousted crusty, fourteen-year incumbent Bill McNichols from Denver's city hall in 1983 with the help of thousands of volunteers. If the campaigns had come in 1976 or 1978, they might well have produced deep community divisions. In the 1980s, however, Peña and Cisneros were able to run on positive platforms as advocates of a new generation of urban growth that would avoid the unnecessary costs of the urban renewal era and make jobs available for all segments of the community.

Peña took the reins in a city with a public leadership vacuum reminiscent of 1947. Like Ben Stapleton a generation before, Bill McNichols had run an administration marked by age, croneyism, and indifference to any but routine services. The energy industry building boom of the late 1970s and early 1980s was largely guided by the private Denver Partnership, representing the major actors in downtown development, rather than by the city. Peña's campaign in 1983 tapped neighborhood activism that had been stifled under McNichols but also enlisted major businesses and developers at the start. His slogan of "Imagine a Great City" could appeal to both groups, as can his theme of growth in the context of long-range planning. Although Peña retained broad popularity, his first major defeat came in October 1985, when voters decisively rejected a $138 million convention center proposed for the northern fringe of downtown. Opposition was based on specific objections to the site, which obviously benefited some landowners more than others, and on a general unwillingness to undertake major new commitments in the midst of the city's lingering recession.[22]

Henry Cisneros has given San Antonio a new political center after the collapse of the Good Government League, the rise of Hispanic influence, and the city-suburban battles of the 1970s. A pragmatic liberal with experience in Washington, he had a record of attention to economic development issues as a city council member from 1975 to 1981. His comfortable election as mayor with 62 percent of the vote in 1981 and his overwhelming reelections in 1983 and 1985 gave him the opportunity to develop a systematic growth strategy first outlined in his own report on "San Antonio's Place in the Technology Environment: A Review of Opportunities and a Blueprint for Action." This "orange book" defined five areas for growth and served as a springboard for Target '90, a consensus goals document involving several hundred civil leaders. Cisneros is described as a "state of the art civic entrepreneur" trying to link government and business and to build a national and international reputation for the city, especially in the area of biotechnology. In a manner analogous to Andrew Young, his essential strategy is to meet the needs of Hispanic residents by expanding job opportunities and building the middle class. However, booming growth on the far north side has yet to create many new jobs downtown or elsewhere in core areas easily accessible to inner neighborhoods. Indeed, the income gap between rich and poor districts widened in the early 1980s.[23] Even in the most up-to-date cities, neighborhoods and suburbs remain essential variables for metropolitan policy and politics.

The history of metropolitan politics in the Sunbelt since 1940 confirms the importance of underlying patterns of social geography. Spatial politics in southern and western cities has meant the development of metropolitan pluralism. A wide range of groups, defined variously by ethnicity, social class, or residential location, have developed the capacity and willingness to pursue parochial goals through formal and informal political entities that are considerably smaller than the metropolis as a whole. The common element in the political geography of many SMSAs is therefore the complexity of competition among central cities, their neighborhoods, and their suburbs. The same metropolitan area may illustrate the problems of neighborhood rivalries, intersuburban competition, sectoral disputes within regional agencies, and traditional city-suburban conflicts.

An irony of sunbelt growth is the convergence of metropolitan politics and problems on northern patterns. The South and West may continue to be centers for economic change, but their systems of metropolitan governance increasingly mirror the divisions of a Chicago or Philadelphia. The Sunbelt's cities emerged from the challenges of World War II with exciting opportunities to build new metropolitan communities without the accumulated mistakes and hostilities that burdened older cities. Their first generation of postwar leaders matched the opportunities with strong ambitions for metropolitan growth under unified direction. Nevertheless, the theme of the last two decades has been the ineffectiveness of integrative institutions, whether the focus is the fate of reform administrations or the rise of intrametropolitan conflict. Despite the promise of common goals, the trend in sunbelt SMSAs has been toward increasing variety and fragmentation in governmental structure. Efforts to sell the entire metropolis on common policies have failed to prevent the proliferation of concern for small areal units. Regional planning, annexation, and deference to core city leadership have all been weakened by the outward tide of population that advanced the status of suburban rings and by smaller eddies that created socioeconomic differences among neighborhoods and among suburbs.

In consequence, the residents of sunbelt SMSAs can expect to face increasingly difficult problems of urban maturity. Their special circumstance of growth gave them a postponement but not an exemption from the defining characteristics of American urban society. Although the urban renewal era lasted longer in the South and West than in the Northeast, the closing years of the century do not necessarily promise the same distinctiveness for the central cities of the Sunbelt that characterized the first postwar generation. Southern and western cities which have lost their battle for continued territorial growth will increasingly find themselves faced with the same problems of obsolescence that haunt New York and Chicago. It is too early to predict the replication of the South Bronx or Chicago's Woodlawn in the Gulf and Pacific cities, but it is not too early to worry about the results of blocked growth for cities such as Atlanta, Richmond, Miami, and New Orleans. Even Los Angeles looks more and more like an older rather than younger city. While the suburban world of Orange and Ventura counties has continued to grow, Los Angeles itself has experienced net outmigration, increasing population densities, a shift toward multifamily housing, and a rising proportion of minority residents.[24] In a symbolic indication of the relative fortunes of the city and its suburbs, the Los Angeles Rams announced a move to Orange County only two years after the New York Giants skipped from the Bronx to New Jersey.

The response of many city dwellers and city politicians to their loss of special status within the metropolis has been to turn in on themselves. Residents defend their own wards and neighborhoods from rapid change while city officials scramble to locate new housing or new factories on remaining parcels of vacant land within the city limits. Unfortunately, the well-publicized return to the city, which was widely hailed in South Atlantic cities such as Baltimore, Washington, Richmond, Charleston, and Savannah and western cities such as Seattle, Portland, and Denver will not have significant long-range impact on the aging process. Beyond the admitted aesthetic attractions of older neighborhoods, the rediscovered advantages of the central city are the availability of housing suitable for one- and two-member households and convenience to downtown office jobs. The former can be supplied just as easily in well-planned suburbs. The latter in itself furnishes a limited market in most cities. In addition, the new rapid-transit systems in Washington, Atlanta, San Francisco, Miami, Portland, and other cities are reducing the competitive advantage of older neighborhoods by enhancing the access of suburbanites to downtown business districts and simultaneously building up rival suburban office nodes.

More broadly, sunbelt citizens can expect that increasing political fragmentation of their metropolitan areas will continue to erode their advantages over older cities and to exacerbate inequities in the intrametropolitan allocation of the benefits of growth and government. When entire SMSAs are considered, sunbelt cities still have resources to provide decent jobs and adequate public services. They can expect another generation of economic prosperity to attract new residents with high levels of education and skills. However, governmental fragmentation and suburban independence will mean that many metropolitan resources will be unavailable for the central cities of these same SMSAs.

Over the past generation, the most exciting aspects of metropolitan politics in the Sunbelt have been the inclusive vision of the 1940s and the willingness to accommodate new interests in the 1970s. In contrast, the 1980s have brought a diminished political vision focused on shorter-term economic development programs for suburbs and central cities. The development efforts themselves have merit, for prosperity is a precondition for effective planning and inclusive public services. However, the underlying economic and political strategies have become increasingly separate and self-interested. The need that remains is to tie the isolated agendas into unified visions of just and prosperous cities. Before the current pattern of intrametropolitan parochialism or conflict becomes a permanent habit, sunbelt cities can continue to seek the institutions and the leadership to build true metropolitan communities.

NOTES

1. Bridges, Amy. "Municipal Reform in the Southwest." Paper delivered at conference on "The Sunbelt: A Region and Regionalism in the Making," Miami, Florida, November 1985; Bernard, Richard. "Municipal Politics in the Sunbelt South." Paper delivered at conference on "The Sunbelt: A Region and Regionalism in the Making," Miami, Florida, November 1985.

2. Salamon, Lester. "Urban Politics, Urban Policy, Case Studies, and Political Theory." *Public Administration Review* 37 (August 1977): 418–28.

3. Jacoway, Elizabeth. "Civil Rights and the Changing South." In *Southern Businessmen and Desegregation*, edited by Elizabeth Jacoway and David Colburn, p. 11. Baton Rouge: Louisiana State University Press, 1982; Goldberg, Robert A. "Racial Change on the Southern Periphery: The Case of San Antonio, Texas, 1960–65." *Journal of Southern History* 49 (August 1983): p. 373; Jennings, M. Kent. *Community Influentials: The Elites of Atlanta*. New York: The Free Press, 1964; Wright, William E. *Memphis Politics: A Study in Racial Bloc Voting*. New York: McGraw-Hill Book Co., 1962.

4. "New Strength in City Hall." *Fortune* 56 (November 1957): 156–59, 251–64; "The Businessmen's City." *Fortune* 57 (February 1958): 93–96.

5. Lowe, Jeanne. *Cities in a Race with Time*. New York: Random House, 1967.; Salisbury, Robert. "Urban Politics: The New Convergence of Power." *Journal of Politics* 26 (November 1964): 775–97.

6. Gelfand, Mark. *A Nation of Cities: The Federal Government and Urban America, 1933–65*. New York: Oxford University Press, 1975, pp. 158–64; Miller, Zane. *The Urbanization of America*. New York: Harcourt, Brace, Jovanovitch, 1973, pp. 181–97; Mollenkopf, John. "The Post-War Politics of Urban Development." *Politics and Society* 5 (1975): 273–80; Barnekov, Timothy, and Rich, Daniel. "Privatism and Urban Development: An Analysis of the Organized Influence of Local Business Elites." *Urban Affairs Quarterly* 12 (June 1977): 431–60.

7. Adrian, Charles. "Metropology: Folklore and Field Research." *Public Administration Review* 21 (Summer 1961): 148–53; Miller, *Urbanization of America*, pp. 196–97.

8. Lubove, Roy. *Twentieth Century Pittsburgh: Government, Business, and Environmental Change*. New York: John Wiley, 1969; Wolfinger, Raymond. *The Politics of Progress*. Englewood Cliffs, N.J.: Prentice-Hall, 1974.

9. Trounstine, Philip J., and Christensen, Terry. *Movers and Shakers: The Study of Community Power*. New York: St. Martin's Press, 1982.

10. Judd, Dennis. "From Cowtown to Sunbelt City: Boosterism and Economic Growth in Denver." In *Restructuring the City: The Political Economy of Urban Development*, edited by Susan Fainstein et al., pp. 189–86. New York: Longman, 1983.

11. San Francisco returned to elections at large in 1980 after experimenting with districts for the 1977 and 1979 elections. Denver modified its electoral system to add "black" and "Hispanic" districts in 1971. San Jose's adoption of districts was pushed more strongly by neighborhood groups than by minorities. Browning, Rufus; Marshall, Dale Rogers; and Tabb, David. *Protest Is Not Enough: The Struggle of Blacks and Hispanics for Equality*. Berkeley: University of California Press, 1984, pp. 19–24, 46–69, 202; Muñoz, Carlos, Jr., and Henry, Charles. "Rainbow Coalitions in Four Cities: San Antonio, Denver, Chicago, and Philadelphia." *PS* 19 (Summer 1986): 604; Heilig, Peggy, and Mundt, Robert J. "Changes in Representational Equity: The Effect of Adopting Districts." *Social Science Quarterly* 64 (June 1983): 393–97; Davidson, Chandler, and Korbel, George. "At Large Elections and Minority Group Representation." *Journal of Politics* 43 (November 1981): 982–1005.

12. Bernard, Richard, and Rice, Bradley R., eds. *Sunbelt Cities: Politics and Growth since World War II*. Austin: University of Texas Press, 1983, pp. 20–26; Bridges, "Municipal Reform."

13. Rice, Bradley R. "If Dixie Were Atlanta." In *Sunbelt Cities*, edited by Richard Bernard and Bradley Rice. Austin: University of Texas Press, 1983, pp. 53–54; Mohl, Raymond. "Miami: The Ethnic Cauldron." In *Sunbelt Cities*, edited by Richard Bernard and Bradley R. Rice, pp. 58–99. Austin: University of Texas Press, 1983.

14. The city of Norfolk managed the first steps toward downtown economic revitalization with a successful waterfront festival market, which opened in 1984. However, fears of white population loss to suburban Virginia Beach and Chesapeake prompted the recent controversial recision of a city-wide plan for school integration through busing that had operated since 1971. The School Board's decision in the spring of 1986 capped six years of political debate and court challenges. The result was a school year that opened in the fall of 1986 with projected enrollment in a quarter of the city's elementary schools over 95 percent black. Such is the indirect political influence of suburban prosperity.

15. Johnson, G. Wesley. "Generations of Elites and Social Change in Phoenix." In *Community Development in the American West*, edited by Jessie Embry and Howard Christy. Provo: Charles Redd Center for Western Studies, 1985, pp. 98–105; Louv, Richard. *America II*. New York: Penguin Books, 1985.

16. Judd, "Cowtown to Sunbelt City," p. 195; Gottlieb, Robert, and Wiley, Peter. *Empires in the Sun*. New York: Putnam, 1982.

17. The stages of political change described here are similar to the model posited by Susan and Norman Fainstein, "Regime Strategies, Communal Resistance, and Economic Forces." In *Restructuring the City: The Political Economy of Urban Redevelopment*, edited by Susan Fainstein, pp. 245–82. New York: Longman, 1983. The Fainsteins describe stages of "directive" municipal politics (before 1965), "concessionary" politics (1965 to 1975), and "conservative" politics (1975 to 1981 or later). Their periodization is somewhat different than mine, however, and the basis of their analysis is class rather than place.

18. Browning, Rufus, and Marshall, Dale Rogers. "Is Anything Enough?" *PS* 19 (Summer 1986): 635–40.

19. Stone, Clarence. "Atlanta: Protest and Elections Are Not Enough." *PS* 19 (Summer 1986): 618–25.

20. *Nation's Cities*, 13 June 1983; New Orleans *Times-Picayune*, 3 March 1986; *Wall Street Journal*, 2 and 25 November 1983.

21. *Nation's Cities*, 25 January 1982; Browning et al., *Protest Is Not Enough*, p. 58; FitzGerald, Frances. "The Castro." *The New Yorker*, 21 July 1986, pp. 47–48.

22. Foster, Richard. "In Downtown Denver, a Civic Group Calls the Shots." *Planning* 49 (January 1983): 18–21; Wittenauer, Cheryl. "Federico Peña: From Dark Horse to Driving Force." *Hispanic Business* 6 (February 1984): 20–23; Muñoz and Henry, "Rainbow Coalitions," p. 606; *Washington Post*, 18 October 1985.

23. Fulton, William. "Henry Cisneros: Mayor as Entrepreneur." *Planning* 51 (February 1985): 4–10; Muñoz and Henry, "Rainbow Coalitions; Broder, David. "San Antonio's Uneven Growth Reflected in Wider Income Gap." *Washington Post*, 11 March 1986.

24. Stanley, David T. *Cities in Trouble*. Columbus, Ohio: Academy for Contemporary Problems, 1976, pp. 1–5; Nathan, Richard, and Adams, Charles. "Understanding Central City Hardship." *Political Science Quarterly* 91 (Spring 1976): 51–62; Nelson, Howard J., and Clark, William A. V. *The Los Angeles Metropolitan Experience: Uniqueness, Generality and the Goal of the Good Life*. Cambridge, Mass.: Ballinger Publishing Co., 1976.

part III

URBAN DEVELOPMENT AND ITS CONSEQUENCES

The decennial census of 1920 marked a milestone in America's national history, showing that for the first time more than half of Americans lived in urban places. For several decades the industrial cities had acted as magnets drawing millions of foreign immigrants and rural migrants in search of jobs in factories, packing houses, docks, and railroad yards. Industrial cities had grown at a startling pace, New York City from a little more than 1 million people in 1860 to more than 5.6 million by 1920, Chicago from 112,000 to 2.7 million in the same sixty-year period, and St. Louis from almost 161,000 to more than 772,000 people. The big cities that sat atop the urban hierarchy constantly were forced to cope with the problems of frenetic population growth.

During the past half-century, these same cities have been forced to cope with the problems of decay. The urban hierarchy of the industrial age has disintegrated. By the 1970s it was apparent that other nations were aggressively competing with the United States in industrial production for domestic and foreign markets. A broad range of economic sectors began to retrench or to disperse their operations around the globe. In all of the advanced Western nations industrial employment fell as a proportion of the workforce; at the same time service-sector employment rose.

For the older industrial cities and regions, the effects of these changes were devastating. The policy options available to local officials were reduced when federal urban programs began to dry up. Local officials desperately cast about for policies that could stimulate new capital investment. The central city revitalization strategies of the 1950s through 1970s, which were underwritten with federal funds, gave way to policies designed to create a "good business climate." Cities found themselves participating in an urban sweepstakes that paralleled the urban competition of the nineteenth century. During that era, cities competed for railroads. In the late twentieth century, cities compete for service-sector growth and for corporate towers, tourism, and downtown malls.

As in the early nineteenth century, the competition has often been frantic, with cities trying to outdo one another to offer incentives to investors. One result of the strategies to promote growth is that public poverty increasingly exists side by side with private plenty. Corporate towers, waterfront recreational development, enclosed shopping malls, luxury hotels, stadiums, and new convention centers have sprung up in cities all across America—while cities struggle to balance budgets, maintain infrastructure, and provide services. Private plenty coexists with private poverty as well. Because of cutbacks in government services and programs, the urban poor have less access to housing, medical care, and other forms of public assistance. Any visitor to an American city who walks down streets filled with homeless people must wonder if American cities are becoming less like cities in other Western nations and more like those in the Third World.

THE POLITICS OF URBAN DEVELOPMENT

As Norman J. Glickman points out in his selection, the politics and policy priorities of cities have changed in step with transformations in the world economy. The loss of manufacturing jobs, together with a continuing decentralization of jobs and population, have hit the older manufacturing centers particularly hard. Corporations have pressured governments at all levels to reduce taxes and regulations to encourage more investment. In the face of the problems already occurring as a result of economic reversals, governments have found it difficult to resist such demands.

In such a context, economic logic easily triumphs over political logic, in part because the language of growth translates into symbolic reassurance that when inducements to investment are offered, surely entrepreneurs will respond. This sort of thinking dominates local politics even though, as Todd Swanstrom's reading suggests, inducements often do not bring growth. The problem for local politics is to somehow achieve a balance between the imperative for growth and a politics that recognizes other values besides those dictated by the marketplace.

Such a balance is very difficult to achieve. Michael Peter Smith, Randy L. Ready, and Dennis R. Judd show in their selection that states and localities are inclined to offer incentives for investment even though there is plenty of evidence that incentives make little difference in the locational investment decisions of firms. The reason for this is that local jurisdictions must not appear to be unfriendly to capital; because other local governments offer incentives, it is difficult for any one local government to resist also doing so.

In response to global economic changes, both the downtown skylines and the neighborhoods within cities have been changing. In cities where the service sector is rapidly expanding, middle-class professionals have taken over neighborhoods with significant architectural features. "Gentrification" creates a bipolar city, split between the prosperous and the poor. Peter

Williams and Neil Smith refer in their selection to the outcome of this process as "social Manhattanization"—a process whereby many cities are becoming like Manhattan, with rich and poor living in uneasy proximity.

THE POLITICS OF FISCAL POLICY

Unlike the position of British and other Western European cities, which derive most of their funds from central government grants, American cities rely mostly on their own tax sources for their revenues, a fact that makes them particularly dependent on local economic growth to supply revenues for the public budget. Because the fiscal health of the city treasury is inescapably connected to the health of the local economy, local budgetary politics is very sensitive to changes in the market position of the city. In their study of postwar budgetary politics in New York City, Paul Kantor and Stephen David describe how local officials constantly struggled to reconcile changes in New York City's economy with the realities and pressures of the city's political system. They demonstrate that New York City's fiscal crisis followed years when city officials attempted to use the budget process to deal with disturbances in the local political system at the cost of major increases in public expenditure and borrowing. When the city's economy declined and access to the capital market was lost, fiscal crisis followed: Economic and political elites took advantage of this to remove the budget from citizen influence, and they shifted budget priorities to favor the promotion of business growth.

The bond market is a powerful constraint on local government policy because cities depend on the private capital market to finance capital projects such as school buildings, highways, bridges, hospitals, sewers, and parks, as well as to meet their short-term "cash-flow" obligations. Alberta Sbragia discusses the complex relationship between cities and the financial institutions and individual investors that make up the municipal bond market. She describes how these relationships limit the autonomy of city officials to define their policy options—though city voters often do not understand how powerful these constraints are. Ultimately, bond ratings institutions can discipline cities that fail to follow prescribed "sound" policies by making it more difficult and expensive for them to borrow money. Sooner or later, this trump card is impossible to ignore, and few cities even make the attempt.

THE INEQUALITY AND SEGREGATED METROPOLIS

It is obvious that cities balance economic logic and political logic only with great difficulty; the imperatives of the market place often win out. Swings of the pendulum, however, do occur from time to time, and local governments can be moved to promote different values. In particular, when social problems mount to such a point that they are given urgent political expression through civil disorders or when the economic well-being of the community is threatened because of neglect of public responsibilities, then city governments are moved to attend to them. Just how and when political authorities respond to collective problems and to what effect is ultimately a matter of political choice. For example, the police may be dispatched to deal with social unrest, or, alternatively, programs can be funded to deal with some of the causes of the unrest (through programs that try to reduce racial discrimination or inequality, for example).

The authors of the *Report of the National Advisory Commission on Civil Disorders*, which was issued in 1967, believed that the urban riots of the 1960s were caused by extreme racial segregation and discrimination. In the selection taken from the report, they urge policy responses that are designed to get at the causes and not merely the effects of the riots. The commission recommended a complex set of policies to break down racial discrimination.

From the perspective of more than two decades later, it is obvious that the problems cited by the commission have not disappeared. William Julius Wilson questions whether race-specific policies such as those advocated by the commission could have been effective in any case. In the selection drawn from an essay he published in *Society*, Wilson puts forth his thesis that, though discrimination undoubtedly still exerts an influence, blacks today are more profoundly affected by shifts in the American economy, combined with the clustering of poverty populations in the central cities, than by overt racism. The new service economy requires levels of training and education that are beyond the reach of most of the young people that make up a portion of what Wilson calls the urban underclass. According to Wilson, lack of access to jobs is directly related to the social problems that beset inner-city blacks. He asserts that far-reaching social policies to provide better opportunities for all individuals in poverty—not race-specific policies—are necessary.

According to John D. Kasarda, the problem goes beyond a mismatch between the skills of poverty populations and the jobs that are being created in the new economy. He asserts that the mismatch that matters is spatial—that minorities in the inner cities live at too great a distance from where the new jobs are located. In his selection, he recommends (among other points) that policies be adopted that would break down patterns of residential segregation and also recommends improved transportation systems so that inner-city residents can commute to the suburban jobs for which they are qualified.

Though the recent concept of the underclass is generally applied very broadly, the urban underclass is sociologically complex, and it is segmented into distinct groups and enclaves. Poverty populations concentrated into inner-city neighborhoods are often labelled the "underclass." An equally visible group, the homeless, also fits the definition. Perhaps because homelessness on a large scale is such a recent phenomenon in American cities, the homeless have become a ubiquitous symbol of the new social problems of the cities.

In his selection, James D. Wright provides a historical and statistical overview of homelessness. He indicates that although homelessness is not a new problem, it has changed substantially; the new homeless are more destitute than the homeless of the past, they are younger, and they are made up of a more complex mixture of groups. In today's cities, he indicates, a "new form of class conflict" is arising between a significant number of people who cannot afford housing—and everyone else.

The selection from Jonathan Kozol's book, *Rachel and Her Children*, conveys an intimate view of the life experiences of homeless people. The daily routine of homeless people revolves around finding safe havens; their lives are filled with desperate insecurities about being arrested, chased out, or subjected to violence. Kozol shows that "We do not know what we want to do with these people," but there is a tendency for hardened attitudes increasingly to dictate public policy. We must, he says, be prepared to "speak the unspeakable," and consider whether we are drifting toward "state terrorism as social welfare policy."

Urban dwellers are becoming more accustomed to seeing poverty side by side with wealth. Indeed, beggars and homeless people on downtown streets have become so ubiquitous that they are taken for granted today; they are usually ignored unless they actually inconvenience someone. No doubt this has occurred because cities, and the people who run them and live in them, have other priorities. As Jon C. Teaford points out, a whole generation of "messiah mayors" have captured the public's imagination with a "gospel of urban hype" about the future of cities. Construction of office towers, luxury hotels, tourist facilities—the renaissance of neighborhoods and waterfronts—all seem to promise a bright future just around the corner. Perhaps the rehabilitated image of the cities explains why people are so tolerant of the terrible tragedies occurring daily on city streets. The constant talk of an urban renaissance makes it appear that the city's problems are transient; we just need to be patient.

In cities in both the Sunbelt and the Frostbelt, a long list of social problems are not being effectively addressed: racism, poverty, homelessness, hunger, health care, and environmental quality. The fiscal and governmental capacities of city governments to respond to these problems are limited, and perhaps that is why urban leaders and citizens alike are so susceptible to a shallow rhetoric of renaissance. Yet the social and political tensions that characterize urban politics may in the future dictate a more substantial response than the one described by Teaford. The present economic logic that guides urban politics is not fixed; our political priorities are, fundamentally, a matter of choice.

The Politics of Urban
Development

39

Cities and the International Division
of Labor*

Norman J. Glickman

INTRODUCTION

In this chapter I shall set out some working hypotheses about the role of
cities in today's changing international division of labor (IDOL), within the
context of more general structural change.[1] In doing so, I shall examine the
complex ways in which cities have evolved over time, how they are centers
for political and economic struggle, and how metropolises are affected by
public policies. I shall discuss the following four major points:

1. There has been a vast transformation of the world economy in that energy
   price increases, new investment and migration patterns, and the inter-
   penetration of markets have had profound and uneven effects on national
   economies. In recent years, economic growth, profits and wages have
   stagnated in most developed countries, while there have been diverse
   impacts on industries, occupations and cities. There have been employment reductions in traditional manufacturing and shifts to the high-technology and service sectors.

*Glickman, Norman J. 1987. "Cities and the International Division of Labor." Pp. 66–86 in ed.
Michael Peter Smith and Joe R. Feagan, *The Capitalist City*, Cambridge, MA: Basil Blackwell.
Copyright © 1987. Reprinted by permission of Basil Blackwell.

2. The "third industrial revolution" (involving electronics, biotechnology and, significantly, information processing) has helped produce two contradictory urban trends. First, it has encouraged deurbanization and the dispersion of the population. This is so because technology and the maturation of product lines have promoted both standardized work and dispersed job sites, and because changing business strategies and organization have allowed firms to seek less urbanized locations. Hence, decline has occurred in traditional manufacturing regions and there has been a continuing decentralization of jobs and population. At the same time, an opposite tendency has produced agglomerations of corporate headquarters functions in a few large cities. These centers of administrative activities maintain control over regions that specialize in production processes that are lower in the urban hierarchy.

3. As a result of economic change, there have been pressures by groups and classes (e.g. income, race, regional, industrial and occupational) who have suffered and who demand policies to cushion themselves from decline. In an era of slow growth, with many groups bringing simultaneous pressures on the state, fiscal problems result. For instance, firms petition the state to increase their profitability via tax cuts, deregulation of markets, relaxed enforcement of health and safety regulations, and reduced social welfare benefits. Corporations have attempted to roll back previously won wage and working conditions directly through bargaining and indirectly through appeals to the state on the grounds that high wages are the prime cause of inflation and low productivity. Workers, on the other hand, fight to maintain their living standards and economic security through the extension of social legislation and urban programs. With slow economic growth, the state cannot meet all of these demands simultaneously. These problems are made more difficult to solve in a more internationalized economy, as external pressures add new dimensions to political conflict.

4. Economic programs trying to re-establish faster growth have geographical side-effects that often aid growing areas and suburbs at the expense of declining regions and central cities. Urban policies, on the other hand, generally try to ameliorate the problems of large cities and declining areas. Therefore, a policy dilemma has resulted that the state cannot easily solve.

In what follows, I shall expand on these points, taking the United States as a case-study.

SOME PHENOMENA

National and International Economic Change

The world economy has changed significantly in the last twenty-five years (see Table 1). The 1970s saw sharp decreases in economic growth rates and increases in inflation. In non-socialist industrialized countries, for example,

TABLE 1. Macroeconomic Performances of Major Country Groups, 1960–81

| | Average Annual Growth Rate of GDP Per Capital[m](%) | | Average Annual Rate of Inflation[m](%) | | Average Annual Growth Rate of Foreign Trade | | | | Exports of goods and Non-factor Services as a Percentage GDP[m] | |
| | | | | | Exports[m,b] | | Imports[m,b] | | | |
	1960–70	1970–81	1960–70	1970–81	1960–70	1970–81	1960–70	1970–81	1960	1981
Low-income countries	4.60	4.50	3.50	11.20	4.90	−0.70	5.30	2.40	7	9
Middle-income countries	6.00	5.60	3.00	13.10	5.40	4.10	6.40	4.80	17	23
Low middle-income	5.00	5.60	2.80	11.10	5.20	3.00	6.50	4.10	15	23
Upper middle-income	6.40	5.60	3.00	18.60	5.40	7.00	5.90	4.70	18	23
Industrialized countries	5.10	3.00	4.30	9.90	8.50	5.40	9.50	4.40	12	20
Capital-surplus oil exporters	13.00	5.30	1.20	18.20	11.00	−1.50	11.00	20.80	—	69
Centrally planned economies[b]	4.90[b]	5.60[b]	—	—	9.40	6.70	8.60	6.10	—	—

w = weighted average, nominal terms.

m = median, nominal terms.

a = real terms, measured from volume indices.

b = 1960–70 and 1970–81.

SOURCE: World Bank (1980, 1983: Tables, 1, 2, 5 and 9).

the average annual Gross Domestic Product (GDP) growth fell from 5.1 per cent to 3 per cent from the 1960s to the 1970s, while inflation rates more than doubled. There have been extraordinary increases in international trade, with the world's exports increasing more than twelve times between 1963 and 1981 (Deardorff and Stern, 1983). The last two columns of Table 1 show the marked increase in trade as a proportion of GDP (e.g. from 12 to 20 per cent developed countries between 1960 and 1981).

To understand changes in the IDOL, it is useful to divide the world into three types of country: (1) *core* countries that make up the leading industrial producers of the Organization for Economic Cooperation and Development (OECD) and that house most corporate centers; (2) *semi-periphery* nations, consisting of the middle-income OECD nations and newly industrializing countries (NICs) that are dependent on core- nation capital investment; and (3) the poor countries and oil exporters of the *periphery* (Wallerstein, 1974).[2]

Two stages of international trade, capital investment and migration patterns can be identified (Glickman and Petras, 1981). During the 1950s and 1960s, labor was imported from the periphery and semi-periphery to the core, capital-intensive exports were sent from the core to the semi-periphery and periphery, most trade and foreign investment was intra-core, and low-cost energy was imported into the core from the peripheral oil-producing nations. After about 1974, however, new trends emerged. As economic growth declined, most labor migration ended, foreign direct investment (FDI) increased from the core to a small number of NICs, more labor-intensive imports came into the core from the NICs, and high-price energy was imported by the core countries. Although reductions of labor importation into the core were accompanied by capital exports to NICS, FDI went to a largely different set of countries from those that were previously labor exporters. Thus, a *triangular* relationship of labor–capital exchange took place: labor had been imported from one set of semi-periphery and periphery countries, but capital exports went to NICs, few of which had been labor exporters.[3] The search for cheap labor in the NICs was largely for assembly operations, especially in the semiconductor, textile, clothing and shoe industries. Relocation of auto, chemical, steel and rubber operations from developed nations were often for marketing purposes or to supply other overseas operations. Importantly, while assembly functions decentralized, control activity remained in the core.

A good example of worldwide industrial dispersion can be seen in the automobile industry. Hill (1983) describes the transition from a US-dominated industry in the 1960s to one now characterized by massive foreign investment by American carmakers and increasing competition from Japanese and European producers. As a result, fierce global competition emerged and the US share of sales dropped sharply. There has been integration of worldwide auto operations, efforts to penetrate European markets by American firms, and penetration of the US market by the Europeans and Japanese. The results have been dramatic: between 1978 and 1982, US firms' car sales declined by 32 per cent while imports rose from 18 to 28 per cent of the domestic market. Employment fell by nearly 300,000 workers. Most recently, there has been massive foreign investment by US car companies (about $80 billion was projected for the period 1980–86) and simultaneous demands for protectionism at home. Global integration of operation has been implemented, involving geographically separate engineering, design, production, assembly and other operations. Ford "World Car" is an example of this strategy. Nearly identical cars are assembled at various sites using components produced in different countries.[4] Firms are thus able to take advantage of local production conditions to maximize worldwide profits.

Castells (1984) shows a similar globalization of the semiconductor industry. Research and management functions, which demand intellectual labor, are located near universities and cities where "quality of life" factors are high. But the other processes—mask-making, wafer fabrication, assembly and testing—may have geographically distinct and separate patterns. Therefore, labor-intensive assembly functions have been locating in Hong Kong, Singapore and Korea, where wages are low. By 1976, "offshore" assembly plants employed twice the number of people working in similar domestic operations. The same lines of geographic development can be seen in the assembly processes of many other industries.

These patterns emerged because of improvements in communications technology and changes in business organization, resulting in the establishment of a "Global Factory" (Barnet, 1980). A large number of people have been brought into this international system of production, exchange and finance. Assembly work can be done nearly anywhere in the world with low-skilled workers. Thus, firms have looked for sites with low-wage, stable and unorganized labor, both within developed nations and in "safe" LDCs (usually those with totalitarian regimes).[5] Crucially, the speed of capital shifts has increased as firms have become better able to disperse production worldwide because of the information revolution (Bluestone and Harrison, 1982; Castells, 1984).

Two spatial phenomena are directly connected to recent global economic change. First, the evolving IDOL has meant that cities have developed new functions. In particular, a few "world cities" (Friedmann and Wolff, 1982) have evolved to organize and manage the far-flung operations of multi-national corporations. Cities such as New York, Tokyo, London and Paris house concentrations of corporate headquarters, high-level corporate services (accountancy, law, etc.), banking, research and government. Supervision of production facilities lower in the urban hierarchy takes place in these conurbantions. Smaller cities assume roles as production, service and consumer centers (Pred, 1977; Cohen, 1981; Noyelle and Stanback, 1984). The higher a city is in the hierarchy, the more control it will have over its own economic destiny. Therefore, we see both a *spatial diffusion* of economic activity and a pronounced *territorial hierarchy* (Castells, 1984).

Second, direct foreign investment has affected regional development. During the early postwar era, most investment was in the core regions of developed nations because of uncertainty about alternative sites and the desire to be near consumer markets. Later, multinational corporations (MNCs) decentralized investment, particularly in assembly operations (Glickman and Woodward, 1984).[6]

International Trade and the US Economy

Within these global patterns, the US economy also changed. There evolved a stagnant economy, a fall in the rate of profit (Nordhaus, 1974; Lovell, 1978), more overseas investment (OECD, 1981), slower productivity growth (Denison, 1979), and stagflation (simultaneous high inflation and unemployment). For example, the GNP growth rate fell from 4.7 per cent per annum (1961–65) to 2.2 per cent (1973–81). On a per capita basis, GNP growth plummeted from 3.1 per cent (1960–73) to only 0.9 per cent (1973–81) (Reich, 1983). Inflation reached 13 per cent in 1980, declining only under President Reagan's deflationary measures of the early 1980s and the deepest postwar recession. After-tax profits fell from 13.7 per cent (1966) to 7.6 per cent (1979).

US investment abroad increased substantially, while direct foreign investment in the US exploded in the 1970s.[7] US assets abroad were $226 billion at the end of 1983, three times the 1970 level. There was also a major shift towards investment in the NICs: 7 per cent of US FDI went to these countries in 1960–68 compared to 19.4 per cent between 1973 and 1978. By 1977, production by US parent companies and majority-owned foreign affiliates overseas was $161 billion, more than one-twelfth of domestic GNP (Howenstine, 1983).[8] Inward FDI grew from $13 billion in 1970 to $134 billion in 1983; the annual growth rate was 8.4 per cent from 1963 to 1973, increasing to 20.5 per cent between 1974 and 1981 (Schoenberger, 1983). Following Dunning (1981), Shoenberger (1983) argues that much inward FDI was by oligopolistic firms seeking access to the large US market in order to exploit their "ownership advantage" in such high-technology sectors as machinery and chemicals.

Trade of US goods and services grew rapidly, as exports increased from $29 billion in 1960 to $348 billion in 1982 (Belli, 1983). Merchandise imports and exports were both about 14 per cent of production in 1970; however, exports rose to 23 per cent and imports increased to 31 per cent of domestic output by 1983. Most significant has been the penetration of US manufacturing goods markets and the decline of the US as a world trade leader.[10] By 1980, nearly three-quarters of all goods produced in the US were in active competition with imports from other countries (Reich, 1983). The US now exports some high-tech items,[11] corporate and financial services, and agricultural products. At the same time, imports are strong in traditional manufactured markets that were previously US-dominated. Major import industries are autos (21 per cent of domestic consumption), consumer electronics (52 per cent), calculators (43 per cent), textile machinery (46 per cent) and cutlery (90 per cent) (Magaziner and Reich, 1982). Significant balance-of-trade problems resulted from declining competitiveness and higher-priced oil.

Trade has had differential effects on occupations and segments of the labor force. Frank and Freeman (1979) show that some 85 per cent of the job losses attributable to US investment abroad has been in blue-collar occupations. Sectors affected adversely by imports have had high union membership and have employed more blue-collar, female and ethnic minority workers. At the same time, export industries tend to have more highly educated, young and managerial employees. Thus, increased imports and outward DFI have adversely affected lower-skilled workers.

IDOL and US Spatial Change

Changes in the IDOL have produced a number of notable consequences for American cities and regions. First, the decline in sales of heavy manufacturing goods in international markets (e.g. transportation equipment, non-electrical and electrical machinery, chemicals) has exacerbated unemployment problems in the industrial heartland of the Northeast and Midwest. Simultaneously, other regions have gained from trade: agricultural sales abroad have helped farming regions in the 1970s, and some of the large cities that lost manufacturing jobs have gained service positions (particularly in corporate headquarters functions). These corporate service jobs are concentrated in the Northeast and other large metropolitan areas (Stanback and Noyelle, 1982).[12]

Second, there has been an uneven pattern of foreign direct investment among US regions. In 1981, employment in non-banking US affiliates of foreign firms was concentrated in the Mid-East (23.4 per cent), Southeast (24.9 per cent), and the Great Lakes (16.2 per cent).[13] But, the fastest employment growth between 1974 and 1981 was in the Southwest (20.1 per cent per year compounded), the Rocky Mountains (16.1 per cent) and Far West (12.8 per cent) regions. McConnell (1980) argued that locations outside the industrial heartland are fast becoming the choice of foreign multinationals. In this sense, foreign affiliates are following the decentralization patterns of US firms. Glickman and Woodward (1985) show that there was significant dispersion from regions with considerable inward FDI directed to those areas that had little in the early 1970s. Their analysis points out that the spatial distribution of foreign firms is becoming similar to that of domestic companies, increasingly favoring the South and West.

Third, international migration (illegal and legal) has had a distinct regional character. Most migrants come from the Caribbean Basin, Central America and (more recently) Asia. Many Hispanic workers (often employed in secondary agricultural and service jobs) reside in the Southwest (e.g. California) and parts of the Northwest (New York, New Jersey). In all, the greater openness of the US economy meant that international forces had more significant effects on urban and regional development than previously.

Returning to the automobile and semiconductor examples discussed earlier, the regional consequences of the industries' transformations have been important. Historically, car assembly and production have been regionally concentrated in Michigan. In 1963, for example, 36 per cent of auto employment was in that state. With the globalization of the car industry, that figure fell to 26 per cent by 1977.[14] Semiconductors have been concentrated in California, Arizona, Texas and Massachusetts, where three-quarters of employment is located. Areas such as Silicon Valley near San Jose and the Route 128 area around Boston dominate research and management locations. Assembly operations that have not been located abroad are in low-wage areas of western states.

Urban and Regional Change in the United States

In addition to the effects of the IDOL, there have been other important spatial ramifications of structural change. On an interregional basis, sharp reversals of long-term regional patterns took place during the 1970s: for the first time the growth of jobs and population was greater in non-metropolitan regions than in metropolitan areas. Cities with large manufacturing bases lost jobs and population[15] to the suburbs (first the inner suburbs, then the outer suburbs, and, finally, the "exurbs" and other non-metropolitan areas) and to the Sunbelt.[16] These phenomena represent more than spillovers across metropolitan boundaries, but encompass growth far from metropolitan areas as well. Part of the non-metropolitan change is due to energy and resource development, and a portion is a result of recreation- and retirement-related employment. However, much non-metropolitan employment growth is also in assembly operations (often in branch plants of large companies) that have relocated from large cities. Most big cities have lost population, independent of region. There has been much continuing migration to the Sunbelt,[17] including the return of blacks who moved to the North two generations ago.[18] In the 1980s, however, long-run patterns were re-established mostly because of the shifts in the IDOL.

The relative importance of industrial location factors has changed. With the decline of manufacturing (particularly heavy manufacturing), the traditional location determinants (transportation availability and costs, agglomeration economies, energy and, to a lesser extent, labor) have less significance or have changed in character. Firms have become more communications- and technology-oriented. Both manufacturing and service firms, for example, are able to decentralize routine operations to low-wage regions (domestically and internationally) and need little unskilled labor near their headquarters. Technological advances in transportation and communications allow greater decentralization, as firms have become more footloose (Malecki, 1979; Markusen, 1982). At the same time, financial reorganization makes decentralization more feasible (Bluestone and Harrison, 1982). Firms, particularly those that hire many white-collar workers, increasingly demand "quality of life" factors. These reasons help explain why many small and medium-sized cities with pleasant living conditions and low taxes have been growing rapidly.

There has been, as a result of these factors, a polarization of the urban system (Hanson, 1983). Cities with concentrations of corporate command functions have a large measure of independence from the rest of the urban system. At the same time, areas that specialize in traditional production or provide consumer services are dependent on corporate centers for investment and finance. Even within metropolitan areas, there is considerable economic segregation—what Friedmann and Wolff (1982) call the "citadel and the ghetto." The gleaming towers of Manhattan coexist with the poverty of nearby Harlem and Bedford-Stuyvesant, although there is little employment for these neighborhoods' residents on Wall Street. Economic and spatial segmentation can also be seen in Silicon Valley, where the homes of researchers and managers are located away from production-line workers (Saxenian, 1984).

SOME TENTATIVE EXPLANATIONS OF ECONOMIC AND POLITICAL CHANGE

Having discussed the IDOL and its effects on the US, we need to tie a number of factors together: the economic slowdown and responses to it, the changing nature of the state, the role of people's movements and corporate initiatives, and fiscal problems at the local level. I provide some tentative explanations in this section.

Three elements of the international postwar corporate system that were put in place in the 1940s and 1950s came back, in a dialectical manner, to haunt the American economy in the 1960s. These were: (1) *Pax Americana*, consisting of the Bretton Woods Agreement and other economic and defense measures, aimed at maintaining American postwar hegemony; (2) *a limited capital–labor accord*, an informal agreement between "Big Capital" and "Big Labor," to share productivity gains in key industries and to pass on higher costs to others; and (3) *a limited capitalist–citizen accord* to provide economic security through social legislation (social security, medical care, etc.) and the reduction of cyclical unemployment through demand management (Bowles, Gorden and Weisskopf, 1983). All parts of this unwritten "social contract" were confined to certain sectors, classes and interest groups. The whole arrangement was predicated on the ability to reward those inside (and, to a lesser degree, outside) the accords by distributing the fruits of economic growth. Wolfe (1981: 10) described the early postwar political situation as "A bipartisan coalition . . . formed to pursue economic expansion at home through growth and overseas through empire. . . . Politics would concern itself with the means—growth—and the ends, or purpose, of social life would take care of themselves."

However, there were exogenous and endogenous forces at play that destroyed this very delicate set of arrangements. Significantly, there came the decline in US economic dominance and the end of the *Pax Americana* in the 1960s. This occurred because of the drain put on the economy in the late 1960s by the support for the military in Vietnam and by competition with the countries that the US had been trying to build up both for markets and for geopolitical purposes (e.g. Germany, Japan and stable LDCs). The growth of social programs and the unwillingness to raise taxes to pay for both the war in Southeast Asia and the "War on Poverty" strained the US fiscal and political capacity. The rise of OPEC and the greater strength of raw material producers also weakened US hegemony. The US economic leadership declined drastically as it was increasingly challenged in its own domestic markets as well as in world markets that it formerly dominated. As a result, stagflation set in, and latent problems in various strata of society surfaced — in production welfare lines and bottom lines. With fewer resources available to keep the accord together, the agreement disintegrated.

Many of America's problems were reinforced by federal policies. For instance, by encouraging the outflow of FDI through tax laws and by other means, domestic jobs were lost. In the 1970s, American firms were competing with their own foreign subsidiaries. Corporations began, as part of a conscious business strategy, to reduce (when practical) production in the United States in many processes and industries (e.g. the assembly operations in the auto industry). Tax and regulatory policy made these corporate strategies easier to carry out. Reagan era monetary policy, in trying to battle against inflation, created high real interest rates and many international trade problems. The resulting overvalued dollar has made foreign investment cheap and exports expensive for American firms.

The domestic "growth coalitions" (Wolfe, 1981; Mollenkopf, 1983), formed to increase economic growth both nationally and locally, fell into disarray. These alignments of corporate, labor and community leaders failed, partly because so many people were not in the coalition to begin with: secondary workers, women, ethnic minorities, consumer groups, environmentalists, and others had been largely powerless from the outset. During the 1960s, these groups put pressure on the state for a bigger slice of the pie. Wage bargaining by workers became much more aggressive, since the cost of being unemployed was very low (due to unemployment benefit and tight labor markets). Women and ethnic minorities also become more important as economic and political forces. These internal factors, combined with the US decline in the international sphere, contributed to the fall in the profit rate and to some of the productivity growth rate decline. Also, even within the growth coalitions, primary workers began negotiating more aggressively on workplace issues (e.g. assembly "speedups" work safety), thereby putting further pressure on profits. Workers were less willing to accept poor working conditions and began to revolt on the production line (Aronowitz, 1973). Finally, there were additional costs placed on the system by the pressures of environmentalists, consumers and others.

The profit squeeze of the late 1960s to early 1970s inevitably brought a counterattack by corporations. As a result, the "people's movements" for greater social welfare (Piven and Cloward, 1971) of the 1960s were superseded by what can be called "corporate movements" in the 1970s. Faced with low profits, businesses took the offensive at the negotiating table, mounted strong anti-union drives, and lobbied hard for restrictive macroeconomic policies in order to reduce wage pressure. At the local level, fiscal limitation efforts (such as California's Proposition 13) received strong corporate backing. Politically, the corporate movement reached its peak with Ronald Reagan's election in 1980 and the passage of the 1981 tax and domestic spending reductions. The deep recession of 1981–2 served to discipline the workforce and to gain wage and shopfloor "give backs"; under this pressure, unions were forced to agree to lower wages and inferior working conditions.

In the light of this corporate offensive, much of the increased international and interregional mobility of capital can be seen both as a way to increase profits by relocating to lower-cost areas (in the conventional, neoclassical economist's view) and as a way of combating labor's gains; in the latter sense, this is a way of crippling the labor movement (Bluestone and Harrison, 1982). Therefore, the movement of branch plants to non-metropolitan areas in 1970s can also be seen as part of an anti-labor strategy (since non-metropolitan areas generally have low union penetration). Relocation to low-wage areas is not only national but international, as indicated earlier.

At the same time, the work process has been changed to reduce the demand for skilled and semi-skilled labor. This has been accomplished by automation, the reorganization of work, and by other methods. Much of this "deskilling" occurs when firms relocate operations to low-wage regions and take advantage of new (and non-union) employees to restructure work (Noble, 1977). This reduces the necessity of employing high-skilled, expensive and independent labor. It helps tip the bargaining scales in favor of management and to increase profits.

CHALLENGES TO THE STATE

In response to some of the effects of structural change, the state has been called upon to do several, often contradictory, things: to take measures to increase profits and fight stagflation; to institute class-based social policies to aid displaced workers; to initiate urban and spatial measures to help depressed areas, and so forth (Friedland, Piven and Alford, 1979; Glickman and Alford, 1982). Since all of these could not be accomplished simultaneously in a slow-growth era, several kinds of conflict resulted.

On one level, the state has been subject increasingly to *external* pressures as trade relations grow more complicated. Assaults have come from other nations (e.g. trade wars, protectionist pressures), multinational corporations (who exact subsidies by threatening to relocate offshore), migrant workers and their employers, and international organizations (the EEC, LAFTA, etc.). All of these groups petition the state to protect their interests.[19] Corporations seek to break down national boundaries and use their full power globally. National governments, as a result, find themselves bargaining with footloose MNCs and, as a result, are less able to formulate effective policy.[20] Pressures build to protect jobs and social services for workers displaced by global shifts. These tugs bring ideological conflicts between free trade and protectionism. We find the US government preaching free trade, yet engaging in protectionism (e.g. the "voluntary quotas" for imported Japanese cars). International conflicts over a variety of products (e.g. steel, wine, pasta) give significant trouble to nation-states.

In addition to these external pressures, the state is faced with *internal* conflicts. These have taken several forms, most often over distributive shares. For example, the corporate ascendancy of the last decade has resulted in sharply lower business tax rates, an increasingly regressive tax code, and real reductions in social spending. This has led to greater tax burdens being placed on consumers and workers. Displaced car, steel and textile workers seek protectionism, restraining and social benefits. Geographically, there are also inherent conflicts between economic policies (e.g. accelerated deprecia-tion allowances) that help expanding areas and urban policies that try to cushion declining cities (Luger, 1983; Glickman, 1984). These conflicts are aggravated by stagflation: as the economy performs poorly, there is more competition among interest groups and classes to try to fight for their shares of the pie. Fiscal strains result from these internal pressures on the state, especially when the economic pie is growing slowly.[21]

In addition, *region*-based demands add another dimension to the prob-lems of the state. That is, coalitions of capital and labor fight for preferences for localities; these groups often transcend class and other alignments, com-ing together for limited purposes when under threat. Examples include a coalition of the Chrysler Corporation, the United Auto Workers Union and the City of Detroit that brought pressure for the 1980 federal loan guarantee to Chrysler.

Just as firms put pressure on the state for tax concessions (accelerated depreciation allowances, etc.) to increase profitability at the national scale, they also do so to increase profitability at the local level. Ronald Reagan's New Federalism, the devolution of other federal programs to the states, enterprise zones and cuts in social spending, are ways of aiding corporate growth. For instance, dispersing the powers of the federal government to the states means that lobbyists for social causes must go to 50 state capitals, where their power is diluted and where corporate power is felt most strongly (Peterson, 1982). Also, one can view tax revolts at the state and local level as corporate/wealthy-led attacks on the social wage; this weakens local tax bases and makes localities more vulnerable to further pressure from firms that induce cities to give greater tax breaks.

These international and domestic pressures result in an increasingly impotent state, since governments cannot deal effectively with internal pres-sures that often lead to fiscal stress. Nor can the state effectively make successful arrangements with the many pressure groups negotiating with it. The combination of internal and external pressures make decision-making very difficult.

Several elements are important to recall at this juncture: (1) the decline in profitability; (2) pressures by corporations on the state to do something to restore profitability (e.g. tax concessions, engineered recessions, deregula-tion); (3) corporate strategies to increase profits, including speedups, increases in supervision, less workplace autonomy, mergers and, significantly, threats to relocate; and (4) pressures by labor, consumers and environmentalists to maintain social and quality of life programs. These factors make the state (at both national and local levels) less able to operate effectively. The international dimension reduces even more the effectiveness of state policy because firms can withdraw capital investment. Capital mobility is a tool used by firms to gain advantage over labor and to extract concessions from the state. And, as we shall see, it makes urban policy more difficult to carry out.

URBAN POLICY

Urban policy (UP) is formulated to correct for market failure brought about by spatial imbalances and to spur economic development. For example, in order to provide space and funds for urban revitalization, UP has consisted of programs such as urban renewal (in the 1950s and 1960s, particularly) and housing. Other things have been done by national governments to reduce the cost of conducting business in cities, including infrastructure grants, loans, small business development efforts, transportation, and water and sewerage programs. An increasing number of programs are undertaken by localities themselves: selling land below market value, infrastructure provision for business, subsidized loans and grants aimed at attracting firms in the spatially competitive environment, noted earlier.

Another flank of urban policy consists of income transfers and public services, including AFDC (Aid to Families with Dependent Children) housing allowances for low-income families, Supplemental Social Insurance, and other income and service programs. These programs are often not for towns but for people and certainly have important urban effects. Some urban programs come about through categorical grants to localities and states, others through less restrictive block grants. The trend since the Nixon Administration has been towards the latter.[22]

Most of the money for these urban programs goes to welfare payments rather than to places. In fact, about $18 is spent on welfare provision (including retirement pensions) for every $1 spent on urban programs. Funds for urban renewal programs have been cut sharply, by 27 per cent in real terms between 1978 and 1984 (Glickman, 1984). Means-tested social programs for the poor were cut by one-sixth during the Reagan administration, about $75 billion (Bawden and Palmer, 1984).

But, in addition to these nominal urban programs, what I call "the *real* urban policy" includes the indirect urban consequences of economic policy: accelerated depreciation allowances, investment tax credits and so forth (Glickman, 1984). The incentives started by these programs are very powerful aids to industrial relocation even though they are not intended for these purposes. For instance, these tax programs try to increase investment by lowering the cost of capital and increasing cash flow. However, in doing so, they also encourage investment in new assets rather than the replacement of existing assets and favor equipment in preference to structures. The result is that the investment that results from these tax write-offs takes place in growing (often Sunbelt) areas, rather than in declining regions. Moreover, there are other non-urban policies that affect the spatial division of labor: the allocation of R & D expenditures, defense appropriations and bases, and other spending to growing, non-union, low-wage areas (Luger, 1983). These non-urban portions of UP constitute the most important part of the real urban policy.

Therefore, we have three branches of urban policy: "place programs," "people programs," and non-urban tax/expenditure policies. Most of these programs are biased towards growth areas that have low wages and "good business climates." Regions, that have strong unions, higher wages, and so forth are being left behind, especially by footloose assembly operations. Therefore, economic policy aimed at increasing investment and production also aids corporations in a spatial sense since capital movements disrupt efforts to organize by workers. As a corollary, the efficiency of most local or national urban development programs is compromised by the mobility of capital. In effect, cities have far less control over local business activity because firms are so easily able to move. Therefore, municipalities find it more difficult to formulate and implement development policies because of the capital mobility and the conflict of urban policies with national economic programs.

For localities, slower economic growth and a more internationalized economy have led to frantic attempts to attract industry through local tax incentives, particularly tax abatements and industrial development bonds for new factories.[23] These local programs have become fundamentally "defensive" in nature: local economic development officers say, "If we don't offer these benefits, our town will be perceived as having a bad business climate." This is "negative sum" game for communities, as subsidies are transferred from them to the corporate sector. As soon as the subsidies run out, or depreciation allowances are taken, firms are free to move on, since they have invested little capital in their plants. Firms can then pit one city against another to win more favourable tax arrangements and create a "reserve army of places" (Walker, 1978). Increasingly, tax incentives are being given when their firms threaten to move elsewhere.[24]

Related is the "capital versus community" theme of Bluestone and Harrison (1982): firms are able to exert their power over communities and impose other social costs related to plant closures. The role of conglomerates (which have a "portfolio of firms" to maximize overall profits) has become more important in the movement of capital as a way of opening new markets, disciplining labor, and taking external control of regional activity.

Fiscal problems have been occurring at the local level, not just in New York and Cleveland, but in growing areas since older areas are "stuck" with old private capital or old public infrastructure and because of conscious disinvestment decisions on the part of corporations. The New York Municipal Assistance Corporation ("BIGMAC") and other (unelected) agencies are instituted to force reductions in services and wage cuts on the public. However, fiscal problems in fast-growth areas (e.g. San Jose and Houston) are also due to the overextension of local capital infrastructure and the refusal of local firms to support public spending on infrastructure or services needed for social reproduction.

CONCLUSIONS

I want to close briefly with some conclusions about the relationship between the IDOL and cities. Despite the rise of conscious and concerted efforts to control and direct growth, the ability of cities to determine their own economic destinies has been sharply limited by increases in capital mobility and by the changes in trade and foreign investment patterns. The ability of firms to rapidly shift production globally makes cities' futures less secure.[25] Moreover, cities continue to be the focus of political struggle over the distribution of income, as they house both modern corporate headquarters and wretched slums. The urban growth coalitions, as Mollenkopf (1983) tells us, have become weaker as a result of the splits between citizens' groups and firms. The hypothesis put forward here is that firms have been using the possibility of international relocation to extract concessions from both workers and cities. In doing so, they are able to tilt economic and political power in their favor.

In the end, cities find themselves less able to deal with their economic problems. Friedmann and Wolff (1982: 327) describe the dilemma as follows:

> A major loser is the local state. Small, isolated without financial power, and encapsulated within the world economy, it is barely able to provide for even the minimal services its population needs. And yet, instead of seeking alliances with neighbouring cities and organized labour, it leaves the real decisions to the higher powers on which it is itself dependent, or to the quasi-independent authorities created by state charter that manage the infrastructure of global capital-system-wide facilities such as ports, airports, rapid transit, water supply, communications, and electric power.

The internationalization of economics, then, poses a number of difficult questions for urban planners:

> How can the economic restructuring taking place at the local level be controlled, when it is often directed by external forces?
> How can local conflicts (over land use, job creation, and the environment) be mediated?
> What new political strategies and institutions need to be developed to gain a measure of autonomy in this ever-changing environment?
> These questions must be answered by planners and local activists if cities are to regain political power.

NOTES

1. Structural change (or economic restructuring) involves long-term shifts in the composition of demand, production and occupational patterns; new technology; a changing international division of labor; shifts in relative prices; and evolving location patterns (both migration and industrial spatial restructuring).

2. Core countries include North-west Europe, North America, Japan and Australia. The semi-periphery consists of lower-income OECD countries such as Ireland and the NICs (including the Republic of Korea, Taiwan, Brazil and Singapore). The NICs have specialized in labor-intensive goods such as clothing, shoes, toys and electronics; many, however, became more capital intensive in the late 1970s, increasing exports of items such as steel to core nations. These categories do not correspond precisely to the World Bank data presented in Table 1 since official data do not differentiate within broad country groupings.

3. Pre-1974 importation of labor to Northern Europe took place largely because of labor shortages in industries such as construction, textiles, metal working, health care and consumer services. The major labor exporters came from the southern tier of Europe, North Africa and from the Caribbean basin. In Europe, a number of institutions were established to recruit and transport laborers for employers. After 1974, investment was directed to NICs such as Brazil, Hong Kong, Korea and Singapore, none of whom had been a major labor exporter previously.

4. For instance, by 1880, 12 per cent of US "Big Three" (GM, Ford and Chrysler) cars were produced by their Latin American affiliates, up from 5.5 per cent only seven years earlier (Trachte and Ross, 1983, cited by Castells, 1984).

5. This industrialization of a few Third World countries has led to rapid urban growth in major cities of these NICs. Although this chapter will concentrate on the developed world, the impact on NICs must be kept in mind.

6. Among the studies of the regional location of direct foreign investment, see Blackbourne (1974: 1982), Dicken and Lloyd (1976), Howenstein (1983), McDermott (1977), McConnell (1980) and Little (1983).

7. Although investment abroad by American firms increased, other countries' investment grew even more quickly. Between 1961 and 1967, the US had 61 per cent of all FDI made by 13 major investing countries (OECD, 1981). By 1974–78, the US share dropped to 30 per cent, while Japan and West Germany increased their combined shares from 9.6 per cent to 29.9 per cent. The share of foreign direct investment by the 13 countries made in the US was only 1.4 per cent in 1961–67, but grew to 24.5 per cent by 1974–78. By 1983, inflows of capital to the US ($82 billion) were far greater than outflows ($50 billion).

8. Viewed in another way, foreign production was three times the value of exports in 1960; by 1977, it was more than five times exports. Twenty-five per cent of outward FDI was in petroleum; other major industries in which US firms had large foreign investment were paper, rubber, textiles, wholesale trade and finance.

9. "Ownership advantage" refers to the ability to exploit superior technology, innovation and product differentiation abroad.

10. The US share of exports of industrialized capitalist countries declined from 21 per cent in 1965 to 16 per cent in 1983. During the same period, the US absorbed an increasing share of the world's imports (20 per cent in 1983 compared to 17 per cent in 1965).

11. According to the 1977 *Annual Survey of Manufactures*, the most export-intensive manufacturing sectors were electrical and non-electrical machinery, instruments, transportation and tobacco products. All but the last (which is small absolutely) have high-technology characteristics.

12. Corporate headquarter activity has been greatest in New York, Los Angeles, Chicago, Cleveland and San Francisco. Cities gaining Fortune 500 corporate headquarters between 1959 and 1976 were Houston and Minneapolis (Noyelle and Stanback, 1984).

13. About a quarter of the book value of property, plant and equipment was in the Southeast, with Louisiana, Florida, South Carolina and Georgia being the largest in that region. Among the states, California, Texas and Alaska had the largest foreign investments (Belli, 1983).

14. Car production has been spatially concentrated in other countries as well. Regions such as Piedmont (Italy), Niedersachsen (FRG), Ile de France (France), and the West Midlands (UK) have been major centers of car production (Hill, 1983). The secondary effects of the decline in car production have been felt in related industries such as steel and tyres. This change in location has been a major factor in serious fiscal problems in car-dominated cities such as Detroit and Flint.

15. For example, between 1970 and 1980, population declined by 18 per cent in St Louis, 24 per cent in Cleveland, and 21 per cent in Detroit (Tabb, 1984).

16. Garnick (1983) reports that metropolitan area population grew at nearly four times the rate of non-metropolitan regions between 1959 and 1969. In the subsequent decade, non-metropolitan areas grew faster. But this reversal of long-term trends was not uniform; in the more urbanized parts of the country (New England, the Mideast, the Great Lakes and the Far West), non-metropolitan areas grew faster in the 1960s and slower in the 1970s compared to metropolitan areas. For less urbanized regions, metropolitan areas grew faster in both decades.

17. Houston and Phoenix grew by more than 25 per cent during the 1970s, for instance.

18. It is critical to understand that often-made "Frostbelt-versus-Sunbelt" categorization is simplistic. There are sections of the Sunbelt that have continued to stagnate (e.g. Mississippi) at the same time that states such as Texas, Florida and Arizona boomed during the 1970s and early 1980s. Similarly, there has been good growth in parts of New England and other Frostbelt areas.

19. Or, at least, not to interfere with their self-perceived prerogatives.

20. Unions also cannot bargain effectively with MNCs because labor is rarely organized internationally. Therefore, firms can play off workers in different countries and reduce wage costs (Bluestone and Harrison, 1982).

21. Although states and localities in the aggregate have run budget surpluses (deficits are generally not permitted by law), there are fiscal problems in many large central cities, intensifying the battle among cities for jobs and tax bases. Fiscal stress is particularly severe in cities with traditional manufacturing bases and large minority populations. Infrastructure is decaying and services have been cut. Fiscal problems make attracting employment more difficult for cash-poor cities.

22. Reasons given for devolution are the desire for greater local autonomy and an interest in reducing federal social expenditures. In reality, the result has been considerably less money going to needy cities and the poor.

23. At the same time, there are moves to create a positive environment for research-based employment (e.g. ties with universities) in order to attract high-tech firms.

24. Essentially, location decisions that were formerly among the best-kept corporate secrets have become among the most public as firms await bids from hard-up cities. In recent years, International Harvester has played off Ohio and Indiania, the Microelectronic and Computer Technology Corporation considered bids from 57 cities, and there has been international bidding for auto plants (e.g. Austria vs. Spain). The implications of these tax losses for local fiscal crisis are obvious and serious (Harrison and Kanter, 1978).

25. This is not to say that cities ever had complete control over their own economic development. My argument is that increased capital mobility and internationalization of the economy result in more external influence.

REFERENCES

Aronowitz, Stanley (1973) *False Promises*, New York: McGraw-Hill.

Barnet, Richard E. (1980) *The Lean Years*, New York: Simon and Schuster.

Bawden, D. Lee, and John L. Palmer (1984) "Social policy: Challenging the welfare state." In John L. Palmer and Isabel V. Sawhill (eds), *The Reagan Record*, Cambridge, Mass.: Ballinger, pp. 177–215.

Belli, R. David (1983) "Foreign direct investment in the United States: Highlights from the 1980 benchmark survey," *Survey of Current Business*, 63 (10): 25–35.

Blackbourn, A. (1972) "The Location of foreign-owned manufacturing plants in the Republic of Ireland," *Tijdschrift voor Economische en Sociale Geografie*, 63 (6): 438–43.

———(1974) "The spatial behavior of American firms in Western Europe." In Hamilton, F. G. (ed.), *Spatial Perspectives on Industrial Organization and Decision-Making* Chichester, Sussex: John Wiley, chapter 9.

———(1978) "Multinational enterprises and regional development: A comment." *Regional Studies* 12: 125–7.

———(1982) "The impact of multinational corporations on the spatial organization of developed nations: a review," in Taylor, Michael and Thrift, Nigel (eds), *The Geography of Multinationals*, New York: St Martin's Press.

Bluestone, Barry and Bennett Harrison (1982) *The Deindustrialization of America*, New York: Basic Books.

Bowles, Samuel, David M. Gordon, and Thomas E. Weisskopf (1983) *Beyond the Wasteland*, New York: Doubleday.

Castells, Manuel (1984) *Towards the Informational City? High Technology, Economic Change, and Spatial Structure: Some Exploratory Hypotheses*, Working Paper no. 430, Berkeley: Institute of Urban and Regional Development, University of California.

Cohen, Robert B. (1981) "The new international division of labor, multinational corporations and urban hierarchy." In Michael Dear and Allen J. Scott (eds), *Urbanization and Urban Planning in Capitalist Society*, London: Methuen, pp. 287–315.

Deardorff, Alan V. and Robert M. Stern (1983) "Current issues in trade policy," mimeo, Ann Arbor, MI: University of Michigan.

Denison, Edward F. (1979) *Accounting for Slower Growth: The United States in the 1970s*, Washington, D.C.: Brookings Institution.

Dicken, Peter and Lloyd, Peter E. (1976) "Geographical perspectives on United States investment in the United Kingdom," *Environment and Planning, A*, 8 (6): 685–705.

Dunning, John H. (1981) *Economic Analysis and the Multinational Enterprise*, London: George Allen and Unwin.

Frank, Robert F. and Richard T. Freeman (1979) "The distributional consequences of direct foreign investment." In William G. Dewald (ed.), *The Impact of International Trade and Investment on Employment*, Washington, D.C.: US Government Printing Office.

Friedland, Roger, Frances Fox Piven and Robert R. Alford (1979) "Political conflict, urban structure, and the fiscal crisis." In Douglas E. Ashford (ed.), *Comparing Public Policies: New Concepts and Methods*, Beverly Hills, Calif.: Sage, pp. 197–225.

Friedmann, John and Goetz Wolff (1982) "World city information: an agenda for research and action," *International Journal of Urban and Regional Research*, 6: 309–44.

Garnick, Daniel H. (1983) "Shifting balances in metropolitan and nonmetropolitan area growth." Paper presented at the 1983 Meeting of the Regional Science Association, Chicago, November.

Glickman, Norman J. (1984) *Economic Policy and the Cities: In Search of Reagan's "Real" Urban Policy*, Working Paper no. 26, Austin: Lyndon B. Johnson School of Public Affairs, University of Texas at Austin, *Journal of the American Planning Association* 50: 471–78.

——and Robert A. Alford (1982), "The state in an internationalized economy," mimeo, Bellagio, Italy.

——and Elizabeth M. Petras (1981) *International Capital and International Labor Flows: Implications for Public Policy*, Working Paper no. 53, Philadelphia: Department of Regional Science, University of Pennsylvania.

——and Douglas F. Woodward (1985) *Direct Foreign Investment and Regional Development: Some Empirical Findings*, Working Paper no. 33, Austin: Lyndon B. Johnson School of Public Affairs, University of Texas at Austin.

Hanson, Royce (ed.) (1983) *Rethinking Urban Policy: Urban Development in an Advanced Economy*, Washington, D.C.: National Academy Press.

Harrison, Bennett and Sandra Kanter (1978) "The political economy of states' job-creation business incentives," *Journal of the American Institute of Planners*, 44: 424–5.

Hill, Richard Child (1983) "The auto-industry in global transition," mimeo, East Lansing, MI: Michigan State University.

Howenstine, Ned G. (1983), "Gross product of US multinational companies, 1977," *Survey of Current Business*, 63 (2): 24–9.

Kemper, N.J. and De Smidt, M. (1980) "Foreign manufacturing establishments in the Netherlands," *Tijdschrift voor Economische en Sociale Geografie*, 71: 21–40.

Law, C.M. (1980) "The foreign company's location investment decision and its role in British regional development," *Tijdschrift voor Economische en Sociale Geografie*, 71; 15–20.

Little, Jane S. (1978), "Locational decisions of foreign investors in the United States," *New England Economic Review* (July/August): 43–63.

Lovell, Michael C. (1978) "The profit picture: trends and cycles," *Brookings Papers on Economic Activity*, no. 3: 769–88.

Luger, Michael (1983) "Federal tax incentives as industrial and urban policy." In William Tabb and Larry Sawers (eds), *Sunbelt–Frostbelt: Regional Change and Industrial Restructuring*, New York: Oxford University Press.

Magaziner, Ira C. and Robert B. Reich (1982) *Minding America's Business*, New York: Vintage.

Malecki, Edward (1979) "Location trends in R & D by large US corporations, 1965–1977," *Economic Geography*, 55: 309–23.

Markusen, Ann R. (1982) "Sectoral differentiation of regional economies." Paper presented at the 1982 Meeting of the Regional Science Association, Pittsburgh.

McConnell, James E. (1980) "Foreign direct investment in the United States," *Annals of the Association of American Geographers*, 70; 259–70.

McDermott, Phillip J. (1977) "Overseas investment and the industrial geography of the United Kingdom," *Area*, 9 (3): 200–7.

Mieszkowski, Peter (1984) "The differential effect of the foreign trade deficit on regions in the U.S.A." Paper presented at the Conference on the Agenda for Metropolitan America, Center for Real Estate and Urban Economics, University of California at Berkeley, September.

Mollenkopf, John H. (1983) *The Contested City*, Princeton: N.J.: Princeton University Press.

Noble, David F. (1977) *America by Design*, New York: Oxford University Press.

Nordhaus, William (1974) "The falling share of profits," *Brookings Papers on Economic Activity*, no. 1: 169–208.

Noyelle, Thierry and Thomas M. Stanback (1984) *Economic Transformation of American Cities*, Totowa, N.J.: Allanheld and Rowman.

OECD (1981) *International and Multinational Enterprises: Recent Direct Investment Trends*, Paris: OECD.

Peterson, George E. (1982) "The state and local sector." In John L. Palmer and Isabel V. Sawhill (eds), *The Reagan Experiment*, Washington, D.C.: Urban Institute Press.

Piven, Frances Fox and Richard Cloward (1971) *Regulating the Poor*, New York: Pantheon.

Pred, Alan (1977) *City Systems in Advanced Economics*, New York: John Wiley.

Reich, Robert M. (1983) *The Next American Frontier*, New York: Times Books.

Saxenian, Annalee (1984) "Urban contradictions of Silicon Valley: Regional growth and the restructuring of the semiconductors industry." In Larry Sawers and William K. Tabb (eds), *Sunbelt/Snowbelt: Urban Development and Regional Restructuring*, New York: Oxford University Press.

Schoenberger, Erica (1983) "The logic of foreign manufacturing investment in the United

States: Implications for the US economy," mimeo, Baltimore, MD: Johns Hopkins University Press.

Stanback, Thomas M. and Thierry Noyelle (1982) *Cities in Transition*, Totowa, N.J.: Allanheld, Osmun.

Tabb, William K. (1984) "Urban development and regional restructuring, an overview." In Larry Sawers and William K. Tabb (eds), *Sunbelt/Snowbelt: Urban Development and Regional Restructuring*, New York: Oxford University Press.

Trachte, Kenneth and Robert Ross (1983) "The crisis of Detroit and the emergence of global capitalism," mimeo.

Walker, Richard (1978) "Two sources of uneven development under advanced capitalism: Spatial differentiation and capital mobility," *Review of Radical Political Economics*, 10(3): 28–37.

Wallerstein, Immanuel (1974) *The Modern World System*, New York: Academic Press.

Watts, H.D. (1980) "The location of European direct investment in the United Kingdom," *Tijdschrift voor Economische en Sociale Geografie*, 71(1): 3–14.

Wolfe, Alan (1981) *America's Impasse*, New York: Pantheon.

World Bank (1980; 1983) *World Development Report*, Washington, D.C.: World Bank.

40
Semisovereign Cities: The Politics of Urban Development*

Todd Swanstrom

Economic theory has invaded political science with a vengeance. A case in point is Paul Peterson's *City Limits*, which applies neoclassical market theory to urban politics.[1] Winner of the 1981 Woodrow Wilson Foundation Award for the best book published in the United States on government, politics, or international affairs, *City Limits* argues that economic forces largely determine urban policy making. Cities must compete for mobile wealth in the intergovernmental marketplace, Peterson says, or face perpetual fiscal crises. The permeability of urban economies places "limits" on redistributive polices for the poor, for such policies "only make the city a

*Swanstrom, Todd. 1989. "Semisovereign Cities: The Politics of Urban Development." *Polity* 21, no. 1 (Fall 1989): 83–110. Copyright © 1989. Reprinted by permission of the Northeastern Political Science Association.

more costly locale for the more productive community members."[2] Instead, Peterson argues, cities must pursue "developmental policies"—policies that provide incentives for investors and higher income residents to locate in the jurisdiction. While developmental policies may harm particular interests in a city, such as homeowners who are displaced by a highway project, all city residents benefit from publicly induced development insofar as it enhances the tax base and increases economic opportunity. Economic growth is a "unitary interest" that all citizens share.

Peterson's account replaces the pluralist image of the decision making process, which is rooted in conflict and bargaining, with a corporate image based on consensus and technical expertise. Peterson leaves room for pluralist politics in what he calls "allocational" policies, policies which do not affect the economy one way or the other. But since most policies do affect the economy, pluralist politics is restricted to a narrow sphere. Developmental policies, which dominate the agenda of urban politics, are decided, for the most part, by an economic elite, dominated by businessmen who possess the technical knowledge needed to design effective developmental policies. In predicting how cities will behave, however, we do not need to know the social background, values, or interests of the decision makers, since they are forced to make decisions by objective economic pressures. At a minimum, political sovereignty means the ability of decision makers to choose from alternative courses of action. In this sense, according to Peterson, cities lack internal sovereignty; unlike nation-states, cities have a limited politics.

Peterson's economic approach to urban politics is not an isolated phenomenon. In many ways, *City Limits* simply sums up, albeit in a brilliant fashion, the trend toward economic approaches to urban politics, both theoretical and practical, in the present period. Public choice theory, for example, has applied economic concepts to urban reform and policy issues with increasing sophistication in recent years.[3] Since the economic troubles and fiscal crises of the 1970s, scholars have become increasingly aware of the market pressures on cities. Some, generally those on the right of the political spectrum, view the increased attention to economic factors as salutary;[4] others, generally on the left, deride the effects.[5] All agree, however, on the importance of economic factors. . . .

Critiques of Peterson's market approach to urban politics have proliferated in recent years. Many challenge the notion that there is a unitary interest in urban economic development. Bryan Jones, for example, asserts that cities must also be concerned with "social order and just government."[6] Susan and Norman Fainstein argue that there is little agreement on goals because the city is "a site for class and racial conflict."[7] Along similar lines, others attack Peterson's assumption that economic development benefits the entire city. Clarence Stone points out that taxes and housing costs go up in high growth cities, the fiscal dividend is often blocked by tax subsidies, and transportation policies frequently serve suburbanites better than city dwellers.[8] Finally, many have criticized Peterson's apolitical image of the decision-making process.[9] John Thomas argues that Peterson's notion of "groupless politics" is wrong; cities have sufficient free floating resources to sustain a rich political life at the neighborhood level.[10] Even in a declining industrial city like Detroit, Bryan Jones and Lynn Bachelor argue, politicians have resources to deal with multinational corporations. Political leadership does make a difference. . . .[11]

. . . The central problem with urban theory today is excessive abstractness. Peterson's theoretical approach is highly deductive: he starts with a set of assumptions derived from neoclassical economics; he then relaxes some of these assumptions to make the theory more "realistic"; finally, he deduces hypotheses from the model and tests them against the real world. While the deductive approach results in parsimonious and elegant theory, strong points of *City Limits*, it cannot do justice to the tremendous variety in urban politics. The abstractions of economic theory must be leavened with the concrete findings of political science.

POLITICS BETWEEN CITIES: SLACK IN THE INTERGOVERNMENTAL MARKETPLACE

Pluralism is essentially a market model of the political process. The market thinking behind pluralism can be clearly seen in the pluralist classic, *Who Governs?*, where Dahl develops a model of the political system based on an exchange relation between producers and consumers. Basically, professional politicians, or political entrepreneurs, offer policies in exchange for voter support at the polls. While most voters are passive consumers, competitive elections guarantee consumer sovereignty in the long run. At the same time, Dahl acknowledges the existence of what he calls "slack" in the political marketplace. Most people are subject to political inertia; they have unused political resources and, on most issues, do not carefully monitor the actions of elected officials. Dahl shows, however, how slack can be functional in the political system. Unused resources can be brought massively to bear if the central interests of voters are threatened, and the existence of slack gives leaders greater flexibility to be creative. Slack leaves room for political leadership.[12]

Like pluralism, Peterson's theory is based on a market model. Only in Peterson's case, instead of voters withdrawing their support at election time, the threat is that investors and residents will "vote with their feet." Peterson portrays the intergovernmental marketplace as taut. While allowing for some slack, Peterson restricts policy discretion to a narrow range of allocational issues which do not influence investment. Empirical research shows, however, that there is more slack than market theory acknowledges; indeed, considerable slack exists even in the area of economic development policy.

The question here is deceptively simple: what causal effect do local public policies have on the location of investment? Even in an experimental science, where all the relevant factors can be controlled, causal inference is extremely difficult. Public policy is not an experimental science. In the real world of public policy, many factors are varying at the same time that the independent variable, public policy, varies. To evaluate the causal effect of public incentive programs on investment, therefore, policy analysts have developed three surrogate methods. One is simply to ask the ultimate decision maker, the investor, what factors entered into the locational decision and see whether the public incentives were an important factor. The second method is to correlate various public policies with investment, controlling, as much as possible, for confounding variables. The third method is to examine the effects of public policies on investor profitability and compare these effects with other factors that vary between cities to see if the public policies could reasonably be expected to make a difference.

In what follows, I review the empirical evidence on the effects of local government policy using these three methods. Local governments can influence investment in three basic ways: through the power to subsidize or tax, the power to regulate, and the power to exhort or inform.[13] I will confine this review to the effect of local taxes and tax incentives. Local tax incentives, it should be noted, are "the most commonly offered municipal development incentive in the country."[14] No matter which method is used, the evidence points overwhelmingly to the conclusion that local taxes and incentives have very little effect on location decisions. Only a small portion of the evidence can be cited here, but I invite the reader to consult various surveys of the literature to confirm this generalization.[15]

Surveys

One of the problems with asking executives about taxes is that they have a conflict of interest: if they think their answers will affect policy, they will have a tendency to say that taxes are important in the hopes of stimulating more tax breaks. Nobody likes to pay taxes. However, numerous surveys have been conducted which effectively eliminate any motivation for self-interested replies. Local taxes are uniformly ranked low. Most surveys rank the accessibility to markets, availability of raw materials, and labor costs near the top. Taxes are ranked near the bottom. A 1958 *Business Week* study found that of 747 references to location decisions, only 5 percent referred to taxation.[16] More recently, Roger Schmenner conducted indepth interviews with eight corporate executives and came to the conclusion that "taxes themselves are merely a minor consideration."[17]

Correlational Studies

Studies which correlate local taxes and incentives with investment have come to a similar negative conclusion. A 1967 study, for example, found "no clearcut relationship between the level of business taxes and manufacturing employment growth rates for states within the same region."[18] Other correlational studies have come to similar conclusions.[19] Some studies have even found a positive relationship between taxes and economic growth.[20] This may not mean that higher taxes cause economic growth, but it certainly does not mean the opposite. At one time, there was a great deal of concern that the cause of the booming economy in the Sunbelt and economic decline in the Northeast was the lower state and local taxes in the former compared to the latter. Actually, taxes had little to do with the matter. Today, the Northeastern economy is outperforming the Sunbelt for reasons that have little to do with taxes. In fact, some of the highest tax jurisdictions, Boston and New York, are experiencing rapid job growth and real estate booms while low tax cities, like Houston, are the doldrums (primarily due to the sharp decline in the price of oil).

Effect of Taxes on Profits

Analyzing the effect of taxes on business profits explains why the correlation between taxes and growth is so low. Local taxes have little effect on business profits, and any effect different tax levels might have on investment is overwhelmed by other, more important, differences between cities. In Wisconsin, for example, local property taxes were estimated to be .68 percent of the value of all shipments for all manufacturing industries combined.[21] Barry Bluestone and Bennett Harrison estimate that total corporate income taxes plus property taxes on business were only 1.69 percent of total business sales for all states in the nation in 1975.[22] Moreover, state and local taxes can be deducted from income for federal taxes and therefore their burden to business is greatly reduced; the federal government subsidizes the payment of state and local taxes. By contrast, the U.S. Department of Labor estimated that labor was the single most important input into the production of a firm in 1977, "accounting for approximately sixty percent of all input payments on a national basis."[23] Not surprisingly, local taxes have only a minor impact on business location decisions, while wage rates have a major impact.

While the evidence for the limited impact of local taxes on investment is overwhelming, most of the evidence cited so far concerns competition *among* regions. What about competition among cities *within* regions? Some argue that within a single metropolitan area local taxes are important in location decisions. Since cities within a region are quite alike on most factors, differences in local taxation can make a difference in intra-regional location decisions. The evidence here is mixed. Some conclude that there is little effect. A study of the Cleveland metropolitan area, for example, found that "tax rates were insignificant in the intra-urban location decision."[24] Some studies, however, point in the other direction. T.E. McMillan argues that if you confine surveys to the question of site location within a single metropolitan area, taxes will be mentioned much more frequently.[25] A correlational analysis of the Cleveland metropolitan area showed that if cities that zone out industry are excluded, there is a significant positive correlation between low taxes and spending on business services and industrial investment.[26] Michael Wasylenko replicated the Cleveland study for the Milwaukee region and concluded that taxes and fiscal variables are significantly related to investment in manufacturing and wholesale but not to investment in construction, retail trade, finance, insurance and real estate, and services.[27]

In short, the evidence on the intrametropolitan effect of local taxing and spending decisions is mixed. There may be some effect with regard to highly footloose industries like routine manufacturing, but the M.I.T. research led by David Birch raises questions about the value of "smoke-stack chasing" as a strategy for economic development. First, very little employment change is due to the migration of firms; almost all the growth in jobs in cities is due to start-ups of new companies.[28] Now, local taxes may affect business start-ups, but almost all the studies have focused on business relocations. Moreover, the Birch study found that two-thirds of the net new jobs came from firms with twenty or fewer employees.[29] On the other hand, local tax incentives almost always go to the largest corporations.[30] In addition, the M.I.T. study found that manufacturing created only 5 percent of the net new jobs in the 1970s; 89 percent were created in services. Finally, other studies have shown that the multiplier effect of corporate industrial growth is less than generally believed.[31] The costs of additional services often outweigh the added tax base.[32] Clearly, smokestack chasing is not a viable long-term strategy for most cities.

Many central cities, realizing that growth in industrial employment is limited, have vigorously pursued white collar employment through various tax-cutting strategies. It is well known, however, that there are strong centripetal forces, independent of local public policy, centralizing high level white collar employment in the downtowns of central cities.[33] In fact, one author estimates, "almost half of the nation's post-1950 gain in office employment and construction was captured by the downtowns of our large cities."[34] The jobs that centralize tend to be high-level professional jobs, or what are sometimes called "advanced corporate services."[35] These advanced corporate services jobs are associated with high-level decision making in our information based economy. They tend to involve highly skilled functions that need downtown locations for the face-to-face contacts available there to aid in high-level decision making.

Although the growth of downtown white collar employment is a positive trend for depressed central cities, numerous studies have concluded that local tax incentives have little effect on boosting white collar employment.[36] In fact, since the service sector is more labor-intensive than is manufacturing, one would expect that local property taxes would play a less significant role in location decisions. A guidebook for local economic development, prepared by the U.S. Department of Housing and Urban Development (H.U.D.), analyzes the effect of a 75 percent tax abatement in a typical office development and concludes that it would only reduce office rents about one dollar per square foot per year (from $12.38 to $11.35).[37] Since office rent is only a small part of the cost of doing business, it is clear that the incentive will have little effect. Moreover, downtowns do not compete directly with suburbs for many types of white collar employment; many firms must locate downtown because of the prestige, business contacts, and specialized business services found there. In a study of the nation's largest tax abatement program, Andrew Parker showed that, even if it is effective in attracting new investment, the costs of office development often outweigh the benefits.[38] Even without tax incentives, there is considerable doubt whether downtown office development is a net fiscal benefit to cities.[39] In short, there is as much reason to suspect the efficacy of the "paper chase" as there is to suspect the effectiveness of smokestack chasing.

The Impression created by Peterson and others, that the economic context of cities is a prison that determines most moves that cities make, is exaggerated. The point is not that the economic context is unimportant but that researchers must examine the particular city and type of mobile wealth before coming to any conclusions about the effect of the economic environment on policy making. Investors do not move from one city to another with the same ease that consumers switch from one brand of toothpaste to another. There is considerable friction in the movement of investment capital. "Transaction costs," to put it in the jargon of the economists, vary from one industry to another, from one locale to another. Some wealth is extremely mobile, as for example, routine manufacturing with low transportation costs, while other investment is not, as for example advanced corporate services that rely on sophisticated business services.

Slack in the intergovernmental marketplace creates room for political discretion. Recognizing the unique pulling power of their downtown areas, cities with strong white collar economies have enacted "linkage" policies that attempt to exploit their locational advantage. The opposite of tax abatement, linkage extracts an extra fee from developers, as a condition for development, in order to compensate for the external costs of growth, such as housing inflation for low income inner city residents. Boston, for example, expects to raise $52 million over a ten-year-period from its linkage fees to fund housing and employment programs. Linkage demonstrates that cities do sometimes possess what political analysts have long attributed to sovereign governments: the power, based on a territorial monopoly, to set policy according to internal political choices and values.[40]

Even where economic imperatives are tightest, however, development policy is never simply a rational response to the facts. No amount of objective and technical analysis can succeed in pinpointing the one best policy for the city as a whole. As we have seen, it is impossible to determine without error the effect of policies on investment. Moreover, information on the effect of policies is uneven.[41] Even if information were perfect, the goals of public sector decision makers are not predetermined; there is no agreed-upon public interest. Should decision makers, for example, seek to maximize jobs and investment next year or five years from now? Who should pay for the incentives to mobilize wealth? All development projects impose costs on part of the public, as in the case of displaced families. Who should pay these costs? Thus, even if policy makers had infinite resources to devote to planning and information gathering, it is unlikely they could agree on the one best policy to enhance the local economy. There is an almost infinite number of trade-offs that need to be evaluated across time, space, classes, and interest groups. Making these trade-offs is the job of politicians.

POLITICS WITHIN CITIES: THE POLITICAL LOGIC OF URBAN DEVELOPMENT

We know the basic structure of economic logic, and Peterson tells us how cities would behave if they followed economic logic. We have learned, however, that the economic pressures on cities are slack and that this leaves room for internal political factors to shape behavior. Urban politics, therefore, is a constant tension between economic and political logic. But what is the structure of political logic?

We could do worse than to begin with Dahl's market conception of pluralist democracy: professional politicians, or political entrepreneurs, compete for the votes of citizens who are for the most part passive consumers of politics. In order to get out the vote, politicians assemble subleaders who mobilize and organize voters in exchange for the prizes and perquisites of office, e.g. patronage and contracts. While the pluralist critique of the possibility of rational comprehensive decision making was correct as far as it went,[42] it would be a mistake to simply return to the internal political marketplace of pluralism, "in which all the active and legitimate groups in the population can make themselves heard at some crucial stage in the process of decision."[43]

While the currency of the political marketplace is votes, not money, it is not a free and fair competition. Slack in the political marketplace gives politicians room to maneuver and be influenced by other pressures, including economic ones. Generally, pluralists overlooked the way the economic context gave business a privileged position and ignored the biasing effect of political-economic structures, or what Clarence Stone calls "systemic power."[44] To simply return to pluralism, at this point, would be to throw out the baby, i.e., the legitimate insights of political economy, with the bathwater, i.e., economic determinism. The truth lies in the interaction between a slack internal political marketplace and a slack external economic marketplace.

While political institutions cannot be understood apart from their economic context, it is still possible to uncover a basic logic of what could be called representative democracy. It is based on the idea that professional politicians must compete for the votes of a basically self-interested, or apathetic, electorate. Political scientists have gradually accumulated knowledge about patterns of behavior in representative democracies, patterns which follow a political logic. Three kinds of political logic can be identified which contrast with economic logic and for which examples can be given of their application to urban development policy. Each of these will be discussed in turn:

The Economics of Growth Versus the Politics of Distribution

Economic analysis of developmental policies is concerned first with the effect of the policies on the overall growth of the city, and only secondarily with the distributive effects. Sometimes the goal seems to be Pareto optimality: at least one person is made better off by the policy and no one is made worse off. Pareto optimality, however, is unrealistic. Seldom is no one hurt by a development project. If a highway is going to be built, some families are going to be displaced; if a city concentrates on attracting one kind of investment (industry), other kinds of investment (tourism) will be hurt. The logic behind the economic model then is the compensation principle, or the so-called Kaldor-Hicks principle: a policy is Kaldor-Hicks efficient if the resulting increase in aggregate wealth is sufficient to compensate the losers fully and still have something left over.[45] Economic logic, therefore, aims at maximizing the fiscal health of city government, even if that means favoring high income residents and corporations over small businesses and the poor.

Political logic, on the other hand, focuses first on the distributive effects of policies, who wins and who loses. Politicians are concerned, of course, with the size of the pie, but they are concerned first and foremost with slicing up the pie in order to feed their political coalition. The question politicians routinely ask themselves is: will supporting this policy increase or decrease my chances of getting reelected? Politically, it does not matter if a new highway will increase the tax base beyond the cost to the public. If the highway will displace residents who are at the heart of a politician's coalition, he or she, following political logic, will oppose the project.

Peterson acknowledges this difference between economic and political logic, but argues that the two logics will be kept separate: economic logic will be applied to developmental policies and political logic will be applied to allocational policies. Peterson develops that Clarence Stone and Heywood Sanders call a "policy determines politics" framework.[46] Developmental policy, because it benefits the whole city, is moved out of the political framework of interest group bargaining and is decided by a business elite using pure economic logic. A central contradiction of Peterson's theory, however, is that, while he bases it on rational decision making, he can give no account of why anyone would rationally participate in formulating urban development policy.

The problem stems from Peterson's identification of urban development policy as a public good. But if the benefits of development are a public good, the question then is how do you avoid the free rider problem?[47] Why should businessmen participate in developmental policy making, if the benefits, an enhanced local economy, are something they would enjoy even if they did not participate?[48] Peterson argues that businessmen participate in developmental policy in order to gain the civic respect that comes from the "halo effect" of benefiting the community as a whole. This solution, however, relies not on an economic theory of motivation but on social psychological assumptions—assumptions that hardly seem adequate to the problem at hand. After all, if public goods could be provided because people felt good about the respect they received for providing them, then there would be no need for the whole coercive apparatus of government.

Aside from coercion, which is not legally applicable to the problem of how to get people to participate in democratic politics, the solution to the free rider problem, preferred by Mancur Olson and others, is "selective incentives." People must be provided with benefits that they will receive only if they participate in the political organization. Professional politicians exercise political discretion over the jobs, contracts, and policies that they control to reward subleaders, who maintain an organization capable of winning elections. The internal political dynamics of how to put together a minimum winning coalition are just as important as the external imperatives of economic growth.

Matthew Crenson once observed that collective goods are not valuable to politicians, because they cannot be used to build a political organization. By definition, public goods can be enjoyed by all; they cannot be restricted to the party faithful. What politicians need are fluid assets, i.e. assets over which they can exercise political discretion to reward their friends and punish their enemies.[49] Development is indeed an excellent source of fluid assets. By its very nature, developmental policy is political. Development is not a public good that benefits everyone equally. Because development is a locational good, it naturally benefits, and harms, some more than others. In the words of David Harvey: "All localized public goods are 'impure' and the externality exists as a 'spatial field' of effects."[50] The spatial effects of developmental policy can be manipulated by professional politicians to enhance their political organization and power.

Two examples from the career of master planner Robert Moses illustrate the political uses of development. In 1925 Hempstead Township refused to cede a portion of its waterfront, thereby effectively killing Moses' dream of creating Jones Beach. According to Robert Caro, Moses met with leaders of the Hempstead Republican machine and gave them advance knowledge of where the causeway and other public improvements would be built. The political leaders subsequently purchased land near the public improvements which they later sold at a great profit. The next year Hempstead Township ceded Moses the land he needed for Jones Beach. In another case, Moses placed the Manhattan terminus of the Triborough Bridge at 125th Street, not at 100th Street, the most rational location, according to Caro. While this action forces thousands of motorists each day to travel an extra 2½ miles every time they cross the bridge, the 125th Street location had the political advantage of benefiting William Randolph Hearst, who sold his deteriorating real estate at 125th Street to Moses for $782,000.[51]

Urban politics is decisively the politics of land use.[52] Real estate interests are key actors in urban political coalitions. The reason is that land values depend crucially on the uses of surrounding land. The most important powers of city government are powers over land use, especially powers over zoning and public improvements. To demonstrate how important city government is for land values, consider how much a parcel of urban land could fetch if it were not for the access provided by city streets. John Logan and Harvey Molotch have coined the term "place entrepreneurs" to refer to people who speculate on the value of land. Many place entrepreneurs are what Logan and Molotch call "structural speculators," real estate interests who shape future locational trends in order to enhance their land values. City government policy is a prime vehicle of structural speculation.[53]

Not only do real estate developers need politicians but politicians need real estate developers. Many of the traditional ways of steering selective benefits to political coalitions have been dried up by civil service laws and other reforms. The great advantage of manipulating the externalities of development projects is that it is a way of paying off political supporters without violating laws against bribery and corruption. George Washington Plunkitt once made the distinction between "honest graft" and "dishonest graft."[54] The externalities of city development policy are a form of honest graft. After all, a politician may reason, if one of our political allies does not make money on rising real estate values, somebody else will. This type of political patronage need not cost the public a single dollar. Moreover, the payments to political supporters are well laundered, so to speak, and hidden from public view.

The Economic Logic of Targeting Versus the Political Logic of Dispersion

An economic approach to urban development policy naturally lends itself to a targeting strategy. The goal in economic policy making is to take advantage of external trends in the most efficient way possible to attract mobile wealth. Efforts should be concentrated in those areas where trends are positive and opportunities are the greatest. The logic is similar to efforts by corporate strategic planners to pick expanding markets and concentrate resources on those where the corporation has a comparative advantage. Success relies on anticipating trends and aggressively targeting resources to take advantage of those trends. Given the limited ability of city governments to affect investment tends, discussed earlier, the need to target in city development policy is even more apparent. Only by targeting subsidies can city governments have a reasonable chance of influencing new private investment.

The political logic of representative democracy, on the other hand, follows what Anthony Downs has called the Law of Political Dispersion.[55] In a democratic system, politicians must spread the fruits of policy around in order to construct a governing coalition. Targeting incentives to a few areas or industries might make economic sense, but it may not attract enough votes to sustain a minimum winning coalition.

The tendency to target or disperse resources is rooted in the different orientations economic and political actors have toward time. Economic analysis is oriented toward future payoffs, disregarding "sunk costs" if they do not make future sense. Politicians, on the other hand, take prior commitments into account and are reluctant to discard them. In economic logic, this is called throwing good money after bad; in political logic, it is known as honoring commitments. Political logic is oriented to the past as well as the future. Economic logic is only future oriented, theoretically willing to make brutal decisions, as in closing down whole factories if they are not profitably aligned with future trends. Presumably, corporations will be eliminated by the marketplace if they do not keep pace with a rapidly changing environment. There is no analogous flushing mechanism in the intergovernmental marketplace. Governments cannot go bankrupt; they have obligations, built up over the years, that cannot be jettisoned overnight. Political logic is conservative, in the strict meaning of the word.

Examples of dispersive political logic abound. James Schlesinger speaks of what he calls the "foot in door techniques" of politicians. "One wishes to attract the support of many groups, but there are limits to the size of the budget. Consequently, resources are applied thinly over a wide array of programs."[56]

One example of the Law of Political Dispersion is experience with the Community Development Block Grants (CDBG). Under the Carter Administration, regulations were written that strongly encouraged cities to target their funding to Neighborhood Strategy Areas (NSAs).[57] The idea was to concentrate block grant spending in order to increase the chances to turn around a neighborhood and attract new investment and residents. If CDBG spending were spread around the entire city, according to economic analysis, it would have little rejuvenating effect. In practice, however, there was a strong tendency to spread the funds to benefit many different areas, and political interests, in the city.[58] In Cleveland, the NSAs started out as relatively defined areas, but as time went on political pressures, including a call from the Council President to the White House, led to expansion of the target areas until they included almost all low and moderate income neighborhoods in Cleveland.[59] Under instrumental rationality, means are valued only as instruments for accomplishing given ends. Economic logic, then, values public policies as instruments for achieving agreed-upon goals. Policies are valued not for themselves but for their effects, which can be measured by cost-benefit analysis. . . .

Political logic is noninstrumental.[60] Policies, of course, are valued for their effects, but they are also valued for what they represent. Policies send messages. In getting policies passed through the political system, it matters as much what they symbolize to voters and politicians as what their effects will be on the world. . . .

Urban development policy is ripe for symbolic politics. Many cities are being buffeted about by economic forces over which they have little control. New production technologies, foreign competition, and the swift transition from a goods-producing to a service-based economy have left many cities with devastating pockets of unemployment and decline. Economic problems abound, yet cities have relatively little leverage, as we have seen, over mobile wealth or economic change. Moreover, knowledge in this area is weak; it is impossible to prove that any particular development policy did not have the desired effect. The temptation to engage in symbolic politics is great. The city is like a ship being so tossed about by the storms and currents that the captain has limited control over its progress. The crew desperately wants to believe that someone is in charge and can steer the ship out of troubled waters. It is not surprising that the captain, concerned about a mutiny, turns to symbolic acts to boost the morale of the crew.

Much local development policy is essentially a form of symbolic reassurance. Local tax abatement programs, for example, have been interpreted as forms of symbolic politics.[61] Even the most depressed industrial cities are enjoying growth in white collar office functions in downtown areas. Local tax abatement programs are an opportunity for politicians to claim credit for the one positive investment trend. As we have seen, the research shows that local taxes are such a small part of the cost of doing business that tax abatements are not effective instruments for influencing business location decisions. The appeal of tax abatement programs, however, lies not in their economic effect but in their political appearance. By giving tax breaks to new investments in the city, politicians can claim that the new jobs and investment would not have occurred without the incentive. It is the political version of the fallacy: *post hoc ergo propter hoc.*

Several characteristics of local property tax abatement programs lend support to this view of them as largely symbolic. As Michael Wolkoff pointed out, one of the odd characteristics of abatement programs is their invariant nature: everyone who applies for an award within the eligible area gets the same award. No effort is made to determine how much incentive is needed to influence the investment location decision, and no assessment of the public benefits from the project, like jobs for city residents, is made.[62] In economic logic, this makes no sense. If tax abatement programs are understood not as instruments for achieving a certain result but as symbols for claiming credit, then the lack of rational planning makes perfect sense. Careful analysis of the costs and benefits of abatements would show that they do not produce new jobs and investment but only create windfall profits for developers. The public benefits do not justify the public costs.[63] Analysis would also show that if cities want to influence investment, they will target their incentives on a few projects. But this will expose the program to charges of political favoritism and will reduce the vaunted leverage ratio of incentives to investment. By drawing a line around an area and giving the same award to every developer, politicians can claim that they are encouraging huge amounts of investment without facing the political problems that would stem from making tough planning decisions.

Tax abatement programs are especially difficult to justify, since all of the subsidy comes out of local revenues. The temptation to engage in programs of symbolic reassurance is even greater, however, when federal grants are conditional upon granting subsidies to mobile wealth. Federal grants lessen the damage of such programs to the local tax base but they do not necessarily overcome the problem of spurious leveraging. Martin Anderson estimates that half of the urban renewal projects would have been built anyway, though perhaps in other areas of the city, without the subsidies.[64] After correlating urban renewal acreage with aggregate investment in housing and industry, Roger Friedland came to the following conclusion: "Urban renewal had no net additive effects on the level of new investment."[65]

More recent programs are not immune to this problem. John Gist points to the possibility that Urban Development Action Grant (UDAG) funds do not cause new investment at all, observing that sometimes the funds are applied for "*after* the private firms have committed themselves."[66] In the case of urban renewal, the federal government picked up two-thirds of the cost, but for UDAG the federal government pays the entire cost. Not only that, but when a developer repays a subsidized loan, the funds usually go to the local government to use as it sees fit within CDBG regulations. Moreover, projects that show a high leverage ratio between subsidy and investment are looked upon more favorably by federal evaluators who determine the grants, even though a high ratio increases the chances of spurious leveraging.[67] Obviously, local officials have little motivation to scrutinize projects to make sure the subsidy is necessary for the investment. In any case, they can use UDAGs to claim credit for new jobs and investment in their city. . . .

The view here is that political logic has its own value. The tendency of democratic politicians to focus on the distribution of growth and to spread the benefits around to put together a minimum winning coalition may be economically inefficient, but it does introduce the value of equality into developmental policy. The bias of economic logic to concentrate resources to maximize growth leads, in urban development, to the tendency to pull out of losing ventures and concentrate on winners. But politicians cannot close down an unprofitable neighborhood the way corporations can close down an unprofitable subsidiary. And a good thing it is. It was neighborhoods organizing through the political system, not the recommendations of economic planners, that eventually stopped the destruction of cities that resulted from urban renewal and highway building.

The symbolic dimension of political logic also has its own value. As John Forrester observes, "Government policy not only produces regulations, incentives, or statements of intention, but it also recommends to its public a praiseworthy attitude to be adopted more generally."[68] Tax abatement programs for downtown office development not only give a false impression that something serious is being done about the problem of jobs and investment, but they signal that the way to do something about those problems is to "bribe" businessmen, who are expected to have only selfish motives, in order to persuade them to invest in the city. Linkage programs, on the other hand, which require downtown developers to contribute to a fund for neighborhood housing, daycare, employment training, or mass transit, send the signal that those who draw on the commonwealth of the city to reap large profits have obligations to contribute to the solution of the problems they helped cause. The lesson is simple yet profound: privileges are linked to obligations, downtown to neighborhoods, office development to housing. Cities are held together by mutual obligations, respect, and commitments—values that are not only overlooked by the economic paradigm but which are drowned "in the icy water of egotistical calculation."[69]

NOTES

1. Paul Peterson, *City Limits* (Chicago: University of Chicago Press, 1981).

2. Ibid., p. 44.

3. See Robert L. Bish and Vincent Ostrom, *Understanding Urban Government: Metropolitan Reform Reconsidered* (Washington, DC: American Enterprise Institute for Public Policy Research, 1979); and Gary J. Miller, *Cities by Contract: The Politics of Municipal Incorporation* (Cambridge, MA: M.I.T. Press, 1981).

4. Irving Kristol, "Sense and Nonsense in Urban Policy," *Wall Street Journal*, 21 December 1977; Gurney Breckenfeld, "Refilling the Metropolitan Doughnut," in *The Rise of the Sunbelt Cities*, ed. David C. Perry and Alfred J. Watkins (Beverly Hills, CA: Sage, 1977); William E. Simon, *A Time for Truth* (New York: Berkley, 1978), ch. V; Donald A. Hicks, "Urban and Economic Adjustment to the Post-Industrial Era," *Hearings Before the Joint Economic Committee, Congress of the United States, Ninety-Seventh Congress, Part 2* (Washington, DC: U.S. Government Printing Office, 1982).

5. Harvey Molotch, "The City as a Growth Machine: Toward a Political Economy of Place," *American Journal of Sociology* 82 (1976): 309–32; Robert Goodman, *The Last Entrepreneurs: America's Regional Wars for Jobs and Dollars* (New York: Simon and Schuster, 1979); Barry Bluestone and Bennett Harrison, *The Deindustrialization of America* (New York: Basic Books, 1982); Roger Friedland, *Power and Crisis in the City: Corporations, Unions and Urban Policy* (New York: Schocken, 1983); Michael D. Kennedy, "The Fiscal Crisis of the City," in *Cities in Transformation: Class, Capital and the State*, ed. Michael P. Smith (Beverly Hills, CA: Sage, 1984).

6. Bryan Jones, "Contracting Limits: An End to City Government?" *Urban Affairs Quarterly* 17, no. 3 (1982): 383.

7. Susan S. Fainstein and Norman I. Fainstein, "Economic Change, National Policy, and the System of Cities," in *Restructuring the City*, ed. Susan Fainstein, et al. (New York: Longman, 1983), pp. 2–3.

8. Clarence Stone, "City Politics and Economic Development: Political Economy Perspectives," *Journal of Politics* 46 (1984): 289. See also Douglas Muzzio and Robert W. Balley, "Economic Development, Housing and Zoning: A Tale of Two Cities," *Journal of Urban Affairs* 8, no. 1 (Winter 1986): 1–18.

9. See Heywood T. Sanders and Clarence Stone, "Developmental Politics Reconsidered," *Urban Affairs Quarterly* 22, no. 4 (June 1987): 521–39.

10. John Clayton Thomas, *Between Citizen and City: Neighborhood Organizations and Urban Politics in Cincinnati* (Lawrence, KS: University Press of Kansas, 1986).

11. Bryan Jones and Lynn Bachelor, *The Sustaining Hand: Community Leadership and Corporate Power* (Lawrence, KS: University Press of Kansas, 1986).

12. Robert Dahl, *Who Governs? Democracy and Power in an American City* (New Haven, CT: Yale University Press, 1961). For a discussion of the value of slack in both economic and political systems, see Hirschman, *Exit, Voice, and Loyalty*.

13. Ernest Sternberg, "A Practitioner's Classification of Economic Development Policy Instruments, With Some Inspirations from Political Economy," *Economic Development Quarterly* 1, no. 2 (1987): 149–61.

14. U.S. Department of Housing and Urban Development, *Local Economic Development Tools and Techniques* (Washington, DC: U.S. Government Printing Office, 1979).

15. John F. Due, "Studies of State-Local Tax Influences on the Location of Industry," *National Tax Journal* 14 (1961): 163–73; David Mulkey and B. L. Dillman, "Location Effects of State and Local Industrial Development Subsidies," *Growth and Change* (April 1976): 37–42; Bennett Harrison and Sandra Kanter, "The Political Economy of State 'Job-Creation' Business Incentives," in *Revitalizing the Northeast*, ed. George Sternlieb and James W. Hughes (New Brunswick, NJ: Center for Urban Policy Research, Rutgers University, 1978); Jerry Jacobs, *Bidding for Business* (Washington, DC: Public Interest Research Group, 1979); Michael J. Wasylenko, "The Location of Firms: The Role of Taxes and Fiscal Incentives," in *Urban Government Finance*, ed. Roy Bahl (Beverly Hills, CA: Sage, 1981); Michael Kieschnick, *Taxes and Growth: Business Incentives and Local Development* (Washington, DC: Council of State Planning Agencies, 1981); Advisory Commission on Intergovernmental Relations, *Regional Growth: Interstate Tax Competition* (Washington, DC: U.S. Government Printing Office, 1981); Roger W. Schmenner, *Making Business Location Decisions* (Englewood Cliffs, NJ: Prentice Hall, 1982).

16. *Business Week*, "Plant Site Preferences of Industry and Factors of Selection," *Business Week Research Report* (1958). See also Survey Research Center, *Industrial Mobility in Michigan* (Ann Arbor: University of Michigan Press, 1950); E. Mueller and J. Morgan, "Location Decisions of Manufacturers," Papers and Proceedings of the 74th Annual Meeting of the American Economics Association (1962); L. Lund, "Factors in Corporate Locational Decisions," Conference Board Information Bulletin Number 66; U.S. Department of Commerce, *Industrial Locations Determinants* (Washington, DC: U.S. Government Printing Office, 1975).

17. Schmenner, *Business Location Decisions*, p. 46.

18. Advisory Commission on Intergovernmental Relations, *State-Local Taxation and Industrial Location* (Washington, DC: U.S. Government Printing Office, 1967).

19. Raymond Struyk, "An Analysis of Tax Structure, Public Service Levels, and Regional Economic Growth," *Journal of Regional Science* (Winter 1967); D. Carlton, "Why Firms Locate Where They Do: An Econometric Model," in *Interregional Movements and Regional Growth*, ed. W. Wheaton (Washington, DC: The Urban Institute, 1979); and Kieschnick, *Taxes and Growth*.

20. C. C. Bloom, *State and Local Tax Differentials* (Iowa City: Bureau of Business Research, State University of Iowa); Thomas R. Plaut and Joseph E. Pluta, "Business Climate, Taxes and Expenditures, and State Industrial Growth in the United States," *Southern Economic Journal* 50 (July 1983): 99–119.

21. Benjamin Bridges, "State and Local Inducements for Industry: Part 2," in *Locational Analysis for Manufacturing* (Cambridge, MA: M.I.T. Press).

22. Barry Bluestone and Bennett Harrison, *The Deindustrialization of America*, p. 186.

For a review of the studies that examine the low impact of local taxes on business profits, see Due, "The Studies of State-Local Tax Influences on the Location of Industry," pp. 165–68; Harrison and Kanter, "The Political Economy of State 'Job Creation' Business Incentives," p. 63; and Susan Olson, *An Evaluation of Tax Incentives as a Means to Encourage Redevelopment* (Cleveland: Cleveland City Planning Commission, 1978), pp. 15–16.

23. Goodman, *The Last Entrepreneurs*, pp. 43–44.

24. C. J. Simon, "Analysis of Manufacturing Location and Relocation In the Cleveland Metropolitan Area: 1966–1971," *American Economist* 24 (1980): 35–42.

25. T. E. McMillan, Jr., "Why Manufacturers Choose Plant Locations vs. Determinants of Plant Locations," *Land Economics* (1965): 239–46.

26. William F. Fox, "Fiscal Differentials and Industrial Location: Some Empirical Evidence," *Urban Studies* 18 (1981): 105–11.

27. Michael Wasylenko, "Evidence of Fiscal Differentials and Intrametropolitan Firm Location," *Land Economics* 56 (1980): 339–49.

28. David L. Birch, "Who Creates Jobs?" *Public Interest* (Fall 1981): 3–14.

29. Ibid., p. 7.

30. Jacobs, *Bidding for Business*.

31. Bluestone and Harrison, *The Deindustrialization of America*.

32. Gene F. Summers and Kristi Branch, "Economic Development and Community Social Change," *Annual Review of Sociology* 10 (1984): 141–66. For a review of studies on the fiscal effects of growth, see John R. Logan and Harvey Molotch, *Urban Fortunes: The Political Economy of Place* (Berkeley, CA: University of California Press, 1987).

33. Thomas M. Stanback, et al, *Services: The New Economy* (Totowa, NJ: Allanheld, Osmun, 1981); Jean Gottman, *The Coming of the Transactional City* (College Park, MD: Institute for Urban Studies, 1983).

34. Alexander Ganz, "Where Has the Urban Crisis Gone?" *Urban Affairs Quarterly* 20, no. 4 (1985): 456.

35. Robert Cohen, *The Corporation and the City* (New York: Conservation of Human Services Project, 1979).

36. New York Office of the Comptroller, Bureau of Performances Analysis, *Performance Audit of the Industrial and Commercial Incentive Board* (New York: Office of the Comptroller, 1979); Todd Swanstrom, "Tax Abatement in Cleveland," *Social Policy* (Winter 1982): 24–30; Andrew Parker, "Local Tax Subsidies as a Stimulus for Development: Are They Cost-Effective? Are They Equitable?" *City Almanac* 17, no. 1 (1983): 8–15. One of the few exceptions is a study of tax abatement in St. Louis: Daniel R. Mandleker, Gary Feder, and Margaret P. Collins, *Reviving Cities with Tax Abatement* (New Brunswick, NJ: Center for Urban Policy Research, 1980). The authors argue that tax abatement produced a huge fiscal surplus for St. Louis, but they never present any convincing evidence that the projects in question would not have been built without the tax incentives.

37. U.S. Department of Housing and Urban Development, *Local Economic Development Tools and Techniques*, p. 51.

38. Parker, "Local Tax Subsidies as a Stimulus for Development."

39. For a review of numerous studies done in San Francisco with mixed results, see Chester Hartman, *The Transformation of San Francisco* (Totowa, NJ: Rowman and Allanheld, 1984), pp. 26–266; and Douglas Muzzio, "Downtown Development: Boon or Bane?" prepared for delivery at the Annual Meeting of the Urban Affairs Association, Akron, Ohio, April 23–25, 1987.

40. The best overviews of linkage policies are Douglas Porter, ed., *Downtown Linkages* (Washington, DC: Urban Land Institute, 1985); and Dennis Keating, "Linking Downtown Development to Broader Community Goals: An Analysis of Linkage Policy in Three Cities," *Journal of the American Planning Association* (Spring 1986): 133–41.

41. John P. Blair, Rudy H. Fichtenbaum, and James A. Swaney, "The Market for Jobs: Locational Decisions and the Competition for Economic Development," *Urban Affairs Quarterly* 20, no. 1 (September 1984): 71; Jones and Bachelor, *The Sustaining Hand*, p. 203.

42. Charles Lindblom, "The Science of 'Muddling Through,'" *Public Administration Review* (Spring 1959): 79–88.

43. Robert A. Dahl, *A Preface to Democratic Theory* (Chicago: University of Chicago Press, 1956), p. 137.

44. Charles Lindblom, *Politics and Markets* (New York: Basic Books, 1977); John Forrester, "Rationality and the Politics of Muddling Through," *Public Administration Review* (Jan./Feb. 1984): 23–31; Clarence Stone, *Economic Growth and Neighborhood Discontent* (Chapel Hill: University of North Carolina Press, 1976).

45. N. Kaldor, "Welfare Propositions and Interpersonal Comparisons of Utility," *Economic Journal* 49 (1939): 549–52. For a critical discussion of the Kaldor-Hicks principle, see Gordon Clark, *Interregional Migration, National Policy, and Social Justice* (Totowa, NJ: Rowman and Allenheld, 1983).

46. Clarence Stone and Heywood T. Sanders, "Development Politics Reconsidered," unpublished manuscript, n.d.

47. Mancur Olson, *The Logic of Collective Action: Public Goods and the Theory of Groups* (New York: Schocken, 1965).

48. Indeed, the paradox of how to get rational individuals to provide collective goods is at the center of contract theory and economic theories of politics generally. In contract theory, the problem is how to move from the state of nature to civil society; economic theories of democracy have long struggled with the problem of how rationally to explain voting participation.

49. Matthew Crenson, *The Unpolitics of Air Pollution: A Study of Nondecisionmaking in the Cities* (Baltimore: Johns Hopkins University Press, 1971), p. 138.

50. David Harvey, *Social Justice and the City* (Baltimore: Johns Hopkins University Press, 1973), p. 60.

51. Robert Caro, *The Power Broker: Robert Moses and the Fall of New York* (New York: Vintage, 1975), pp. 209–10 and 390–91.

52. Stephen L. Elkin, *City and Regime in the American Republic* (Chicago: University of Chicago Press, 1987).

53. Logan and Molotch, *Urban Fortunes*.

54. William L. Riordan, *Plunkitt of Tammany Hall* (New York: E. P. Dutton, 1963).

55. Anthony Downs, "Using the Lessons of Experience to Allocate Resources in the Community Development Program," in *Housing Urban America*, ed. Jon Pynoos, Robert Schafer, and Chester W. Hartman (New York: Aldine, 1980), p. 530.

56. James R. Schlesinger, "Systems Analysis and the Political Process," *Journal of Law and Economics* XI (1968): 286.

57. *Code of Federal Regulations* (1978), 570.301.

58. For evidence on the CDBG dispersion effect, see Jack Fyock, "The Housing and Community Development Act of 1974: A Study of Policy Formulation, Administration, and Impact," paper delivered at the 1978 Meeting of the American Political Science Association, New York; Donald F. Kettl, *Managing Community Development in the New Federalism* (New York: Praeger, 1980).

59. Todd Swanstrom, *The Crisis of Growth Politics: Cleveland, Kucinich, and the Challenge of Urban Populism* (Philadelphia: Temple University Press, 1985), p. 200.

60. For an insightful discussion of the contrast between economic and political rationality, including the noninstrumental, or "constitutive," nature of the latter, see Stephen Elkin, "Economic and Political Rationality," *Polity* 18, no. 2 (1985): 253–71.

61. Swanstrom, "Tax Abatement in Cleveland"; and *The Crisis of Growth Politics*, ch. 6; Richard C. Feiock and James Clingermayer, "Municipal Representation, Executive Power, and Economic Development Policy," paper presented at the 1985 Southern Political Science Association Meeting; Irene S. Rubin and Herbert J. Rubin, "Economic Incentives: The Poor (Cities) Pay More," *Urban Affairs Quarterly* 2, no. 1 (September 1987): 37–62.

62. Michael J. Wolkoff, "The Nature of Property Tax Abatement Awards," *American Planning Association Journal* (Winter 1983): 77–84.

63. Parker, "Local Tax Abatements as a Stimulus for Development."

64. Martin Anderson, *The Federal Bulldozer* (New York: McGraw-Hill, 1964), p. 167.

65. Roger O. Friedland, *Class, Power and the Central City: The Contradictions of Urban Growth* (PhD. Dissertation, University of Wisconsin-Milwaukee, 1977).

66. John R. Gist, "Urban Development Action Grants: Design and Implementation," in *Urban Revitalization*, ed. Donald B. Rosenthal (Beverly Hills, CA: Sage, 1980), p. 243.

67. David Cordish, "Overview of UDAG," in *The Urban Development Action Grant Program*, ed. Richard P. Nathan and Jerry Webman (Princeton, NJ: Princeton Urban and Regional Research Center, 1980).

68. John Forrester, "Public Policy and Respect," *democracy* (Fall 1982): 94.

69. Karl Marx and Friedrich Engels, *The Communist Manifesto* (New York: Appleton-Century-Crofts, 1955), p. 12.

41

Capital Flight, Tax Incentives and the Marginalization of American States and Localities*

Michael Peter Smith, Randy L. Ready,

and Dennis R. Judd

The most significant forces affecting contemporary urban American are macro-level economic shifts in capital investment. Cities are dependent on global and national trends that shape their fate.

Probably because economic development is overwhelmingly important to localities and states, their political leaders are keen to grab their "fair" share of national economic growth. but they are handicapped in this attempt, for states and localities have become marginalized actors within the federal system. They have been granted the responsibility for the social and economic welfare of citizens within their borders, and President Reagan wants to grant them still more responsibility, yet they have neither the resources nor the political power sufficient to fulfill their responsibilities. Perhaps for this reason public officials sometimes desperately pursue economic growth as the panacea for all the problems that confront them. As noted by Theodore Lowi, "most cities [find] themselves literally too small to handle their policy problems but politically too weak to resist trying." (Lowi, 1979:47).

This tendency has been strongly encouraged by the Reagan Administration, which wants to replace direct public expenditures to solve social problems with a strategy to revitalize private enterprise. Supply side economics is offered as the necessary stimulus for private initiative, without regard for geographic location. Private market solutions are also proposed to solve problems of urban disinvestment and uneven regional development. For example, in 1982 the U.S. Department of Housing and Urban Development (HUD) asserted that:

> It is State governments that are capable of mobilizing the broad bases of support to tackle the economic, financial and social problems that affect the well-being of the State as a whole as it competes with others to attract and retain residences and businesses (HUD, 1982:57).

*Smith, Michael Peter, Randy L. Ready, and Dennis R. Judd. 1985. "Capital Flight, Tax Incentives and the Marginalization of American States and Localities." Pp. 181–183 and 188–201 in *Public Policy across States and Communities*, ed. Dennis R. Judd. Greenwich, CT: JAI Press. Copyright © 1985. Reprinted by permission of JAI Press Inc.

This policy casts cities and states as competitors in an "open market" scheme, each responsible for securing its share of national economic growth. It is important to note that such a competition is hardly new. Well before the 1980 election, state and local governments had developed and participated in a wide array of strategies designed to give them a competitive advantage in attracting capital investment.

During the 1970s economic development agencies and programs proliferated. At first, most programs were designed to promote particular cities and regions as having a "healthy business climate" (Libassi and Hausner, 1977:178). But the state of the art soon advanced to embrace an array of inducement techniques to attract investment to a given location or, similarly, to retain economic enterprises already located there. In 1975, 100,000 people in about 20,000 state and local organizations were attempting to promote economic development (Miller, 1977:122). Development campaigns became "internecine and aggressive" (Vaughan, 1979:98) as states and municipalities attempted to outbid their neighbors for economic growth. Promotional advertising by states alone amounted to over $12 million in 1975 (Miller, 1977:123).

Journals such as *Plant Location* were developed specifically to facilitate the competitive process. New York City's advertisement in a 1980 issue claimed "no other city in America offers more incentives for business or relocation." Virginia promoted itself as "not only a right-to-work state. It's a want-to-work state." "Mississippi is number one in business climate," while Springfield, Missouri is "The Promised Land." Aurora, Colorado boasted "a new labor force each month," but "there's a lot to like about Illinois." "Profitable, Oklahoma" got into the act with a grinning baby proclaiming "you'd grin too if you had my energy," against a background of power lines. Whether or not Chicago was actually "fund city," or San Diego "zoned for success," the promotion of economic development had become a big business, and states and municipalities had become development entrepreneurs.

States and localities have attempted to influence private investment decisions through three principal avenues: fiscal/tax policy, regulatory policy, and expenditure policy (Peirce, Hagstrom, and Steinbach, 1979:12; NAPA, 1980:35; Daniels, 1982:68; Litvak and Daniels, 1979:27). Fiscal/tax policy embraces all tax laws, exemptions and abatements. Regulatory policy includes regulations of such matters as land use (zoning), environmental policy, and water and sewage provisions; the chartering of banks and the issuing of licenses and permits. Expenditure policy refers to direct outlays by governments. Expenditure policies also encapsulate state policies regarding the siting of state facilities and the use of budgetary resources for education and highway construction.

Jurisdictions use these governmental powers in an attempt to improve their investment environment. The most popular of all the available incentive programs are those concerning taxes and finance. A vast assortment of such incentive tools are utilized: property tax holidays, abatements and rollbacks; tax increment financing; income tax breaks; sales tax exemptions;

loss carry-forwards; manpower training assistance; guaranteed loans; industrial revenue bonding; subsidized interest payments; lease financing; depreciation allowances; and the list goes on.

Often these programs are administered by non-profit and quasi-public development organizations at state and local levels, variously called Economic Development Corporations (EDCs), Local Development Companies (LDCs) or Downtown Development Authorities (DDAs). These organizations are now well established political institutions. They legitimate and organize an overt alliance between state and capital under the rubric "public-private partnerships." Along with corporate tax concessions, industrial revenue bonds, regulatory "relief," and state absorption of the costs of education, training, and physical infrastructure, they are the primary institutions through which local jurisdictions have fostered the process of economic growth and capital accumulation. Development corporations usually implement their decisions without referendums or legislative approval even though they have a great deal of discretion over the use of public funds. Taken together, public-private "partnerships" intensify the conditions of competition among geographically fixed political jurisdictions for increasingly concentrated and globally portable capital investment.

Because of the long history of intergovernmental competition (see Cook, 1982 for the historical development of this phenomenon), it is possible to assess the principal economic and political effects of state and local policies aimed at influencing capital investment decisions. . . .

TAX CONCESSIONS AND CORPORATE LOCATION

Urban and regional scholars have produced a large amount of research concerning locational decisions by firms. Recent research has been prompted by the much publicized conflict between the Frostbelt and the Sunbelt and by the "urban crisis" literature.

The locational decision of a new firm or the decision to move by an established business (either to relocate or to open a new branch facility) is among the most complex and demanding decisions that managers face: "imbedded in that decision is concern for the firm's capacity, its supply and logistics, its production, planning and control policies, and its process technology" (Schmenner, 1980:448).

David Smith, the British economic geographer, identifies the major factors in determining location to be some measure of: land and its attributes; capital (both finance and equipment); raw materials and power availability; cost and skill-level of the labor force; access to an expanding market; transportation and freight rates; agglomeration economies and interindustry linkages; public policy and planning; and the attitudes, personal considerations, or unique circumstances of the decision-makers themselves (Smith, 1981:45–64). Vaughan (1979:20) places all of these factors into three general categories: demand for output, input costs and availability, and local characteristics. Economically, each factor's importance depends upon its specific influence on a firm's costs or revenues and the degree to which that influence varies geographically (Litvak and Daniels, 1979:15).

The consideration of these factors is important for this analysis only insofar as it reveals much about the relative importance of taxation and financial incentives within the web of economic locational determinants. Neo-classical locational theory is based on the assumption that firms select the location that maximizes their total profit (Moriarity et al., 1980; Smith, 1981; Miller, 1977). Thus, if tax concessions and financial incentives affect total profits at alternative locations, they may influence locational decisions. But how much do they do so?

Most analysts agree that *labor* is the single largest cost and most important factor in influencing firm location for most industries (Vaughan, 1979:24–25; Moriarity et al., 1980:181; Daniels, 1982:59). Daniels estimates that labor accounts for 66 cents of each dollar of value added costs for an average industry — more for service industries (Daniels, 1982:59). Firms are most often influenced by such labor force characteristics as its size, unemployment rate, skill level, and degree of unionization (Moriarity et al., 1980:181–203; Vaughan, 1979:25–28).

Obviously, differences in fiscal incentives or tax levels among jurisdictions would have to be very significant to influence the location of business activity. The cost of labor, market considerations, and major production inputs drastically outweigh tax variations among jurisdictions. For example, businesses pay an average of one dollar in state and local taxes for every twenty dollars paid out in wages and salaries. Consequently, "a two percent difference in unit labor cost could offset as much as a forty percent difference in taxes among states" (Litvak and Daniels, 1979:28).

The research on business location has shown overwhelmingly that:

> Taxes and fiscal inducements have little, if any, affect on industrial location decisions. Thus, state and local policies designed to attract business are generally wasted government resources, since businesses that ultimately locate in a jurisdiction would have made the same decision with or without the fiscal incentive (Wasylenko, 1981:155).

Michael Wasylenko reached this conclusion on the basis of a comprehensive review of economic geographical location studies conducted since the 1920s. These studies were not partisan policy analyses, as is the case with some of the recent literature, but utilized theoretical, survey, or econometric data. The consensus in this literature is overwhelming: as economic incentives, tax concessions are ineffectual give-aways of public resources.

Moriarity et al. (1980) conducted a rigorous review of empirical studies concerning the role of taxation in corporate industrial location and concluded that "state and local tax differentials carry little weight in determining locational choices." In his review, Moriarity encountered three studies (Alyea, 1967; Ross, 1953; and Morgan and Hackbart, 1974) that maintained that the empirical evidence had "not proven that, *ceteris paribux* tax incentives or other inducements considerations are not significant marginal factors in attracting business to a community" (Alyea, quoted in Moriarity et al., 1980: 253). The qualification offered by these studies was that locations which are otherwise similar may be differentially attractive depending upon rates of taxation. Indeed, this is the one exception to the general research finding which has sometimes been suggested in recent studies. For example, Litvak and Daniels (1979) suggest that tax differentials may influence location decisions along border areas, between cities within a certain state, or within particular metropolitan areas. Survey results collected from 201 firms from the Fortune 500 list also suggest that one factor contributing to the decline of central cities as industrial locations may have been that business taxes (especially local property taxes) were excessive, in light of the level of services in those cities, as compared with taxes and services in surrounding suburbs (Subcommittee on the City, 1978:V–VI).

Moriarity et al. (1980:254) dismisses these contentions as unsupported by empirical evidence: "These studies imply that firms are footloose within metropolitan areas and that profitability does not vary with location. In fact, the profitability of most firms in metropolitan areas may be significantly affected by their location." His assertion is supported by an exhaustive study of the intraregional location decisions made by firms in New England and Cincinnati. In his comparative study of these two regions, Schmenner (1980:455) found that the primary reason for firm relocation was space limitation. Over 80 percent of those firms which relocated in Cincinnati did so in order to expand their space. His survey results revealed that only a quarter to a third of the relocating plants moved to new locations with lower tax rates. Most—40 to 50 percent—moved to locations with very similar tax rates. Interestingly, 25 percent even moved to jurisdictions with *higher* property tax rates. These findings applied to both capital intensive and labor intensive enterprises.

INTERREGIONAL LOCATION: MYTHS AND REALITIES

Research evidence makes it obvious that financial incentives and tax concessions that attempt to affect the interregional competition for large corporations are ineffectual. Although major relocations are highly publicized, the dynamic of corporate location and investment policies is often misunderstood. Only 554 of the 140,093 large manufacturing firms (those with more than 20 employees) actually moved interregionally between 1969 and 1976. That entails only ½ of 1 percent of all the new jobs created during that period (Litvak, 1981:5). Among the largest multinational corporations employing more than 500 employees, their investment policies created under 15 percent of all new employment in the 1970s. From 1970–1977 the rate of employment growth among the top 100 corporations was only 3.9 percent in contrast to an overall private sector growth rate of 6.5 percent during that same period (Friedland, 1982:49). Many researchers have noted that "the overwhelming majority of new jobs come from the birth and expansion of young, small and independent corporations, not from branch plants, headquarters, or the relocation of multiplant operations" (Peirce, Hagstrom and Steinbach, 1979:17).

Major interregional industrial relocations, such as that of the textile industry in the middle part of this century, are unlikely to occur under current economic conditions. The internationalization of the world economic system has made it difficult or impossible for underdeveloped regions within the United States to outbid emerging Third World industrial location sites. The low wage structures there more than offset any possible U.S. tax incentive effects on production costs.

In a recent insightful study, Friedland (1983:43) has observed that large, multilocational, multinational corporations tend to shift locations incrementally rather than all at once. Their size, market power, and diversification of operations allow such incremental investment and disinvestment practices. Accordingly, plants can be maintained in one place and allowed to depreciate (to take full advantage of federal tax policies) while new investment is channeled elsewhere. Therefore, wholesale plant relocation accounts for a very small proportion of relocation decisions.

The cumulative global effect of this incremental disinvestment should not be underestimated. A growing body of data (Sassen-Koob, 1981a, 1981b, 1983; Frobel, Heinrichs, and Kyere, 1980) documents the extent to which there has been a relocation of manufacturing activities *as a whole* from the United States domestic locations in all regions to Third World assembly and production sites like Mexico, Taiwan, the Philippines, Malaysia, Argentina, and other countries in Latin America and the Middle East. This shift has been sectoral rather than interregional. The transfer of industries producing for the world market to free trade zones, like Singapore; locations recently experiencing favorable capital flows, such as Saudi Arabia; and Third World sites that offer cheap labor, often with limited political rights like Chile and Brazil, has become a problem for *both* the Frostbelt and the Sunbelt (see Mollenkopf, 1977).

To compete with the Third World, states and local governments would have to create wages in the industrial sector that conform to Third World wage rates, but within a First World price structure. Now that many types of manufacturing have become globalized, monopoly sector firms can take full advantage of systemic differences among national economies and labor markets. This enables them to pay top dollar to buy labor peace in the Third World at a small fraction of unionized wage levels in developed societies. With regard to labor policies, American states and localities are politically unable to impose wage rates. And by manipulating tax policies they cannot hope to offset the huge differences in labor costs, by even the most extremely regressive tax measures.

In view of the transnational character of corporate industrial investment during the 1970s and early 1980s, the increased birthrate of smaller firms in the Sunbelt as compared to the deteriorating market conditions and firm deaths in the Frostbelt appear to be the most significant factor in explaining uneven regional development within the United States (Schmenner, 1980; Peirce, Hagstrom and Steinbach, 1979; Watkins and Perry, 1977). Significantly, innovative small firms which account for a large share of employment growth in all regions, tend to pay relatively low wages and offer limited fringe benefits to their workers. Often undercapitalized, they have high death as well as high birth rates. They often seek new categories of workers like women and youth who, being new to the labor market, are easily attracted to low wage work (Friedland, 1983:49).

Small firms in this growth sector often lack both capital and, initially, the profit rates that might make favorable tax incentive policies an important locational inducement. Tax incentive policies are structurally geared not toward small independent firms but to the monopoly fraction of capital. Being undercapitalized, small firms often "require years to generate significant profits or capital gains" that could be substantially enhanced by favorable tax policies (Walton, 1982:16). Accordingly, public policies that made a sizable pool of start-up capital available to innovative firms on favorable credit terms might do far more to generate stable jobs, under conditions that would enable such firms to be less exploitative of their labor force, than do tax incentives, the lion's share of which are claimed by monopoly capital.

Furthermore, when corporate relocation, rather than small firm birth or death, does take place within the continental United States, eighty to ninety percent of all company moves are to other locations within the same metropolitan area (Schmenner, 1980:465). This finding, when considered together with the fact that large firm interregional migration does not account for uneven regional development, strongly suggests that local and state efforts to affect locational decisions of large firms are misguided, expensive, and doomed to failure:

> Areas suffering from high unemployment often blame their difficulties on the outmigration of firms, and regard as a panacea an aggressive promotional campaign to attract new footloose firms. The myth of a rich vein of large, non-polluting firms that can be mined by state development offering free land and access roads, subsidized buildings, and tax abatements, has distorted state development efforts for years. A rational economic development policy cannot be developed until this myth is dispelled and the true components of employment change identified (Vaughan, 1979:19).

Even if various tax incentive devices could affect corporate locational decisions, they would be ineffectual because both actual "differences" among localities and regions and true "incentives" are, in fact, nonexistent. That is, there is a general tendency for actual tax payments that similar firms incur to converge regardless of region. As for financial incentives, they are so universally available that they tend to cancel each other out. As a consequence, the firms which receive subsidies would usually receive them regardless of where they locate.

Additionally, state and local business taxes account for such a small proportion of total production costs (estimated at 4.4 percent by the Federal Reserve Bank of Boston), that taxes are essentially inconsequential cost factors given the current small differentials among areas (Carlton, 1979:28; Moriarity, 1980:249). The small tax variations from region to region are further reduced by the Federal corporate tax deduction which is allowed for state and local taxes. In effect, about one-third of the state and local tax obligation of the average company is paid for by the federal government (Carlton, 1979:28).

State legislatures attempt to keep their taxes in line with neighboring states by following either a "direct matching method" or a "trade-off" approach. The former procedure involves keeping each state tax rate in line with neighboring states' rates. The latter method amounts to the states keeping their overall tax level in line with adjacent states without regard to matching each tax rate (Wasylenko, 1981:168–186). Such conscious efforts by state governments to maintain a corporate tax equilibrium with nearby states leaves little possibility that tax incentives can play much of an economic leveraging role as a locational determinant.

To the extent that tax rates do vary among localities and states, the differences may well be offset by other factors. For instance, higher tax levels may correspond to a greater quality and quantity of public services that a firm receives (for example, public education of the work force, police and fire protection, garbage collection and water supply). Such services may offset any extra tax costs which are incurred (Carlton, 1979:37; ACIR, 1980:44; Moriarity et al., 1980:248), a factor perhaps helping to explain the finding that 25 percent of intrametropolitan locational shifts in Cincinnati were to jurisdictions with higher tax rates.

There is also evidence that the incidence of differential business taxes may, in effect, be passed on to consumers in the form of higher prices for a firm's product. Of course, this depends on a number of market features such as the degree of competitiveness facing a firm and the extent to which a firm's supply and demand are sensitive to price changes. It is certain that monopoly sector firms are best situated to shift their state and local tax burdens forward to consumers or to capitalize the tax differences in higher land values (Carlton, 1979:28–29; ACIR, 1980:44).

This is not the only burden that ordinary citizens must bear. The cumulative effect of state and local tax incentive policies in the past three decades has been a dramatic shift in the burden of governmental revenue production from corporations to households. In 1950, businesses paid 20 percent of all state and local property taxes; by late 1983 their share had declined to 8 percent. As Friedland (1983:45) has concluded, "The increased power of [multilocational] corporations to play the market for public goods forces a lowering of subnational corporate tax burdens."

"BEGGARING THY NEIGHBOR"

Economic growth sometimes occurs, or seems to occur, in places which offer incentives. When this happens in a slow growth environment, such as that confronting the advanced capitalist societies today, employment and investment are displaced from one area to another. Resources are incrementally transferred from one location to another with no increase in the total amount of national resources and jobs available: a zero-sum game takes place in which no net national economic growth occurs because of locational decisions (Subcommittee on Oversight, 1981:232; Peirce, Hagstrom, and Steinbach, 1979:2; Litvak and Daniels, 1979:60; Leone and Meyer, 1977:53; Bearse, 1982:35).

Subsidizing new industry through the use of tax concessions or financial incentives also distorts the national economy by creating artificial advantages for firms that receive subsidies as compared to those that do not (USGAO, 1979; Peirce, Hagstrom and Steinbach, 1979). Thus, "beggaring thy neighbor" applies not only to inter-jurisdictional rivalries but to competition among business firms. The effects of this "beggaring they neighbor" approach mainly fall negatively upon state and local governments but positively advantage corporations which know how to play the game:

> a policy which makes capital available to certain firms, not suffering from capital unavailability, at below market rates in order to make their location or expansion in certain areas more attractive . . . can only produce jobs at the expense of another state. . . . Such a policy will provoke retaliation as well as cost state governments much more than they can afford to pay (Litvak and Daniels, 1979:60).

In this sort of predatory context, all jurisdictions that want to play in the zero-sum competition must face the basic fact that many of the same programs and policies have become universally available. Thus, the inducement packages offered by competing jurisdictions tend to cancel each other out (Libassi and Hausner, 1977; Litvak and Daniels, 1979:60; Prescott and Lewis, 1979:172; Subcommittee on Oversight, 1981:231). Even if differentials hypothetically existed between states and localities before the new financial incentives, these have been narrowed or erased by the national popularity of such incentives. The result is a subsidy to multilocational industry for locating where it wishes and a sizeable, needless expense to nearly all state and local governments.

State and local politicians are enmeshed in a classical instance of the tragedy of the commons. They are loathe to criticize the argument that tax incentives are beneficial, or to question the effectiveness of the other instruments which attempt to promote economic development, for fear that the first to say "no" will be excluded from whatever growth does take place in the national economy. Perhaps it is no accident that one of the few political figures willing to assume a critical stance was former Governor Milliken of

Michigan, where corporate disinvestment has devastated the economic base. Milliken has said: "We are just outbidding each other. We are vying for the same companies. Each state is trying to put in more incentives, more tax abatement programs, and the like. There has to be some point of marginal utility . . . where it becomes counterproductive within the country" (in Peirce, Hagstrom, and Steinbach, 1979:2). Yet, until that point reaches crisis proportions, very few state and local political elites are willing to jump off the treadmill (for notable exceptions see Feagin, 1983). . . .

ECONOMIC GROWTH OR ECONOMIC DEVELOPMENT?

By now it should be clear that solutions to the "urban crisis" and the "reindustrialization of America" are not to be found in fiscal and tax policies. Those policies have not been successful in generating a stable economic base for the social development of the working population. Economic growth obtained through locational inducements that weaken the political capacity to place democratic controls upon private power is not the same as economic development. The former must not be confused with the latter. As Ledebur (1977:5) has pointed out, *economic growth* "refers to increases in the total value of goods and services produced . . . and the aggregative income generated within a region." In contrast, *economic development* is concerned with the collective welfare of individuals rather than with the expansion of aggregate wealth, independently of its distributional effects. Usually, proponents of economic growth through tax inducements express little or no interest in those social indicators which make up a human needs-based concept of economic development. . . .

Perhaps the only immediate alternative to the costly locational incentive techniques which accompany but do not cause economic growth, while ignoring the need for economic development, is to completely eliminate them. At present only a national policy would be capable of abolishing these costly state and local revenue giveaway programs. Despite some promising instances of effective grassroots political mobilization to resist the prevailing domination of economic growth and decline by multilocational capital in California and Vermont localities (see Feagin, 1983; Kann, 1983), most state and local governments are too caught up in the fierce competition for jobs and investment to act unilaterally to demand genuine economic development as a precondition of investment (see Subcommittee on Urban and Rural Economic Development, 1981).

In view of the globalization of locational competition in the past decade, even national policy to curb the wastefully competitive struggle cannot effectively address the transnational dimension of rapid capital mobility, runaway plants, and uneven development. Nevertheless, working to abolish an important political tool in the struggle for democratic control is a useful starting point. Once the first step is taken to redefine the axis of economic development policy, subsequent political strategies can be formulated and acted upon to insure that capital investment is made "the servant of society, not its master" (Smith, 1981:456).

REFERENCES

Advisory Commission on Intergovernmental Relations (1980) Regional Growth: Historical Perspectives. Washington, DC: Advisory Commission on Intergovernmental Relations.

Advisory Commission on Intergovernmental Relations and the National Academy of Public Administration (1982) The States and Distressed Communities: The 1981 Report. Washington, DC: HUD Office of Community Planning and Development.

Alyea, P. E. (1967) "Property tax inducements to attract industry." Pp. 139–158 in R. W. Lindholm (ed.), Property Taxation USA. Madison, WI: University of Wisconsin Press.

Bearse, P. J. (1982) "Institutional innovation and the changing public/private interface in development finance: overall perspectives." Pp. 3–39 in P. J. Bearse (ed.), Mobilizing Capital: Program Innovation and the Changing Public/Private Interface of Development Finance. New York: Elsevier Science Publishing Co.

Carlton, D. W. (1979) "Why new firms locate where they do: an econometric model." In W. C. Wheaton (ed.), Interregional Movements and Regional Growth. Washington, DC: The Urban Institute.

Castells, M. (1975) "Immigrant workers and class struggles in advanced capitalism: the Western European experience." Politics and Society 5(1):33–66.

Contese, C. F. and B. Jones (1977) "The sociological analysis of boom towns." Western Sociological Review 8(1):76–90.

Cook, T. E. (1982) "The courtship of capital: political implications of increasingly portable capital and fixed territorial jurisdictions of government." Paper delivered at the Annual Meeting of the American Political Science Association, Denver, CO, September 2–5.

Daniels, B. (1982) "Capital is only part of the problem." Pp. 53–76 in P. J. Bearse (ed.), Mobilizing Capital: Program Innovation and the Changing Public/Private Interface in Development Finance. New York: Elsevier Science Publishing Co.

Ecker-Racz, L. L. (1970) The Politics and Economics of State-Local Finance. Englewood Cliffs, NJ: Prentice-Hall.

Edwards, R. (1979) Contested Terrain: The Transformation of the Workplace in the Twentieth Century. New York: Basic Books.

Feagin, J. R. (1983) The Urban Real Estate Game. Englewood Cliffs, NJ: Prentice-Hall.

Firestine, R. F. (1977) "Economic growth and inequality: demographic change and the public sector response." Pp. 191–210 in D. C. Perry and A. J. Watkins (eds.), The Rise of the Sunbelt Cities, Vol. 14, Urban Affairs Annual Reviews. Beverly Hills, CA: Sage Publications.

Friedland, R. (1983) "The politics of profit and the geography of growth." Urban Affairs Quarterly 19(September):41–54.

Frobel, F., J. Heinrichs and O. Kreye (1980) The New International Division of Labor. Cambridge University Press.

Gordon, D. M. (1977) "Class struggle and stages of American urban development." In D. C. Perry and A. J. Watkins (eds.), The Rise of the Sunbelt Cities, Vol. 14, Urban Affairs Annual Reviews. Beverly Hills, CA: Sage Publications.

Hellman, D. A., G. H. Wassall and L. H. Falk (1976) State Financial Incentives to Industry. Lexington, MA: D. C. Heath.

Hubbell, L. K. (1979) "Development banking and financial incentives for the private sector." In K. L. Hubbell (ed.), Fiscal Crisis in American Cities: The Federal Response. Cambridge, MA: Ballinger.

Kann, M. E. (1983) "Radicals in power: lessons from Santa Monica." Socialist Review 13(May-June):81–101.

Lamb, Robert and Stephen Rappaport (1980) Municipal Bonds: The Comprehensive Review of Tax-Exempt Securities and Public Finance. New York: McGraw-Hill.

Ledebur, L. C. (1977) "Regional economic development and human resource requirements." In P. V. Braden (ed.), Human Resource and Regional Economic Development. Washington, DC: Economic Development Administration.

Leone, R. A. and J. A. Meyer (1977) "Tax exemption and the local property tax." In J. R. Meyer and J. M. Quigley (eds.), Local Public Finance and the Fiscal Squeeze: A Case Study. Cambridge, MA: Ballinger.

Libassi, P. and V. A. Hausner (1977) "Public policy options to encourage investment in central cities." In P. E. Braden (ed.), Human Resource and Regional Economic Development. Washington, DC: Economic Development Administration.

Litvak, L. (1981) "Questions arise as the popularity of bonds grows." Nation's Cities' Weekly 5:8.

Litvak, L. and B. Daniels (1979) Innovations in Development Finance. Washington, DC: The Council of State Planning Agencies.

Lowi, T. J. (1979) "The state of cities in the second republic." Pp. 43–513 in J. P. Blair and D. Nachmias (eds.), Fiscal Retrenchment and Urban Policy, Vol. 17, Urban Affairs Annual Reviews. Beverly Hills, CA: Sage Publications.

Maxwell, J. A. and J. R. Aronson (1977) Financing State and Local Governments, 3rd ed. Washington, DC: The Brookings Institution.

Miller, W. E. (1977) Manufacturing: A Study of Industrial Location. University Park, PA: The Pennsylvania University Press.

Mollenkopf, J. H. (1977a) "The post-war politics of urban development." In J. Walton and D. E. Carns (eds.), Cities in Change: Studies on the Urban Condition, 2nd ed. Boston: Allyn and Bacon.

——— (1977b) "The rise of the southwest: problem and promise." Washington, DC: Urban Technical Assistance Office, Economic Development Administration (April).

Morgan, W. E. and M. M. Hackbart (1974) "An analysis of state and local industrial tax exemption programs." Southern Economic Journal 41(2):201–205.

Moriarty, B. M. et al. (1980) Industrial Location and Community Development. Chapel Hill, NC: University of North Carolina Press.

National Academy of Public Administration (1980) The States and Urban Strategies: A Comparative Analysis. Washington, DC: U.S. Government Printing Office.

Peirce, N. R., J. Hagstrom and C. Steinbach (1979) Economic Development: The Challenge of the 1980s. Washington, DC: The Council of State Planning Agencies.

Perry, D. C. and A. J. Watkins, eds. (1977) The Rise of the Sunbelt Cities, Vol. 14, Urban Affairs Annual Reviews. Beverly Hills, CA: Sage Publications.

Prescott, J. R. and W. C. Lewis (1975) Urban-Regional Economic Growth and Policy. Ann Arbor, MI: Ann Arbor Science Publishers, Inc.

Ross, W. D. (1953) "Tax exemptions in Louisiana as a device for encouraging industrial development." Southwestern Social Science Quarterly 34(June):14–22.

Sassen-Koob, S. (1981a) "Exporting capital and importing labor." Occasional Paper 28, Center for Latin American and Caribbean Studies, New York University.

――― (1981b) "Recomposition and perpheralization at the core." In M. Dixon and S. Dixon (eds.), The New Nomads: From Immigrant Labor to Transnational Working Class. San Francisco: Synthesis Publications.

――― (1983) "The new labor demand in global cities." In M. P. Smith (ed.), Cities in Transformation: Class, Capital, and the State, Vol. 26, Urban Affairs Annual Reviews. Berkeley, CA: Sage Publications.

Schmenner, R. W. (1980) "Industrial location and urban public management." Pp. 446–468 in A. P. Solomon (ed.), The Prospective City: Economy, Population, Energy, and Environmental Development. Cambridge, MA: MIT Press.

Smith, D. M. (1981) Industrial Location: An Economic-Geographical Analysis, 2nd ed. New York: John Wiley and Sons.

Smith, M. P. and M. Keller (1983) "'Managed growth' and the politics of uneven development in New Orleans." Pp. 126–166 in S. S. Fainstein and N. I. Fainstein (eds.), Restructuring the City: The Political Economy of Urban Redevelopment. New York: Longman.

Stuart, R. (1983) "Business said to have barred new plants in largely black communities." New York Times (February):9.

Subcommittee on the City of the Committee on Banking, Finance, and Urban Affairs, House of Representatives, 95th Congress, Second Session (1978) Large Corporations and Urban Employment. Washington, DC: U.S. Government Printing Office.

Subcommittee on Oversight of the Committee on Ways and Means of the House of Representatives, 97th Congress, First Session (1981) 'Small Issue' Industrial Development Bonds. Washington, DC: U.S. Government Printing Office.

Subcommittee on Urban and Rural Economic Development (1981).

U.S. Department of Housing and Urban Development (1982) The President's National Urban Policy Report: 1982. Washington, D.C. U.S. Government Printing Office.

U.S. Department of the Treasury and the Joint Committee on Internal Revenue Taxation (1975) Estimates of Federal Tax Expenditures. Washington, DC: U.S. Government Printing Office.

U.S. General Accounting Office (1982) Revitalizing Distressed Areas Through Enterprise

Zones: Many Uncertainties Exist. Washington, D.C.: U.S. Government Printing Office.

Vaughan, R. J. (1979) State Taxation and Economic Development. Washington, DC: The Council of State Planning Agencies.

Walton, J. (1983) "Cities and jobs and politics." Urban Affairs Quarterly 19(September):5–17.

Watkins, A. J. and D. C. Perry (1977) "Regional change and the impact of uneven urban development." In D. C. Perry and A. J. Watkins (eds.), The Rise of the Sunbelt Cities, Vol. 14, Urban Affairs Annual Reviews. Beverly Hills, CA: Sage Publications.

Wasylenko, M. (1981) "The location of firms: the roles of taxes and fiscal incentives." Pp. 155–190 in R. Bahl (ed.), Urban Government Finance: Emerging Trends, Vol. 20, Urban Affairs Annual Reviews. Beverly Hills, CA: Sage Publications.

42

From "Renaissance" to Restructuring: The Dynamics of Contemporary Urban Development*

Peter Williams and Neil Smith

The notion that gentrification represents some sort of urban renaissance or revival is widespread, particularly in the United States (Gruen 1964, Alpern 1979, Sumka 1979, DeVito 1980, Demarest 1981). This perspective would imply some kind of prior secular decline and now a reversal of established trends. That is really the meaning of renaissance and it was the explicit symbolism behind the naming of Detroit's Ford-inspired Renaissance Center, the spiritual renewal after the fall. The popularity of the renaissance/revival theme lies in its inherent optimism and the belief that squalor is being expunged and the city is being reclaimed for the respectable classes. As such it is a sharply partisan view of contemporary urban change and one which negates the real history of urban development and change. There was no such simple fall and there is no such simple rebirth.

The history of urban development is a story of the constant patterning

*Williams, Peter, and Neil Smith. 1986. "From 'Renaissance' to Restructuring: The Dynamics of Contemporary Urban Development." Pp. 204–224 in Gentrification of the City. Winchester, MA: Allen and Unwin. Copyright © 1986. Reprinted by permission of Allen and Unwin.

and transformation of the city landscape. More rapid and more institutionalized with the advent of capitalism, this transformation process can be seen as a constant structuring and restructuring of urban space with nothing remaining untouched for very long. Although such changes in urban form and structure are always taking place, they do not occur at a constant pace, nor proceed in a uniform direction. Rather, like the larger patterns of change in capitalist society itself, this tends to be a cyclical process. There are periods in which new spatial patterns are set in a relatively rapid restructuring, and other periods in which established patterns become more entrenched, rather than new ones set. Of course, there is no clean historical break between these different kinds of process, since to a considerable extent they occur simultaneously. Thus if we examine the period from 1945 to 1973 in most advanced capitalist societies, it is evident that the most profound transformation in urban structure revolved around the suburbanization process. This represented a dramatic consummation of processes that had originated much earlier in the 20th century and even in the late 19th century. At the same time, the suburbanization of the postwar period was laying the foundation for the restructuring that would come to dominate in the 1970s. The important question is this: if the history of cities is one of constant structuring and restructuring, why is gentrification and the contemporary restructuring of urban space so significant, if indeed it is?

In the first place, it cannot be claimed that the process is without precedent. Even if most urban restructuring has involved an outward expansion of the capitalist city, there are more than a few historical examples of the "redevelopment" of central-city areas. The most obvious example, albeit an unintentional predicament, is the rebuilding of cities, from London to San Francisco, after their devastation by fire. More important is the kind of transformation accomplished largely by the private market in most 19th-century cities. In London, for example,

> the City was transformed from a residential–industrial area into a depopulated conglomeration of banks, offices, warehouses, and railway stations. Its poorer inhabitants were unceremoniously evicted to make way for this glittering symbol of late Victorian capitalism. (Stedman Jones 1971:151–3)

Engels (1973 edn.) observed the same process in Manchester, documenting its effect on the working class, and in a now-famous passage, Marx (1967 edn, vol. I, 657) observed the general effect of so-called improvements, as they were known at the time in Britain:

> "Improvements" of towns, accompanying the increase of wealth, by the demolition of badly built quarters, the erection of palaces for banks, warehouses, etc., the widening of streets for business traffic, for the carriages of luxury, and for the introduction of tramways, etc., drive away the poor into even worse and more crowded hiding places.

If Haussmann's rebuilding of Paris in the 1850s and 1860s was more planned, with military and political purposes playing a considerable role, the results were virtually the same for the working class (Pinkney 1958).

The prior occurrence of "improvements" and renewal in the central city is sometimes construed to minimize the importance of the contemporary gentrification process. It is viewed by some as a periodic feature in the "natural" life cycle of cities. We do not accept this naturalistic interpretation of the market or of urban social processes. The major problem with this approach is its ahistorical treatment of urban growth and urban processes (see, for example, Jacobs 1969, 1984), contending that the earliest cities and the most modern are governed by the same laws and generalizations. We hold, on the contrary, that urban processes are quite specific to different societies, different periods, and especially different modes of production, and that the contemporary process of gentrification is quintessentially a feature of the advanced capitalist city. Gentrification would be impossible in cities where there was no well-developed geographical division of residential location by class. Previous societies certainly incorporated class divisions, but these were not expressed in a systematic differentiation of urban residential space. Medieval cities, as is well known, were divided by horizontal distance in individual buildings, not by geographical location.[1] In reality, gentrification as we know it could only appear on the agenda after the industrial revolution had led to the dramatic expansion of cities, and the suburbanization process accomplished an increasingly acute geographical differentiation as part of this expansion. As society expanded and restructured, so its spatial manifestations changed. The creation of exclusive domains, such as the suburbs, meant that gentrification became feasible.

What we are arguing here is that although 19th-century clearances had a very similar effect on working-class housing, namely a reduction in available units and even an increase in prices (Allan 1965, Rodger 1982), these "improvements" were not responsible for such a significant restructuring as we seem to be experiencing today. We are not arguing that the contemporary rebuilding and restructuring of the central and inner urban areas represents an end to suburbanization; nor are we arguing that it represents such a profound change in urban structure as occurred with the advent of suburbanization. Rather, we *are* arguing that just as suburbanization was the spatial expression of a larger social and economic process (Harvey 1978, Aglietta 1979), so too gentrification is a highly visible spatial process deeply rooted in current patterns of social and economic differentiation. The task for us here is to attempt to assess the immediate direction and consequences of this urban restructuring. How substantial will the changes be? What kind of urban areas will be fashioned in the immediate future? What will be the effects of the process on today's city residents and on urban politics and conflict? These are our concerns in this concluding essay.

Throughout the book different authors have sought to penetrate the imagery of gentrification and expose the essential processes at work. Thus we have exposed the inadequacies of much current commentary on this process and have attempted a more deep-seated and rounded understanding of its form, causes, and immediate consequences. What we seek to do here is to look ahead and project this understanding onto our knowledge of the unfolding of capitalist societies so that we can begin to grasp the contemporary and future significance of gentrification.

THE FUTURE OF THE CENTRAL CITY

In the heady days following World War II, it became increasingly fashionable, given seemingly unlimited economic and technological expansion, to study and anticipate the urban future. It was an optimistic era; the future not only looked bright, but, more than that, it seemed almost controllable. We anticipated the end of business cycles, the end of poverty (at least in the developed world) and the end of ideology. This passion for futurism was especially intense in the United States, which then still represented the most forward pioneer in many social, economic and cultural trends. Today, this kind of futurism has virtually disappeared (but see Gappert & Knight 1982). Its demise was not simply the result of changing academic fashions, but was very closely related to specific social, political and economic changes that emerged between the late 1960s and 1973 and which rendered futurism a difficult and increasingly utopian pursuit. Even economic forecasters now acknowledge that it is no longer possible to predict with any accuracy the course of events.

The fundamental problem with these kinds of attempts to forecast (and sometimes even predict) the future lay in their methodology. So constant were the upward trends at the time (or so it appeared) that there seemed to be no major objection to forecasting the future through what we might call speculative extrapolation. Current trends were plotted, the trajectory extrapolated, and the results were interpreted, with a modicum of respectable speculation, for given futures: 1990, 2000 and 2025 (see, for example, Berry 1970). Already losing its appeal with the political uprisings of the late 1960s and the beginnings of financial crisis in the world money markets, this methodology was quickly rendered obsolete with the full onslaught of world economic crisis in 1973. Speculative extrapolation provides no tools for comprehending widespread and rapid reversals of established trends. More than that, the emergence of a complex and interlinked world economy means there are no longer any sheltered national systems.

Discussions today of the future of the city are more cautious, less speculative, and suffer less from the naive linearity of extrapolative futurism (Davies & Champion 1983). It remains vital to understand the direction and pace of social trends, but these are increasingly treated in the context of multiple tendencies that are often contradictory; the future is treated as more and more contingent. A certain amount of speculation is inevitable in considering the future of the central city, but today that speculation tends to be based on a more sophisticated understanding of the substantive forces involved. Much effort has therefore been devoted to explaining the different facets of physical decay and social deprivation in the urban center (see, for example, Anderson *et al.* 1983), and it is upon this kind of explanatory analysis that discussion of the future must be based. We isolate here four sets of forces, or agents of change, which will be among the most crucial in determining the future landscape of the central city. These are as follows: the new international division of labor, the changing function of cities, the economic crisis, and the role of the state. These should be seen not as separate "factors" determining urban development, but as elements of a larger, integrated whole. Nor should they be viewed as exclusive; separating out these four agents of change, we have also omitted others that will help substantially to shape the future. For example we have set aside questions of demographic change, the sexual division of labor, and the rise of new technology, either because we feel their effects are largely covered in the above headings, or because their effect is likely to be secondary.

What we are arguing is that we can only discuss the future of gentrification within a broader understanding of what is happening to cities and societies. We begin by briefly discussing the new international division of labor which now dominates the world economy.

The New International Division of Labor

We would argue that the continuing development of a new international division of labor will be the major determinant, at the regional scale, of urban restructuring. Cities in so-called declining regions, from Glasgow and Gary to Newcastle, Australia, can expect relatively low investments of capital in the built environment, whereas others, such as Boston, Bristol and Toronto, are likely to experience increases, or at least no relative decrease, in capital investments. The reasons for this are in part complex, in part intuitively obvious. The major impetus behind the new international division of labor (Fröebel *et al.* 1980) comes from the internationalization of capital: not commodity capital, which has been internationalized for centuries in the form of trading companies, nor finance capital which has been internationalized for decades in the form of multinational corporations, but *productive* capital in the form of capital invested directly in the production process.

Whereas previous production processes tended to be organized at the subnational regional level (thus the old regional geography distinguished regions on the basis of the production of specialized commodities) industrial production today is increasingly organized across international boundaries and more on the basis of differential wage rates. The "world car" is only the most obvious illustration; from textiles to electronic games, steel products to computer systems, the final product is assembled from components produced in several or more countries. The insularity of regions within national economics is no more, and this has led to a restructuring of geographical space at the regional level which impresses certain patterns on urban centers (Massey, 1979, Carney *et al.* 1980, Smith 1985). New international regions are being created; Clydeside, Merseyside, and the Ruhr share an experience at odds with that of south-east England, Queensland, and California. Certainly all of the latter have themselves experienced downturns, and some major centers within them have lost jobs and population, but the regions as a whole remain prosperous and vibrant.

In many cities that were the old industrial core of advanced capitalism, the new international division of labor has brought a dramatic deindustrialization of the productive base. Capital has been withdrawn in part or in whole from the basic manufacturing infrastructure of these cities, and as a result it is also withdrawn from other land uses, residential, commercial, retail, and so on. This pattern of economic decline, broadly related to industrial decline in older centers, is resulting in a cruel dialectic of decay and opportunity. In cities such as Liverpool, England, and Gary, Indiana, it is decay that dominates the present and immediate future, whereas in Baltimore and perhaps Pittsburgh the drastic cheapening of central locations brought on by this decay has been capitalized (quite literally) as a means of reconstructing and restructuring the urban center.

The new international division of labor has also resulted in the concentration of modern industrial and nonindustrial activities, leading to strong economic growth in certain cities, from the American sunbelt and the Japanese industrial centers to the "European arc" stretching from the East Midlands of England, through the Netherlands, to Frankfurt. Although many of the cities in these areas are also experiencing economic and physical decline in the center, this is generally less intense than in the deindustrialized regions, and the consequent restructuring at the center is often masked by the general prosperity. Much of the growth in these cities is in peripheral areas and beyond, in the small towns surrounding the metropolitan area.

In summary, then, we can expect that as the new international division of labor develops further, many predominantly older cities will continue to experience an outflow of capital and a consequent decline in economic and physical conditions. This need not be universal; rather it will be highly uneven. Decline, however, engenders profitable opportunity in so far as central locations are available at low prices. The extent to which these opportunities will be capitalized upon is much more difficult to estimate since it immediately involves a consideration of alternative competitive investment opportunities, and this in turn leads us to the question of economic crisis and the pattern of economic growth and depression in the next decade. Before broaching this question, however, let us examine the changing function of the city.

Urban Hierarchy and City Function

In the wake of deindustrialization and the disproportionate increase in "service" jobs, it has become conventional wisdom that cities have been transformed from industrial centers into service centers. This is correct, but far too general to provide an understanding of the complex hierarchy of cities and city functions that is evolving. In the last few years, several authors have suggested that we are witnessing, for the first time, the emergence of truly global cities and a closely articulated hierarchy of urban areas in the world economy. This is part of the process of regional transformation and the development of the new international division of labor discussed earlier. Cohen (1981) suggests that in the last few decades we have witnessed the decline of the "metropolis and region" structure which dominated the United States, and other advanced capitalist nations, in the first part of the 20th century. As national economies were increasingly wrenched into the international economy, the urban areas that operated as national-level centers in these economies were increasingly bifurcated into international and simply national centers. A further layer of regional centers was also expanded. He argues that New York, London and Tokyo have already emerged as global cities in the sense that their largest financial and corporate enterprises are involved more in international than in national transactions (Cohen 1981:308; see also *Business Week* 1984:100).

Many of the other large cities have suffered a relative demise, losing some of their international functions but retaining considerable corporate administrative activity. Even such large metropolises as Chicago, Amsterdam – Rotterdam, Manchester, and Melbourne seem to fall into this category. Other smaller urban areas have been separated out as merely regional centers. This pattern, of course, is not static, and Cohen suggests that cities like Frankfurt and San Francisco (and Sydney and Toronto, we would add) may well be vying for international status. Noyelle (1983) and Noyelle and Stanback (1981) come to similar conclusions about a new urban hierarchy, but since their analysis has a narrower, more national focus, they provide a different categorization of cities.

The point here is not the argument over which cities fit where in the hierarchy. Rather, it is to recognize that the development of this new urban hierarchy is simultaneously creating a new hierarchy of urban functions. If the late feudal city was defined by the concentration for commercial capital (in market "towns"), and the early capitalist city by the concentration of productive capital in industry, the late capitalist city is defined differently again. For the international and most of the national cities, it is the concentration of money capital and the gamut of financial, administrative and professional services that lubricate the money flow; it is this function that defines the late capitalist cities at the top of the new urban hierarchy. The situation of the regional centers and smaller cities is more ambiguous. Although their economies are also changing toward certain kinds of services, many of them are likely to remain local manufacturing centers, producing goods for which there is no effective international or national market.

Now it is reasonable to expect that central urban areas will be differentially affected according to their place in this emerging hierarchy and their changing function. Cohen (1981:307) argues that the difference between international- and national-level urban centers is reflected in "higher prices for rents and services which result from the pronounced agglomeration of corporate and corporate-related activities" in the global cities. Indeed, if one looks at the housing market in the centers of these global cities, it seems likely that this market would remain buoyant even in the face of any further economic recession which adversely affects housing. The Manhattan real-estate market, for example, as transacted by brokers or in the pages of *The Times* or the *New York Times*, is geared not to local or even national but to international trends and demands.

Thus it would seem that we can expect a Manhattanization of the international city. By this we mean not simply an architectural Manhattanization with the clustering of skyscrapers in the center; that is already largely accomplished. Rather, we can expect a *social Manhattanization* whereby the agglomeration of corporate and corporate-related activities at the center leads to a further agglomeration of upper-income residential neighborhoods and of lavish recreation and entertainment facilities. The main question here is the extent to which this type of gentrification will permeate down the urban hierarchy. Since they too harbor considerable concentrations of corporate and related activities, many national centers are likely to experience a continued Manhattanization, if more selective *vis-à-vis* geographical neighborhoods. Regional centers (such as Dublin and Baltimore, Vancouver and Adelaide) have already experienced gentrification, but the continuation of this process in the face of economic crisis will be more contingent upon local conditions and policies.

Certainly we are not suggesting that the extreme wealth and indulgence of New York's Manhattan, or of Mayfair or Belgravia in London will reach out into all the presently gentrified inner areas. However, we would suggest that there are important connections between this process of social Manhattanization and the more mundane restratification process which is taking place in the inner suburbs. The creation of corporate financial and service economies is achieved not simply by the establishment of global headquarters buildings in one selected center, but also by the creation of a network of activities across the globe. That network reaches down into a large number of urban centers. Alongside this new administrative economy come all the elements necessary to maintain it: advanced education centers, cultural facilities, science parks, and the whole panoply of recreational and life-style accompaniments.

Just as the new urban hierarchy is interconnected, so the new social hierarchy that derives from the emergence of administrative economies is both connected and dispersed across space. Manhattan and Mayfair provide homes for the elite in accessible and relatively safe environments. The executives, professionals and public servants who service the economy cannot live in such close proximity, but they can easily displace an increasingly residualized working class from the inner areas of those cities where this new economy concentrates. Indeed, in conjunction with the demand for office space, such groups are able to transform the old working hearts of such cities into office, home and leisure centers, e.g. the transformation of the dock areas of Bristol, Vancouver and London. Thus, when we talk of Manhattanization, it is essential to think of the spread effects. Manhattan symbolizes the transformation of economies, but the impact of that transformation does not simply remain there.

Economic Crisis

The continued economic crisis is likely to have the most profound effect on the immediate future of the central city. The reason for this, quite simply, is that changes in urban form are brought about by investments of capital in the built environment, and investment patterns are dramatically different in periods of crisis than in periods of expansion. In quantitative terms, there is no simple equation between economic crisis and levels of investment in the built environment. A number of authors have discussed the tendency for massive quantities of capital to move into construction on the eve of crisis (Ambrose & Colenutt, 1975, Harvey 1978). Thus the office boom in London in the early 1970s preceded an economic slump beginning in 1973, and reinvestment in 1978 preceded the slump of the late 1970s and early 1980s. Housing starts in the US have varied wildly in the late 1970s and early 1980s (from 1.07 million in 1982 to over 2 million in 1983) with the end of one "recession," then a hiatus, the beginning of another recession, and then a short but dramatic recovery. The astonishing rise in new office construction in 1983 and 1984 in most US cities undoubtedly presages another sharp economic decline.

The temporality of investment has therefore been cyclical and highly uneven in spatial terms. The sharp oscillations typical of the American economy in recent years have not been experienced in the United Kingdom, where the economy has been depressed throughout since 1979, with only small and occasional periods of growth. Even more important, there have been significant spatial changes in the pattern of investment at the urban scale. Whereas, in previous decades, the suburbs and the outer city have claimed the vast majority of new investment in the built environment, these outer areas no longer dominate so thoroughly. According to Data Resources Inc., an estimated 42 percent of total construction capital in the United States in 1983 ($54 billion) was committed to renovation and remodeling, much of it located in the central city (*Business Week* 1983). Rehabilitation is much less sensitive to changes in the interest rate. This suggests a significant spatial countercyclical trend. Although in general the volume of construction declines considerably during crisis, within this decline we appear to be seeing a considerable transfer of capital from suburban new starts to central and inner-city rehabilitation efforts.[2]

Of course the latter still lags behind the former in absolute terms, and although central area investment increased in relative terms, as a result of the most recent recession, it is not clear how vital a countercyclical tendency gentrification actually is. Indeed the impressionistic evidence suggests that in most US cities, central city rehabilitation stayed "up" through the first 12 months of recession until the first half of 1982, but declined in late 1982, only to increase again rapidly in 1983. In conclusion it is not clear how representative the American experience actually is. We would expect that in Britain, mainland Europe, even Australia, where to different degrees the state is more involved in the land and housing markets, gentrification will be less susceptible to the booms and troughs of the private market.

Obviously, then, there is no simple way to forecast the effect of economic crisis on gentrification and urban restructuring. The most immediate influences on the level of activity are the mortgage and interest rates, and to the extent that there is a sustained rise in these rates, or that they remain high, as part of the recurrence of economic crisis, then central urban restructuring is likely to be adversely affected; capital will be invested elsewhere, if at all, and would-be buyers will delay their purchase of residential and commercial space. More broadly, relationships between gentrification and the administrative economy are relatively clear. Any factors that restrict the expansion of that economy, in total and in specific locations (for example high interest rates, which inhibit new office construction, or a fall in market rents, which leads to the postponement of new schemes), can reduce the pressures that are ultimately expressed through gentrification. The residential choices of the people who occupy the professional and managerial posts arising from the development of this economy are in turn heavily conditioned by those forces. Thus, in that it affects the production as well as the consumption of the gentrified landscape, the advent of deeper economic crisis is probably the most salient potential barrier to the present momentum of urban restructuring.

The Role of the State

Thus far, the state's involvement in urban restructuring has been essentially reactive. This is not to diminish the importance of the state's role but to place it in context. The mid-century slum clearance and urban renewal programs initiated by many governments represent the most direct and far-reaching attempts at intervention by the state in this sector. These were attempts to reverse the decay of centrally located residential, industrial and commercial areas where property had become obsolete. The conventional lament that these programs were often social failures, rehousing fewer people than they displaced, mistakes the proclaimed justification of slum clearance for its real goal. These programs were more economic in motivation than social, and in that respect were successful. State intervention both provided new opportunities for private investment and reduced the risk involved.

In the 1970s and 1980s, the state has been less involved in the process. In Britain, the 1977 Inner City White Paper marked the attempt to codify an urban policy and continue the state's centrality (Home 1982), but even before the election of Thatcher it was clear that little would come of the White Paper. Since then, the major urban initiatives have been the Enterprise Zones and privatization campaigns, both of which attempt to reduce the role of the state in urban reconstruction. In the United States there has been a similar pattern of the state extricating itself from direct responsibility for redevelopment. From 1949 to 1974 the Federal Government had become increasingly involved in redevelopment efforts, but with the Nixon moratorium on new public housing (1971) and the installation of the Community Development Block Grant (CDBG) program (1974), the Federal Government pulled back from direct involvement. Carter's UDAG programme (Urban Development Action Grant), implemented in late 1977, and his ill-fated National Urban Plan of 1979, represented a temporary and only partly effective attempt to reinstigate federally planned urban redevelopment. In the 1980s, the Reagan administration has pulled back dramatically, declaring that urban redevelopment is a job for the private market. Some federal funding remains and there are limited local sources, but these are increasingly divided between tax incentives for large corporate projects and small-scale ancillary projects such as street lighting, neighborhood spruce-up projects, and sidewalk herringbone paving.

The reduction in state funds has affected different cities differently. In the United Kingdom it has led to a considerable slowdown in rehabilitation and redevelopment, although this is less noticeable in London, as one might expect. In the United States, so far, the process has been more vulnerable to the vagaries of the economy. However, the full impact of federal cuts may not yet have been felt. Only since 1982 have local governments begun to reorganize their plans for gentrification, citing the Reagan cuts. To take one prominent but not necessarily representative example, the New York City plan to redevelop Harlem (City of New York 1982) explicitly cites federal cutbacks and emphasizes the need to reorient plans for the gentrification of Harlem (Schaffer & Smith 1984) toward the private sector. The role of the public sector here will essentially involve the supply of seed money and seed projects, as well as the packaging of larger private undertakings. Nonetheless, because of the perceived risk of trying to gentrify Harlem, and because the City owns over 35 percent of housing stock in the area, it is likely that the success or failure of the city government's plans will be central to the future of the area.

Although the present trend toward privatization suggests a diminished role for the state, the latter's plans will remain important determinants of change. But there is also no guarantee that the state will maintain its selective involvement in the restructuring process. It is possible, indeed likely, that, in response to economic crisis and its effects on urban areas, the state will be forced to revert to a heavily interventionist role. This is already the direction of British Labour Party policy, and the intent of the Democrats' "New New Deal." To the extent that these "Public Works" programs lead to increased public investment in construction, the central urban areas are the most likely focus, especially in the United States where physical and economic decay at the centre is much more advanced than in other countries, and much greater than at the time of the original New Deal.

Thus, although the direct role of the state in the restructuring process is presently secondary to private capital, this might not be so with the recurrence of economic downturn. If the state becomes more directly involved, the issues of urban restructuring will become much more highly politicized. At local as well as national levels, the state will be forced to defend and legitimate its active role in gentrification. In Britain and to a lesser extent Australia this is already occurring, but in the United States it has been possible for the state to come out unabashedly in support of gentrification. Further, with greater state involvement, the forward momentum and the limitations of the process are made more contingent. Large fiscal deficits notwithstanding, the state's freedom from constraints of short-term profitability will provide a wide arena of action in which the outcomes are dominated by political struggles rather than economic investment decisions.

Although direct involvement in the restructuring of urban space is presently limited (grand plans are no longer fashionable or feasible), there are also many indirect routes by which the state assists both reconstruction in general and gentrification in particular. The structure of the taxation and subsidy systems, joint initiatives, and the creation of an investment climate favorable to restructuring are all part of the ways in which the state assists such changes. Gentrification poses a particularly interesting example. Although it is recognized to have negative effects on what is viewed as a residual population, governments of all complexions are viewing its effects in an increasingly favorable light because of the extent of private capital involved. In Britain the state provided improvement grants that were seen to have contributed to gentrification, but these may now be more restricted to low-income groups. This is a reflection of budgetary restrictions rather than any opposition to gentrification. Indeed there are many other ways in which the state in Britain, in the form of central and local government, is creating a favorable investment climate: maintenance of a buoyant home-ownership market, conservation policies, the sale of public housing, mortgage-interest relief, and a sheltered circuit of housing finance.

Gentrification contributes substantially to the imagery of success. The very act of renewal, recovery and rehabilitation in which individuals engage has enormous appeal to governments at all levels, and particularly to those taking the view that it is the suppression of the individual by the state that brought about economic decline. Others who place faith in the efforts of communities are often equally receptive to gentrification because they see the steady infusion of middle-class people into an area as one way of ensuring that the community will exercise its rights; it will break the cycle of deprivation and bring about general renewal. Of course, the originators and supporters of such policies either do not comprehend that "success" and "social balance" generally lead to the replacement of one population by another, or else they comprehend it and support this displacement.

SOCIAL MANHATTANIZATION:
THE POLARIZATION OF THE CITY?

The trends we have identified suggest a continued momentum toward a gentrified central and inner city. The direction of this change is toward a new central city dominated by middle-class residential areas, a concentration of professional, administrative and managerial employment, and the upmarket recreational and entertainment facilities that cater to this population (as well as to tourists). Though relatively central enclaves of working-class residents will surely remain, the momentum of the present restructuring points to a more peripheralized working class, in geographical terms. Of course, as we have stressed, this remains a tendency. The "bourgeois playground" at the centre is as yet partial and selective; it is not happening in all cities, nor are all affected cities already a replica of Manhattan. This is why we have tried to emphasize the possible limits and obstacles to the process.

This apparent geographical polarization of the city is not simply an isolated "spatial process," but rather the spatial result of a deeper social restructuring. In fact, there is remarkable agreement across the political spectrum that this polarization is taking place. On the left, we saw in the mid-1970s the emergence of labor-market segmentation theory (Edwards *et al.* 1975). According to this body of theory, which has become almost conventional wisdom among radical economists, the capitalist economy creates a "dual labor market" with primary and secondary sectors. The primary sector is dominated by white males who enjoy reasonable wages, job security, and union representation. The secondary sector is dominated by "women and minorities," where pay scales are calibrated to the minimum wage, conditions are bad, work hours are erratic and union representation is rare.

On the right, the discussion in this period was of structural unemployment and its effect on the so-called middle class, by which was generally meant white workers and professionals with stable and relatively well-paying employment. In the wake of ten years either in or between recessions, the reality of polarization has penetrated right-wing visions of the city. Implicitly recognized in the Enterprise Zone proposals, this polarization is given explicit formulation in the American context by George Sternlieb:

> Thus the vision of the city becomes strikingly bipolar: on the one hand the city of the poor, with anywhere from a quarter (Boston) to a seventh (New York) of the population on welfare; with crime rates that stagger the imagination even when appropriate allowance is made for their vagaries; and with truancy levels vastly understated by the official reporting techniques, which make a mockery of the traditional role of public education as a homogenizing influence and ladder upward for the urban proletariat.
>
> Separate and distinct from this—though frequently in physical proximity, it is psychologically and fiscally at a vast distance—is the city of the elite. Varying in scale from a very few select blocks in some municipalities to substantial and growing population thresholds in others is the city in which inhabitants are matched to the new postmanufacturing job base, peopled by groups who do not require or utilize the local service base. (Sternlieb & Hughes 1983:463)

This polarization has probably been sharpest in the United States, where economic fluctuations have been sharper, workers are less organized against the employers' offensive, and the welfare system is so meager in its coverage. At the national level, 1983 was a year of rapid economic growth and declining unemployment, yet the rate of poverty actually increased to over 15 percent of the total population; 6 million have been added to the ranks of the official poor since 1980. The poverty rate for blacks increased to 35.7 percent, the highest level since such figures were first collected in 1966; for households headed by women the figure rose to 36 percent (Pear 1984). The selectivity of the so-called economic recovery is even clearer at the urban scale. Although New York City is again gaining jobs, the level of unemployment is up, since a large proportion of the new jobs has gone to commuters. The city budget is again registering a surplus after the default of 1975, yet poverty is up: "More people than at any time since the Depression are . . . hungry and homeless, and about one of every four New Yorkers is below the poverty level." The "recovery" is making New York a "city of haves and have-nots" (Goodwin 1984).

This social polarization is matched spatially with the expansion of elite enclaves near the center, and the development of a siege mentality at the "frontier" of gentrification. Census data reveal that Manhattan was the 14th richest county in the United States in 1979 with a per capita income of $10,889, whereas the Bronx, just across the Harlem river, was 2280th out of 3132, with a per capita income of only $2943. At the census tract level, the polarization is even more dramatic; by some measures the richest and poorest census tracts in the entire country are less than five miles apart (in Manhattan and the Bronx, respectively). The polarization of New York City is probably more extreme than in many other cities in the advanced capitalist world, but the same general pattern is repeated from Washington, DC to Edinburgh. The Manhattanization of central areas into elite enclaves is matched by a sharper ghettoization of minorities, the poor, and parts of the working class.

In light of the rapid changes that have ensued since 1973, the dual-economy thesis appears too static to capture the kind of restructuring that is taking place. The reduction of living standards has affected not only the secondary sector, but also workers in the primary sector; deindustrialization and employers' demands for productivity increases along with wage reduction have cut sharply into the power and "privileges" of primary-sector workers. Even in the midst of a strong recovery in the United states and a lackluster one elsewhere, the polarization of society is eroding any duality of the labor market and placing more and more workers in low-paying, insecure jobs. In the depression following recovery, we can expect this trend to be accelerated and the social and spatial polarization accentuated. This is the immediate prospect.

POLICIES AND STRATEGIES

The conservative approach to these questions is essentially to support the restructuring process as one of renaissance while lamenting the polarization. "From this point of view," according to Sternlieb and Hughes (1983:467), gentrification is a "triumph" since it leads to higher property-tax returns and

greater "economic vigor" in the city. They issue an appeal for class cooperation, arguing that this is the only realistic approach: "If cities are to be
reconstructed, a reconciliation between the two warring parties is going to be
required. *The poor need the rich.*" We are arguing the exact opposite. First,
the restructuring process is already established, and required no social reconciliation of the kind sought. Secondly, the restructuring process itself is partly
responsible for the polarization of rich and poor, and simply to appeal for
reconciliation in the face of that reality is utterly utopian. As polarization
proceeds, conflict is almost inevitable (Hargreaves, undated).[3] When and
where are the only questions. Thirdly, the poor only need the rich so long as
the society's resources are owned and controlled by "the rich," and access to
these resources for the poor depends on selling one's labor power for a wage
(assuming the availability of jobs), presumably to "the rich." Yet it is precisely their control of society's resources and the outflux of capital in search
of higher profits that has contributed to the dilapidated urban landscapes of
the central city. That is how much "the poor need the rich." We can hardly
be satisfied with formulaic apologies for the status quo in place of serious
analysis.

It is often further argued that the benefits of gentrification are far greater
than the costs (Schill & Nathan 1983). Whether this is true is doubtful, but
more important it is beside the point. The benefits and costs are so unevenly
distributed that one has to look not at some overall equation but at different
segments of the population. There are distinct losers as well as winners, and
the consistent losers are the poor and working class who will be displaced as
gentrification proceeds, and who will confront higher housing costs in tight
markets (Hartman 1983). In New York City the vacancy rate is below 2
percent, and a housing emergency is generally considered to exist when
vacancies fall below 5 percent. It is against this background that the city has
launched its plan to gentrify Harlem. Mayor Edward Koch is on record as
having said that he sees no problem with Manhattan becoming a place where
only those earning $40,000 or more can live.

Many residents of targeted neighborhoods feel the threat acutely.
Others, especially homeowners (some of whom will be working class) or
small business owners, anticipate substantial economic gains, but many of
these end up disappointed. There is considerable conflict over gentrification,
but, in the English-speaking world at least, these have usually been small-
scale, isolated and fragmented struggles. Further, the results have not been
encouraging. There have been fights against state-subsidized hotel projects,
new roads destroying old communities, the influx of speculators into workingclass neighborhoods, the building of luxury flats, and so on. But none of
these has sparked a movement or reaction comparable to the situation in
Amsterdam or Berlin, where hundreds of thousands of people have rioted
in the late 1970s and early 1980s over both the shortage and expense of
housing.

Indeed it may not be possible to prevent gentrification. In so far as it is
mainly a private-market phenomenon, its occurrence is unplanned and only

partly predictable at the neighborhood level. Fighting it is like fighting a brush fire, and takes considerable organization. If it is difficult to stop head-on, can the process somehow be deflected in such a way as to benefit or at least minimize the costs for workingclass residents? This has been the effect of state involvement in the United Kingdom, where some local authorities have rehabilitated dwellings and reinstalled the old tenants. This was only achieved as the result of pressure put on local councils, and does not in any case apply to a large proportion of renovated properties. Moreover, the cutback in spending means few local authorities now do this while all are required to sell their properties to tenants. Ultimately this will enhance the gentrification process. In the United States, there has been little interest yet in this approach. Gentrification is still seen by most city governments, as well as the Federal Government, not as the cause but as the solution to the city's "housing problem", a "triumph", in the words of Sternlieb and Hughes (1983). . . .

What then is the likely future? There are clearly a variety of forces at work. The gentrifying middle classes are themselves becoming politically important. The emergence of so-called "Yuppies" (young, upwardly mobile, urban professionals), and the seriousness with which they are being taken by politicians, demonstrate the capacities of that group. It is unclear whether they will attempt to form alliances with the people they are potentially displacing. Certainly we can cite examples where this has occurred, but it is not apparent that this has slowed displacement. Indeed there is a certain irony that their attempts to promote the provision of social services in gentrifying areas have resulted in higher tax bills, which have in turn helped force out industries employing the people they were seeking to defend. The working-class populations in these areas are under attack with respect to both jobs and homes, and it is not at all clear that they will survive the onslaught except in much reduced numbers.

It might also be that the seeds of disruption lie in the instability of home-ownership and the service economy, as well as in the worn-out infrastructure in the areas being gentrified. These areas will require increasingly large investments to redevelop and maintain them adequately. Can the economy deliver such funds via government grants and wage packets? It is uncertain to say the least, particularly in Britain, where peripheralization in the world economy is most advanced.

Although it is possible to forecast a collapse in the office market, and a change in the administrative economy through the use of high technology leading to the residualization of all but a few urban centers, it would seem that, for the next 25 years, we are likely to witness an intensification of the gentrification process. But nothing is certain and the exercise of political power by different classes and groups could lead to a very different outcome. One of the most salient checks may well be the increase in violence and crime as well as political organization that will come about as more and more of the urban population in centers throughout the world are marginalized and pushed outside the mainstream of social and economic life. Although gentrifiers may collectively mobilize the police in their support, and successfully so, the very threat of uprisings is highly inimical to continued gentrification.

We have already entered the realm of speculation. What is apparent, however, is that the answer to whether gentrification will continue to spread and intensify will not be found in an analysis of the process itself. Whether the future brings an extension of the present market-led process and the displacement of the poor will depend on economic changes in that market and political interventions that push the market one way or another. This in turn depends on the success of different classes and groups organizing in defence of their own interests.

NOTES

1. Horizontal differentiation still occurs in some European cities as a relic, but the pattern has changed substantially.

2. It is notoriously difficult to identify the incidence of gentrification—central and inner-city rehabilitation and rebuilding by middle- and upper-class inmovers—from physical and economic housing data at the national level. The figures used here are necessarily rough indicators, with very obvious limitations. See Gale (1984) for some thoughts on this.

3. This prediction has already gained a horrifying credibility in the riots in Britain in 1985. There is evidence that in one area, Brixton, the pressure created by gentrification was *one* of the elements at work.

REFERENCES

Aglietta, M. 1979. *A theory of capitalist regulation: the U.S. experience.* London: New Left Books.

Allan, C. M. 1965. The genesis of British urban redevelopment with regard to Glasgow. *Papers and Proceedings of the Regional Science Association* 6, 149–57.

Alpern, D. M. 1979. A city revival? *Newsweek* 97 (3) (January 15), 28–35.

Althusser, L. 1977. *For Marx.* London: Verso.

Ambrose, P. and B. Colenutt 1975. *The property machine.* Harmondsworth: Penguin.

Anderson, J., S. Duncan and R. Hudson (eds.) 1983. *Redundant spaces in cities and regions? Studies in industrial decline and social change.* London: Academic Press.

Berry, B. J. L. 1970. The geography of the United States in the year 2000. *Transactions of the Institute of British Geographers* 51, 21–54.

Business Week 1984. The New York colossus. *Business Week* (July 23).

Business Week 1983. Remodeling: small builders hammer out a profitable niche. *Business Week* (November 7).

City of New York 1982. *Redevelopment strategy for central Harlem.* Unpublished report by the Task Force for the Mayor, August.

Cohen, R. B. 1981. The new international division of labor, multinational corporations and urban hierarchy. In *Urbanization and urban planning in capitalist society,* M. Dear and A. Scott (eds.), 289–315. London: Methuen.

Davies, R. L. and A. G. Champion (eds.) 1983. *The future for the city centre.* London: Academic Press.

Demarest, M. 1981. He digs downtown. *Time* 118 (8), 42–53.

DeVito, M. J. 1980. Retailing plays key role in downtown renaissance. *Journal of Housing* 37 (4), 197–200.

Edwards, R., M. Reich and D. Gordon (eds.) 1975. *Labor market segmentation.* Lexington, Mass.: Lexington Books.

Engels, F. 1975 edn. *The housing question.* Moscow: Progress Publishers.

Fröebel, F., J. Heenrichs and O. Kreye 1980. *The new international division of labour.* Cambridge: Cambridge University Press.

Gappert, G. and R. Knight (eds.) 1982. *Cities in the 21st century. Urban affairs annual review* vol. 23. Beverly Hills: Sage Pulications.

Goodwin, M. 1984. Recovery making New York city of haves and have-nots. *New York Times* (July 28).

Gruen, V. 1964. *The heart of our cities.* New York: Simon & Schuster.

Hartman, C. (ed.) 1983. *America's housing crisis—what is to be done?* London: Routledge & Kegan Paul.

Harvey, D. 1978. The urban process under capitalism: a framework for analysis. *International Journal of Urban and Regional Research* 2 (1), 100–31.

Home, R. 1982. *Inner city regeneration.* London: E. & F. N. Spon.

Jacobs, J. 1969. *The economy of cities.* New York: Vintage.

Jacobs, J. 1984. *Cities and the wealth of nations.* New York: Random House.

Marx, K. 1967 edn. *Capital* (3 volumes). New York: International Publishers.

Massey, D. 1979. In what sense a regional problem? *Regional Studies* 13, 233–43.

Noyelle, T. 1983. The implications of industry restructuring for spatial organization in the United States. In *Regional analysis and the new international division of labor,* F. Moulaert and P. Salinas (eds.), 115–33. Boston: Kluwer Nijhoff.

Noyelle, T. and T. Stanback 1981. *The economic transformation of American cities.* New York: Conservation of Human Resources.

Pear, R. 1984. Rate of poverty found to persist in face of gains. *New York Times* (August 3).

Pinkney, D. H. 1958. *Napoleon III and the rebuilding of Paris.* Princeton: Princeton University Press.

Rodger, R. 1982. Rents and ground rents: housing and the land market in nineteenth-century Britain. In *The structure of nineteenth-century cities,* J. H. Johnson and C. G. Pooley (eds.), 39–74. London: Croom Helm.

Schill, M. H. and R. P. Nathan 1983. *Revitalizing America's cities: neighborhood reinvestment and displacement.* Albany: State University of New York Press.

Smith, N. 1985. Deindustrialization and regionalization: class alliance and class struggle. *Journal of the Regional Science Association* 55.

Stedman Jones, G. 1971. *Outcast London. A study in the relationship between classes.* Oxford: Clarendon Press.

Sternlieb, G. and J. W. Hughes 1983. The uncertain future of the central city. *Urban Affairs Quarterly* 18 (4), 455–72.

Sumka, H. 1979. Neighborhood revitalization and displacement: a review of the evidence. *Journal of the American Planning Association* 45 (4) (October), 480–7.

The Politics of
Fiscal Policy

43
The Political Economy of Change in Urban Budgetary Politics: A Framework for Analysis and a Case Study*

Paul Kantor and Stephen David

POLITICS, ECONOMICS AND BUDGETING: AN
ANALYTICAL FRAMEWORK

In order to explore the changing dynamics of local budgetary politics, one must take into account the relationships between the political and economic forces which affect cities over time. While we cannot provide an integrated theory of urban budgeting at a high level of refinement, we do propose a framework that relates changes in the political economy of cities to modes of urban budgeting. We begin by focusing on the structure that operates at the city-wide level, which acts to constrain the behaviours of budgetary participants. This structure limits the autonomy of actors within the budgetary arena in the same way that market systems constrain business firms and international systems affect the nation-state.[1] Business firms that fail to adjust to market conditions suffer a loss in profits; similarly, nation-states place their regimes in greater danger if they fail to adjust to changes in the power relations among nations. The structural context operates indirectly by rewarding some activities and punishing others; it simply defines constraining conditions, which, in turn, influence the expectations and behaviour of competing participants.

*Kantor, Paul, and Stephen David. 1983. "The Political Economy of Change in Urban Budgetary Politics: A Framework for Analysis and a Case Study." *British Journal of Political Science* 13 (1983): 254–274. Copyright © 1983 by Cambridge University Press. Reprinted by permission of Cambridge University Press.

As a result, our framework involves three levels of analysis—structure, actors' expectations and actors' behaviour. The middle layer is essential, for its signifies the indirect effect of structure and the possibility of choice for participants. Participant choices will be determined by the interplay between structural and internal forces. However, since the impact of structural factors will be considerable, we can expect the behaviour of most budget makers and the resulting policy outcomes to be altered as contextual changes occur.

But what forces at the city-wide level are of such magnitude that they are likely to alter budgetary decision processes and policies? To answer this fully it would be necessary to identify all the major political and economic forces that shape budget policies in cities and constrain the political choices of actors. While this cannot be attempted, it is possible to indicate two important features of the urban political economy that have such relevance to the politics of budgeting.

One set of constraints springs from the particular position of cities in a market economy. As Tiebout has suggested, the position of cities in a national market order is different from that of higher government units.[2] Unlike the national government, cities cannot control the movement of people and wealth across their borders. Although the differences between the economic contexts of cities and the nation-state should not be exaggerated,[3] the inability of cities to regulate capital movements, immigration, the import and export of commodities and to manipulate other economies through foreign policy and military strategy is distinctive. Cities face a highly competitive economic environment due to pressures generated by inter-city rivalry for people and wealth and they are highly vulnerable to the winds of economic change.

Consequently, cities are constrained to promote their communities' economic well-being by competing against each other for "productive capital and labor."[4] As Peterson argues, promotion of the community's economic well-being is an objective that city officials can neglect only at great political and economic risk to themselves and their communities. To act otherwise would mean ignoring those very sources of wealth that provide the base from which public services are financed and that enable the politician to satisfy competing interests.[5] These considerations necessarily have profound implications for city budgeting because tax and expenditure policies are among the most significant means by which cities can promote the objective of community prosperity. The budget may be used to influence locational decisions by enhancing the city's "business climate," attracting a work force and otherwise promoting the city's economic development through taxing and spending. As long as cities confront the constraint of inter-city economic rivalry, a locality's competitive position *vis à vis* other cities is likely to influence the expectations of participants in the budgetary arena.

Over the long run, however, expectations about a city's market position can change. Throughout American history uneven patterns of urban economic development have been the norm because the competitive position of some cities has grown over time while other cities have not grown or have diminished.[6] For example, we are currently witnessing the growing market power of the cities of the Sun Belt at the same time as cities located in the older industrial heartland of the United States are experiencing slower growth and even decline. Because cities differ in their market positions over time, city budget makers confront a changing set of constraints in dealing with budget choices. With growing economic power, budget participants can anticipate greater freedom in the allocation of slack resources. Alternatively, cities with weaker market positions may be forced to operate under more severe constraints in their budgeting, making participants less independent in their choices. Thus, changes in the local economic system are a continuous constraint on budgetary politics.

Another source of constraint on budgeting arises from forces within the locality's political system. Major changes in the patterns of group support can generate political instability and endanger public support for local officialdom. Political stability is an important objective of all cities, if only to enable a locality to secure social order, attract and maintain a productive citizenry. Maintaining public support is essential in a democratic polity, because public officials must secure election. Over the long run the entry of new groups or the changing interests of old participants are likely to generate new conflicts, thereby undermining existing alignments. Consequently, budget makers are likely to view the budget differently in a context where political support cannot be taken for granted and changing group demands must be bargained out. In this instance there are greater incentives to utilize slack resources to restore political quiescence and generate support for local authorities.

However, cities operate under special constraints in utilizing the budget to cope with political instability. At the national level citizens cannot leave the political unit except with great difficulty; consequently, political demands must be bargained out and all must accept the outcome. In the case of local government, however, if the process of bargaining over group differences proves too costly or produces unfavourable outcomes, certain groups may be able to choose the "exit" option, i.e., resolve the conflict by moving to another political unit.[7] As a result, the use of budget remedies to bargain out conflicts is always subject to the consequences these outcomes have on private sector locational decisions—particularly the "exit" or relocation of the revenue-producer segment of the population.[8] If this is so, then the willingness of public officials to allocate material resources of the city in response to threats to social stability is limited. If budget makers are severely constrained by widespread threats by revenue producing groups to move, policy response to social instability may become more symbolic, non-material or even coercive. In essence, the use of the budget arena as a forum for generating political support can be expected to vary with the demands of some groups and the relocational threats of others.

In effect, changing assessments of the city's competitive economic position and changing patterns of political support within cities can alter the expectations and behaviour of budgetary participants. In Table 1 we show

TABLE 1. City Economic Systems, Political Systems and Types of Budgetary Arenas

		Political support	
		Stable	Unstable
City economic system	Growth	Incemental budgeting	Pluralistic budgeting
	Decline	Elite budgeting	Command budgeting

four distinct types of budgetary arena.[9] As expectations change in response to different political and economic environments, incremental, pluralist, elite and command budgeting emerge. The discussion below and the case of New York City that follows suggest that these patterns are far from minor variations on the theme of incrementalism; rather, they are distinct political arenas, which differ in respect to the participants, the distribution of power, decision-making processes and policy outputs.[10]

Incremental Budgeting

Certain economic and political conditions facilitate the routinization of budget politics to a point where political actors expect to utilize the budget largely for maintaining the status quo via incremental adjustments, much as Wildavsky has described. Among the most significant constraints favouring this pattern are urban economic expansion and political quiescence. Such conditions were often achieved by today's older urban centres during the late nineteenth century and first half of the twentieth century. During this period America's major cities won a pre-eminent economic position as they steadily attracted wealth and people in a period of rapid economic growth. The city constituted an essential growth point of industrialization, where the forces of production were efficiently organized to take advantage of mechanization, technological change and economies of scale in production.

The city's superior market position had at least two important political ramifications for budgetary decisions. Firstly, given the steady inward flow of wealth during this period of urban growth, the financial viability of the metropolis could be taken for granted; local officials could turn inward and view most fiscal decisions in terms of piecemeal concerns and particularistic goals.

Secondly, relatively sustained economic growth functioned to minimize the importance of class conflicts[11] in the political process. City growth provided increasing amounts of revenue which could be distributed to service demanding groups within the city without imposing severe burdens on revenue-providing interests. Thus, conflicts over the distribution of resources to various classes could remain latent or at least be minimized by adept city leaders. Lower status groups who entered the city's political process could expect to accumulate rewards steadily from party leaders who had the means of co-opting potentially hostile participants.[12]

The strategies followed by the city's dominant political institution at the time — the political machine — illustrate the effect of these favourable economic circumstances. The machine served to limit the demands of disadvantaged groups for costly social services by acting to represent their individual or particularistic interests through the distribution of jobs, favours and other rewards in exchange for votes.[13] The machine's interactions with the business community primarily involved those businesses, such as utilities, which were in need of local franchises or particular favours. It was unnecessary to use the budget as a means of inducing the revenue producing sectors to remain within the locality. In short, the machine did not have to "bribe" businesses to remain within the locale; it merely had to impose order on the giving of favours to local businesses from the politicians.[14]

These historical considerations suggest the economic and political context within which incremental budgeting is likely to emerge. Economic growth which accompanies a dominant market position enables budgetary participants to forgo harnessing the budget to the goal of promoting the local economy; political quiescence ensures that demands upon budget makers for costly public services, particularly those of a redistributive nature, will be limited and more easily satisfied through growth of the city's revenue base. Consequently, in this kind of political economy the primary focus of budgeting is the management of narrow and particularistic claims — be they from the advantaged or disadvantaged sectors of the population.

Since there is widespread consensus among political actors about the basic pattern of public resource distribution, there are few incentives for making major departures in public expenditure patterns. Log-rolling, shifting alliances, segmental and specialized arenas become basic characteristics of decision making, as the availability of highly divisible outputs encourages autonomous political activity. In effect, the purpose of the budget will tend to be one of system maintenance. It is precisely this kind of context that facilitates the routinization of budgetary decisions and the elaboration of widely accepted budgetary rules. Over time these political relations become stable enough to produce predictable, incremental patterns of budget outputs.

Pluralist Budgeting

The largesse occasioned by a city's favourable market position can be a powerful mechanism for co-opting service-demanding groups and routinizing the use of public expenditures. But even under conditions favouring growth in city resources, incremental expectations can be shattered by upheaval within a community's political system, which results in declining support for political authorities, challenging existing patterns of distribution. To the extent that political authorities find their traditional bases of support shaken or disrupted, there are powerful incentives to abandon many past budgetary commitments in order to use the budget as a means of knitting together new supportive alliances and securing social order. By the same token, the existence of slack resources and uncertainty in the city's political system encourages various claimants—both old and new ones—to form alliances in order to press their demands on officials and to bargain out their differences.

As a result, it is unlikely that budgetary decision making can proceed in as incremental a fashion as when the budget had largely a maintenance function; the budgetary decisional processes will probably become pluralist in nature. Service-demanding groups will seek to enlarge their share of public resources while revenue-producing interests will be attempting to minimize the costs upon them and to obtain a new equilibrium. The latter can be expected to use the threat to move in the ensuing bargaining. Log-rolling within the constraints of stable rules and routines is likely to be abandoned in favour of a game of pluralistic bargaining. As such, budget decisions are most likely to be a result of building winning group coalitions in a highly fluid process of negotiation and compromise.

Given the budget's functions of building political support, it is doubtful whether budgetary outputs can remain very incremental. In particular, the size of the budget is unlikely to be closely geared to past revenue constraints because political leaders recognize the advantages of bargaining out conflicts of interest in terms of material benefits. As Clark and Wilson have suggested, differing interests are more easily reconciled if they can be framed in terms of material rather than non-material benefits, for the former "are readily divisible and the propriety of comprising dollar benefits is widely accepted."[15] By increasing revenues the budget can be used to reconcile group conflicts. To avoid or minimize relocational consequences, political leaders will seek to obtain funding from external sources. Thus, the "orthodox" order of budgetary calculation—determining available revenue and then fulfilling priority commitments—is likely to be reversed. The dominant fiscal constraint will tend to be one of meeting the expenditure demands of key supporters and interests and then redefining the revenue constraint in light of these political commitments.

Elite Budgeting

In a city that is losing its advantageous market position, the local government comes under severe pressure to protect and revitalize its economic base. Consequently, expectations among participants are likely to become influenced by the strategic planning role which the budget must invariably play in achieving goals that serve to enhance the city's economic position. All interests with any significant stake in the city, whether those making private investment in the locale or dependent groups who view the city as an important provider of services, recognize a shared interest in the city's economic viability. Attempts to utilize the budgetary arena as a venue for realizing group objectives are constrained by the market impact of such outcomes on the city's competitive position. Thus, the need to achieve city-wide fiscal objectives cannot be ignored by even the most powerful interests within the city without suffering in the long run.

This change in the function of the budget towards strategic economic planning transforms decision making on taxing and spending issues. Rather than an arena characterized by log-rolling or pluralist bargaining, fiscal decision making tends toward centralized co-ordination by economic elites. New dependency relationships are created that shift power over the budget to those who are in a position to enhance the city's market position.

Firstly, greater central co-ordination of the budgetary process arises because declining cities are more dependent on the decisions of political and economic actors outside the city. Economic decline diminishes local autonomy. Cities in weak market positions are more dependent on those decision makers at other levels of government and in the private sector who are able directly or indirectly to influence the competitive status of the city or minimize the disruptive consequences of declining revenues. State and federal office holders as well as potential private-sector investors are in such a position and are liab'e to impose fiscal objectives on the budget in exchange for their financial and political assistance. This type of dependency relationship puts a premium on the city's ability to close ranks in order to compensate for a weak negotiating position and to demonstrate the ability to implement budget objectives demanded by those outside of the city.

Secondly, elite co-ordination arises because decisions over the budget are highly dependent on the demands of revenue producers whose commercial, industrial and financial activities directly influence the city's market position. As Hirschman suggests, the dominant issue in a declining organization is the future of the collectivity—whether to voice the demand for revitalization or to exit and relocate elsewhere.[16] The bargaining power of these groups in city fiscal decisions is immeasurably strengthened by the community's economic deterioration. As a result of their threat to relocate, they are in a position to demand and to receive a privileged role in determining budget outcomes.

Finally, pressure for more centralized co-ordination is likely to arise from the inability of coalition building to resolve conflicts over the issues of redistribution that dominate politics in a declining city. Attempts to improve the city's competitive status are likely to entail increased conflict over the distribution of resources among the city's revenue producers and service users. For example, business groups which have a major stake in protecting their immovable investments in the central business district are likely to have different interests in the city's survival than ghetto residents who are more dependent on the municipal payroll. Cuts in major services are unlikely to affect both of these groups equally. As these conflicts between the city's service users and revenue producers involve disagreement over very high stakes, they are difficult to resolve by bargaining and are likely to require a more hierarchical decision process than coalition building.

In essence, pressures for greater central co-ordination spring from the need to orchestrate the city's dependency relations, i.e., to conduct *simultaneously* the "foreign relations" of economic dependency, influence the relocational decisions of producers and resolve conflicts over economic burdens that are occasioned by falling public expenditure. All this transforms the budget into a system of city-wide economic planning in which power accrues to elites whom Mills has described in another context as owning "command post" positions in major executive institutions.[17] Almost invariably this would include banking, real estate and other business elites who share a "coincidence of objective interests,"[18] and who are capable of achieving them. Budgeting as strategic planning becomes largely removed from the so-called "middle levels of power" to places where those in political and economic command posts set the agendas.

Command Budgeting

Although the fiscal scarcity brought about by urban economic deterioration can revolutionize power and process in the budgetary arena, a different kind of political order is also possible. Budgeting under the dual constraints of scarcity and intense conflict may emerge if those who are relegated to inferior positions under conditions of decline fail to accept their diminished status and rewards. Such a prospect is not remote since elite budgeting puts political power into the hands of those who are often opposed to the interests of so many previously influential groups, and the unavailability of slack resources limits opportunities for obtaining political support through the skillful distribution of material rewards.

Amidst scarcity and political instability, budgetary strategies for obtaining market objectives must be imposed on dissident groups or be abandoned despite the economic consequences they might entail for the city. But so long as market decline continues in a city, those businesses with substantial investments in the locale cannot be expected to yield control of the budget easily. Instead, confronted with political opposition to their rule, they are more likely to rely on techniques of social control in order to manage political opposition while they retain the budget's economic objectives. In this way minimal resources are allocated to restoring the orderly functioning of the city's political system, while the substance of budget policy goes to encouraging revitalization of the city's economic base.

The budgetary elites can respond to political discontent with a variety of strategems. These would include limited changes in budgetary allocations, attempts to co-opt potential opponents, and the potential use of coercive sanctions, if necessary.[19] An increase in budgetary expenditures for particular groups, particularly those who are in positions to frustrate the city's economic objectives, is most likely to be employed. For example, pay differentials for city employees who are in the uniformed services (i.e. police, fire, sanitation) would induce support from those municipal employees who are strategically situated to undermine the most essential housekeeping services. Similarly, it is possible to fund a limited number of the demands of neighbourhood groups for improvements to services. The widespread use of such techniques could prevent opposition groups from coalescing. At the same time, these policies would not involve substantial changes in budgetary expenditures. In addition, the time-honoured device of inviting representatives of dissident elements to serve in official positions may be used with similar results; through co-optation city leaders can smooth the path for the implementation of policies which might otherwise provoke vigorous opposition.

Alternatively, more coercive sanctions may be utilized for limited purposes against isolated groups if strategies for diffusing opposition require further reinforcement. Should the use of these control techniques fail, budgetary leaders can still resist making major concessions; state authority can supplant local officials for periods of time when threats to social order in the city become unmanageable. It is probable, however, that local elites can avoid resorting to such coercive measures. The history of American cities suggests that the management of political support via the distribution of individual rewards and sanctions is likely to be a very workable strategy of social control.

THE CHANGING POLITICS OF CITY BUDGETING: NEW YORK CITY AS A CASE STUDY

In order to illustrate the usefulness of relating changes in the political economy of cities to urban budgetary politics, we draw upon the experience of New York City since 1945. While New York is hardly a typical American city, many of its experiences are likely to be duplicated elsewhere. New York's great wealth and large public sector distinguishes it from many other cities, perhaps making retrenchment more difficult when the city did undergo a major decline. Although other troubled major cities, such as Chicago, Cleveland and Detroit have since appeared to share many of New York City's budgetary experiences, these and other large cities may not experience all the transformations found in New York.

Nevertheless, New York, like most other major urban centres in the North East and Mid West, has had to deal with many similar long-run economic and political changes. Firstly, budget makers in these older cities have witnessed a pattern of slow growth and then eventual decline in their local economies.[20] As we document below, New York's large size, economic complexity and other unique characteristics did not spare it from the forces which have affected America's older metropolitan areas.

Secondly, many of these cities experienced periods of social disturbance and political conflict. Initially, post-war politics in America's older urban centres was characterized by relative calm and stability as many traditional power broker groups maintained their ascendancy in city political systems. Even though shifting demographic patterns within urban areas and the decline of the machine in city politics created new problems for big city mayors, mayoral electoral coalitions displayed remarkable stability in New York, Chicago, New Haven, and many other large cities prior to the 1960s.[21] But as a result of the race issue, the civil rights movement, ethnic awareness and other factors, big city politics frequently became more strife-ridden during the late 1960s. City officials found that "politics as usual" had disappeared, as new issues, new demands and new participants triggered threats of electoral realignment and social disorder.[22] The decline of historically prosperous urban economies and the emergence of sustained periods of urban political disorder together constitute major themes of change in the post-war political economies of American cities, including New York.

Incremental Budgeting in New York City, 1945–62

The logic of incremental budgeting is evident during the seventeen post-war years in which New York City experienced relatively steady economic growth and political stability. While New York City was experiencing many of the economic changes found in other central cities during this period, its development as a corporate headquarters centre seemed to guarantee continued prosperity. Even though the city suffered a decline of nearly 190,000 manufacturing jobs between 1952 and 1964 as part of a national pattern of industrial dispersal, the rise in private sector white-collar employment, particularly in growth industries, such as finance, services and communications, helped balance this manufacturing loss.[23]

Steady, if slow, economic growth was paralleled by years of remarkable political quiescence, particularly among potential service-demanding groups in the city. Notably absent were stable coalitions of groups seeking major changes in public services. For example, city employees lacked the unity needed to win major influence in determining salaries and wages. Similarly, the city's growing minority community had yet to enter the local political system to make major demands. Post-war New York was dominated by participants whose major efforts were devoted to promoting their particular interests by shifting back and forth between what Sayre and Kaufman called the "service demanding and money provider" camps.[24]

As numerous studies have shown, budgeting in post-war New York City was dominated by essentially incremental practices and thinking.[25] Holding a commanding position within city government, the Board of Estimate dominated budgetary decisions in a process described as "encumbered by past decisions and commitments and with procedures which [were] slow to change."[26] The dominant alliance within the Board comprised the comptroller and the five borough presidents whose combined voting power limited mayoral influence and almost invariably dampened attempts to increase spending for new programmes or services. The prevailing bargains were most often struck by these six officials in a continuous log-rolling process which largely resulted in incremental budget increases designed to keep pace with inflation and contain growing union power through marginal improvements in wage and working conditions.[27]

Two practices of the Board of Estimate enhanced their ability to maintain an incremental pattern of budgeting. First, the Board depoliticized the question of the availability of revenue. Rather than bargaining about this issue on any continuous basis, the Board simply regarded the existing revenue constraint as the inviolate basis for making spending decisions. Since growth in the city's economy was providing increasing revenues year after year, the Board could make incremental adjustments in spending without opening up the revenue side of city fiscal policy. Secondly, the Board concerned itself more with exercising tight controls on how money was spent than on programme management. Working closely with the Bureau of the Budget, the Board imposed various procedures which provided tight control over expenditures and allowed constant Board modification of the budget throughout the course of the fiscal year.[28]

In essence, the growing availability of resources and the limited claims emanating from service-demanding groups permitted city officials to deal with these demands when they were still formulated in particularistic terms. In the absence of stable coalitions sharing broader concerns, budgetary politics largely reinforced the status quo.

Pluralist Budgeting in New York City, 1962–75

Transformation of budgetary politics along pluralist lines became evident in New York City during the decade after 1962. These changes, however, cannot be attributed to the course of the city's economic development, for the 1960s witnessed few departures from New York's post-war pattern of relatively stable economic growth. Maintaining its market position as the nation's leading business headquarters city, New York City enjoyed a total gain of over 200,000 new jobs during this period as a result of steady expansion in both the public and private employment sectors.[29] While the recession which began in 1969 precipitated a sharp reversal of these trends, it did not lead to a transformation of the budgetary arena until the bankruptcy crisis of 1975.

Instead, the change in budgetary politics must be credited to events in the political system that were dramatic departures from the earlier years of political stability. As a result of events at the national and local level, the previously quiescent minority community became highly politicized and sought to become a major contender in the city's political system. The emergence of the minority community as a major participant was matched by the city's public servants. Confronted by a mayor who sought to diminish their power, the civil service unions successfully fought against his attempts to mobilize public opinion, to stand fast against strikes and, in one instance, to call for the use of the national guard.

The impact of these two groups of claimants was such that the basic pattern of political reckoning in the city's budgetary affairs changed.[30] The demands on the budget could not be accommodated by particularistic responses since neither established revenue constraints nor past patterns of resource allocation were accepted by major participants in the budgetary process. On the one hand, the mayor was caught between demands of the minority community for a major expansion of public services and jobs and the power of service providers whose co-operation he needed. On the other hand, the consensus among revenue provider groups in holding down city expenditures was shaken by the social turmoil and disorder that seemed to accompany the militancy of minorities and unions in the city's political affairs. Consequently, the pressures for utilizing the budgetary arena as a venue for bargaining out the differences among all these contenders became irresistible. By expanding the pool of scarce resources, abandoning past constraints and opening up budget decisions in order to facilitate bargaining among these groups, officials worked toward utilizing the budget for building political support.

These shifts brought about an arena of budget decision making which centred upon the mayor who played a major role in using the city's money to deal with the management of group conflict. Under pressure from their service-demanding constituencies, Mayors Wagner and Lindsay used newly gained authority from the 1963 Charter revision to transform the process of budgetary decision making, by separating decisions which involved mandated or recurring expenditures from those associated with new programmes. The latter decisions were made by City Hall during the course of the year; the budget was then modified to reflect the fiscal implications of the decisions.[31]

Unlike the previous period, there were major budgetary changes made during the year as the mayor embarked on new policies. When collective bargaining agreements were reached with public employee unions, the mayor used budget modifications, unallocated monies and accruals to finance the agreements. Innovative programmes initiated by new federal and state monies generated hosts of budget modifications. To meet the matching fund requirements of these inter-governmental aid programmes, the mayor diverted local tax monies away from traditional housekeeping departments (e.g., police, fire, sanitation) and raised city taxes.[32] In short, City Hall changed the character of budgetary decision making from a routine and predictable process to a more open, fluid, unpatterned pluralist process.[33]

Not only did the decisional component shed its incremental character, but budgetary outputs exhibited non-incremental features that mirrored these major political changes. Firstly, the growth in the size of the budget was unparalleled; for example, from 1966 to 1971 operating expenditures increased at almost double the growth rate of the previous five-year period.[34] While the inflation that began in the late 1960s explains part of this growth of expenditure, the increased rate of spending was seven times the rise of the consumer price index for New York City during most of the years of this period.[35]

Secondly, non-incremental patterns of allocating budgetary resources to various claimants became a key feature of budget politics. . . . After 1962–63 the budgets of various departments no longer showed very predictable growth patterns. For three major city services — fire, police and education — it is clear that the Board of Estimate's treatment of each (as expressed in simple percentage changes in annual budget allotments) shows notable continuity prior to 1962. After this year, however, considerable divergence and discontinuity in the funding patterns among these services became the norm, indicating a decline in incremental budget responses. Of the three departments, two — police and fire — were funded almost entirely from local monies while education did receive substantial inter-governmental transfers. Unpredictable expenditure was the pattern for most city departments, irrespective of the different funding sources.[36]

The singling out of particular groups of claimants for favoured treatment by city authorities is evident during the whole of this period. Initially, city employees and the minority community were major beneficiaries of change in the budgetary system. During 1966–71 the three municipal programmes with the largest rate of increase were higher education (251 per cent), welfare (225 per cent) and hospitals (123 per cent).[37] The open admissions programme, aimed directly at the city's minorities and ethnic groups, accounts for the extraordinary increase in the higher education budget, while non-whites made up most of the clients for the other two programmes. Similarly, city employment grew at twice the rate of the 1950s while fringe benefits also rose rapidly,[38] reflecting the new public sector jobs made available to minorities and increased remuneration to the providers of municipal services. However, as tighter budgets were imposed during the later years of this period as a result of the decline in the city's economy and smaller growth levels in inter-governmental aid, only the city's civil servants continued to receive substantial benefits. In fact, controlling for inflation, compensation for most city employees increased more rapidly after 1970.[39] The decline in overall expenditure growth was primarily borne by minority interests.

Thirdly, the revenue constraint which authorities previously considered sacrosanct was largely abandoned as a control on budgetary growth after 1962. In fact budget growth outstripped revenues so much that by the end of the 1965–75 decade a deficit of more than $3 billion had accumulated. All three major sources of finance — inter-governmental aid, local non-property taxes and real-estate taxes — were extensively altered in order to fund this growth in expenditure. An enormous increase in state and federal aid took place, mainly in the area of social welfare. At the same time the city carried out major changes in the local taxes it imposed, gaining increased yields from non-property taxes and charges greater than those from real-estate taxes. The net result was a significant restructuring of the budget's financial base, with inter-governmental transfers replacing the property tax as the city's primary sources of revenue. As a result of the increases in city taxes, revenue yields from local sources rose faster than the growth in personal income of city residents.[40]

Finally, city officials departed from the revenue constraint in order to balance the city's budget by yet another method; namely, the issue of short-term revenue and tax anticipation notes to roll over (or refinance) deficits in the expense budget. This practice of rolling over deficits to the subsequent fiscal year began with Wagner's last budget and was continued throughout the remainder of the period, allowing city officials to comply technically with charter requirements of a balanced budget.

New York's budget politics exhibited the characteristics of a locality encouraged by its growing revenue base and increased inter-governmental aid to use its largesse to deal with disruptions in its political system. Consequently, previously inviolate revenue constraints, rule-bound procedures and well established patterns of public resource distribution were no longer key features of New York City's budget politics.

Elite Budgeting in New York City, 1975–80

The collapse of pluralism and the rise of elite budgeting in New York City was precipitated by the city's declining economic position. Beginning with the recession of 1969, the city lost a considerable number of jobs, reflecting an unprecedented decline of jobs in manufacturing and non-manufacturing sectors. Despite the fact that New York has long been spared the spectre of city-centre economic decline by virtue of its function as headquarters for corporations, there was no reversal of the city's adverse economic trends.[41]

New York's deteriorating fiscal condition did not go unnoticed by its major creditors, who began to reassess their New York City bond portfolios.[42] Since anticipated growth in the city's revenue base was now dismissed as unlikely, only an absolute but orderly cut in city expenditures could offer much chance of repayment of the enormous credit extended to the city.

Working within the constraints upon the city's pluralist budgetary system, however, city political leaders were unable to plan a strategy for recovery. Despite attempts to place controls on spending, the participants who gained entrance to the city's political system during Lindsay's reign—the public employees' unions and minorities—were not expelled; their claims continued to receive recognition during Lindsay's last years and by his successor, Abe Beame.[43] As a result, budgetary expenditures continued to exceed available revenues, and the city continued borrowing at even higher levels than before.

In the face of such pluralist stalemate, the large New York commercial banks, and later other banks across the country, dumped approximately 2.3 billion of their New York City holdings between the summer of 1974 and spring of 1975, precipitating the fiscal crisis.[44] In March 1975 the market for New York City securities collapsed, leading to intervention by the state and federal government.

Since the fiscal crisis the real locus of power in the budgetary process has shifted to financial and business elites who virtually set up and then came to dominate new government institutions established at the state and federal levels.[45] These institutions have the authority to supervise the city's finances.

The state government established the Financial Control Board (FCB), the Municipal Assistance Corporation (MAC) and the Office of the Special Deputy Comptroller for the City of New York, while the national government set up the office of New York City Affairs in the United States Department of the Treasury. Collectively, their authority includes approving the city's expense and capital budgets and city contracts with municipal employee unions and outside businesses. They also monitor and certify whether or not the city government is taking appropriate steps to balance its budget according to generally accepted accounting principles and is taking whatever steps are necessary to re-enter and remain in the capital market.

During the early days of the fiscal crisis the city's most prominent business leaders were directly involved in day-to-day management of city budgetary operations as they served on these institutions. While leading businessmen have continued to dominate the membership of these structures, the latter's functions have shifted in recent years from one of management to watchdog.

This shift has occurred as the result of the election of a mayor, Edward Koch, who has been highly responsive to the concerns of the business community. Koch reversed the pattern of most New York City politicians since the end of the Second World War by publicly allying with the revenue providers rather than the service demanding sectors of his constituency. He has been most proud of his achievements in promoting the city's fiscal solvency, even at the expense of a decline in services. Confronted with these elite-dominated state and federal structures, which gave him little choice, Koch has successfully changed the city's political climate.

In return, elite interests have been highly active in promoting support for Koch's efforts. New York's largest banks and corporations established a peak organization—the New York City Partnership—to represent their interests. The Partnership and the Central Trades and Labor Council (the peak association of private sector labour) formed a joint committee to promote programmes to improve the city's private economy. The uniformed city employees split from the rest of the municipal labour movement, claiming that their functions were essential jobs performed by the City. This coalition—with its near dominance over political campaign contributions and access to the media—has provided Koch with consistent and sustained support. In addition, Koch has gone out of his way to provoke verbal confrontations with minority spokesmen. This tactic has made him extremely popular with white working-class and middle-class voters in the outer boroughs, who have been more accepting of reduced city services from a mayor expressing some of their deepest resentments. As a result, the Democratic, Republican and Conservative party organizations were compelled to support Koch for re-election in 1981; their electorate gave them little choice.

Under new fiscal leaders, the primary purpose of budgeting has changed to one of economic planning in an attempt to restore the city's market position. The growth of local spending has been dramatically reduced, enabling the city to pursue policies intended to induce private investment. Controlling for inflation, city expenditures actually fell by 20 per cent since the fiscal crisis. Between 1975 and 1979 the city's budget grew at an annual rate of only 0·6 per cent; this compares with an annual growth rate in the expense budget of 12·2 per cent between 1971 and 1975. As a result of this real reduction in city government, the expense budget makes up only one-sixth of the city's GNP in 1981. It had been one quarter in 1975.[46] With shrinkage in the size of city government, local taxes on business and property have been reduced in an attempt to promote the investment of private capital. Moreover, the city administration has reinforced this policy by promoting private capital investment in many other areas—e.g., constructing a convention centre, planning new commercial and office facilities as well as vast luxury housing complexes and subsidizing town-centre building rehabilitation.

This deployment of the budget to improve the city's competitive position has been largely at the expense of the two groups which were primary beneficiaries of pluralist budgeting—the public employee unions and the minority community. There has been a 35 per cent reduction in the number of city employees as a result of layoffs and a policy of job attrition. Collective bargaining settlements have left the city's work-force with wage freezes and wage increases below the rate of inflation. In addition, city employee unions have been forced to commit as much as 40 per cent of their pension funds for the purchase of MAC and New York City bonds (this compares with much smaller amounts invested by the city's major financial institutions since the fiscal crisis). This development has had the impact of moderating wage demands and making the strike threat a weak weapon.

The city's minority community has suffered even more than municipal employees under budgetary retrenchment. Unlike the previous decade, it has not been difficult for budgetary elites to take advantage of the relative political weakness of the city's racial minorities. With the assistance of the State, grant levels for welfare have been frozen since 1974 (during the period in which the consumer price index increased by almost 51 per cent).[47] There have also been significant cuts in services such as Medicaid, addiction programmes and compensatory higher education. Moreover, as last hired among city personnel, Blacks and Puerto Ricans have borne the brunt of city job layoffs.

If New York City's economy had continued to decline, there was a distinct possibility that the fourth type of budgetary arena—command budgeting—would have emerged. . . .

This scenario was avoided, however, with an unexpected upturn in the city's economic fortunes. . . . As the capital market begins to open up, the city can again borrow money for rebuilding and maintaining its infrastructure. If the present pattern of growing local economy and a stable local political system . . . continue[s] we can expect New York City's budgeting to undergo yet another transformation; namely, the re-emergence of incremental budgeting.

NOTES

1. Paul Kantor, *The Dependent City* (New York: Harper Collins, 1988); Peterson, *City Limits*; Kenneth N. Waltz, *Theory of International Politics* (Reading, Mass.; Addison-Wesley, 1979).

2. Charles M. Tiebout, "A Pure Theory of Local Expenditure" in Scott Greer *et al.*, ed., *The New Urbanization* (New York: St Martin's Press, 1968), pp. 355–66.

3. Clearly, the international context imposes on nation states important economic and political constraints, which are likely to be reflected in domestic policy. Nation states struggling for power and wealth in the international order have been considered to behave along the lines we are suggesting in the case of cities. See, Graham T. Allison, *Essence of Decision* (Boston: Little Brown, 1971). As we argue below, however, our framework of analysis does not assume the unified pursuit of "rational" interests, a point suggested by Allison.

4. Peterson, *City Limits*, p. 151.

5. Peterson, *City Limits*, pp. 150–1.

6. Alfred J. Watkins, *The Practice of Urban Economics* (Beverly Hills, Calif.: Sage, 1980).

7. "Exit" and "relocation" as social processes are discussed in Albert O. Hirschman, *Exit, Voice, and Loyalty* (Cambridge: Harvard University Press, 1971) and Kevin R. Cox, *Conflict, Power and Politics in the City* (New York: McGraw Hill, 1973), respectively.

8. Clarence N. Stone, "Systematic Power in Community Decision Making: A Restatement of Stratification Theory," *American Political Science Review*, LXXIV (1980), 978 90.

9. We are utilizing fairly crude indicators of the market position and political support of cities in our table in absence of widely accepted theories which explain these forces. For example, in urban economics there are micro-level locational theories, which focus on the actions of individual units (firms, industries) as they adjust to market changes. There are also various macro-level approaches seeking to explain urban economic development—e.g., stages of urban development, the relationship of export to service sectors, etc. Watkins, *Practice of Urban Economics* and Wilber R. Thompson, *A Preface to Urban Economics* (Baltimore: Johns Hopkins Press, 1965), Chap. 1. But all this is far from a theory of urban economic development. Consequently, we are employing urban growth/decline as an indicator of city market position since it appears so strongly related to urban prosperity in the end.

10. The concept of policy arenas, in general, and budget arenas in particular, can be found in at least two streams of the literature. Works which seek to generalize on the basis of governmental policy functions are Paul Kantor, "Elites, Pluralists and Policy Arenas in London: Toward A Comparative Theory of City Policy Formation," *British Journal of Political Science*, VI (1976), 311–34; Lowi, "American Business"; and Peterson, *City Limits*. Literature which distinguishes among different types of budgetary decisional processes include Wildavsky, *Budgeting* and his related works.

11. This might also include other categories of conflicts over social status, such as race. See Lowi, "American Business."

12. For a description of this process in the case of New York City see Theodore J. Lowi, *At the Pleasure of the Mayor* (Glencoe, Ill.: The Free Press, 1964), especially Chap. 4.

13. Martin Shefter, "The Emergence of the Machine: An Alternative View," and Ira Katznelson, "The Crisis of the Capitalist City: Urban Politics and Social Control," in Willis D. Hawley, *et al., Theoretical Perspectives on Urban Politics* (Englewood Cliffs, N.J.: Prentice-Hall, 1976), pp. 14–44 and 214–29.

14. Norman and Susan Fainstein, *Urban Political Movements* (Englewood Cliffs, N.J.: Prentice-Hall, 1974), pp. 16–18.

15. P. B. Clark and J. Q. Wilson, "Incentive Systems: A Theory of Organizations," *Administrative Science Quarterly*, VI (1961), 129–66, p. 141.

16. *Exit, Voice, and Loyalty.* We are also indebted to Paul E. Peterson for calling our attention to some of the relationships we discussed.

17. C. Wright Mills, *The Power Elite* (New York: Oxford University Press, 1956).

18. Mills, *Power Elite*, p. 296.

19. For a discussion of some of these techniques see Michael Lipsky, *Protest in City Politics* (Chicago: Rand McNally, 1970) and Ira Katznelson, *Black Men, White Cities* (New York: Oxford University Press, 1973).

20. For a succinct analysis of the structural factors which have promoted this development, see Report of the Twentieth Century Fund Task Force on the future of New York City, *New York: World City*, background and paper by Masha Sinnreich (Cambridge, Mass.: Oelgeshlager, Gunn. and Hain, 1980), pp. 48–53. As regards national urban trends see Advisory Commission on Intergovernmental Relations. *Trends in Metropolitan Government* (Washington, D.C.: US Government Printing Office, 1977); David C. Perry and Alfred J. Watkins, eds, *The Rise of the Sunbelt Cities* (Beverly Hills, California: Sage, 1978); and William Gorham and Nathan Glazer, eds, *The Urban Predicament* (Washington, D.C.: The Urban Institute, 1976).

21. See W. Sayre and H. Kaufman, *Governing New York City: Politics in the Metropolis* (New York: Russell Sage, 1960); E. Banfield, *Political Influence* (Glencoe, Ill.: The Free Press, 1969); and Dahl, *Who Governs?*

22. The literature describing these events is voluminous. Among the most relevant are Walter Dean Burnham, *Critical Elections and the Mainsprings of American Politics* (New York: W. W. Norton, 1970); Francis F. Piven and Richard A. Cloward, *Regulating the Poor* (New York: Vintage, 1971); and Jewel Bellush and Stephen M. David, *Race and Politics in New York City* (New York: Praeger, 1971).

23. E. Tobier, "Economic Development Strategy for the City," in L. C. Smith and A. M. H. Walsh, eds, *Agenda for the City: Issues Confronting New York* (Beverly Hills: Sage, 1970), pp. 27–84.

24. This description of New York City's political system during this period relies heavily on the classic study done by Sayre and Kaufman, *Governing New York City: Politics in the Metropolis* (New York: Russell Sage, 1960), especially Chap. XIII.

25. The best known management study of the city government during this period concluded that increases in the city budget were due to inflation rather than "an excessively high standard of municipal living." (Report of the Mayor's Committee

on Management Survey, *Modern Management for the City of New York* (New York: The Committee, 1953), Vol. I., p. 176.)

26. A. Schick, *Central Budget Issues Under the New York City Charter*, report prepared for the State Charter Revision Commission for New York City (New York: State Charter Revision Commission, 1974), p. 67.

27. David and Kantor, "Political Theory and Transformations," p. 198.

28. David and Kantor, "Political Theory and Transformations," pp. 198–200.

29. R. W. Bahl, A. K. Campbell, and D. Greytak, *Taxes, Expenditures and the Economic Base: Case Study of New York City* (New York: Praeger, 1974).

30. The impact of these groups is discussed in detail in Bellush and David, *Race and Politics in New York City*, Piven and Cloward, *Regulating the Poor*, David Greenstone and Paul E. Peterson, *Race and Authority in Urban Politics* (New York: Russell Sage, 1973) and Francis Piven. "The Urban Crisis: Who Got What and Why," in Robert P. Wolff, ed., *1984 Revisited* (New York, Random House, 1972), pp. 165–201.

31. Schick, *Central Budget Issues*, pp. 7–8.

32. D. Haider, "Sayre and Kaufman Revisited: New York City Government Since 1965," *Urban Affairs Quarterly*, xv (1979), pp. 138–9.

33. Schick, *Central Budget Issues*, pp. 67, 49–52, and 64–6.

34. Schick, *Central Budget Issues*, p. 42.

35. D. Bernstein, "Financing the City Government," in R. H. Connery and D. Caraley, eds, *Governing the City: Challenges and Options for New York* (New York: Praeger, 1969), pp. 78–9.

36. The primary impact of the increased state and federal aid was programmatic; the bulk of these monies went to agencies performing social welfare functions. See Haider, "Sayre and Kaufman Revisited," p. 131.

37. M. Shefter, "New York City's Fiscal Crisis: The Politics of Inflation and Retrenchment," *Public Interest*, XLVIII (1977), 98–127, reprinted in C. Levine, *Managing Fiscal Stress: The Crisis in the Public Sector* (Chatham, N.J.: Chatham House Publishers, 1980), p. 78.

38. Bahl, Campbell and Greytak, *Taxes, Expenditures and the Economic Base*, p. 5.

39. Haider, "Sayre and Kaufman Revisited," pp. 138–9.

40. Bernstein, "Financing the City Government," pp. 83–6. In the fiscal year 1958–59, the city received 47 per cent of its revenue from the real estate tax, 30 per cent from other local taxes, and 23 per cent from intergovernmental aid. A decade later, 29 per cent of the city's revenue came from the real estate tax, the same percentage from other local taxes and charges, and 42 per cent from inter-governmental aid.

41. Congressional Budget Office, "The Causes of New York City's Fiscal Crisis," *Political Science Quarterly*, xc (1975–76), p. 668.

42. Jack Newfield and Paul Dubrul, *The Abuse of Power* (New York: Viking, 1977), pp. 37–8.

43. Haider, "Sayre and Kaufman Revisited," pp. 137–9.

44. Shefter, "New York City's Fiscal Crisis," p. 82.

45. Of the nine original members of MAC five were chosen by the governor and four by the mayor; all but one of these appointees had banking or brokerage connections.

Haider reached a somewhat similar conclusion in his study of New York's budgetary arena during this period. Haider concluded that the "dominant actors" came from the business and financial community, as well as the federal government and the municipal unions. See Haider, "Sayer and Kaufman Revisited," p. 149. Cf. Shefter, "New York City's Fiscal Crisis," pp. 81–4.

46. Charles Brecher and Raymond D. Horton, eds, *Setting Municipal Priorities* (Montclair, N.J.: Landmark Studies, 1981), p. 2.

47. Brecher and Horton, *Setting Municipal Priorities*, p. 2.

44
Politics, Local Government, and the Municipal Bond Market*

Alberta M. Sbragia

The investment community has an important role in local government finance, as became apparent when it precipitated New York City's fiscal crisis by refusing to lend the city more funds. Because local governments borrow much of the money they need both to construct buildings and to attract private sector employers, complex relationships have developed between local governments in their capacity as borrowers and the network of financial institutions, securities dealers, and individual investors that act as lenders. These relationships provide opportunities for, and set constraints upon, local officials; under certain conditions, they establish the limits within which the officials may act. . . .

Yet another reason for borrowing is to have the cash on hand required to pay day-to-day bills. Such borrowing is intended to improve cash flow and generally is backed by revenue (from the property tax, for instance) that the city knows it is going to receive. The loans allow the city to spend from anticipated revenues as the bills come in, and city finances thereby run more smoothly. Sometimes, however, such borrowing is used to make up an actual shortfall in revenue, a situation often indicating that the borrower is in fairly serious trouble.[1]

Funds borrowed for capital facilities and for the use of the private sector are repaid over a long period of time—commonly from fifteen to thirty

*Sbragia, Alberta M. 1983. "Politics, Local Government, and the Municipal Bond Market." Pp. 67–69, 73, 95–107, and 110–111 in *The Municipal Money Chase: The Politics of Municipal Finance*. Boulder: Westview Press. Copyright © 1983. Reprinted by permission of Alberta M. Sbragia.

years, although even forty-year loans are not unknown. Although borrowing for these purposes is typically long-term, officials deal with cash flow problems by borrowing funds that they repay within a year. Because local governments collect their various types of revenue (such as property tax payments) at least once a year, short-term borrowing allows them to borrow money that carries them from one collection date to the next. Short-term borrowing is also often used to provide "working capital" for a capital project until long-term funds are acquired. . . .

Municipal notes and bonds are brought and sold in what is called the municipal bond market. That market, simply put, is the forum within which state and local governments borrow by selling their notes and bonds and in which investors lend by buying the securities. Perhaps the best description of this market for the layperson was that given by the Twentieth Century Fund Task Force on Municipal Bond Credit Ratings:

> The municipal bond market is not confined to a single location such as an exchange for listed securities. Rather, it is a nation-wide network of investors, investment institutions, securities dealers, and governmental borrowers. In this setting, hundreds of new and outstanding municipal securities are traded each business day. . . .[2]

POLITICS, LOCAL GOVERNMENT, AND THE MARKET

Analysis of the interdependence between local government, on the one hand, and the municipal bond market, on the other, is an excellent way to begin understanding the intersection between the various "systems" — economic, financial, intergovernmental, metropolitan, political, and administrative — to which a local government is related. The bond market represents one point at which these systems intersect. Moreover, because such analysis forces us to take a close look at special-purpose governments such as public authorities (which are often ignored in discussing, for example, urban politics or urban policymaking), it raises questions about the different types of governance that characterize the geographic area we call a city and the implications of such differences for policymaking.

A study of the market may not give us the details of what is normally considered the "stuff" of city politics, but it does indicate where and how that stuff fits into the larger picture. Although it is obvious that municipal government does not exist in isolation, it is nonetheless difficult to get a grip on the *multiple* relations in which city (as well as other local) officials are involved. Studies of intergovernmental relations, for example, necessarily focus on one set of relationships. Similarly, scholars examining the impact of capitalism on the city focus on the development of corporate capital, capital accumulation, and/or conflict and legitimacy.[3] In contrast, by focusing on the bond market, we are compelled to think about numerous intersecting relationships: those between the city government and the public authorities that operate within its boundaries, as well as those between city government and the larger economic world within which city government exists.

In the section to come, I shall very briefly consider four sets of relationships between the market and local borrowers. The discussion here is exploratory, but it will indicate the types of issues raised by an inquiry into the links between the municipal bond market and the major political and administrative processes characteristic of urban areas.

1. The operations of the municipal bond market are shaped in three major ways by the intergovernmental system within which local, especially municipal, officials operate.

First, the market, using risk as its criterion, must discriminate among local borrowers primarily because neither Washington nor the state capitols, with few exceptions, give any kind of guarantees to lenders. The lack of either state or federal loan guarantees leaves local governments without the kind of uniform protection that more central involvement often brings. That is, the market could conceivably lend to local governments *as a class* if all localities had some kind of "floor" provided by Washington or the state government. In Great Britain, for example, all local governments are generally considered credit-worthy, and they are therefore not judged on their individual fiscal vices and virtues. The reasons for such uniformity of treatment stem from the application of more standardized audit procedures than those used in the United States, and especially from the fact that borrowing has to be approved by the central government (which will also lend money to local governments if they cannot borrow in the market). British lenders are thus assured that if a borrower defaults, London will lend it funds to cover the deficit; further, the requirement that local authorities be rigorously audited reassures lenders that default is unlikely to happen in the first place.[4]

In the United States, by contrast, the federal government does not approve loans, require comprehensive audits, or guarantee that loans to local governments will be repaid (in the case of loan guarantees given to New York City, Congress made it very clear that it did not intend to establish a precedent). Washington, for the most part, stays out of local borrowing. State governments do impose limits, but they then dilute them: State audits are often sporadic and incomplete, whereas state legislatures pass legislation allowing constitutional limits and restrictions on debt to be circumvented. The lack of active federal and state oversight forces the market to use risk as the basis for its investment decisions and, therefore, to discriminate between local borrowers. Both the individual fiscal conditions of cities and their revenue-producing projects are exposed to the full force of market judgment. Local governments are, within certain limits, free to borrow without state or federal approval, but they pay for their discretionary powers by exposure to calculations based on risk.

Second, the market responds to a city's borrowing needs according, in part, to that city's treatment by the federal and state government. Monies from both sources are important in giving cities and other governments the financial capacity needed for borrowing purposes. Federal money has been particularly useful in this respect. In essence, the combination of aid for capital and operating expenditures that has come from Washington has helped maintain many Frostbelt cities as *viable risks*.[5]

To the extent that federal aid has maintained the solvency and the economic viability of local governments, the market has benefited. Lenders, after all, depend on borrowers for their profits. The market thus has a direct interest in Washington's urban policies: Cities that slip into such poor fiscal shape that they become an unacceptably bad risk represent lost "customers." The older securities of such cities also tend to plummet in value, resulting in severe loss to investors trying to sell them in the secondary market. Because it is not really in the market's interest to be forced to exercise frequently its ultimate weapon — namely, the refusal of further loans — cuts in federal aid that threaten the financial viability of cities are potentially damaging to investors as well.

Third, both lenders and borrowers will try to use the intergovernmental system to prevent default and/or bankruptcy by lobbying for various types of assistance from other levels of government. These efforts will be more successful for some cities than for others. New York City was able to get both state and federal help because of the huge amounts of money involved, the power of the banks holding city securities, and the symbolic value of New York City in the international markets as the seat of U.S. financial power. Cleveland was not so fortunate, however; although the state did exercise some powers of oversight and did offer some financial help, this city had to deal with its default largely on its own.

Although our sample of defaults is exceedingly small, it is probably safe to say that federal assistance will not be repeated, certainly not on the scale offered to New York City. It is more difficult, however, to say whether New York City will prove unique in winning sizable help from state authorities or whether Cleveland will subsequently appear exceptionally unfortunate in having been unable to mobilize more help from the state capitol. Nonetheless, the existence of the state-local intergovernmental system, characterized by the state's powers to regulate local finance, makes that system a possible actor in the relationship between a city and bondholders in the case of default. The importance of this system is perhaps best illustrated by the jitters caused on Wall Street over the possibility of a state government default, for a state in such a case could not turn to a higher level of government with expectations of the constitutionally clear-cut relationships that exist between state and local government. Certainly, the New York City case showed that bondholders — banks, in particular — will try to use the power of the state government both to protect their investments in municipal securities and to impose fiscal discipline on a city. But the case of Cleveland suggests that such a strategy is not always completely effective.

2. The bond market's treatment of a city reflects that city's success in attracting federal money or private sector jobs, or both, and reinforces prospects for further success.

. . . [C]ity governments compete for federal aid and for private sector jobs. Some of the federal aid has been used to help attract jobs, and . . . the bond market has also been used to attract jobs through the issuance of IRBs. The more successful cities are in getting federal money and private sector jobs, the better their relative position in the bond market. And the better they do in the market, the less money they have to pay for interest costs, the more attractive they seem to businessmen as places to move to or stay in, and (at least in the case of declining cities) the stronger become their claims on Washington for continued help in attracting jobs, insofar as they can argue that federal money is already being used effectively. Conversely, a city that is unable to attract private jobs and sufficient federal aid will do badly in the market, thereby increasing its interest costs and burdening its already overloaded budget.

Because risk is the determinant of investment behavior, the market does not serve as a redistributive or compensatory mechanism; rather, it penalizes the weak and rewards the strong. It also reinforces the process of economic decline and boom. It must be emphasized that this situation is not the result of a deliberate strategy on the part of investors; on the contrary, it is an imperative flowing from the logic of investment based on risk.

It has been suggested that a national public bank should be established that, by lending to local governments out of favor with the market, would compensate for the effects of the vicious cycle mentioned earlier and thus protect weak local governments from being further weakened by the financial market. The market, however, imposes a form of fiscal discipline that is seen by borrowers and lenders alike to be more impartial and therefore more authoritative than any exercised by government. Many officials are therefore reluctant to renounce a process that, while hurting weak governments, nevertheless forces them to live within their means at the risk of being cut off from credit.

3. The process of circumventing state restrictions on municipal borrowing in order to obtain capital for urban development has involved a proliferation of authorities, and such proliferation inhibits the ability of city governments to control the provision of services within their boundaries.

Students of urban politics used to spend much of their time arguing about who governed in cities, but this issue has now become much less relevant. Whoever does govern — through city-wide institutions, at least — is able to choose among relatively few options. The ability of special districts and public authorities to obtain credit separately from city or county government has fragmented power within the metropolitan area, and within city boundaries, to the point that merely understanding the distribution of formal authority, much less influence, has become a gigantic task.

It has been suggested that, even without the complications entailed by examining special-purpose authorities and districts, the fragmentation of power within city government *itself* has made many big cities ungovernable. That is, the cities' policymaking system is structurally incapable of providing "coherent policy-making and service delivery."[6] Big city governments have difficulty in making coherent policy even in those areas over which officials have control, but they obviously have even more difficulty affecting the many functions outside their jurisdiction. The problem of fragmentation is therefore more serious than the incapacity of city-wide institutions. Officials in many cities, large and small, suburbs as well as central cities (and those in rural as well as in urban areas), often have relatively little control over the capital infrastructure that shapes a city and the opportunities enjoyed by its residents. Even if a city does have a policymaking system capable of formulating and implementing coherent policy, it is generally unable to act in many policy areas that are vital to city life.

Special districts and public authorities crisscross almost all cities, except perhaps the very smallest. The power to control what happens within a city is thereby fragmented. As long as twenty-five years ago, John Bollens recognized the problem, which has since grown far worse. He remarked that the "uncoordinated, splintered efforts" of special districts dispersed policymaking among many governmental bodies.[7] Bollens' analysis would apply even more strongly today, for special districts and public authorities[8] are the main contributors to the extreme fragmentation of formal power, not to mention influence, in urban areas. Insulated from the public (because their boards are usually appointed rather than elected) and autonomous in policy-making, these authorities shape the entire urban area; as a result, city officials are often unable to exercise even coordination, much less control, over their operations. Annmarie Hauck Walsh, after conducting the most exhaustive study to date of public authorities, concludes that "the primary question concerning public authorities today is how to direct their financial and management resources toward broad governmental goals." This question arises, she argues, because "government control . . . is weak and uneven."[9]

Especially because special-purpose governments usually deal with capital facilities, their actions may literally transform the landscape of both central and suburban cities. And the facilities built, as Walsh points out, are usually chosen on the basis of financial return, for the bond market more strongly emphasizes financial criteria for authorities than for general-purpose governments with the right to tax. Walsh finds, for example, that authorities favor "highways over rail transportation, water supply and power production over pollution abatement and recreational use of water resources, school building over expansion of student counseling, sports arenas over open spaces, industrial parks over small business assistance," and so on.[10]

In short, city officialdom does not control much of the capital infrastructure on which the city's most basic functions depend, and it therefore exercises much less control over the kinds of recreational, transportation, and even business opportunities that residents will have than most voters assume. Although city residents may be dissatisfied with the bus system, sewer problems, or airport noise, there is generally little that their elected officials can do about such complaints. Furthermore, the city government, when internally divided, is in a weak position even to negotiate with individual authority boards, each of which has a relatively clear idea of its mission, a fairly straightforward calculus for achieving it, and an insulation from the public that frees it from worrying about citizen input or hostile interest groups.

The distribution of power in the urban/metropolitan area, then, is directly affected by strategies for increasing access to the municipal bond market. Like the sorcerer's apprentice, city governments have employed a formula to help them in their tasks that has run out of their control; but there is not sorcerer in sight to end the chaos caused by this process.

4. In times of "normal politics," the market serves as an outer boundary within which a city's political choices take place; in times of fiscal crisis, lenders occupy a central place in the municipal political process.

The market generally acts as a de facto "outer boundary" for political choices made by city officials about service levels, tax rates, and economic development. I use the term "outer boundary" because lenders are not usually concerned with specific policies of borrowers—as long as the latter maintain credit-worthiness. Just as lenders have not been concerned per se with the working conditions offered by corporations that have borrowed funds in the taxable financial markets, so they are not concerned with the kinds of policies pursued by local officials—that is, as long as such policies do not stop officials from meeting debt payment deadlines.

Because lenders are mainly concerned with getting their money back, they evaluate a city's performance according to strictly financial criteria, rather than according to its politics or to the kinds of social goals it may (or may not) have chosen to pursue. Lenders are interested in cash flow, the match between revenue and expenditure, and the health of a city's economic base—not in whether the city government is providing for its poor, trying to reduce inequality, or providing avenues of political participation. The fact that New York City came by its fiscal problems through its generosity to the poor was irrelevant to the market. Once it became clear that New York City was living far beyond its means, lenders would not lend. The calculation of risk is paramount—but indifferent to "good intentions."

However, this indifference works both ways. As long as borrowers satisfy lenders' criteria, the market will not penalize them for also being generous to the poor. For example, although California has been a high-tax, high-service state, the state's credit rating has been excellent. Its booming economy has been able to support a high level of services without suffering erosion; lenders have therefore considered the state government a good risk.

The market—and the fears of those controlling it—forces cities to maintain a minimal level of solvency and to regain solvency once it has been lost. In the absence of such solvency, the risk of lending to cities will be too high, and the cities will be denied access to the market. Officials usually try to avoid, even at high political cost, any budgetary situation that might provoke a denial of credit. Indeed, they will avoid even approaching such a situation. The worried reactions of city officials to lowered ratings indicate that such officials recognize the tacit threat posed by the market.

Although the market sets the broad limits within which local officials operate and although it exerts various pressures, implicit and explicit, upon a city's management of its finances, it does not enter directly into the political arena unless there is a crisis. The representatives of the financial community —bankers, for example—do not usually take a public stance in clashes or publicly participate in coalitions between the various groups that engage in "city politics" as conventionally understood. Although bankers are often consulted by city officials about a wide range of financial matters, such bankers usually become news-worthy only when lenders show signs of refusing to support a city.

This is not to say that the principles of the market are absent from political debate. The logic used by lenders in assessing risk—and the criteria they deem important—is also often expressed by groups (business and taxpayer groups especially) that see a city more as a financial enterprise than as a dispenser of services. Such groups stress the same factors as do lenders: They want a city, above all, to live within its economic and financial means, and they generally desire enlargement of the tax base. Conversely, they do not wish that tax base to be unduly burdened, nor do they wish the city to spend more than it receives.[11]

When a city is declining economically, such an emphasis on defending (or expanding) the tax base and on balancing the budget nearly always results in a downgrading of those services used primarily by the poor. Such services, whatever their other virtues, do not enhance a city's credit-worthiness; instead, they represent a burden on the budget that does not, at least directly, enhance a city's tax base by helping economic development. Furthermore, services for the poor are primarily paid for by the nonpoor—those most likely to move out of the municipality, thereby weakening its tax base. The logic of the financial market thus discourages both redistributive policies in times of decline as well as the use of operating deficits to provide services beyond the city's budgetary capability.

The market actually dominates the making of political decisions when a city is on the brink of default or has actually defaulted. At that point, the interest of bondholders becomes an explicit and highly visible force; to the extent that this interest is harmed, penalties will be imposed by lenders on the city. Political leaders do not have the margins for maneuver otherwise available to them in times of routine politics; the conflicts are obvious, and clear-cut choices have to be made. The fundamental choice is not merely one between cutting services and having the city's rating dropped, but rather one between retrenchment and being cut off from the market altogether. In the cases of both New York City and Cleveland, officials cut services and increased taxes rather than cause the cities to be permanently cut off from the market.[12]

Even if those groups demanding fiscal prudence are not heeded prior to a crisis, the market itself will in the end, however crudely and with whatever mistakes of timing, force local officials to listen. If the local officials fail to "live within their means," however elastic and ambiguous the definition of that term might be, sooner or later they will be penalized. The arguments of the market are represented in all cities by at least a few groups. If they are heeded, a crisis is unlikely to occur; if they are not, the market will force city officials to listen.

Officials have, in fact, little choice but to listen to the counsels of lenders. Once a borrowing government has been perceived to be so high a risk that lenders will not lend at any interest rate, local officials either have to make their government a better risk or else give up borrowing—and the prospect of future borrowing—altogether. The latter option is, of course, a very difficult one, given that a city in crisis may be unable even to meet its current payroll without borrowing, and certainly will be incapable of providing further capital facilities from its own funds. Simply put, over the long term, a city government would find it nearly impossible to continue providing the services demanded by its citizens if it were cut off from credit.

Substantial power (although . . . not complete power) is thus directly exercised by the financial community over cities in trouble and indirectly exercised over others wanting to stay out of trouble. Two features of such power make it extremely problematic for city governments. First, it is power exercised in such a way as to be unaccountable to voters. Voters cannot force lenders to lend to their city government, nor can they impose a lowering of the interest rate charged. The city is therefore subject to strong sanctions over which local voters have no control.

Second, it is power exercised in a way that is usually invisible or unintelligible to voters; even when its workings *are* seen, their effects are often unacceptable to significant elements of the population. This situation does not come as a great surprise. The burden of interest rates and their link to bond ratings, for example, do not usually play a major part in political debate. Furthermore, the ultimate sanction—long-term denial of credit— has never had to be exercised in the post-war period (Cleveland was in default for only twenty-two months), so there exists no dramatic case that can be used to illustrate the consequences. Citizens are therefore unlikely to understand why bond ratings are important or why access to the municipal bond market is necessary for city government. The specialized language of the investment banker is simply not a normal part of political debate in cities.

Considering the arcane nature of the financial world and the fact that the consequences of default or of declining ratings are not felt immediately, it is actually easy to see why citizens are sometimes baffled by their officials' fears of being cut off from credit. Liberals and the poor, especially, are apt to resent the priority given to keeping up a city's reputation on Wall Street, particularly when the cost of such respectability is a cutback in services. They tend to argue that even if a city cannot meet its debt payments, it should maintain services to the poor, rather than cut such services in order to repay debt. Robert Lekachman articulated this view most clearly during New York City's fiscal crisis. After analyzing the effects of budget cutbacks on hospitals, transit fares, schools, and parks, he put forth the following argument:

> In sum, we are experiencing a substantial redistribution of resources from families in average or worse circumstances to affluent investors, bank stockholders and other unneedy citizens. . . . I find it hard to believe the average resident of New York would be worse off now and in the near future if the city defaulted on some of its debt. Given a choice, I would rather go broke in good company than suffer the Egyptian captivity of Ma Bell, the banks and the life insurance companies. But nobody asked me or any of the other voters.[13]

Many city residents probably feel the same way, although it is worth noting that voters in Cleveland supported the raising of taxes to help balance the budget; in New York City, moreover, voters generally accepted Mayor Koch's argument that it was necessary to reduce services. Still, it is not immediately obvious to some that repayment of debt is so important as to justify the dismissal of city employees and substantial cutbacks in service. The importance of maintaining or regaining access to the market is another matter that remains unclear. As one resident of Cleveland put it on the day the city came to an agreement with the banks holding its notes, "I guess it's a good thing they did it, but I don't know that it's going to make much difference to me. Things have just been going without it, you know."[14]

The views expressed by Lekachman and by this Cleveland resident are very different from those of most local officials. The latter generally attempt to anticipate the market's reaction and to fashion policies that will keep them in good standing or at least secure the minimum approval necessary for borrowing to continue. The market rarely has to deny credit, simply because local officials try so hard to keep their cities credit-worthy. As Raymond Owen points out . . . "government" is concerned with continuity, stability, and predictability. The bond market is crucial to that kind of stability, since its monies are essential for the kinds of long-term capital projects and economic development that government has to undertake. Moreover, politicians depend on that stable presence, for it gives them the slack, flexibility, to provide services that will help them politically.

At times, however, the gap between the perceptions of officials and those of voters makes it difficult for the former to convince the latter that a financial crisis will be as damaging to a city as officials fear. The peril of being denied credit is real for city officials, but it is often too ambiguous to be fully understood by many citizens. When the prospect of a crisis does occur, as in Cleveland, voters may be willing to approve a tax increase that they had previously rejected when it is proposed as a way to *prevent* the crisis. Officials may well feel caught between the demands of the market and those of their voters when they try to prevent a crisis, given that the voters may not see the market's relevance for the city. When a crisis does occur, however, many of the market's demands are almost bound to prevail, sooner or later.

The Director of Ohio's Budget and Management Office succinctly analyzed the relationship between voters, the bond market, and city government as follows: "What's important is not what the public thinks. It's what the people in the New York bond rating agencies think."[15] The leader of Cleveland's police union seemed to agree when he said, "You can only go so long without getting back into the bond market."[16] Finally, the finance director of Cleveland pointed out that the city will have to spend more than $400 million over six years to repair collapsing bridges and streets, with still more to be spent in the future to upgrade a rapidly deteriorating water and sewer system. Although the federal and state government contributed substantially to the initial $400 million expenditure, $60 million had to be found by the city itself. As the director ironically put it, "Sixty million dollars, when you don't even have a bond rating, is a lot of money."[17] His comment sums up the point of this [essay].

NOTES

1. For giving me a sense of market dynamics, I am grateful to my interviewees: municipal finance officers, investment and commercial bankers, and officials at both the Treasury Department and the Office of the Comptroller of the Currency. I would also like to thank the Faculty of Arts and Sciences and the University Center for Urban Research of the University of Pittsburgh for the grants that funded this research.

1. Advisory Commission on Intergovernmental Relations, *City Financial Emergencies: The Intergovernmental Dimension* (Washington, D.C.: Government Printing Office, 1973), pp. 61–63.

2. *The Rating Game: Report of the Twentieth Century Fund Task Force on Municipal Bond Credit Ratings* (New York: The Twentieth Century Fund, 1974), p. 1.

3. See, for example, O'Connor, *The Fiscal Crisis of the State*; David Harvey, *Social Justice and the City* (Baltimore: Johns Hopkins, 1973); Ira Katznelson, "The Crisis of the Capitalist City: Urban Politics and Social Control," in *Theoretical Perspectives on Urban Politics*, eds. Willis D. Hawley et al. (Englewood Cliffs, N.J.: Prentice-Hall, 1976), pp. 214–229; Manuel Castells, *City, Class, and Power* (New York: St. Martin's Press, 1978).

4. See Alberta Sbragia, "Cities, Capital, and Banks: The Politics of Debt in the U.S.A., U.K., and France," in *Urban Political Economy*, ed. Kenneth Newton (London: Frances Pinter, 1981), pp. 200–220, and "The Politics of Local Borrowing: A Comparative Analysis," *Studies In Public Policy*, no. 37, Centre for the Study of Public Policy, University of Strathclyde, Glasgow.

5. See Advisory Commission on Intergovernmental Relations, *Understanding the Market for State and Local Debt*, pp. 23–24; U.S., Congress, Senate, Committee on Finance, *Targeted Fiscal Assistance to State and Local Governments, Hearings*

before the Subcommittee on Revenue Sharing, Intergovernmental Revenue Impact, and Economic Problems, 96th Cong., 1st sess., 1979, p. 131; John E. Petersen, "Big City Borrowing Costs," in *Cities Under Stress: The Fiscal Crises of Urban America*, eds. Robert W. Burchell and David Listokin (Piscataway, N.J.: The Center for Urban Policy Research, Rutgers, The State University of New Jersey, 1981), pp. 245–246.

6. Douglas Yates, *The Ungovernable City: The Politics of Urban Problems and Policy Making* (Cambridge: MIT Press, 1977), p. 30.

7. John C. Bollens, *Special District Governments in the United States* (Berkeley, Calif.: University of California Press, 1957), p. 255; see also Advisory Commission on Intergovernmental Relations, *The Problem of Special Districts in American Government* (Washington, D.C.: Government Printing Office, 1964).

8. There is some debate about which units should be called "public authorities" and which should be known as "special districts." The two terms are often used interchangeably.

9. Walsh, *The Public's Business*, p. 259.

10. Ibid., p. 338.

11. For a historical perspective on when and why business groups developed these views, see Martin Shefter, "The Emergence of the Political Machine: An Alternative View," in *Theoretical Perspectives on Urban Politics*, eds. Willis D. Hawley et al. (Englewood Cliffs, N.J.: Prentice-Hall, 1976).

12. For an excellent discussion of how the process of expansionary spending followed by retrenchment has historically worked in New York City, see Martin Shefter, "New York City's Fiscal Crisis: The Politics of Inflation and Retrenchment," in *Managing Fiscal Stress: The Crisis in the Public Sector*, ed. Charles H. Levine (Chatham, N.J.: Chatham House, 1980), pp. 71–94.

13. Robert Lekachman, "Swallowing Big Mac: Banks and Beggars in New York City," *The New Leader*, 1 September 1975, p. 9.

14. Iver Peterson, "Cleveland's Council Clears Pact Ending City's Default," *New York Times*, 9 October 1980, p. A22.

15. "Cleveland Striving To Polish Its Image," *New York Times*, 12 October 1980, p. 59.

16. Peterson, "Cleveland's Council Clears Pact Ending City's Default," p. A22.

17. Ibid.

Inequality and the
Segregated Metropolis

45

Report of the National Advisory Commission on Civil Disorders*

INTRODUCTION

The summer of 1967 again brought racial disorders to American cities, and with them shock, fear and bewilderment to the nation.

The worst came during a two-week period in July, first in Newark and then in Detroit. Each set off a chain reaction in neighboring communities.

On July 28, 1967, the President of the United States established this Commission and directed us to answer three basic questions:

What happened?
Why did it happen?
What can be done to prevent it from happening again?

To respond to these questions, we have undertaken a broad range of studies and investigations. We have visited the riot cities; we have heard many witnesses; we have sought the counsel of experts across the country.

This is our basic conclusion: Our nation is moving toward two societies, one black, one white—separate and unequal.

Reaction to last summer's disorders has quickened the movement and deepened the division. Discrimination and segregation have long permeated much of American life; they now threaten the future of every American.

This deepening racial division is not inevitable. The movement apart

---

* *Report of the National Advisory Commission on Civil Disorders*. 1968. Pp. 1, 9–11, and 21–29.
New York: Bantam Books.

can be reversed. Choice is still possible. Our principal task is to define that choice and to press for a national resolution.

To pursue our present course will involve the continuing polarization of the American community and, ultimately, the destruction of basic democratic values.

The alternative is not blind repression or capitulation to lawlessness. It is the realization of common opportunities for all within a single society. . . .

The Basic Causes

In addressing the question "Why did it happen?" we shift our focus from the local to the national scene, from the particular events of the summer of 1967 to the factors within the society at large that created a mood of violence among many urban Negroes.

These factors are complex and interacting; they vary significantly in their effect from city to city and from year to year; and the consequences of one disorder, generating new grievances and new demands, become the causes of the next. Thus was created the "thicket of tension, conflicting evidence and extreme opinions" cited by the President.

Despite these complexities, certain fundamental matters are clear. Of these, the most fundamental is the racial attitude and behavior of white Americans toward black Americans.

Race prejudice has shaped our history decisively; it now threatens to affect our future.

White racism is essentially responsible for the explosive mixture which has been accumulating in our cities since the end of World War II. Among the ingredients of this mixture are:

- *Pervasive discrimination and segregation* in employment, education and housing, which have resulted in the continuing exclusion of great numbers of Negroes from the benefits of economic progress.
- *Black in-migration and white exodus*, which have produced the massive and growing concentrations of impoverished Negroes in our major cities, creating a growing crisis of deteriorating facilities and services and unmet human needs.
- *The black ghettos* where segregation and poverty converge on the young to destroy opportunity and enforce failure. Crime, drug addiction, dependency on welfare, and bitterness and resentment against society in general and white society in particular are the result.

At the same time, most whites and some Negroes outside the ghetto have prospered to a degree unparalleled in the history of civilization. Through television and other media, this affluence has been flaunted before the eyes of the Negro poor and the jobless ghetto youth.

Yet these facts alone cannot be said to have caused the disorders. Recently, other powerful ingredients have begun to catalyze the mixture:

- *Frustrated hopes* are the residue of the unfulfilled expectations aroused by the great judicial and legislative victories of the Civil Rights Movement and the dramatic struggle for equal rights in the South.
- *A climate that tends toward approval and encouragement of violence* as a form of protest has been created by white terrorism directed against non-violent protest; by the open defiance of law and federal authority by state and local officials resisting desegregation; and by some protest groups engaging in civil disobedience who turn their backs on nonviolence, go beyond the constitutionally protected rights of petition and free assembly, and resort to violence to attempt to compel alteration of laws and policies with which they disagree.
- *The frustrations of powerlessness* have led some Negroes to the conviction that there is no effective alternative to violence as a means of achieving redress of grievances, and of "moving the system." These frustrations are reflected in alienation and hostility toward the institutions of law and government and the white society which controls them, and in the reach toward racial consciousness and solidarity reflected in the slogan "Black Power."
- *A new mood* has sprung up among Negroes, particularly among the young, in which self-esteem and enhanced racial pride are replacing apathy and submission to "the system."
- *The police are not merely a "spark" factor.* To some Negroes police have come to symbolize white power, white racism and white repression. And the fact is that many police do reflect and express these white attitudes. The atmosphere of hostility and cynicism is reinforced by a widespread belief among Negroes in the existence of police brutality and in a "double standard" of justice and protection—one for Negroes and one for whites.

To this point, we have attempted to identify the prime components of the "explosive mixture." In the chapters that follow we seek to analyze them in the perspective of history. Their meaning, however, is clear:

In the summer of 1967, we have seen in our cities a chain reaction of racial violence. If we are heedless, none of us shall escape the consequences. . . .

The Future of the Cities

By 1985, the Negro population in central cities is expected to increase by 68 percent to approximately 20.3 million. Coupled with the continued exodus of white families to the suburbs, this growth will produce majority Negro populations in many of the nation's largest cities.

The future of these cities, and of their burgeoning Negro populations, is grim. Most new employment opportunities are being created in suburbs and outlying areas. This trend will continue unless important changes in public policy are made.

In prospect, therefore, is further deterioration of already inadequate municipal tax bases in the face of increasing demands for public services, and continuing unemployment and poverty among the urban Negro population:

- We can maintain present policies, continuing both the proportion of the nation's resources now allocated to programs for the unemployed and the disadvantaged, and the inadequate and failing effort to achieve an integrated society.
- We can adopt a policy of "enrichment" aimed at improving dramatically the quality of ghetto life while abandoning integration as a goal.
- We can pursue integration by combining ghetto "enrichment" with policies which will encourage Negro movement out of central city areas.

The first choice, continuance of present policies, has ominous consequences for our society. The share of the nation's resources now allocated to programs for the disadvantaged is insufficient to arrest the deterioration of life in central city ghettos. Under such conditions, a rising proportion of Negroes may come to see in the deprivation and segregation they experience, a justification for violent protest, or for extending support to now isolated extremists who advocate civil disruption. Large-scale and continuing violence could result, followed by white retaliation, and, ultimately, the separation of the two communities in a garrison state.

Even if violence does not occur, the consequences are unacceptable. Development of a racially integrated society, extraordinarily difficult today, will be virtually impossible when the present black central city population of 12.1 million has grown to almost 21 million.

To continue present policies is to make permanent the division of our country into two societies; one, largely Negro and poor, located in the central cities; the other, predominantly white and affluent, located in the suburbs and in outlying areas.

The second choice, ghetto enrichment coupled with abandonment of integration, is also unacceptable. It is another way of choosing a permanently divided country. Moreover, equality cannot be achieved under conditions of nearly complete separation. In a country where the economy, and particularly the resources of employment, are predominantly white, a policy of separation can only relegate Negroes to a permanently inferior economic status.

We believe that the only possible choice for America is the third—a policy which combines ghetto enrichment with programs designed to encourage integration of substantial numbers of Negroes into the society outside the ghetto.

Enrichment must be an important adjunct to integration, for no matter how ambitious or energetic the program, few Negroes now living in central cities can be quickly integrated. In the meantime, large-scale improvement in the quality of ghetto life is essential.

But this can be no more than an interim strategy. Programs must be developed which will permit substantial Negro movement out of the ghettos.

The primary goal must be a single society, in which every citizen will be free to live and work according to his capabilities and desires, not his color.

Recommendations for National Action

Introduction. No American—white or black—can escape the consequences of the continuing social and economic decay of our major cities.

Only a commitment to national action on an unprecedented scale can shape a future compatible with the historic ideals of American society.

The great productivity of our economy, and a federal revenue system which is highly responsive to economic growth, can provide the resources.

The major need is to generate new will—the will to tax ourselves to the extent necessary to meet the vital needs of the nation.

We have set forth goals and proposed strategies to reach those goals. We discuss and recommend programs not to commit each of us to specific parts of such programs but to illustrate the type and dimension of action needed.

The major goal is the creation of a true union—a single society and a single American identity. Toward that goal, we propose the following objectives for national action:

- Opening up opportunities to those who are restricted by racial segregation and discrimination, and eliminating all barriers to their choice of jobs, education and housing.
- Removing the frustration of powerlessness among the disadvantaged by providing the means for them to deal with the problems that affect their own lives and by increasing the capacity of our public and private institutions to respond to these problems.
- Increasing communication across racial lines to destroy stereotypes, to halt polarization, end distrust and hostility, and create common ground for efforts toward public order and social justice.

We propose these aims to fulfill our pledge of equality and to meet the fundamental needs of a democratic and civilized society—domestic peace and social justice.

Pervasive unemployment and underemployment are the most persistent and serious grievances in minority areas. They are inextricably linked to the problem of civil disorder.

Despite growing federal expenditures for manpower development and training programs, and sustained general economic prosperity and increasing demands for skilled workers, about two million—white and nonwhite—are permanently unemployed. About ten million are underemployed, of whom 6.5 million work full time for wages below the poverty line.

The 500,000 "hard-core" unemployed in the central cities who lack a basic education and are unable to hold a steady job are made up in large part of Negro males between the ages of 18 and 25. In the riot cities which we surveyed, Negroes were three times as likely as whites to hold unskilled jobs, which are often part time, seasonal, low-paying and "dead end."

Negro males between the ages of 15 and 25 predominated among the rioters. More than 20 percent of the rioters were unemployed, and many who were employed held intermittent, low status, unskilled jobs which they regarded as below their education and ability.

The Commission recommends that the federal government:

- Undertake joint efforts with cities and states to consolidate existing manpower programs to avoid fragmentation and duplication.
- Take immediate action to create 2,000,000 new jobs over the next three years—one million in the public sector and one million in the private sector—to absorb the hard-core unemployed and materially reduce the level of underemployment for all workers, black and white. We propose 250,000 public sector and 300,000 private sector jobs in the first year.
- Provide on-the-job training by both public and private employers with reimbursement to private employers for the extra costs of training the hard-core unemployed, by contract or by tax credits.
- Provide tax and other incentives to investment in rural as well as urban poverty areas in order to offer to the rural poor an alternative to migration to urban centers.
- Take new and vigorous action to remove artificial barriers to employment and promotion, including not only racial discrimination but, in certain cases, arrest records or lack of a high school diploma. Strengthen those agencies such as the Equal Employment Opportunity Commission, charged with eliminating discriminatory practices, and provide full support for Title VI of the 1964 Civil Rights Act allowing federal grant-in-aid funds to be withheld from activities which discriminate on grounds of color or race.

The Commission commends the recent public commitment of the National Council of the Building and Construction Trades Unions, AFL-CIO, to encourage and recruit Negro membership in apprenticeship programs. This commitment should be intensified and implemented.

Education.   Education in a democratic society must equip children to develop their potential and to participate fully in American life. For the community at large, the schools have discharged this responsibility well. But for many minorities, and particularly for the children of the ghetto, the schools have failed to provide the educational experience which could overcome the effects of discrimination and deprivation.

This failure is one of the persistent sources of grievance and resentment within the Negro community. The hostility of Negro parents and students toward the school system is generating increasing conflict and causing disruption within many city school districts. But the most dramatic evidence of the relationship between educational practices and civil disorders lies in the high incidence of riot participation by ghetto youth who have not completed high school.

The bleak record of public education for ghetto children is growing worse. In the critical skills — verbal and reading ability — Negro students are falling further behind whites with each year of school completed. The high unemployment and underemployment rate for Negro youth is evidence, in part, of the growing educational crisis.

We support integration as the priority education strategy; it is essential to the future of American society. In this last summer's disorders we have seen the consequences of racial isolation at all levels, and of attitudes toward race, on both sides, produced by three centuries of myth, ignorance and bias. It is indispensable that opportunities for interaction between the races be expanded.

We recognize that the growing dominance of pupils from disadvantaged minorities in city school populations will not soon be reversed. No matter how great the effort toward desegregation, many children of the ghetto will not, within their school careers, attend integrated schools.

If existing disadvantages are not to be perpetuated, we must drastically improve the quality of ghetto education. Equality of results with all-white schools must be the goal.

To implement these strategies, the Commission recommends:

- Sharply increased efforts to eliminate de facto segregation in our schools through substantial federal aid to school systems seeking to desegregate either within the system or in cooperation with neighboring school systems.
- Elimination of racial discrimination in Northern as well as Southern schools by vigorous application of Title VI of the Civil Rights Act of 1964.
- Extension of quality early childhood education to every disadvantaged child in the country.
- Efforts to improve dramatically schools serving disadvantaged children through substantial federal funding of year-round compensatory education programs, improved teaching, and expanded experimentation and research.
- Elimination of illiteracy through greater federal support for adult basic education.
- Enlarged opportunities for parent and community participation in the public schools.
- Reoriented vocational education emphasizing work-experience training and the involvement of business and industry.
- Expanded opportunities for higher education through increased federal assistance to disadvantaged students.
- Revision of state aid formulas to assure more per student aid to districts having a high proportion of disadvantaged school-age children.

The Welfare System.   Our present system of public welfare is designed to save money instead of people, and tragically ends up doing neither. This system has two critical deficiencies:

First, it excludes large numbers of persons who are in great need, and who, if provided a decent level of support, might be able to become more productive and self-sufficient. No federal funds are available for millions of unemployed and underemployed men and women who are needy but neither aged, handicapped nor the parents of minor children.

Second, for those included, the system provides assistance well below the minimum necessary for a decent level of existence, and imposes restrictions that encourage continued dependency on welfare and undermine self-respect.

A welter of statutory requirements and administrative practices and regulations operate to remind recipients that they are considered untrustworthy, promiscuous and lazy. Residence requirements prevent assistance to people in need who are newly arrived in the state. Searches of recipients' homes violate privacy. Inadequate social services compound the problems.

The Commission recommends that the federal government, acting with state and local governments where necessary, reform the existing welfare system to:

- Establish, for recipients in existing welfare categories, uniform national standards of assistance at least as high as the annual "poverty level" of income, now set by the Social Security Administration at $3,335 per year for an urban family of four.
- Require that all states receiving federal welfare contributions participate in the Aid to Families with Dependent Children—Unemployed Parents program (AFDC-UP) that permits assistance to families with both father and mother in the home, thus aiding the family while it is still intact.
- Bear a substantially greater portion of all welfare costs—at least 90 percent of total payments.
- Increase incentives for seeking employment and job training, but remove restrictions recently enacted by the Congress that would compel mothers of young children to work.
- Provide more adequate social services through neighborhood centers and family-planning programs.
- Remove the freeze placed by the 1967 welfare amendments on the percentage of children in a state that can be covered by federal assistance.
- Eliminate residence requirements.

As a long-range goal, the Commission recommends that the federal government seek to develop a national system of income supplementation based strictly on need with two broad and basic purposes:

- To provide, for those who can work or who do work, any necessary supplements in such a way as to develop incentives for fuller employment;
- To provide, for those who cannot work and for mothers who decide to remain with their children, a minimum standard of decent living, and to aid in the saving of children from the prison of poverty that has held their parents.

A broad system of supplementation would involve substantially greater federal expenditures than anything now contemplated. The cost will range widely depending on the standard of need accepted as the "basic allowance" to individuals and families, and on the rate at which additional income above this level is taxed. Yet if the deepening cycle of poverty and dependence on welfare can be broken, if the children of the poor can be given the opportunity to scale the wall that now separates them from the rest of society, the return on this investment will be great indeed.

Housing. After more than three decades of fragmented and grossly underfunded federal housing programs, nearly six million substandard housing units remain occupied in the United States.

The housing problem is particularly acute in the minority ghettos. Nearly two-thirds of all non-white families living in the central cities today live in neighborhoods marked with substandard housing and general urban blight. Two major factors are responsible.

First: Many ghetto residents simply cannot pay the rent necessary to support decent housing. In Detroit, for example, over 40 percent of the non-white occupied units in 1960 required rent of over 35 percent of the tenants' income.

Second: Discrimination prevents access to many non-slum areas, particularly the suburbs, where good housing exists. In addition, by creating a "back pressure" in the racial ghettos, it makes it possible for landlords to break up apartments for denser occupancy, and keeps prices and rents of deteriorated ghetto housing higher than they would be in a truly free market.

To date, federal programs have been able to do comparatively little to provide housing for the disadvantaged. In the 31-year history of subsidized federal housing, only about 800,000 units have been constructed, with recent production averaging about 50,000 units a year. By comparison, over a period only three years longer, FHA insurance guarantees have made possible the construction of over ten million middle and upper-income units.

Two points are fundamental to the Commission's recommendations:

First: Federal housing programs must be given a new thrust aimed at overcoming the prevailing patterns of racial segregation. If this is not done, those programs will continue to concentrate the most impoverished and dependent segments of the population into the central-city ghettos where there is already a critical gap between the needs of the population and the public resources to deal with them.

Second: The private sector must be brought into the production and financing of low and moderate rental housing to supply the capabilities and capital necessary to meet the housing needs of the nation.

The Commission recommends that the federal government:

- Enact a comprehensive and enforceable federal open housing law to cover the sale or rental of all housing, including single family homes.

- Reorient federal housing programs to place more low and moderate income housing outside of ghetto areas.
- Bring within the reach of low and moderate income families within the next five years six million new and existing units of decent housing, beginning with 600,000 units in the next year.
- Expansion and modification of the rent supplement program to permit use of supplements for existing housing, thus greatly increasing the reach of the program.
- Expansion and modification of the below-market interest rate program to enlarge the interest subsidy to all sponsors and provide interest-free loans to nonprofit sponsors to cover pre-construction costs, and permit sale of projects to nonprofit corporations, cooperatives, or condominiums.
- Creation of an ownership supplement program similar to present rent supplements, to make home ownership possible for low-income families.
- Federal writedown of interest rates on loans to private builders constructing moderate-rent housing.
- Expansion of the public housing program, with emphasis on small units on scattered sites, and leasing and "turnkey" programs.
- Expansion of the Model Cities program.
- Expansion and reorientation of the urban renewal program to give priority to projects directly assisting low-income households to obtain adequate housing.

Conclusion.   One of the first witnesses to be invited to appear before this Commission was Dr. Kenneth B. Clark, a distinguished and perceptive scholar. Referring to the reports of earlier riot commissions, he said:

> I read that report . . . of the 1919 riot in Chicago, and it is as if I were reading the report of the investigating committee on the Harlem riot of '35, the report of the investigating committee on the Harlem riot of '43, the report of the McCone Commission on the Watts riot.
>
> I must again in candor say to you members of this Commission — it is a kind of Alice in Wonderland — with the same moving picture re-shown over and over again, the same analysis, the same recommendations, and the same inaction.

These words come to our minds as we conclude this report.

We have provided an honest beginning. We have learned much. But we have uncovered no startling truths, no unique insights, no simple solutions. The destruction and the bitterness of racial disorder, the harsh polemics of black revolt and white repression have been seen and heard before in this country.

It is time now to end the destruction and the violence, not only in the streets of the ghetto but in the lives of people.

46
Inner-City Dislocations*

William Julius Wilson

The social problems of urban life in advanced industrial America are, in large measure, viewed as problems of race. Joblessness, urban crime, addiction, out-of-wedlock births, female-headed families, and welfare dependency have risen dramatically in the past several decades. Moreover, as several of the essays in this special issue have clearly demonstrated, the rates reflect an amazingly uneven distribution by race. These problems are heavily concentrated in urban areas, but it would be a mistake to assume that they afflict all segments of the urban minority community. Rather, as some of the essays have also correctly pointed out, these problems disproportionately plague the urban underclass—a heterogeneous grouping of families and individuals in the inner city that are outside the mainstream of the American occupational system and that consequently represent the very bottom of the economic hierarchy. It is my view that the increasing rates of social dislocation in the inner city cannot be explained simply in terms of racial discrimination or in terms of a "culture of poverty," but should be viewed as having complex and interrelated sociological antecedents, ranging from demographic changes to the problems of societal organization.

Racial discrimination is the most frequently invoked explanation of racial variation in certain forms of urban social dislocation. Proponents of the discrimination thesis, however, often fail to make a distinction between the effects of historical discrimination and the effects of contemporary discrimination.

There is no doubt that contemporary discrimination has contributed to or aggravated the social and economic problems of the black poor. But is discrimination greater today than it was in 1948, when black unemployment (5.9%) was less than half the rate in 1980 (12.3%), and when the black/white unemployment ratio (1.7) was almost a quarter less than the ratio in 1980 (2.1)? There are obviously many reasons for the higher levels of black joblessness since the mid-1950s, but to suggest contemporary discrimination as the main factor is, as I shall soon show, to obscure the impact of major demographic and economic changes and to leave unanswered the question of why black unemployment was lower not after, but prior to, the mid-1950s.

It should also be pointed out that, contrary to prevailing opinion, the black family showed signs of deterioration not before, but after, the mid-twentieth century. Until the publication of Herbert Gutman's impressive

*Wilson, William Julius. 1983. "Inner-City Dislocations." *Society* (November-December 1983): 80–86. Copyright © 1983 Transaction Publishers. Reprinted by permission of Transaction Publishers.

historical study of the black family, it had been widely assumed that the contemporary problems of the black family could be traced back to slavery. Gutman, however, produced data demonstrating that the black family was not particularly disorganized either during slavery or during the early years of their first migration to the urban North, thereby suggesting that the present problems of black family disorganization are a product of more recent forces. But are these problems mainly a consequence of contemporary discrimination, or are they related to other factors that ostensibly have little to do with race? If contemporary discrimination is the main culprit, why have its nefarious effects produced the most severe problems of inner-city social dislocation—including joblessness—during the *1970s,* a decade that followed an unprecedented period of antidiscrimination legislation and that ushered in the proliferation of affirmative-action programs.

To repeat, the problem is to unravel the effects of contemporary discrimination, on the one hand, and historical discrimination, on the other. Even if all contemporary discrimination were eliminated, the problems of social dislocation in the inner city would persist for many years, until the effects of historical discrimination disappeared. However, a full appreciation of the legacy of historical discrimination is impossible without taking into account other historical and contemporary forces that have helped shape the experiences and behavior of impoverished urban minorities.

One of the major consequences of historical discrimination is the presence of a large black underclass in our central cities, plagued by problems of joblessness and other forms of social dislocation. Whereas blacks made up 23 percent of the population of central cities in 1977, they constituted 46 percent of the poor in those cities. In accounting for the historical developments that contributed to this concentration of urban black poverty, I will draw briefly upon Stanley Lieberson's recent and original study *A Piece of the Pie: Black and White Immigrants since 1880.* On the basis of a systematic analysis of early U.S. censuses and various other data sources, Lieberson showed that in many areas of life, including the labor market, blacks in the early twentieth century were discriminated against far more severely than the new immigrants from Southern, Central, and Eastern Europe. However, he cautions against attributing this solely to racial bias. The disadvantage of skin color—the fact that the dominant white population preferred whites over nonwhites—is one that blacks have certainly shared with the Chinese, Japanese, American Indians, and other nonwhite groups. Nonetheless, even though blacks have experienced greater discrimination, the contrast with the Asians does reveal that skin color per se was "not an insurmountable obstacle." Indeed, Lieberson argues that the greater success enjoyed by Asians may well be explained largely by the different context of their contact with whites. Because changes in immigration policy cut off Asian migration to America in the late-nineteenth and earlier-twentieth century, the Japanese and Chinese populations—in sharp contrast to blacks—did not reach large numbers and therefore did not pose as great a threat to the white population. Lieberson concedes that the "response of whites to Chinese and Japanese was of the same violent and savage character in areas where they were concentrated," but he also notes that "the threat was quickly stopped through changes in immigration policy."

Furthermore, the discontinuation of large-scale immigration from Japan and China enabled these groups to solidify networks of ethnic contact and to occupy particular occupational niches. The 1970 census records 22,580,000 blacks and only 435,000 Chinese and 591,000 Japanese. "Imagine," Lieberson exclaims, "22 million Japanese Americans trying to carve out initial niches through truck farming!"

THE IMPORTANCE OF MIGRANT FLOWS

If different population sizes accounted for a good deal of the difference in the economic success of blacks versus Asians, they also helped determine the dissimilar rates of progress of urban blacks and the new Europeans. The dynamic factor behind these differences, and perhaps the most important single contributor to the varying rates of urban ethnic progress in the twentieth century, is the flow of migrants. Changes in U.S. policy first halted Asian immigration to America and then curtailed the new European immigration. However, black migration to the urban North continued in substantial numbers several decades after the new European immigration had ceased. Accordingly, the percentage of northern blacks who are recent migrants substantially exceeds the dwindling percentage of Europeans who are recent migrants.

In this connection, Lieberson theorizes that the changes in race relations that accompany shifts in racial composition are not caused by any radical alteration in white dispositions but, rather, that shifts in composition activate dispositions that were present all along. "In other words," writes Lieberson, "there is a latent structure to the race relations pattern in a given setting, with only certain parts of this structure observed at a given time." The sizable and continuous migration of blacks from the South to the North, coupled with the cessation of immigration from Eastern, Central, and Southern Europe, created a situation in which other whites muffled their negative disposition toward the new Europeans and focused antagonism toward blacks. In the words of Lieberson, "the presence of blacks made it harder to discriminate against the new Europeans because the alternative was viewed less favorably."

The flow of migrants made it much more difficult for blacks to follow the path of the Asians and new Europeans, who had overcome the negative effects of discrimination by finding special occupational niches. Only a small percentage of a group's total work force can be absorbed in such specialties when the group's population increases rapidly or is a sizable proportion of the total population. Furthermore, the flow of migrants had a harmful effect on the earlier-arriving or longer-standing black residents of the North. Lieberson insightfully points out that sizable numbers of newcomers raise the level of ethnic and/or racial consciousness on the part of others in the city; moreover, if these newcomers are less able to compete for more desirable positions than are the longer-standing residents, they will tend to undercut the position of other members of the group. This is because the older residents and those of higher socioeconomic status cannot totally avoid the newcomers, although they work at it through subgroup residential isolation. Hence, there is some deterioration in the quality of residential areas, schools, and the like for those earlier residents who might otherwise enjoy more fully the rewards of their mobility. Beyond this, from the point of view of the dominant outsiders, the newcomers may reinforce stereotypes and negative dispositions that affect all members of the group.

In sum, because substantial black migration to the North continued several decades after the new European and Asian migration ceased, urban blacks, having their ranks constantly replenished with poor migrants, found it much more difficult to follow the path of the new Europeans and the Asian immigrants in overcoming the effects of discrimination. The net result is that as the nation entered the last quarter century, its large urban areas continued to have a disproportionate concentration of poor blacks who, as I shall show, have been especially vulnerable to recent structural changes in the economy.

It should also be emphasized, however, that black migration to urban areas has been minimal in recent years. Indeed, between 1970 and 1977, blacks actually experienced a net outmigration of 653,000 from the central cities. In most large cities, the number of blacks increased only moderately; in some, in fact, the number declined. As the demographer Philip Hauser pointed out, increases in the urban black population during the 1970s were "mainly due to births." This would indicate that, for the first time in the twentieth century, the ranks of blacks in our central cities are no longer being replenished by poor migrants. This strongly suggests, other things being equal, that urban blacks will experience a steady decrease in joblessness, crime, out-of-wedlock births, single-parent homes, and welfare dependency. In other words, just as the Asian and new European immigrants benefited from a cessation of migration, there is now reason to expect that the cessation of black migration will help to upgrade urban black communities. In making this observation, however, I am in no way overlooking other factors that affect the differential rate of ethnic progress at different periods of time, such as structural changes in the economy, population size, and discrimination. Nonetheless, one of the major obstacles to urban black advancement —the constant flow of migrants—has been removed.

Hispanics, on the other hand, appear to be migrating to urban centers in increasing numbers. The status of Hispanics vis-à-vis other ethnic groups is not entirely clear because there are no useful figures for 1970 on their type of residence. But data collected since 1974 indicate that their numbers are increasingly rapidly in central cities, as a consequence of immigration as well as births. Indeed, in several large cities (including New York, Los Angeles, San Francisco, San Diego, Phoenix, and Denver) Hispanics apparently outnumber black Americans. Accordingly, the rapid growth of the Hispanic population in urban areas, accompanied by the opposite trend for black Americans, could contribute significantly to different outcomes for these two groups in the last two decades of the twentieth century. Specifically, whereas blacks could very well experience a decrease in their rates of joblessness, crime, out-of-wedlock births, single-parent homes, and welfare dependency, Hispanics could show a steady increase in each of these problems. Moreover, whereas blacks could experience a decrease in the ethnic hostility directed toward them, Hispanics, with their increasing visibility, could become victims of increasing ethnic antagonism.

The flow of migrants also has implications for the average age of an ethnic group. The higher the median age of a group, the greater its representation in the higher-income and professional categories where older individuals are more heavily represented. It is not mere coincidence, then, that younger ethnic groups, such as blacks and Hispanics, who are highly concentrated in age groups where unemployment and violent crime are prevalent, also tend to have high unemployment and crime rates, even if other factors are considered. In 1980, ethnic groups differed significantly in median age, ranging from 23.2 years for blacks and Hispanics to 31.3 years for whites. Only 21.3 percent of all American whites were under age 15, compared with 28.7 percent for blacks and 32 percent for Hispanics.

In the nation's central cities in 1977, the median age was 30.3 years for whites, 23.9 for blacks, and 21.8 for Hispanics. One cannot overemphasize the importance of the sudden increase of young minorities in the central cities. The number of central-city black teenagers (16–19 years old) increased by almost 75 percent from 1960 to 1969, compared with an increase of only 14 percent for whites in the same age group. Furthermore, young black adults (ages 20 to 24) in the central city increased in number by two-thirds during the same period — three times the increase for comparable whites. From 1970 to 1977, the increase in the number of young blacks slackened off somewhat but was still substantial. For example, the number of young blacks (ages 14 to 24) in the central cities of our large metropolitan areas (populations above 1 million) increased by 22 percent from 1970 to 1977; young Hispanics, by 26 percent. The number of young whites in these central cities, however, decreased by 7 percent.

On the basis of these demographic changes alone, one would expect blacks and Hispanics to account disproportionately for the increasing social problems of the central city. Indeed, in 1980, 55 percent of all those arrested for violent and property crimes in American cities were younger than 21.

Age is also related to out-of-wedlock births, female-headed homes, and welfare dependency. Teenagers accounted for almost half of out-of-wedlock births in 1978. Moreover, 80 percent of all out-of-wedlock black births in 1978 were to teenage and young-adult (ages 20 to 24) women. Further, the median age of female householders has decreased significantly in recent years because of the sharp rise in teenage and young-adult female householders. (In 1970, young black-female householders, ages 14 to 24, having children under 18 years old constituted 30.9 percent of all black female householders with children under age 18; by 1979, their proportion had increased to 37.2 percent, compared with increases from 22.4 to 27.9 percent for comparable white families and from 29.9 to 38.3 percent for comparable Hispanic families.) Finally, the explosion of teenage births has contributed significantly to an increase in the number of children on AFDC (aid to families with dependent children) from 35 per 1,000 children under age 18 in 1960 to 113 per 1,000 in 1979.

In short, recent increases in crime, out-of-wedlock births, female-headed homes, and welfare dependency are related to the explosion in numbers of young people, especially among minorities. However, as James Q. Wilson pointed out in his analysis of the proliferation of social problems in the 1960s, a decade of general economic prosperity, "changes in the age structure of the population cannot alone account for the social dislocations" in those years. Wilson argues, for instance, that from 1960 to 1970 the rate of serious crime in the District of Columbia increased by more than 400 percent, heroin addiction by more than 1,000 percent, welfare rates by 100 percent, and unemployment rates by 100 percent; yet the number of young persons between 16 and 21 years of age increased by only 32 percent. Also, the number of murders in Detroit increased from 100 in 1960 to 500 in 1971, "yet the number of young persons did not quintuple."

Wilson, drawing from published research, notes that the "increase in the murder rate during the 1960s was more than ten times greater than what one would have expected from the changing age structure of the population alone," and that "only 13.4 percent of the increase in arrests for robbery between 1950 and 1965 could be accounted for by the increase in the numbers of persons between the ages of ten and twenty-four." Speculating on this problem, Wilson advances the hypothesis that the abrupt increase in the number of young persons had an "exponential effect on the rate of certain social problems." In other words, there may be a "critical mass" of young persons such that when that mass is reached or is increased suddenly and substantially, "a self-sustaining chain reaction is set off that creates an explosive increase in the amount of crime, addiction, and welfare dependency."

This hypothesis seems to be especially relevant to densely populated inner-city neighborhoods, especially those with large public housing projects. The 1937 United States Housing Act provided federal money for the construction of housing for the poor. But, as Roncek and colleagues pointed out in a recent article in *Social Problems*, opposition from organized community groups trying to prevent public housing construction in their neighborhoods "led to massive, segregated housing projects, which become ghettos for minorities and the economically disadvantaged." As large poor families were placed in high-density housing projects in the inner city, both family and neighborhood life suffered. Family deterioration, high crime rates, and vandalism flourished in these projects. In St. Louis, for example, the Pruitt-Igoe project, which housed about 10,000 children and adults, developed serious problems only five years after it opened and became so unlivable that it was closed in 1976, less than a quarter-century after it was built.

If James Q. Wilson's critical-mass theory has any validity, it would seem to be readily demonstrated in densely populated inner-city neighborhoods having a heavy concentration of teenagers and young adults. As Oscar Newman showed in *Defensible Space*, the population concentration in these projects, the types of housing, and the surrounding population concentration have interactive effects on the occurrence and types of crimes. In other words, the crime problem, generally high in inner-city neighborhoods, is exacerbated by conditions in the housing projects. But as Lee Rainwater has suggested, in his book *Behind Ghetto Walls*, the character of family life in the federal housing projects "shares much with the family life of lower-class Negroes" elsewhere. The population explosion of young minorities in already densely settled inner-city neighborhoods over the past two decades has created a situation whereby life in inner-city neighborhoods closely approximates life in the projects. In both cases, residents have greater difficulty recognizing their neighbors and, therefore, are less likely to be concerned for them or to engage in reciprocal guardian behavior. The more densely a neighborhood or block is populated, the less contact and interaction among neighbors and the less likely the potential offenders can be detected or distinguished. Events in one part of the neighborhood or block tend to be of little concern to those residing in other parts. And it hardly needs emphasizing that what observers call "the central city crisis" derives in part from the unprecedented increase in these neighborhoods of younger blacks, many of whom are not enrolled in school, are jobless, and are a source of delinquency, crime, and ghetto unrest.

It should be pointed out, however, that the cessation of black migration to the central cities and the steady black outmigration to the suburbs will help relieve the population pressures in the inner city. Perhaps even more significant is the fact that in 1977 there were overall 6 percent fewer blacks in the age group 13 and under than there were in 1970. In metropolitan areas there were likewise 6 percent fewer blacks in that age group; and in the central cities, there were 13 percent fewer black children age 13 or younger. Similarly, between 1970 and 1977, white children in this age group decreased by 14 percent overall, by 17 percent in metropolitan areas, and by 24 percent in the central cities. By contrast, Hispanic children age 13 or younger *increased* during this period—18 percent overall, 16 percent in metropolitan areas, and 12 percent in the central cities. Thus, just as the change in migration flow could contribute to differential rates of ethnic involvement in certain types of social problems, so too could changes in the age structure. In short, whereas whites and blacks—all other things being equal—are likely to experience a decrease in such problems as joblessness, crime, out-of-wedlock births, family dissolution, and welfare dependency in the near future, the growing Hispanic population is more likely to show increasing rates of social dislocation.

ECONOMIC CHANGES AND ETHNIC CULTURE

Problems of social dislocation in the inner city have also been profoundly exacerbated by recent structural changes in the economy. Indeed, the population explosion among young minorities in recent years occurred at a time when changes in the economy are posing serious problems for unskilled workers, both in and out of the labor force.

Urban minorities are particularly vulnerable to structural economic changes: the shift from goods-producing to service-producing industries, the increasing segmentation of the labor market, the growing use of industrial technology, and the relocation of manufacturing industries out of the central cities. Such economic changes serve to remind us, as John Kasarda notes in this issue, that for several decades America's urban areas have been undergoing what appears to be an irreversible structural transformation—from centers of production and distribution of material goods to centers of administration, information exchange, finance, trade, and government services. This process has effectively eliminated millions of manufacturing, wholesale, and retail jobs since 1948, a process that has accelerated since 1967. At the same time, there has been an increase in "postindustrial society" occupational positions that usually require levels of training and education beyond the reach of disadvantaged inner-city residents. These changing employment patterns have accompanied shifts in the demographic composition of our central cities—from predominantly European white to predominantly black, Hispanic, and other minorities—leading to a decrease both in the total population size of the central cities and in aggregate personal-income levels.

The cumulative effect of these technological-employment and population changes, as Kasarda points out, has been a growing mismatch between the level of skill or training of city residents and the formal prerequisites for urban jobs. Thus we have deeper "ghettoization," solidification of high levels of urban poverty, increased institutional problems in the inner city (e.g., the declining quality of public schools, poorer municipal services), and a rise in such social dislocations as joblessness, crime, single-parent homes, and welfare dependency.

The changes brought about by the cessation of migration to the central cities and by the sharp drop in the number of black children under age 13 seem to make it more likely that the economic situation of urban blacks as a group will noticeably improve in the near future. However, the present problems of black joblessness are so overwhelming (less than 30 percent of all black-male teenagers and only 62 percent of all black young-adult males [ages 20 to 24] were employed in 1978) that perhaps only an extraordinary program of economic reform can possibly prevent a significant segment of the urban underclass from being permanently locked out of the mainstream of the American occupational system.

In focusing on different explanations of the social dislocation in the inner city, I have yet to say anything about the role of ethnic culture. Even after considering racial discrimination, migrant flows, changes in ethnic demography, and structural changes in the economy, a number of readers will still maintain that ethnic cultural differences account in large measure for the disproportionate and rising rates of social dislocation in the inner city. But any cultural explanation of group behavioral differences must deal with, among other things, the often considerable variation within groups on several aspects of behavior. For example, whereas only 7 percent of urban black families having incomes of $25,000 or more in 1978 were headed by women, 85 percent of those having incomes below $4,000 were headed by women. The higher the economic position of black families, the greater the percentage of two-parent households. Moreover, the proportion of black children born out of wedlock (See Diana Pearce's article in this issue) is partly a function of the sharp decrease in fertility among married blacks (i.e., two-parent families) who have a higher economic status in the black community. By treating blacks and other ethnics as monolithic groups, we lose sight of the fact that *high-income* blacks, Hispanics, and Indians have *even fewer* children than their counterparts in the general population.

Nonetheless, in the face of some puzzling facts concerning rates of welfare and crime in the 1960s, the cultural explanation seems to hold validity for some observers. From the Great Depression to 1960, for example, unemployment accounted in large measure for welfare dependency. During this period, the correlation between the nonwhite-male unemployment and the rate of new AFDC cases was very nearly perfect. As the nonwhite-male unemployment rate increased, the rate of new AFDC cases increased; as the former decreased, the latter correspondingly decreased. Commenting on this relationship in his book *The Politics of a Guaranteed Income*, Daniel P. Moynihan stated that "the correlation was among the strongest known to social science. It could not be established that the men who lost their jobs were the ones who left their families, but the mathematical relationship of the two statistical series—unemployment rates and new AFDC cases—was astonishingly close." However, the relationship suddenly began to weaken at the beginning of the 1960s, had vanished by 1963, and had completely reversed itself by the end of the decade—a steady decline in the rate of nonwhite-male unemployment and a steady increase in the number of new AFDC cases.

Some observers quickly seized on these figures. Welfare dependency, they argued, had become a cultural trait; even during an economic upswing, welfare rates among minorities were increasing. Upon closer inspection, though, one sees that even though nonwhite-male unemployment did drop during the 1960s, the percentage of nonwhite males who dropped out of the labor force increased steadily throughout the decade, thereby maintaining the association between economic dislocation and welfare dependency. The importance of labor-force participation in explaining certain types of social problems was also demonstrated in a recent empirical study relating labor-market opportunities to the increasing rate of crime among youths, reported in the *Journal of Political Economy.*

The labor force/not-in-the-labor-force formulation has greater explanatory power than the non-working formulation, demonstrating the importance of participation rates relative to unemployment rates in explaining crime rates. This point is reinforced when one observes that during the middle and later sixties, crime rates rose while unemployment rates declined. It is the decline in the participation rate which provides an explanation of the rise in crime during this period.

A well-founded sociological assumption is that different ethnic behaviors and different ethnic outcomes largely reflect different opportunities for, and external obstacles against, advancement—experiences that are in turn determined by different historical and material circumstances and by different times of arrival and patterns of settlement. In addition, even if one can show that different values are related to differences in ethnic group behavior, mobility, and success, this hardly constitutes a full explanation. By revealing cultural differences, we reach only the first step in a proper sociological investigation; analysis of the social and historical basis of those differences remains to be done. In the words of Stephen Steinberg, "only by adopting a theoretical approach that explores the interaction between cultural and material factors is it possible to assess the role of values in ethnic mobility without mystifying culture and imputing a cultural superiority to groups that have enjoyed disproportionate success."

In short, cultural values do not *determine* behavior or success. Rather, cultural values grow out of specific circumstances and life chances and reflect one's position in the class structure. Thus, if lower-class blacks have low aspirations or do not plan for the future, this is not ultimately because of different cultural norms but because the group is responding to restricted opportunities, a bleak future, and feelings of resignation originating from bitter personal experience. Accordingly, as Steinberg persuasively argues, behavior described as social-pathological and associated with lower-class ethnics should not be analyzed as a cultural aberration but as a symptom of class inequality. If impoverished conditions produced exceedingly high rates of crime among first-generation Irish, Italians, and Jews, what would have been the outcome of these groups had they been mired in poverty for five to ten generations like so many black families in the United States?

Adaptive responses to recurrent situations take the form of behavior patterns, norms, and aspirations. As economic and social opportunities change, new behavioral solutions originate, form patterns, and are later upheld and complemented by norms. If new conditions emerge, both the behavior patterns and the norms eventually undergo change. As Herbert Gans has put it: "some behavioral norms are more persistent than others, but over the long run, all of the norms and aspirations by which people live are nonpersistent: they rise and fall with changes in situations."

ALLIES NEEDED

To suggest that changes in social and economic situations will bring about changes in behavior patterns and norms raises the issue of public policy: how to deal effectively with the social dislocations that have plagued the urban underclass over the past several decades. Space does not permit a detailed discussion of public policy and social dislocations in the inner city, but it must be emphasized that any significant reduction of inner-city joblessness, and of the related problems of crime, out-of-wedlock births, single-parent homes, and welfare dependency, will call for a program of socioeconomic reform far more comprehensive than what Americans have usually regarded as appropriate or desirable.

A shift away from the convenient focus on "racism" would probably result in a greater appreciation and understanding of the complex factors that account for recent increases in the social dislocations of the inner city. Although discrimination undoubtedly still contributes to these problems, in the past twenty years they have been more profoundly affected by shifts in the American economy that have both produced massive joblessness among low-income urban minorities and exacerbated conditions stemming from historical discrimination, the continuous flow of migrants to the large metropolises, changes in the urban-minority age structure, and population changes in the central city. For all these reasons, the urban underclass has not significantly benefited from race-specific policy programs (e.g., affirmative action) that are designed only to combat discrimination. Indeed, the economic and social plight of the underclass calls for public policies that benefit all the poor, not just poor minorities. I have in mind policies that address the broader, and more difficult to confront, problems of societal organization, including the problems of generating full employment, achieving effective welfare reform, and developing a comprehensive economic policy to promote sustained and balanced urban economic growth. Unless these problems are seriously addressed, we have little hope that public policy can significantly reduce social dislocation in the inner city.

I am reminded, in this connection, of Bayard Rustin's plea in the early 1960s—that blacks ought recognize the importance of *fundamental* economic reform and the need for an effective and broad-based interracial coalition to achieve it. It is evident—more now than at any time in the last half of twentieth century—that blacks and other minorities will need allies to affect a program of reform that can improve the conditions of the underclass. And since an effective political coalition will partly depend upon how the issues are defined, the political message must underscore the need for socioeconomic reform that benefits *all* groups in society. Civil rights organizations, as one important example, will have to change or expand their definition of racial problems in America and broaden the scope of their policy recommendations. They would, of course, continue to stress the immediate goal of eliminating racial discrimination; but they will have to recognize that low-income minorities are also profoundly affected by problems in social organization that go beyond race (such as structural changes in the economy) and that the dislocations which follow often include increased joblessness, rising crime, family deterioration, and welfare dependency.

47

Urban Employment Change and Minority Skills Mismatch*

John D. Kasarda

America's cities are much different today from what they were in the 1960s, when many of our assumptions about poverty were formed. Perhaps most striking have been the dramatic changes during the past two decades in the education required for employment in our largest northern cities, where the growth of concentrated poverty has been most severe. This chapter highlights how the loss of low-education-requisite jobs placed the residential and employment bases of major northern cities on a collision course that fundamentally altered opportunity ladders for their disadvantaged minority residents and contributed to the rise of a subgroup that has come to be labeled the "urban underclass."

To set the stage, I summarize research on the growth of urban poverty concentrations and outline my working theses. I then document weakening demands for lesser-educated labor residing in the cities, as well as emerging skills mismatches. Next, the consequences of these changes for post-1970 increases in inner-city Black joblessness are illustrated. I conclude with some suggestions to improve employment opportunities for disadvantaged urban Blacks and reduce their isolation from areas where jobs better matched to their skills are expanding.

THE SPATIAL REDISTRIBUTION OF POVERTY POPULATIONS

The nation's poverty population, once predominantly rural, has become increasingly urbanized. In 1959, only 27 percent of our poor resided in metropolitan central cities. By 1985, central cities housed 43 percent of the U.S. poverty population. During this same period, the percentage of poor Blacks living in the central cities rose from 38 percent to 61 percent (U.S. Bureau of the Census, 1982, 1985a). In addition to the shift of the nation's poverty population from rural to urban areas, there was a growth in its spatial concentration within these major urban centers. Mary Jo Bane and Paul Jargowsky document that the number of central-city poor people living in extreme poverty tracts (i.e., census tracts where more than 40% of the

*Kasarda, John D. "Urban Employment Change and Minority Skills Mismatch." Pp. 65–89 in *Creating Jobs, Creating Workers: Economic Development and Employment in Metropolitan Chicago,* ed. Lawrence B Joseph. Chicago: Center for Urban Research and Policy Studies. Copyright © 1990. Reprinted by permission of the Center for Urban Research and Policy Studies.

residents fall below the poverty line) expanded by 66 percent between 1970 and 1980, from 975,000 to 1,615,000. Moreover, four northern cities (New York, Chicago, Philadelphia, and Detroit) accounted for fully three-quarters of this increase (Bane and Jargowsky, 1988).

Using an identical definition of extreme poverty tracts, Green (1988) found that 30 large American cities added 527 such tracts between 1970 to 1980. Similar to Bane and Jargowsky, he discovered that 492 (or 91%) of these additional extreme poverty tracts were located in his 15 sampled cities from the Northeast and Midwest. Whereas nearly half (13 out of 30) of the sampled cities were in the South, they had a combined increase of only 36 extreme poverty tracts (17%), while the two large cities of the West, Los Angeles and Phoenix, together added only 9 extreme poverty tracts between 1970 and 1980. Clearly, then, the rise of concentrated poverty appears most severe in the older industrial cities of the North.

Ronald Mincy further documents that concentrated poverty is almost exclusively a minority problem. His analysis of extreme poverty tracts in the 100 largest central cities in 1980 showed that of 1.8 million poor people residing in these tracts, fewer than 10 percent were non-Hispanic White, while nearly 70 percent were Black. Nearly all of the remainder were Hispanic (Mincy, 1988).

The concept of "underclass" is not synonymous with poverty population, however. It also incorporates certain behavioral characteristics — such as joblessness, out-of-wedlock births, welfare dependency, dropping out of school, and illicit activities — that conflict with mainstream societal values. In addition, there is often a spatial criterion included. The underclass is thought to reside in segregated, deprived neighborhoods where social problems are highly concentrated, resulting in mutually reinforcing contagion effects through imitative behavior and peer pressure.

While considerable debate continues to surround definitions (or even the existence) of the underclass population, attempts have been made to measure its size by using "behavioral" indicators derived from census data. Erol Ricketts and Isabel Sawhill measured the underclass as people living in neighborhoods whose residents in 1980 simultaneously exhibited disproportionately high rates of school dropout, joblessness, female-headed families, and welfare dependency.[1] They found that approximately 2.5 million people lived in such tracts and that these tracts are disproportionately located in major cities in the Northeast and Midwest. They report that in underclass tracts, on average, 63 percent of the resident adults had less than a high school education, 60 percent of the families with children were headed by women, 56 percent of the adult men were not regularly employed, and 34 percent of the households were receiving public assistance. Their research also revealed that, although the total poverty population only grew by 8 percent between 1970 and 1980, the number of people living in underclass areas grew by 230 percent, from 752,000 to 2,484,000 (Ricketts and Sawhill, 1988).

Mark Alan Hughes shows an enormous increase between 1970 and

1980 in the isolation and deprivation of ghetto neighborhoods in eight distressed cities. Hughes' mapping of the location and spread of predominantly Black census tracts in these cities revealed a substantial growth in the number of poor Black neighborhoods that did not border on integrated or non-Black neighborhoods. During the 1970s, many Black census tracts became surrounded by other Black census tracts, limiting the potential for contact with non-Black residents for those who resided in increasingly isolated tracts at the ghetto core (Hughes, 1988).

Hughes also compared absolute changes between 1970 and 1980 in the number of tracts with high coincident levels of adult male joblessness, mother-only families, and welfare recipiency. He found that these tracts, which he labeled "deprivation neighborhoods," mushroomed over the ten-year period. In Chicago, for example, deprivation neighborhoods increased by 150 percent, from 120 tracts to 299 tracts, while the population living in these tracts expanded by 132 percent, from 445,000 to 1,034,000. Similarly, in Detroit, deprivation tracts expanded from 60 to 197 (228%), and the population residing in these tracts increased from 193,880 to 708,593 (265%). Just as remarkable, the ratio of Black non-deprivation tracts to deprivation tracts completely reversed in both cities during the decade; in Chicago, from 3 to 2 in 1970 to 2 to 5 in 1980, and in Detroit, from 5 to 2 in 1970 to 1 to 4 in 1980 (Hughes, 1988).

In sum, there is considerable evidence that the size of the urban underclass grew substantially after 1970 and that it became more spatially isolated. Underclass growth and isolation have been especially acute in the older industrialized cities of the Northeast and Midwest. In the next section, I outline a thesis of conflicting urban economic and demographic changes that partially accounts for the marked increases of urban underclass population. I also raise some related theses apropos spatial mobility and employment selectivity of Blacks and varying socioeconomic status that also contributed to the problem.

WORKING THESES

Poverty areas and underclass populations expanded in large northern cities despite targeted infusions of public assistance, affirmative action programs, and civil rights legislation (programs traditionally supported by liberals) and have persisted in the face of national and urban economic recovery (solutions espoused by many conservatives). One reason why neither liberal nor conservative prescriptions worked, I propose, is that both were overwhelmed by fundamental changes in the structure of the economies of these cities, which affected the employment prospects of their disadvantaged Black residents.

Modern advances in transportation, communication, and industrial technologies, interacting with the changing structure of national and global economic organization, have transformed major northern cities from centers of goods production and distribution to centers of information exchange and higher-order service provision (Kasarda, 1976, 1988). As a result, many goods-processing establishments (e.g., in manufacturing, warehousing, retail trade) that once constituted the economic backbones of these cities—and provided employment opportunities for lesser-educated residents—either vanished or relocated. Blue-collar and other jobs with lower education requisites have been replaced, in part, by knowledge-intensive white-collar jobs that typically require education beyond high school. These expanding white-collar jobs are not *functionally* accessible to most disadvantaged urban Blacks, even though they are relatively close to the core ghettos (that is, they are *spatially* accessible).

Aggravating blue-collar employment declines in the cities' traditional goods-producing industries was the urban exodus of White middle-income residents and the neighborhood business establishments that once served them. This exodus drained the city tax base and further diminished the number of blue-collar service jobs such as domestic workers, gas station attendants, and local delivery personnel. Concurrently, many secondary commercial areas of cities withered; they could not be economically sustained by the lower income levels of minority residential groups that replaced suburban-bound Whites (Kasarda, 1978).

Economic distress created by urban industrial transformation and White flight tells only part of the story, however. With important civil rights gains during the 1960s and 1970s, selective "Black flight" from the ghettos accelerated, resulting in a socioeconomic and spatial bifurcation of urban Black communities. As William J. Wilson points out, prior to the 1960s Black inner-city communities were far more heterogeneous in socioeconomic mix and family structure because de facto and de jure segregation bound together Blacks of all income levels. The presence of working-class and middle-income Blacks within or nearby the ghettos sustained essential local institutions such as neighborhood clubs, churches, schools, and organized recreational activities for youth. Working-class and middle-income Black residents also provided community leadership, mainstream role models for youth, greater familial stability, and sanctions against deviant behavior (Wilson, 1987).

Yet, as Wilson argues, it was these more economically stable Blacks who disproportionately benefited from civil rights gains, such as affirmative action and open housing, that removed artificial barriers to job access and facilitated their exodus from ghetto neighborhoods. Left behind in increasingly isolated concentrations were the most disadvantaged with the least to offer in marketable skills, role models, and economic and familial stability. Under such conditions, ghetto problems became magnified and socialization of their younger residents to mainstream values and positive work ethics atrophied.

Let me add four extensions to Wilson's thesis. First, with the flight of working- and middle-class Blacks from the ghettos, not only were mainstream role models, normative guidance, and neighborhood leadership resources lost, but it also became extremely difficult for most small Black-owned stores and shops that served ghetto residents to survive. It was often these locally-owned neighborhood establishments that provided ghetto youth with their initial job experience and in so doing also offered visible models of employed teenagers. When these establishments closed, both important functions were lost.

Second, prior to the 1960s, de jure and de facto racial segregation in business and shopping patterns resulted in "protected markets," with Black earnings expended primarily in Black-owned establishments. Money earned by Blacks who worked in White-owned businesses was much more likely to be funneled to a Black-owned neighborhood establishment or local Black professional than was the case in the 1970s and 1980s. Black income thus was multiplied through Black chains of exchange rather than flowing out of the Black community, as is more likely the case today.[2] As a result, not only was aggregate Black community income diminished but, in turn, the number of Blacks who could be employed in the neighborhood was substantially reduced.

Third, it is well documented that affirmative action programs were far more effective in the public sector than the private sector. My analysis of changes in white-collar employment in major northern cities between 1970 and 1980 shows that upper-echelon white-collar employment gains by central-city Blacks were skewed toward the public sector, whereas such gains by non-Hispanic Whites and others were almost exclusively in the private sector.[3] By the mid-1970s, administrative growth in the public sector had already begun to slow, especially in the major cities, and it slowed even further during the 1980s era of urban fiscal austerity (Moss, 1988). At the same time, a burst of entrepreneurship and small-business growth commenced that bypassed Blacks. In contrast to dramatic gains by most other racial and ethnic groups, the number of Black-owned firms with employees actually declined (Boyd, 1989; U.S. Bureau of the Census, 1979, 1985b). It seems plausible that the differential success in affirmative action in the public sector disproportionately attracted better educated, more talented Blacks from private sector pursuits in which most upper-income growth opportunities emerged in the past 15 years. Entering the more secure public sector, I propose, also reduces the prospects of these persons starting their own businesses and thus economically bolstering the Black community by providing additional employment opportunities for Blacks.

Fourth, since the early 1970s, certain federal policies have been guided by the reasonable principle that government assistance should be targeted to areas where the needs are the greatest, as measured by such factors as job loss, poverty rate, and persistence of unemployment (U.S. Department of Housing and Urban Development, 1978, 1980; Swanson and Vogel, 1986). The idea is that the most distressed areas should receive the largest allocation of government funds for subsistence and local support services for the economically displaced and others left behind. While these policies unquestionably helped relieve pressing problems such as the inability of the unemployed to afford private-sector housing or obtain adequate nutrition and health care, they did nothing to reduce the skills mismatch between the resident labor force and available urban jobs. In fact, spatially concentrated assistance may have inadvertently increased the mismatch and the plight of educationally disadvantaged residents by binding them to inner-city areas of severe blue-collar job decline and to areas that, by program definition, are the most distressed.

For those individuals with some resources and for the fortunate proportion whose efforts to break the bonds of poverty succeed, spatially concentrated government assistance will not impede their mobility. But for many inner-city poor who lack skills and have few economic options, local concentrations of government assistance and community services can be "sticking" forces. Given their lack of skills, the opportunity cost of moving and giving up their in-place assistance would be too high. They may see themselves as better off with their marginal, but secure, in-place government assistance than taking a chance and moving in search of a minimum-wage, entry-level job, often in an unknown environment.

I will return to the above issues later in this chapter. First, let me document the immense employment restructuring that has occurred in our largest northern cities in terms of education levels of jobholders.

RISING EDUCATIONAL REQUISITES FOR EMPLOYMENT

The decline in jobs that require little education and the corresponding increase in the importance of higher education for working in economically transforming northern cities in clearly manifested by Table 1. This table, based on data from the three largest northeastern cities and three largest midwestern cities, presents changes between 1970 and 1980 in the number of central-city jobs in terms of the education level of jobholders. Most striking is the fact that these cities experienced not only substantial declines in jobs held by those who did not complete high school, but also considerable declines in jobs held by those who have only a high school degree. At the same time, the number of city jobs held by those with higher education mushroomed.

The four cities that accounted for the lion's share of the *increases* in concentrated poverty populations during the 1970s (New York, Chicago, Philadelphia, and Detroit) also experienced the lion's share of *declines* in jobs held by high school dropouts and by those with only a high school degree. In 1980, as compared with 1970, there were 211,400 fewer workers in Chicago who did not have a high school degree. The number of workers with only 12 years of schooling also declined by 81,020 during the decade, while the number of jobholders with some college and college completed increased by 91,320 and 112,500, respectively. Similar patterns are exhibited by the other large northern cities, with major increases in jobs held by those with education beyond high school and even greater declines in employment by those with a high school degree or less.

TABLE 1. Change in Number of Central-City Jobs, by Education Level of Jobholders, Selected Central Cities, 1970–1980

	Less than H.S.	H.S. Only	Some College	College Graduate	Total
Boston	−80,260	−48,980	25,700	58,280	−45,260
	(−58.7%)	(−28.9%)	(32.9%)	(71.4%)	(−9.7%)
Chicago	−211,400	−81,020	91,320	112,500	−88,600
	(−41.8%)	(−18.6%)	(43.9%)	(56.7%)	(−6.5%)
Cleveland	−64,600	−20,220	26,300	15,980	−42,600
	(−48.2%)	(−14.0%)	(53.5%)	(31.0%)	(−11.2%)
Detroit	−107,300	−55,460	35,320	22,320	−105,120
	(−55.0%)	(−28.7%)	(48.4%)	(35.3%)	(−20.0%)
New York	−443,800	−161,180	237,580	266,360	−101,040
	(−40.4%)	(−15.8%)	(61.0%)	(47.3%)	(−3.2%)
Philadelphia	−144,060	−31,640	48,280	55,540	−71,880
	(−47.2%)	(−11.1%)	(60.5%)	(57.4%)	(−9.3%)

SOURCES: U.S. Bureau of the Census, Machine Readable Public Use Microdata Sample File, 5% A Sample, 1980; ibid., 15% County Group Sample, 1970.

Note: Figures in parentheses denote percentage change.

Portions of the decrease in city jobs occupied by those without a high school degree and growth in jobs held by those with higher education reflect improvements in the overall educational attainment of the city labor force, including Blacks, during the 1970s. These improvements, however, were not nearly as great as the concurrent upward shifts in the education levels of city jobholders. As a result, much of the job increase in the some-college or college-graduate categories for each city was absorbed by suburban commuters, while many job losses in the less-than-high-school or high-school-only category were absorbed by city residents. Moreover, general improvements in city residents' education levels meant that lesser-educated jobless Blacks fell further behind in the hiring queue (Lieberson, 1980). Particularly affected were those large numbers of urban Blacks who had not completed high school, especially younger ones. For central-city minority youth, school drop-out rates during the 1970s and 1980s ranged from 30 to 50 percent. Case studies of the most impoverished neighborhoods and underclass schools in Chicago and New York suggest even higher drop-out rates (Hess, 1986; Kornblum, 1985).

Table 2 illustrates the structural dilemma facing sizable portions of the Black urban labor force. This table compares the 1980 educational distributions of those employed by city industries, including the self-employed, with the educational distributions of all out-of-school Black males ages 16–64 and out-of-school Black males aged 16–64 who are not working. The educational disparities between Black residents and jobs are dramatic. Despite educational gains, Black urban labor remains highly concentrated in the

TABLE 2. Educational Distribution of Jobholders and Out-of-School Black Males, Aged 16–64, Selected Central Cities, 1980

	Less than H.S.	H.S. Only	Some College	College Only
Baltimore:				
City Jobholders	29.6%	32.3%	19.4%	18.6%
Black Males	54.4	26.9	14.2	4.4
Black Males Not Working	67.5	20.0	10.0	2.1
Boston:				
City Jobholders	13.4	28.6	24.7	33.2
Black Males	35.4	38.6	17.4	8.6
Black Males Not Working	47.6	34.7	12.0	5.8
Chicago:				
City Jobholders	23.4	28.2	23.8	24.7
Black Males	44.7	29.2	19.6	6.6
Black Males Not Working	58.1	26.6	12.8	2.5
Cleveland:				
City Jobholders	20.7	36.8	22.5	20.1
Black Males	46.4	34.1	15.1	4.4
Black Males Not Working	56.7	30.8	11.0	1.5
Detroit:				
City Jobholders	21.1	32.8	25.8	20.3
Black Males	43.3	30.5	20.3	5.9
Black Males Not Working	56.1	28.9	13.6	1.3
New York:				
City Jobholders	22.0	28.8	21.2	28.0
Black Males	39.3	33.2	18.8	8.7
Black Males Not Working	52.5	28.3	14.9	4.4
Philadelphia:				
City Jobholders	23.2	36.3	18.4	22.0
Black Males	46.9	35.1	13.3	5.6
Black Males Not Working	60.1	28.8	9.2	1.9
St. Louis:				
City Jobholders	25.4	33.5	22.1	19.0
Black Males	50.9	28.1	15.5	5.5
Black Males Not Working	63.8	24.7	9.3	2.2

SOURCE: U.S. Bureau of the Census, Machine Readable Public Use Microdata Sample File, 5% A Sample, 1980.

education category in which city employment has rapidly declined since 1970 — the category in which people have not completed high school — and greatly underrepresented in the educational attainment categories in which city employment is rapidly rising, especially the category of college graduate. As late as 1980, the modal education-completed category for out-of-school Black male residents in all cities except Boston was less than 12 years.

Those out-of-school Black males who are jobless display even lower levels of educational attainment. In Chicago, for example, while 44.7 percent of all Black males who were out of school had less than 12 years of education in 1980, 58.1 percent of Black males who were out of school *and* jobless had not completed high school. With the exception of Boston, where 47.6 percent of jobless Black males did not complete high school, more than 50 percent of jobless Black males in all cities had completed less than 12 years of schooling, including a remarkable 60+ percent in Philadelphia, St. Louis, and Baltimore. Comparing these figures with the percentage of city jobs filled in 1980 by those with less than a high school degree (top left figure of each city panel) and with changes in city jobs occupied by the poorly educated between 1970 and 1980 (Table 1) exemplifies the substantial educational disparity (and corresponding skills mismatch) faced by urban Blacks in general and jobless Blacks in particular.

This educational disparity between city jobs and Black residents poses a serious structural impediment to major improvements in urban Black employment prospects. It may be the case that any *individual* Black male who has not completed high school can secure employment in the city — some vacancies almost always exist, even in declining employment sectors. But, given the demographic-employment distributions shown in Table 2, if large *portions* of out-of-work urban Blacks all sought the jobs available, they would simply overwhelm vacancies at the lower end of the education continuum.

The structural mismatch between city jobs and Black labor that is displayed at the higher-education end of the continuum helps explain why policies based primarily on urban economic development have had limited success in reducing urban Black joblessness. Most Blacks simply lack the education to participate in the new growth sectors of the urban economy. While city jobs taken by college graduates have skyrocketed, the percentage of urban Black males who have completed college remains extremely small (only 6.6 percent in Chicago as of 1980). For those who are out of work, the disparity at the higher-education end is even greater.

Confinement of poorly educated blacks in cities that are rapidly losing jobs that require only a high school education poses another serious impediment to lowering their unemployment rates. As blue-collar and other less knowledge-intensive jobs dispersed to the suburbs, working class Whites were able to relocate much more easily than Blacks (Kain and Zax, 1987). For example, data from the U.S. Census of Manufacturers show that between 1972 and 1982 New York City lost 30 percent of its manufacturing jobs, Chicago lost 36 percent, and Detroit lost 41 percent. During approximately the same period, 1970–1980, the non-Hispanic White population declined by 1.4 million in New York, 700,000 in Chicago, and 420,000 in Detroit, while the Black populations of these three cities actually *increased* by 180,000, 111,000, and 102,000, respectively (Kasarda, 1985).

RESIDENTIAL AND TRANSPORTATION CONSTRAINTS

Since John Kain's seminal article on the effects of metropolitan job decentralization and housing segregation on Black employment, spirited debate has surrounded the question of whether spatial factors play a role in the rise of joblessness among urban Blacks (Kain, 1968; Offner and Saks, 1971; Strazheim, 1980; Price and Mills, 1985; Ellwood, 1986; Hughes, 1987; Leonard, 1987; Jencks and Mayer, 1988; Holzer, 1989). At issue is whether the suburbanization of blue-collar and other lower-skilled jobs has worked to the economic disadvantage of Blacks who remain residentially constrained to inner-city housing.

Jonathan Leonard, for example, reports that distance of business establishments from the ghetto is the most significant determinant of Blacks' employment share. The farther the establishment is from the ghetto, the fewer Blacks it employs and the more slowly it adds Black employees over time (Leonard, 1987). Since most lower-education-requisite job growth in metropolitan areas is located at their peripheries, those concentrated in the urban core are at a "spatial" disadvantage (Kain, 1968; Kasarda, 1976). This disadvantage is reflected in the longer commuting times of Blacks to suburban jobs. This is illustrated in Table 3, which presents Black-White differences in commuting times among lesser-educated central-city residents working in the suburbs of nine major metropolitan areas. In every city, Blacks have longer average commuting times than Whites, regardless of whether one compares those without a high school degree or those with only a high school education. Additional analysis revealed that racial differences are not accounted for by transit mode, since nearly the same percentages of Blacks who work in the suburbs commute by private automobile as do Whites. . . .

Transportation constraints are even more striking when one looks at those who are jobless. Complementary analysis was conducted on unemployed Black males, aged 16–64, and out-of-the-labor-force, out-of-school Black males, aged 16–64 (U.S. Bureau of the Census, 1980). The figures were remarkable. In New York, for example, 72 percent of the Black males

TABLE 3. Mean Travel Time to Suburban Jobs by Central-City Males, Aged 16–64 and Employed Full-Time, by Education and Race, 1980

| | Mean One-Way Travel Time (minutes) | | | |
| | Less than H.S. | | H.S. Degree Only | |
	Blacks	Whites	Blacks	Whites
Baltimore	41.0	29.4	37.2	34.1
Boston	36.2	32.3	39.0	29.3
Chicago	46.2	35.9	46.3	33.3
Cleveland	31.6	24.0	32.7	22.9
Detroit	29.2	23.9	28.2	23.5
New York	54.4	44.1	53.2	44.4
Philadelphia	40.3	36.4	44.8	34.8
St. Louis	33.4	29.2	35.9	27.7

SOURCE: U.S. Bureau of the Census, Machine Readable Public Use Microdata Sample File, 5% A Sample, 1980.

who were unemployed resided in a household with no private vehicle, and 78 percent of those who were not in school or in the labor force resided in households with no private vehicle. Corresponding figures for Philadelphia were 54 percent and 60 percent, respectively; for Chicago, 45 percent and 55 percent, respectively. I then analyzed automobile availability in Chicago's low-income Black census tracts. In the Near West Side, more than three out of four households in these tracts did not have an automobile in 1980. In Chicago's south side ghetto of Oakland, the figure was the same. In those Black census tracts with the greatest joblessness, more than 80 percent of the households did not possess a private vehicle in 1980. Residential confinement of disadvantaged Blacks in areas of blue-collar job decline together with their limited automobile ownership—the latter increasingly necessary to obtain employment in a dispersing metropolitan economy—would surely seem to contribute to their high rates of unemployment, reinforcing problems of their skills mismatch with nearby urban growth industries. . . .

REDUCING SKILL AND SPATIAL MISMATCHES

We have seen that as northern cities have been functionally transformed from centers of goods processing to centers of information processing, education levels associated with urban jobs have risen much faster than the education levels of their Black labor pools, resulting in high rates of structural unemployment among the least educated. Not only do older Black residents have few prospects of gaining additional schooling (their educational distributions are essentially fixed), but approximately 40 percent of younger inner-city Blacks are failing to finish high school, with much higher dropout rates in underclass areas (Hess, 1986; Wilson, 1987).

Mismatches between education levels and job opportunities are particularly acute in those cities where declines in traditional blue-collar industries and the growth of information-processing industries have been most substantial since 1970. So different are the skills used and the education required in these growing urban industrial sectors that adaptation by the poorly educated is exceedingly difficult. This difficulty is concretely represented in the exceptionally high jobless rates of those central-city residents who have not completed high school, *regardless of race*, and rapid rises since 1970 in jobless rates of poorly educated residents, again regardless of race.

Exacerbating the mismatches between labor pools and job opportunities have been recent demographic trends in these cities. During the past two decades, northern cities that lost the largest numbers of blue-collar and other jobs with lower educational requisites simultaneously added large numbers of Blacks with no education beyond high school to their working-age populations. Most of these new labor force entrants were offspring of the massive numbers of Blacks who migrated to northern cities during the 1950s and 1960s, when inner-city jobs requiring only limited education and fewer skills were far more plentiful. As those jobs dispersed to the suburbs and exurbs, relatively few Blacks followed, resulting in serious labor imbalances in many metropolitan areas, with excesses of jobless minorities in the inner cities while suburban businesses face shortages of lesser-skilled labor.

This demographic disequilibrium, which contrasts sharply with that anticipated on the basis of traditional labor market mobility models, leads to an important policy question: What is continuing to hold lesser-educated, jobless minorities in urban centers while employment opportunities appropriate to their skills are dispersing? To be sure, such factors as racial discrimination, a lack of sufficient low-income housing in outlying areas, and the dependence of low-income minorities on public transportation account for much of the explanation. Moreover, I suggested earlier that certain public policies may be unintentionally anchoring disadvantaged persons in areas of substantial blue-collar job decline. There is also the vast urban underground economy that enables many of those displaced from the mainstream economy to survive. Indeed, for some who lack the educational, technical, or interpersonal skills for employment in mainstream institutions, inner-city ghettos may provide the only environment in which they can stay afloat economically. Yet, large concentrations of those who have become dependent on the urban underground economy pose serious problems (crime, drug abuse, loitering, vandalism) that dissuade businesses from locating nearby and push out more economically stable families and others who eschew such behaviors. As a consequence, not only do local employment opportunities further deteriorate, reinforcing neighborhood economic decline, but also selective out-migration of more mainstream-oriented residents spatially isolates the most disadvantaged.

To revitalize inner-city areas of decline, some have suggested a national development bank, a new Reconstruction Finance Corporation, enterprise zones, or government-business-labor partnerships that might help rebuild their historic employment bases (see Butler, 1981; Hanson, 1983; Rohatyn, 1979, 1981; U.S. Department of Housing and Urban Development, 1978, 1980, 1984). The government subsidies, tax incentives, and regulatory relief contained in existing and proposed urban policies are not nearly sufficient, however, to overcome technological and market forces (both national and global) that are redistributing urban blue-collar jobs and shaping the economies of our major cities. It is becoming recognized that economic advancement of large cities and maximum job creation will most likely be accomplished through private and public initiatives that promote information-processing and other advanced service-sector industries whose functions are consistent with the roles that computer-age cities most effectively perform in an increasingly globalized economy (Kasarda, 1980).

Northern cities that are pro-active in capitalizing on their new advanced service-sector roles should experience overall employment growth, as occurred during the 1980s in Boston, Chicago, and New York City. But if large portions of their residents lack the appropriate education to be hired by information-processing and other white-collar service industries beginning to dominate urban employment bases, the plight of the poorly educated could further deteriorate. For this reason and because demographic forces portend potential shortages of educationally qualified resident labor for white-collar service industries expanding in the cities, there have been cogent calls from both the public and private sectors to upgrade city schools, reduce Black youth drop-out rates, and increase the proportion who continue on to higher education. Only with substantial educational upgrading of urban Blacks will the skills mismatch problem be reduced.

Such policies, however, are unlikely to alleviate the unemployment problems currently facing large numbers of economically displaced older Blacks and yet-to-be-placed younger ones with serious educational deficiencies—those caught in the web of urban change. Their unemployment will persist because the educational qualifications and skills demanded by most of today's urban growth industries are difficult to impart through short-term, non-traditional programs (Kasarda, 1988). Educational challenges become even more daunting when one realizes that even jobs held by high school graduates are rapidly declining in most major northern cities, with net employment growth restricted to job holders with at least some higher education (see Table 1). Simply put, a high school degree will not be enough to prevent many from slipping further down the hiring queue in our information-age cities.

The implausibility of rebuilding urban blue-collar job bases or of providing sufficient education to large numbers of displaced Black workers so that they may be re-employed in expanding white-collar industries necessitates a renewed look at the traditional means by which Americans have adapted to economic displacement—that is, spatial mobility. Despite the mass loss of lower-skilled jobs in many cities during the past decade, there have been substantial increases in these jobs nationwide. For example, between 1975 and 1985, more than 2.1 million non-administrative jobs were *added* in eating and drinking establishments, which is more than the total number of production jobs that existed in 1985 in America's automobile, primary metals, and textile industries combined (U.S. Bureau of Labor Statistics, 1986). Unfortunately, essentially all of the net national growth in jobs with lower educational requisites has occurred in the suburbs, exurbs, and non-metropolitan areas, which are far removed from large concentrations of poorly educated minorities.

To reduce this spatial mismatch, a number of strategies should be considered, including: (1) a computerized job-opportunity network that would provide up-to-date information on available jobs throughout the particular metropolitan area, the region, and the nation; (2) partial underwriting of more distant job searches by the unemployed; (3) need-based temporary relocation and rental assistance once a job has been secured; (4) housing vouchers for those whose income levels require such assistance, as opposed to additional spatially fixed public housing complexes; (5) stricter enforcement of existing fair-housing and fair-hiring laws; (6) public-private cooperative efforts to transport unemployed inner-city residents to suburban businesses facing labor shortages; and (7) a thorough review of all spatially targeted government programs to ensure that they are not inadvertently anchoring those with limited resources to distressed inner-city areas where there are few prospects for permanent or meaningful employment.

These policies should be complemented with programs that improve opportunities for ghetto youths to live in household and neighborhood environments where adult work is the norm and to attend public schools that will provide them with necessary skills and social networks for employment in a rapidly transforming economy. In this regard, it has been shown that low-income Black youths who moved from inner-city Chicago to predominantly White suburbs as part of a subsidized housing experiment performed remarkably well, both academically and socially (Rosenbaum et al., 1987).

The spatial mobility strategies noted above are not suggested as replacements for efforts to make cities more attractive to blue-collar industries or imperative programs to improve inner-city schools and the educational qualifications of city residents, but rather as complements to them. All three general strategies (jobs-to-people, people-to-jobs, and educational upgrading) must be further complemented by national economic development policies that foster sustained private sector employment growth. The economic health of cities and industry demand for blue-collar labor are inexorably interwoven with the health of the national economy. Moreover, programs assisting the education, retraining, or relocation of the structurally unemployed will prove fruitless unless there are new and enduring jobs at the end of the training programs or moves.

NOTES

1. They used a composite definition in which census tracts must fall at least one standard deviation above the national mean on *all* four characteristics (Ricketts and Sawhill, 1988).

2. A San Francisco study found that a dollar turns over five to six times in the Chinese business community, while in most inner-city Black communities dollars leave before they turn over even once (Kotkin, 1986; Wartzman, 1988).

3. This analysis was based on the U.S. Census Bureau's Public Use Microdata Sample files.

REFERENCES

Bane, Mary Jo, and Paul A. Jargowsky (1988). "Urban Poverty Areas: Basic Questions Concerning Prevalence, Growth, and Dynamics." In Michael G. H. McGeary and Laurence E. Lynn, Jr., eds., *Urban Change and Poverty.* Washington, D.C.: National Academy Press.

Boyd, Robert L. (1989). *Ethnic Entrepreneurs in the New Economy: Business Enterprise Among Asian Americans and Blacks in a Changing Urban Environment.* Ph.D. Dissertation, University of North Carolina, Chapel Hill.

Butler, Stuart M. (1981). *Enterprise Zones: Greenlining the Inner Cities.* New York: Universe Books.

Ellwood, David T. (1986). "The Spatial Mismatch Hypothesis: Are There Teenage Jobs Missing in the Ghetto?" In Richard B. Freeman and Harry J. Holzer, eds., *The Black Youth Employment Crisis*. Chicago: University of Chicago Press.

Green, Richard P. (1988). "Changes in the Spatial Dispersion of Extreme Poverty Areas in Large American Cities." Paper presented at the annual meeting of the Regional Science Association. Toronto, Canada, November 1988.

Hanson, Royce, ed. (1983). *Rethinking Urban Policy: Urban Development in an Advanced Economy*. Report prepared for the Committee on National Urban Policy, Commission on Behavioral and Social Sciences and Education. Washington, D.C.: National Academy Press.

Hess, G. Alfred Jr. (1986). "Educational Triage in an Urban School Setting," *Metropolitan Education*, Fall 1986, pp. 39–52.

Holzer, Harry (1989). "The Empirical Status of the Spatial Mismatch Hypothesis." Department of Economics, Michigan State University.

Hughes, Mark Alan (1987). "Moving Up and Moving Out: Confusing Ends and Means about Ghetto Dispersal," *Urban Studies* vol. 24, no. 5 (Oct. 1987), pp. 503–517.

—————— (1988). "The 'Underclass' Fallacy." Unpublished manuscript, Woodrow Wilson School of Public and International Affairs, Princeton University.

Jencks, Christopher, and Susan E. Mayer (1988). "Residential Segregation, Job Proximity, and Black Job Opportunities: The Empirical Status of the Spatial Mismatch Hypothesis." In Michael McGeary and Laurence E. Lynn, Jr., eds., *Urban Change and Poverty*. Washington, D.C.: National Academy Press.

Kain, John (1968). "Housing Segregation, Negro Employment, and Metropolitan Decentralization," *Quarterly Journal of Economics*, vol. 82 (May 1968), pp. 175–197.

Kain, John, and Jeffrey Zax (1987). "Quits, Moves, and Employer Relocation in Segregated Housing Markets." Unpublished paper, Department of Economics, Harvard University.

Kasarda, John D. (1976). "The Changing Occupational Structure of the American Metropolis: Apropos the Urban Problem." In Barry Schwartz, ed., *The Changing Face of the Suburbs*. Chicago: University of Chicago Press.

—————— (1978). "Urbanization, Community, and the Metropolitan Problem." In David Street and Associates, *Handbook of Contemporary Urban Life*. San Francisco: Jossey-Bass.

—————— (1980). "The Implications of Contemporary Redistribution Trends for National Urban Policy," *Social Science Quarterly*, vol. 61, nos. 3 & 4 (December, 1980), pp. 373–400.

—————— (1985). "Urban Change and Minority Opportunities." In Paul E. Peterson, ed., *The New Urban Reality*. Washington, D.C.: Brookings Institution.

—————— (1988). "Jobs, Migration, and Emerging Urban Mismatches." In Michael G. H. McGeary and Laurence E. Lynn, Jr., eds., *Urban Change and Poverty*. Washington, D.C.: National Academy Press.

Kornblum, William S. (1985). "Institution Building in the Urban High School." In Gerald Suttles and Mayer N. Zald, eds., *The Challenge of Social Control: Citizenship and Institution Building in Modern Society*. Norwood, N.J.: Albex.

Kotkin, Joel (1986). "The Reluctant Entrepreneurs," *Inc.*, vol. 8, no. 9 (September 1986), pp. 81–86.

Leonard, Jonathan S. (1987). "The Interaction of Residential Segregation and Employment Discrimination," *Journal of Urban Economics*, vol. 21 (1987), pp. 323–346.

Lieberson, Stanley (1980). *A Piece of the Pie: Blacks and White Immigrants Since 1880.* Berkeley: University of California Press.

Massey, Douglas S., and Nancy A. Denton (1987). "Trends in Residential Segregation of Blacks, Hispanics, and Asians: 1970–1980," *American Sociological Review*, vol. 52 (December 1987), pp. 802–825.

Mincy, Ronald B. (1988). "Industrial Restructuring, Dynamic Events, and the Racial Composition of Concentrated Poverty." Paper prepared for Planning Meeting of Social Science Research Council on Industrial Restructuring, Local Political Economies, and Communities and Neighborhoods. New York, September 21–23, 1988.

Moss, Philip I. (1988). "Employment Gains by Minorities, Women in Large City Government, 1976–83," *Monthly Labor Review*, November 1988, pp. 18–24.

Offner, Paul, and Daniel Saks (1971). "A Note on John Kain's 'Housing Segregation, Negro Employment, and Metropolitan Decentralization,'" *Quarterly Journal of Economics*, vol. 85, no. 1 (Feb. 1971), pp. 147–160.

Price, Richard, and Edwin S. Mills (1985). "Race and Residence in Earnings Determination," *Journal of Urban Economics*, vol. 17 (1985), pp. 1–18.

Ricketts, Erol R., and Isabel V. Sawhill (1988). "Defining and Measuring the Underclass," *Journal of Policy Analysis and Management*, vol. 7, no. 2 (Winter 1988), pp. 316–340.

Rohatyn, Felix (1979). "Public-Private Partnerships to Stave Off Disaster," *Harvard Business Review*, vol. 57, no. 6 (November–December 1979), pp. 6–9.

—— (1981). "The Older America: Can It Survive?" *New York Review of Books*, vol. 27, no. 21 (1981), pp. 13–16.

Rosenbaum, James E., Marilyn J. Kulieke, and Leonard S. Rubinowitz (1987). "Low Income Black Children in White Suburban Schools: A Study of School and Student Responses," *Journal of Negro Education*, vol. 56, No. 1 (Winter 1987) pp. 35–43.

Sawhill, Isabel V. (1987). "Anti-Poverty Strategies for the 1980s." In Center for National Policy, *Work and Welfare: The Case for New Directions in National Policy.* Alternatives for the 1980s, No. 22. Washington, D.C.: Center for National Policy.

Strazheim, Mahlon (1980). "Discrimination and the Spatial Characteristics of the Urban Labor Market for Black Workers," *Journal of Urban Economics*, vol. 7, no. 1 (Jan. 1980), pp. 119–140.

Swanson, Bert E., and Ronald K. Vogel (1986). "Rating America's Cities—Credit Risk, Urban Distress, and the Quality of Life," *Journal of Urban Affairs*, vol. 8, no. 2 (Spring 1986), pp. 67–84.

U.S. Bureau of Labor Statistics (1986). Establishment Data 1939–1986, Machine Readable Files. Washington, D.C.

U.S. Bureau of the Census (1979). *The 1977 Survey of Minority-Owned Business Enterprises: Black, MB77-1.* Washington, D.C.: U.S. Government Printing Office.

———— (1980). Machine Readable Public Use Microdata Sample File, 5% A Sample.

———— (1982). "Characteristics of Population Below Poverty Levels: 1980," *CPS Reports*. Washington, D.C.

———— (1985a). "Money Income and Poverty Status of Families and Person in the United States: 1985," *CPS Reports*. Washington, D.C.

———— (1985b). *The 1982 Survey of Minority-Owned Business Enterprises: Black, MB82-1*. Washington, D.C.: U.S. Government Printing Office.

U.S. Department of Housing and Urban Development (1978). *The President's National Urban Policy Report, 1978*. Washington, D.C.: U.S. Department of Housing and Urban Development.

———— (1980). *The President's National Urban Policy Report, 1980*. Washington, D.C.: U.S. Department of Housing and Urban Development.

———— (1984). *The President's National Urban Policy Report, 1984*. Washington, D.C.: U.S. Department of Housing and Urban Development.

Wartzman, Rick (1988). "St. Louis Blues: A Blighted Inner City Bespeaks the Sad State of Black Commerce," *Wall Street Journal*, May 10, 1988, p. 1, col. 1.

Wilson, William Julius (1987). *The Truly Disadvantaged: The Inner City, the Underclass, and Public Policy*. Chicago: University of Chicago Press.

48

Address Unknown: Homelessness in Contemporary America*

James D. Wright

The past decade has witnessed the growth of a disturbing and largely unexpected new problem in American cities: the rise of what has been called the "new homeless." Homeless derelicts, broken-down alcoholics, and skid row bums have existed in most times and places throughout our history. But the seemingly sudden appearance of homeless young men, women, children, and whole families on the streets and in the shelters was, in retrospect, a clear signal that something had gone very seriously wrong.

The sudden intensity and new visibility of the homelessness problem took most observers by surprise. Ten or fifteen years ago, a walk along the

*Wright, James D. 1989. "Address Unknown: Homelessness in Contemporary America." *Society* 26 (September–October 1989): 45–53. Copyright © 1989 Transaction Publishers. Reprinted by permission of Transaction Publishers.

twenty-odd blocks from Madison Square Gardens to Greenwich Village would have been largely uneventful, a pleasant outing in an interesting part of New York City. The same walk today brings one across an assortment of derelict and indigent people—old women rummaging in the trash for bottles and cans, young kids swilling cheap wine from paper bags, seedy men ranting meaninglessly at all who venture near. Who are these people? Where did they come from? What, if anything, can or should be done to help?

Many stereotypes about the homeless have sprung up in the last decade. One of the most popular is that they are all crazy people who have been let loose from mental hospitals. A variation is that they are all broken-down old drunks. One writer has described them as the "drunk, the addicted, and the just plain shiftless"; the implication is that most of the homeless could do better for themselves if they really wanted to. Still another view is that they are welfare leeches, living off the dole. A particularly popular view that sprang up during the Reagan years was that most of the homeless are, as Reagan put it, "well, we might say, homeless by choice," people who have been chosen to give up on the rat race of modern society and to live unfettered by bills, taxes, mortgage payments, and related worries. In truth, all of these stereotypes are true of some homeless people, and none of them are true of all homeless people. As with any other large group in the American population, the homeless are a diverse, heterogeneous lot. No single catch phrase or easy myth can possibly describe them all.

As in times past, most homeless people in America today are men, but a sizable fraction are women and a smaller but still significant fraction are the children of homeless adults. All told, the women and children add up to between one-third and two-fifths of the homeless population. Indifference to the plight of homeless adult men comes easily in an illiberal era, but indifference to the plight of homeless women and children, groups society has traditionally obligated itself to protect, comes easily only to the coldhearted.

Likewise, alcohol abuse and homelessness are tightly linked in the popular stereotype, but recent studies confirm that less than 40 percent of the homeless population abuses alcohol to excess; the majority, the remaining 60 percent, do not. Focusing just on the adult men, the studies show that alcohol abuse still runs only to about 50 percent: about half the men are chronic alcoholics, but then, the other half are not.

In like fashion, mental illness is certainly a significant problem within the homeless population, but severe chronic psychiatric disorder characterizes only about a third; the remaining two-thirds are not mentally ill, at least not according to any meaningful clinical standard.

Being among the poorest of the poor, it is also true that many homeless people receive governmental assistance in the form of general assistance (welfare), food stamps, disability pensions, and the like. Yet, nationwide, the studies show that only about half the homeless receive any form of social welfare assistance; the remaining half survive on their own devices, without government aid of any sort.

And so: Some of the homeless *are* broken-down alcoholics, but most are not. Some *are* mentally impaired, but most are not. Some *are* living off the benefit programs made available through the social welfare system, but most are not. Clearly, the popular mythologies do not provide an adequate portrait of the homeless in America today.

ON DEFINITIONS AND NUMBERS

Defining homelessness for either research or operational purposes has proven to be a rather sticky business. It is easy to agree on the extremes of a definition: an old man who sleeps under a bridge down by the river and has nowhere else to go would obviously be considered homeless in any conceivable definition of the term. But there are also many ambiguous cases. What of persons who live in rooming houses or flophouses? Even if they have lived in the same room for years, we might still want to consider them homeless in at least some senses of the term. What of persons who live in abandoned buildings? In tents or shacks made from scrap materials? In cars and vans? What of a divorced woman with children who can no longer afford rent on the apartment and who has an offer from her family "to live with us for as long as you need"? What of people who would be homeless except that they have temporarily secured shelter in the homes of their families or friends? Or those that would be homeless except that they are temporarily "housed" in jails, prisons, hospitals, or other institutions? What of the person on a fixed income who rents a cheap hotel room three weeks a month and lives on the streets or in the shelters for the fourth week because the pension is adequate to cover only three-quarters of the monthly room rent?

Clearly, to be homeless is to lack regular and customary access to a conventional dwelling unit. The ambiguities arise in trying to define "regular and customary access" and "conventional dwelling unit."

These examples demonstrate that *homelessness is not and cannot be a precisely defined condition.* A family who sleeps in its pickup truck and has nowhere else to go would be considered homeless by almost everyone. A long-distance trucker who sleeps regularly—perhaps three or four nights a week—in the cab of his $1000,000 rig, who earns $30,000 or $40,000 a year, and who has a nice home where he sleeps when he is not on the road, would not be considered "homeless" by anyone. Our long-distance trucker has options; our homeless family living in its pickup does not.

Thus, choice is implied in any definition of homelessness. In general, people who choose to live the way they do are not to be considered homeless, however inadequate their housing may appear to be, while those who live in objectively inadequate housing—in makeshift quarters or cheap flophouses or in the shelters and missions—because they do not have the resources to do otherwise *would* be considered homeless in most definitions, clearly in mine.

"The resources to do otherwise" implies yet another aspect of my definition of homelessness: that true homelessness results from extreme poverty. One hears from time to time of "street people" who are found to have a locker in the bus station stuffed with cash, or of vagabonds who, in a former life, traded stock on Wall Street but cashed in for the unfettered romance of life on the road. In some sense, these people are "homeless," but they are homeless by choice. Ronald Reagan notwithstanding, they comprise no important part of the homeless problem in this nation and I shall say nothing further about them.

Poor people living in objectively inadequate housing because they lack the means to do otherwise number in the tens of millions. Indeed, if we adopt a sufficiently inclusive definition of "objectively inadequate housing," we would capture virtually the entire poverty population of the country, some 35 million people, within the homeless category. And yet, surely, being homeless is more than just being poor, although, just as surely, being poor has a lot to do with it.

My colleagues and I have therefore found it useful to distinguish between the *literally homeless* and the *marginally housed*. By "literally homeless" I mean those who, on a given night, have nowhere to go — no rented room, no friend's apartment, no flophouse — people who sleep out on the streets or who *would* sleep out on the streets except that they avail themselves of beds in shelters, missions, and other facilities set up to provide space for otherwise homeless people. And by "marginally housed" I mean those who have a more or less reasonable claim to more or less stable housing of more or less minimal adequacy, being closer to the "less" than the "more" on one or all criteria. This distinction certainly does not solve the definitional problem, but it does specify more clearly the subgroups of interest.

This discussion should be adequate to confirm that there is no single, best, correct, easily agreed upon definition of "homelessness," and thus, no single correct answer to the question: "How many homeless people are there?" There is, rather, a continuum of housing adequacy or housing stability, with actual cases to be found everywhere along the continuum. Just where in the continuum one draws the line, defining those above as adequately if marginally housed and those below as homeless, is of necessity a somewhat arbitrary and therefore disputable decision.

Nonetheless, despite the unavoidable arbitrariness, the discussion calls attention to three pertinent groups: (1) the poverty population as a whole, (2) the subset of the poverty population that is marginally housed, and (3) the subset of the poverty population that is literally homeless. It is useful to get some feel for the relative sizes of these three groups.

I focus in this brief discussion on the city of Chicago. According to U.S. government statistics and definitions, the poverty population of the city of Chicago amounts to about 600,000 persons. Of these, approximately 100,000 are poor enough to qualify for General Assistance under the rather strict Illinois guidelines. A recent study of General Assistance recipients in Chicago found that fully half resided with relatives and friends — that is, were not literally homeless (mainly because of the largess of their social networks) but who were at high risk of literal homelessness in the face of the merest misfortune. Certainly, we shall not be too far off if we let this group, some 50,000 persons, represent the "marginally housed."

The most recent, systematic, and sophisticated attempt to tally the literally homeless population of Chicago reports about 3,000 literally homeless persons on any given night. Taking these numbers at face value, the ratio of poor persons to marginally housed persons to literally homeless persons, at least in one large American city, is on the order of 600 to 50 to 3.

It is transparent that homelessness is only a small part, indeed, a very small part, of the larger poverty problem in the nation. Most poor people, even most of the very poor, manage to avoid literal homelessness and secure for themselves some sort of reasonably stable housing. Just how they manage to do this given recent trends in the housing economy is an important question that is yet to be successfully answered.

Also, the number of literally homeless at any one time is much lower than the number of potentially homeless (or marginally housed) people. The evidence from Chicago suggests a pool of 50,000 persons who might easily become homeless on any given day; the actual pool at risk is no doubt even larger. Even with a literally homeless count of 3,000, Chicago is hard-pressed to come up with sufficient shelter space. The point is that however bad the homelessness problem has become, it could easily be worse by one or two orders of magnitude. The *potential* homelessness problem in contemporary America, in short, is many times worse than the *actual* problem being confronted today.

It is also worth stressing that the number of literally homeless *on any given night* is not a true indication of the magnitude of the problem since that number is by definition smaller than the number of homeless *in any given month* or over the span of *any given year*. To illustrate, in the Chicago census of the literally homeless, 31 percent were found to have been homeless less than two months, whereas 25 percent had been homeless for more than two years. Homelessness, that is, is a heterogeneous mixture of transitory short-term and chronic long-term housing problems. Some people became homeless only to reclaim a stable housing arrangement in a matter of days, weeks, or months; some became homeless and remain homeless for the rest of their lives.

The transitory or situational component adds even more ambiguity to the numbers question. The estimate in Chicago, to illustrate, is that the number ever homeless in the span of a year exceeds the number homeless on any given night approximately by a factor of three. A recent study by the Rand Corporation in California gives similar results. Three separate counties were included in that study; the estimated ratios of annual to nighttime homeless in the three counties were about 2 to 1, 3 to 1, and 4 to 1.

Nevertheless, it is still important to have some sense of the approximate dimensions of the homeless problem in America today. Unfortunately, there is no national study that provides this information. However, Martha Burt has published results from a national probability sample of shelter and soup kitchen users suggesting that roughly 200,000 homeless adults used shelters and soup kitchens in the large U.S. cities in a typical week in March, 1987. To provide a *complete* estimate of the "single point in time" number of homeless, one would need to add to this figure all homeless children (who comprise perhaps a tenth of the total), all homeless adults who did not use shelters or soup kitchens during the week in question (an unknown number), and all homeless persons living outside cities with populations of 100,000 or more (also an unknown number). These additions, I think, would bring the final estimate somewhere respectably close to the "best guess" figure given later.

I have reviewed the results from a number of studies done in single cities, discarding those that I felt were obviously deficient and giving the greatest weight to those that I felt had been the most scientifically respectable. Based on these studies and the usual simplifying assumptions, my conclusion is that the total literally homeless population of the nation on any given night numbers in the hundreds of thousands, although probably not in the millions. As a rule of thumb, we can speak of a half million homeless people in America at any one time. And if the ratio of one-night to annual homelessness estimated for the city of Chicago (about 3 to 1) is generally true, then the *annual* homeless population of the nation is on the order of one-and-a-half millions.

"Reasoned guesses" by advocacy groups invariably posit much larger numbers than these. None of the studies that go into my estimates could be considered definitive, and so it is certainly possible that the true numbers are very much larger than the numbers I have cited. Most of the researchers whose results I have summarized above, however, began their studies expecting to find many more homeless people than they actually found, and almost all of them would have been more satisfied with their results had they done so. In any case, I am aware of no compelling *evidence* that implies numbers of literally homeless people substantially larger than those I have cited.

WORTHY AND UNWORTHY HOMELESS

What have we learned in the research of the past decade about these half-million or so Americans who are homeless on any given night? We have learned, first of all, that they are a very diverse group of unfortunates: men and women, adults and children, young and old, black and white. We have also learned that relatively few of them are chronically homeless. Indeed, only a quarter to a third would be considered chronically or permanently homeless. The majority are *episodically* homeless; that is, they become homeless now and again, with the episodes of literal homelessness punctuated by periods of more or less stable housing situations. And of course, many homeless people on any given night are recently homeless for the first time, so that no pattern is yet established.

Let me digress briefly to a personal reminiscence. A few years ago, I was having dinner with my mother. In the course of our conversation, the subject of my research on the homeless came up, and my mother asked me, "Who are these homeless people anyway?" I began to respond with my standard litany—the average age, the proportion white, the proportion of women, and such—when I was stopped short. "That is not what I want to know," Mother said. "What I want to know is, how many of these people should I really feel sorry for and how many are just bums who could do better for themselves if they tried?" This abrupt question got directly to the heart of the matter.

At the time of this conversation, I was engaged in the national evaluation of the Health Care for the Homeless (HCH) program, a demonstration project that had established clinics to provide health care for the homeless in nineteen large U.S. cities. At the time, we had data on nearly thirty thousand people who had received health care services through this program, and so I tried to tease an answer to my mother's question from these data.

I began with the homeless families, the lone homeless women, and the homeless adolescents already out on their own, figuring that anybody, even Mother, would find it easy to sympathize with these people. It took her aback to learn that about 15 percent of the HCH clients were children or adolescents aged nineteen or less, and that an additional 23 percent were adult women; the women and children, that is, added up to three-eights of the total. She allowed as how all of these were to be counted among the "deserving homeless." And so I then turned to the lone adult men.

Among the remaining five-eighths of the clients who are adult men, some 3 percent are elderly persons over sixty-five. Being close to sixty-five herself, Mother had no difficulty in adding these to the "deserving" group. Of the remaining non-elderly adult men—and we were now down to about 56 or 57 percent of the client base—fully a third turn out to be veterans of the U.S. armed services. Mother served in the Navy in World War II and found this to be a shocking figure; she just *assumed* that the Veteran's Administration took care of the people who had served their country. And so these too went into the pile of "deserving homeless."

Without the veterans, the elderly, the homeless families, the women, and the children, we were only left with about three-eighths of the client base. Among this three-eighths, I pointed out, fully a third are disabled by psychiatric impairments ranging from the moderate to the profound, and among those without disabling psychiatric impairments, more than a tenth are *physically* disabled and incapable of work. Mother readily agreed that the disabled, either physically or mentally, also deserved our compassion; and we were thus left with fewer than a quarter of the original client base, 22 percent to be precise.

I then pointed out that among this 22 percent—the nonelderly, nonveteran, nondisabled lone adult men—more than half had some sort of job—full-time employment in a few cases, part-time or sporadic employment in most cases, but in all cases jobs whose earnings were not adequate to sustain a stable housing situation. And of those not currently employed, more than half were in fact looking for work. Thus, of the 22 percent of clients remaining at this point, more than 80 percent either had work or were at least looking for work, and Mother, living in a section of Indiana that has been hard hit by the economic developments of the last decade, found it within herself to be sympathetic to these men as well.

We were then left with what she and I both agreed were the "undeserving" or "unworthy" homeless—not members of homeless families, not women or children or youth, not elderly, not veterans, not mentally or physically disabled, not currently working, and not looking for work. My mother's attitude about homelessness in America was altered dramatically when she realized that this group comprised less than 5 percent of the total, barely one homeless person in twenty.

IS HOMELESSNESS A "NEW" PROBLEM?

I began this article by referring to "the growth of a disturbing and largely unexpected new problem." But it is worth asking whether this is a new problem, and whether this is a growing problem.

Strictly speaking, homelessness is definitely *not* a "new problem," in that homeless people have always existed in American society (and, for that matter, in most other societies as well). In the recent past, the homeless were seen to consist mainly of "hobos" (transient men who "rode the rails" and whose style of life was frequently romanticized in the pulp novels of an earlier era) and "skid row bums" (older, usually white, men whose capacity for independent existence had been comprised by the ravages of chronic alcoholism). Scholarly interest in skid row spawned a large academic literature on the topic, but the homeless received no sustained policy attention; they and their problems were largely invisible to social-policy makers and to the American public at large.

Rather surprisingly, even during the War on Poverty of the middle 1960s, little or nothing was written about the *homeless* poor, although one must assume they existed even then. The most influential book ever written about poverty is probably Michael Harrington's *The Other America*, published initially in 1962. Despite several readings of that fine, sensitive volume, I am unable to find a single word about the homeless poor. Many of the processes that I think have contributed directly to today's homelessness problem, particularly the displacement of the poor to make way for urban renewal and the revitalization of downtown, are taken up by Harrington in considerable detail, but the apparent implication, that some of the displaced would become *permanently* displaced, and therefore *homeless*, goes unstated.

Recent historical research on homelessness confirms that the problem dates back at least to the colonial era, when there were sufficient numbers of "wandering poor" at least to raise popular alarms and enact legal measures to deal with them. In Massachusetts, the chosen mechanism was the process of "warning out." Names of transients, along with information on their former residences, were presented to the colonial courts. Upon judicial review, the person or family could then be "warned out" (that is, told to leave town). Some of the more populous towns actually hired persons to go door-to-door seeking out strangers.

These methods were to the end of controlling the relief rolls; up until 1739, a person was eligible for poor relief in Massachusetts if he or she had not been warned out within the first three months of residency. The modern-day equivalent has come to be known as "Greyhound therapy," whereby transients and derelicts are given a bus ticket that will take them and their problems elsewhere. Transients could also be "bound out," in essence, indentured to families needing laborers or servants: a colonial-era version, perhaps of what we call "workfare." These methods were used to control homelessness in Massachusetts until they were ended by law in 1794.

As in the present day, the wandering poor of colonial times were largely single men and women, although two-parent families were surprisingly common (comprising between 28 and 68 percent of those warned out across the towns and years covered in these studies). Also as in the present day, the wandering poor were drawn from the bottom of the social hierarchy: the men were artisans, mariners, or laborers, and the women were domestic servants for the most part. Except for the overseas immigrants (mostly Irish), they came from towns within a ten-mile radius. Interestingly, there were as many women as men among those warned out. Similar findings appear in several historical studies of indigent and homeless populations throughout the nineteenth and early-twentieth centuries.

The Great Depression marked the last great wave of homelessness in this country. Peter Rossi has pointed out that in 1933, the Federal Emergency Relief Administration housed something like 125,000 people in its transient camps around the country. Another survey of the time, also cited by Rossi, estimated that the homelessness population of 765 select cities and towns was on the order of 200,000, with estimates for the entire nation ranging upward to perhaps one-and-a-half million (much as the estimates of today). Most of the homeless of the depression were younger men and women moving from place to place in search of jobs.

The outbreak of World War II in essence ended the depression and created immense employment opportunities for men and women alike, an economic boom that continued throughout the post-war decades, certainly well into the middle of the 1960s, and that caused the virtual extinction of homelessness. Certainly, residual pockets of homelessness remained in the skid row areas, but the residents of skid row came less and less to be the economically down-and-out and more and more to be debilitated alcoholic males. Based on the urban renewal efforts of the 1960s and the obvious aging of the residual skid row population, the impending demise of skid row was widely and confidently predicted.

The postwar real growth in personal income ended in 1966, as the Vietnam war heated up. Between the war-related inflation and decay of living standards, the 1973 Arab oil embargo, and other related developments in the world economy, the country entered an economic slump that was to last until 1980. During this period, double-digit inflation *and* double-digit unemployment were not uncommon, and the national poverty rate, which had been steadily declining, began, just as steadily, to climb back up. By 1983, the poverty level was the highest recorded in any year since 1966, and while the rate has dipped back down again slightly since 1983, it is still very much higher than anything witnessed in the 1970s. And thus, by the late 1970s and certainly by the early 1980s, homelessness—the most extreme manifestation of poverty—reappeared as a problem on the national scene.

Homelessness, in short, is not a new problem in the larger historical sweep of things, but the current rash of homelessness certainly exceeds anything witnessed in this country in the last half-century. More to the point, the last major outbreak occurred as a consequence of the worst economic crisis in American history; the current situation exists in the midst of national prosperity literally unparalleled in the entire history of the world.

Not only did homelessness make a "comeback" in the early 1980s, but the character of homelessness also changed; this is another sense in which today's problem could be described as "new." In 1985, my colleagues and I had occasion to review medical records of men seen in a health clinic at the New York City Men's Shelter, in the very heart of the Bowery, for the period 1969–1984. Among the men seen in the early years of this period (1969–1972), almost half (49 percent) were white, 49 percent were documented alcohol or drug abusers, and the average age was forty-four. Among men seen at the end of the period (1981–1984), only 15 percent were white, only 28 percent were documented alcohol or drug abusers, and the average age was thirty-six. Thus, during the 1970s and early 1980s, the homeless population changed from largely white, older, and alcohol-abusive, into a population dominated by younger, non-substance-abusive, nonwhite men. Between the Great Depression and the 1980s, the road to homelessness was paved with alcohol abuse; today, quite clearly, many alternative routes have been opened.

In *Without Shelter* Peter Rossi presents a detailed comparison of results from studies of the homeless done in the 1950s and early 1960s with those undertaken in the 1980s, thus contrasting the "old" homeless and the "new." The first point of contrast is that the homeless of today suffer a more severe form of housing deprivation than did the homeless of twenty or thirty years past. Bogue's 1958 study in Chicago found only about a hundred homeless men sleeping, literally, out on the streets, out of a total homeless population estimated at twelve thousand. Rossi's 1986 survey found nearly fourteen hundred homeless persons sleeping out of doors in a total population estimated at about three thousand. Nearly all of the old homeless somehow found nightly shelter indoors (usually in flophouses and cubicle hotels, most of which have disappeared), unlike the new homeless, sizable fractions of whom sleep in the streets.

A second major difference is the presence of sizable numbers of women among today's homeless. Bogue's estimate in 1958 was that women comprised no more than 3 percent of the city's skid row population; in the middle 1980s, one homeless person in four is a woman. A third important contrast concerns the age distribution, the elderly having disappeared almost entirely from the ranks of the new homeless. Studies of the 1950s and 1960s routinely reported the average age of homeless persons to be somewhere in the middle fifties. Today, it is in the middle thirties.

Rossi points out two further differences: the substantially more straitened economic circumstances and the changing racial and ethnic composition of the new homeless. In 1958, Bogue estimated the average annual income of Chicago's homeless to be $1,058; Rossi's estimate for 1986 is $1,198. Converted to constant dollars, the average income of today's homeless is barely a third of the income of the homeless in 1958. Thus, the new homeless suffer a much more profound degree of economic destitution, often surviving on 40 percent or less of a poverty-level income.

Finally, the old homeless were mostly white — 70 percent in Bahr and Caplow's well-known study of the Bowery, 82 percent in Bogue's study of Chicago. Among the new homeless, racial and ethnic minorities are heavily overrepresented.

We speak, then, of the "new face of homelessness" and of the "new homeless" to signify the very dramatic transformation of the nature of the homeless population that has occurred in the past decade.

IS HOMELESSNESS A GROWING PROBLEM?

Granted that the character of homelessness has changed, what evidence is there that the magnitude of the problem has in fact been increasing? Certainly, the amount of attention being devoted to the topic has grown, but what of the problem itself?

Since, as I have already stressed, we do not know very precisely just how many homeless people there are in America today, it is very difficult to say whether that number is higher, lower, or the same as the number of homeless five or ten or twenty years ago. The case that homeless is in fact a growing problem is therefore largely inferential. The pertinent evidence has been reviewed in some detail by the U.S. General Accounting Office (GAO). Rather than cover the same ground here, let me simply quote GAO's conclusions:

> In summary, no one knows how many homeless people there are in America because of the many difficulties [in] locating and counting them. As a result, there is considerable disagreement over the size of the homeless population. However, there is agreement in the studies we reviewed and among shelter providers, researchers, and agency officials we interviewed that the homeless population is growing. Current estimates of annual increases in the growth of homelessness vary between 10 and 38 percent.

The most recent evidence on the upward trend in homelessness in the 1980s has been reviewed by economists Richard Freeman and Brian Hall. Between 1983 and 1985, they report, the shelter population of New York City increased by 28 percent, and that of Boston by 20 percent. Early in

1986, the U.S. Conference of Mayors released a study of twenty-five major U.S. cities, concluding that in twenty-two of the twenty-five, homelessness had indeed increased. There has also been a parallel increase in the numbers seeking food from soup kitchens, food banks, and the like. Thus, while all indicators are indirect and inferential, none suggest that the size of the homeless population is stable or declining; to the contrary, all suggest that the problem is growing rapidly.

HOW DID IT COME TO BE?

To ask how it came to be is to ask of the causes of homelessness, a topic about which everyone seems to have some opinion. *My* opinion is that many of the most commonly cited and much-discussed "causes" of contemporary homelessness are, in fact, not very important after all.

Chief among these not-very-important factors is the ongoing movement to deinstitutionalize the mentally ill. I do not mean to make light of the very serious mental health problems faced by many homeless people, but it is simply wrong to suggest that most, or even many, people are homeless because they have recently been released from a mental hospital.

What is sometimes overlooked in discussions of homelessness and deinstitutionalization is that we began deinstitutionalizing the mentally ill in the 1950s. The movement accelerated in the 1960s, owing largely to some favorable court orders concerning less-restrictive treatments. By the late 1970s, most of the people destined ever to be "deinstitutionalized" already had been. So as a direct contributing factor to the rise of homelessness in the 1980s, deinstitutionalization cannot be that important.

Many also seem to think that the rise of homelessness in the 1980s was the direct responsibility of Ronald Reagan particularly the result of the many cutbacks that Reagan engineered in human-services spending. This, like the deinstitutionalization theme, is at best a half-truth. Certainly, the Reagan years were not kind or gentle to the nation's poor, destitute, and homeless. A particular problem has been the federal government's absolute bail-out from its commitment to the subsidized construction of low-income housing units, a point that I will return to shortly. But at the same time, many of the factors that have worked to increase or exacerbate the problem of homelessness in the 1980s are rooted in the larger workings of the political economy, not in specific political decisions made by the Reagan administration.

What, then, *has* been the cause of this growing problem? Like most other social problems, homelessness has many complex causes that are sometimes difficult to disentangle. We can begin to get a handle on the complexity, however, by stating an obvious although often overlooked point: homeless people are people without housing, and thus, the *ultimate* cause of the problem is an insufficient supply of housing suitable to the needs of homeless people. Although this means, principally, an inadequate supply of low-income housing suitable to single individuals, the housing problem cuts even more deeply.

In twelve large U.S. cities, between the late 1970s and the early 1980s, the number of low-income housing units dropped from 1.6 million units to 1.1 million units, a decline of about 30 percent. Many of these "lost" units have been taken from the single room occupancy hotels or flophouse hotels and rooming houses, those that have always served as the "housing of last resort" for the socially and economically marginal segments of the urban poverty population. Many likewise have been lost through arson or abandonment. And many have disappeared as low-income housing only to reappear as housing for the affluent upper-middle class, in a process that has come to be known as gentrification.

Saying that the homeless lack housing, however, is like saying that the poor lack money: the point is a correct one, even a valuable one, but it is by no means the whole story. A second critical factor has been the recent increase in the poverty rate and the growing size of the "population at risk" for homelessness, the urban poor. In the same twelve cities mentioned above, over the same time frame, the poverty population increased from about 2.5 million poor people to 3.4 million, an increase of 36 percent. Dividing poor people into low-income units, these twelve cities averaged 1.6 poor people per unit in the late 1970s, and 3.1 poor people per unit in the early 1980s. In a five-year span, in short, the low-income housing "squeeze" tightened by a factor of two. Less low-income housing for more low-income persons necessarily predestines a rise in the numbers without housing, as indeed we have dramatically witnessed in the early years of the decade.

My argument is that these large scale housing and economic trends have conspired to create a housing "game" that increasingly large numbers are destined to lose. Who, specifically, will in fact lose at the housing game is a separate question, and on this point, attention turns to various personal characteristics of the homeless population that cause them to compete poorly in this game. Their extreme poverty, social disaffiliation, and high levels of personal disability are, of course, the principal problems. Thus, it is not entirely *wrong* to say that people are homeless because they are alcoholic or mentally ill or socially estranged — just as it is not entirely wrong to blame "bad luck" for losing at cards. Given a game that some are destined to lose, it is appropriate to ask who the losers turn out to be. But it is wrong, I think, to mistake an analysis of the losers for an analysis of the game itself.

Another important factor that is often overlooked in discussions of the homeless is the seemingly endless deterioration of the purchasing power of welfare and related benefits. Converted to constant dollars, the value of welfare, aid to families with dependent children (AFDC), and most other social benefit payments today is about half that of twenty years ago. Twenty years ago, or so it would seem, these payments were at least adequate to maintain persons and families in stable housing situations, even in the face of the loss of other income. Today, clearly, they are not. To cite one recent example, the state of Massachusetts has one of the more generous AFDC programs of any state in the country, and yet the state has been ordered by the courts twice in the past few years to increase AFDC payments. Why? The court compared the average AFDC payment in the state to the average cost of rental housing in the Boston area and concluded that the payment levels, although already generous by national standards, could only be contributing to the homelessness problem among AFDC recipeints.

What we witness in the rise of the new homeless is a new form of class conflict — a conflict over housing in the urban areas between that class in the population whose income is adequate to cover its housing costs, and that class whose income is not. In the past, this conflict was held largely in check by the aversion of the middle class to downtown living and by the federal government's commitment to subsidized housing for the poor. As the cities are made more attractive to the middle class, as revitalization and gentrification lure the urban tax base back to the central cities, and as the federal commitment to subsidized housing fades, the intensity of this conflict grows —and with it, the roster of casualties, the urban homeless.

No problem that is ultimately rooted in the large-scale workings of the political economy can be solved easily or cheaply, and this problem is no exception. Based on my analysis, the solution has two essential steps: the federal government must massively intervene in the private housing market, to halt the loss of additional low-income units and to underwrite the construction of many more; and the benefits paid to the welfare-dependent population — AFDC, general assistance, Veterans Administration income benefits, Social Security, and so on — must approximately double.

Either of the above will easily add a few tens of billions to the annual federal expenditure, and thus, neither is the least bit likely to happen in the current political environment, where lowering the federal deficit and reducing federal spending are seen as a Doxology of Political Faith, widely subscribed to by politicians of all ideological persuasions. Thus, in the short run, which is probably to say for the rest of this century, the focus will be on amelioration, not on solutions. We will do what we can to improve the lives of homeless people — more and better temporary shelters, more adequate nutrition, better and more accessible health care, and so on. In the process, we will make the lives of many homeless people more comfortable, perhaps, but we will not rid ourselves of this national disgrace.

READINGS SUGGESTED BY THE AUTHOR

Rossi, Peter et al. "The Urban Homeless: Estimating Composition and Size." *Science* 235:4794 (1987).

Rossi, Peter H. *Without Shelter: Homelessness in the 1980s.* New York: Priority Press Publications, 1989.

Rossi, Peter, and Wright, James. "The Determinants of Homelessness." *Health Affairs* 6:1 (1987).

U.S. GAO. *Homelessness: A Complex Problem and the Federal Response.* Washington DC: General Accounting Office, 1985.

Wright, James. "The Worthy and Unworthy Homeless." *Society* 25:5 (1988).

49
Untouchables*

Jonathan Kozol

On some nights, after a visit to the Martinique, I have returned to a hotel and steamed myself in a hot shower. Part of the reason is sheer physical exhaustion after walking up long flights of stairs, sitting cross-legged for several hours on a floor within a room in which there are no chairs, remaining sometimes until 3:00 or 4:00 A.M. in order to untangle complicated stories and to be quite sure I have the details right.

But another reason, which I feel some hesitation to confess, is the recognition of so much pathology, so much infection and contagious illness in the homeless population. The little girl that I call Raisin likes to put her fingers on my mouth to win herself a chance to talk. When she's in a thoughtful mood, she puts her fingers in her own mouth and she rests her head against my chest. When I get up to leave she holds her arms around my legs. It is impossible to wish to keep her at a distance. I feel ashamed when, later the same night, I scrub myself with a determination I associate with doctors in a Third World clinic.

So, in an undeniable and awful sense, even the children do become untouchables. Michael Ignatieff reflects on the responsibilities that bind us to the outcasts of a social order: "What are our obligations to those strangers at our gates? Take one step outside our zone of safety. . . . There they are, hands outstretched. . . ."[1] He is too generous to note that even our most natural inclinations may be thwarted by a practical consideration like the fear of illness.

The nightmare of the powerless, . . . "is that one day they will make their claim and the powerful will demand a reason, one day the look of entreaty will be met with the unknowing stare of force." That nightmare exists already in our nation. We do demand a reason for the claims made by the homeless families of our cities, and the reasons that they give do not always convince us. Ignatieff cites King Lear upon the heath: "O, reason not the need! . . . Allow not nature more than nature needs, man's life is cheap as beasts." We will return to this because it runs precisely counter to a currently held view that "basic needs"—food, roof or burial ditch—are all the poor have any right to ask and all they may expect. It may be enough for now to note that, in the cases we have just observed, even nature's minimal needs have not been met.

I think of a mother in the Allerton Hotel, twelve blocks from the

Martinique, who is forced to choose, when she goes shopping, between food or diapers for her children. Documentation gathered by David Beseda of the Coalition for the Homeless identifies the substitution of newspapers for diapers by the mothers of small children who must spend all of their allocated funds for concentrated formula and food for other children. Ignatieff's nightmare is made real each day within Manhattan's zone of danger. Once we escape that zone, the wish to wash ourselves — to scrub away the filth — may be more than a health precaution.

Richard Lazarus, an educated, thirty-six-year-old Vietnam veteran I met two days after Thanksgiving in the subway underneath Grand Central Station, tells me he had never been without a job until the recent summer. In July he underwent the loss of job, children and wife, all in a single stroke. As in almost all these situations, it was the simultaneous occurrence of a number of emergencies, any one of which he might sustain alone but not all at the same time, that suddenly removed him from his home

"Always, up until last summer, I have found a job that paid at least $300. Now I couldn't find a job that paid $200. When I found an opening at a department store they said that I was overqualified. If someone had asked me a year ago who are the homeless, I would not have known what to reply. Now I know the answer. They are people like myself. I went to Catholic elementary school. I had my secondary education in a private military school. I joined the service and was sent to Thailand as an airman." He has a trade. It's known as "inventory data processing." He had held a single job in data processing for seven years until last summer when the company shut down, without a warning, and moved out of state.

"When the company left I could find nothing. I looked everywhere. I got one job for two months in the summer. Part-time, as a security guard in one of the hotels for homeless families."

When I ask which one it was, he says the Martinique. "I clocked the floors for fire check. From the top floor to the lobby I swore to myself: rat infested, roach infested, drug infested, filth infested, garbage everywhere, and little children playing in the stairs. Innocent people, women, children, boxed in by their misery. Most people are permitted to make more than one mistake. Not when you're poor."

In September he was sick. "I was guarding homeless people and I didn't have a home. I slept in Washington Square and Central Park." He's living now in a run-down hotel operated in conjunction with the Third Street Shelter on the Bowery. "When you come in at night the guards wear gloves. They check you with a metal detector. They're afraid to touch me."

While we talk we watch an old man nearby who is standing flat and motionless against the wall, surrounded by two dozen bright-red shopping bags from Macy's. Every so often, someone stops to put a coin into his hand. I notice the care with which the people drop their coins, in order that their hands do not touch his. When I pass that spot some hours later he will still be there. I'll do the same. I'll look at his hand — the fingers worn and swollen and the nails curled in like claws—and I will drop a quarter and extract my hand and move off quickly.

After standing with Lazarus for two hours before a hot-dog stand, I ask him if he'd like to leave the station to sit down with me and get a decent meal. He's awkward about accepting this. When I press him, he explains he had only one subway token and has no more money. If he leaves the station he will need a dollar to get back inside. He agrees to leave when I assure him I can spare a dollar. Outside on Forty-second Street, we're facing the Grand Hyatt. He looks at it with fear.

"The first thing that you see when you come out of there is power."

At a delicatessen next to the Grand Hyatt he explains about the subway tokens. Each morning at the shelter you get in a line in order to receive two subway tokens. This is to enable you to look for jobs; the job search is required. But, in order to get the tokens, you have got to prove that you already have a job appointment. "It's a long line. By the time you get the tokens you have missed the job appointment. You wait in line for everything. I get the feeling that the point is not to find a job but to teach us something about who we are. Getting us in line is the idea."

In the restaurant he orders a chicken sandwich and, although he's nervous and his hands are shaking, he eats fast; he's almost done before I've put a paper napkin in my lap. He apologizes but he tells me that this is the first thing he has had to eat since 8:00 A.M. It's now about 8:30 in the evening.

"Before I got into this place I was sleeping in the parks. When it got colder I would sleep all night in an X-rated movie or the subway or the Port Authority. I'd spend most of my time just walking. I would try to bathe each day in public toilets. I'd wash my clothes and lay them outside in the sun to dry. I didn't want to feel like a pariah that nobody would get near. I used to talk with people like yourself so that I would not begin to feel cut off. I invested all my strength in fighting off depression. I was scared that I would fall apart.

"During this time I tried to reunite with my old lady. For me, the loss of work and loss of wife had left me rocking. Then the welfare regulations hit me. I began to feel that I would be reduced to trash. You're never prepared for this. It's like there isn't any bottom. It's not like cracks in a safety net. It's like a black hole sucking you inside. Half the people that I know are suffering from chest infections and sleep deprivation. The lack of sleep leaves you debilitated, shaky. You exaggerate your fears. If a psychiatrist came along he'd say that I was crazy. But I was an ordinary man. There was nothing wrong with me. I lost my wife. I lost my kids. I lost my home. Now would you say that I was crazy if I told you I was feeling sad?

"I was a pretty stable man. Now I tremble when I meet somebody in the ordinary world. I'm trembling right now. One reason that I didn't want to leave the subway was that I feel safer underground. When you asked if I would come outside and get something to eat, my first thought was that you would see me shaking if we sat down for a meal and you'd think I was an alcoholic.

"I've had a bad cold for two weeks. When you're sick there's no way to get better. You cannot sleep in at the shelter. You have *got* to go outside and show that you are looking for a job. I had asthma as a kid. It was gone for twenty years. Now it's back. I'm always swallowing for air. Before I got into the shelter, I did not have Medicaid or welfare. If you don't have an address it's very hard. I scrambled to get into the computer.

"Asthma's common at the shelter. There's a lot of dust. That may be why. Edema [swollen feet]—you get it from sitting up so much and walking all day long. If you're very hungry and you want a meal you can get it at St. Francis. You can get a sandwich at Grand Central every night at ten o'clock. So if you want to keep from starving you are always on the move. If you have no subway tokens then you jump the stile. So you're always breaking rules and so you start to have this sense of premonition: 'Sooner or later I'll be caught.' You live in constant fear.

"The welfare workers are imperious and punctual. No matter how desperate you are, they're short of time. I ask them: 'Will my records go upstairs?' They snap at me: 'Can't you see that we're about to close?' All I asked them was a simple question.

"A year ago I never thought that somebody like me would end up in a shelter. Nothing you've ever undergone prepares you. You walk into the place—the smell of sweat and urine hits you like a wall. Unwashed bodies and the look of absolute despair on many, many faces there would make you think you were in Dante's Hell. Abandon hope. I read a lot. I'm not a lazy man.

"I slept with my clothes on the first night that I was there. I was given a cot but they were out of sheets. I lay awake. I heard men crying in their sleep. They're sound asleep and they are *crying*. What you fear is that you will be here forever. You do not know if it's ever going to end. You think to yourself: It is a dream and I will wake. Sometimes I think: It's an experiment. They are watching you to find out how much you can take. Someone will come someday and say: 'Okay, this guy has suffered long enough. Now we'll take him back into our world.' Then you wake up and get in line. . . .

"Listen to me: I've always worked. I need to work! I'm not a lazy man." His voices rises and the people at the other tables stare. "If I thought that I could never work again I'd want to die."

He explains to me that you can work inside the shelter for a token salary. For twenty hours' work they pay $12.50. He has done this. "Even sixty cents an hour makes you feel that you are not completely dead. It may be slave labor but it gets you certain privileges, like being first in line for meals. I'm one of the residents they like because I follow all the rules. Those rules are very important. If you make a single error you are out. More than that, you lose your benefits. You put your welfare card in the machine. 'NO BENEFITS. YOUR CASE IS CLOSED.' You're dead. It's thirty days before your case can be reopened.

"When I'm very scared I go into the public library to read. You have to stay awake. They throw you out the minute that you close your eyes. When I was at rockbottom I went to a priest. It was the first time I had asked to be confessed in twenty years. Alone in that big beautiful church, it occurred to me that the Creator had been teaching me a lesson that I'd never learned. 'I've given you a couple of gifts. Now share them with your brothers.' I would ask if there could be a God. Then I'd say: 'We have free will. God did not do this to me.' That's all. That's my theology.

"My only relatives alive in New York City are my father and my children and my wife. My father's in the Hebrew Home for the Aged. He's eighty-three. He's had several strokes. So I can't tell him what has happened. When I go there I put on the cleanest clothes I have. He asks about the children and I tell him everything is fine.

"The worst thing I have ever undergone was when I lost my wife. She was my guidance system. If I can ever get a job I'll save up money for a while. I'll stay in the shelter so that I can save enough to put down money for a home."

I ask him if he can save money.

"Not officially. You do it off the books."

He tells me his wife is doubled up for now in somebody's apartment with his children. At ten o'clock he says he has to get back to the shelter. "Curfew's at eleven. If you miss it, then you sleep outside." I ask for his address. He writes it out: Kenton Hotel, 8 East Third Street. Bed number 135.

"I'm a number. When I was evicted I was given a court docket number. When I got on welfare I received another number. Now I'm in the shelter I have a bed number. If my wife and I can get our kids in a hotel someday, we'll have another number, a room number. I have to keep repeating to myself: I have a name. I was born. I have a mother and a father. I am not a number.

"When you go to welfare the first thing you have to do is show them that you have a birth certificate. Many people lost their birth certificate when they were dispossessed. Or you lose it in the streets or in the shelter if somebody steals your clothes. But you have to prove that you were born in order to receive a check. Why do they do this? How much can you stand?"

We say good-bye outside the subway ramp on Forty-second Street. I give him the dollar — he refuses to take more — and we shake hands. I write to him later but I've never gotten a response. It's possible that, in my haste, I got the wrong bed number. Back in the zone of safety in my clean hotel I wash my hands.

Many homeless people, unable to get into shelters, frightened of disease or violence, or else intimidated by the regulations, look for refuge in such public places as train stations and church doorways.

Scores of people sleep in the active subway tunnels of Manhattan, inches from 600-volt live rails. Many more sleep on the ramps and station platforms. Go into the subway station under Herald Square on a December night at twelve o'clock and you will see what scarce accommodations mean at the rockbottom. Emerging from the subway, walk on Thirty-second Street to Penn Station. There you will see another form of scarce accommodations: Hot-air grates in the area are highly prized. Homeless people who arrive late often find there is no vacancy, even in a cardboard box over a grate.

A man who's taken shelter from the wind that sweeps Fifth Avenue by sleeping beneath the outstretched arms of Jesus on the bronze doors of St. Patrick's Cathedral tells a reporter he can't sleep there anymore because shopkeepers feel that he is hurting business. He moves to the south side of the church where he will be less visible.

Stories like these are heard in every state and city of the nation. A twenty-year-old man in Florida tells me that he ran away when he was nine years old from a juvenile detention home in Michigan. He found that he was small enough to slip his body through the deposit slot of a Good Will box. Getting in was easy, he explains, and it was warm because of the clothes and quilts and other gifts that people dropped into the box. "Getting out," he says, "was not so easy. I had to reach my arms above my head, grab hold of the metal edge, twist my body into an *S*, and pull myself out slowly through the slot. When I was fourteen I was too big to fit into the slot. I believe I am the only person in America who has lived for five years in a Good Will box."

Thousands of American people live in dumpsters behind restaurants, hotels, and groceries. A woman describes the unimaginable experience of being awakened in the middle of a winter's night by several late-arriving garbage trucks. She nearly drowned beneath two tons of rotting vegetables and fruit.

A thirty-four-year-old man in Chicago found his sanctuary in a broken trash compactor. This offered perhaps the ultimate concealment, and the rotting food which generated heat may have protected him against the freezing weather of Chicago. One night, not knowing that the trash compactor had in his absence been repaired, he fell asleep. When the engine was turned on, he was compressed into a cube of refuse.

People in many cities speak of spending nights in phone booths. I have seen this only in New York. Public telephones in Grand Central Station are aligned in recessed areas outside the main concourse. On almost any night before one-thirty, visitors will see a score of people stuffed into these booths with their belongings. Even phone-booth vacancies are scarce in New York City. As in public housing, people are sometimes obliged to double up. One night I stood for an hour and observed three people — man, woman, and child — jammed into a single booth. All three were asleep.

Officials have tried a number of times to drive the homeless from Grand Central Station. In order to make conditions less attractive, benches have been removed throughout the terminal. One set of benches has been left there, I am told, because they have been judged "historic landmarks." The terminal's 300 lockers, used in former times by homeless people to secure their few belongings, were removed in 1986. Authorities were forced to justify this action by declaring them, in the words of the city council, "a threat to public safety." Shaving, cleaning of clothes, and other forms of hygiene are prohibited in the men's room of Grand Central. A fast-food chain that wanted to distribute unsold donuts in the terminal was denied the right to do so on the grounds that this would draw more hungry people.

At one-thirty every morning, homeless people are ejected from Grand Central. Many have attempted to take refuge on the ramp that leads to Forty-second Street. The ramp initially provided a degree of warmth because it was protected from the street by wooden doors. The station management responded to this challenge in two ways. First, the ramp was mopped with a strong mixture of ammonia to produce a noxious smell. When the people sleeping there brought cardboard boxes and newspapers to protect them from the fumes, the entrance doors were chained wide open. Temperatures dropped some nights to ten degrees.

In a case that won brief press attention in December 1985, an elderly woman who had been living in Grand Central on one of the few remaining benches was removed night after night during the weeks preceding Christmas. On Christmas Eve she became ill. No ambulance was called. At one-thirty the police compelled her to move to the ramp outside. At dawn she came inside, climbed back on bench number 9 to sleep, and died that morning of pneumonia.

At Penn Station, fifteen blocks away, homeless women are denied use of the bathroom. Amtrak police come by and herd them off each hour on the hour. In June of 1985, Amtrak officials issued this directive to police: "It is the policy of Amtrak to not allow the homeless and undesirables to remain. . . . Officers are encouraged to eject all undesirables. . . . Now is the time to train and educate them that their presence will not be tolerated as cold weather sets in." In an internal memo, according to CBS, an Amtrak official later went beyond this language and asked flatly: "Can't we get rid of this trash?"

In a surprising action, the union representing the police resisted this directive and brought suit against Penn Station's management in 1986. Nonetheless, as temperatures plunged during the nights after Thanksgiving, homeless men and women were ejected from the station. At 2:00 A.M. I watched a man about my age carry his cardboard box outside the station and try to construct a barricade against the wind that tore across Eighth Avenue. The man was so cold his fingers shook and, when I spoke to him, he tried but could not answer.

Driving women from the toilets in a railroad station raises questions that go far beyond the issue of "deterrence." It may surprise the reader to be told that many of these women are quite young. Few are dressed in the familiar rags that are suggested by the term "bag ladies." Some are dressed so neatly and conceal their packages and bags so skillfully that one finds it hard to differentiate them from commuters waiting for a train. Given the denial of hygienic opportunities, it is difficult to know how they are able to remain presentable. The sight of clusters of police officials, mostly male, guarding a women's toilet from its use by homeless females does not speak well for the public conscience of New York.

Where do these women defecate? How do they bathe? What will we do when, in her physical distress, a woman finally disrobes in public and begins to urinate right on the floor? We may regard her as an animal. She may by then begin to view herself in the same way.

Several cities have devised unusual measures to assure that homeless people will learn quickly that they are not welcome. In Laramie, Wyoming, they are given one night's shelter. On the next morning, an organization called "The Good Samaritan Fund" gives them one-way tickets to another town. The college town of Lancaster, Ohio, offers homeless families one-way tickets to Columbus.

In a number of states and cities, homeless people have been murdered, knifed, or set on fire. Two high school students in California have been tried for the knife murder of a homeless man whom they found sleeping in a park. The man, an unemployed house painter, was stabbed seventeen times before his throat was slashed.

In Chicago a man was set ablaze while sleeping on a bench in early morning, opposite a popular restaurant. Rush-hour commuters passed him and his charred possessions for four hours before someone called police at noon. A man who watched him burning from a third-floor room above the bench refused to notify police. The purpose was "to get him out," according to a local record-store employee. A resident told reporters that the problem of the homeless was akin to that of "nuclear waste."

In Tucson, where police use German shepherds to hunt for the homeless in the skid-row neighborhoods, a mayor was recently elected on the promise that he'd drive the homeless out of town. "We're tired of it. Tired of feeling guilty about these people," said an anti-homeless activist in Phoenix.

In several cities it is a crime to sleep in public; in some, armrests have been inserted in the middle of park benches to make it impossible for homeless people to lie down. In others, trash has been defined as "public property," making it a felony to forage in the rotted food.

Grocers in Santa Barbara sprinkled bleach on food discarded in their dumpsters. In Portland, Oregon, owners of some shops in redeveloped Old Town have designed slow-dripping gutters (they are known as "drip lines") to prevent the homeless from attempting to take shelter underneath their awnings.

Harsher tactics have been recommended in Fort Launderdale. A city council member offered a proposal to spray trash containers with rat poison to discourage foraging by homeless families. The way to "get rid of vermin," he observed, is to cut their food supply. Some of these policies have been defeated, but the inclination to sequester, punish and conceal the homeless has attracted wide support.

"We are the rejected waste of the society," said Lazarus. "They use us, if they think we have some use, maybe for sweeping leaves or scrubbing off graffiti in the subway stations. They don't object if we donate our blood. I've given plasma. That's one way that even worthless people can do something for democracy. We may serve another function too. Perhaps we help to scare the people who still have a home — even a place that's got no heat, that's rat infested, filthy. If they see us in the streets, maybe they are scared enough so they will learn not to complain. If they were thinking about asking for a better heater or a better stove, they're going to think twice. It's like farmers posting scarecrows in the fields. People see these terrifying figures in Penn Station and they know, with one false step, that they could be here too. They think: 'I better not complain.' " . . .

What startles most observers is not simply that such tragedies persist in the United States, but that almost all have been well documented and that even the most solid documentation does not bring about corrective action. Instead of action, a common response in New York, as elsewhere, is the forming of a "task force" to investigate. This is frequently the last we hear of it. Another substitute for action is a press event at which a city official seems to overlap immediate concerns by the unveiling of a plan to build a thousand, or a hundred thousand, homes over the course of ten or twenty years at an expense of several billion dollars. The sweep of these announcements tends to dwarf the urgency of the initial issue. When, after a year or so, we learn that little has been done and that the problem has grown worse, we tend to feel not outrage but exhaustion. Exhaustion, however, as we have seen, turns easily to a less generous reaction.

"I am about to be heartless," wrote a columnist in *Newsweek* in December 1986. "There are people living on the streets . . . turning sidewalks into dormitories. They are called the homeless. . . . Often they are called worse. They are America's living nightmare. . . . They have got to go."

The author notes that it is his taxes which pay for the paving and the cleaning of the streets they call their home. "That makes me their landlord. I want to evict them."

A senior at Boston University sees homeless people on the streets not far from where he goes to class. He complains that measures taken recently to drive them from the area have not been sufficiently aggressive: "I would very much like to see actions more severe . . ." Perhaps, he admits, it isn't possible to have them all arrested, though this notion seems to hold appeal for him; perhaps "a more suitable middle ground" may be arrived at to prevent this "nauseating . . . element" from being permitted to "run free so close to my home."

"Our response," says one Bostonian, "has gone from indifference to pitying . . . to hatred." I think this is coming to be true and that it marks an incremental stage in our capacity to view the frail, the ill, the dispossessed, the unsuccessful not as people who have certain human qualities we share but as an outcaste entity. From harsh deterrence to punitive incarceration to the willful cutting off of life supports is an increasingly short journey. "I am proposing triage of a sort, triage by self-selection," writes Charles Murray. "The patient always has the right to fail. Society always has the right to let him."

Why is it that writings which present these hardened attitudes seem to prevail so easily in public policy? It may be that kindly voices are more easily derided. Callous attitudes are never subject to the charge of being sentimental. It is a recurrent theme in *King Lear*, writes Ignatieff, that "there is a truth in the brutal simplicities of the merciless which the more complicated truth of the merciful is helpless to refute." A rich man, he observes, "never lacks for arguments to deny the poor his charity. 'Basest beggars' can always be found to be 'in the poorest things superfluous.'"

"They are a nightmare. I evict them. They will have to go."

So from pity we graduate to weariness; from weariness to impatience; from impatience to annoyance; from annoyance to dislike and sometimes to contempt.

"No excuses are good enough," the *New York Times* observed in reference to the Holland Hotel in 1985, a year before I spoke with Mrs. Andrews of her stay in that hotel. But, in the event, excuses did suffice. The city did, and does, continue to send children to the Holland and to many similar hotels. Nearly 200 families, with 450 children, are stilling living in the Holland as I write.

Can it be these children have by now become not simply noxious or unclean in our imagination but something like an ulcer to society, a cancer, a malignant growth?

"If the point is to dispose of us most economically," said Lazarus, "why do they need to go to all this trouble and expense? Why not end this misery efficiently? Why not a lethal injection?"

This question, voiced in panic and despair, is one perhaps that he would not have posed if he were in a less tormented state of mind. There is an answer. I believe it should be stated here because the rhetoric of desperation may be taken, otherwise, for a realistic vision of America as it exists today. The answer is that we have failed in many ways to do what conscience and American ideals demand but have yet to fall so far as to wish anyone's demise. Despite the grave injustices that we allow, or lack the power to confront, we do not in fact want to "dispose" of *any* people—or "compact" them into concentration camps or any other institutions of internment. The truth is: We do not know what we want to do with these poor people. We leave them, therefore, in a limbo and, while waiting in that limbo, many who are very young do cease to be a burden to society.

But the question of this shaken man emerging from the underground of New York's subway system to gaze up at the Grand Hyatt may suggest a slightly different question: Might a day come in the not-too-distant future when a notion of this sort may be proposed and not regarded as abhorrent? It has happened in other advanced societies. We know this, and we also know that no society is totally exempt from entertaining "rational" solutions of this kind.

State terrorism as social welfare policy—which is, I think, a fair description of what Lazarus, a credible witness of life at the bottom in Manhattan, has perceived—has not yet achieved acceptance in our social order; but it may no longer be regarded as beyond imagination. When we speak the unspeakable, think the unthinkable, and permit the impermissible, we are not far from a final darkness.

NOTE

1. Michael Ignatieff, *The Needs of Strangers: An Essay on Privacy, Solidarity, and the Politics of Being Human* (New York: Penguin Books, 1984).

50
The Messiah Mayors*
Jon C. Teaford

. . . [D]uring the 1980s, the older [cities] were . . . benefiting from a nationwide boom in office employment and business and professional services. Though new office buildings meant good news for central-city mayors in search of tax dollars, the inventory of suburban office space was expanding at a more rapid rate than that in the urban core, and the growth in suburban office employment far outpaced that of New York, Chicago, or Philadelphia. Many major corporations were relocating their back-office operations outside of the city, moving thousands of employees to suburbia or beyond.

For example, Citicorp shifted its credit card operations from New York City to South Dakota; Mutual of New York transferred back-office workers to suburban Westchester County; Bankers Trust likewise moved 1,200 to 1,400 employees to Jersey City; and Morgan Bank built its data processing and operations center on a 158-acre site in suburban Delaware.[1] Between 1977 and 1986 insurance companies cut the number of their employees in New York City from 75,000 to 65,000, whereas the surrounding suburban counties in New York State recorded a gain of 5,700 insurance jobs, and northeastern New Jersey had almost 7,000 additional workers in this industry.[2] Between 1982 and 1985 Manhattan's share of office space in the New York City metropolitan area dropped from 67 percent to 60 percent, and in 1986 developers added 16.1 million square feet of offices to the suburban supply whereas Manhattan gained 7.6 million square feet.[3] By the late 1980s Michigan's suburban Oakland County could claim more office

*Teaford, Jon C. 1990. "The Messiah Mayors." Pp. 295–307 in *The Rough Road to Renaissance: Urban Revitalization in America, 1940–1985*. Baltimore: Johns Hopkins University Press. Copyright © 1990 by Johns Hopkins University. Reprinted by permission of Johns Hopkins University Press.

space than the central city of Detroit. In fact, the two suburban communities of Southfield and Troy had a combined office inventory virtually equal to that of the Motor City.[4]

Overall employment figures also demonstrated that suburbia was outpacing the central cities during the late 1970s and the early 1980s. For example, employment in Mayor Koch's New York was growing at a considerably slower rate than in nearby suburbia. In 1977 New York City accounted for nearly half the jobs in the metropolitan area, but during the ensuing decade, it could claim only about 30 percent of the new employment.[5] Similarly, Boston proudly boasted of a 16 percent rise in employment between 1976 and 1985, but during these same years, New England as a whole recorded a 27 percent gain in the number of jobs and the national rate was 23 percent.[6] Meanwhile, between 1980 and 1986 the renaissance city of Baltimore recorded a net loss of 7,700 jobs, a weak showing compared with nearby Washington, D.C., or suburban Maryland.[7] Philadelphia's annual employment growth rate for 1980–86 was −0.6 percent compared with +1.2 percent for the metropolitan area as a whole and +1.5 percent for the United States.[8] The annual rate in Mayor Schoemehl's Saint Louis was −1.8 percent from 1980 through 1985, actually worse than the −0.9 percent average for the 1970s.[9]

America's urban renaissance was, then, only a relative phenomenon. The central-city economy of the mid-1980s was generally better than it had been in the mid-1970s, but compared with suburbia or the nation as a whole, even the most prosperous of the older central cities seemed sluggish at best. Moreover, the central-city office construction boom of the 1980s was no greater than that of the late 1960s and early 1970s. At the close of the 1980s no soaring giants had topped such creations of the early 1970s as Chicago's Sears Tower or New York City's World Trade Center. Instead, the 1980s office construction bonanza could be seen as a continuation of an office boom that had been in progress since the late 1950s and had suffered only a momentary interruption in the mid-1970s. If new office towers and an expanding business and professional service sector were symptoms of urban rebirth, then the gestation period for this new life had begun at least a quarter of a century earlier.

But the office sector was not the only sign of economic hope for the central city. The much-publicized growth in tourism and convention business and the accompanying boom in hotel construction also signaled revitalization. In Boston more than 4,000 new hotel rooms opened for visitors between 1980 and 1985, more than the total constructed during the entire half century from 1930 to 1980. Moreover, Boston's hotel employment soared 109 percent between 1976 and 1985.[10] In downtown Baltimore the number of available hotel rooms tripled between 1980 and 1986 as did the figures for tourist visits and expenditures.[11] Unknown to convention goers prior to 1980, Baltimore was capturing an increasing share of the meeting business, and the Saint Louis "Meeting Place" campaign also seemed to be placing the Missouri metropolis on the convention map. With newly fashioned "fun" images, former models of dullness and despair like Baltimore and Saint Louis were reaping financial rewards.

But for every older central city winning in the convention game, there was a loser. For example, tourism and convention business was not fueling a rebirth in Philadelphia; instead, the hotel business in the City of Brotherly Love was as dismal as ever. In 1985 downtown Philadelphia had 6,200 hotel rooms compared with 6,300 a decade earlier. Despite charging the lowest room prices in the Northeast, the occupancy rate in 1985 dropped below 55 percent, the worst in the Boston-Washington megalopolis. Between July 1, 1984, and June 30, 1985, the fifteen major downtown hotels lost a total of $36.5 million, leading the *Philadelphia Inquirer* to pronounce the local lodging industry "desperately ill."[12] Moreover, the immediate future held little promise. An expert on the lodging business observed: "The city's hotel industry faces a bleak future. Some hotels are going to down-size or go out of business. Business is dead for the remainder of this decade."[13] Among the casualties was the historic Bellevue Stratford, which closed in 1986, only eight years after a $25 million remodeling.[14]

Many attributed the Bellevue Stratford's fate to the absence of a modern convention center in the Pennsylvania metropolis, and throughout the 1980s Philadelphia leaders fought over the construction of a new meeting facility to replace the outmoded Civic Center. After its formation in 1982, a convention-center steering committee proceeded to hire a consulting firm and in 1983 selected the site of the Reading Railroad terminal adjacent to the Gallery shopping mall as the best location for the new center. A successful campaign for state aid ensued, and construction of the facility seemed imminent in 1986. At that time a spokesman for the Philadelphia Convention and Visitors Bureau confidently reported, "Everything's in place . . . We're very optimistic."[15] But dispute over the site revived in 1987 with the architecture critic for the *Philadelphia Inquirer* attacking it, and a coalition of neighborhood groups brought suit to halt the project. In January 1988 one observer of the struggle reported, "Philadelphia is still far from having a new convention center."[16]

Philadelphia was not, then, to receive its fair share of the revitalizing bounty of America's convention business. And some visitors felt the city's ill fortune was well deserved. In the mid-1980s one participant at a beauty care and hair salon convention held in Philadelphia was so angered by the experience that he placed a full-page ad in a trade journal expressing his views. According to this outraged visitor: "Some of the hotels were without a doubt the worst we had encountered. If we had had a choice, we'd have picked tents and sleeping bags . . . The food at the Convention Center was right out of the Hanoi prison system." "What can I say about this city?" the ad continued. "Beirut is cleaner. There must be a city ordinance against cutting the grass and picking up the refuse."[17] Moreover, the editor of *Philadelphia* magazine agreed, responding to the complaints by calling the city "shabby, dirty and unappealing."[18] In a nationwide survey a convention-center consulting firm found that people throughout the country shared this impression. In the 1980s as in the 1940s, Philadelphia had a reputation as a "dirty, boring city."[19] Mayor Schaefer's Baltimore may have successfully repackaged itself in flashy new wrappings, but Philadelphia was still deemed dismal and deteriorating.

Philadelphia was not the only loser in the convention game. All the efforts of Mayor Voinovich and his fellow boosters could not transform Cleveland into a meeting mecca. In 1987 the owner of two of Cleveland's four downtown hotels attacked the local convention bureau for failure to attract meetings; he claimed that his establishments had only a 35 percent to 40 percent occupancy rate and had lost $3 million in the past four years. When asked by the *Plain Dealer* whether Cleveland was a comeback city, the hotel owner responded: "You might say that anyone who believes that . . . is either on marijuana or heroin. It's [that] far away from reality."[20] In reply, the convention bureau president admitted that his agency was not as successful in attracting conventions and hotel bookings as it had been ten years earlier, but he blamed this partially on the lack of adequate hotel space for large meetings.[21] Actually, in the first half of the 1980s no major hotel chain had been willing to make a commitment to downtown Cleveland. Despite all the positive rhetoric and the attempts at image refurbishing, Hyatt and Hilton knew that investing in Cleveland would be a mistake.

Buffalo could boast a Hilton and a Hyatt, but it proved equally unattractive to convention planners. In 1979 the city constructed a $22 million convention center that four years later the *Washington Post* described as "something of an embarrassment." The facility attracted only four major events in 1982, losing $400,000 and drawing fewer than five thousand visitors. In 1983 a spokesman for the Chamber of Commerce admitted, "We have an image problem," but with the optimism of a good booster he proclaimed, "Without a doubt, conventions and tourism are the most encouraging light on the horizon for this community."[22] Only in dismally depressed Buffalo could a $400,000 deficit rank as the most encouraging light on the horizon.

Overall, the older central cities were doing better than Buffalo, but they were not proving inordinately successful in the competition for the convention trade. By 1986 New York City and Chicago headed the list of convention destinations, hosting more delegates than any other cities. Not one of the ten other older central cities, however, ranked among the top ten gathering places. Instead, Sunbelt communities such as Dallas, Houston, Las Vegas, and Anaheim followed New York and Chicago on the list and were acquiring a growing share of meeting business.[23]

Not even the most applauded tourist draw of the older central cities proved a total success. Baltimore's Inner Harbor with its festival marketplace and aquarium was the envy of places like Cleveland and Philadelphia, but one element of Mayor Schaefer's complex proved a bomb. To add to the fun in downtown Baltimore, in 1985 the Six Flags corporation transformed a derelict power plant adjacent to the harbor into an attraction that was billed as "the nation's first urban theme park."[24] According to the Urban Land

Institute, it was "designed to attract affluent 25- to 40-year-old adults" and to provide employment for two hundred Baltimore residents.[25] The power plant's marketing director stated, "[I don't] think there's any way it won't work," and press releases proclaimed it "the most spectacular indoor entertainment facility ever imagined."[26] The theme park, however, never made money and closed in January 1987. Amid all the upbeat publicity, the failure of the Six Flags Power Plant received little notice. Just as the media hyped the success of Boston's Quincy Market and ignored the failure of nearby Lafayette Place, the shortcomings of Baltimore and the erroneous investments at Inner Harbor were overlooked. During the late 1970s and the 1980s, Cleveland had to be proclaimed a comeback city even if it was not, and Baltimore had to be painted pink by image makers even though much of it was dull gray.

Like convention centers, mass transit had been touted as a leading panacea for central-city woes in the 1970s, but by the mid-1980s transit realities also seemed to fall short of the promoters' hype. Generally, the much-awaited transit projects proved more expensive than expected, attracted less patronage, and reaped fewer benefits. Perhaps no city placed greater faith in the miracle-working propensities of rail transit than had Buffalo. Since the early 1970s, local advocates of a rail system envisioned it as the stimulus for a resurgent city. Optimism gradually waned, however, as the scheme's price soared, the miles of proposed trackage shrank, and construction delays mounted. Though Mayor Griffin continued to count on the new subway to ignite a downtown renaissance, in 1983 an expert at the Brookings Institution expressed less sanguine sentiments. He argued, "The main advantage of a subway is that it's a gigantic public works project," but he noted, "Once it's built, it doesn't pay for itself."[27]

This observation proved accurate, for in 1986 the *New York Times* reported that according to a state study group, "Buffalo's year-old rapid-transit line might be forced to shut down unless a new source of revenue is found to cover its operating deficits."[28] The Buffalo line was carrying only twenty-one thousand to twenty-three thousand riders per day as compared to the projected forty-five thousand, and fares covered less than 20 percent of operating costs. Confronted by budget woes, transit officials were forced to delay completion of the downtown pedestrian mall that was expected to be the capstone of the scheme. Instead, the chief retailing thoroughfare remained torn up, causing the transit authority's executive director to call downtown Buffalo "Beirut."[29] In 1986 the subway's superintendent still insisted, "There is all the potential in the world for this system to be a very big asset to Buffalo," and completion of the line to the south campus of the state university was expected to boost ridership. But others were fed up with the scheme. A suburban councilman organized Citizens Against Rapid Transit Extensions and argued that "the whole thing [had] been a perfect 10 in bad decision-making."[30]

Meanwhile, Detroit was the scene of an even more publicized and more troubled transit initiative. By the early 1980s Detroit's hopes for a regional rapid transit system had produced only plans for a 2.9-mile People Mover looping around downtown on an elevated track. Seemingly this mini-line should have proved a manageable endeavor, but its construction was fraught with difficulties. When it was discovered that the concrete guideway beams were cracking and prone to shattering, the whole project seemed threatened. By 1985 the chairman of the Southeastern Michigan Transportation Authority was admitting, "Ever since we began this project, all we have had is pain on top of pain," and the unsympathetic director of the federal Urban Mass Transportation Administration had nicknamed the costly scheme "the price mover."[31] Moreover, in 1986 a journalist with the *Detroit News* complained that the People Mover's $210 million expenditure "could have purchased 1,000 new buses, 12,000 vans for transporting the poor, elderly, and handicapped, or a new subcompact auto for every low-income household that now lacks a car."[32]

Finally, in the summer of 1987 Detroit's People Mover opened to passengers, a year and a half behind schedule and with a price tag that was $73 million above the original estimate. After a preview ride, a *Detroit Free Press* columnist called the Mover a "$200.3 million carnival ride," but his newspaper's editorial board looked forward to further transit projects, announcing optimistically, "The People Mover may get plans for rail transit back on track."[33] By the beginning of 1988, however, the People Mover was transporting only about eleven thousand people daily compared with the original prediction of seventy-five thousand. And a visiting Chicago journalist found that most of the passengers were not downtown workers as expected but "wide-eyed gawkers, curious tourists and nostalgic city residents."[34] Given the massive investment, eleven thousand curiosity seekers hardly seemed an adequate dividend. As one *Free Press* journalist commented: "The cost of this spiffy, super-tech transit system demands that it be much more than a tourist attraction."[35]

Elsewhere transit expenditures produced better returns but also reaped many critics. Baltimore opened its first rapid transit line without suffering Detroit's manifold embarrassments. But when Governor Schaefer sought state funding for an extension of the system, a *Baltimore Sun* poll found that only 15.7 percent of the respondents in the metropolitan area said they would ever use the proposed rail line. Moreover, representatives from the Maryland suburbs of Washington, D.C., attacked the scheme as a "boondoggle."[36] In fact, boondoggle was a word used increasingly when referring to rapid transit projects, and in 1983 *Harper's* printed an article that referred to rail schemes as "the billion-dollar boondoggle that can't beat the bus."[37] In some cities with long-established rapid transit systems, billions of additional dollars also did not solve transportation problems or end the chorus of criticisms. At the close of 1986 an article on New York's subways complained, "Cities like Toronto and Paris have quiet, clean trains, but New Yorkers have to endure delays, breakdowns, filth, crimes, fires, graffiti, faulty signs and air conditioners, and, now, a triple-digit fare."[38] When asked to compare the New York transit system in 1986 with that of ten years earlier, one New Yorker expressed a typical sentiment, "I don't care whether it's better or worse, but it's terrible the way it is."[39]

Though some cities were still attempting to dun the federal government for money to build rail systems, by the mid-1980s, the rapid transit boom seemed to have passed. Baltimore and Buffalo had completed functioning rail lines, but many questioned whether the benefits justified the costs. Boston and New York had made transit improvements, though not enough to satisfy their steadfast patrons or lure many additional passengers. Transit schemes might aid downtowns and reinforce the central-city economies, yet they would not revolutionize urban America. In 1985 Americans still lived in an automobile age just as they had in 1975 and 1965.

Thus in the 1980s the United States was not experiencing a transportation revolution, though it was in the midst of an economic transformation that had both positive and negative consequences for the older urban hubs. Those central cities fortunate enough to attract conventions could boast of new hotel and restaurant jobs, and the employment figures for financial institutions and business and professional services proved that one city after another did have some economic future. Jobs were being created in the central cities, and they were not doomed to be welfare wastelands. Yet the economic transformation of the late 1970s and 1980s also created employment problems. As central-city factories closed, blue-collar workers lost good-paying jobs and seemingly had little hope of success in the new service economy of the postindustrial city. The unskilled jobs in the convention hotels, burgeoning fast-food restaurants, or the expanding hospital complexes paid little more than minimum wage, far less than the manufacturing jobs that were migrating to the suburbs, the American South or Southwest, or to Asia. In addition, displaced factory workers had little chance of landing well-paying positions in business services or the professions. One could not move readily from the assembly line to the offices of Arthur Andersen. Accounting firms needed trained personnel as did law offices. Those workers who could operate a welding iron or wrench but not a computer seemed destined for unemployment or the counter of McDonalds.

This growing mismatch of skills between city residents and new job openings was especially serious because of the failure of central-city schools to adequately train youths and the high dropout rate among inner-city teenagers. In New York City the dropout rate was nearly 50 percent, in Chicago it was 45 percent, and in Boston 43 percent.[40] Moreover, on a typical day one-third of the students in Chicago's schools were absent. Judged by national standards, the central-city educational record was dismal with only one-third of Chicago's pupils reading at or above their grade level. By 1988 one-half of the Windy City's public high schools ranked in the lowest 1 percent in the performance of their students on the national ACT tests. That year a local journalist warned, "The situation has deteriorated so badly that exasperated businessmen . . . complain that Chicago students lack the basic reading and writing skills for even minimum-wage employment."[41] Neither the rising office towers downtown nor the newly opened

Neiman-Marcus store on North Michigan Avenue offered any economic hope for these teenagers. The reborn city was a dead-end for them.

In fact, suburban commuters were the chief beneficiaries of the growing supply of downtown office jobs. The number of jobs in New York City rose 7 percent between 1977 and 1984, but the number of employed city residents increased only 1 percent.[42] Most of the new jobs were going to suburbanites with the requisite skills. The same trend was evident in other cities. Between 1969 and 1979 in downtown Baltimore the proportion of workers who lived in the city dropped from 58 percent to 46 percent, and the highest-paying positions went to suburban dwellers.[43]

Meanwhile, despite all the rhetoric of revitalization, central-city residents remained disproportionately poor. In 1984 after thirteen years of Mayor Schaefer's leadership, Baltimore's unemployment rate was 7.4 percent, or more than 40 percent higher that the state average of 5.2 percent.[44] Every year from 1977 through 1985 the unemployment rate for Boston stood well above the Massachusetts figure.[45] Moreover, the number of those falling below the poverty level fixed by the federal government was increasing in the New England metropolis. Sixteen percent of Bostonians had an income below the poverty line in 1970; by 1985 the figure was 20 percent, and the Boston Redevelopment Authority estimated that it would rise to 23 percent in 1990.[46] The fate of central-city minority groups was particularly gloomy. With too many dropouts and too few jobs in manufacturing, blacks and Hispanics did not benefit from the purported renaissance as much as non-Hispanic whites. In 1987 in New York City the unemployment rate for non-Hispanic whites was 3.1 percent but for minorities it was 8.5 percent.[47] A year earlier an extraordinary 20 percent of Pittsburgh blacks were jobless compared with less than 4 percent of the city's whites.[48]

Everywhere the signs of continued decay vied with symptoms of revival. Infant mortality rates among inner-city blacks remained far above the national average. Violent crime was still a source of fear, and tales of muggings continued to keep city dwellers and suburbanites alike off many inner-city streets after dark. In the tenth year of Mayor Schaefer's reign, the *Baltimore Sun* reported that with only one-half the population of strife-torn Northern Ireland, Baltimore had three times as many murders.[49] Lamenting the decline of white blue-collar neighborhoods in Philadelphia and the departure of factory jobs, in 1985 a local journalist wrote: "The area east of Hunting Park is populated by zombie armies of crack dealers and users, by 15-year-old Puerto Rican Scarfaces who pump energy and money in the only remaining industry in the neighborhood: cocaine."[50] Such a description fit New York, Chicago, Boston, or Saint Louis as well as the City of Brotherly Love. One did not need to read a costly foundation report to discover there was "rot beneath the glitter." A drive through the city streets beyond the central business district would yield the same conclusion.

Moreover, slums persisted, and housing, if anything, was a more serious problem than it had been before. Public housing units were decaying, and the federal government was opposed to increasing appropriations for such projects. In Chicago, public housing was a perennial and seemingly insoluble problem. At the close of 1986 the *Chicago Tribune* ran a series of articles that referred to the projects' "crime, graffiti, garbage, urine-stained stairwells and broken elevators" and described the giant high-rise apartment buildings as "almost universally viewed as failures that devour human lives and tax dollars."[51] According to the *Tribune*, the local housing authority's finances were "falling apart as quickly as its buildings," and the newspaper concluded, "In the future, as in the past, all the stereotypes, all the fears, all the frustrations that have come to be associated with public housing in Chicago are likely to block significant change."[52]

Rehabilitation of housing was occurring in the older cities, but it produced more publicity than dwelling units. The neighborhood development corporations may have proudly turned out a few hundred housing units annually, but in the meantime thousands of dwellings were deteriorating and thousands of poor residents needed improved shelter. By the mid-1980s Chicago could claim 960 new or rehabilitated low-income units each year, yet 3,500 units, most of them inner-city slums, were demolished annually. The executive director of the Chicago Rehab Network admitted that his organization's efforts were "a Band-Aid approach to saving neighborhood housing," and the *Tribune* referred to the community development corporations' rehabilitation efforts as "drops of salvation in [a] housing drought."[53] A Cincinnati councilman expressed much the same opinion when he complained of appropriating money to neighborhood development corporations: "Three years pass, and you ask how many housing units they've produced and usually you can count them on one hand."[54]

Gentrification seemed to offer hope to middle- and upper-income Americans in search of central-city dwellings, and the media frequently focused on comeback neighborhoods with their renovated townhouses and charming boutiques. Yet there were only slight glimmers of gentrification in such cities as Cleveland and Detroit, and in revived Pittsburgh, city boosters could point to merely a few gentrified streets. Even where the return of the middle class seemed more pronounced, it was deemed a mixed blessing, driving up housing costs for the poor and displacing lower-income residents with few housing alternatives. To stem the supposed tide of gentrification in Baltimore, in 1986 working-class residents of Upper Fells Point banded together to block a proposal to add their neighborhood to the Fells Point Historic District. Designation as a historic district would ensure state and federal tax credits for people investing in the renovation or restoration of properties, and thus gentrification would probably ensue. The leader of the working-class opposition warned: "This is going to be nothing but another Georgetown. The rich are going to be in and the poor are going to be out."[55]

During the 1980s, Boston probably suffered the greatest housing pressure owing to an influx of middle-class residents. Conversion of rental properties to condominiums for the affluent was a leading political issue. In the 1987 municipal election mayoral challenger Joseph Tierney asked incumbent Raymond Flynn, "What has the city of Boston done under your leadership to provide and build and encourage the construction of affordable housing . . . your record speaks for itself and it's dismally poor."[56] Moreover, when the *Boston Globe* asked city council candidates "what [was] the single most critical issue facing the city of Boston," one respondent after another replied "affordable housing."[57]

Focusing attention on the low-income housing problem were frequent media reports on the homeless in America's cities. Though figures differed on the number of homeless, it seemed as if their numbers were increasing in many renaissance cities. This was in part owing to the deinstitutionalization of the mentally ill, a policy that added new recruits to the army of street people and "crazies" found in every central city. But especially troubling was evidence that a growing number of families, especially female-headed families, were without shelter. In 1984 New York City was caring for 2,354 homeless families in hotels and shelters, a 148 percent rise over July 1982, and by September 1986 the figure was up to 4,365 families, or about fifteen thousand people. As of 1986 New York City had sixty-five hotels, motels, and city-run shelters to house the homeless.[58] That same year Chicago authorities estimated that there were twenty-five thousand homeless in the Windy City, and to handle the problem, the city government provided 1,400 additional beds in the public shelters.[59] Whatever the reasons for this phenomenon, it was hardly a sign of renewed economic vitality in the older central cities.

Homelessness, continued poverty, the skills mismatch, and the high dropout rates all were evidence of the shortcomings of the supposed urban renaissance. Perhaps some were profiting from a revived Baltimore or Pittsburgh, but much seemed to remain the same for those at the bottom of the social ladder. Commenting on this inequitable distribution of the benefits of prosperity, some observers began to warn of the development of two cities within the central city, one rich and the other poor. In 1984 Robert F. Wagner, Jr., son of the former mayor and himself deputy mayor under Edward Koch, spoke of the emergence of "two New Yorks." The New York below Ninety-sixth Street in Manhattan was "made up of people with jobs and opportunities," whereas the other New York consisted of "blacks, Hispanics, and the elderly, who are often unemployed and poor."[60]

Moreover, three years later a commission on the city's future chaired by Wagner warned that "without a response to the problem of poverty, the New York of the 21st century [would] be not just a city divided, not just a city excluding those at the bottom from the fullness of opportunity, but a city in which peace and social harmony [might] not be possible."[61] Articles referred to life in New York as "a tale of two cities," and Irving Howe claimed, "The signs of social and economic polarization seem more visible, more gross than in earlier years." "Those sleek, dark-curtained limos," Howe wrote, "driving through streets in which thousands of people are homeless on winter nights" were among the signs, as was "the glitz of midtown contrasted with the devastation of large sweeps of Brooklyn and the Bronx."[62]

Such devotees of renaissance rhetoric as Baltimore's Mayor Schaefer would tolerate none of this carping; for him Baltimore was back, and he had an aquarium to prove it. Yet by the late 1980s it was apparent to any objective observer that America's older central cities had not yet triumphed wholly over the forces of blight and decentralization that they had been battling for five decades. Flashy new skylines proved that central-city downtowns had not died as the founders of the Urban Land Institute had feared they would. There were millions of feet of additional office space in the central business districts, and millions of workers congregated there each weekday. But in most of the older hubs suburban shoppers were a relatively rare sight, and the first-run movie houses had long before switched off their marquee lights. Some film palaces survived as performing arts centers, but most were gone as was much of the downtown nightlife. The function of the central business district had narrowed. In the 1980s it was the center of business and professional services and finance, but no longer the hub of shopping or amusement.

Moreover, beyond the central business districts, vacant lots and abandoned buildings were constant reminders of the scars inflicted by persistent blight and decentralization. Some neighborhoods were gentrified, but these were, in the words of one urban expert, "islands of renewal in seas of decay."[63] A number of residential areas had survived the preceding half century relatively unscathed, and others seemed to be sprouting new life after the long battle against decline. Yet no city lacked its wastelands that lent credence to the worst fears of those who had warned of urban decay decades before. A visitor to those no-man's-lands could only conclude that America's cities had taken a wrong turn along the road to renaissance and become irretrievably lost.

Yet, if nothing else, the messiah mayors had boosted the spirits of many urban dwellers and made them proud of their cities. They had also rehabilitated the bleak images of the older cities and convinced many Americans that places like Baltimore were fun and cities like Pittsburgh were highly livable. Further, the messiah mayors had seemingly overcome some of the political problems that had undermined the efforts of earlier executives. They had fashioned enough of an urban consensus to keep themselves in power year after year and had made the formerly ungovernable cities governable. Whereas the disruption of traditional political patterns had made the road to renaissance rougher for earlier mayors, the Kochs, Schaefers, and Youngs filled some of the dangerous potholes and eliminated some of the obstacles in the way of revitalization. These messiahs may not have worked as many miracles as they claimed, but they were generally adept enough at political sleight-of-hand to keep up the illusion of success.

NOTES

1. Marilyn Rubin, "Back-Office Activity—An Overview," *City Almanac* 18 (June–August 1984): 3; and "Back-Office Locations: Some Corporate Views," ibid. 18 (June–August 1984): 20–21.

2. Samuel M. Ehrenhalt, "New York City's Economy: New Risks and a Changing Outlook," *Citizens Budget Commission Quarterly* 8 (Winter 1988): 3.

3. Christopher B. Leinberger and Charles Lockwood, "How Business Is Reshaping America," *Atlantic Monthly* 258 (October 1986): 48.

4. Joe T. Darden, Richard Child Hill, Jane Thomas, and Richard Thomas, *Detroit: Race and Uneven Development* (Philadelphia: Temple University Press, 1987), p. 34.

5. Ehrenhalt, "New York City's Economy," p. 3.

6. Rachelle L. Levitt, ed., *Cities Reborn* (Washington, D.C.: Urban Land Institute, 1987), p. 18.

7. *Washington Post*, 25 January 1988, p. WB3.

8. Anita A. Summers and Thomas F. Luce, *Economic Development within the Philadelphia Metropolitan Area* (Philadelphia: University of Pennsylvania Press, 1987), p. 13.

9. Levitt, *Cities Reborn*, p. 153.

10. Ibid., pp. 18, 21.

11. Marc V. Levine, "Downtown Redevelopment as an Urban Growth Strategy: A Critical Appraisal of the Baltimore Renaissance," *Journal of Urban Affairs* 9, no. 2 (1987) p. 109.

12. Gregory R. Barnes, "Philly Hotels Face Survival Struggle," *Hotel and Motel Management* 201 (13 January 1986): 3, 48.

13. Ibid.

14. Bill Gillette, "Philly Bids Adieu to Historic Bellevue," ibid. 201 (7 April 1986): 1, 22–23; Susan Kossoy, "Bellevue Closes; Staff Scrambles to Move Groups," *Meeting News* 10 (April 1986): 10; and Edward Watkins, "Philadelphia's Fairmont: The New Grand Dame of Broad Street," *Lodging Hospitality* 36 (May 1980): 32–34.

15. Gillette, "Philly Bids Adieu," p. 23; Loren Feldman, "Center of the Storm," *Philadelphia Magazine* 75 (April 1984): 142–46, 177–93.

16. Patrick Starr, "Philadelphia: Reading Reevaluated," *Planning* 54 (January 1988): 28.

17. D. Herbert Lipson, "Off the Cuff," *Philadelphia Magazine* 78 (March 1987): 1.

18. Ibid.

19. Feldman, "Center of the Storm," p. 146.

20. *Cleveland Plain Dealer*, 7 November 1987, pp. 1A, 12A.

21. Ibid., p. 12A.

22. *Washington Post*, 18 April 1983, p. A4.

23. *Wall Street Journal*, 16 September 1987, p. 37.

24. *Washington Post*, 12 January 1987, Business section, p. 10.

25. Harold R. Snedcof, *Cultural Facilities in Mixed-Use Development* (Washington, D.C.: Urban Land Institute, 1985), pp. 248–49.

26. Tim Wheeler, "The Tourists Are Coming!" *Baltimore Magazine* 78 (May 1985): 72.

27. *Washington Post*, 18 April 1983, p. A4.

28. *New York Times*, 1 June 1986, sec. 1, p. 39.

29. Michael Desmond, "Trying to Make Buffalo's Ends Meet," *Mass Transit* 13 (October 1986): 28.

30. *New York Times*, 1 June 1986, sec. 1, p. 39.

31. Katharine Blood, "The Price Mover," *Forbes* 135 (22 April 1985): 76. See also Ed Bas, "Detroits Troubled People Mover," *Mass Transit* 13 (October 1986): 8–9, 56–57; "A Railway That Won't," *Maclean's* 98 (24 June 1985): 57; and Luther Jackson, "Detroit's People Mover Finally off the Ground," *Mass Transit* 11 (September 1984): 112–13, 115–16.

32. Tony Snow, "The Great Train Robbery," *Policy Review* 36 (Spring 1986): 44.

33. *Detroit Free Press*, 26 July 1987, p. 7G; and 9 August 1987, p. 2C.

34. *Chicago Tribune*, 7 January 1988, sec. 1, p. 28.

35. *Detroit Free Press*, 26 July 1987, p. 7G.

36. *Washington Post*, 23 January 1988, p. D5; and 10 February 1988, p. C6.

37. Michael Berryhill, "Railroading the Cities," *Harper's* 267 (December 1983): 2, 8, 10, 12, 14, 16.

38. Marilyn Webb, "Paradise Postponed," *New York* 19 (17 November 1986): 46.

39. Ibid., p. 50. See also Michael C. D. MacDonald, *America's Cities: A Report on the Myth of Urban Renaissance* (New York: Simon and Schuster, 1984), pp. 357–62.

40. *Boston Globe*, 24 January 1988, p. 23.

41. Ben Joravsky, "The Chicago School Mess," *Illinois Issues* 14 (April 1988): 13.

42. Daniel E. Chall, "New York City's 'Skills Mismatch,'" *Federal Reserve Bank of New York Quarterly Review* 10 (Spring 1985): 21.

43. Levine, "Downtown Redevelopment," pp. 113–14.

44. *Washington Post*, 24 November 1984, p. A8.

45. Levitt, *Cities Reborn*, p. 19.

46. *Boston Globe*, 24 January 1988, p. 23.

47. Ehrenhalt, "New York City's Economy," p. 5.

48. Alberta Sbragia, "The Pittsburgh Model of Economic Development: Partnership, Responsiveness, and Indifference," in Gregory Squires, ed., *Unequal Partnerships: Urban Economic Development in Postwar America* (New Brunswick, N.J.: Rutgers University Press, forthcoming).

49. Hal Riedl, "Don Shaefer's Town," *New Republic* 185 (25 November 1981): 27.

50. Mike Mallowe, "Notes from the New White Ghetto," *Philadelphia Magazine* 77 (December 1986): 245.

51. *Chicago Tribune*, 2 December 1986, sec. 1, pp. 1, 12.

52. Ibid., 5 December 1986, sec. 1, p. 1; and 30 November 1986, sec. 1, p. 11. See also ibid., 1 December 1986, sec. 1, pp. 1, 9; 4 December 1986, sec. 1, pp. 1, 11; 10 December 1986, sec. 1, pp. 1, 8, and 12 December 1986, sec. 1, pp. 1, 8.

53. Ibid., 8 December 1986, sec. 1, pp. 1, 10.

54. Susan Morse, "Neighborhood Spirit Shapes a City," *Historic Preservation* 40 (July–August 1988): 27.

55. *Washington Post*, 19 June 1986, p. Mdl. See also Mark Cohen, "The Most Complicated Neighborhood in America," *Baltimore Magazine* 81 (August 1988): 44–49, 93–94; *Washington Post*, 31 May 1986, p. A23; and ibid., 8 June 1986, p. H7.

56. *Boston Globe*, 27 October 1987, p. 8.

57. Ibid., 26 October 1987, p. 20.

58. Thomas J. Main, "The Homeless Families of New York," *Public Interest*, no. 85 (Fall 1986): 4.

59. *Chicago Tribune*, 12 December 1986, sec. 1, p. 8.

60. *Christian Science Monitor*, 12 October 1984, p. 10.

61. Commission on the Year 2000, *New York Ascendant* (New York: City of New York, 1987), p. 7.

62. David Blum, "One Block: A Tale of Two Cities on West Eightieth Street," *New York Magazine* 20 (9 February 1987): 24–32; and Irving Howe, "Social Retreat and the Tumler," *Dissent* 34 (Fall 1987): 409.

63. Brian J. L. Berry, "Islands of Renewal in Seas of Decay," in Paul E. Peterson, ed., *The New Urban Reality* (Washington, D.C.: Brookings Institution, 1985), p. 69.